THE ECONOMICS
AND POLITICS
OF REGULATION

THE ECONOMICS AND POLITICS OF REGULATION
A Behavioral Approach

Douglas Needham
Western Kentucky University

Little, Brown and Company
Boston   Toronto

Library of Congress Cataloging in Publication Data

Needham, Douglas.
  The economics and politics of regulation.

   1. Industry and state—United States.
2. Trade regulation—United States.   I. Title.
HD3616.U46N37   1982   338.973   82-82211
ISBN 0-316-59975-1

Library of Congress Catalog Card No. 82-82211

ISBN 0-316-59975-1

9 8 7 6 5 4 3 2 1

MV

Published simultaneously in Canada
by Little, Brown & Company (Canada) Limited

Printed in the United States of America

Preface

In this book I attempt to overcome a number of weaknesses in currently available textbooks on government regulation. Some books dealing with government policies toward business tend to be focused mainly on the institutional and legal aspects of these policies. Other books that are more analytical and attempt to present the economic theory underlying government regulation suffer from incomplete presentations of the reasons for regulation, of the issue of whose goals are served by regulation, and of the effects of regulation on all members of society.

I adopt a broad behavioral approach, focusing on the determinants of people's perceptions and evaluations of regulation's effects. This approach is used to develop a framework that integrates a number of factors underlying the existence and effects of government regulation that are often either omitted or treated separately in the literature.

This book is intended to serve the needs of upper-level undergraduate and introductory graduate courses dealing with government regulation of business in colleges and universities, business schools, and law schools. It also provides a comprehensive, forward-looking overview of the determinants and effects of government regulation that will prove useful for professionals actively engaged in the regulatory process, including government officials, regulators, lawyers, business people, and other types of decision makers confronted by government regulations.

Familiarity with elementary principles of microeconomics will be helpful to the reader but is not mandatory, because the book has been made as self-contained as possible. A number of recent developments in the professional economics literature, connected with incentive systems, distributional considerations in cost-benefit analysis, and methodology of economic analysis, have been integrated into the book. These developments are explained and diagrams are provided when their use will enhance the reader's understanding. Symbols are used only occasionally to summarize relationships among the factors discussed. Carefully selected reference works for each chapter are provided in the References preceding the Index, to permit instructors and readers to deal with individual topics in greater depth. When the book is used at the graduate level, it should be extensively supplemented by these works.

Two major elements of all government regulations are welded together in this book: the "politics" of regulation, emphasizing whose interests are served and the process that produces regulation; and economic analysis of the complex set of factors that determines the effects of regulation on regulated and unregulated segments of society.

These include, for example, individuals, regulated and unregulated; interest groups; legislators; regulators; and organizations; all are participants in the regulatory process. Their behavior jointly determines the nature and effects of regulation. I explain both the manner in which the behavior of these groups is related and the implications of these relationships for the form and effects of regulation.

Participants in the regulatory process operate in an environment that shapes their individual and collective behavior. This environment includes a number of constraints, including personal ideologies and values, limitations on available resources, an inherited institutional structure, and uncertainty about the effects of existing and proposed regulations. These and other constraints jointly influence the behavior of the participants in the regulatory process. When their implications for the form and effects of regulation are considered, they must therefore be viewed jointly, rather than separately. Such a view is achieved by the framework presented in this book.

Government regulation is only one type of instrument that individuals may use to further their aims. A myopic focus on government regulation of business alone fails to capture the range of possible substitute instruments available to governments and individuals and does not provide a suitable framework either for understanding people's choices among instruments or for evaluating them. This book provides a framework for understanding and evaluating alternatives to regulation.

The unifying framework presented in this book is important. The behaviors of participants in the regulatory process are interrelated and cannot be satisfactorily analyzed separately. Also, different types of regulation are related to each other. These relationships exist both on the demand side of regulation, owing to factors linking the types of regulation demanded by various interest groups, and also on the supply side of regulation, owing to factors linking the behaviors of regulatory agencies and regulated firms. It will be shown that failure to take account of these interactions among different types of regulation underlies many failures of current types of regulation to achieve their intended objectives.

The traditional tools of economic analysis also need to be broadened in several ways. For example, the weights that participants in the regulatory process attribute to people's evaluations of regulation's effects need to be explicitly considered in both descriptive and normative analyses of regulation. Also, people's evaluations should be viewed as endogenous, or variable, rather than as fixed factors, for several related reasons. For example, evaluations of regulations are influenced by information regarding its effects from a variety of sources, and this information can change; and experience with regulation may indicate that its effects are different from those anticipated.

Another major reason for viewing evaluations of regulation as variable is connected with the distinction between subjective and revealed evaluations. In a satisfactory analysis of government regulation, it must be explicitly recognized that revealed and subjective evaluations may differ. This difference applies to all participants in the regulatory process — to regulators and interest groups as well as to regulated decision makers. If revealed and subjective evaluations are not the same, the normative significance that can be placed on revealed evaluations is severely limited.

Revealed evaluations constitute a tool that people employ to further their objectives. The extent to which individuals will honestly reveal their subjective evaluations depends on the incentives that confront them, because this will determine the consequences of honest versus misrepresented revelations of preferences. These incentives, and hence the nature of revealed evaluations, depend in part on the form of existing regulatory constraints. Examination of the types of incentive that motivate people to reveal their evaluations and other kinds of information truthfully are relatively recent in the professional economics literature. Because they are crucial in a satisfactory normative analysis of regulation, these developments are integrated into the analytical framework employed in this book.

Another dimension that needs to be added to traditional economic analyses of regulation is the disequilibrium behavior of participants in the regulatory process. Owing to uncertainty regarding the outcome of any type of regulation, participants will not generally be able to immediately adopt forms of behavior that simultaneously achieve all their respective goals or targets. The disequilibrium behavior rules the participants adopt whenever their targets are not being achieved will influence the ensuing time path of the behavior of all the participants.

Trade-offs are unavoidable, and the omission from this book of detailed consideration of historical, institutional, and legal material on various types of government regulation is not intended to minimize the possible importance of these factors as an influence on the conduct of regulation in practice. To obtain a clear understanding of the causes and consequences of regulation in practice, however, a flexible analytical framework that shows how the many dimensions of regulation are related, and the process that generates them, is indispensable. This kind of framework affords a perspective on the conflicting perceptions and value systems that permeate issues in regulation. The solution to any problem depends on the manner in which the problem is formulated; many issues in regulation are connected with the problem-formulation stage, and can be properly understood only within a flexible analytical framework.

I would like to thank a number of persons whose efforts contributed to the completion of this project. Lee E. Preston, University of Maryland, read an earlier version of the manuscript and made many constructive suggestions for improving the exposition. Bruce Caldwell, University of

North Carolina, provided enlightening discussions on methodology in the social sciences, and reviewed Section 2.4, which deals with methodology and theory choice. Others who read all or part of the manuscript and made constructive comments were W. Bruce Erickson, University of Minnesota, and Kevin C. Sontheimer, University of Pittsburgh. Ruth Turner performed miracles typing the manuscript under severe time constraints. Naturally, responsibility for the final form of the book is solely mine, including any deficiencies that may remain. The permission of Holt-Saunders Ltd. to include material from my book, *The Economics of Industrial Structure, Conduct and Performance* in two sections of Chapters 8 and 9, and permission of the *American Economic Review* and William A. Niskanen and Thomas C. Schelling to include material is also gratefully acknowledged.

It is hoped that readers of the book will find the issues related to government regulation as stimulating and challenging as the author does.

Douglas Needham

IN MEMORIAM
Douglas Needham
Born 1940   Died 1982

Doug Needham died on August 13, 1982. He had completed the bulk of the work on this book before his untimely death.

My small contribution to this work was to read the galley proofs, make some minor, technical corrections, and prepare the index. In reviewing Doug's work I tried to put myself into his Weltanschauung and make only the minimum of changes, so that his ideas were not altered in a substantive way.

Doug had a very fertile mind and never stopped subjecting ideas, whether conventional wisdom or his own novel views, to constant examination. To improve our understanding of public policy issues in general and regulatory issues in particular was a never-ending quest for him. His objective shines through in this and his other published works. It was also an outlook that he successfully transmitted to students. The profession and his students will sorely miss his presence.

John C. Wassom
Western Kentucky University

Contents

CHAPTER ONE

Introduction

1.1 REGULATION IN THE UNITED STATES

The term "regulation" can be defined in many ways. Any definition will influence one's conceptualization of what is meant by regulation and how it relates to other factors. Attempts to measure characteristics of regulation will produce results that depend on the way the term is defined. Assumptions about the nature of regulation will influence the conclusions anyone reaches when thinking about regulatory issues.

Although regulation takes many forms, and has varying characteristics, it generally involves a conscious attempt by an individual or a group to influence the behavior of other individuals or organizations. The fact that regulation attempts to restrict people's behavior does not necessarily imply that the restrictions are unwarranted or undesirable. Most people agree that governments should impose restraints on human conduct in such forms as laws against theft, violence and murder, fraud, and similar activities. There is less agreement on the desirability of other types of regulation, including restraints on business activities. One's views on the desirability of any type of regulation depend in part on the perceived objectives regulation is designed to achieve, and these perceived objectives can vary greatly (see Section 1.2). One's views may also be influenced by the type of regulatory instruments employed, such as monitoring and enforcement activities, penalties, rewards, or other types of remedy employed by regulatory agencies, such as licensing, certification, or inspection. The concept of regulation as a restraint on people's behavior must not be confused with the objectives or instruments of regulation, though all three aspects of regulation are related and are needed in understanding and evaluating regulation. The major focus of this book will be upon the decision-making process of individuals and the implications of regulatory constraints for their behavior. The many characteristics of government regulation are linked via the process of decision making by individuals who demand government regulation, legislators and regulators who formulate and administer regulations, regulated decision makers, and

1

unregulated decision makers who are indirectly affected by regulation. The interactions among these decision makers result in the process that creates government regulation and its effects.

Although this book focuses on government regulations aimed at the behavior of business enterprises in the United States, the methodology employed and many of the major conclusions reached can also be applied to other types of government regulation. Moreover, it is not always possible to separate different types of government regulation: all types of government regulation — all laws, taxes and subsidies, and many government activities not usually considered as regulation — are functionally equivalent in the sense that they influence the opportunities, consequences, penalties, and rewards associated with alternative courses of action considered by decision makers. Individuals' behavior will depend on *all* the government regulations and other types of constraint that collectively determine the opportunity set confronting each individual decision maker. Regulations aimed at business behavior will also generally affect other dimensions of people's behavior; for example, regulations that affect individuals' incomes may affect their childbearing behavior. Similarly, regulations aimed at other areas of people's behavior may affect business behavior. Thus, criminal laws prohibiting kinds of behavior such as marijuana growing and prostitution may channel human activities into economic activities of a more (or possibly less) socially acceptable kind. Regulations affecting political campaign spending, the geographic boundaries of legislative districts, and other aspects of political behavior may also have implications for business behavior. These political constraints are often intimately connected with factors underlying legislators' behavior and the type of regulatory legislation that is enacted.

Just as government regulation of business behavior consists of only a portion of government regulations, "government" regulations, which are given legislative sanction, constitute only a portion of the regulations that confront individuals and organizations. Ethical and moral codes of conduct associated with people's religious beliefs, professional affiliation, social customs, and other behaviorial restraints often deeply affect the way people behave. Although the institutions and organizations involved in the creation and enforcement of these codes of conduct differ from government, the methodology employed in this book and many of the conclusions that apply to government regulations affecting business behavior can also be applied to these other types of restraint. Human behavior depends on the *joint* effect of all these restraints and regulations. This fact is extremely important; the effects on behavior of any particular type of regulatory constraint will generally depend on, and vary with, differences in other existing types of restraint on people's behavior.

Even when the type of regulation we are considering is limited to government regulation of business behavior, a meaningful idea of the scope and magnitude of this type of regulation in the United States is difficult to grasp. Government regulation of business takes many forms; each form has many dimensions; and there are correspondingly many possible measures of its scope and magnitude. One measure is the number of regulations directed at businesses that are listed in the Federal Register, which contains the rules and regulations promulgated by federal agencies. In the almost forty-year period between 1937, when federal agencies were first required to publish their regulations in the Register, and 1975, the size of the Register expanded from approximately 3,400 pages to more than 60,000 pages. A quarter of this increase occurred between 1974 and 1975 alone. The accelerated expansion of the Federal Register continued until the Reagan administration instituted measures to deregulate aspects of a few selected industries.

State and local government regulations aimed at business behavior must also be taken into account to gain a proper perspective over the extent of regulation. These regulations have tended to exhibit growth similar to that of federal regulations. The expansion in federal and state regulation of business behavior is related (see Chapter 11). To a considerable extent, such growth reflects conscious and unconscious competition among regulatory agencies intent on enforcing their own regulatory constraints on different facets of business behavior.

The growth in the number of government regulations actually understates the growth of regulation because it neglects the greater detail and complexity of regulations added in each successive time period. Again, this increased complexity often reflects attempts by regulatory agencies to enforce their regulations successfully and to prevent the frustration of the desired effects of their regulations by the response of regulated decision makers and other regulatory agencies. McKie (1960) has aptly called this the "tar-baby effect" of regulation, since it usually entangles the regulatory agency in control efforts of increasing complexity with little impact except a growing feeling of frustration on the part of the regulators.

Another way to measure the extent of regulation is to list all the regulatory agencies, and their budgets or number of employees, or some other index of the agencies' size. This requires a definition of the term "regulatory agency," which is not difficult in the case of agencies that perform only regulatory functions, such as the Interstate Commerce Commission, Civil Aeronautics Board, Securities and Exchange Commission, Federal Trade Commission, Consumer Product Safety Commission, Environmental Protection Agency, Food and Drug Administration, Equal Employment Opportunity Commission, and Federal Communications Commission. These are only a sample of the many government agencies that specialize in administering and enforcing regulations. It is more difficult to draw a line between regulatory agencies and other types of government units in the case of agencies that perform both regulatory and other functions. For example, in addition to its other functions, the

Department of Labor administers employment and job safety standards; the Department of Agriculture administers food inspection programs; and the Department of Justice, the Treasury, and the Internal Revenue Service each has mixed regulatory and nonregulatory functions. Many agencies with mixed functions have larger budgets and allocate more of their budgets to regulatory functions than do agencies that specialize in regulation.

Table 1.1 lists the major federal regulatory agencies. The number of such agencies, their budgets, and the number of their employees have grown at an accelerating pace in recent years. Weidenbaum (1981) has estimated that between 1974 and 1980 the combined operating expenses

Table 1.1. Federal Regulatory Agencies

I. *Agencies Specializing in Regulatory Functions*
Civil Aeronautics Board
Commodity Futures Trading Commission
Comptroller of the Currency
Consumer Product Safety Commission
Environmental Protection Agency
Equal Employment Opportunity Commission
Federal Communications Commission
Federal Deposit Insurance Corporation
Federal Energy Regulatory Commission
Federal Trade Commission
International Trade Commission
Interstate Commerce Commission
National Labor Relations Board
National Transportation Safety Board
Nuclear Regulatory Commission
Securities and Exchange Commission

II. *Agencies with Regulatory plus other Functions*
Department of Agriculture
Department of Commerce
Department of Defense
Department of Energy
Department of Human Resources (formerly Department of Health, Education, and Welfare)
Department of the Interior
Department of Justice
Department of Labor (Occupational Health and Safety Administration)
Department of Transportation (National Highway Traffic Safety Administration)
Department of the Treasury

of the major federal regulatory agencies increased from $2.8 billion to $6 billion, while those agencies' total employment increased from approximately 66,000 to more than 80,000 employees in the same period. Moreover, regulatory agencies have been growing not only in absolute terms but also in terms of the fraction of total economic activity they occupy, measured either as a fraction of the gross national product produced in regulated industries or in terms of the total labor force employed in regulatory agencies.

The budget figures understate the great extent of the total costs of administering federal regulations, because much of the cost of providing information to regulatory agencies is borne by individuals and organizations in the private sector. In a report published by the comptroller general of the United States in 1978 it was estimated that businesses alone expended 69 million hours annually at an estimated cost of more than $1 billion to respond to more than 2,100 federal reporting requirements, excluding IRS forms. The same report cites an IRS estimate that its reporting and recording requirements result in some 613 million hours of effort by businesses and individuals. Another report by the U.S. Commission on Federal Paperwork (1977) estimated that whereas the burden of federal government paperwork cost the government $45 billion in 1977, the total cost including the burden placed on individuals and businesses amounted to $100 billion, or about $500 for each person in the country. These figures and estimates apply only to federal regulatory agencies.

Still another way to measure the scope of regulation is to focus on individuals and organizations whose behavior is regulated. Variants of government regulation of business have existed at least since medieval times, when European rulers granted charters containing rights and obligations to individuals and organizations engaging in shipping and other trades. In contrast, regulation of business activities is a relatively recent phenomenon in the United States. Although some limited forms of local regulation existed in the early 1800s, the origin of federal regulation of business on a national scale dates back only to the creation of the Interstate Commerce Commission in 1887. Creation of the ICC was in part a response to the growth of the monopoly power of transcontinental railroads, but it also received support from eastern railroads anxious to limit price competition in the railroad industry. The ICC's jurisdiction over interstate railroad rates and service was later extended to include control over rates and entry into highway transportation.

The passage of the Sherman Act in 1890 marked the beginning of federal regulation of monopoly and competition in the United States. Chapters 6 and 7 explain why regulation of monopoly and competition by agencies such as the Federal Trade Commission and Department of Justice can be viewed as a form of regulation. In markets and industries where monopoly was considered to be unavoidable or desirable for efficiency or other reasons, federal, state, and local governments often adopted the traditional "public utility regulation" approach to dealing with monopoly power. Thus, in such industries as electricity, gas, telephone, and other types of communication, independent state or federal commissions were established to regulate the profits and certain other aspects of the firms composing the industry (see Chapters 8 and 9). This form of regulation was generally confined to a single industry, and to only a very small fraction of the industries in the United States. MacAvoy (1979) has estimated that the fraction of the nation's output produced by industries that were regulated by independent federal and state regulatory commissions amounted to 8 percent of the gross national product in 1965, and increased to approximately 11 percent when regulation was extended to petroleum production, refining, and marketing in the mid-1970s.

The largest extension of regulation occurred in the 1970s with the creation of agencies such as the Occupational Health and Safety Administration, the Environmental Protection Agency, the Consumer Product Safety Commission, and the National Highway Traffic Safety Administration. Except for the latter, the regulations administered by these newer agencies apply to all industries, though the actual impact of the regulations differs from industry to industry and, in practice, is confined to a few industries such as mining, construction, chemicals, petroleum, paper, primary metals, and motor vehicles. MacAvoy (1979) has estimated that these industries together produce about 12 percent of the GNP, which implies that the "new wave" of regulation in the 1970s has extended the regulated sector of the economy to industries that produce approximately a quarter of the nation's total output.

Even a doubling of the scope of government regulation of business activities may seem modest compared with its scope in everyday life. A moment's reflection on the events of a normal day will confirm this impression for many readers. The regulations that influence the ingredients listed on your cereal box or bacon packaging, the Building Code specifications that determine many of the features of your home or apartment, the antipollution devices on the car you drive to work, the regulations relating to the safety of your workplace or the features of the products and services that you help to produce, and the amount of pollutants emitted by the plant or building in which you work are a few of those affecting us from cradle to grave. This pervasiveness of regulation contrasts markedly with the size of the regulated sector of the economy and with the number and size of regulatory agencies.

No human activity escapes the direct or indirect effects of regulation. Focusing only on the decision makers whose behavior is the target of regulations can in no way indicate the scope or magnitude of the effects of regulation on those decision makers and on other members of society and organizations that are not directly regulated. This is so because all regulated decision makers enter into transactions with unregulated decision makers, and regulation also generally has effects on regulated decision makers' behavior that are far broader than the effects intended.

The effects of regulation can be divided into its "benefits" and "costs" (see Chapters 3 and 4), concepts and measures that are indispensable for evaluating regulation. Many studies on the costs of regulation, and fewer estimates of its benefits, have been published in the past ten years or so. The reader is cautioned against uncritical acceptance of these estimates, for a number of reasons. First, all cost and benefit estimates are implicitly or explicitly based on models that show how regulation affects regulated decision makers and others. These models sometimes omit relationships that influence the effects of regulation in the real world. Second, all such benefit-cost studies make implicit or explicit assumptions about whose evaluations of the effects of regulation should be considered. The assumptions made do not always include all the evaluations that might be considered relevant in the real world. All existing measures of the costs of regulation omit important dimensions of the costs of regulations, and many studies merge certain cost concepts with benefit measures in an illegitimate process of aggregating incommensurable benefit and cost concepts (see Chapter 4).

A third and generally neglected reason for treating benefit and cost measures of regulation with skepticism is that regulation is a means by which individuals and interest groups attempt to further their own interests. The kinds of incentive that would motivate individuals to honestly reveal their evaluations of the costs and benefits of regulation do not exist at present (see Chapters 12 and 13). As a result, little reliance can be placed on the cost and benefit information that forms the basis of empirical studies conducted even by relatively unbiased observers and analysts. Attempts to correct data for possible information distortion amount to little more than substituting the analyst's value judgments concerning the benefits and costs of regulation and as such are no more reliable than the raw data.

Benefit-cost studies of regulation are included in the references listed for several chapters of this book, and the reader is encouraged to devote some time to reading them, but only after developing a framework for understanding the methodology that forms the basis of all benefit-cost studies of regulation. Two elements of any "problem of regulation" — a model of regulation and a value system used to evaluate regulation — automatically determine the conclusions reached regarding regulation's effects, benefits, and costs. Not surprisingly, there is considerable competition between individuals and interest groups for the right to define these two elements and the nature of specific problems of regulation. This right conveys the ability to formulate a problem of regulation in such a manner that the conclusions correspond to those desired by the problem formulator: the right to define a problem automatically conveys the ability to influence the prescribed solution to the problem. This is the way to win wars without ever going into battle, as Chinese philosophers of old were well aware. We hope that this book will prevent you from unconsciously turning over your right to formulate problems to other people whose interests and motivations conflict with yours.

1.2   DISAGREEMENTS ON REGULATION

Most disagreements about issues connected with regulation can be traced to one of two kinds of disagreement. They are implicitly or explicitly either (1) disagreements about the effects of regulation on individuals and organizations or (2) disagreements about evaluations of those effects. Although both kinds of disagreement may occur simultaneously, the distinction between effects of regulation and evaluations of those effects is a useful one.

Whether particular effects of regulation are judged to be good or bad will depend on the value system used to evaluate these effects. Evaluations of the effects of regulation (or of any other aspect of the human environment) are necessarily subjective. Disagreements about evaluations therefore ultimately boil down to issues about *whose* evaluations are appropriate for evaluating perceived effects of regulation. Traditional economic analysis has generally assumed that it is appropriate to use the evaluations of persons who experience effects of regulation to evaluate those effects. Although traditional economic analysis of government activities has long recognized that people might be unwilling to directly reveal their evaluations of the effects of government activities, until recently the problem of purposeful distortion of people's evaluations, and methods of overcoming this problem, received inadequate attention. In addition, the economics literature has still not adequately dealt with the information flows that initially create people's perceptions of the effects of regulation and other government activities.

Perceived effects of regulation and evaluations of those effects can be separated in the following sense: the people whose explicit or implicit models of regulation are used to determine the effects of regulation may be different from the people whose evaluations are used to judge those effects. Economists, for example, generally build analytical models of regulation that predict certain effects of regulation and then proceed to use other people's evaluations of those effects as a basis for making judgments about regulation. As already noted, a change in the identity of the people whose evaluations are used by economists will generally result in different evaluations of the same effects.

Even in the preceding situation, the separation of effects of regulation from the evaluation of those effects is somewhat illusory, for the following reasons. To predict the effects of regulation on regulated and unregulated decision makers, economists, and other researchers must attribute goals and constraints to these decision makers. Effects of regulation are the result of responses by individuals to changes in one or more of the constraints that collectively determine their perceived environment. Any predictions about how individuals will react to changes in their environment attributable to regulation will depend on the nature of the goals they are assumed to pursue. In other words, effects of regulation in terms of people's responses to regulation will be influenced by their personal perceptions and evaluations of the way regulation affects their environment and opportunities. These factors emphasize that although the distinction between effects and evaluations of the effects of regulation is often useful in clarifying one's thinking, this does not mean that these two aspects can always be neatly separated. People's perceptions and evaluations of changes in their environment tend to develop together and often interact. In Chapter 3, for example, we shall emphasize that a person's monetary evaluation of the benefits and costs of some effects of regulation on that person or on other individuals will be influenced by the effect of regulation on that person's money income.

Any notion that a completely objective and value-free analysis of regulatory issues can be made should be discarded at an early stage; recognizing this strengthens one's ability to understand many issues connected with regulation. For example, it helps to cure the erroneous notion that there is a single best solution to regulatory problems. There may be many different optimal solutions, depending on whose perceptions and value systems are adopted in solving the problem. Indeed, whether a problem exists at all depends on whose perceptions and value systems are adopted as a standard of reference. Even specialists in regulation are not immune to adopting assumptions and conclusions that bear little resemblance to reality. Furthermore, the problems, models, and prescribed solutions that occupy the time and efforts of scientists in any field are endogenously determined by the preferences, rewards, and penalties that form part of the scientists' environment (see Section 2.4).

Throughout this book we shall attempt to make the value systems and evaluation criteria that are implicit in particular models and solutions to regulatory problems as explicit as possible. We shall also make every effort possible to use expository devices that permit the reader to vary the value systems that are implicit in particular models of regulation, and the models themselves, and to understand the consequences of such variations for regulatory problems and solutions.

Most specialists in the field of regulation now generally agree that a satisfactory treatment of regulation must include the behavior of at least the following four types of decision maker: legislators and regulators whose decisions and behavior determine the nature of regulatory constraints; regulated decision makers subject to those constraints; and unregulated decision makers whose behavior either influences, or is influenced by, the behavior of the three preceding types of decision maker.

The behavior of each type of decision maker and the resulting implications for regulation depend on the objectives and constraints confronting that type. However, some aspects of the behavior of the other three types of decision maker will represent a constraint for each type. Thus, the behavior of all four types of decision maker is interdependent, and the consequences of that behavior for any aspect of regulation are jointly determined by all the interacting objectives and constraints.

In order to deal with these complexities of regulation, the chapters that follow proceed in stages. The determinants and consequences of different types of decision-maker behavior will be examined in isolation first; this will be followed by explanations of the consequences of interactions among the behaviors of the different types of decision makers. Throughout, we shall attempt to provide an expository framework that is flexible and capable of dealing with a wide range of possible decision-maker objectives and constraints. This framework will be employed, not only to explain the models of decision-maker behavior that are used in traditional analyses of regulation but also to highlight the impact, on conclusions regarding regulation, of changing the traditional models.

CHAPTER TWO

Reasons for Regulation

2.1 THEORIES ON THE ORIGIN OF REGULATION

Until the early 1960s most of the emphasis on the economics of regulation focused on the question of how regulated decision makers and other members of society are affected by regulatory constraints on their behavior. Since that time there has been a surge of interest in the reasons why regulation comes into existence and on the process that determines the kind of regulatory constraints that exist in practice. This shift of emphasis has led to increased knowledge of the process that produces regulatory legislation and the forces that shape the way in which regulatory legislation is administered. Controversies persist, however, and a number of theories have been advanced to explain why regulation comes into existence and the forms it takes in practice. In the remainder of this section we shall provide some perspective on these matters by first briefly outlining the major alternative types of explanation that have been advanced for the existence of regulation. The relationship among these theories and their relationship to a general model of the way regulatory objectives and instruments and the effects of regulation are related will then be explained.

(a) Market Failure and Transactions Failure

The reason for regulation advanced by traditional economic analysis is the existence of some type of "market failure," a situation in which the prices, quantities, or other characteristics of transactions between buyers and sellers in a market differ from like characteristics that are judged to be desirable from the point of view of achieving certain objectives. Market failures take many forms and have many causes. One important type of market failure may result from monopoly of the selling side of a market.

11

In certain circumstances, monopolistic pricing behavior may reduce the efficiency of the nation's resources in producing and allocating goods and services (see Chapter 6). Another type of market failure occurs when transactions between buyers and sellers in a market have "external effects" on third parties not directly involved in those transactions (e.g., environmental pollution).

The concept of market failure has recently been extended by economists to include many types of situation that result from constraints confronting parties to market transactions that have been neglected or omitted from traditional economic analysis. Examples of such constraints are information flow characteristics such as uncertainty and asymmetry in the information possessed by different individuals. Another constraint ignored by traditional economic analysis is the fact that parties to many types of transaction act as agents for other individuals (see Chapter 10).

Another recent development in the economics literature is the adoption of a much broader concept of transactions between individuals, including not only market exchanges of goods and services or assets for money but also other types of exchange. Political transactions that involve exchanges of money, votes, or other resources for promises, support, or future votes are included in this broader concept. Also included are social aspects of transactions between individuals, such as the right to equality of opportunity in education, jobs, and housing. These other types of transaction may also exhibit "transactions failures" analogous to market failures, and regulation may be an appropriate means of attempting to remedy such transactions failures.

Accompanying this broader view of the nature of transactions between individuals, and the associated extension of the concept of market failure to a more general concept of transactions failure, there is increasing recognition that regulation itself is capable of creating or enlarging transactions failures. The personal objectives and constraints that determine the rewards and penalties associated with alternative courses of action by regulators need not correspond to those which produce the kind of behavior by regulators that is necessary to reduce or eliminate market or transactions failures in the economy. In this respect, as Wolfe (1979) has emphasized, regulators and public sector decision makers in general are no different from decision makers in the private sector. In Chapter 4 (Section 4.4) we shall explain why it will always be necessary to regulate the behavior of regulators themselves.

Regulation is not the only possible instrument to use in attempting to remedy market or other types of transactions failure. However, as Shaffer (1979) has lucidly emphasized, all markets and transactions are in practice regulated by some kind of government laws or regulations, and without regulations of any kind, most markets and types of transaction would cease to exist. Without laws, the terms of many types of agreement and transaction between individuals would be unenforceable and would cease. The choice facing individuals and society is not between regulation and no regulation; rather, it is how much regulation and what kinds of regulation are desirable. In making this choice, it is necessary to take into account the other types of instruments available for dealing with transactions failures and other perceived objectives of regulation. The best choices will generally involve a mix of regulatory and other instruments for achieving particular objectives of individuals and society as a whole (see Chapter 15).

(b) Interest-Group Theories

Until the early 1960s the generally accepted view of why regulation comes into existence was the "public interest" theory, which assumed that regulation was a government response to public demands for the rectification of inefficient or inequitable practices by individuals and organizations. The view that government regulation was instituted primarily for the protection and benefit of the public at large, or some large segment of the public, was usually implicitly assumed rather than explicitly documented. As shall be explained in later chapters, it is difficult to identify the "public interest" on any public policy issue, and this difficulty is one of the major elements of the problem of regulation.

Economists have traditionally focused on a very narrow class of government policies, namely those which are capable of increasing the satisfaction of some members of society without simultaneously reducing the satisfaction of any members of society, and these policies are obviously in the public interest. In practice, however, very few government policies, including regulatory policies, are of this so-called Pareto-optimal kind. Usually, some people benefit and some are harmed by any policy measure, and the problem of defining what is meant by the "public interest" in these cases boils down to a value judgment about whose interests and evaluations of the policy measures should be taken into account by policymakers (see Chapter 3). It will be shown that even when using the time-honored Pareto-optimal criterion of policies that are in the public interest, economists make implicit value judgments about whose interests and evaluations should count in defining the public interest. Also, a major weakness of the traditional public interest theory is that it does not explain the mechanism by which any particular perception of the public interest is translated into public sector decisions.

Following a seminal article by Stigler (1961), a number of writers have argued that regulation is a government response to demands for regulation by particular interest groups and segments of society that seek to advance their perceived self-interest, sometimes at the expense of others.

The really important element in Stigler's theory is the emphasis on the need to consider determinants of the relative political power of different interest groups, not his conclusion that regulation benefits producers at the expense of consumers. Stigler's producer-protection thesis may be consistent with regulation in some of the older regulated industries, such as trucking, airlines, and railroads, but seems inconsistent with some of the more recent types of regulation in areas like consumer protection, safety, and health. Sometimes the interests served by regulatory legislation and agencies are those of consumer rather than producer groups. Many recent types of regulation of business cross industry boundaries, and many of these regulations increase firms' operating costs and reduce profits. Evidence that certain types of regulation harm producers in some industries implies that the consumer or other interest groups that lobbied for these regulations were more organized and politically powerful than the producer groups. This, in turn, implies that the relative political power and ability of interest groups to obtain the types of regulation they demand depends on factors other than those cited by Stigler, such as the size of interest groups and the costs of organizing individuals into effective political pressure groups.

Producers and consumers are not the only interest groups that may be affected by regulation, and regulation need not necessarily advance the interests of one of these groups at the expense of the other. Lee (1980) views regulation as a mutually beneficial exchange between consumers and producers. For example, in Lee's model of regulation, enforcement of the monopoly-cartel enforcement function is transferred from producers to society. In exchange, producers agree to surrender the power of product-price determination to a third-party regulatory agency, which sets product prices on the basis of an attempt to balance different interests of members of society. Other theories place primary emphasis on regulators as the motivating force underlying the overall level of regulation and the number of regulatory agencies in existence (McKenzie and Macaulay, 1980). Some of these theories view regulation as mainly serving the interests of regulators; others see some version of the public interest being served. For example, Owen and Braeutigam (1978) view regulation as a desirable mechanism that reduces the speed and severity of disequilibrium adjustments in the private market system, providing some protection to victims of economic change, in the form of a longer period of adjustment for amortizing fixed physical and human capital and skills.

A satisfactory theory of the factors that explain the relative political power of interest groups and the kinds of regulation actually in force must include more detailed analysis of the process by which interest-group demands for regulation are formulated and articulated to legislators responsible for regulatory legislation. Even if attention is confined to producers in one industry, for example, differences in the personal goals and constraints that confront individual producers generally imply differences in the extent to which any type of regulation serves the interest of these producers. Some may perceive opportunities to acquire greater political strength by entering into a coalition with owners of inputs, consumers, or other types of interest group and demanding types of regulation favoring the coalition's joint interests, rather than joining a coalition that consists only of producers in the same industry. Migue (1977) has demonstrated that it is possible for consumers of an industry's product and owners of certain inputs that are in inelastic supply to the industry to benefit jointly from regulations that subsidize the industry. Similarly, Mieszkowski (1967) has shown that the owners of some inputs employed by an industry can gain from regulations that restrict demand for the industry's product.

A good deal of empirical evidence appears to be inconsistent with theories of regulation that view regulation as a response by government decision makers to demands of well-defined interest groups, such as producers, consumers, environmentalists, and regulators. Part of the explanation may be that regulation can have effects that are different from those anticipated by groups that demand regulation. Another possibility is that existing theories of regulation may pay insufficient attention to the factors that determine how legislators and regulators respond to competing demands for regulation by different interest groups. The personal goals and other constraints that underlie the behavior of decision makers on the "supply side" of regulation are fundamental here. Peltzman (1972) has argued that instead of giving an interest group with dominant political power the kind of regulation it demands, regulators may maximize their own political support for other objectives by *balancing* the demands of competing interest groups for different types of regulation when carrying out regulatory policy. If this balancing of demands were an accurate representation of how legislators and regulators behave in practice, one would not observe a close correlation between the characteristics of regulation in practice and the interests of a single interest group. Chapter 5 examines the factors that influence the behavior of regulators and legislators in detail.

The idea of existing forms of regulation as a compromise among demands for regulation by competing interest groups can be used to unify the interest-group theories and explanations for the existence of regulation. Useful perspective may be gained by viewing each theory as a special case in a general interest-group theory of the demand for regulation. All these theories have a common element: each assumes that regulation is the result of attempts by individuals to further personal objectives and ambitions. The type of regulation that will be demanded by an individual or interest group will depend on the nature of these objectives and of the constraints that confront the individual or interest group. The strength with which these various demands are registered on legislators and regulators will similarly depend on a number of factors, such as the number of people composing an interest group; their money, time, and other resources; the process by which individual demands for regulation are transformed into interest-group demands; and the nature of the channels through which these demands are expressed, such as direct lobbying, campaign contributions, and other methods of persuasion.

The interest-group theories of why regulation exists, and its form, reach different conclusions because of differences in their respective assumptions about the personal goals and constraints facing individuals. In addition, all the existing variants of a general interest-group theory of regulation omit a number of constraints that face decision makers in practice and that have important implications for descriptive and pre-scriptive aspects of regulation. For example, the absence of incentives for individuals to provide accurate information permeates all facets of regulation and has not been adequately recognized in the theory or practice of regulation (see Chapter 12). Many other examples of weak-nesses of particular versions of the interest-group theory of regulation examined in this book do not invalidate the general approach they share; they merely imply that the theories need to be modified to take into account possibly important factors underlying demands for, and supplies of, regulation in practice.

(c) The Relationship Between "Transactions Failure" and "Interest-Group" Theories

There are major differences between transactions failure and interest-group explanations for the existence of regulation. Despite these differ-ences, we must understand that these two types of explanation are not necessarily incompatible. A major difference between them is that interest-group theories make explicit whose interests lie behind demands for regulation, whereas in the market failure and transactions failure theories the interests to be served by regulation are only implied within the defi-nition of the specific "failure" to be corrected. The following considera-tions will clarify this difference.

The central features of any variant of market failure and transactions failure explanations for regulation are (1) a concept of "desirable trans-actions characteristics" and (2) a transactions "failure" in the form of a divergence between the actual characteristics and the desirable characteris-tics of a transaction. The reasons for this divergence, and its exact form, depend on the personal objectives and constraints that influence the be-havior of individuals affected by the transaction.

In order to define the concept of desirable characteristics that any particular type of transaction should exhibit, someone's evaluations of its characteristics must be employed. A wide range of perspectives exists for assessing any transaction, including evaluations by one or more of the parties to the transaction, and evaluations by nonparticipants who themselves may or may not be affected by the transaction. Examples of nonparticipants who are affected by the terms of transactions are principals who are represented by an agent and people who experience external effects (e.g., pollution) as a result of the transaction. The concept of desirable characteristics of any given type of transaction will generally vary depending on which of the many perspectives is adopted for appraising the transaction. No matter which perspective is employed and whose evaluations are adopted as the basis of defining the concept of desirable characteristics of a particular type of transaction, that concept and the associated concept of "transactions failure" will reflect the perceptions and personal values of the individual or individuals responsible for the evaluation.

The self-interest of a person who evaluates a transaction need not be the sole or major criterion used to evaluate the transaction. That person may estimate a transaction not only on the basis of its effects on himself but also by its perceived effects on others. Yet, the weights that the evaluator assigns to the perceived effects of the transaction on different people will determine the weights that are assigned to their interests. Therefore, any concept of desirable transactions characteristics, and the associated concept of transactions failure, will necessarily reflect implicit weights that are based on someone's evaluation of whose interests "should" count in evaluating the transaction in question.

The preceding discussion indicates that the traditional view of regulation as a remedy for "failures" of the market system of providing goods and services is an oversimplification. Similarly, the traditional view that the rationale of government intervention and regulation of private sector economic activities is determined by the innate characteristics of goods and services — and in particular whether "externalities" occur in the production or consumption of those goods and services — is no longer tenable. It is now well established in the economics literature that defects in the demand-revealing mechanism for goods and services exhibiting external effects may preclude more efficient public sector solutions to market imperfections. Also, the behavior of legislators and bureaucrats in response to even properly revealed demands for goods and services with externalities can result in public sector solutions that are inferior to private sector provision of those goods and services (see Chapters 5 and 13).

The notion that there exists an intrinsic distinction between "private" goods and services and goods and services with external effects is not tenable once one recognizes that most goods and services can be produced by a number of methods, or technologies. These technologies affect the degree to which a product or service exhibits "private" and "externality" characteristics. For example, fire protection can be obtained by purchasing private goods such as fire extinguishers, alarms, and sprinkler systems, or by purchasing the services of a local fire department that is also available to other individuals. If there is a choice between alternative technologies that determines the degree of private and external effects exhibited by a product or service, Auster and Silver (1973) have pointed out that the real issue is not whether the product or service should be regulated or provided by the government. Rather, the important question is why consumer and producer decisions sometimes result in a choice of technologies that result in an absence of external effects and market provision of goods and services, whereas in other cases these decisions choose technologies that result in external effects and government intervention in private sector markets.

The profit motive, bogeyman and favorite whipping boy of many people who wish to change business behavior to suit their own ends, cannot totally explain why firms select production technologies that result in external effects. A business that fails to use a production technology that reduces pollution or other externalities risks government regulation or even public ownership. Each of these possibilities might have more disastrous consequences for the firm's profits than would the use of a higher-cost technology that reduces external effects of the firm's activities. The choice of technology and the characteristics of a firm's products, including the degree and type of external effects associated with those products, are just as much a matter of conscious choice by business decision makers as is any other facet of business behavior. A rather extreme view of the rationale of regulation has been offered by Smythe (1979), who argues that the whole apparatus of regulation in the United States was created with the approval of private enterprise, as a means of heading off public ownership between the 1880s and 1920s. This view is of course only a hypothesis, but it is thought-provoking and helps to provide an early warning against adopting many of the stereotyped approaches that can be found on all sides of the issue of regulation.

Government regulation of business activities and other aspects of human behavior is as much a political as an economic phenomenon, and the theory of regulation cannot be separated from the theory of representative government. Regulation of business can extend modes of competition between firms' decision makers in economic markets to the political sphere, and it may be viewed as an additional means by which individuals and organizations attempt to further their respective interests via legislative and public sector actions. Regulation should not be viewed only as a method of changing the rules of permissible behavior relating to market transactions, however. Regulations that change these rules in political transactions will also influence the nature and outcome of the regulatory process. Economic and political aspects of people's behavior are both instruments that an individual or a group may employ to further its perceived interests and objectives. Often, the best strategy may involve a mixture of resources and efforts devoted to both economic and political activities. In such situations, market activities and government regulation may be complementary rather than alternative activities.

2.2   THE DEMAND FOR REGULATION

In this section some characteristics of the demand for government regulation that have not yet been adequately dealt with in existing theories of regulation are briefly outlined. A problem with most theories of regulation is that they do not explain how group demands for particular regulations are initially formulated or how these demands are transmitted to legislators and regulators. These factors need to be taken into account in order to develop a more satisfactory explanation of the process that generates demands for government regulation in practice.

(a)   Factors Underlying Individual Preferences and Demands

A satisfactory theory of demands for regulation must begin with the behavior of individual decision makers rather than with that of groups of decision makers. A fundamental principle in economics and behavioral science in general is that how a group of individuals will behave depends on how each member of the group expects other group members to behave. This principle applies to an individual's decision to join an interest group, the choice among different interest groups, and the way the individual behaves as a member of any one interest group. Existing interest-group theories of regulation are unsatisfactory, since they do not explain how interest groups are formed or how individual members reach group demands for regulation.

People demand certain effects of regulation, such as cleaner air and water, safer products and working environments, and greater access of minorities to job opportunities, rather than regulation itself. Moreover, regulation is only one of a number of instruments that can be used in attempts to achieve these results. Which effects are desired, which instruments are preferred for achieving these results, and which types of regulatory instrument are demanded at a specific time by an individual will depend on the personal objectives and the perceived constraints confronting that individual. All individuals are confronted by several major types of constraint, which will be described briefly before the implications of these constraints for a person's demands for regulation are examined.

(1) Everyone faces personal time, income, and wealth constraints. An individual's producing, consuming, and leisure activities cannot exceed twenty-four hours a day. The income constraint takes the form of a stipulation that the total sources of income an individual earns cannot exceed the individual's total expenditure of income. This constraint includes saving, which can be viewed as the purchase of claims on future income, and borrowing, which we may see as the sale of claims on future income. At any specific time a person also has wealth in the form of

human and nonhuman capital assets with income-producing potential. Human capital consists of the knowledge and skills of the individual. Nonhuman capital includes assets such as money balances, stocks or bonds, equity in a home, tools, or any other form of property rights.

(2) A second major type of constraint that confronts any individual consists of the behavior of other individuals and organizations with whom the individual may engage in transactions. These acts include sales of the individual's skills and assets, purchases of goods and services, political deals such as the exchange of votes or other kinds of support for promises from political candidates, and a variety of agreements with other individuals to cooperate in order to achieve collective goals in both the private and the public sector. The actual and prospective behavior of other individuals with whom an individual enters into transactions will largely determine the actual and prospective terms of those exchanges. These terms will, in turn, determine the consequences, rewards, and penalties associated with alternative uses of an individual's time and other personal resources and will therefore influence the individual's decisions regarding uses of these resources and the individual's behavior.

(3) A third major type of constraint is a set of laws and other rules that relate to permissible forms of behavior. Violations of these laws or rules generally lead to some kind of penalties or sanctions. These rules include not only government laws and regulations but also rules established by private sector decision makers, such as rules established by employers for employees and broad social or religious customs.

Taken together, these three types of constraint determine both the opportunities confronting an individual at any particular time and the consequences of alternative uses of the individual's time and other resources. In attempting to achieve their personal goals, ambitions, and satisfaction, individuals may decide to allocate some time and other personal resources to changing these constraints. For example, an individual owner of input A may attempt to increase his income by raising the market price buyers must pay per unit of the input supplied. This will generally lead to some reduction in the quantity of input A demanded, as some users of A substitute other relatively inexpensive inputs for A in their production process. The individual may also attempt to change the behavior of individuals with whom he engages in transactions in an effort to change the terms of the transactions in the individual's favor. Thus, the owner of input A may provide users of the input with advertising messages or other types of information designed to reduce the extent to which input A is replaced by other inputs when the price of input A is raised. A third possibility is that an individual may attempt to change the laws and rules that govern permissible behavior in transactions between individuals. The owner of input A may devote time and other resources to demanding passage of a law that prevents or reduces the extent to which input A can be replaced by other inputs when the price of A increases. A law or regulation requiring certain input mixes to be employed would effectively prevent substitution of other inputs for input A, for example.

Owners of other inputs can be expected to engage in the same kind of activities designed to change constraints and terms of transactions in their favor, and economic and political competition among owners of different inputs, skills, and other resources is likely to be a normal part of human activity. It is in such a context that regulation must be viewed. Moreover, regulation must not simply be viewed as an instrument for changing the rules of behavior and terms of transactions in conventionally defined economic markets. The activities of owners of different inputs will not be confined to demands for regulatory legislation that affects private sector transactions. Such demands will also generally include demands for regulations which affect political decision processes and which give different individuals and groups of individuals an edge over rivals engaging in political competition. Participants in this competitive process may, for example, attempt to secure passage of regulatory legislation that limits their opponents' lobbying activities relative to their own. In addition, individuals and groups may seek passage of regulatory legislation that increases their power relative to public sector decision makers; an overall limit on campaign contributions, or a constitutional amendment requiring a balanced federal budget, are examples.

In viewing the process of individual decision making that underlies demands for regulation, we must recognize that individuals play many roles simultaneously. Most individuals are input sellers, consumers, shareholders, voters, taxpayers, and members of numerous economic, political, and social interest groups. Any theory of regulation that fails to take this simultaneity into account may be seriously deficient as a basis for understanding the type of regulations demanded in practice. A person's attitude toward, support for, or opposition to, any regulatory policy will not usually be determined by the effect of that policy on a single role or aspect of the individual's behavior. Rather, it will depend on the perceived net effect of the policy on all the roles occupied by the individual. For example, a consumer might not object to regulations that raise the price of a product without improving any quality of the product if that consumer is also a shareholder in the firm producing the product. Some taxpayers might not mind their taxes being increased to pay for regulatory policies if they work in regulatory agencies.

Not only do individuals occupy different roles simultaneously, but different people exhibit these roles in varying degrees. One implication of these role differences is that one would not generally expect to find a close association between support for, or opposition to, particular regulations and groups of individuals who are classified on the basis of single roles, such as consumers, producers, taxpayers, or any other homogeneous classification criterion that focuses on a narrow aspect of human behavior. Whether one is attempting to explain economic, political, or other dimensions of human behavior, models that take into account interactions between the dimensions of an individual's behavior are required. This is especially true in government regulation, which represents an interface between economic and political dimensions of human behavior.

(b) How Individual Preferences Are Transformed into Group Demands

Most individuals are unable to exert sufficient influence over public policies on their own and must either join or form coalitions with others in order to implement mutual interests effectively. As was noted in Section 2.2(a), existing interest-group theories of regulation are unsatisfactory, since they do not explain how interest groups are created or the process by which individual members' preferences are transformed into agreed group demands for regulation.

Many factors influence any individual's decision to join or form an interest group; some factors have been analyzed by economists in connection with the economic theory of clubs, which deals with the behavior of individuals cooperating for mutual advantage. In a review article of the current state of the economic theory of clubs, Sandler and Tschirhart (1980) have emphasized that coalition formation in politics is a special case of the general theory of group formation. Similarities between the preferences and objectives of an individual and other members of interest groups will not be the only factor that influences the individual to become a member of particular groups. In any group, differences in the objectives and constraints that confront individual group members will generally exist and often result in preferences for different types of effects and instruments of regulation. In these circumstances, it is necessary to explain how different preferences are transformed into group demands. This group decision process itself may influence an individual's choice between groups, since it will generally determine how much weight is assigned to any person's preferences in reaching the group decision.

Factors that influence the outcome of group decision processes, notably committee decision making, have received increasing attention in the economics literature in recent years. The results of some of these analyses are sometimes unexpected and contrary to conventional wisdom. For example, in an analysis of power in voting bodies, Fisher and Schotter (1978) have indicated that the number or percentage of votes a member of a voting body controls is not a reliable index of that member's voting power measured in terms of a member's ability to turn a losing coalition into a winning coalition, and therefore to influence the outcome of the voting body's decision. They demonstrate that irrespective of the decision rule, such as majority rule that is used by a voting body, an increase in the proportion of votes controlled by a member of that body may *reduce* that person's voting power. Conversely, members whose voting weight is reduced may experience an increase in voting power.

Another factor that has not been sufficiently stressed in the literature on group formation and behavior has been noted by Shibata (1979): group formation and behavior may be based on the threat of competition from other individuals and groups rather than on any independent predisposition to cooperate with other members of a group. A person's expectations regarding the reactions of others to his or her own behavior are extremely important in determining individual and group behavior. This fact has long been recognized in connection with the behavior of firms, as Archibald (1959) and Needham (1978) have emphasized. Although the same principles apply to any aspect of human behavior, including a person's choice of interest groups and behavior as a member of those groups, these principles have not received sufficient attention. Limited space precludes a more detailed discussion of group decision processes at this stage.

(c) The Nature of Demand-Revealing Activities

Given certain preferences, or demands, for regulation by individuals and interest groups, the ways in which they attempt to transmit these preferences and demands to legislators and regulators will henceforth be referred to as "demand-revealing activities." These activities will play an important role in determining the rewards and penalties associated with alternative courses of action by public sector decision makers. These penalties and rewards, together with the personal preferences and goals of legislators and regulators, will in turn influence the kinds of decisions they make and the kinds of regulatory legislation and administration that are supplied.

The demand-revealing mechanism for regulation and public sector activities in general is complex. Individuals and groups may reveal their demands for regulation in a number of ways, such as votes, financial support for political candidates, promises of future support or other considerations, and a variety of lobbying activities involving the expenditure of time and money aimed at influencing the decisions of legislators and regulators. An individual may simultaneously engage in a number of types of demand-revealing activities designed to achieve the same result. Individuals and organizations may simultaneously support a number of public sector decision makers with divergent viewpoints. Backing all the horses in a race may be a more reliable method of ensuring a return on one's investment than backing one horse with the highest probability of winning the race. An empirical study by Welch (1980) suggests that economic interest groups contribute to political candidates for office in order to secure political favors rather than to influence election outcomes. Silberman and Yochum (1980) have also emphasized that in attempting to explain special-interest campaign contributions, it is necessary to take into account the demand side of the market for these contributions, in the form of candidates' preferences for different types of contribution and demand-revealing activities in general.

Individuals' and interest groups' lobbying activities will not necessarily be restricted to efforts to directly influence public sector decision makers. Mobilizing others to direct their time and resources to a cause is as much a part of lobbying as is direct contact with legislators or bureaucrats responsible for administering regulations. Voting is neither the only nor the most desirable way for individuals and interest groups to reveal their demands for public sector activities. Feldman (1979) has emphasized that any voting system can be manipulated by misrepresentation of voter preferences.

Financial contributions to public sector decision makers are not necessarily undesirable elements in the demand-revealing process. From the perspective of entry-barrier theory, it is possible to demonstrate that limitations on political campaign contributions or any other type of lobbying activities may worsen rather than improve public sector performance in certain circumstances. It is necessary to explicitly recognize the multiplicity of demand-revealing activities existing in practice, and the multidimensional nature of any particular individual's demand-revealing activities, in order to improve one's understanding of descriptive and normative aspects of the process that underlies people's demands for regulation.

The total amount of resources actually employed by individuals and interest groups in attempts to influence legislators and other public sector decision makers will depend on the nature and magnitude of "political competition" among interest groups. Competing interest groups may allocate an amount of resources to demand-revealing and lobbying activities that is equal to or even exceeds the total expected value of the benefits they expect to receive from influencing public sector decisions. There is an analogy here with firms who compete so vigorously that they make no profits. Who gets the benefit from all the resources devoted to these kinds of political competition? The main recipients will be the owners of inputs employed in activities aimed at influencing private- and public-sector decision makers. The legislators and regulators whose favor is sought so ardently by groups demanding regulation and other public policies may capture some of the largesse directly, in campaign contributions or other perquisites. This bounty is only a fraction of the resources allocated to competitive activities aimed at influencing public sector decisions, however. Economists have always distinguished between resources used to produce private sector goods and services and those used to produce goods and services that are consumed collectively, such as national defense and resources used by government agencies administering regulatory policies. Economists have also extensively analyzed problems of allocating the nation's scarce resources between private- and public-sector activities. In contrast, resources used to gain control over public sector decisions have received relatively little attention from economists. This is unfortunate, because the larger the share of the nation's resources expended on competition for the right to decide who shall bake the national cake, the smaller the share of resources remaining for the cake. Determining the optimal level of resources that should be devoted to political competition is no different, and no less important in principle, from determining the optimal allocation of resources between private and public goods and services. Unfortunately, neglect of this important issue can only be noted in this work.

(d) Nature and Sources of Information Underlying Demands

An individual's demands for regulation are based on that person's perceptions and expectations regarding effects of regulation. These perceptions will in turn reflect the person's own knowledge and experience and information obtained from a variety of sources. These sources include information provided by other individuals and interest groups who support or oppose particular types or effects of regulation. In this connection, legislators and regulators should not be omitted from the list of possible interest groups. Like members of any interest group, legislators and regulators may engage in activities that provide information about regulation and that may intentionally or unintentionally influence other people's demands for regulation. It is not sufficient, therefore, to assume that legislators' and regulators' interests and desires will be reflected in how they react to "given" demands for regulation expressed by other individuals and interest groups. To the extent that legislators and regulators provide information that influences other people's demands for regulation, the demand and supply sides of the political market for regulation will be interdependent. In addition to such interdependence, demands for regulation expressed by interest groups may also be interdependent in the sense that the nature and intensity of demands expressed by one group may depend in part on the nature and intensity of demands expressed by members of other groups. These interdependent preferences may be created, or reinforced, by information provided by interest groups attempting to influence other people's perceptions regarding the effects or other aspects of regulation.

The importance of information as an influence on people's perceptions of the effects and other aspects of regulation provides perspective for introducing one of the major characteristics and problems of regulation and human transactions in general, possible misrepresentation of information. If, by misrepresenting information, an individual expects to secure an outcome that is preferred to the expected outcome when the individual is truthful, misrepresentation may occur. Incentives for truthful revelation are not present in most existing transactions between individuals (see Chapter 12). As a result, the information provided by parties to many types of transaction will not reflect the parties' truthful evaluation of the situation the information describes.

Possible misrepresentation of information is not confined to regulated decision makers or to sellers engaging in market transactions. It can occur in private- or public-sector transactions and may be a characteristic of the behavior of regulators, consumers, voters, legislators, or any other type of decision maker. Once it is recognized that incentives for truthful revelation of information is a general problem that applies to all types of transaction, the next logical step is to attempt to identify the characteristics of these incentives for any given type of transaction. This search for so-called incentive-compatible characteristics of transactions between individuals is a relatively recent development, dating back little more than ten years in the economics literature. Original developments were associated with specific types of transaction, such as the demand-revealing process for public goods (Clark, 1971) and the Soviet incentive system for managers of factories (Weitzman, 1976). It is only relatively recently that a surge of articles in the economics journals has extended the search for incentive-compatible characteristics to other types of transaction, such as agent-principal relationships, auditing, and interdivision relationships within firms and other organizations (see references to Chapters 12 and 13). As a result, a general theory of incentive-compatible characteristics of transactions is beginning to develop, and many of the principles are directly relevant in a number of regulatory contexts (see Chapters 12 and 13). Failure to recognize and deal with possible misrepresentation of information by individuals has implications that are much broader than problems of regulation. To the extent that information is misrepresented, especially information regarding people's preferences and their revealed evaluations of the benefits and costs of aspects of their environment, such information is of limited value, either for descriptive analyses dealing with how people actually behave, or for normative analyses of how people should behave in order to achieve their objectives.

(e) Uncertainty and Expected versus Actual Effects

Even in the absence of any attempts to misrepresent information regarding the effects of regulation, the actual effects of regulation may differ from people's perceptions and expectations. This is not too surprising, since experts in the field of regulation often disagree on the effects of regulation, and even when they agree on certain effects, these effects are generally the result of a complex process that the average person could not be expected to understand without the expenditure of considerable time and effort.

If the actual effects of government regulation turn out to be different from the effects people expected and desired, they may revise their demands for particular forms and instruments of regulation and may even revise their choice between regulation and other approaches and instruments for achieving desired effects (e.g., cleaner environment, safer products). Existing analyses of regulation have generally omitted the influence of feedback of information regarding the effects of existing regulatory instruments on the process by which demands for regulation are formed.

When people do revise their demands for regulation, regulation becomes a dynamic process. In these circumstances, the effects of regulation are not only an output of regulation but, in addition, are also a major input into an evolving process where demands for regulation change through time as individuals and interest groups attempt to select regulatory and other instruments that achieve desired effects. In addition, if experience with existing regulatory instruments indicates that certain desired effects are not attainable, the desired effects that are the targets of regulatory policies may also be changed as time passes.

Regulation must be viewed as a dynamic process that results from people's attempts to improve their personal satisfaction in a world of uncertainty regarding the effects of regulatory and other instruments. The shift of emphasis from a static to a dynamic view of regulation increases the number of factors that are relevant in determining the characteristics of the regulatory process at any point in time. In addition to the desired effects that are the *targets of regulation,* such as cleaner air or safer products, and *regulatory instruments,* such as pollution and product safety standards, monetary and other types of penalties or rewards for violating or exceeding regulatory standards, and monitoring and enforcement policies of regulatory agencies, a third factor of importance must be added. Also relevant are the *disequilibrium adjustment rules* that describe the ways people react when information about the effects of existing regulatory instruments indicates that regulatory targets are not being achieved. These disequilibrium adjustment rules, together with the factors that underly people's choice of desired effects of regulation, are the two key aspects of human behavior that determine the dynamic time sequence of demands for, and actual effects of, regulation.

2.3   THE SUPPLY OF REGULATION: LEGISLATORS' AND REGULATORS' BEHAVIOR

In this section I briefly outline factors that are relevant in determining the supply of regulatory legislation and the manner in which that body of law is administered. The main objective here is to emphasize certain aspects of the supply side of regulation that are frequently overlooked.

At any given time, legislators will be faced with demands for regulatory legislation that will be expressed in various ways (e.g., votes, campaign contributions, and direct lobbying). In deciding how to respond to these demands, legislators will weigh the demands in terms of votes, campaign contributions, and the extent to which the demands conform to the legislators' personal concepts of the kinds of regulation that are appropriate. In most situations the response of a legislator will involve balancing different interest groups' demands rather than meeting the demands of a single interest group (see Chapter 5). Also, as noted in the previous section, the legislator is usually in a position to influence demands for regulation by providing information about the nature and effects of alternative types of regulation. The situation is therefore analogous to the ability of firms to influence consumer behavior and demands for their products by advertising activities.

The behavior of regulators who are responsible for administering regulatory laws is generally assumed to be relevant only after the passage of such legislation. It is a mistake to omit regulatory agencies as a potential influence on the behavior of legislators engaged in framing regulatory legislation, however, even in situations where the legislation creates a new regulatory agency and does not simply change the responsibilities and powers of an existing agency. Existing agencies will generally be affected by the behavior of a new regulatory agency in a number of ways. A new regulatory agency will be an additional claim on the government's overall budget, and some existing agencies may fear that this will result in a reduction in their budgets. They may attempt to reduce this possibility by trying to ensure that a new agency's responsibilities and powers, as defined in the legislation that creates the new agency, do not overlap with theirs. Existing agencies may also try to ensure that a new agency's area of responsibility is complementary to their own responsibilities, in the sense that an expansion in the new agency will lead to increased demands for the services of the existing agencies.

Still other possible relationships may be perceived by decision makers in existing regulatory agencies when a new agency is being contemplated at the legislative stage. No generalizations or conclusions in any particular case are possible without explicitly considering the goals and constraints that confront decision makers in existing agencies and their perceptions regarding the future behavior of the new agency. Yet it is clear that regulatory agencies may exert a significant impact on regulatory legislation. This impact may be exerted either directly on legislators or indirectly by providing information to individuals and interest groups who influence legislators' behavior. Owing to differences in goals and constraints facing individual existing agencies, one would not generally expect these agencies to adopt a common position on any new piece of regulatory legislation and to present a united "regulators' lobby."

Once regulatory legislation has been passed, it must be administered by a regulatory agency, and the determinants of agency behavior become the appropriate focus of attention in attempting to explain the manner in which regulatory constraints are created and applied in practice. In the existing literature, legislators' behavior is considered to be an important influence on regulatory agency behavior in connection with the budget allocation and monitoring of these agencies. There is considerable controversy, however, regarding the determinants and nature of legislators' budget allocation and monitoring activities and the implications of these activities for regulators' behavior. For example, even if legislators are motivated to spend time monitoring regulatory activities, they must often rely on information provided by regulators for purposes of determining effects of regulation and the costs of regulatory agency activities. As noted earlier, regulators may also be in a position to influence legislators' behavior indirectly by providing information to legislators' constituents or other interest groups. In these circumstances, some writers have questioned whether legislators can legitimately be considered to be a constraining influence on regulators' behavior.

Fiorina and Noll (1978), for example, have argued that a legislator's constituents who are affected by, or require the services of, certain regulatory agencies may use legislators as one method of trying to obtain information or action from the agency. Legislators who need a favorable response from a regulatory agency in order to provide "facilitation services" to their constituents and who are not members of the agency's legislative review committee may support rather than constrain an agency's preferred behavior.

Although generalizations are impossible without explicit examination of the goals and constraints of both legislators and regulators, two possible general forms of the relationship between their behavior may emerge, for any dimension of regulation. One possibility is that legislators' and regulatory agency decision makers' behavior is complementary in that an increase or decrease in some dimension of regulation will contribute to the goals of both. The other possible relationship is one in which an increase or decrease in some dimension of regulation will influence the goals of regulators and legislators in opposite directions. This second situation, which could be described as a competitive or adversary relationship between regulators and legislators, is the only one in which legislators' behavior can be said to constrain regulatory agency behavior, and vice versa. Even in this situation, however, the constraint need not be effective if the information on which either type of decision maker bases its behavior is an inaccurate description of the way the other type of decision maker behaves.

The literature has extensively examined the influence of the goals of regulatory agency decision makers, legislators' behavior, and various characteristics of regulated decision makers on the behavior of regulators and the kind of regulatory policies that will be adopted. In contrast, the influence of other regulatory agencies on the behavior of individual regulatory agencies has been virtually ignored. This situation may be changing, as indicated by articles like the one by McGuire, Coiner, and Spancake (1979) that consider the influence of introducing rivalrous agencies as a means of improving government sector performance. Even where monopoly agencies regulate different kinds of individual and business behavior, the behavior of other regulatory agencies cannot legitimately be ignored as a determinant of individual agencies' behavior. If attention is confined to regulation of business behavior, it is not difficult to understand why the behavior of individual regulatory agencies will generally be affected by other regulatory agencies' behavior. The characteristics of a firm's product, or any other dimension of the firm's behavior, that achieves the objectives of the firm's decision makers will depend on all the constraints that confront the firm. Different dimensions of a firm's behavior are interdependent; that is, a change in any single dimension of that behavior will generally also change the optimal level of other dimensions of the firm's behavior.

For example, if a regulatory constraint changes the price of a firm's product, the level of advertising that achieves the highest feasible level of the firm's goals will also usually be changed. If a second regulatory constraint is imposed on the level of the firm's advertising, this constraint will affect the demand conditions for the firm's product and will normally change the level of product price that achieves the highest feasible level of the firm's objective. Other areas of the firm's activities may also change. If a regulatory constraint fixes the price of a firm's product at a certain level, for example, the firm's decision makers may respond by reducing the amount of one or more of the inputs used to produce the product, resulting in a reduction in some features of the quality of the product. This change will effectively raise the price of a given quality of the product and violate the price regulation. To prevent such a situation, the regulatory agency responsible for regulating the price of the firm's product would have to step up its monitoring and enforcement activities in order to restore the appropriate degree of compliance of the firm with the price regulations. Even if the agency is temporarily successful, changes in the regulatory constraints administered by other regulatory agencies may alter the firm's behavior and the extent to which it is possible or profitable for the firm to comply with the price regulations.

The preceding examples emphasize that, whether individual regulatory agencies recognize it or not, the nature of the response of a regulated firm to any specific regulatory constraint will generally be influenced by all the other regulatory constraints that confront the firm. If individual agencies do not recognize and take into account the influence of other regulatory agencies, two types of situation may occur. If regulatory constraints administered by individual agencies are of the type that tend to work against, and offset, the efforts of other regulatory agencies to influence particular dimensions of firms' behavior, the result may be a divergent process of regulation. In other words, increasing efforts by individual agencies to regulate particular dimensions of business behavior may produce a situation in which firms' behavior departs increasingly from that which is desired by regulatory agencies. This result is not inevitable, however, and a convergent process is possible even in situations where the actions of individual agencies tend to offset the efforts of other agencies.

A second possibility is that regulatory constraints administered by different agencies might reinforce the efforts of other regulatory agencies to influence different dimensions of firms' behavior. Even in this case, however, it is desirable for individual agencies to recognize and to try to take these relationships into account; otherwise there will be a tendency for firms' behavior to overshoot the levels desired by individual agencies. In principle, the latter result can be just as undesirable as underattainment of regulatory targets in the form of desired characteristics of business behavior. For example, a product will exhibit "too much" safety, although the product exceeds regulatory standards of safety, if the resources that were used to bring the product's safety above the regulatory standard could have been used instead for other purposes that are more highly valued than the extra safety by consumers of the product and by members of society in general.

2.4 DESCRIPTIVE VERSUS NORMATIVE ASPECTS OF THEORIES

A theory, or model, of regulation is a set of propositions or hypotheses about how certain characteristics of regulation are related to each other and to other characteristics of the environment within which regulation occurs. The models people use when thinking about regulation may take the form of simple verbal or complex mathematical relationships. As noted in Section 2.1, many models of regulation exist in the literature, with differences in the number of variables, the nature of the relationships involved, and the implications and predictions associated with particular models. Even when participants in the regulatory process analyze their own behavior, their theories of regulation need not be accurate representations of either the causes or the consequences of that behavior, for reasons explained by Nisbett and Wilson (1977) and Argyris (1978). In these circumstances, it is helpful to outline considerations that are appropriate in choosing between different theories, models, and methodological approaches to regulation. A brief discussion of the appropriate criteria for theory or model choice and evaluation is much more than a matter of academic interest for anyone who is interested in understanding regulation. Choice of model will affect one's thinking about regulation and the nature of one's prescriptions for dealing with any regulatory issue.

One cannot evaluate a theory or model of regulation or any other phenomenon without reference to the purpose it is intended to serve. An incorrect model may serve the purpose of some individuals adequately if it is in their interests to mislead others concerning the nature and effects of regulation. In science it is widely acknowledged that a major purpose of theorizing and model building is to provide insights and information that improve our knowledge of processes that underlie observed phenomena in the real world. The set of hypothesized relationships that constitute any one model automatically implies a set of predictions about how the phenomenon under study will behave in specified circumstances. One can evaluate a theory or model by reference to how well its predictions are consistent with observed facts, or "data," in the real world. Indeed, scientists in many disciplines, and most economists, consider the predictive adequacy or accuracy of a theory or model as the main criterion for choosing and evaluating the theory or model. Milton Friedman's view (1953) that the goal of science is to discover hypotheses and models that predict well and that the realism of the assumptions of a model or theory is irrelevant has been the dominant methodological position in economic analysis for some time. The situation is now changing, however, as many economists recognize that Friedman's view is only one of many possible normative goals of economic analysis (Mason, 1980–81). A growing number of articles in economics journals have recently emphasized that the goal of science may include objectives other than prediction. For example, science may attempt to explain which one of a number of models with equal predictive adequacy is a more accurate representation of the process that actually underlies the predicted phenomenon. Caldwell (1980a) has emphasized that philosophers of science since the 1940s have been unanimous in their rejection of the notion that the only goal of science is prediction and that, from this perspective, the adherence of the economics profession to Friedman's methodology may be viewed as anachronistic.

The appropriate criteria for choosing and evaluating theories and models in science will vary with the assumed purpose of science, and this may differ among individuals, disciplines, and periods in time. The issue of how scientists choose among different methodologies, theories, and models was once the exclusive concern of philosophers of science but is now being considered by some economists. As a result, an improved understanding of the nature of and relationship between alternative methodological positions in economics, and between criteria of theory choice, is likely to develop in the economics profession. At present, there is still much confusion owing to a failure to define clearly the meaning of key concepts such as "predictive adequacy," "realism," "testability," "simplicity," "facts," and "truth" when discussing criteria of theory choice. Each of these terms has been used in many ways by different writers on the subject of methodology and theory choice; often, different concepts are incorrectly used as though they were interchangeable. For example, Caldwell (1980a) has pointed out that the terms "realistic," "testable," "empirically confirmed," and "true" are often confused in the literature.

"Predictive adequacy" really consists of a number of distinguishable criteria of theory and model choice, such as testability, degree of empirical confirmation, and criterion of empirical confirmation. "Testability" refers to the capability of a hypothesis to be subjected to test; "degree of empirical confirmation" refers to the extent to which a hypothesis is accepted or rejected by empirical testing. Empirical tests of hypotheses permit "the facts" to determine whether the predictions of a hypothesis, theory, or model are inconsistent with the facts and therefore whether the hypothesis should be rejected. The implicit notion that "the facts do not lie" is naive; we have already mentioned the problem of information distortion and the fact that it is an almost universal characteristic of transactions among humans. This incentive-compatible problem is being increasingly acknowledged in a surge of recent papers in the professional economics journals (see Chapter 12). If available facts distort the actual nature of phenomena they describe, it is a strange kind of logic that dictates that the facts should be the ultimate arbiter of models that attempt to explain reality.

In addition, to use the extent to which a model's predictions are consistent with "the facts" as a criterion of model selection leaves unanswered the ambiguity that exists regarding which facts are to be considered appropriate. Even in the absence of purposeful information distortion by individuals, facts, like beauty, are in the eye of the beholder, and different people's perceptions of the same situation may result in reports of completely different facts by those individuals. Ask any two persons to describe an automobile accident they have just witnessed!

Even if models of regulation were limited to empirically tested models, and there were no distortion of the data used to test the models, one would be left with a large number of models, some with conflicting predictions, yet all equally consistent with available data. Whether a given model will be rejected or tentatively accepted as consistent with the facts will depend on the choice of empirical data used to test the model's predictions, the choice of statistical methodology employed to transform the data into a form that may be compared with the model's predictions, and the choice of an inferential rule for accepting or rejecting the model. There is no objective way to determine which empirical data, which statistical methodology, or which inferential rule should be selected from a number of possible alternatives. Scientists and researchers adopt conventions, such as the convention of rejecting a model if there is more than a 1 percent, or alternatively more than a 5 percent, probability that its predictions will be inconsistent with the data. However, as Caldwell (1980a) has emphasized, a theory or model can be testable, empirically tested, accepted as inconsistent with the facts according to the inferential rule employed, and yet may not be a true representation of the process it purports to describe. Mayer (1980) has also emphasized major weaknesses in existing methods of testing hypotheses in economics.

The concept of "realism" can also be defined in a number of ways, with correspondingly different criteria of theory choice and evaluation. The term has been used to describe both the assumptions and the predictions of a theory. If the purpose of a theory is to describe how people actually behave, rather than to derive predictions regarding that behavior, the realism of the assumptions regarding the determinants of people's behavior may be an appropriate criterion of theory choice. It should perhaps be added that trying to make a model of human behavior correspond more closely to the way in which people actually make decisions may be very difficult, especially if they purposely distort their actual decision-making behavior. In contrast, if the purpose of a theory is to predict people's behavior, the realism of the behavioral assumptions may be irrelevant as a criterion of theory choice.

Considerable perspective on the problem of theory choice and evaluation can be gained by recognizing that theories and models have many characteristics and that the problem of theory choice is the problem of assigning weights to these various characteristics. Viewed from this perspective, the problem of theory choice is simply one instance of the general theory of human choice. Economists especially should have little difficulty in accepting the proposition that the appropriate weights, and criteria of theory choice, depend on the purpose or objectives of the theory or model. These objectives may often be much narrower than the purpose of science or of a particular discipline, and characteristics such as predictive adequacy or realism of assumptions may be appropriate criteria of theory choice and evaluation for some purposes. In addition, it is necessary to recognize that the weighting system and criteria of theory choice actually employed by an individual or discipline cannot be divorced from the constraints that determine the incentive system of penalties and rewards that face the researcher or members of a discipline at any point in time.

It is important also to understand the distinction between "descriptive" models and "normative," or prescriptive, models of regulation (or any other phenomenon). Descriptive models deal with "what is," normative models with "what ought to be." In the context of regulation, a descriptive model would describe the factors that determine the kind of regulation that actually exists, or the effects of existing or planned forms of regulation on individuals and on society. A normative model would describe the characteristics and effects that regulation *should* exhibit. The fundamental difference between the two types is that the normative model includes an additional "value system" or objective that is used to evaluate various effects of regulation predicted by the descriptive model (see Chapter 3). The main point to understand at this stage is that the use of different value systems results in different evaluations of particular effects predicted by any descriptive model. In other words, the benchmark that is used to describe what the characteristics of regulation "should" be depends critically on the value system or objective used to evaluate it. It is desirable that these value systems be made explicit and be displayed in a clear manner to enable one to evaluate any proposals for regulation or regulatory reform. Unfortunately, this prescription is rarely followed in practice, since it would often reveal too much about the real intentions of the persons making the proposals. One should always be suspicious of analysts who are reluctant to reveal the value system that is implicit in their conclusions and prescriptions.

Any normative model of human behavior is implicitly or explicitly based on an underlying descriptive model of the behavior being evaluated. In other words, in order to know what kind of regulation is best for achieving the maximum feasible level of a particular objective (e.g., maximizing the satisfaction of the community), it is necessary to take into account the constraints within which this maximization process takes place. It is especially necessary to know what determines the behavior of decision makers in the absence of regulation, since these factors will influence how they react to any set of regulatory constraints. Therefore, descriptive and normative models are closely related. Also, note that the distinction between normative and descriptive analysis is not confined to issues that confront society as a whole. In the case of a business firm, for example, managers interested in profit maximization, sales maximization, or any other goal need to know what kind of behavior is necessary to achieve these goals in order to evaluate either their own decisions or those of others within the organization.

In contrast to normative models, descriptive models are often described as being "value free," and many economists pretend — or actually believe — that their descriptive models are "purely scientific" and independent of ethical or normative judgments. This is not so, since the analyst chooses which problems he or she will investigate, the methodology employed, the nature of the constraints included or excluded from consideration, and so on. The analyst's values, perceptions, and personal constraints are involved in all these choices, and to suggest otherwise is misleading. We have already emphasized that the predictions of any model depend critically on the assumptions of the model, and in choosing to employ any given model the analyst is necessarily exercising his or her personal evaluations, as Tarascio and Caldwell (1979) have reminded us.

Even the fundamental assumption that individuals attempt to maximize their personal satisfaction, which is present in all orthodox economic analysis, has normative implications, as Brennan (1979) has pointed out. Any model that assumes that individuals try to maximize their satisfaction

will yield conclusions and predictions regarding what is "optimal" behavior by individuals and organizations that are different from the predictions yielded by a model that assumes some other kind of objective
is pursued by individuals. Utility maximization is a hypothesis regarding
how individuals actually behave and is not the only possible assumption
regarding human motivation. Kapteyn, Wansbeck, and Buyze (1979)
studied individual utility functions empirically and found evidence that
provided no support for the utility-maximization hypothesis and that
suggested that the adoption of an alternative satisficing hypothesis would
be more appropriate in models of individual behavior.

Value judgments are unavoidable in model selection. Ideally, value
judgments should be made explicit, and the sensitivity of a model's major
predictions to the choice of the underlying value system should be indicated, in order to permit proper evaluation of the model. As Brennan
(1979), Fusfeld (1980), and Elliot (1980) have emphasized, however, values
and normative elements also enter the process of descriptive economic
analysis and model building in a number of other ways and are often
inextricably related. For example, facts or consequences that are revealed
by descriptive analysis may subsequently become values if they are perceived to contribute to a desired objective. Also, people's value judgments
are the result of both knowledge and objectives, and these two elements
evolve together and continually interact and affect each other. For these
and other reasons cited by the authors just named, it may be difficult or
even impossible to separate descriptive and normative elements of a
model. The unavoidable presence of normative elements in models does
not, however, reduce the potential contribution of model building to
increasing knowledge and also to understanding and evaluating normative evaluation criteria and objectives themselves. It is failure to recognize normative elements in models, or failure to subject these elements
to critical examination and comparison with the implications of alternative normative criteria, that reduces model building's contribution to
knowledge and the development of human values.

We shall emphasize, on numerous occasions throughout this book,
the nature of the implicit value systems that underlie existing models of
regulation and will indicate the implications of alternative value systems.
The problem of choosing between value systems is one of the fundamental
aspects of the problem of regulation that, like the information distortion
problem, has been grossly neglected. It is futile to suggest that there is
one correct methodology, or model, for analyzing regulation. Such an
idea tends to breed inflexibility into people's thinking about any problem, and such a tendency already exists, since it is always easier to try
to apply one's existing knowledge and methodology to a problem than
to learn about new ways of approaching the problem. Unfortunately, at
present the many-model approach to problems is not carried far enough,
owing to time and other constraints that determine the incentive system
confronting researchers in most disciplines.

When one is considering existing descriptive and normative models of regulation, in addition to the influence of the perceptions and values of the analysts who engage in the process of model building and analysis, one must not overlook the environment in which these models are constructed and the system of penalties and rewards that confronts individual analysts. Even if we could define what is "ultimate truth" or "reality," it would be a mistake to assume that the competition of ideas among researchers would weed out bad models and reveal the implicit assumptions in all models, leading inexorably to the ultimate truth. Researchers are no different from any other type of decision maker; their research behavior and resulting types of competition will depend on their personal goals and the penalty-reward system they face. R. B. McKenzie (1979) has explained how competition for a fixed fund of faculty wages or promotions might lead to predatory rather than productive faculty behavior. In addition, Garner (1979) has emphasized that when publication is the primary signal of professional ability, research decisions may be biased toward orthodox, low-risk projects, denying science the bold hypotheses and vigorous competition necessary for significant advances in human understanding. L. V. Blankenship (1977) has pointed out that research done for paying clients will generally be influenced by a number of characteristics of the analyst-client relationship. The general problem of information distortion applies to researchers and their subjects, clients, or peers, no less than to other types of decision maker. Each party to a transaction engages in a complex game in which each seeks to influence the other party's behavior. The behavior of scientists and researchers may often exhibit many of the characteristics that result in "transactions failures" similar to the traditional reasons given for regulation mentioned in Section 7.2. The appropriate solutions to these problems are very similar, in terms of the kinds of incentive system required to elicit desirable characteristics of behavior on the part of researchers and regulated decision makers. The idea that researchers may just as legitimately be considered candidates for regulation as business or other types of decision maker will not go down well in the halls of academe and contract research. The idea that the scientific community or its sponsors alone are qualified to define the research agenda and that others must unquestioningly accept their choice of methodology and provide the needed resources is equally repugnant to many members of society.

Scientists and specialists concerned with human behavior and institutions are separated by disciplinary boundaries. To some extent, specialization is unavoidable, since it takes considerable time and effort to learn the methodology and literature in each discipline. However, specialization causes problems, since all dimensions of human behavior are linked and are often interdependent; that is, specific dimensions of behavior are influenced by other dimensions of behavior. Predictions made by individual disciplines regarding certain aspects of human behavior that ignore this interdependence may be erroneous. Disciplinary specialization is particularly troublesome if one is interested in understanding regulation, because the voters, legislators, regulators, and regulated decision makers whose behavior interacts to produce regulation and its effects are often the subjects of study in different disciplines, such as political science, economics, and law. Each discipline tends to ignore the results of the others' efforts, partly as a consequence of disciplinary methodological and language barriers. Even when members of one discipline attempt to deal with types of decisions and aspects of human behavior that are traditionally within the province of another discipline, they employ their own methodology. Economists have recently extended their methodology to studying aspects of human behavior such as voting, legislators' behavior, marriage, childbearing, and crime, areas traditionally reserved by other disciplines. Whether this extension will yield improved insights into human behavior in these areas remains to be seen. One thing seems clear, however: until members of different disciplines begin to learn about the methodologies of other disciplines, a significant opportunity for each discipline to understand and benefit from the others will be lost. The ability of individual researchers to carry the burden of acquiring interdisciplinary methodology and knowledge may be too great, and the existing incentives make it far easier for researchers to use their own discipline's methodology to publish and gain promotion than to cross disciplinary boundaries. The prospects for interdisciplinary research conducted by teams of researchers from different disciplines are brighter, but the incentives are still lacking that will produce such a development on any large scale. Efforts to understand and improve regulation will be slower if the interdisciplinary nature of many regulatory problems, and their solutions, are not recognized and adequately taken into account. The lack of suitable incentives required to speed our knowledge of regulation is, however, a special case of the general problem of regulating human behavior that this book attempts to clarify.

There is a close analogy between normative theories, or models, and "problems." A problem can be viewed as a situation that differs in some respects from what "ought" to be. Problems are therefore normative; they imply a value system or objective that is being used to compare two situations. Moreover, just as the predictions of any model depend on the exact nature of the assumptions of the model, the appropriate solution to any problem depends on how it is defined. It is just as easy to invent problems that do not exist in the real world as it is to build models that bear no relationship to the real world. Similarly, it is just as easy to define any problem in such a manner that the desired solution corresponds to the solution one prefers as it is to build a model that yields desired conclusions. It follows that there is a tremendous advantage to those who can monopolize the problem formulation stage in dealing with any given issue, since they can thereby obtain the solution they prefer, while appealing to "science" for a justification for the solution. One would therefore expect to find considerable competition among the various sides to any issue for control of the problem formulation stage. In practice, we do observe this, though the parties involved often take great pains to disguise this fact. Problem formulation, not problem solving, is the critical stage in dealing with any issue. Just as one should be skeptical of the suggestion that "we must let the facts decide," uncritical acceptance of a particular formulation of any problem should be avoided, even if it is formulated by "experts" in the field. Remember that the perceptions, value system, and reward-and-penalty system facing the experts will, in addition to their abilities, influence the way they formulate problems. If these prescriptions are ignored, at least be prepared to reach for your wallet or some other facet of your self-interest. Model building cannot be divorced from the list of means by which individuals and interest groups attempt to attain their respective aims.

CHAPTER THREE

Benefits of Regulation

3.1 EFFECTS AND EVALUATIONS OF REGULATION

Discussions and evaluations of regulation are frequently conducted within a cost-benefit framework. This is true not only at the relatively sophisticated level of analysis conducted by economists and other specialists; cost-benefit analysis also often occurs, consciously or unconsciously, whenever people think about regulation's effects on themselves or others. Whether one is for or against any form of regulation depends on a mental process of listing perceived "effects" of regulation and then evaluating them positively or negatively. "Benefits" are simply perceived effects of regulation that someone evaluates positively; "costs" are perceived effects of regulation that someone evaluates negatively.

The main purpose of this chapter is to clarify the methodology involved in cost-benefit analysis and to pinpoint aspects of this methodology that are critical to the conclusions reached by using such analysis. Cost-benefit analysis can be a useful tool for organizing one's thoughts and for clarifying complex issues. Unless the assumptions that underlie this technique are clearly understood, however, its use in any application may obscure more than it reveals. In the hands of unscrupulous individuals, it can become a subtle weapon for foisting their interests on others in the guise of a "scientific" or "objective" tool of analysis.

Following development of a general expository framework indicating the factors that underlie all benefit and cost evaluations of regulation, Section 3.2 will examine problems encountered in aggregating different effects of regulation and evaluations of those effects by different individuals. Section 3.3 explains the meaning of, and relationship between, "efficiency" and "equity" criteria for evaluating regulation and their relationship to benefit and cost concepts. The digressions involved in these sections are necessary because many of the issues connected with cost-benefit analysis are still controversial in the economics literature. Also,

40

this literature consists mainly of journal articles that focus on specific facets or applications of cost-benefit analysis. These articles do not provide a comprehensive framework — one that links all the factors that influence cost-benefit estimates in any application.

As we have noted, a cost-benefit approach to regulation involves two central elements: (1) a listing of certain effects of regulation and (2) an evaluation of these effects as costs or benefits. Table 3.1 summarizes such a process and typifies the kind of approach that is usually adopted in cost-benefit analyses in general. What is not obvious from the table is that any cost-benefit analysis involves a conscious decision regarding *which* "effects" and *whose* evaluations of those effects are included in the table. Effects of regulation are numerous and depend on whose perceptions are adopted. Even experts disagree about the nature and magnitude of these effects. These disagreements are based on differences in the models of regulation the experts believe to be accurate representations of reality. It must therefore be explicitly recognized at the outset that the outcome of any cost-benefit analysis will hinge critically on the decision of which effects to include in the table. For regulations affecting pollution, many other effects than those included in the table might be perceived to occur, and might be considered relevant by the persons performing a cost-benefit analysis of those regulations. For example, higher expenditures by regulated firms on pollution control equipment might have the additional effect of increasing research and development efforts by firms that produce pollution control equipment.

Even when different people perceive the same effects, their evaluations of them may differ in magnitude; and the same effect of regulation may

Table 3.1.   Evaluations of Effects of Regulation

	Regulatory Effects	*Benefit*[a]	*Cost*[a]
A	Pollution-control expenditures	—	\$ (firm)
B	Compliance-monitoring expenditures	—	\$ (regulatory agency)
C	Reduced pollution	Amount x (value) (community residents)	
D	Facility relocation	Reduced blight x (value) (residents)	Lost jobs x (value) (workers)
	Totals	\$	\$
	Net benefit-cost balance	?	?

[a] Relevant evaluations are indicated in parentheses.

be evaluated positively by some and negatively by others. In Table 3.1, for example, the relocation of a firm's facilities may be regarded as a benefit by residents who will experience reduced congestion and urban blight because a factory in their area is being relocated and as a cost by workers who will lose their jobs as a result of the relocation.

A change in the identity of the person or persons whose evaluations of particular perceived effects of regulation are taken into account will generally change the magnitude of the resulting benefits and costs. Therefore, to interpret any cost-benefit study of regulation properly, it is necessary to know *whose* evaluations of the effects of regulation were used. If a cost-benefit study originated from, or was paid for by, someone who stands to gain or lose from the results of the study, special caution is required in interpreting its results.

Table 3.2 is more useful than Table 3.1 in emphasizing the importance of whose evaluations of effects of regulation are adopted, for the outcome of any cost-benefit analysis. The top row of Table 3.2 lists the organizations and individuals whose evaluations of the effects of regulation could be considered in any cost-benefit analysis. Table 3.2 is also more general than Table 3.1; the first column of the table lists all possible effects of some dimension of regulation. Each element in the body of the table represents a specific person's (or organization's) evaluation of a particular effect of regulation. Effects that are evaluated positively are benefits (B), and effects that are evaluated negatively are costs (C), from the point of view of the party making the evaluation.

Some elements in Table 3.2 may be zero if individuals or organizations do not perceive certain effects of regulation or if a particular effect does not change the level of their satisfaction. In the third column of the table only the firm's pollution control expenditures attributable to regulation are evaluated by the firm's decision makers. In practice, regulation will also generally have effects on other dimensions of regulated firms' behavior, as explained in Chapter 11. Also, in principle, a firm's decision

Table 3.2.   Evaluations of Effects of Regulation

Effects of Regulation	Regulatory Agency	Regulated Firm(s)	Unregulated Firm(s)	Person 1	Person 2 ... Person n
A		C			
B	C				
C			B	B	B B
D				B	C
.					
.					
.					

makers could evaluate reductions in pollution (effect C) positively. For regulation of pollution control to be necessary, however, the benefits of reduced pollution to the firm's decision makers would have to be less than the pollution control expenditures.

Table 3.2 is compatible with a wide variety of models of the effects of regulation and with a broad range of criteria for evaluating those effects. Failure to use such a flexible and general expository framework would create a bias in readers' minds toward acceptance of particular models of effects of regulation or of particular value systems for evaluating those effects. This result is undesirable, since our purpose is to help readers to acquire the necessary mental tools to permit them to decide regulatory issues for themselves.

One can derive whatever conclusions one wishes from cost-benefit analyses of regulation merely by using those evaluation systems and models of effects of regulation that produce the desired results. This should serve as a caution to readers who might otherwise regard particular cost-benefit studies as providing definitive answers about an issue. As has been emphasized, the conclusions of any analysis can be properly interpreted only by focusing on the assumptions that underlie those conclusions. In the context of cost-benefit analysis, attention must focus on the choice of effects and evaluations employed.

Anticipated versus Actual Effects. Which effects of regulation and whose evaluations of those effects "should" be used in cost-benefit analyses of regulation or other aspects of people's environment? The answer depends on the purpose the analysis is intended to achieve. It is possible to use cost-benefit approaches to regulation either for descriptive purposes, such as describing the factors that underlie people's behavior and evaluations, or for normative purposes, concerned with problems of how people should behave. For example, it is the *anticipated effects* of regulation that are relevant in influencing people's initial support for, or opposition to, one type of regulation. People's evaluations of such effects will therefore underlie and determine the strength of their demands for, or opposition to, the regulation in question.

Actual effects of regulation may differ from anticipated effects. Regulation will generally have unanticipated effects on the behavior of regulated decision makers (see Chapter 11). In addition, effects of regulation on regulated decision makers' behavior will also ordinarily influence unregulated decision makers' behavior, so that the overall effects of regulation spread throughout the economic system like ripples from a stone thrown into a pond.

From the normative perspective of attempting to base public policies on actual rather than anticipated effects, the actual effects are the appropriate ones to include in Table 3.2. Actual effects of regulation will, however, also generally have implications for anticipated effects and for people's behavior. Whenever the actual effects of regulation are perceived to differ substantially from the anticipated effects, people will often revise their anticipations regarding the effects, benefits, and costs of regulation. Such a development results in a dynamic process of regulation, where anticipated effects change in the light of feedback of information regarding the actual effects of existing characteristics of regulation.

Revealed versus Subjectively Perceived Evaluations. The distinction between descriptive and normative purposes of cost-benefit analyses is also relevant to the choice of the appropriate evaluation criteria for Table 3.2. For descriptive purposes of understanding and explaining demands for regulation in practice, it is evaluations of effects of regulation that people *reveal* to policymakers and other members of society that determine the nature of demands for regulation. These revealed evaluations may differ from the *true subjective evaluations* if people think that over- or underestimation of the benefits and costs they subjectively experience from regulation's effects will be more likely to achieve their goals. One of the major problems of attempting to implement regulatory policies in accordance with people's true subjective evaluations of benefits and costs is that of devising incentives for people to reveal their true subjective evaluations (examined in Chapters 12 and 13).

It is important to recognize the possible existence of differences between people's subjectively perceived and their revealed evaluations and to realize that revealed benefit and cost evaluations are a tool individuals may use to advance their interests. Nonetheless, it is the revealed evaluations that are relevant for descriptive purposes of understanding the response and behavior of persons to whom these evaluations are revealed (e.g., legislators and regulators). In contrast, from the normative perspective of devising standards for evaluating legislators' and regulators' behavior, it is people's true subjective evaluations that are relevant.

These comments regarding unanticipated and actual effects of regulation, and revealed versus subjective evaluations of those effects, apply irrespective of whose evaluations of the effects of regulation (i.e., which columns) are adopted in Table 3.2. The final important question is *whose* evaluations of the effects of regulation should be included in the columns of the table. The answer to this question depends, in the final analysis, on whose interests are considered "relevant." Since individuals naturally consider their own interests to be relevant, and their evaluations of effects of regulation underlie their demands for regulation, the interests and evaluations of all persons who perceive themselves to be affected by a type of regulation should in principle be included in the table if it is used as a basis for describing people's actual behavior.

Economists have also generally adopted individual evaluations as the proper normative criteria for evaluating effects of regulation and consider that the evaluations of "all members of society" who are affected by regulation as appropriate for inclusion in the table. However, by (1) limiting individual evaluations to monetary benefit and cost concepts and (2) aggregating the monetary benefit and cost evaluations of different people, economists' traditional cost-benefit analyses in fact (a) rule out the evaluations of some people affected by regulation, (b) implicitly give greater weight to some people's evaluations than to others, and (c) frequently result in cost-benefit evaluations of policies that are not in the interests of the people whose interests are ostensibly taken into account.

These matters can be clarified within the framework of Table 3.2, since the cost-benefit analyses of traditional economic analysis are simply a special case of adopting certain evaluations and evaluation practices. The consequences of alternative possible approaches can easily be contrasted within the framework of the table. These alternatives may be more appropriate both for descriptive purposes of understanding people's behavior in practice and for devising appropriate normative standards for regulatory policies and regulators' behavior. Mishan (1980) has suggested that the evaluation concepts and methods employed by traditional economic analysis and cost-benefit analyses do not appear to be acceptable to a majority of people. This suggestion implies that there is little chance that economists' prescriptions for public policies that are based on the traditional evaluation methods will be adopted in practice.

3.2   PROBLEMS OF AGGREGATING EVALUATIONS OF EFFECTS OF REGULATION

To arrive at any kind of overall evaluation of any regulatory policy, the evaluations of different effects by different individuals and organizations, as depicted in Table 3.2, must somehow be aggregated. Aggregating the preferences and evaluations of individuals is standard practice in theoretical and applied economic analysis in general. The results of the following detailed examination of this practice therefore also have implications for a much broader area than regulation. The following discussion is divided into four sections that deal, respectively, with:

(a) valuing and aggregating effects perceived by an individual
(b) aggregating people's evaluations of effects
(c) valuing and aggregating effects that occur at different times
(d) interdependence between perceived effects and people's evaluations

(a) Valuing and Aggregating Effects Perceived by an Individual

The effects of regulation will generally influence an individual's satisfaction in a number of ways. Regulation may change the prices or other characteristics of a number of products the person buys or sells. Some of these effects may tend to increase the individual's satisfaction whereas others may tend to reduce it.

A person's evaluation of any aspect of regulation will depend on the perceived net impact of all the effects of regulation on the individual's satisfaction. This fact implies that there must be some means by which the different effects of regulation on the individual's satisfaction can be compared and aggregated. In other words, the individual's evaluations of effects of regulation depicted in Table 3.2 must be capable of being expressed in a common denominator, or "numeraire."

Two features of Table 3.2 require emphasis at this stage. First, the benefit (B) and cost (C) evaluations of effects of regulation can in principle be expressed in many ways (e.g., changes in satisfaction, money values, votes). Second, it is the vertical summation of elements in each column, representing a *particular person's* evaluations of *all effects* of regulation, that is relevant as a determinant of that person's overall evaluation of regulation and of his or her behavior in terms of support for, or opposition to, the regulation. Horizontal summation of the elements indicates the overall evaluation of a *particular effect* of regulation by *all members of society*. Although this aspect frequently receives attention in many cost-benefit studies, it is not relevant from the behavioral point of view of determining the support for or opposition to regulation, unless regulation has only one effect on every person whose evaluations are included in the table.

The change in a person's satisfaction as a result of any one effect of regulation is termed the "marginal utility" (MU) of that effect by economists. The marginal utility of any single effect of regulation cannot be expressed in any way that is operationally measurable, since the change in satisfaction experienced by any individual is a subjective psychological phenomenon. The *ratio* between the marginal utility of any two effects *is* operationally measurable, however, and has a precise meaning. If MU_A is the change in a person's satisfaction resulting from a change in some aspect of the person's environment (effect A), and MU_B is the change in the same person's satisfaction resulting from another change in the person's environment (effect B), the expression MU_A/MU_B represents the person's evaluation of effect A, measured in terms of the number of units of effect B that yield that person an amount of satisfaction exactly equal to the satisfaction the person gets from effect A. Similarly, the reciprocal of the preceding expression, MU_B/MU_A, measures the value of effect B, expressed in terms of the number of units of effect A, which the person in question considers "equivalent" to effect B, in terms of the satisfaction he or she experiences from the two effects.

If the marginal utilities of a number of effects of regulation on an individual are divided by the *same* marginal utility measure, the result will be a "value" for each effect, expressed in terms of a *common* measure of value. The separate effects of regulation on the individual can then be compared, or aggregated, using an operational measure of value. In principle, the MU of *any* aspect of the person's environment could be used as a numeraire for this purpose. For example, if the marginal utilities of each of the effects of regulation on an individual were divided by the MU of bananas, the value of each effect would be expressed in terms of a "banana equivalent." The banana equivalents, positive or negative, of the effects of regulation could then be aggregated to obtain a measure of the net change in satisfaction of the individual as a result of regulation. This net change would be expressed in terms of the number of bananas the individual considers equivalent to the net effect of all the effects of regulation on his or her satisfaction. Thus, measures of value expressed in money terms are by no means the only way in which people's evaluations can be expressed. Monetary measures of value result from a decision to use the MU of a person's money income instead of the MU of bananas, to express a person's evaluations in terms of a common measure of value. For example, $MU_A / MU_{money\ income}$ expresses the amount of money income a person considers equivalent, in terms of the satisfaction it yields that person, to a unit of effect A. The following general expression represents the money-income equivalent of the net change in a person's satisfaction that results from all the perceived effects of regulation on that individual:

$$\$Value = \frac{MU_A}{MU_{income}} \Delta A + \frac{MU_B}{MU_{income}} \Delta B$$
$$+ \frac{MU_c}{MU_{income}} \Delta C + \cdots + \frac{MU_n}{MU_{income}} \Delta_n$$

The MU ratios in this summation are the money-income equivalents of the positive ("benefits") and negative ("costs") changes in satisfaction experienced by a person as a result of a single unit of each type of effect of regulation, $A, B, C \ldots n$. The symbols $\Delta A, \Delta B, \Delta C, \Delta n$ are the number of units of each type of effect of regulation that affects that person's satisfaction. The change in satisfaction experienced by the person as a result of one unit of any particular type of effect of regulation must be multiplied by the number of units of that effect to obtain the total change in satisfaction resulting from that effect. The units of different types of effect of regulation themselves will not generally be commensurable. Thus, effect A may be a change in the price of a regulated firm's product, and effect B may be a change in pollution associated with production of the product.

"Putting a money value on everything" is sometimes viewed as a sordid activity, engaged in only by economists and other excessively mercenary individuals. We hope it is clear that whenever human evaluations of anything occur, the same valuation process is involved whether or not money income is used as the common denominator of value. For human evaluations of different factors to be comparable, they must necessarily be expressed in terms of a common measure of value. Use of money income or other monetary indexes to express evaluations is a widely adopted convention. Other indexes, such as bananas, could be used as a common measure of value; the point is that *some* common measure is needed in order to obtain operationally measurable human evaluations.

Two features of the evaluation of the effects of regulation should be noted with special care. One is that we are at present assuming that all effects of regulation occur in the same time period, so that the MU of money income in that time period is the relevant denominator that is used in the marginal utility ratios that express the monetary equivalents of the effects of regulation on the individual. If effects of regulation occur in different time periods, the MU of income in different time periods may differ, so that the person's evaluations of effects of regulation that occur in different time periods would no longer be expressed in terms of a common denominator, even though they would still be expressed in money terms. We shall deal with this problem in Section 3.2(c).

The second important aspect of this method of evaluating the effects of regulation is the obvious dependence of the evaluation on a person's perceptions of those effects and on his or her tastes and preferences regarding these effects. There is a tendency in economics and other behavioral sciences that emphasize the behavior of individuals to accept an individual's preferences as the proper ultimate source of evaluations. This means accepting the process by which people's perceptions and tastes are formed. If this process is influenced in any way by the aspects of the person's environment that are being evaluated, such as the free enterprise system, government, or regulatory institutions, people's evaluations are themselves in part determined by the object of the evaluation and are of dubious normative significance as a guide to individual or social actions. Thus, to search for normative criteria of evaluation, it becomes necessary to look beyond people's perceptions and preferences at any given time to the process that underlies and influences these perceptions and preferences.

(b) Aggregating People's Evaluations of Effects

Comparing and aggregating different people's evaluations of effects of regulation means comparing and aggregating elements along the rows of Table 3.2. Attention may be focused either on individual rows of the table (representing people's evaluations of individual effects of regulation) or on the vertical summation of each column (representing each person's overall evaluation of all the effects of regulation). As was noted at the beginning of Section 3.2(a), it is a person's overall evaluation of a policy that is relevant in determining his or her support for, or opposition to, the policy. However, this does not preclude the possibility that individuals may lobby for changes in the policy that are directed at particular effects of the policy.

People who evaluate a particular regulation negatively are likely to oppose it, and those who evaluate the regulation positively will favor it. These two groups may be willing to invest time and other resources in attempting to influence decision makers who decide whether or not the regulation will be implemented. Although individuals will not plan to use more resources for this purpose than an amount that is equivalent in value to the gains or losses they expect to result from regulation, it is possible for the total amount of resources used by all individuals in such efforts to exceed the difference between the total benefits and total costs of regulation. From a normative point of view, it may be appropriate to inquire whether there is a better solution to the problem of regulation. For example, could those who expect to experience reductions in satisfaction as a result of some aspect of regulation be compensated by those who stand to gain, or vice versa?

We have seen that evaluations of the effects of regulation by any individual can, in principle, always be expressed in monetary terms. Economists have also traditionally assumed that if it is possible for potential gainers from a policy to compensate potential losers in monetary terms, the policy is in the interests of "society as a whole." Conversely, if those who stand to lose from some policy could compensate potential gainers in monetary terms, the policy is assumed to be adverse from the point of view of society as a whole. To determine whether it is possible for potential gainers to compensate potential losers, economists have generally used the aggregated monetary evaluations of the effects of the policy by individual members of society.

This practice has been criticized for several reasons. It has frequently been pointed out that unless compensation of potential losers by potential gainers *actually occurs,* society as a whole cannot be said to be better off as a result of a policy that results in these anticipated gains and losses. Instead, some would gain and others would lose as a result of the policy. In practice, compensation rarely occurs when policies adversely affect some members of society. Unfortunately, this fact has not deterred generations of economists from engaging in cost-benefit analyses of policies and adding up different people's monetary evaluations of the costs and benefits of policies to decide whether the policies are in the interests of society as a whole.

Some economists believe that as long as the total monetary evaluations of benefits of a policy exceed the total monetary evaluations of the costs of the policy, it is possible for the potential gainers to compensate the potential losers and that any failure to implement compensation policies is a failure of political will rather than of economic analysis. Articles in economics journals (Boadway, 1974, 1976), have further clarified what some economists have always known, namely that a situation in which total monetary evaluations of the benefits of a policy exceed the total monetary evaluations of its costs does not guarantee that compensation of losers by gainers is *possible*. Nor is an excess of total monetary evaluations of benefits of a policy over total monetary evaluations of the costs of the policy *necessary* in some situation in which compensation of losers by gainers is possible.

These conclusions can be understood by reference to a simple example within the marginal utility framework. Suppose that it *were* possible to measure the change in a person's psychological satisfaction resulting from a particular effect of regulation and that increases or decreases in satisfaction could be measured in "utils" of satisfaction. The marginal utilities of the effect of regulating activity A and the marginal utilities of money income for two persons are shown in the following example. Person 1's marginal utility of the effect of regulation on activity A ($- MU_A$) indicates that person 1 experiences a decline in satisfaction owing to the effect of regulation on activity A.

Person 1

$$\frac{-MU_A}{MU_{income}} = \frac{-10 \text{ utils}}{1 \text{ util}} = -10 \text{ units of person 1's income that yield equivalent satisfaction to effect } A \text{ of regulation on activity } A$$

Person 2

$$\frac{MU_A}{MU_{income}} = \frac{5 \text{ utils}}{\frac{1}{3} \text{ util}} = +15 \text{ units of person 2's income that yield equivalent satisfaction to effect } A \text{ of regulation on activity } A$$

The example shows that person 1 experiences a reduction in satisfaction that he or she values as equivalent to a $10 reduction in income. Person 2 experiences an increase in satisfaction that he or she values as equivalent to a $15 increase in income. Obviously, the total benefits of the regulation of activity A are greater than the total costs. Yet, if activity A is regulated, person 2 experiences an increase in satisfaction equal to 5 utils of pleasure, while person 1 experiences a decrease in pleasure of 10 utils — a net reduction in the total satisfaction of society as a whole of 5 utils.

It may not be possible for person 2 to compensate person 1 despite the fact that person 2 values the change at $15 while person 1 values the change only at −$10. The reason for this is that *compensation involves a change in income* for both parties. When income changes, this change will generally alter the magnitude of MU_{income}, the amount of satisfaction a person derives from a change in income. This in turn will affect the monetary evaluation of the benefits or costs a person experiences as a result of a particular effect.

In this example, if person 2's MU_{income} remained unchanged at 1/3 util, a \$10 transfer of income from person 2 to person 1 would reduce person 2's satisfaction by $(10 \times \frac{1}{3}) = 3\frac{1}{3}$ utils. Similarly, if person 1's MU_{income} remained unchanged at 1 util, the \$10 increase in person 1's income would tend to raise person 1's satisfaction $(10 \times 1) = 10$ utils. On balance, person 1 would be no worse off, and person 2 would have experienced a net increase in satisfaction of $(5 - 3\frac{1}{3}) = 1\frac{2}{3}$ utils. In this case, compensation would be possible, leaving no member of society worse off. If MU_{income} of person 2 rose and/or MU_{income} of person 1 declined as income was transferred from person 2 to person 1 following the regulatory change, clearly, compensation may be impossible.

Changes in the MU_{income} that are responsible for creating the impossibility of compensation in certain circumstances despite an excess of the monetary evaluation of gainers' benefits over losers' costs may also create paradoxical situations. Prior to a policy change, monetary benefits can exceed costs; after the change, the monetary evaluations of benefits by gainers are less than the costs of the losers! In other words, gainers are estimated to be able to compensate losers before the policy change, and after the change losers are estimated to be able to compensate gainers for reversing the policy! The explanation, again, is the effect of the policy change on incomes and MU_{income}.

Some economists have suggested that to justify a policy change gainers must be able to compensate losers before the change, and after the change losers must not be able to compensate gainers for reversing the policy. But this argument misses the point: unless compensation actually occurs, some people lose; and the possibility of compensation cannot be determined by reference to the relative level of total monetary benefits and costs, either before or after a policy change.

Where does all this leave us in terms of evaluating any particular effect of regulation? Clearly, people's monetary evaluations of the benefits or costs of an effect will accurately reflect the relative level of satisfaction they experience as a result of that effect only if the MU_{income} is the *same* for different people. Conversely, by adding or comparing the monetary evaluations of an effect by different people, and using the resulting figures as a measure of people's aggregate or relative satisfaction, economists are implicitly assuming that the marginal utility of income is the same for different people.

If we rearrange the relationship between a person's monetary evaluation of any particular effect from

Person 1's monetary evaluation of one unit of effect $A = \dfrac{MU_A}{MU_{income}}$

to the expression

MU_A = Person 1's monetary evaluation of one unit of effect $A \times MU_{income}$

it can readily be seen that the change in satisfaction experienced by different individuals as the result of one unit of effect A (MU_A) will not be proportional to their monetary evaluations of the benefits or costs of one unit of effect A unless MU_{income} is the same for everyone.

The idea of employing monetary evaluations is itself not objectionable, provided that those evaluations of different people are weighted by their respective MU_{income}. Assuming that the MU_{income} is the same for different people is a convenient way of trying to avoid what economists call "interpersonal utility comparisons." This term means *direct* measurement and comparison of the change in satisfaction, or "marginal utility" of a particular effect itself, which is not possible. It is unavoidable, however, if one wishes to compare people's evaluations of anything. Moreover, as we shall demonstrate next, the fundamental problem (and the dimensions of its possible solution) is much broader than is suggested by concentrating on monetary evaluations and marginal utilities of income.

It was emphasized earlier in this section that the marginal utility of *any* item may, in principle, be used as the numeraire in expressing an individual's evaluations of different effects. Use of the marginal utility of money income is merely a convention adopted in traditional economic analysis. In comparing the evaluations of different people, a different numeraire than the MU_{income} is similarly permissible, such as "banana equivalents." Once again, however, if the evaluations are to accurately reflect different people's *satisfaction* from effect A, each person's banana valuations of effect A would have to be multiplied by the $MU_{bananas}$ for each person. If we knew that the $MU_{bananas}$ was the same for different people, we could forget about the MU of money in comparing people's evaluations of effect A or anything else! In fact, anyone who could discover an item that *everyone* derived the same amount of satisfaction from would become famous, for its use as a numeraire would permit direct comparison of people's evaluations of anything, expressed in terms of that item, as a guide to their relative satisfaction! Of course, the catch is that such a discovery would entail a direct comparison of the satisfaction, or utility, derived by different people from that item.

Since interpersonal utility comparisons are unavoidable if one wishes to measure and compare different people's evaluations of anything, the best way to proceed is to recognize this fact and make explicit instead of implicit assumptions about the marginal utility of income (or some other numeraire). People's monetary evaluations of any change in their environment *must* be weighted by some index of the relative level of their marginal utility of income if a reliable guide to the implications of that effect for their satisfaction is to be obtained. The fact that we might not know what the marginal utilities of money income are for different people is no different from the situation that usually exists regarding any other aspect of their behavior. We do not generally assume, without evidence, that some aspect of human behavior or taste is identical for everyone, and we should not do so in the case of the marginal utility of income.

To test hypotheses concerning the MU income of different people, data on income distribution and aspects of human behavior are required. As we shall explain in more detail in Section 3.3, economists have largely ignored income distribution issues. Explicit rather than implicit assumptions about MU_{income} of different people and groups, and a willingness to attempt to refine these assumptions on the basis of observed data, are necessary to improve normative cost-benefit studies of regulation or any other policies that affect more than one person.

Many individuals reject cost-benefit approaches to policy questions because of some of the deficiencies we have been discussing, and they might reject this approach even if the modifications we have indicated as necessary were made. Even a good analysis does not necessarily mean a generally accepted one, and as Williams (1972) has pointed out, many people reject imperfect approaches to a problem even if no perfect approach exists. Fundamentally, cost-benefit analysis is an exercise in setting out people's thought processes and evaluations systematically. It can be applied to enlighten or to obfuscate; it can be used as a learning device or as a device for clothing a predetermined set of conclusions. None of these aspects alone is sufficient to indict the methodology involved, and the same arguments that are often used as a basis for rejecting cost-benefit analysis could be applied with equal force to almost any aspect of the logical positivist tradition of scientific endeavor.

A sense of proportion is therefore needed when examining weaknesses of cost-benefit analysis such as the implicit assumption that the marginal utility of income is the same for different people. After one introduces various assumptions about the marginal utility of income, the major conclusions of the analysis need not necessarily be changed. Moreover, focusing on this assumption is rather like insisting that a skydiver wear a helmet when jumping sans parachute, because the evaluations of benefits and costs people reveal will often be misrepresentations of their true preferences (see Chapter 12). Introducing the kind of incentives that induce honest revelation of preferences and other information should logically take priority over empirical research that tries to determine how these evaluations are related to the respondents' marginal utility of income.

In viewing the cost-benefit technique of analysis, the crucial question is: What are the alternatives? We have pointed out that people who perceive themselves to be affected positively or adversely by a particular type of regulation may have incentives to engage in political activities designed to influence appropriate decision makers. One cannot simply assume that the results of such behavior will be superior, from anyone's point of view, to the results of efforts to determine, by means of cost-benefit analysis, whether some compromise solution might be preferred by all parties affected by regulation. The parties involved may well expend more resources on political competition designed to influence regulation than would be necessary if a cooperative cost-benefit analysis of the actual effects of regulation were undertaken.

(c) Valuing and Aggregating Effects
That Occur at Different Times

If the effects of regulation occur at different points in time (as is generally the case), a number of additional considerations are relevant in valuing these effects, even when attention is confined to a single decision maker's valuations of them. This is so because (1) the marginal utility of money income may be different in different time periods and (2) the individual's valuation of a specific change in satisfaction may vary with the time at which the satisfaction occurs. The way these two complications should be handled can be explained by reference to the following expression representing the monetary value of regulation's effects on an individual:

$$\$\text{Value} = \frac{MU_1}{MU_{Y1}} \cdot \Delta 1 + \frac{MU_2}{MU_{Y2}} \cdot \Delta 2 + \frac{MU_3}{MU_{Y3}} \cdot \Delta 3 + \cdots \frac{MU_n}{MU_{Yn}} \cdot \Delta n \quad (1)$$

As before, the numerators MU_1, MU_2 ... MU_n show the actual changes in the person's satisfaction owing to the effect of regulation of some aspect of the individual's environment. The only difference is that these changes in satisfaction are now assumed to occur at different periods of time instead of during the same time period.

By dividing the change in satisfaction resulting from regulation's effect in any given time period, i, by MU_{Yi}, the marginal utility of income in that period, a money value measure of the benefits or costs of the effect of regulation in that period is obtained. In contrast to the cases discussed in Sections 3.2(a)(b), however, these terms cannot simply be added together to obtain an accurate measure of the total effect of regulation on a person's satisfaction. For one thing, doing so implicitly assumes that $1 of income in any period yields the same satisfaction to the person as $1 income in any other period, so that $MU_{Y1} = MU_{Y2} = MU_{Y3} = MU_{Yn}$.

If the marginal utility of income differs in different periods, a $1 money valuation of satisfaction experienced in one period implies a different amount of satisfaction, or utility, from a $1 money evaluation of satisfaction experienced in another period. In order for monetary evaluations of satisfaction experienced in different periods to reflect satisfaction experienced in different periods accurately, a numeraire that will make it possible to express the monetary evaluations of satisfaction in different periods in terms of a common measure of value is needed.

The problem is exactly analogous to that involved in aggregating valuations of different effects of regulation discussed in Section 3.2(a), and the solution is similar. In principle, the marginal utility of income in *any* period could be used as the numeraire, but we shall use the marginal utility of income in the first period, MU_{Y1}, in illustrating the principle involved: each of the terms in expression (1) would be divided by MU_{Y1}, and the resulting expression for each period would be a monetary expression of the change in satisfaction experienced in that period, *expressed in terms of a period 1 income equivalent.* This can be understood more easily by recognizing that, for example,

$$\frac{MU_2 / MU_{Y2}}{MU_{Y1}} = MU_2 \times \frac{MU_{Y1}}{MU_{Y2}}$$

and the expression MU_{Y1}/MU_{Y2} is the number of units of income in period 2 that are equivalent to a unit of income in period 1, in terms of satisfaction yielded to the individual. Multiplying this last expression by MU_2 therefore yields a money value measure of the change in the individual's satisfaction in period 2, expressed in terms of a period 1 income equivalent.

This adjustment *only* takes care of the problem of allowing for differences in the marginal utility of income in different periods. Although the resulting monetary measures of satisfaction in each period are expressed in terms of a common measure of value, they *still* cannot legitimately be added together. To do so would be to assume implicitly that a unit of satisfaction experienced in any period of time is valued exactly the same by the individual, no matter when that unit of satisfaction is experienced. As has been indicated, this assumption is not generally true of most individuals. The method of dealing with this problem is analogous to that involved in any "investment-type" decision where the effects of the decision are spread over a number of periods into the future. Each of the future anticipated effects is "discounted" and expressed in terms of a common "present value." In the finance and capital-budgeting literature, this present-value calculation is usually expressed as follows:

$$\text{Present value} = \frac{F_1}{(1 + d)^1} + \frac{F_2}{(1 + d)^2} + \frac{F_3}{(1 + d)^3} + \cdots + \frac{F_n}{(1 + d)^n}$$

where $1/(1 + d)^i$ is the "discount rate" that must be applied to the effect that occurs in the ith period of time. In terms of this example, the F's would be the monetary values of changes in satisfaction caused by effects of regulation that occur in each time period, expressed in terms of period i income equivalents. The expression $(1 + d)^i$ is equal to MU_1/MU_i, which represents the number of units of satisfaction in time period i that are regarded as being equivalent to one unit of satisfaction in period 1 by the decision maker whose evaluations are being considered.

In the finance and capital-budgeting literature $(1 + d)$ is usually assumed to be greater than one, indicating that money expected in the future has a smaller present value. This is so because the decision maker is assumed to be able to borrow or lend money at a positive interest rate. When dealing with individual and consumer behavior it is also generally assumed that people will prefer a unit of satisfaction now to a unit of satisfaction in the future, so that the expression MU_1/MU_i is also greater than unity. Such positive "time preference" is not always an accurate representation of human behavior; individuals may sometimes prefer a unit of satisfaction at some time in the future to a unit of satisfaction now.

If the reader is wondering what all this has to do with regulation, it should be noted that almost every type of regulation has effects that occur in a number of time periods. Valuing these effects on any individual's satisfaction is unavoidable if one wishes to determine whether the regulation "benefits" or "costs" the individual. Conversely, although it is not always either recognized or explicitly acknowledged, the use of any discount rate $(1 + d)$ in discounting the future benefits and costs of regulation automatically implies an assumption about MU_1/MU_t, the rate at which individuals are willing to trade satisfaction in different periods.

In the area of public health and safety, regulation even has effects on the expected length of an individual's lifetime. In such cases, in order to value regulation's effects, it becomes necessary to value human life itself! What, for example, is the value to an individual of an increase in the probability of living to a certain age? In principle, the answer depends on the individual's evaluation of the increased satisfaction he or she expects to experience by living until that age.

This evaluation of the benefits from greater life expectancy depends in part on the constraints that person faces, including the costs of increasing the probability of living longer. Contrary to popular notions of mortality, the value of human life is not infinite; most of us cannot afford that sum to extend our life expectancy, and many of us would not want to do so even if we could. For example, if longer life could be guaranteed as a result of complete abstinence from smoking, drinking, and sex, we would not observe everyone abstaining from these activities. As Thomas Schelling (1978) has reminded us:

Everybody behaves like two people, one who wants clean lungs and long life and another who adores tobacco, or one who wants a lean body and another who wants dessert. The two are in a continual contest for control; the "straight" one often in command most of the time, but the wayward one needing only to get occasional control to spoil the other's best laid plan.

The preceding examples illustrate an important point. In valuing human life, length of life is not the only variable that affects individual satisfaction. The amounts of satisfaction derived from consumption, leisure, and even work activities are also important to most people. Some individuals may even prefer to "live dangerously and die young." Even those who prefer a more moderate approach to living may consider the timing of their consumption, leisure, or work activities just as important as the total lifetime amounts of these activities. This possibility is totally ignored by the conventionally accepted formula for calculating the present value of a stream of future effects that was outlined earlier. As I have explained elsewhere (Needham, 1978), this formula implicitly assumes that decision makers performing the evaluations wish to maximize the total terminal value of the stream of future effects without regard to the timing of those effects.

To date, many cost-benefit studies that attempt to measure the value of human life are generally based on models of human behavior that ignore important aspects of the objective function that describes the factors that people derive pleasure from, and the constraints within which they attempt to maximize the pleasure they derive from life. As a result, many existing models and empirical estimates of the value individuals place on human life are unreliable guides for private or public policy decisions (Linnertooth, 1979; Lane, 1978).

(d) Interdependence Between Perceived Effects and People's Evaluations

Differences in perceived effects of regulation, and in people's evaluations of them, are both relevant in explaining why different members of society often differ in their attitudes toward, and evaluations of, regulation. Although the perceived effects of regulation and the evaluation of these effects may be distinguished conceptually, in practice they are often related and are jointly determined by the personal goals and constraints that confront the person making the evaluation.

For example, the marginal utilities of income in the denominators of the following monetary evaluation of the effects of regulation by an individual are not usually independent of the effects of regulation, listed in

$$\$V = \frac{MU_A}{MU_{income}} \cdot \Delta A + \frac{MU_B}{MU_{income}} \cdot \Delta B + \frac{MU_C}{MU_{income}} \cdot \Delta C +$$
$$\cdots \frac{MU_n}{MU_{income}} \cdot \Delta n$$

the numerator of each ratio. This can be explained by reference to an example where regulation's effects are on the prices of several goods consumed by the individual. The precise order in which these prices are changed will determine the resulting path of the individual's consumption and real income, or purchasing power of income, through time. Changes in the level of the individual's real income will generally affect the magnitude of the marginal utility of income, which in turn is used to express the monetary equivalent of the changes in satisfaction resulting from changes in the quantities of goods and services the individual consumes.

This means that a *different* monetary evaluation of the total change in satisfaction resulting from a particular set of price changes attributable to regulation will result from differences in the time sequence of the price changes! See Burns (1963), Mohring (1971), and Silberberg (1972) for a fuller discussion of this "path dependence" characteristic of evaluations of any combination of effects on an individual's satisfaction.

Since there can be no evaluation of a change in satisfaction from effects of regulation without assuming a particular order or sequence of these effects, any evaluation of regulation's effects must include consideration of the time path of those effects. This means abandoning what economists call "comparative static" methods of analysis, which focus only on "equilibrium" changes in the variables under analysis, and adopting disequilibrium methods of analysis. Disequilibrium analysis considers the time path of variables as they move from one equilibrium position to another.

For present purposes, it is sufficient to note that this disequilibrium analysis requires an additional set of assumptions to those of comparative static analysis, which deals with decision makers' objectives and constraints that affect their equilibrium behavior. This set of assumptions describes the way decision makers adjust their behavior when their objectives are not being met. In terms of the present analysis, these "disequilibrium adjustment rules" will determine the order in which the various "effects" of regulation occur in any given setting. As already explained, this will influence the magnitude of the marginal utility of income measures in the expression that describes the value of these effects to an individual or a group.

Another type of interdependence occurs whenever the changes in satisfaction associated with particular effects of regulation represented by the MU_A, MU_B terms in the numerator of valuation equation (p. 57) are related to each other. Whether this occurs will depend on the precise form of the preferences or "utility function" of the evaluator. For example, if the person's satisfaction is related to the level of A and B in the manner

$$\text{Total satisfaction} = U = aA + bB + \cdots$$

the change in satisfaction owing to a one-unit change in effect A will be a. In this case, MU_A will not be related to MU_B, which equals b. If, instead, the person's preferences are described by the relationship

$$\text{Total satisfaction} = U = A^S B^{(1-S)}$$

it can easily be demonstrated that

$$MU_A = \frac{S \cdot MU_B}{(1 - S)}$$

In this last case, the magnitudes of MU_A and MU_B are interrelated, owing to the form of the decision maker's preferences. This distinction between a situation in which the marginal utilities of different effects of regulation are additive, and a situation where the marginal utilities are interactive, is not necessarily explained only by the features of the decision maker's preference function; it can also result from other constraints confronting the decision maker. This is analogous to the distinction between complementary and substitute goods on the "demand" and production or "cost" side in traditional economic theory.

3.3   EFFICIENCY AND EQUITY
BENEFIT CONCEPTS

This section will clarify the meaning and relationship between concepts of "efficiency" and "equity," and the implications of these concepts for analyses of the effects and evaluations of regulation. Each concept can be defined in a number of ways, and the issues involved in attempting to apply them are quite complex. Fortunately, Table 3.2 provides an expository framework capable of integrating efficiency and equity concepts and of indicating the consequences of adopting various definitions of equity for evaluations of regulation and other public policies.

The equity, or fairness, of private and public policies often dominates discussions of their desirability; yet these terms are rarely defined, and until relatively recently economists themselves have attempted to avoid issues of equity. Some economists continue to insist that distributional and equity aspects of private and public policies are outside their professional domain and should be left to the "political system." They are wrong on all counts, as will be demonstrated. Efficiency and equity are unavoidably related in all evaluations of private and public policies, including the formal evaluation framework of cost-benefit analysis.

Economists have professional expertise in the determination of distributional consequences of private and public policies and in pointing out the implications of using different equity concepts in private and public decision making. The economist of course has no right to impose his or her value judgments regarding which equity concepts and resulting distributional weights *should* be used in evaluating these policies. Yet, leaving such judgments to the "political system" of decision making does not guarantee that the political decision makers' equity concepts will in any sense be improvements over the economists' concepts. This is especially true if the political decision makers — whether voters, lobbyists, legislators, or bureaucrats — are unaware of the implications of using particular equity concepts in their own decision making. In such circumstances, even "self-interested" equity concepts need not produce results that are in the decision makers' own interests.

The fundamental reason why it is necessary to study equity concepts, and their implications for people's evaluations and behavior, does not rest on controversial normative issues connected with these concepts.

Rather, it is necessary because these concepts undoubtedly *do* in practice influence people's evaluations of private and public aspects of their environment. If models in behavioral science are to explain real-world human behavior, then distributional considerations and their associated equity concepts must be included in those models. As we shall see, the means of accomplishing this are already available in existing methodological approaches in economics and the behavioral sciences. The medicine is less painful than one might imagine from all the furor about whether or not it should be taken. The results may not please everyone, however, because analysis of distributional considerations makes explicit many value judgments that are hidden by current approaches to private- and public-policy analyses. Yet, it is these value judgments that motivate and guide people's behavior, and exposing them can only improve our understanding of human behavior.

Traditional Efficiency Concept. In Table 3.3, which is an amended version of Table 3.2, only the evaluations of effects of regulation by individuals are represented by the columns, for expository convenience. The elements in the row of Table 3.3 labeled $(B - C)_i$ indicate the algebraic sum of the positive benefit and negative cost evaluations in each column. As already explained, this sum represents a particular individual's overall evaluation of the net benefits or costs that result from all the effects of regulation.

If the benefit (B) and cost (C) evaluations in the body of the table are expressed in *monetary* terms, it is necessary to multiply a person's monetary evaluations of the net benefits of regulation $(B - C)_i$, by that

Table 3.3. Evaluations of Effects of Regulation

Effects of regulation	*Person 1*	*Person 2 ...*		*Person n*	
A	B	B		C	
B	B	C		C	
C	B	C		B	
.	.	.		.	
.	.	.		.	
.	.	.		.	
$(B - C)_i$					$\dfrac{\Sigma (B - C)_i}{\Sigma s_i}$
MU_{Yi}	MU_{Y1}	MU_{Y2}	. . .	MU_{Yn}	
s_i	s_1	s_2	. . .		

person's marginal utility of income to obtain a measure of the change in *satisfaction* experienced by that person, as explained in Section 3.2(a). Each element in the row of Table 3.2 labeled MU_{Yi} indicates the marginal utility of income of the person whose evaluations are contained in the corresponding column.[1] Each element in the row of Table 3.2 labeled s_i indicates the change in satisfaction experienced by an individual as a result of all the effects of regulation.

We are now in a position to explain the meaning of efficiency and equity concepts and to relate them to Table 3.3. Economists have traditionally evaluated a wide range of private and public decisions by reference to three efficiency concepts termed, respectively, "allocative," "technical," and "distributive" efficiency.[2] In terms of Table 3.3, the allocative efficiency concept is concerned with the level of $\Sigma (B - C)_i$, the *summation* of monetary evaluations by different members of society of the effects of regulation or other policies. If total monetary benefits of regulation or some other policy exceed total monetary costs of that policy, traditional economic analysis concludes that the policy has "positive net benefits" and is "in the interests of society."

Traditional analysis recognized that some individuals might experience reductions in satisfaction from a particular policy and that some of the $(B - C)_i$ evaluations in Table 3.3 might be negative. But, as explained in Section 3.2(b), most economists assumed that as long as total net monetary benefits to society, $\Sigma (B - C)_i$, is positive, it is possible for gainers to compensate losers, so that no one need suffer as a result of the policy and some people gain. More recently (Boadway, 1974, 1976) it has been recognized that a situation in which $\Sigma (B - C)_i$ is positive does not guarantee that compensation of losers by gainers is possible, nor would it be necessary in some situations in which compensation would be possible. It is quite possible for the aggregate level of satisfaction experienced by members of society to decline even though $\Sigma (B - C)_i$ is positive!

Importance of Marginal Utilities of Income. The key to understanding the preceding conclusions is provided by the row of Table 3.3 that indicates the marginal utilities of income of different individuals. These terms refer to the change in satisfaction experienced by a person as the result of a one-unit change in that person's income. Like the changes in satisfaction due to all effects of regulation indicated by the s_i row of the table, these subjective and psychological indices of a person's welfare are not

---

[1] If effects of regulation and changes in people's satisfaction occur in different time periods, it was explained that monetary evaluations of these changes in satisfaction must be multiplied by a "discount factor" $1/(1 + d)^n$ in addition to marginal utilities of income. For expositional convenience we shall ignore such complexities, since they do not change the major conclusions of this section.

[2] Detailed treatment of the logic that underlies these efficiency concepts is contained in Chapter 6.

directly measurable. Despite this, the use of different people's monetary evaluations of benefits and costs of any policy as a guide to changes in their satisfaction *necessarily involves the use of implicit or explicit assumptions about the magnitude of these marginal utilities of income.*

In addition, only if MU_Y is the same for different people will monetary benefit and cost evaluations accurately reflect the relative magnitude of changes in satisfaction experienced by different people. If MU_Y is not the same for different people, it is clear from Table 3.3 that in a situation with larger MU_Y weights for people with negative $(B - C)_i$ evaluations than for people with positive $(B - C)_i$ evaluations, this could result in changes in satisfaction in the s_i row that add up to a negative figure for $\Sigma\, s_i$, *despite* the existence of a positive figure for the sum of monetary benefits and costs $\Sigma\, (B - C)_i$.

The use of people's monetary evaluations of benefits and costs as a guide to people's satisfaction *automatically* implies the assumption that the marginal utility of income is the same for different people. For a long time, many economists assumed that they could avoid making direct comparisons of changes in satisfaction experienced by different people by using these monetary evaluations. Such "interpersonal utility comparisons" are unavoidable, however, and take the form of implicit assumptions about marginal utilities of income whenever monetary evaluations alone are used.

The next crucially important point is that, whether or not marginal utilities of income are the same for different individuals, the use of MU_Y's as weights for monetary evaluations *implicitly accepts the distribution of income between different individuals that prevails at the time the monetary evaluations are expressed.* The change in satisfaction any individual experiences as a result of a one-unit change in income will generally depend on the level of that person's income, and perhaps also on the person's income relative to that of other individuals. In fact, accepting people's monetary evaluations of benefits and costs implies accepting much more than the prevailing distribution of income; it also implies acceptance of *every other aspect* of people's environment that underlies their monetary evaluations.

The strange logic of evaluating all policies that change the status quo solely by reference to evaluations that implicitly accept the status quo will not escape the reader as easily as it has escaped many economists. *Some* basis of evaluation has to be used, admittedly, but the status quo is not the only alternative available. One might argue that since we are essentially interested in whether the status quo can be improved, it represents a justifiable basis for evaluations. However, as was explained in Section 3.2(b), a policy that looks like an improvement before it is implemented may look like a deterioration afterward, owing to a change in factors that underlie evaluation criteria, such as the distribution of income.

It is often claimed that because traditional economic analysis aggregates the monetary benefit and cost evaluations of different people without regard to how those benefits and costs are distributed between them, it *ignores* equity and distributional implications. It would be more accurate to say that by using monetary evaluations that reflect the prevailing income distribution, and by making implicit assumptions about the magnitude of different people's marginal utilities of income, *traditional economic cost-benefit analysis implicitly adopts a particular system of distributional weights attached to different people's evaluations.* Any notion that the traditional allocative efficiency criterion is value free is clearly inappropriate and should be discarded.

Once it is recognized that the use of people's monetary evaluations of benefits and costs implicitly accepts the prevailing distribution of income between individuals and necessarily involves implicit interpersonal comparisons of the marginal utility of income between different people, the stage is set for incorporating explicit distributional and equity considerations into benefit-cost analyses of regulation and other policies.

Distribution of Benefits and Costs. Before turning to the normative issue of equity concepts, it is necessary to clarify what is meant by the term "distributional considerations" of regulatory and other policies. This term encompasses a number of different characteristics of Table 3.3. Most people who talk about the distributional effects of government or other policies are referring to the distribution of benefits and costs of those policies among different individuals or groups of individuals. This means focusing attention on the distribution of the B and C elements between the columns of Table 3.3, instead of looking only at the summation of the elements $\Sigma (B - C)_i$ representing the net benefits to society.

There are several reasons for being concerned with the distribution of benefits and costs among individuals. One reason is that the net benefit figure for each person $(B - C)_i$, must be weighted by that person's marginal utility of income in order to compare the effects of a policy on the relative amount of satisfaction experienced by different people. A second reason is that this same figure represents the income equivalent of the change in satisfaction experienced by the person as a result of the policy. This change in income will therefore imply a corresponding change in income distribution, and possible changes in the MU_Y of different people. Third, the sign and size of the net benefit figure for each individual will influence the direction and magnitude of the individual's political activities designed to support or oppose the policy change in question.

For all these reasons, it is not surprising that the existing literature that considers distributional implications of policies has focused on *income distribution* implications. This perspective does not cover all the distributional aspects of regulatory or other policies however. The

$(B - C)_i$ row in Table 3.3 includes for each person only a single benefit, cost, or zero figure that indicates the net effect of the policy on any individual's satisfaction. This net effect is determined by the benefits and costs of all the effects on the individual's satisfaction listed in the column that corresponds to the individual's evaluations.

These individual effects of regulatory or other policies on a person's satisfaction cannot possibly be inferred from the net benefit figure $(B - C)_i$ alone. It would not tell us, for example, whether a person who experiences a net benefit experiences any costs, or whether a person experiencing a net cost enjoys any benefits. Similarly, a zero net benefit is compatible with innumerable benefit and cost levels of equal size experienced by the individual whose net benefit is zero. For these and other reasons, information on the distribution of benefits and costs of individual effects between different persons (indicated by each row in the table) and the distribution of these effects for any particular person (indicated by each column of the table) may be very important.

For example, although an individual's support for, or opposition to, a policy depends on the net effect of the policy on the person's satisfaction, some of the policy's effects may be more important than others. Changing certain aspects of the regulatory policy measure may eliminate or reduce certain cost effects on a person's satisfaction, so that a person who has opposed a policy may switch and support it. In contrast, the elimination of some effects may not be pivotal, in the sense that they turn a policy measure that creates net costs for an individual into one that creates net benefits, or vice versa. When combined with information regarding the costs of changing some features of a policy measure, information on the benefits and costs of individual effects of the policy may be useful in improving the degree of the policy measure's acceptability.

Alternative Concepts of Equity. So far, we have dealt almost exclusively with purely *descriptive* aspects of the distribution of the benefits and costs of effects of regulatory or other policies. "Equity" is a *normative* concept, and equity issues are concerned with the question of how these distributional effects "should" be weighted. An evaluation of the equity of a regulatory or other type of policy involves a comparison of the observed distribution of its benefits and costs among individuals and some normative standard of desirable or "fair" distribution of them. Actually, in the descriptive analysis of distributional considerations we have already encountered an equity concept that is so well disguised that it has eluded many people, including some economists, for a long time. This is the notion that people's monetary evaluations of the benefits and costs of a policy's effects on them should be weighted by their marginal utilities of income. As has been explained, such weighting is necessary if correct estimates of the changes in different people's satisfaction are to be obtained; it has also been emphasized that the marginal utility of income weights implicitly accepts the distribution of income that underlies those weights.

Useful perspective may be gained by viewing all equity considerations as an additional set of weights that are introduced to the evaluation of the effects of regulatory or other types of policy. *These weights take the form of an additional weight that is used to multiply every benefit and cost coefficient in Table 3.3.* For example, in the case of marginal utility of income weights, every coefficient in each row is multiplied by the same weight, corresponding to that person's marginal utility of income. Other equity concepts may involve different weights for different coefficients in each row, or zero weights for some coefficients. If people's monetary evaluations were entirely rejected — perhaps on the ground of rejecting income as an appropriate index of people's evaluations — only the equity weights would remain in Table 3.3. In this case, equity considerations alone would determine evaluations of the effects of particular regulatory or other policies, and efficiency considerations as traditionally defined would be given zero weight.

If one observes evaluations of public policies in practice, it is very clear that economists' efficiency considerations are often ignored in these policies' evaluation. In other cases, efficiency and equity considerations are combined. As these examples suggest, the framework of Table 3.3 may be used as a basis for trying to infer which kind of weights were implicitly used in evaluating and deciding on particular private or public policy measures.

The practice of giving everyone a single vote on any policy or issue has interesting implications, since it assigns a weight that is the same for everyone: this practice implicitly assumes that the issue being voted on will have equal effects on different people's satisfaction. One can readily see that this assumption is equivalent to the assumption that marginal utilities of income for different people are *inversely proportional* to their monetary evaluations of the effects of the policy, so that the expression $(B - C)_i \cdot MU_{Yi}$ is exactly the same for everyone. When used as indices of people's satisfaction, all voting systems make implicit assumptions about the marginal utility of income for different people, as does the use of unweighted monetary benefit-cost evaluations of policies.

In principle, equity weights can be assigned to the evaluations of various individuals, or to a single person's evaluations of different effects, in an indefinite number of ways, each resulting in differing evaluations of any regulatory policy. Most discussions of equity imply that weights should be assigned so that "equals should be treated equally," but this concept of "horizontal" equity is deceptively simple. In order to make it operational, "equality" among people must be defined.

People have innumerable personal and environmental characteristics, such as skin color, intelligence, geographical location, income, sex, age, and nationality. It would be difficult to find two persons for whom all conceivable characteristics are identical. Choice of an index of "equality" inevitably means selecting characteristics that are sufficiently alike for them to be grouped together into a subset of characteristics, but these people will still differ with respect to many other characteristics.

Even if one characteristic, such as income, is chosen as an index of "equality," there are still problems involved in trying to define operationally who is an "equal." For example, "income" may be current period money income, the purchasing power of that income, lifetime income, or some other measure of income. Depending on which measure of income is used, one's evaluation of the distributional consequences of any policy will be different. For example, an evaluation of the income-distributional effects of benefits and costs of education will show quite different results, depending on whether lifetime income or income within some lesser time period is considered the relevant index for purpose of defining "equals" and "unequals," as demonstrated by Crean (1975).

An index of horizontal equity implies that unequals should be treated "unequally." Again, an index of what is meant by "unequal" is required, with weights for different degrees of "inequality," in order to implement the implied concept of "vertical equity." Any one concept of horizontal equity is quite compatible with innumerable weights and corresponding concepts of vertical equity, each one implying a different evaluation for any given policy.

Moreover, as Pauly and Willet (1976) have pointed out, any concept of horizontal or vertical equity may be interpreted in two ways, which they term ex ante and ex post equity. In the context of the military draft, a concept of ex post equity would regard the draft "fair" if everyone were required to serve for an equal period of time, since each person would end up paying an equal share of the human time cost of defense. In contrast, an ex ante concept would consider the draft fair if a lottery were employed that guaranteed every person an equal chance of incurring the obligation to pay the human cost of defense. People may not be indifferent to these two methods, even though the expected value of their share of the cost is the same in both cases and is equal to Total cost/No people. People who dislike risks, defined as probabilistic situations, will prefer the ex post to the ex ante concept of equity, for example. The actual share of the cost borne by different people under the lottery method will differ, so that the method that exhibits ex ante equity will not be equitable ex post.

Consequences of Introducing Equity Concepts. Whatever concept of equity is employed, and the associated set of weights for evaluating the distribution of effects of regulatory or other policies between different individuals, certain very important implications are shared by all evaluation systems that include equity weights. Perhaps the most important of these is the fact that *policies that increase or maximize efficiency will no*

longer be socially optimal policies in most situations (Harberger, 1978).
This perhaps surprising conclusion can easily be understood. If a regulatory policy (or any other aspect of the human environment) is evaluated by any set of weights that includes both efficiency and equity concepts,

Total evaluation of policy =
    Evaluation of efficiency effects + Evaluation of equity effects

the dimensions of the regulatory policy that maximize the evaluation measure must satisfy the condition

Change in total evaluation =
    Change in efficiency effects + Change in equity effects = 0

Maximizing efficiency means adopting a policy that makes the first term before the equals sign zero. In general, the second term after the equals sign will not be zero when such a policy is adopted: the policy change will have equity effects that are valued positively or negatively at the efficiency-maximizing level. This, in turn, implies that the dimensions of a policy that maximize the evaluation of that policy in terms of efficiency and equity criteria will not require efficiency to be maximized. There is, in other words, usually an automatic trade-off between efficiency and equity whenever equity weights are used to evaluate policies. Moreover, this trade-off will tend to work against efficiency considerations, the larger the equity weights are relative to efficiency weights.

The conclusion that equity considerations will usually involve reductions in the efficiency characteristics of optimal social policies greatly disturbs some economists. They do not always seem to recognize that their traditional efficiency concepts are themselves based on an equity concept — the acceptance of the prevailing income distribution and its implications for monetary evaluations of efficiency. In fact, *any* set of equity weights that is proportional to people's marginal utilities of income will yield different evaluations but will also yield optimal characteristics of policies that are identical to policies based on economists' traditional efficiency concepts. In terms of the equation, this situation would mean that the efficiency and equity evaluations of a policy were proportional, and policy dimensions that maximize efficiency considerations would also maximize equity considerations.

Some economists who find the implications of introducing equity weights into evaluations of the effects of private and public policies disquieting have proposed that equity considerations be introduced into policy evaluations in the form of a constraint describing desired distributional consequences, rather than as weights in the objective function that is used to evaluate public policies (Harberger, 1978). These proposals would have the opposite of the effect intended by the proponent, however, since they would have the actual effect of *increasing* rather than reducing the relative impact of equity considerations compared with efficiency considerations in policy evaluations.

In Chapter 2, Section 2.4, it was explained that when variables are introduced into a problem in the form of a constraint that must be met, the importance of choosing values of decision variables that meet the constraint is elevated *above* the importance of choosing values of decision variables that increase the level of the decision maker's objective function. In the present context, introducing equity considerations as a constraint would give these considerations priority over any considerations of efficiency until those equity constraints had been met.

Equity considerations — like any other variables or constraints that are added to an analysis — change the nature of the conclusions that are appropriate. One may understand the reluctance of those who understand and are familiar with efficiency concepts to learn about equity concepts and introduce them into their analyses, but doing this is necessary if one is to understand the way decision makers evaluate and determine policies in practice.

Efficiency considerations are often given scant regard in private and public decision making, even when they are understood by the decision makers. In contrast, decision makers in practice *do* often weight different people differently when making their decisions, and these weights are not always proportional to people's monetary evaluations, as is assumed in traditional economic models of the firm and other rational-actor models of decision making.

Unfortunately, we do not yet know very much about the kind of distributional weights decision makers use or why they use them. In part, this is because many of the possible criteria for grouping people (e.g., income, wealth, power) are positively associated, making it difficult to determine which of these characteristics decision makers use to group people. If we do not know how decision makers group people, it is difficult to infer the weights decision makers apply to different groups from observation of decision-maker behavior.

Another problem is the general presence of misrepresentations of preferences and evaluations by all parties to transactions. In the absence of the kind of incentive systems encouraging truthful revelation of evaluations, accurately inferring any kind of evaluation weights from observed data is likely to be impossible.

Interactions Among Distributional Effects and People's Evaluations. There is one other aspect of distributional effects of private and public policies that needs to be stated explicitly. In evaluating the effects of regulatory or other policies, a person's satisfaction may depend in part on how those policies affect others, in addition to the direct effects on that person. This means that the distributional effects of the policies enter directly into that person's utility function and influence the person's evaluations.

We cannot generalize about *which* particular distributional effects will affect any individual's satisfaction directly. In some cases, it may be distributional effects on particular individuals, such as the person's neighbors or friends that directly affect a person's satisfaction. This situation is exemplified by the "keeping up with the Joneses" syndrome. In other cases, a person may be more concerned with the distributional effects on a general class of individuals, such as people in his or her income or social class, without regard to their identity.

The kind of distributional effects on others that affect a person's satisfaction may vary similarly. The effects of a policy on income distribution may be a major factor that influences some people's satisfaction. For other people, the distribution of some other effect may be more important. Even where the effect of policies on others' income directly affects a person's satisfaction, he or she may be concerned with the absolute effects on others' income, or with the effect relative to the effect on his or her own income.

Any of these distributional effects can be easily incorporated into the framework of analysis presented in Table 3.3. Each distributional effect of a policy that may directly affect a person's satisfaction will simply require an additional "Effect" row in the table. Coefficients in that row will, as before, represent different people's monetary evaluations of those effects. No major changes in methodology are required, because all we have done is to add one or more variables representing distributional effects to a person's preference function.

As we have repeatedly emphasized, the effects of any policy on a person's satisfaction depend on the precise form of the person's preference function and on all the other constraints confronting the individual. The conclusions of the analysis will of course change, because the evaluations of a policy by one or more individuals will be changed. Moreover, these evaluations will now be interdependent, in that one person's evaluations of the effects of a policy will now depend on how other people are affected by and evaluate the policy change.

A simple example illustrates the way a person's evaluations of a policy will be changed if distributional effects on others enter into his or her evaluations. If the individual were concerned only with the effects of a policy on himself or herself, changes in the distribution of effects of the policy among other people will not change the individual's evaluation. In contrast, if the distribution of the effects of the policy among others does concern the individual, he or she will value the policy differently, even if the effects on the individual are the same, depending on the precise way in which these other effects are distributed among others.

When distributional effects of a policy on others directly affect a person's evaluations of that policy, the characteristics of "socially optimal" policies will also be changed, irrespective of the precise magnitude of the efficiency and equity weights used to evaluate those policies. This is the case because the characteristics of socially optimal policies always depend in part on the nature and magnitude of the unweighted monetary benefit and cost evaluation of those policies, in addition to the efficiency and equity weights. But all these things also happen whenever *any* new variable is added to the preference function or constraints that confront one or more members of society. When viewed from this perspective, there is nothing special about adding distributional effects as a separate factor into people's evaluations of private or public policies.

Equity Weights and the Political Process. Since equity weights determine the relative weight given to the monetary evaluations of individuals, it is obvious that people will not in general be indifferent to the equity weights used in regulatory or other public policy decisions. Each person's influence on those decisions will be the greater the larger the weight given to their monetary or other evaluation of the outcomes of the decision.

People with low monetary evaluations, perhaps because of low current incomes, will concentrate on trying to increase their equity weights in decision makers' evaluation processes as a means to increasing their influence on private and public policy decisions. Individuals may enter into coalitions with others to try to collectively influence the equity weights assigned to that group. All these considerations suggest that the actual process of determining which equity weights will be used by private or public decision makers is little different from the general political process of trying to influence regulatory constraints and other outcomes of individual or of collective decision processes.

Viewed from this perspective — and recognizing that any change in equity weights will increase some people's satisfaction relative to others — it is clear that one would not expect to find general agreement about equity weights. The search for a normative set of equity weights that "make every member of society better off" is clearly an attempt to perform the impossible.

Equity issues are unavoidable in dealing with regulation, whether or not a formal benefit-cost framework is used to clarify the issues. Choice of equity weights determines whose evaluations of private and public policies will count in decisions regarding those policies. This is an unavoidable trade-off — except in a society of clones with identical preference functions and identical personal environments; in such circumstances, any individual's decisions would duplicate those of everyone else.

CHAPTER FOUR

Costs of Regulation

4.1 COST CONCEPTS AND REGULATION

Costs, like benefits, are inherently subjective, and the issue of appropriate cost concepts in analyses of regulation cannot be separated from the issue of whose evaluations of costs of regulation are employed or from the objectives and constraints that confront the person or persons whose evaluations are being considered. Once it is recognized that all cost and benefit concepts are subjective evaluations made by specific individuals, it is possible to avoid many of the major pitfalls that await the unwary interpreter of specific cost and benefit concepts and measures. Emphasis is properly shifted from the concepts and measures to the two crucial issues underlying all cost and benefit measures. First, whose evaluations actually underlie, or should underlie, these measures in any particular case? Second, what are the factors that determine people's evaluations of any particular aspects of their environment?

People's evaluations of aspects of their environment are determined by their personal preferences, objectives, and the perceived constraints that confront them. The cost and benefit concepts used by businessmen, accountants, economists, regulators, other government decision makers, and by individual members of society often differ because the objectives or constraints that confront these types of decision maker and individuals are often different. Traditional economic analysis is largely concerned with situations in which decision makers are required to make choices between alternatives. In such a context, the concept of "opportunity cost," which refers to the alternatives that are rejected when a decision maker selects one of a number of alternatives, is an important cost concept.

Controversies still exist in the economics literature concerning whether opportunity costs can be observed and measured by persons other than the one who makes a choice among any set of alternatives. Buchanan and Faith (1979) and other writers have correctly emphasized that rejected alternatives, and their anticipated consequences, are subjective. Also, the actual consequences of people's decisions may differ

71

from those anticipated at the time people make choices among alternative courses of action. The costs and benefits associated with the actual consequences of people's choices and decisions may not, therefore, accurately reflect the anticipated costs and benefits of those choices and decisions. It is the anticipated consequences of alternative choices that determine people's decisions and behavior. The actual consequences influence people's decisions to the extent that anticipated future consequences of particular choices are based on the actual consequences of past decisions, or they may lead to revisions of previously held perceptions and evaluations.

Despite the validity of these observations, it is incorrect to argue that the subjective opportunity costs associated with individuals' choices between alternatives are not observable and measurable by persons other than the one making the choice. Even subjective cost or benefit concepts can be measured by other people if the person who evaluates the costs or benefits can be motivated to truthfully reveal his or her subjective evaluations. The issue of accurate cost and benefit estimation is inseparably connected with the problem of providing incentives for truthful revelation of information.

In situations where people's revealed evaluations of the costs and benefits of certain aspects of their environment can affect the choices that are available, there may be incentives for individuals to misrepresent their subjective cost and benefit evaluations. Individuals who do not like a particular type of regulation may overstate their subjective evaluations of the costs and understate the benefits they anticipate will result from that type of regulation. As Vaughn (1980) has emphasized, if costs and benefits are incorrectly estimated by persons who do not themselves experience the costs and benefits, public policies may have perverse effects on individuals affected by those policies. The solution is not to abandon efforts to measure the costs and benefits of public policies, however, but to devote greater effort to providing incentives that motivate individuals to truthfully reveal their evaluations of the policies' costs and benefits.

A second important cost or benefit concept is the effect on the level of a person's satisfaction, or other objective, of a change in one of the constraints confronting that individual. Constraints influence the nature and consequences of the alternatives that confront the individual. If a change in one constraint enables an individual to reach a higher level of satisfaction, or some other objective, the individual will view the increase in the level of satisfaction as a benefit of the change in the constraint. Conversely, if such a change lowers the individual's satisfaction, or level of attainment of some other objective, the individual will view the reduced satisfaction as a cost of the change in the constraint.[1]

----

[1] For readers who are familiar with constrained optimization techniques and calculus, this second cost or benefit concept is the same as the Lagrangian multiplier, which represents the effect of relaxing one of the constraints that confronts an individual, on the level of the individual's objective.

Although these two concepts are not the same, they are related. A change in one of the constraints confronting an individual may change the alternatives selected, and rejected, by the individual. Costs in the sense of a person's evaluation of the effect of a change in one of the constraints the person faces is as relevant to cost and benefit evaluations of effects of regulation as is the concept of opportunity cost, since regulation changes constraints that confront a number of different types of decision maker. Also, irrespective of which of the subjective cost concepts one is concerned with, both can be measured by other observers, provided that individuals can be motivated to reveal their subjective evaluations truthfully.

These two cost concepts by no means exhaust all the cost concepts that may be relevant in analyzing the effects of regulation on people's behavior and its consequences. When dealing with most issues connected with regulation, a number of cost concepts need to be carefully distinguished. The remainder of this section will examine the following five cost concepts connected with government regulation of business.

1. expenditures by regulatory agencies
2. expenditures by firms that are attributable to regulation
3. reductions in satisfaction experienced by some members of society as a result of regulation
4. ignored or unintended effects of regulation
5. costs of demand-revealing activities

Although these five cost concepts are different, they are interrelated, and all are generally relevant in any satisfactory analysis of regulation. Fortunately, this multidimensional characteristic of the cost concept that is appropriate for analyzing regulation need not cause the reader more than a momentary spasm of apprehension, since we can employ the expository framework of Tables 3.2 and 3.3 to clarify the relationships between these different dimensions of the costs of regulation. (Table 4.1, presented here, is a modified version of Table 3.2.)

1. *Expenditures by Regulatory Agencies.* These are expenditures that result from the agencies' efforts to change some dimension of firms' behavior, depicted by the C term in the column of Table 4.1 that refers to evaluations of effects of regulation by regulatory agencies. This C term could be further divided into various types of expenditure by the agency, such as compliance-monitoring and enforcement expenditures. Notice that it is possible for regulatory expenditures to be large even if regulation has no effects on regulated decision makers' behavior because of regulators' lack of knowledge regarding what kind of regulatory constraints are needed to change regulated decision makers' behavior.

2. *Expenditures by Regulated Firms That Are Attributable to Regulation.* These are depicted by the C terms in the column of Table 4.1 that

Table 4-1.   Evaluations of Effects of Regulation

Effects of regulation	Regulatory agency	Regulated firm(s)	Unregulated firm(s)	Person 1 ... Person n	
A		C			
B	C			B	
C					
D					
E		C		B	
F		C			B
.					
.					
.					
$(B - C)_i$					$\Sigma\,(B - C)_i$

refers to regulated firms' evaluations of effects of regulation. These terms do not include only expenditures directly involved in meeting regulatory standards, such as increased pollution-control expenditures. They may also include costs of providing information to regulatory agencies and legal expenses incurred by regulated firms that are defending themselves against charges of violating regulatory standards. If a firm is successful in such a defense, the firm's total expenditures and costs may still be higher even though its pollution control or other expenditures are not changed by regulation.

Sections 4.2 and 4.3 will discuss concepts (2) and (1) and the factors that determine their magnitude in more detail. These two concepts cover most conventional treatments of the "costs of regulation." Note that the magnitude of both cost elements will depend on the nature of the regulatory constraint used to influence the level of activity A. In addition, certain costs of regulation, such as the costs of obtaining information about aspects of regulated firms' behavior, may be distributed between regulatory agencies and regulated firms. The share of these information costs that is borne by each party will also depend on the nature of the regulatory constraint. A common misconception is that regulated firms "should not" bear the costs of information required by regulatory agencies. The most efficient and effective method of collecting this information may require firms to bear part or all these costs, depending on the circumstances involved.

Cost concepts (1) and (2) may be viewed either from a descriptive viewpoint, which is concerned with the levels of these cost components existing in practice, or from a normative viewpoint, which is concerned with what the desirable levels and characteristics of these cost concepts "should" be. In both cases, because the two concepts are interdependent and are jointly determined by factors that influence the behavior of regulated firms and regulatory agencies, both cost concepts must be analyzed simultaneously in order to derive correct conclusions. We shall elaborate on these points in Section 4.3. (See also Chapters 12 and 13.)

3. *Reductions in Satisfaction Experienced by Some Members of Society as a Result of Regulation.* As explained in Chapter 3, each of the individual elements in the $(B - C)_i$ row of Table 4.1 indicates a particular individual's monetary evaluation of the net benefits or costs of all effects of regulation. The sum of the elements in this row $(B - C)_i$, expresses the summation of monetary evaluations of effects of regulation by all members of society. Costs of regulation in the sense of negative evaluations of particular effects of regulatory policies will generally exist; to ignore them is to obtain only a partial view of the effects of regulation.

4. *Ignored or Unintended Effects of Regulation.* If these effects are evaluated negatively, they are costs; ignored positive effects of regulation are benefits. These omitted effects of regulation include effects that are genuinely overlooked as well as effects that are purposely ignored for any reason. Chapter 3 emphasized that there are many possible models of the effects of regulation and many criteria for evaluating them. These models and evaluation criteria will tend to vary with the goals and constraints that confront the person or persons performing the cost-benefit evaluation. Differences in goals or constraints confronting these individuals can lead to omitted effects of regulation.

Omitted benefits and costs have several dimensions:

a. *Omitted Evaluations of Changes in Satisfaction Experienced by People Who Are Not Listed in the Columns of Table 4.1.* We emphasized in Chapter 3 the crucial importance of *whose* evaluations of regulation's effects are included as a determinant of the resulting benefit and cost evaluations of regulation. If some people's evaluations are omitted, which is equivalent to attributing zero equity weights to those people's evaluations of the effects of regulation on their own satisfaction, this will obviously omit some benefits and costs of regulation. The reader may imagine a table such as Table 4.1 including *every* member of society. If one then eliminates from consideration one or more of the columns in the table, the resulting benefit and cost measures of regulation will obviously generally differ.

b. *Omitted Effects of Regulation.* Omitting some effects of regulation from consideration is equivalent to allocating a zero weight to people's evaluations of those effects. It is also equivalent to eliminating one of the rows of Table 4.1. This omission will clearly result in different measures of the benefits and costs of regulation from those that would obtain if these effects were included in the table.

c. *Omitted Time Periods.* As emphasized in Chapter 3, there is always also a *time* dimension to effects of regulation, and their benefits and costs. Lengthening the time dimension to which Table 4.1 applies may change the benefits and costs of regulating the level of activity A in a number of ways.

For example, it may result in the addition of more columns to the table, representing additional people who are affected by regulation of activity A in later time periods than those originally considered by the table. Suppose that regulation resulted in a failure of existing generations to replace human or physical capital stock. The resulting cost, in the form of a reduction in the future output level because of the capital stock reduction, might not be felt for several generations. If the time period to which Table 4.1 applies does not extend sufficiently into the future to include the evaluations of the reduction in capital stock by future generations, it would omit this "cost" of regulation.

Lengthening the time period to which the table applies may also add rows to the table that represent effects of regulating activity A that do not occur until a later time period. For example, regulating the form in which nuclear waste is packaged might reduce pollution in earlier periods and prolong existing life spans; but when the packaging eventually deteriorates, the pollution may occur anyway and destroy everyone and everything alive at the time.

The reader is reminded that when adding benefits and costs that apply to effects in future time periods, it is necessary to "discount" these evaluations and express them in terms of current period equivalents, as explained in Chapter 3, Section 3.2(b).

5. *Costs of Demand-Revealing Activities.* There is another type of cost associated with regulation that has been virtually ignored in the traditional economics literature. To provide the proper perspective for introducing this facet of regulatory costs, it is necessary to emphasize several important features of the benefit and cost evaluations in Table 4.1. This framework can be used either for descriptive analyses, which are concerned with how regulatory or other government policies are actually evaluated, or for normative analyses, which are concerned with how these policies "should" be evaluated. In either situation, it needs to be more adequately recognized that individuals who compose society are not indifferent to the way government policies are evaluated and generally are not passive bystanders in the evaluation process.

People have a number of means for revealing their preferences and evaluations to the decision makers responsible for making government policies. These means include the use of time, money, and other resources by individuals on various types of "evaluation-revealing" activities; some of these means, such as voting, are not correlated with income and wealth. Despite this, time or income used to reveal a person's evaluations of some aspect of his or her environment, termed "demand-revealing" activities in the economics literature, could be used for other purposes. Even votes cast in support of a candidate or government policy have other uses, since these votes could be traded and used to support another candidate or policy in exchange for the promise of future votes and support for the individual's future choices. All resources used for demand-revealing activities have opportunity costs, therefore, in the form of forgone opportunities to use those resources for other purposes, which may or may not be connected with demand-revealing activities. These costs will *not be included* in conventional cost-benefit analyses of regulation or other policies, as depicted by Table 4.1.

The implications of regulation for costs in the sense of scarce resources devoted by members of society to demand-revealing activities that generate the kinds of benefit and cost information contained in Table 4.1 should be taken into account in evaluating regulation. However, the *magnitude* of these costs is not the only aspect of the demand-revealing process that matters. Perhaps even more important is the effect of regulation on the *degree of misrepresentation of the benefits and costs* that result from the demand-revealing process.

Individuals will misrepresent their evaluations of the benefits or costs of particular government policies or other aspects of their environment whenever they believe that doing so will further their personal interests in comparison with the consequences of truthful revelation. One of the major virtues of a market price system is that in a certain limited class of transactions between individuals, truthful demand revelation in bidding for inputs or outputs occurs. Economists have long recognized that securing such truthful revelations may be a problem when goods or services have "external effects," which means effects on more than one person. Moreover, these problems exist whether people's demands and evaluations are revealed by traditional market bidding or by voting, as Feldman (1979) has emphasized.

The lack of incentives for truthful revelation of evaluations is a major problem in all types of transactions among individuals and is not solved simply by moving responsibility for making certain decisions from individuals to public sector decision makers who act as agents for a group that is affected by those decisions. (See Chapter 12.) In the present context it is necessary to recognize that the effect of any regulatory constraint on incentives for people to truthfully reveal their evaluations of the benefits and costs of regulatory activities is a very important effect of regulation that is not revealed by the benefit and cost figures in Table 4.1. In addition, these figures do not include either the total costs or the changes in total costs of demand-revealing activities engaged in by individuals.

Although demand-revealing activities themselves entail costs, regulation could either increase or reduce these costs. An increase in total resources used for such activities attributable to regulation represents a cost of regulation, whereas a reduction in total resources used for these activities represents a benefit. In either case, the degree of misrepresentation of evaluations revealed by members of society could increase, decrease, or remain unchanged.

Costs of revealing people's evaluations will always exist whether or not there is any government regulation. Individuals will always reveal their evaluations of policies, activities, and aspects of the transactions they engage in whenever they expect such revelations to contribute to their personal objectives. When viewed from this perspective, *the benefit and cost evaluations depicted in Table 4.1 are also a tool individuals may use to advance their interests.* This, we suggest, is a more appropriate perspective for viewing evaluations of the impact of regulation on society than approaches that implicitly or explicitly assume "given" preferences and benefit and cost information that accurately reflects these preferences.

Viewed from this perspective, the frequent assertion that matters of valuation should be left to the political system is obviously no solution at all to the problem of determining values. At best, it is an evasion of the fundamental issues involved in the determination of societal values. At worst, it is an abdication that leaves open opportunities for "the political system" to be the cloak for particular persons and interests to advance their narrow self-interests.

Irrespective of whether the struggle between individuals or interest groups to advance their respective aims takes place in the marketplace or in the political forum, ultimately the struggle is one of a confrontation of different people's evaluations. Battles over evaluation — whether or not they are called "benefit-cost" issues or are analyzed within a formal framework — are essentially attempts by different groups to influence the magnitudes of the benefit-cost coefficients as shown in Table 4.1 in private and public decision makers' minds. For example, adding columns to Table 4.1 means taking additional people's evaluations into account, and adding rows means taking additional effects of a particular policy into account. These "evaluation games" obviously change the influence of particular individuals in any evaluation and decision process.

Whenever a regulatory constraint is introduced, people will be affected in different ways and will experience changes in satisfaction. Irrespective of whether, and how, they reveal their evaluations, these changes could, in principle, be depicted by Table 4.1, but they are not directly observable. Economists, political scientists, and other analysts who approach societal issues within a benefit-cost framework should try to remember that they are implicitly dealing with the value systems of individuals.

Whenever a weight is assigned to an individual's evaluation of a policy — whether it is a vote, a monetary evaluation of that policy by that person, or some other equity weight — this automatically constitutes a statement about how much that person's evaluation of the policy "should" count in the overall evaluation of that policy. Recognizing this should introduce some humility into the cost-benefit analyst's approach to societal problems. The analyst is, in effect, purporting to introduce other people's perceptions and valuations of the policy's effects into the analysis.

This is unavoidable because *someone's* perception and valuations of the effects of the policy must be used. It is desirable that the opinions of people whose perceptions and evaluations are included be made as explicit as possible, however. On these grounds, a disaggregated benefit-analysis framework that, like Table 3.1, shows the distribution of benefits and costs between different members of society, is preferable to one that aggregates the evaluations of different individuals. As we have emphasized, net benefit totals can tell us nothing about the composition of the benefits and costs that result in those net benefits.

Unfortunately, it is very difficult to implement these prescriptions for cost-benefit analyses in practice. This is so because researchers themselves do not work in a value-free environment, and we have amply demonstrated that benefit-cost evaluations of particular policies are a weapon that can be used to further the interests of individuals and groups in society.

Some misconceptions exist in the literature about the role of the economist in the valuation process, which constitutes the essence of benefit-cost analysis. Valuations of policy effects are unavoidable, and the economist is no better equipped than anyone else to say whose evaluations should be employed to evaluate policies. Economists are, however, particularly well equipped by their training in model building to indicate how the effects of particular policies depend on the precise models of individual and organizational behavior employed in a cost-benefit analysis. The same training also makes them especially well qualified both to determine the implications of using different valuation systems for evaluating policies and to infer the kind of valuations that are implicit in policy decisions. Finally, as the recent surge of articles in the economics journals dealing with incentive systems indicates, economists are in the forefront of recognizing and attempting to overcome the fundamental problem of misrepresentation of information in transactions between people. This problem is pervasive and is one of the basic features of all regulatory issues.

4.2 IMPACT OF REGULATION ON REGULATED FIRMS' COSTS

The effect of regulation on regulated firms' costs is often emphasized in discussions of regulation. It is often automatically assumed that regulation of any aspect of a firm's behavior increases the cost of the firm's products or services, even in situations where regulation reduces the prices consumers pay or has beneficial effects on other dimensions of the firm's behavior. Acquiring a clear understanding of the impact of regulation on firms' costs is complicated by the fact that there are many different dimensions to the concept of a firm's costs. This section will therefore examine the relationship between regulation and regulated firms' costs within a framework that encompasses different dimensions of a firm's costs and their relationship to other dimensions of the firm's behavior.

Dimensions of a Firm's Costs. A firm's total costs are usually defined as the sum of its expenditures on inputs, as follows:

$$\text{Total costs} = \text{TC} = \Sigma \text{ input quantity}_i \times \text{price of input } i \cdots \quad (1)$$

Dividing TC by the firm's total output yields a measure of the *average cost* (AC), or unit cost, of the firm's output. If the change in TC associated with a change in the level of the firm's output is divided by that change in output, the result is a measure of the *marginal cost* (MC) of the firm's output. Even in a firm that produces a single product or service, there are a number of different AC and MC concepts, since the "output" of a firm has different dimensions.

The relationship among the total, average, and marginal costs of any *particular* dimension of the firm's output is shown in Figure 4.1. The shape of the firm's total cost curve, which shows how the firm's total costs vary as the level of that dimension of output is changed, determines the shape of the AC and MC curves for that same dimension of output. Three

Figure 4.1

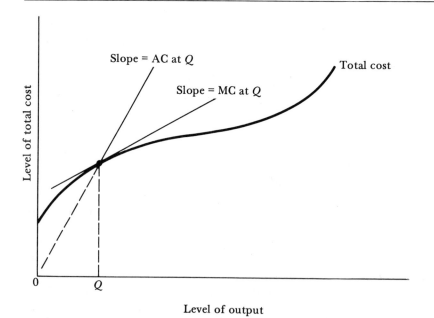

Level of output

Figure 4.2

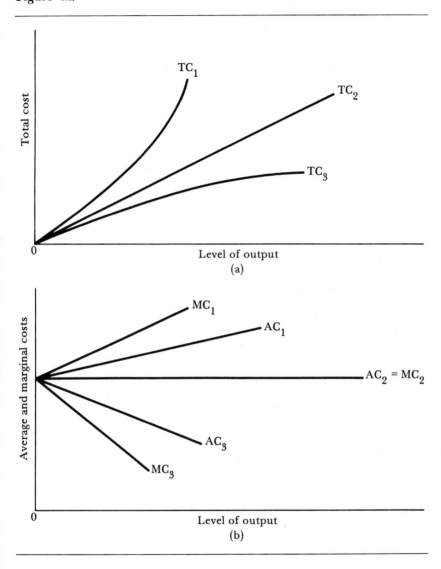

types of relationship among total, average, and marginal costs are possible; these are depicted in Figure 4.2. Different dimensions of the firm's output, such as the volume and rate of output, may have different-shaped total, average, and marginal cost curves.[2]

2 See Needham (1978, chap. 2) for more detailed treatment of these matters.

If a firm purchases an input, such as a piece of capital equipment, which produces output in a number of time periods, the price of this so-called fixed input must be allocated between different units of output in order to calculate AC and MC of output concepts. The fraction of the total price of the input allocated to output produced in different time periods corresponds to the businessman's and accountant's concept of "depreciation" expense. In practice, a variety of conventions are adopted for allocating the cost of long-lived inputs between output produced by the inputs in different time periods.

The cost allocation rule that is adopted by a firm's decision makers for allocating the cost of long-lived inputs between output produced in different time periods will affect the AC and MC concepts associated with output produced in different time periods. Moreover, since estimates of how much future output will be produced by a particular input necessarily imply assumptions about future demand for output, these cost concepts are not entirely independent of the firm's decision-makers' estimates of future demand for output.

Additional considerations become relevant in determining the firm's cost concepts if it produces more than one kind of product or service. When the firm's total input cost figure is divided by different types of output, there is a cost allocation problem very similar to that which is involved in allocating the cost of long-lived inputs between outputs produced in different time periods. The only difference is that the "different types of output" being considered are now produced in the same time period.

If particular inputs produce particular types of output, there is no problem; the cost of each input is simply allocated to the product it produces. A more likely situation is that a particular input or group of inputs simultaneously produce more than one product. How, for example, should the cost of a cow be allocated between hides and beef? Once again, a firm's decision makers will adopt some kind of decision rules, or weights, for allocating input costs between different joint products. Our concern here is not with the particular cost allocation decision rules (or weights) adopted in any particular case but with the general proposition that the firm's cost concepts will depend on the nature of these decision rules in addition to other factors that underlie the firm's costs.

Since there are many dimensions to a firm's costs, effects of regulation on these costs may also be multidimensional. The overall net impact of regulation on a firm's total costs, measured by the net change in input quantities purchased by the firm multiplied by their prices, may mask a host of effects on the total, average, and marginal cost concepts associated with different dimensions of the firm's output and behavior.

Determinants of a Firm's Costs. It is not possible to determine the effect of regulation on regulated firms' costs without taking into account the various factors that determine these costs in the absence of regulation. The effects of regulation on a regulated firm depend on (1) the firm's objectives and constraints, which determine the firm's choice of input levels and various output and cost dimensions in the absence of regulation, and (2) the characteristics of the regulatory constraint that is added to the preceding factors influencing the firm's decision making. It is impossible to understand or to predict the impact of regulation on a firm's costs without reference to both factors.

The major determinants of a firm's behavior and cost concepts in the absence of regulation are as follows:

i. the prices or supply conditions of the firm's inputs
ii. the firm's production function, which describes the relationship between quantities of various inputs and the resulting quantities of output produced
iii. the demand conditions for the firm's products and services
iv. the objectives of the firm's decision makers

These factors jointly determine both the amount of inputs purchased by the firm's decision makers and the amount of output produced. As already noted, the cost-allocation rules the firm's decision makers employ for allocating input prices between different types of output, or between output produced in different time periods, will also be relevant in determining the implications of any particular selected input-and-output mix for the firm's various cost concepts.

In traditional economic analysis, the firm's production function is assumed to be a technological constraint, determined by available knowledge regarding alternative methods of producing particular outputs, and generally outside the control of the firm's decision makers. Following the seminal work of Leibenstein (1966), it is now recognized that a firm's production function depends also on the objectives and constraints facing human inputs employed by the firm. Policing and incentive systems internal to the firm can influence the amount of output produced by particular human inputs in a given time period. The firm's production function is, therefore, partly under the control of the firm's decision makers who are responsible for choosing internal policing and incentive systems.

Another important consideration is that the level of a firm's total costs may be higher than the minimum level necessary to produce particular outputs, even in the absence of regulation. A number of factors may be responsible for such a result. The objectives of a firm's decision makers may be incompatible with cost-minimizing input mixes, for example. While profit, sales revenue, and growth-maximizing objectives imply cost minimization, managerial preferences for certain types of input will generally motivate managers to select input mixes that do not minimize the total costs of particular outputs. Lack of appropriate incentives to prevent such a situation represents a special case of Leibenstein's more general analysis of reasons for the existence of "X-inefficiency," a failure to adopt feasible cost-minimizing methods of producing particular outputs in organizations.

Effects of Regulation on a Regulated Firm's Costs. The effects of regulation on a regulated firm's input and output choices, and therefore on its various cost concepts, will also depend on the characteristics of the regulatory constraint. A regulatory constraint may take the form of limitations on the firm's absolute profits, or on the rate of profit in relation to capital or sales revenue. Alternatively, the constraint may directly limit one or more of the firm's average cost or marginal cost concepts, or the input mix that may be used to produce the firm's products, the firm's cost allocation rules, the decision rules the firm uses when hiring inputs, or any other aspect of the firm's operations.

Different types of regulatory constraint will affect the firm's costs in different ways, and different effects on the firm's costs will result from a particular regulatory constraint depending on the precise form of all the factors previously discussed. Generalizations about the effects of regulation on a regulated firm's costs are therefore impossible. The facile notion that "regulation increases firms' costs" may be useful propaganda for opponents of regulation, but it is of little use as a guide to descriptive or normative analyses of the relationship that exists between regulation and regulated firms' costs. In Chapter 8 we shall examine the impact of a regulatory constraint that limits the amount of profit per unit of capital a firm may earn on a regulated firm's costs and efficiency. This is the traditional method of regulating public utility industries in the United States.

A general perspective on the effects of regulation on a firm's costs may be obtained by reference to the definition of total costs as the sum of input quantities purchased by the firm multiplied by the prices of the inputs. At one extreme, if a firm faces a budgetary restriction on the total amount of money that can be spent on inputs, regulation will not affect the firm's total costs. It may, however, result in changes in the firm's input mix and output mix and in level of average and marginal costs of individual products the firm produces.

At the other extreme, regulation may increase or decrease a firm's total costs without changing its input-and-output mix; this will occur if regulation raises or lowers the height of the total cost curve in Figure 4.1 by exactly the same amount at different levels of the firm's output. Since the slope of the total cost curve will not be changed, the magnitude of marginal cost will not be changed at any output level of the firm. For profit-maximizing firms, it is marginal cost, not total or average cost, that determines the level of output and other dimensions of the firm's behavior. It is quite possible, in other words, for regulation to increase a firm's total costs sufficiently to cause losses and even bankruptcy before the behavior of the firm is changed.

It must be emphasized that in certain circumstances regulation can also reduce regulated firms' total, average, and marginal costs. These circumstances generally involve the introduction of or changes in existing policing systems that increase the productivity of a firm's inputs. These policing systems may be either internal or external to the firm, and the manner in which they are affected by regulation depends critically on the form of the regulatory constraint. For example, by insulating regulated firms from competition with established or potential rival firms, regulation might reduce the pressure for individual firms to adopt cost-minimizing policing and production methods. On the other hand, if an agency adopts the average costs of the most efficient firms in a regulated industry as a criterion for determining industry pricing and allowed profit rates, doing so might increase efficiency in less efficient firms that would earn lower profits than other firms on the basis of their existing cost levels. In a study of United States domestic trunk airlines, Pustay (1978) estimated that major cost savings — on the order of 12 to 15 percent of total industry costs — would have been obtainable from 1965 to 1974 if all carriers had performed as efficiently as the most efficient airline in the industry.

Implications of Changes of Costs for Efficiency. The magnitude and direction of a change in a regulated firm's total costs, or in the average and marginal costs of individual products that are attributable to regulation cannot by themselves be used as an index of the effect on the firm's efficiency. "Efficiency" is generally defined as the ratio of output to input, and where a firm produces more than one type of output, or uses more than one type of input, individual inputs and outputs must be weighted and aggregated in order to obtain a measure of the firm's overall efficiency, as follows:

$$\text{Efficiency} = \frac{\Sigma w_i \times \text{output}_i}{\Sigma w_j \times \text{input}_j}$$

In profit-maximizing firms, the w_i weights are market prices of output, and the w_j weights are market prices of inputs. The numerator of the efficiency condition therefore represents the firm's total revenues, and the denominator represents the firm's total costs. Any increase in total revenue, or reduction in total costs, will increase the firm's profits. Thus, the concept of efficiency is directly related to the firm's objectives. More generally, the input and output concepts and the weights that are appropriate in measuring the efficiency of *any* firm, or other type of organization, depend on the objectives that are considered appropriate for that firm or organization.

The perceived objectives of any organization depend on whose perceptions are adopted as the relevant criterion for judging those objectives.

Profit-maximizing businessmen will adopt input and output measures, and corresponding weights, which may differ from the input, output, and weights considered appropriate by people outside the organization. The *essence* of the rationale for regulating business firms or other organizations may usefully be viewed as a difference between (1) the input, output, or weight concepts viewed as relevant from the point of view of decision makers in those organizations, and (2) the input, output, and weight concepts considered relevant by some other person or group. It follows that the concepts of efficiency that these groups consider to be appropriate for the organization will also differ. Efficiency in a firm or other organization may simultaneously increase and decrease as a result of regulation that changes the firm's input and/or output mix, depending on whose perceptions of the proper input, output, and weight concepts are adopted.

Irrespective of which concept is adopted as an appropriate criterion for judging efficiency in regulated firms or other organizations, *both* the numerator and denominator of the efficiency expression are relevant in determining the effects of regulation on efficiency. Changes in the denominator of the efficiency expression, which refer to changes in the total costs of the firm or other organization, cannot themselves indicate the effects of regulation on the firm's efficiency. Changes in the numerator of the expression, which refers to output mix and weights indicating relative evaluations of different outputs, must also be considered. This is a particular case of a more general prescription for considering all costs and benefits of regulation jointly. The reasoning that underlies this prescription is contained in Section 4.4.

4.3   REGULATORY AGENCY COST
AND EFFICIENCY CONCEPTS

This section will explain the determinants of the C term in Table 4.1 that represents the total expenditures, or total costs, of a regulatory agency. It will also examine the nature and determinants of concepts of regulatory agency efficiency.

The total expenditures of a regulatory agency, like a firm's total costs, equals the sum of the quantities of each input employed by the agency multiplied by the price of the input. The issue of whether one should use market prices of regulatory agency inputs, or the value of those inputs in alternative uses, to measure the agency's total costs depends on the purpose of the cost calculation. If one is concerned with the question of whether regulatory agency input and output policies maximize the value society derives from its limited stock of scarce resources, the value of agency inputs in alternative uses is the proper valuation criterion for those inputs.

In contrast, if one is concerned with descriptive or normative analysis of the agency's efforts to change particular dimensions of regulated firms' behavior, and the agency's hiring decisions, the agency's inputs should be valued at their market prices. This is because it is the market prices of the inputs, not their value in alternative uses, that influences the behavior of the agency's decision makers. Market prices have to be paid to acquire the services of regulatory agency inputs whether or not those inputs have a lower value in alternative uses.

Another similarity between firms and regulatory agencies is that the input choices of an agency will depend on the three following considerations:

i. input prices or supply conditions
ii. the "production function" linking regulatory inputs and outputs
iii. the objectives or "utility function" of regulatory agency decision makers

The utility function describes the satisfaction agency decision makers responsible for input-hiring decisions derive directly or indirectly from various characteristics of the agency's operations. Unlike a firm's decision makers, sales revenues and profits will not be arguments in these functions. This is a minor difference, however, since budget allocations to the agency may depend on agency inputs or outputs, and such budget allocations are analogous to sales revenues in a firm. A leading hypothesis concerning the motivations of public sector bureaucrats is the "budget-maximization" hypothesis (see Chapter 5); this is identical to the sales-revenue-maximization hypothesis of traditional economic analysis of firms' behavior.

There is even a bureaucratic analogue to the profit-maximization hypothesis. If the difference between an agency's budget allocation and the total costs of producing certain agency outputs is defined as "discretionary budget," agency decision makers who try to maximize the amount of discretionary budget will behave exactly like a profit-maximizing decision maker would in selecting input and output levels of the agency.

One can readily see that (Total revenues − Total costs) = Profit = "Discretionary budget." There may even be stronger motivations for an agency's decision makers to act in a "profit-maximizing" manner than do managers in business firms, such as when the amount of discretionary budget that can be appropriated by the agency managers, in the form of inputs that yield managers satisfaction without adding anything to agency output, is greater than in business firms.

In the present context, however, our main concern is not with the precise nature of agency decision makers' objectives. It is to point out that the inputs hired by a regulatory agency, and therefore the agency's total costs, outputs, and the average and marginal costs of various agency output concepts, will depend on, and vary with, the nature of these objectives.

Regulatory Agency Production Functions. Our main goal in this section is to focus on item (ii) in the preceding list, the regulatory agency production function and its implications for agency cost and efficiency concepts. It is here that the existing literature on regulatory agency behavior and costs is at its weakest. Much more care is needed in specifying the nature of regulatory agency production functions, both from the perspective of describing agency behavior in practice, and also in terms of the kind of production functions and resulting agency cost concepts that are appropriate for achieving specific agency goals, such as changing regulated firms' behavior.

For purposes of describing the factors that underlie regulatory agency decision makers' behavior in practice, the "relevant" production function will be the input-output relationships that those decision makers consider when making input- and output-level decisions. These behaviorally relevant concepts will be related to each decision maker's preference function and reward system. That is, from all the input and output concepts agency decision makers could adopt, they will generally focus on those concepts which have a perceived impact on their personal satisfaction, either directly or indirectly via effects on the rewards and penalties accruing to them.

Although the input and output concepts that actually underlie the decisions of regulatory agency decision makers depend on their preferences and the penalty-and-reward systems that confront them, from a normative point of view the important question is which input and output concepts regulatory agency decision makers *should* consider in their decision making.

From a normative point of view, the primary function of regulatory agencies is to influence the behavior of individuals or organizations, irrespective of one's model of regulation or the evaluation criteria used to evaluate agency behavior and performance. *It is logical, therefore, to regard the behavior of the regulated decision makers as the appropriate "output" concept for purposes of regulation.*

Once attention is focused on changes in the behavior of regulated firms as the appropriate concept of the "output" of regulatory agencies, one can point to the factors that determine the regulatory agency's "production function" linking agency inputs to this output concept: (1) the goals and constraints facing decision makers in regulated firms that determine the firm's behavior in the absence of regulation and (2) the nature of the "regulatory constraint."

The term "regulatory constraint" is vague. In the literature this term is sometimes equated with the behavior of regulatory agencies, which is unfortunate, for a regulatory agency's behavior is not the only determinant of a regulatory constraint. A quantum leap in one's perceptions and understanding of the relationship between agency behavior and regulated firms' behavior may be gained by viewing any regulatory constraint as a penalty or reward of some kind, multiplied by a probability that the penalty or reward will be experienced by the regulated decision maker.

The penalty or reward, and the probability of its occurrence, may vary with some dimension of the regulated decision maker's behavior. For example, as Figure 4.3 shows, at low levels of pollution there may be no penalty for pollution, but beyond some maximum permitted level of pollution penalties may be applied to polluting firms, and these penalties may rise with increases in pollution beyond that level.

The existence of penalties for certain kinds of firms' behavior does not necessarily mean that they will be effective in changing the behavior. Violations of regulatory standards of behavior must be detected, and this requires monitoring firms' behavior and prosecuting violators. Some regulatory agencies have authority to vary the level of penalties or rewards for certain kinds of behavior by regulated decision makers. In most cases, however, the major impact of agency activities on a firm's behavior will operate via the influence of these activities for the probability of detecting and successfully prosecuting firms that violate regulatory standards of behavior. The magnitude of this probability will therefore play a crucial role in determining the height and shape of the curve in Figure 4.3.

The overall "probability" of detection and successful prosecution can be divided into a number of component probabilities. For present purposes, we shall consider three of these, as follows:

i. P_d, the probability that a firm's behavior will be monitored and that violations of required standards of behavior will be detected by regulatory agencies

Figure 4.3

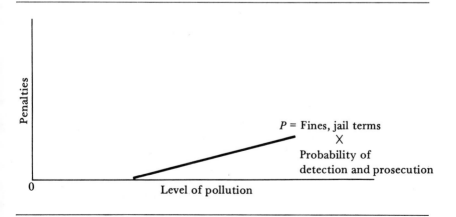

   ii. P_p, the probability that a firm whose behavior is in violation of required standards will be prosecuted by the regulatory agency

   iii. P_f, the probability that a firm that is prosecuted will fail in its defense, lose the case, and be subject to the penalties prescribed by law

The level of these probabilities *in the minds of regulated firms' decision makers* is relevant for determining their behavior, not the "objective" probabilities, or the probabilities viewed from the point of view of the regulatory agency. Also, the three probabilities must be multiplied in order to obtain the probability of detection and successful prosecution. This probability must then in turn be multiplied by the penalties prescribed by law in order to obtain the P curve in Figure 4.4.

Regulatory agency inputs and activities may affect each of these probabilities. Scarcity of resources will generally prevent a regulatory agency from monitoring the behavior of all firms, except in industries with a small number of firms. The decision rules and monitoring practices used by a regulatory agency will influence P_d. Limited resources will also generally prevent regulatory agencies from prosecuting all firms found to be violating regulatory standards; again, the precise nature of the agency's case selection criteria will influence P_p. For example, P_p may be higher for firms that are larger in overall size than for smaller firms committing the same violations.

The probability that the regulatory agency will win a case, P_f, will depend on the amount and quality of the legal and other resources the agency devotes to a case. Again, limited resources will compel agencies to use decision rules for allocating these resources among cases.

These P_d, P_p, and P_f probabilities do not depend solely on agency behavior. Regulated firms may engage in activities, including information distortion, that affect P_d. Similarly, given the case selection policies of regulatory agencies, the dimensions of certain aspects of a regulated firm's behavior will influence whether a firm that has violated regulatory standards will be prosecuted. Information regarding agency decision rules is quite valuable to regulated firms, for it enables them to adopt policies that reduce P_d or P_p. We have already mentioned that P_f will depend on the amount and quality of legal and other resources that firms spend in defending themselves against cases brought by regulatory agencies.

Firms are not the only organizations whose behavior will affect these three probabilities. The behavior of the courts will also exert considerable impact. Legal precedents will influence regulatory agency case selection policies and also the amount that regulated firms spend to defend themselves, for example. For these reasons, the regulatory agency production function that describes the relationship between agency inputs and the resulting effects on a regulated firms' behavior will be quite complex.

The situation is analogous to that involved in Leibenstein's concept of X inefficiency. The outputs from particular regulatory agency inputs depend on the goals and constraints facing those inputs. The ability of

Figure 4.4

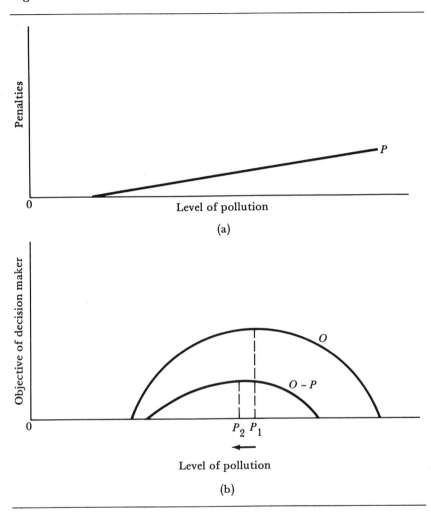

agency inputs to influence a regulated firm's behavior depends not only on constraints within, but also on constraints external to, the agency, such as determinants of a regulated firm's behavior and the behavior of the courts. Changes in any of these external constraints will change the regulatory agency production function with respect to the effect of given regulatory inputs on a regulated firm's behavior.

The penalties and probability of successful prosecution and the resulting constraint, depicted in Figure 4.3, provide a framework for linking agency inputs and their effects on regulated firms' behavior. The

nature of the connection between regulatory agency inputs and regulated
firms' behavior is the essence of the "regulatory production function,"
whether one is dealing with descriptive or normative aspects of agency
behavior. Conceptualizing this critical link is a necessary first step to both
theoretical and empirical studies of regulatory agency production functions in practice. Unfortunately, the existing literature on regulation has
been slow in realizing this.

Figure 4.4(a) depicts the penalties for pollution by a firm, multiplied
by the probability that the firm will be detected and will have to pay the
penalty, at different levels of pollution by the firm. The curve labeled
O in part (b) of the figure shows the level of a regulated firm's objective,
expressed in the same dimensions as the penalty curve, at different levels
of pollution by the firm in the absence of regulation. The shape and position of curve O depends on all the constraints that confront the regulated firm's decision makers in the absence of regulation, as well as on
their objectives (see Chapter 12).

The curve $O - P$ in Figure 4.4(b) shows the effect of subtracting the
penalty curve from the firm's objective curve. If the penalty curve in
part (a) of the figure were a horizontal line, curve O would be shifted
down *by the same amount at different levels* of the firm's behavior, here
exemplified as pollution activities. This would reduce the level of the
firm's objective function at all levels of pollution but would *not* change
the level of polluting activity that *maximizes* the firm's objective function
including the effects of regulation. Before regulation, the level of polluting activity that maximized the firm's objective function was P_1. This
level will *still* maximize the firm's objective function even in the presence
of regulation if the penalty function is a horizontal line, which will occur
if the penalties multiplied by probabilities of being detected and paying
those penalties do not vary with the level of pollution.

In contrast, if the probabilistic penalty function slopes up from left
to right, one can readily confirm that because a larger amount is being
subtracted from O as the level of polluting activity increases, the $O - P$
curve will now reach its highest point at a level of polluting activity
lower than P_1. In this case, regulation will reduce the optimal level of
the firm's polluting activities.

If the penalty function sloped *down* from left to right, similar reasoning will demonstrate that the optimal level of polluting activities is
increased above P_1 — regulation will provide incentives for *increased* pollution activities. If the reader thinks that this situation is unlikely, an
example may convince him or her otherwise. Even if penalties for pollution increase with level of polluting activities, and even if regulatory
agencies monitor large polluters more than small ones so that the probability of detecting violations is greater for large polluters, large polluters
may spend more to defend themselves against prosecution, resulting in a
smaller probability of successful prosecution than occurs for firms with

smaller levels of pollution. Larger levels of pollution may mean larger profits, or greater costs of trying to reduce pollution. If the reduced probability of successful prosecution at higher levels of pollution is greater than any increases in probability of detection, the result may be a downward-sloping penalty function in Figure 4.4, providing incentives for greater pollution.

It is clear, then, that the impact of the regulatory penalty curve on a regulated firm's behavior depends on the *slope* of the penalty curve. A similar conclusion also applies to *changes* in the penalty curve that occur because of changes in penalties and/or in the probability of successful prosecution of violators of regulatory standards. An upward or a downward shift in the penalty curve will change the height of the $O - P$ curve but will not change the optimal level of the regulated firm's behavior unless the slope of the penalty curve, and therefore the slope of the $O - P$ curve, is changed *at the previous optimal level of the regulated firm's behavior.*

The italicized phrase is important, because changes in the slope of the penalty curve may occur at some levels of pollution activities and not at others. To change the regulated firm's behavior, the slope of $O - P$ at the unregulated level of the firm's pollution activities must be changed. The slope of the $O - P$ curve shows the effect of a change in the level of the regulated firm's activity on the level of its objective. Unless this slope is changed, the firm cannot raise the attained level of its objective by changing the level of that activity.

Regulatory Agency Efficiency Concepts. The total output of a regulatory agency, measured in terms of the effect of regulatory agency activities on some dimension of regulated firms' behavior, could in principle be divided by the total input costs of the agency, resulting in a measure of the "average" cost of agency activities per unit of changes in regulated firms' behavior. Similarly, the ratio of changes in the behavior of regulated firms resulting from changes in agency input levels could be expressed in terms of "marginal costs" of agency output.

If the regulatory agency is responsible for regulating more than one dimension of regulated firms' behavior, the same problems of allocating the cost of particular inputs between different types of output that are encountered in multiproduct firms and other types of organization will be encountered. The cost allocation decision rules adopted by the agency would influence the average and marginal cost measures associated with any particular dimension of the agency's output.

Combinations of regulatory agency inputs that minimize the total costs of producing particular regulatory agency outputs, such as desired changes in regulated firms' behavior, can in principle be defined and used as bench marks of "efficient" regulatory agency input mixes. Again, however, whenever a regulatory agency is responsible for regulating more than one dimension of regulated firms' behavior, the usual problems of defining "efficiency" in multiproduct firms are encountered. Defining "efficiency" in terms of the ratio

$$\frac{\Sigma \text{ outputs}}{\Sigma \text{ inputs}}$$

requires weights to be assigned to different outputs and different inputs. In the case of profit-maximizing firms, the use of market prices of outputs and inputs will mean that any increase in the ratio implies an increase in profits. An increase in efficiency is, in other words, synonymous with an increase in the level of the profit-maximizing firm's objective function. In the case of a regulatory agency, the appropriate weights to be assigned to outputs and inputs depend on the agency's objective function. As we have emphasized many times, this depends essentially on *whose* evaluations of the "changes in regulated firms' behavior" and "prices of regulatory agency inputs" are used to evaluate agency behavior.

Irrespective of whose evaluations are used, the criteria that should be used to evaluate regulation of a dimension of a firm's activity, or change in regulation, involve a comparison of the *combined* changes in total costs of the regulatory agency and regulated firm, and $\Sigma (B - C)_i$ — the sum of the positive and negative evaluations of the effects of regulating the firm's behavior — by all those persons whose evaluations are considered "relevant." The reader is reminded that regulation may have effects on regulated and unregulated firms that regulators did not anticipate or intend. In principle, these effects should also be included in evaluating the efficiency of regulatory agency activities. Also, since the benefit (B) and cost (C) evaluation criteria may include any equity weights that are considered relevant, the preceding efficiency criterion is applicable to any model of the effects of regulation and to any set of normative evaluation criteria.

If the combined costs of a regulatory agency and regulation-induced changes in regulated firms' costs appear in the denominator of the regulatory agency efficiency measure, and the $\Sigma (B - C)_i$ term appears in the numerator, "increases in regulatory agency efficiency," so defined, will imply an increase in the performance of the agency by those persons whose evaluations are considered relevant. An alternative approach would be to include only the costs of the regulatory agency in the denominator of the efficiency measure, and to include effects of regulation on regulated firms' costs in the numerator together with the $(B - C)_i$ evaluations of effects of regulation on regulated and unregulated firms' behavior. In either case, the efficiency of the regulatory agency cannot be adequately expressed solely in terms of the agency's costs and resulting changes in regulated firms' behavior.

Multiple Regulatory Agencies and Efficiency Concepts. An additional complication exists if the attempts of individual regulatory agencies to change some dimension of regulated firms' behavior causes changes in the expenditures and costs of other regulatory agencies. Regulation of pollution may, for example, divert firms' resources from investments in worker safety. This change may cause agencies responsible for worker safety to increase their monitoring and enforcement activities and the amount of inputs they employ. Such changes as these should in principle be included in the denominator, or subtracted from the numerator, of the first agency's efficiency measure: the effects and output concepts of individual regulatory agencies are interrelated, and efficiency concepts for individual regulatory agencies will generally depend on the behavior of other regulatory agencies, no matter how these efficiency concepts are defined. (See Chapter 11.)

By broadening the range of effects of regulation that are considered appropriate indices of the "output" of regulatory agencies, one is in effect changing the production function that is considered appropriate for judging the regulatory agency's efficiency and performance. For this reason, the issue of what the appropriate production function for an agency is, and the issue of what agency objectives should be, cannot be separated in practice, though of course they may be distinguished conceptually as separate influences on agency behavior.

The foregoing illustrates again that the effects and evaluations of regulation cannot be separated from the issue of whose interests and evaluations are to be considered relevant normative indices for judging regulation. Instead of viewing production functions as technically determined input-output relationships, as is the usual practice in the literature of economics and business, it is more appropriate to regard them as behaviorally determined by decision makers' objectives and constraints, as Leibenstein has emphasized (1966, 1972, 1975, 1978b).

Similarly, the conventional practice of treating production functions as a fixed constraint faced by decision makers needs to be revised. Like other aspects of the decision maker's behavior, production functions are endogenously determined by interactions between a decision maker's objectives and the various constraints that are outside the decision maker's control. In other words, we should regard production functions as part of the solution in a decision maker's optimization process, rather than as something determined outside the analysis.

4.4 THE NEED TO CONSIDER COSTS AND BENEFITS OF REGULATION JOINTLY

Sections 4.1–4.3 have focused on the meaning, determinants, and relationship among a number of different components of the costs of regulation. This final section will draw together the common threads that link cost and benefit concepts of regulation. Emphasis will be on the reasons why cost and benefit evaluations must be considered jointly rather than separately. Although the major principles have already been expounded in this and the preceding chapter, it is easy to lose sight of the fundamentals when discussing individual cost and benefit concepts. In addition, some features that costs of regulation share in common with benefits have not been mentioned in this chapter.

Determination of Benefit and Cost Evaluations. Evaluations of the costs and benefits of regulation (or anything else) are jointly determined by the value systems and constraints that confront the people making the cost and benefit evaluations. This principle has a number of important implications, some of which are overlooked or ignored in conventional approaches to cost-benefit analysis. As a result, incorrect or misleading interpretations may be placed on particular cost-benefit studies of regulation or other aspects of the human environment. We shall outline these implications and relate them to the expository framework presented in Table 4.1.

The personal value systems and constraints confronting particular individuals, which determine their perceptions and evaluations of the effects of regulation, also determine the following important characteristics of the resulting cost and benefit evaluations:

(a) One characteristic concerns whether or not those individuals will disclose or *"reveal"* their evaluations of the personal benefits and costs of regulation, and the manner in which they will reveal these evaluations. Some individuals may prefer to reveal their evaluations by voting, by making monetary contributions to decision makers capable of influencing regulation, by personal lobbying of such decision makers, by engaging in a wide variety of activities designed to influence the perceptions of a wider class of citizens whose behavior is considered capable of influencing regulation, or through some combination of these activities.

(b) The second characteristic concerns whether or not individuals will *misrepresent* their evaluations of the benefits and costs of regulation. Individuals can be expected to misrepresent their evaluations of particular benefits and costs of regulation whenever they believe that doing so will result in an outcome that is preferred to the outcome expected when they reveal their evaluations honestly. Misrepresentation can occur in voting behavior or in any other method of revealing evaluations and is not confined to misrepresentation of individuals' monetary evaluations of benefits and costs.

The fact that benefit and cost evaluations are jointly determined by the value system and constraints facing the individuals responsible for those evaluations also implies that *benefit and cost evaluations can be changed, either by changing the value system and/or constraints confront-*

ing those individuals or, alternatively, by changing the identity of individuals whose evaluations are taken into consideration. In either case, focusing on costs, or benefits, alone is inappropriate, since both will generally be changed simultaneously.

Monetary benefit and cost evaluations in Table 4.1 may be weighted by equity weights, as explained in Chapter 3. These weights can take many forms, and their magnitude will determine the weight given to the evaluations of particular individuals, and to particular effects of regulation, in any overall evaluation of those effects. In the present context, the costs and benefits associated with an individual's evaluation of regulation must be weighted by the *same* factor whenever those costs and benefits occur in the same time period. It would be inappropriate to apply one weight to an individual's evaluation of the costs of regulation, and a different weight to that individual's evaluation of the benefits of regulation occurring in the same time period.

Alternative Uses for Table 4.1. Table 4.1 may be used as a framework either for *descriptive* analyses of how people actually evaluate regulation or any other aspect of their environment, or for *normative* analyses of how people "should" evaluate regulation. Although the table does not indicate the nature of people's objectives and constraints that underlie the benefit or cost elements in the table, it does clearly illustrate the relationship among a number of dimensions of cost-benefit analysis. For example, it shows how the outcome of any cost-benefit analysis hinges critically on the identity of persons whose evaluations are considered relevant (the columns of Table 4.1), the effects that are considered relevant (the rows of Table 4.1), and the weights assigned (or not assigned) to particular rows, columns, or individual benefit and cost elements in the table.

In the following chapters we shall examine the objectives and constraints that confront certain strategic types of decision maker, such as regulatory agency decision makers, legislators, voters, and regulated decision makers. It is these decision-makers' behavior that generates the effects of regulation and evaluation of those effects depicted by the benefit and cost elements in Table 4.1.

The use of Table 4.1 as an expository framework is not restricted to matters of regulation alone. In principle, any type of decision that is based on an evaluation of benefits and costs of alternative courses of action may be depicted within the multiple-reference-group and multiple-effects framework of Table 4.1. It can be applied, for example, to the decisions of a legislator who is considering the consequences of different dimensions of his or her behavior and voters' evaluations of those consequences. Or it can be applied to a firm's decision makers considering the consequences of multiple-product dimensions for different individuals and markets.

The relevant dimensions of the benefit and cost elements for these other types of decision maker may be different. Firms' decision makers may be concerned only with revealed monetary evaluations of the benefits of their products and services, in the form of market demands; legislators may be concerned only with votes. These traditional assumptions are merely special cases, however, and do not necessarily describe reality. Legislators may be concerned with monetary sources of funds for campaign expenditures as well as with votes, and firms' decision makers may be concerned about evaluations of their behavior by groups other than the purchasers of their products. This is especially true once it is recognized that people who are not happy with firms' behavior may engage in political activities aimed at securing regulatory legislation designed to change that behavior.

As the following chapters demonstrate, traditional analyses of the behavior of business firms, legislators, and regulators have been far too restrictive in terms of the assumed objectives of these decision makers and the reference groups whose evaluations influence their behavior. The required modifications of traditional theories of decision-maker behavior can readily be explained in terms of adding to Table 4.1 rows and columns that depict the benefits and costs considered by the decision maker whose behavior is being analyzed.

The References for this chapter include a selection of cost-benefit studies of different types of regulation, including trucking, milk, and crude oil price regulations, and mandatory deposits on beverage containers. The reader may test his or her understanding of the principles of cost-benefit analysis contained in this and the preceding chapter by reading these studies from a critical perspective, concentrating on the explicit and implicit assumptions contained in the studies and on the implications of varying these assumptions for the results and conclusions reached by the authors.

CHAPTER FIVE

Regulatory Agency Behavior

5.1 IMPORTANCE OF REGULATORY AGENCY BEHAVIOR

The behavior of regulatory agencies entrusted with responsibility for administering and enforcing regulatory legislation is important in any descriptive or normative study of regulation. It is these agencies which largely determine the nature of the regulatory constraint which confronts regulated decision makers. Although regulatory legislation may prescribe the nature and magnitude of penalties or rewards for certain types of behavior, it is the regulatory agency that determines the type of monitoring activities that are used to detect violation of required standards of behavior. Similarly, it is the regulatory agency that decides whether to prosecute all violations detected, or only a subset of these violations, and that establishes the criteria for selecting which violators will be prosecuted. The amount of resources expended on prosecuting individual violators is another important factor entirely within the discretion of the regulatory agency.

By controlling monitoring and enforcement activities that affect the probability of detection and successful prosecution of violators, a regulatory agency influences the expected level of the penalties or rewards confronting regulated decision makers (see Chapter 12). It is sufficient here to point out that, owing to its control of monitoring and enforcement, a regulatory agency in effect has wide discretion over the magnitude of penalties and rewards for specific behavior, even where penalties are ostensibly fixed by regulatory legislation.

In addition, the "standards of behavior" prescribed by regulatory legislation are usually sufficiently imprecise to permit agencies a broad range of discretion in interpreting what is meant by those standards. In other words, holding penalties and the probability of detecting certain

99

standards of behavior constant, a change in the probability that a regulated decision maker's behavior will result in penalties can be achieved by varying the agency's interpretation of what is meant by "required standards of behavior" in regulatory legislation. Similarly, in the case of agencies with responsibility for allocating "rewards," such as licenses to engage in activities like television or radio broadcasting, trucking, dentistry, medicine, or the operation of a taxicab, the criteria prescribed by legislation will generally be in vague terms, such as "serving the public interest," "providing adequate service," or "providing service at reasonable cost." This vagueness leaves wide discretion for the agency in selecting the criteria it will use for allocating licenses or other rewards.

Regulatory agency behavior is not entirely without constraints. In addition to any limitations contained in regulatory legislation, agencies operate within budgetary limitations on the overall size of their operations. These budget limitations are related to the behavior of the legislative or administrative sponsor responsible for making these budget allocations. Agency behavior that displeases the sponsors will generally be avoided. In theory, if the sponsors are themselves elected representatives, budgetary restraints on agency behavior will reflect the interests of some members of society.

For a variety of reasons, legislators may be neither motivated nor able to reflect the desires of the people they "represent." The reader might pause to reflect on how he or she would "represent" two or more people who want their representative to behave in two or more ways. The "democratic restraints" thesis also ignores the fact that much of the information on regulators' behavior that must serve as the basis for monitoring and evaluating that behavior is provided by regulators themselves. The kind of incentives that would motivate regulators to supply honest information regarding their activities do not exist in the real world — and neither do the kind of incentives that are required to elicit honest evaluations of regulators' performance.

Even budgetary restraints on regulators are not as effective as one might suppose, since it is possible for regulators, by controlling the characteristics of the regulatory constraint, to force or motivate regulated decision makers to bear a major portion of the administrative costs of regulation. Information-gathering activities are an obvious example of a situation where most of the cost is borne by regulated decision makers. We hasten to add that this situation is not necessarily undesirable; as was emphasized in Chapter 3, regulatory agency costs and regulated decision-maker costs are jointly determined by the nature of the regulatory constraint. An optional regulatory constraint may require regulated decision makers to be responsible for providing and bearing the cost of information supplied to regulators regarding certain facets of their behavior. In the present context, we merely wish to point out that the budget of an agency does not adequately reflect, or limit, the total amount of resources involved in the administration of the agency's responsibilities.

Another important constraint on agency behavior in practice is its "production function," which describes the relationship between the agency's inputs and outputs. The terms "input" and "output" are a matter of perspective, and in practice regulators may use a variety of input and output concepts other than the concept of output that is relevant if one is concerned with the effects of regulation on regulated decision makers and on society. From a normative point of view, the effect of regulation on the behavior of regulated decision makers is the relevant concept of regulators' output. This output depends on (1) the objectives and other constraints that confront these decision makers and (2) the form of the regulatory constraint that confronts regulated decision makers. The regulatory constraint depends, in turn, on the penalties or rewards for certain kinds of behavior, and on the probability that a regulated decision maker exhibiting these kinds of behavior will be detected and successfully prosecuted or rewarded.

The probability of successful detection and rewards or penalties being applied to regulated decision makers depends only partly on regulatory inputs and activities. The behavior of regulated firms and the courts also determines the magnitude of this probability. Therefore, the output of agency activities — defined in terms of resulting changes in regulated decision makers' behavior that occur in response to particular regulatory inputs — depends on a number of complex relationships.

An agency that is not aware of the underlying production function linking its inputs to regulated decision makers' behavior may be totally ineffective in changing that behavior. In practice, few agencies have adequate knowledge of their production function, and much regulatory "failure" can be attributed to this inadequacy. Regulatory agencies themselves cannot be blamed for this state of affairs. Only relatively recently have developments in theory of regulation clarified the nature of the relationship that exists between regulatory inputs, regulatory constraints, and regulated decision-maker behavior.

Part of the problem of determining a regulatory agency's production function is that much of the information on the goals and constraints facing regulated decision makers must be obtained, directly or indirectly, from the regulated decision makers themselves. Incentives for these decision makers to reveal this information honestly are lacking and need to be built into regulatory constraints (explained in Chapter 12). In addition, even when regulated decision makers honestly reveal information, their behavior in response to a regulatory constraint may in part depend on how they expect regulators to change the regulatory constraint in response to this behavior. This factor greatly complicates the problem of determining the nature of the regulatory agency production function in the sense in which we are defining that term.

Even if a regulatory agency knows its production function, when combined with the agency's budget restraint, it may be unable to perform the functions mandated by the regulatory legislation: the budget may not be sufficient to permit the agency to hire the quantities and qualities of inputs required to produce the mandated effects on regulated decision-maker behavior.

As noted in Chapter 2, it is a mistake to assume that regulatory agency behavior becomes important only after regulatory legislation is enacted. An existing agency may initiate demands for additional legislation that expands its functions or powers. This may be a response to what James McKie (1970) has aptly termed the "tar-baby effect" of regulation. Regulating any single dimension of individual or organizational behavior will result in changes in other dimensions of the regulated decision maker's behavior (see Chapter 11). These changes may weaken or frustrate the ability of a regulatory agency to influence the regulated dimension of behavior and lead the agency to attempt to extend regulation to other dimensions of the regulated decision maker's behavior.

The tar-baby effect refers to extensions of regulatory control in response to decision-maker reactions that reduce or evade earlier regulation. It may lead to ever expanding control and to increasing frustration on the part of the regulators. This is especially true in situations in which regulatory control is distributed among separate regulatory agencies acting independently (see Chapter 11). A regulatory agency may initiate regulatory legislation either by approaching legislators directly or by providing information to voters and other groups that leads indirectly to pressure on legislators for regulatory reform.

Even in situations in which a new regulatory agency is being created, existing agencies will rarely be indifferent to the content of the legislation that creates the new agency and defines its responsibilities and the scope of its powers. The strength and direction of the influence of existing agencies on new regulatory legislation depend on a variety of factors, and no generalizations are possible. At one extreme, existing agencies may seek to limit the power of a new agency that they perceive as a competitor, either for scarce budget resources, or for the services of clients or sponsors of the existing agencies. In contrast, some existing regulatory agencies might prefer a new agency with ill-defined and wide powers if they perceive their relationship with the new agency to be one of "complementarity," a situation in which the activities of one agency contribute toward increased demand for the services of another. Regulators may provide information to voters and legislators that may influence their behavior. In addition, as Fiorina and Noll (1978) have emphasized, legislators may require the support of regulators as much as regulators need the support of legislators.

In any event, whether or not legislation governing regulatory agency behavior is narrowly defined, the inalienable discretion agencies possess over monitoring and enforcement activities will leave a large element of discretion of the precise form of the constraint that confronts regulated decision makers. Avoiding this discretion would be impossible without eliminating the need for the regulatory agency. Moreover, regulatory discretion in monitoring and enforcement activities is desirable because *the nature of an optimal regulatory constraint depends on aspects of regulated decision makers' behavior that cannot be determined in advance.* It will generally be necessary to determine the nature of an optimal regulatory constraint by observing the effects of specific monitoring and enforcement policies on regulated decision-maker behavior and by varying these policies and the associated regulatory constraint in response to information feedback. Without discretion in monitoring and enforcement, it would be impossible to approach the optimal regulatory constraint by a series of iterations, as will generally be required in practice.

5.2 DETERMINANTS OF BUREAUCRATIC BEHAVIOR

The behavior of regulatory agencies depends both on the goals of decision makers within the agencies and on the constraints that confront them. The relevant constraints include the legislation that established the agency and defined its responsibilities and methods of operation, the factors that determine the agency's budget, the production function that describes the relationship between the agency's inputs and outputs, the prices of the agency's inputs, and other constraints that will be discussed in this and subsequent sections. The goals of the agency's decision makers, and each of the constraints, can take a variety of forms, each with different implications for the agency's behavior.

Knowledge of the objectives and constraints confronting agency decision makers is therefore essential in order to understand and to predict agency behavior accurately. Such knowledge is also necessary to effect a change in regulatory agency behavior in any desired manner. Moreover, decision-maker objectives and *all* the constraints considered relevant by the decision maker interact to determine his or her behavior. It is legitimate to focus on the decision maker's objectives, or on one of the constraints, and to consider the consequences of changing the form of the objectives or the constraint for the decision maker's behavior. This is standard practice in the literature. It must never be forgotten, however, that the resulting consequences for the decision maker's behavior depend not only on the constraint that is changed but also on the form of all the other constraints. In other words, the same change in objectives, or in a particular constraint, will have *different* consequences for the decision maker's behavior if one or more of the other constraints is changed.

We emphasize this factor because it is vital to interpreting correctly the results of studies that attempt to determine the nature of decision-maker objectives, or particular constraints, in practice. Many statistical studies of whether business firms' decision makers pursued profit maximization or sales revenue maximization have been based on the correct assumption that these objectives lead to different behavior if all other constraints facing the decision makers are the same. What the studies often failed to do was to try to ensure that the decision makers in the firms included in the statistical studies *did* face the same constraints. If they do not face the same constraints, then very little can be concluded about the objectives of decision makers from their observed behavior.

Niskanen's Model of Bureaucratic Behavior. A logical starting point for trying to understand the way in which decision makers' objectives and constraints interact in determining regulatory agency behavior is the model of bureaucratic behavior associated with William Niskanen, which has attracted considerable attention in the literature of public sector decision making. The model has been considerably refined and extended since Niskanen's earliest contributions but remains the paradigm of bureaucratic behavior in the economics literature. In Figure 5.1, the horizontal axis represents the level of output of a bureaucratic agency, and

Figure 5.1

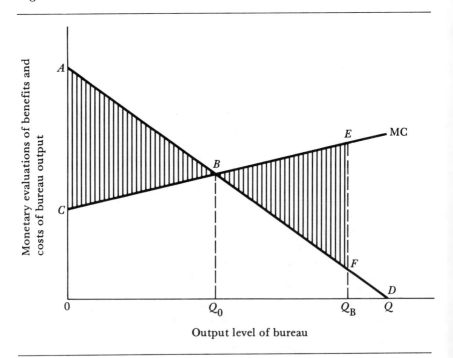

the vertical axis measures in money terms the benefits and costs of the agency's output. The marginal cost of the agency's output at different output levels is shown by the curve labeled MC. Curve AD shows the value placed by the agency's sponsor (budget allocator) on each incremental unit of the agency's output. The total amount the sponsor is willing to pay for any given quantity of the agency's output Q is shown by the area under curve AD up to that output level Q.

In his earlier model of bureaucratic behavior, Niskanen (1968) assumed that the goal of the head bureaucratic decision maker was to maximize the agency's budget, arguing that income perquisites, prestige, and other factors that yield the decision maker satisfaction directly would be correlated positively with the size of an agency's budget. Niskanen's second central hypothesis was that the agency was in a position to select its output level and obtain from its sponsor the budget allocation corresponding to the total value the sponsor placed on that level. In these circumstances, the agency will select an output level that maximizes the agency's budget, subject only to the constraint that the total costs of supplying the selected output level must not exceed the budget.

The selected output level would be point D_0 in Figure 5.1, where the value of an extra unit of output to the sponsor is zero and would add nothing to the agency's budget, and the budget would be the entire area under the "demand" curve D, unless the total cost of that output, represented by the area under the MC curve at output level D, exceeded the maximum budget (OAD). In the latter circumstances, the bureaucrat will select a level of output such as Q_B, where the shaded area BEF equals the shaded area ABC. Area ABC equals the excess of total revenue over total cost generated by output level Q_0. Area BEF equals the excess of total cost over total revenue generated by output levels beyond Q_0. Beyond output level Q_0, increases in output will yield increases in budget, but the increases in total cost necessary to produce the extra output are greater than the increases in the budget. The agency can expand output beyond Q_0 only up to the point at which area ABC is "used up" by the area BEF.

The implications of this earliest of Niskanen's models of bureaucratic behavior for the efficiency with which the agency produces its output are interesting. At output levels up to D the agency will never produce its output inefficiently, which would result in an MC curve above the minimum possible level. If the agency were producing its output inefficiently, an increase in efficiency would shift the MC curve down, and the total costs of the agency's current output would be less than the total budget. This would enable the agency to increase its budget by selecting a higher output level. In contrast, if minimum total costs of output D are less than the budget at D, the agency has an incentive to be inefficient, since it can produce output D at higher costs without reducing the budget.

The most important conclusion of Niskanen's analysis is that the agency will produce an output level that is higher than Q_0, the output level that maximizes society's satisfaction assuming that the sponsors' preferences accurately reflect the preferences of all citizens, an assumption that will be retained for the moment.

In later versions of his model, Niskanen (1975) replaced the assumption that bureaucrats attempt to maximize the size of the agency's total budget by an assumption that they attempt to maximize their satisfaction, which is assumed to depend on income and on nonmonetary perquisites, which in turn are assumed to be positively related to the level of the agency's output and its "discretionary budget." The discretionary budget is defined as the difference between the maximum budget that would be approved by the government review group that comprises the agency's sponsor and the minimum total cost of producing the agency's selected output level.

This reformulation avoids the possibility that the agency will be efficient over some ranges of output and inefficient over others, a feature that seems inconsistent with observations of real-world bureaucratic behavior. This reformulated objective function leads to a general conclusion that a bureau's budget is always too large, that the output is generally larger than Q_0, and that output will generally be produced inefficiently by the agency. At one limit, if bureaucrats do not value the discretionary budget, the agency's output level will be produced efficiently but will be above Q_0. At the other limit, if bureaucrats do not derive satisfaction directly or indirectly from the bureau's output, they will produce an output level like Q_0, but it will be produced inefficiently.

Explicit and implicit assumptions regarding information flows are crucial in Niskanen's model. The bureaucrat is assumed to have information about the sponsor's "demand" curve (AD), yet the sponsor is assumed not to know the MC curve. If the sponsor knows the MC curve, it can allocate budget that is just sufficient to enable Q_0 to be produced. Q_0 is the output level which achieves allocative efficiency, in traditional economic analysis. Technical efficiency, resulting in MC higher than the minimum possible level, would still be possible, unless the sponsor has information on the regulatory agency's production function and input-supply prices.

The sponsor may use a variety of monitoring and other techniques designed to obtain information about the agency's cost function. For example, where there is more than one agency, or a private sector organization, capable of producing the output, budgets may be allocated on the basis of competitive bids. Or attempts may be made to obtain cost information from sources at lower levels of the agency itself; in certain circumstances competition for jobs within the same agency may be used as a device for eliciting information regarding the agency's minimum cost function.

Because all methods of obtaining information involve costs to the sponsor, it will not, however, generally be desirable to obtain enough information to eliminate allocative and technical inefficiency on the part of the agency. The "optimal" level of monitoring activities by the sponsor will be where the marginal cost of monitoring equals the value to the sponsor of the resulting reductions in allocative and/or technical inefficiency in the agency. Because the costs of monitoring and preventing technical and allocative inefficiency may differ, the optimal level at which the two types of control mechanism should be operated is where their marginal effects on inefficiency are proportional to their respective marginal costs.

Importance of Agency Sponsors' Behavior. Whether these prescriptions will be implemented depends on the motivations and behavior of the sponsors. Until now we have assumed that the sponsor's evaluation of the agency's output accurately reflects the preferences and evaluations of the median voter, or some other criterion of "society's" preferences. This does not necessarily imply that legislators will engage in the level and type of monitoring activities that are socially optimal. (See Chapter 13.) Here, it is sufficient to point out that the kind of incentives that are required to induce legislative decision makers to undertake socially optimal types and levels of monitoring behavior in regard to regulatory agencies will not result from the existing kinds of objectives and constraints currently facing legislators. Section 5.4 will deal with the determinants of legislators' behavior in more detail.

Normative Aspects of Evaluations of Regulators' Output. If the legislative review committee's evaluations of the bureau's output depicted by curve AD are different from the evaluations of society as a whole, little normative significance can be attached to the conclusion that bureaus will produce a larger level of agency output than Q_0. Niskanen argues that, at least in the United States, most legislative committees are dominated by legislators who have higher demands for the service of the bureaucratic agency they review than the median demand in the whole legislature, and that the committee decisions are very seldom amended. Therefore, even if the preferences of the legislature as a whole accurately reflect the preferences of society, the legislative committees will value the agency's output more highly than will society as a whole. According to Niskanen (1971), the reason review committees are weighted in favor of legislative committees who have higher demands for the outputs they are reviewing than society as a whole is that legislators prefer to serve on committees that deal with agency services that are most important to their regional constituencies. If this argument is a correct depiction of reality, the result would be a tendency for the review committee's curve AD in Figure 5.1 to lie to the right of the AD curve, which would reflect society's preferences. This would reinforce a tendency for the bureau to produce "too much" output, even in a limiting situation in which bureaucrats do not value output and produce Q_0

Niskanen's argument that committees reviewing and allocating budgets to bureaucratic agencies will value agency output higher than society as a whole does not necessarily apply in all circumstances, however (Mackay and Weaver, 1979). If the review committee's evaluation of the agency's output is biased in the opposite direction, and is lower than the evaluation of those outputs by society as a whole, agency output may be lower than the level that would maximize society's satisfaction, despite any tendency for the agency to produce an output level higher than Q_0, the output that maximizes the satisfaction of the review committee/ budget allocator.

Even if legislative review committees and curve AD in Figure 5.1 faithfully reflect the evaluations of an agency's output by society, no normative significance can be attached to the conclusion that agencies will produce an output level greater than Q_0 if the evaluations of society are not *correct* evaluations of society's true preferences. There are several reasons why individuals may not reveal their true evaluations of agency output correctly. First, it is well known in the public goods literature that individuals will not generally reveal true evaluations of public goods whose effects apply to them irrespective of the amount they contribute to the cost of those goods. The kind of incentive systems that overcome incentives for the untruthful reporting of information will be examined in Chapter 12.

Second, since society's monetary evaluations of any particular activity depend critically on *whose* evaluations are taken to represent those of society, the theoretical expedient of using *every* member of society's preferences does not overcome this problem, even if members of society are restricted to the generations alive at any point in time. The distribution of income, wealth, power, and other factors will affect people's monetary evaluation of a particular activity, so that the same people will evaluate a particular activity differently, depending on these distributions. The distributions of income and power will often be related to, and depend on, levels of the activity in question, so that the monetary evaluations might vary with the level of the activity itself. Finally, if the purpose of the activity is to change the distribution of income or other factors, monetary evaluations based on particular income distributions become irrelevant as a guide to the desirability of particular activities. All these issues are relevant in interpreting "society's" monetary evaluations of an activity as a normative bench mark for judging agency behavior. In short, the criteria of "correct" budget size, level of output, or degree of technical efficiency exhibited by public sector bureaucrats depend critically on unavoidable normative judgments.

Third, even if a set of criteria is adopted as an appropriate normative index of society's preferences, and even if people do not distort their true evaluations of an activity performed by a government bureau, relatively little attention has been focused in the literature on the process by which these evaluations are formed. To place a monetary value on a particular activity or output, people have to have some idea of what the effects of that output are, both on themselves and on others. If the activity has not been performed, *no one* may know what its effects are. Alternatively, some members of society may "know" what the effects of an activity are; others may not know or not have the same information or perceptions. If the decision maker actually producing the output is one, or perhaps the only, source of information regarding the effects of the output, another dimension is added to the problem of placing normative connotations on some concept of "society's" preferences.

Other Dimensions of Bureau Behavior. The size of agency budgets, and the degree of technical and allocative efficiency exhibited by government agencies, are not the only features of bureaucratic behavior that have received attention in the literature. For example, Bennett and Johnson (1979a,b) have indicated the dimensions of the mountain of paperwork created by the federal government bureaucracy.

Irrespective of whether it is measured in physical terms of the amount of paperwork generated, the hours required to produce the paperwork, or the monetary cost of these activities, the amount is staggering. This includes only the tip of the mountain, because it does not include the costs imposed on the private sector in responding to federal demands for information. Even this statistic understates the magnitude of the paperwork burden imposed by government, since it excludes state and local governments.

By 1980 the paperwork burden had grown steadily, despite recommendations to control federal paperwork by innumerable agencies, boards, bureaus, committees, commissions, departments, and presidential task forces since the late 1880s, and despite executive orders and legislation to control government forms. The latest attempt to curb growth of federal paperwork is the Paperwork Reduction Act, passed in December 1980. This act is intended to eliminate a number of weaknesses in the 1942 Federal Reports Act, which created a review process for government forms, administered by the Office of Management and Budget (OMB). The 1942 act exempted a number of federal agencies, including the Internal Revenue Service, which has been estimated to generate one third of the federal forms involving the general public, and the OMB disapproved only a small percentage of agencies' applications for federal forms (Bennett and Johnson 1979a). The 1980 act amended the 1942 act to include virtually all federal agencies including the IRS, created within the OMB an Office of Information and Regulatory Affairs with responsibility for clearance of all new federal paperwork, and established a federal information locator system to discover duplication of federal forms and to help agencies locate existing sources of information.

It remains to be seen whether this latest attempt to reduce the federal paperwork burden will be more successful than previous attempts. An example may be sufficient to introduce some skepticism in this matter. When President Lyndon Johnson ordered the number of forms in use to be reduced by 10 percent compared with the number in use in October 1975, the federal bureaucracy achieved this reduction but increased the man-hours required to complete the remaining forms in doing so!

To try to explain the federal paperwork phenomenon's resistance to attempts at reduction, Bennett and Johnson (1979a) attempted to integrate paperwork into a theory of bureaucratic behavior. According to their analysis, when agencies lack easily quantifiable measures of output, paperwork becomes the tangible evidence that they are performing some activity; moreover, it is a weapon agencies can use to inflate the cost of output above its true value, thereby increasing the bureaucrats' "discretionary budget." If, as their analysis requires, paperwork is positively associated in an agency's budgetary sponsor's mind with the total cost of producing a given level of output, increases in paperwork at a given level of agency output will increase both the total budget allocated to the agency and its discretionary budget, which is the amount by which the total budget exceeds the actual minimum cost of producing that level of output. There is a second phase of agency behavior in which paperwork is involved in Bennett and Johnson's model. In this phase, the federal bureaucrat takes the budget actually authorized by its sponsor as given and attempts to increase the discretionary budget by reducing its actual cost of production. This can be accomplished by shifting some of the cost of processing paperwork to the private sector or to state and local governments.

Evaluations of Bureau Behavior from Other Sources. The legislative review committee is not the only mechanism by which evaluations of a public sector agency's behavior may be obtained, even though such committees may be the main factor underlying the agency's budget allocation. In addition to the legislative sponsor's evaluations, evaluations of agency behavior by client groups or other interest groups may directly and indirectly affect agency decision makers' behavior. Studies of "bureaucratic responsiveness" to a variety of client and other interest-group concepts have been made (Rycroft, 1978; Ermer, 1979) and generally conclude that bureaucrats are "unresponsive." Indeed, it is virtually impossible to find any theoretical or empirical evidence in the literature that suggests that bureaucrats do anything right. Our purpose here is not to suggest that they do, since this would invite a bolt of lightning from the social pundits of our time and the legions of people who derive gainful employment from discovering and attempting to remedy perceived deficiencies in public- and private-sector behavior. Rather, it is to emphasize that it is impossible to judge bureaucratic behavior without some explicit or implicit notion of "correct behavior" and that this notion of correct behavior should take into account the real-world nature of the constraints that confront public sector decision makers.

Even when the Niskanen type of model of public sector agency behavior is applied to agencies producing "public goods" of the traditional kind, there are a number of descriptive and normative aspects of the model that are inadequate. These inadequacies are greatly multiplied when an attempt is made to apply the model to the behavior of a regulatory agency. Moreover, since many government agencies of the more traditional variety also perform certain regulatory functions, this further diminishes the descriptive relevance or normative significance of the conventional models of agency behavior that have been discussed in this section.

One may be appalled by the estimate that businesses take about 69 million hours annually at an estimated cost of over $1 billion to respond to more than 2,100 United States reporting requirements (excluding the IRS) contained in a 1978 Report by the Comptroller General of the United States entitled *Federal Paperwork: Its Impact on American Businesses*. One may feel dismayed that regulators rely on regulated firms for much of their information and seem to employ ex-employees of regulated industries who often later return to those regulated industries. Yet whether or how to correct these situations cannot be determined without determining the characteristics of "socially optimal" decision-maker behavior within a realistic model of goals and constraints facing those decision makers in practice.

As we shall discover, this requires analysis of the behavior, not only of regulatory agencies, but also regulated industries, legislators, and individuals. Part of the solution to improving regulatory agency behavior, as will be shown, consists of improving the behavior of other decision makers also. Moreover, it will be found that the characteristics of socially optimal behavior of different decision makers are interdependent *and* cannot be determined in advance. That is, the search for criteria of socially optimal behavior and the attempt to ensure such behavior on the part of decision makers are problems that must be solved simultaneously. The assumption that it is possible to determine criteria of socially optimal behavior in advance is naive and overlooks the fact that most of the constraints that confront both regulated decision makers and regulators are unknown. Yet, it is these constraints, together with normative concepts of "desired" behavior, that determine what kind of regulatory constraints will be required to elicit specific desired forms of behavior.

5.3 INADEQUACIES OF EXISTING MODELS OF BUREAUCRATIC BEHAVIOR

In this section we focus on a number of weaknesses in existing models of bureaucratic behavior and discuss the implications for models of regulatory agency behavior. These weaknesses fall into two categories.

First, existing models exhibit an unnecessarily restrictive approach to the forms of some of the constraints that are included and often omit constraints that may influence bureaucratic decision makers' behavior and materially change the conclusions of descriptive analyses of bureaucratic behavior. Second, in the literature that deals with normative aspects of bureaucratic behavior, judgments concerning the performance of bureaucrats often involve implicit assumptions on the part of those persons making the judgments that are questionable, and should be made explicit. In addition, a number of normative issues that *should* be included are ignored in the existing literature. A prime example of this is the question of what the "output" dimension(s) of regulatory agencies' behavior should be, apart from its level and the efficiency with which it is produced.

For convenience of exposition, these various unsatisfactory features of the existing literature on bureaucratic behavior in general and regulatory agency behavior in particular will be discussed under the three following headings:

a. the nature of agency decision makers' goals
b. the nature of agency production and cost functions
c. the nature of demand for agency output

(a) Nature of Agency Decision Makers' Goals

Even in the case of public sector agencies that produce traditional "public goods" like defense, health, or education services, one should not accept uncritically the Niskanen assumption of budget-maximizing goals on the part of agency decision makers as a description of the objective of all bureaucrats. Admittedly, it is difficult to refute the hypothesis, because agency budgets tend to increase automatically as a result of an income tax system that generates added tax revenues for the government sector as the value of the nation's output grows. It is not clear what the behavior of budgets would be if government revenues were not increasing automatically as the value of the nation's total output of goods and services increases. Also, the level of an agency's budget tends to be positively associated with most of the variables that might yield satisfaction to agency decision makers directly or indirectly (e.g., income, particular inputs in the agency, agency output, self-esteem). Nonetheless, examples can be found where agency decision makers have furthered their careers by cutting agency budgets.

More important, whereas in business organizations the executives with the fastest career advancement remained with one organization, the fastest career advancement in government organizations is shown by political appointees and career civil servants who moved among bureaus (Margolis,

1975). These moves often include moving from the head of a relatively large bureau to the head of a small one, and also moves from administrative to political careers. The managers of bureaus consist of a mixed variety of people with different career aspirations and incentive patterns that cast doubt on the adequacy of the budget-maximization hypothesis as a general description of their objectives.

Any attempt to determine the objectives of decision makers must consider the relevant time frame the individual decision maker uses in making decisions. This time frame may depend on the characteristics of the position itself. For example, Eckert (1973) has shown that there are significant differences in the behavior of regulators in local governments, depending on whether they hold positions as civil servants in administrative bureaus, who may have incentives to consider the longer-run consequences of their decisions, or as commissioners who are appointed for a shorter period of time.

Whose Goals Are the Agency's Goals? A different type of problem involved in trying to determine the nature of the objectives pursued by both private- and public-sector organizations' decision makers is deciding *which* decision maker's goals should be considered relevant in determining the organization's characteristics.

All organizations, including regulatory agencies, consist of a number of individuals with generally different preferences and objectives. Two approaches to the concept of an organizational goal that are relevant in determining organizational behavior can be distinguished in the literature. In one approach, the diverse objectives of individuals in the organization are somehow pooled, or aggregated, to form a single organizational goal, a collective intent that the individual decision makers share. The process of aggregation that is envisaged by different writers can vary and may involve unanimity, majority opinion, or a coalition view of goal formation (Mohr, 1973; Duncan, 1976).

The second approach recognizes the limited span of control and decision-making capacity of individual decision makers in any organization and retains the diversity of objectives of different decision makers within the organization. Each decision maker has responsibility for some aspect of the firm's operations, and the decisions of all the decision makers in the organization interact to produce the organization's behavior and characteristics at any point in time. In this approach there is no formal process of collective goal formation that needs to be investigated to determine the behavior of individual decision makers in the organization. It is sufficient to investigate the goals and constraints facing individual decision makers; these constraints include the system of authority, rewards, and penalties within the organization.

The second approach leaves open the important and interesting question of how these internal incentives can be altered to produce improvements in characteristics of the organization's operations, such as productivity, efficiency, and so on. It emphasizes the fact that the issue of determining an organization's behavior cannot be divorced from the structure of decision making within the organization or from the system of penalties and rewards that faces the organization's individual decision makers. Admittedly, this tends to blur the distinction between the organization's "objectives" and "constraints." For example, individual decision makers may be allocated certain "targets" and given responsibility for varying certain decision variables as a means of attempting to solve the organization's overall decision problem by a decentralized decision process. These targets are "intermediate" objectives, best regarded as constraints, and are not the "ultimate" objective the organization may be attempting to achieve. This obviously complicates the process of attempting to infer an organization's "ultimate" objectives from observations of decision-maker behavior. Nonetheless, the behavior of the organization's decision makers, and the characteristics of the organization as a whole, will depend on the nature of these intermediate targets.

The second approach to behaviorally relevant organizational goals has the virtue of emphasizing that constraints internal to an organization can be just as important as external constraints in determining the organization's behavior. With a few exceptions, such as the seminal work of Williamson (1975, 1977), recognition of this fact has been rather slow in dawning on economists. This situation is partly attributable to the traditional practice of assuming that a single decision maker is responsible for the behavior of the business "firm." An important corollary of this, in the context of regulation of business or other organizational behavior, is that the form of regulatory constraints that is necessary in order to elicit certain forms of organizational behavior will depend on the nature of constraints *internal* to the regulated organization as well as on the external constraints facing the organization.

In attempting to explain regulatory agency behavior, an approach that emphasizes the decision rules and procedures within the agency may contribute more to an understanding of the agency's overall behavior than information about the personal objectives of the head of the agency.

(b) Nature of Agency Production and Cost Functions

The dimensions of the output concept on the horizontal axis of Figure 5.1 are obviously crucial in determining the demand and cost curves in the diagram. The output concept must be measurable in order for these curves even to exist. Moreover, if the output concept and model are to have any relevance in describing real-world behavior, the output concept must be one that is relevant to agency decision makers in practice, not simply a concept created by analysts. Niskanen's model of bureaucratic behavior implicitly assumes that the agency's sponsors can measure and monitor agency output; if this were not possible, the agency could obtain a larger budget simply by promising more than it could produce, and there would be no constraint in the form of a need to cover the total costs of the output level the agency promised sponsors it would deliver.

Many people, Niskanen included, see greater difficulty of measuring output in public sector organizations than private sector organizations as a major distinguishing feature of these organizations, often resulting in the use of indices of input rather than output to measure bureaucratic performance in the public sector. This is especially true of regulatory agencies. If one accepts the normative proposition that the major goal of regulatory agencies should be to change the behavior of the regulated firms or decision makers in those firms, it is exceedingly difficult to obtain measures of agency output in terms of the resulting changes in regulated firms' behavior. Observed changes in firms' behavior may occur because of changes in the objectives or other constraints that confront the firms' decision makers, in addition to changes resulting from regulatory constraints. The influence of changes in these other factors on regulated firms' behavior must therefore be eliminated in order to obtain a measure of the impact of regulators' behavior on regulated firms' behavior (see Chapter 12).

In practice, regulatory agencies and those who monitor their activities use indices of the agency's monitoring and enforcement activities as a measure of the agency's "output." These indices may not be associated with agency output measured in terms of the agency's impact on regulated firms' behavior. The agency's monitoring and enforcement activities may even influence regulated firms' behavior in the opposite way to that desired by the agency.

The Output Concept Implies a Production Function. The choice of a particular activity to represent an organization's output *automatically* implies choice of the "production function" for the organization. This production function is the relationship between the output concept that is selected and the inputs required to produce the output. Together with the prices of the inputs, this production function determines the total cost of producing any level of the organization's output.

The important point, from our perspective, is that a crucial normative element is involved in the choice of any organization's output concept. Traditional economic analysis of organizations in general and existing models of bureaucratic behavior ignore this element and are concerned merely with the technical and allocative efficiency of "given" outputs, not with whether the "given" outputs are the most suitable outputs concepts from the point of view of achieving the organization's goals, or wider goals such as the goals of society. When dealing with the problem of regulation, this question has to be faced and answered explicitly. When it comes to asking what the output concepts of a regulatory agency "should" be, however, the literature is silent.

If one adopts dimensions of regulatory agency behavior such as monitoring and enforcement activities as measures of output, rather than the effect of these activities on regulated firms' behavior, "monitoring" and "enforcement" are activities with innumerable possible dimensions, each with possibly different and underlying production functions and cost functions. Which of the many possible monitoring and enforcement concepts is *actually* adopted will influence the regulatory agency's behavior. Which of the concepts *should* be adopted requires analysis of the impact of each alternative on the extent to which the agency achieves its goals, defined in terms of desired effects on regulated firms' behavior. In Chapter 12 we shall synthesize scattered developments in the literature into a framework for devising optimal monitoring and enforcement mechanisms for regulatory agencies in general.

No normative significance can be attached to the conclusion that the agency will produce more output than Q_0 in Figure 5.1 if the output concept used by the decision makers is not the output concept they "should" be using, viewed from the perspective of selecting organizational output concepts that maximize society's satisfaction.

The implications of the choice of an organization's output concept for the demand and cost functions that face a regulatory agency include the possibility that the traditional shape of the cost function in Figure 5.1 may be completely changed. Suppose that regulatory agency output is measured in terms of the effect of agency behavior on some feature of regulated firms' behavior, say product safety. An increase in the level of the agency's monitoring activities, and total costs, may produce no effect, or even a reduction, in product safety in regulated firms (explained in Chapter 12). Or a reduction in the agency's monitoring activities, combined with a change in the structure of penalties or rewards applied to regulated firms with regard to meeting certain product safety standards, may result in an *increase* in product safety in regulated firms. In other words, a reduction in total costs of the agency may increase agency "output" measured in terms of the effect of agency behavior on regulated firms' behavior! These examples are not extreme possibilities but are highly likely outcomes under certain conditions (which are described in Chapter 12).

As these examples suggest, the form of a regulatory agency's cost function depends intimately both on what the agency's output is conceived to be and on the associated production function attached to the output concept. The production function may depend on characteristics of the regulated firms; for example, it may take more regulatory staff to monitor 100 firms than 10, more staff to monitor 10 firms in 10 states than to monitor 10 firms in a single state, and so on. The regulated firm's propensity to defend itself against charges of violating agency standards will also affect how many enforcement resources are required to get a given probability of successful enforcement.

A regulatory agency's production function will also depend on characteristics of the legal system, such as the specificity with which a regulated firm's behavior is defined in legislation administered by the regulatory agency, or the methods used by the courts to deal with cases brought before them by the agency. None of these complexities is dealt with in analyses of bureaucratic behavior that assume a "given" cost function and proceed to analyze the decision makers' behavior based on this cost function. Much more care is needed in specifying the nature of agency production and cost functions, both from the perspective of describing agency behavior in practice, and from the normative perspective of determining the kind of output concepts, productions, functions, and cost concepts that are appropriate for achieving specific regulatory agency purposes.

(c) Nature of Demand for Agency Output

In the theory of bureaucratic behavior outlined in Section 5.2 the demand curve AD in Figure 5.1 reflects the evaluations of the agency's output by the legislative committee or sponsor that allocates the agency's budget. In Section 5.2 it was explained that normative judgments may not be made if curve AD, although based on society's revealed evaluations of the agency's output, does not reflect the "true" evaluations of society. This may occur because of purposeful distortion; because of ignorance of the true effects of the output on the individuals making the evaluation; or where the agency's purpose is to change factors, such as income or wealth or power distributions, that underlie society's evaluations. Even abstracting from these complications, however, the model is seriously deficient for purposes of descriptive or normative analysis of bureaucratic behavior, for the following reason: the sponsor's demand curve is not the *only* evaluation curve that may affect the bureaucrat's choice of output level. This observation remains true even if the sponsor's evaluation curve *does* coincide with society's "true" evaluation curve.

At this point, it is necessary to focus more closely on the concept of "society's" evaluation of the agency's output. In the economics literature the demand curve for a firm's product is the horizontal summation of the demand functions of different individuals, whose valuations of the output of the firm reflect the consumption benefits they may experience from the output, expressed in money terms. Horizontal summation of individual demand curves is necessary whenever a particular unit of output can be consumed only by one person. The resulting demand curve reflects the firm's budget constraint and is the only demand curve that is relevant to the firm's decision makers if they pursue profit maximization as a goal.

Even in the case of such "private" goods, the outputs may have effects on individuals other than consumers; such effects are termed "externalities" in the economics literature and may be valued either positively or negatively by those individuals. Assuming that the externalities are valued positively by those persons affected, these external benefits at each output level should be added vertically to the consumers' total demand curve at that output level in order to obtain society's evaluation of the firm's output level. The externalities need not, of course, affect every member of society or be valued equally by those who are affected.

In the case of public sector organizations producing outputs that affect more than one person simultaneously (e.g., national defense, foreign relations, laws, regulatory policies), the demand or evaluation curve of each member of society affected by the output must be added vertically to obtain society's evaluation or demand curve. Again, some people may value a specific public sector output, or a specific level of public sector output, negatively.

In the process of vertical aggregation of individuals' evaluations of a given type of public sector output, a very important assumption is made in the literature of economics. Specifically, the evaluations of different people are weighted in proportion to the money values those people place on the public outputs. It is well known that this means accepting the existing distribution of money income in society, since a change in its distribution would change each individual's monetary evaluation of the satisfaction associated with a particular public sector output level. More important for our purposes is the fact that *no other characteristics of the individuals composing society* are relevant in aggregating their respective preferences. Thus, for example, the evaluations of a hippie and an environmental engineer who both value an increment of pollution control at $X are treated equally in the evaluation of "society's" preferences.

We are not suggesting that this principle of weighting different people's evaluations only in money terms is wrong. We merely wish to make it explicit, and consider the implications, for models of organizational behavior, of alternative principles. In the final analysis, how one should weight individuals' evaluations is a value judgment; the economist cannot solve this issue anymore than anyone else can. But economists can and should make clear important assumptions in their analysis of decision maker behavior and institutional forms and the consequences of varying those assumptions. This is especially necessary if the assumption is clouding their own understanding of decision-maker behavior in public- and private-sector organizations.

Common observation suggests that, in practice, decision makers do not weigh different individuals' evaluations equally, irrespective of whether their evaluations are expressed in money terms or otherwise, such as votes. In general, decision makers in public- and private-sector organizations alike weigh the evaluations of different individuals or groups differently. This fact has several important implications for the behavior of those decision makers. First, the evaluations of an organization's "sponsors," defined as those people responsible for allocating the organization's budget, are not the only, or necessarily the most important, "demand curve" the decision maker takes into account in deciding characteristics of the organization, such as the output level. The assumption of profit maximization in business firms automatically *implies* that the sponsor's demand curve (i.e., consumers' evaluations) is the only relevant evaluation curve. This does not mean that in practice business firms ignore the evaluations of their output by other "interest" groups who perceive themselves to be affected by the firm's output or other dimensions. Indeed, it is illuminating to consider the problem of social responsibility of business as, essentially, the problem of which of these interest groups *should* be considered by business (see Chapter 15). And there is no doubt that much observed business behavior is evidence of a response by business decision makers to other interest-group evaluations in addition to consumer demand curves.

Similar principles apply to analysis of bureaucratic behavior in public-good-producing organizations. The evaluation curves of different individuals or groups affected by any particular dimension of the organization's behavior may be weighted differently by any regulatory agency decision maker. The resulting vertical addition of these curves to obtain the "overall" evaluation of the agency's output by different groups will generally result in agency decision makers adopting a pattern of behavior that is different from that which would be adopted if they considered only the organization's sponsors' evaluation curve, which represents the "budget constraint" facing the organization. An agency's decisions may, in other words, be the result of an attempt by the agency to balance the interests of different individuals or groups in society by applying the agency decision maker's own weights to the evaluations of different individuals and interest groups. A similar concept of regulatory agency behavior has been expounded by Peltzman (1976), who emphasizes the regulator's attempt to strike a balance between the marginal benefits and costs of different interest groups affected.

The assumption of bureaucratic budget maximization in Niskanen's model is analogous to the assumption of profit or sales revenue maximization in the theory of the firm, in that it implicitly assumes away any effect on agency decision-maker behavior resulting from evaluations of the agency's behavior by groups other than those responsible for allocating budgets to the agency. The extent to which evaluations by other groups affect decision-maker behavior is an empirical matter, not a theoretical matter; nonetheless, their consequences for descriptive and normative analyses of bureaucratic behavior in general should be taken into account. In the case of regulatory agencies, the need for this is even stronger, since the interest groups affected by regulation are often likely to have an even stronger impact on the regulatory agency's behavior than are the evaluations of the agency by its legislative sponsors.

We have assumed that the evaluations of the agency's output by different individuals or interest groups are independent of one another. A further step in the direction of practical relevance must be taken by recognizing that they are likely to be interdependent. What this means, in simple terms, is that person or group A's evaluation of an agency's behavior is affected by person or group B's evaluation of the agency's behavior. One reason for this is rather obvious: the sponsors' evaluation of the agency will tend to be affected by the evaluations of interest groups and the pressures they bring to bear on the sponsors, in addition to any pressure directly brought to bear by the interest groups on the agency itself. Less obvious but equally relevant is the fact that individual interest groups may engage in activities designed to influence the perceptions and evaluations of the agency by other interest groups. For example, environmentalists may try to (1) directly influence an agency's decisions, (2) influence the agency's decisions by bringing pressure to bear on the agency's sponsors, and (3) influence the perceptions and evaluations of the agency by other members of society.

A further step in the direction of realism is to recognize that the regulatory agency itself may alter the perceptions and evaluations of its activities by members of society, interest groups, and its sponsors. Public relations activities analogous to the advertising activities of business firms may be one means of doing this. Such activities need not necessarily mislead people regarding the agency's output and its consequences. They could just as easily correct mistaken impressions based on information from other sources.

The possibility that the agency may affect the perceptions of its sponsors and other evaluators of its activities greatly complicates the problem of devising normative standards of agency behavior. What significance can be attached, for example, to a situation in which the agency produces output level Q_0 in Figure 5.1 if society's evaluations of agency output are partly the result of the agency's efforts to influence those evaluations? Also, it needs to be recognized that individuals, interest groups, and even sponsors may have just as much incentive to report inaccurate information or evaluations of the agency's activities as the agency itself.

Competition Between Bureaus. The final unsatisfactory aspect of existing analyses of demand conditions facing bureaucratic decision makers in general, and regulatory agencies in particular, is connected with the vexed subject of competition among bureaus. As Niskanen himself recognizes (1975, p. 620), the demand curve facing a specific bureau is not the total demand for the service provided by the bureau. It is the total demand for the service *minus* the output that the bureau's decision makers expect "rival" bureaus, or private sector organizations, to supply. The relationship between the total demand for the kind of output supplied by the bureau (D_T), demand for the bureau's output (D_S), and the expected output level supplied by other bureaus or organizations (Q), is shown in Figure 5.2. Curve D_S is that portion of curve D_T which lies to the right of the quantity of output Q supplied by other bureaus or organizations.

Niskanen is incorrect, however, in concluding that increases in the number of bureaus or overlapping functions of existing agencies, or allowing private sector organizations to compete for government contracts, will result in "improved" agency performance in terms of either output level or level of cost. Economic theory indicates that the number of rivals is less important as a determinant of a firm's behavior than the firm's expectations regarding its rivals' reactions to variations in its own behavior (see Chapter 7). These expected reactions can produce variations in the behavior of a group of firms that range all the way from the behavior which a single-firm monopoly would exhibit to that exhibited by "perfectly competitive" firms, irrespective of the number of firms in

Figure 5.2

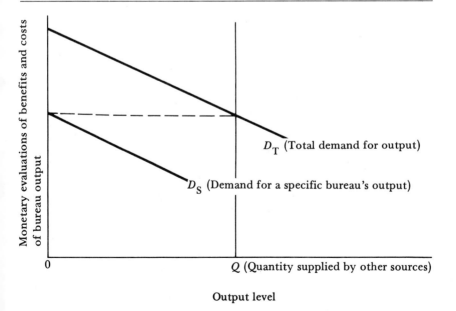

the group and independently of any explicit collusion by the firms in the group. To date, the factors that determine a firm's expectations regarding its rivals' reactions remain controversial in the economics literature. Yet, it is precisely these reactions which determine how "competitors" affect individual firms' behavior.

The same principles that are applicable to determining the effect of rival firms' behavior on the behavior of individual firms apply to the effect of the existence of other bureaus on the behavior of an individual bureau. The position of curve D_g, representing demand for the output of a specific bureau, in Figure 5.2 depends on the quantity of output supplied by other bureaus. This diagram is in fact identical to the diagram that is applicable in determining the behavior of potential entrant firms into an industry (discussed in Chapter 14), and the analysis and conclusions presented there are directly applicable to the issue of how other bureaus affect the behavior of a specific bureau. Unfortunately, the factors that determine how a specific bureau expects other bureaus to react, in terms of changes in their output levels or other dimensions of behavior that affect the demand for the first bureau's output, are less well known than in the case of rival firms. Again, it is precisely these factors that are relevant in determining how a bureau will be affected by the behavior of other bureaus and which of the possible behavior patterns — ranging from perfect "cooperation" to extreme "conflict" — will result in any particular case. Some writers, such as Goodin (1975), hypothesize that bureaucratic "backscratching" is a more likely phenomenon than bureaucratic conflict and competition. The issue cannot be settled, however, without explicit models of bureaucratic behavior incorporating the factors that determine whether cooperation or conflict will pay off for individual bureaus.

If other bureaus base their behavior in part on how they expect the first bureau to behave, there is a further parallel between the behavior of firms and the behavior of bureaus. In these circumstances, the bureau may recognize that it can influence other bureaus' behavior by its own actions, and take into account the "reaction function" that describes how it expects other bureaus to behave in response to its own behavior, in selecting "optimal" levels of its own decision variables. In effect, this extends our earlier conclusion, that the agency may be able to influence the evaluations of its actions by sponsors and other interest groups, and therefore the demand curve it faces, to include the effect of other bureaus' behavior on the agency's demand curve.

Ineffective Constraints on Bureau Behavior. Our discussion of the weaknesses in existing models of bureaucratic behavior has emphasized the omission of constraints that may be relevant in determining agency behavior. Before concluding this section, it is necessary to point out that the opposite situation is also possible. That is, factors generally assumed to be constraints on bureaucratic behavior may not in fact be effective in influencing it.

An example is provided by OMB's failure to disapprove requests from agencies for additional forms, cited in Bennett and Johnson (1979a). Other writers have questioned the ability of the president and his politically appointed cabinet officers to exert much influence on the career bureaucrats in the agencies they head. Heclo (1977), for example, paints a picture of cabinet officers who are largely ineffective in changing the behavior of the career bureaucrats in their agencies. Appointees and bureaucrats each maximize their own objectives without requiring much of the other. Political appointees may, for example, create their own personal teams to replace career civil servants. Heclo argues that this state of affairs will reduce the overall quality of performance of democratic institutions. Civil servants have knowledge and experience of "supply side" constraints confronting their agencies, while political appointees may have knowledge of the "demand side." Both types of information need to be coordinated; decision makers of each type should not be pursuing their own goals in ignorance of one half of the information needed to solve the problem.

A word of caution is in order regarding the implications of a failure of perceived constraints to affect decision-maker behavior. For example, before concluding that a lack of political constraints on bureaucratic behavior, either from legislative or presidential sources, is bad for public sector performance, it is necessary to investigate carefully the characteristics of politicians' behavior. If the objectives and constraints that confront legislators, cabinet officers, or other political decision makers are likely to produce behavior that is not in the public interest, strengthening the impact of these constraints on bureaucratic behavior may be undesirable. Thus, if political appointees who head agencies are concerned with dramatic policies and flashy changes readily intelligible to the public but with little real substance, bureaucratic foot-dragging in response to these policies may be in the public interest.

The fundamental problem involved in legislative, presidential, and bureaucratic decision making is that each type of decision maker has a different piece of knowledge regarding relevant constraints. Thus, the real task is to weld these different pieces of knowledge into an overall set of policy decisions that are "optimal" according to some criterion of society's goals. To focus upon the behavior of only one actor in this process, whether regulatory agencies, legislators, or administration officials, is too narrow a perspective. *Each* actor must somehow be motivated to reveal accurately the knowledge he or she possesses, and some type of decision mechanism or incentive facing individual decision makers must be devised that will tend to produce the best solution to the problem that is possible, given the information and other constraints that face different decision makers.

Incentive systems facing individual decision makers that tend to produce these results will be developed in Chapters 12 and 13. For the present, it is necessary to emphasize that the argument that the behavior of regulatory agency decision makers "should" be constrained by political decision makers is based on an implicit assumption that may not be warranted — that the behavior of the political decision makers is responsive to what is conceived to be the "proper" evaluation system for evaluating society's interests. Similarly, we should not be too quick to blame particular types of decision makers for their actions without first examining the nature of the constraints that determine the rewards and penalties applicable to actions by those decision makers.

For example, if the Congressional Budget Office or its administrative counterpart, OMB, is found to be largely ineffective in ensuring that certain aspects of bureaucratic behavior conform to congressional or administrative policies and edicts, this may be because the ability, in terms of resources available, is inadequate, or because the motivation to enforce these policies is lacking. If OMB is too hard on a particular agency, for example, the cabinet head may appeal to the president, and this may reflect adversely on OMB. Without better knowledge of the relevant constraints that confront OMB decision makers, it is impossible to determine the reasons for certain aspects of their behavior, or how the situation could be improved. Presidential or other reorganization plans or techniques such as management by objectives, planning-programming-budgeting, and zero-based budgeting will not change bureaucratic behavior unless they simultaneously change the rewards and penalties for bureaucratic behavior.

5.4 LEGISLATORS' BEHAVIOR AND REGULATION

The behavior of legislators must be included in any satisfactory treatment of regulation, for a number of reasons. Legislators are largely responsible for enacting regulatory legislation, and the form of this legislation often defines the responsibilities and constrains the behavior of regulatory agencies. If the goals of the regulatory agency and the methods that may be used to implement those goals are spelled out in detail in the regulatory legislation, this will reduce the amount of discretion that is open to regulatory agencies in their subsequent administration of the legislative mandate.

Legislators' behavior also influences agency behavior through the allocation of budgets to the agency and by monitoring agency behavior. Legislative monitoring activities may occur continually rather than only at budget allocation time, and they may involve a larger number of legislators than members of the agency's review and budget allocation committee in the Congress or state and local legislatures. A legislator's constituents who are affected by or wish to influence a regulatory agency may use legislators as one method of trying to obtain information regarding the agency or influencing its behavior.

These "facilitation services" involve a two-way flow of influence between legislators and regulators (Fiorina and Noll, 1978). The legislator needs a favorable response from the regulatory agency in order to please constituents, and legislators who are not members of the legislative review committee or are otherwise unable to influence the committee may lack power to influence agency behavior. The net result may be that, rather than legislators acting as a constraint on regulatory agency behavior, legislators' behavior may be influenced by the need to please regulators in order to obtain favors in the form of positive response to their constituents' requests. Actually, the relationship between legislators and regulators may be even more complex than this "who-controls-whom" example suggests, and it may take a number of forms.

It should not be assumed that this two-way flow of influence between legislators and regulators occurs only at the monitoring stage. As we emphasized in the opening section of this chapter, existing regulatory agencies may bring pressure to bear on legislators when new regulatory agencies or regulations are being formulated by Congress.

In order to examine the impact of legislators' behavior on any aspect of regulatory agency behavior, it is necessary to analyze legislators' behavior within a model of all the determinants of their behavior.

Unfortunately, a satisfactory model of legislators' behavior has not yet been developed, despite a large number of contributions in the political science and economics literature. The situation is very similar to that involved in the literature dealing with bureaucratic behavior. Researchers and writers focus on legislators' objectives or on a subset of the constraints they believe confront legislators. They then derive conclusions about legislators' behavior that have little predictive relevance or normative significance, because other important constraints that might reasonably be expected to influence legislators' behavior are omitted from the theoretical models and statistical counterparts.

In the brief space available, we cannot remedy this situation entirely. What we can do is outline the major constraints and the relationship among them that should be included in any serious attempt to explain the determinants of legislators' behavior and its implications for regulation in the real world. Fortunately, our task and the demands on the reader are lightened by the fact that, from an analytical point of view, the major constraints that determine legislators' behavior, and the principles that are applicable in determining their implications for legislators' behavior, are very similar to those discussed in the preceding two sections dealing with regulatory agency behavior. Only the dimensions of legislators' behavior and the forms of the constraints are different.

Voters' Behavior as a Constraint on Legislators. The first major constraint confronting legislators is the need to get elected. This generally requires the legislator to get a majority of the votes cast. Notice that it does not necessarily require the legislator to maximize the number of votes he or she could get. If the total number of votes cast, termed "voter participation" in the literature, varies with the platform selected by the legislator, there may be a large number of platforms, each resulting in a different number of votes cast, that earn the legislator a majority of the votes and enable the legislator to be elected. In these circumstances, the goal of getting elected may still leave a legislator considerable discretion in the choice of political platforms.

The literature of political science and economics has made much of the fact that a vote-maximizing legislator will select a platform that is preferred by the median voter. This does not mean that legislators in practice will attempt to maximize the number of votes they get, since other platforms may enable them to reach higher levels of their objectives, measured in terms of the platform each legislator prefers. Wittman (1977) has emphasized that when candidates view winning merely as a means to implementing platforms they prefer, not as an objective itself, to be able to predict which platforms candidates will offer voters, one must know the candidates' preferences and objectives. Romer and Rosenthal (1979) concluded that studies fail to indicate that actual government expenditures correspond in general to those desired by the median voter.

In addition to the candidate's platform and the level of his or her campaign expenditures, the constraint that describes the factors that determine how many votes will be cast in an election, and the number of votes cast for a particular legislator, depends on (1) voter behavior and (2) the behavior of rival legislators. Determinants of voter participation and voting behavior have been extensively analyzed in the political science and economics literature but are still controversial. It is recognized that voter perceptions of how they are affected by the various platforms presented by candidates, and how they stand to gain or lose as a result of these platforms, will affect their voting behavior. Similarly, it is recognized that information about platforms may be imparted to voters by candidates' campaign expenditures and also by TV and other media.

What has not been adequately recognized in the voting behavior models is that individuals can attempt to influence legislators' behavior by means other than voting. Campaign contributions and direct lobbying of a legislator after election may be considered a much more effective means of influencing a legislator's behavior than voting. If a voter does not expect his or her vote to affect the election outcome, the voter may not vote, even though the consequences of the outcome of the election for his or her welfare are very large; legislative platforms are not sacrosanct, and the individual may plan to lobby to change the elected legislator's policies after election instead of voting.

Normative Implications of Voters' Behavior. Before leaving the implications of voter behavior for legislators' behavior, several comments are appropriate regarding the normative significance that is usually attributed to voter behavior in general and to the median voter's preferences in particular. It is generally assumed, either explicitly or implicitly, that legislators' behavior "should" reflect voter preferences. This conclusion is not warranted in any of the three following circumstances. First, it is not warranted if voters purposely misrepresent their preferences and evaluations of public sector activities; this situation can be expected to occur whenever a person expects to secure an outcome he or she prefers to be the outcome expected to result from being honest. Gibbard (1973) and Satterthwaite (1975) independently proved that *no voting system is non-manipulable or cheatproof,* that is, it is *never* possible for individual voters to secure a preferred outcome by misrepresenting their true preferences. However, the argument (Feldman, 1979) that the Gibbard-Satterthwaite theorem ought to end a 200-year search for an ideal voting procedure is unwarranted. The conclusion that it is always *possible* for some voters to obtain a preferred outcome by misrepresenting their true preferences abstracts from the nature of the incentives that determine whether it is in their best interests to misrepresent rather than report information accurately.

Second, the assumption that legislators should respond to voter preferences is not warranted if voters are ignorant of the true nature and effects of public sector activities. It is inappropriate to regard the voter-legislator relationship as a situation in which the legislators respond to the "given" preferences of the voter. Part of the function of legislators is to provide information about the consequences of public sector resource uses to voters, and this will influence voter perceptions and evaluations. A more appropriate characterization of the voter-legislator relationship is one of principal and agent, where the agent (legislator) has information about the effects of public sector resource uses, and the principal (voter) forms his or her evaluations of those effects in part on the basis of information provided by the agent. It is neither possible nor desirable for legislators to provide voters with all the information the legislator possesses regarding these effects. Doing so would be extremely costly, and voters might not be motivated to divert their scarce time to becoming informed and revealing evaluations based on the improved information. Even if they were so affected, their evaluations of the effects might still be incorrect perceptions of the effects of the public sector resource uses because these perceptions are also affected by information about the public sector activities obtained from other sources.

Legislators and other sources of information regarding the effects of public policies may have incentives to distort the true effects of these policies, leading to voter evaluations that are not the same as those based on correct information. Even if there is no distortion of information about the effects of public policies, different people, including experts, will often have completely different perceptions of those effects. In other words, there may be no such thing as a unique, "correctly" perceived set of effects of a particular public sector resource use for voters, or anyone else, to evaluate. Consequently, attributing normative significance to the evaluations of a particular group, voters or otherwise, is ultimately a value judgment.

Third, if individuals express their preferences for public sector activities *by means other than voting*, such as direct lobbying or other methods of influencing public sector decision makers, the strength of an individual's preferences for particular public activities can be gauged *only* by reference to *all* these activities viewed collectively, not simply by reference to voting behavior. Votes alone cannot, and do not, reveal the intensity of different people's evaluations of public sector resource uses. Niskanen has accurately characterized the nature of the choices between candidates in an election as follows: "A two-candidate election provides about as much information on the population preferences as would the selection of a fixed diet for a several-year period from a menu which includes only two diets, where the price and some of the elements of the diet are obscure, the capability of the chef is uncertain, a bar girl and a rock group are distracting one's attention, and there is only one place to eat in a very large region."

A number of writers have pointed out that a theory of individual voter behavior is inappropriate as the basis of a model of group voter behavior if it ignores the influence of factors such as coalition formation and an individual voter's expectations regarding other voters' behavior. Guttman (1978), for example, shows that if individual voters with identical preferences expect other voters to match their monetary contributions to a public good, individuals will behave in such a manner that the satisfaction of the group as a whole will be maximized. Also, models of demand-revealing mechanisms for public sector activities that are based *solely* on voter behavior are incomplete. Models of voter behavior need to be linked with models of lobbying and with all methods by which individuals and interest groups seek to influence public sector decision makers in order to develop a model of the demand-revealing mechanism for public sector activities that is satisfactory for both descriptive and normative purposes.

When different methods individuals can use to influence legislators' behavior are considered, a negative view of lobbying activities, political contributions, and other activities may be inappropriate. In contrast to lobbying and other activities, voting does not enable an individual to weight his or her preferences higher or lower than anyone else's, since each person has only one vote. This apparently egalitarian view attributes the same weight to the preference of a person who has bothered to become informed about the consequences of his or her vote as to the uninformed voter; it gives the same weight to each person's evaluation even though they may be affected very differently by the outcome of the matter they are voting on, and independently of *any* characteristic of the people voting. In Chapter 3 it was pointed out that there are innumerable criteria that could be used as an index of equity, and that the choice between them is ultimately a value judgment and reflects a particular person's judgment, interests, and environment. This is equally true of the one-person, one-vote concept.

Anticipated Behavior of Rival Legislators. The behavior of rival legislators is the second major influence on legislators' choice of platform and other aspects of campaign strategy. At one extreme, if each legislator expects his or her rivals for office to adopt vote-maximizing platforms, he or she will also be forced to offer vote-maximizing platforms. This, in turn, implies that legislators will offer platforms preferred by the median voter, a situation that is often considered to be the political analogue of perfect competition in economic markets. There is, however, absolutely no reason why individual legislators should necessarily expect their rivals to adopt vote-maximizing platforms. Such platforms may be far from the one the candidate prefers.

Wittman (1978) has emphasized that a political party might prefer to lose an election while retaining its ability to adopt policies it prefers rather than to win an election by promising a platform that maximizes votes but departs from the party's ideology or that reduces the party's "legislative profit." In the case of individual legislators, we have pointed out that there may be a number of platforms which the legislator expects would win an election, yet which do not maximize the number of votes obtained. Candidates may purposely avoid controversial issues that would increase voter turnout and the number of votes obtained if they expect the additional votes to be equally distributed between the candidates. Ferejohn and Noll (1978) have demonstrated that legislators' uncertainty about voter preferences can profoundly affect electoral strategies and may even induce candidates to collude rather than compete in selecting platforms. On the basis of data for state legislators, Crain (1977) suggests that in most settings the gains from increased rivalry between incumbent politicians do not appear to offer the gains from cooperation between them.

At the federal level, Abrams and Settle (1978) examined the 1974 amendments to the Federal Election Campaign Act that introduced public financing of presidential elections and set limits on campaign spending. They suggest that this legislation was motivated more by a desire on the part of incumbent politicians to control entry of potential opponents and/or to sustain the power of the ruling majority party by establishing campaign regulations adverse to the current minority party than to serve the public interest by increasing access to public office by people with limited financial means. The authors present evidence suggesting that the 1974 amendments, which were passed by a heavily Democratic Congress over opposition from Republicans, were quite likely to have been responsible for the Democratic victory in the 1976 presidential election.

It is the *expected reactions and behavior of rival legislators* in response to a legislator's own behavior that are relevant in determining the optimal platform, campaign expenditures, and other dimensions of the individual legislator's behavior. These expectations need not be correlated with the current behavior of rival legislators and may not be correlated with particular "structural" characteristics of the political market, such as the number of rival legislators (see Chapter 7). Here, we wish to emphasize that irrespective of the particular institutional setting or the number of legislators, different behavior may be exhibited by individual legislators and groups of legislators depending on each legislator's expectations regarding the response of other legislators to his or her behavior.

The same conclusion is applicable if the "rival legislators" whose behavior is taken into account is expanded to include *potential* rivals. Whether or not "entry barriers" exist in political "markets" or other decision-making situations, their implications for the behavior of the potential entrant and of established decision makers can vary widely, depending on how these entry barriers affect the expectations of each decision maker regarding his or her rivals' behavior. This requires emphasis, for the literature of economics and political science often contains explicit or implicit assumptions that "entry barriers" are necessarily "bad" for the behavior of established decision makers. This assumption is not warranted (see Chapter 15). The effect of adding another rival, actual or potential, on established decision makers' behavior cannot be determined without knowing the established decision makers' expectations regarding the new rival's behavior. Johnson (1978) gives examples where the addition of more candidates to an election reduced rather than increased campaign spending by existing candidates, for example.

A number of writers (Niskanen, 1975; Crain, 1977) have argued that incumbents have advantages over potential candidates in congressional and other elections. These advantages take the form of higher levels of campaign expenditure required to inform voters of new candidates; "free" access of incumbents to television, postal facilities, and other media during their terms of office; and similar factors that result in a cost differential between the incumbent and potential candidate in reaching and informing a given number of voters. Again, the implications of these factors for the behavior of potential candidates or incumbents are impossible to determine without taking into account the rivals' anticipated reactions.

The treatment of entry barriers in the literature dealing with political behavior is unsatisfactory. The theoretical concept of entry barriers requires refinement before empirical measurement is possible. There are many unwarranted assumptions about what constitutes an entry barrier in politics, and there are erroneous conclusions regarding the impact of entry barriers on politicians' behavior. This is hardly surprising, since it is only recently that the theory of entry barriers, which originated in connection with the pricing behavior of business firms, has reached a stage of refinement that recognizes that any satisfactory definition of entry barriers is multidimensional in character and is intimately connected with rivals' anticipated reactions. (See Chapters 7, 15.)

The foregoing discussion clearly indicates that a constraint in the form of the need to get elected implies no unique form of legislators' behavior in terms of platform adopted, campaign expenditure, or any dimensions of behavior either before or after election to office. In addition, dimensions of a legislator's behavior that are relevant to getting elected, and the platform selected to win election, are not the same things as the behavior and platform actually carried out by the legislator after his or her election.

There is a direct analogy in this respect between legislators' behavior and regulated firms' behavior (discussed in Chapter 12). The promised or "target" behavior of the legislator may differ from the legislator's actual behavior after election, and the discrepancy may be either purposeful or the result of unforeseen circumstances. Therefore, when legislators include legislative platforms containing regulatory legislation, incentives such as those discussed in Chapter 12 may be required to encourage truthful revelation of the regulatory intent of the legislator, and incentives for the legislator to obtain information about the regulatory problem he or she plans to deal with. Otherwise, legislators may have the same incentives as regulated firms and regulatory agencies to overstate the true estimated cost of public programs to increase the probability of being able to deliver promised programs.

A Model of Legislators' Behavior. For the passage and form of regulatory legislation, the factors that determine an individual legislator's behavior with respect to a piece of regulatory legislation can be analyzed in a framework that is very similar to that previously employed to explain the determinants of bureaucrats' behavior. We must first recognize that several dimensions of the legislator's behavior may be involved in dealing with regulatory or any other type of legislation, such as the amount of time the legislator spends studying the problem, participating in the formulation of the legislation, and lobbying for its success or defeat both inside and outside the legislature.

For each of these dimensions of the legislator's behavior there are constraints facing the legislator on the "cost side" in the form of limitations on the legislator's ability and time plus other resources such as staff and money, and the opportunity cost of not using these scarce resources for other legislative projects. Similarly, on the "demand side," each dimension of the legislator's behavior will be evaluated by a variety of individuals and interest groups.

One of these groups will be the legislator's constituents, and their evaluations of the legislator's behavior will influence the probability of reelection in the future. This does not mean that the evaluations of constituents will necessarily be given the greatest weight in the legislator's process of aggregating various groups' evaluations of his or her activities, and in the resulting behavior adopted by the legislator. The evaluations of other interest groups, expressed in direct lobbying activities, campaign contributions, or other perquisites that yield satisfaction to the legislator (e.g., the promise of lucrative job offers after the legislator's term of office expires) may influence the legislator more. The important point is that *all* these evaluations will play some part in determining the legislator's adopted course of behavior.

This extremely important point can be clarified diagrammatically as follows. The legislator can be visualized as adding vertically the "demand" curve representing the perceived evaluation of his or her behavior by each individual or group attempting to influence the legislator's behavior. In this aggregation process, each component demand curve will be weighted by its contribution to the legislator's own objectives. The point where the resulting vertically aggregated demand curve D intersects a curve showing the marginal cost of a change in behavior to the legislator determines the level of behavior that maximizes the legislator's own personal satisfaction.

This is demonstrated in Figure 5.3, where for convenience the evaluation of the legislator's behavior by only three persons or groups is assumed. The expression B_0 is the level of behavior that maximizes the legislator's objective function. It should be noted that the reason why the intersection of the demand and marginal cost curves represents the behavior adopted by the legislator (in contrast to the conclusions of the previous discussion of budget-maximizing bureaucrats) is that the legislator's objective function has been taken into account in the form of the weights attached to the various evaluation curves by the legislator. In the case of Figure 5.1 the objectives of the regulatory decision maker were separated from the evaluation curve.

It should be clear from Figure 5.3 that the evaluations of all the groups considered relevant by the legislator determine the course of action he or she selects. Suppose that a fourth evaluation curve were added to Figure 5.3 in the negative region of the diagram below the horizontal axis, which indicates evaluations of persons who dislike the particular dimension of behavior depicted by the diagram and whose evaluations are considered relevant by the legislator. This would shift the vertically aggregated total evaluation curve downward and reduce the level of behavior that maximizes the legislator's objective function.

Figure 5.3

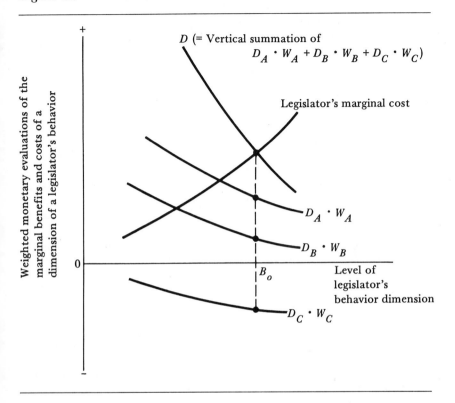

The conclusion that legislators will not generally base their behavior on the evaluations of a single reference group has important implications for politicians' behavior in a large number of contexts. It is relevant in connection with studies of the responsiveness of legislators to their constituents, for example. In addition to the finding of many studies that legislators are not particularly responsive to constituents' demands, statistical studies have focused on the correlation between politicians' responsiveness to constituents' demands and various characteristics of the constituency, such as the number of constituents, the homogeneity of constituents' preferences, the closeness of the vote in elections, the number of candidates for election, and so on. Since constituents are only one of the groups whose evaluations affect a legislator's behavior, there is no reason why any of the characteristics of this group should be correlated either with the degree of responsiveness of the legislator to constituents or with any dimension of the legislator's behavior.

A second context in which the conclusion that legislators' behavior will not generally reflect the evaluations and demands of only a single reference group is as important as legislators' response to demands of various groups for regulatory legislation. The same conclusions also apply to the behavior of regulators faced by demands from a variety of interest groups, and this casts considerable doubt on the practical relevance of any particular version of single-interest-group theories of regulation or regulatory agency behavior. The failure of statistical studies to support any of the single-interest-group theories of regulation reinforces this view.

The multiple-reference-group model of decision-maker behavior is not restricted to legislators and regulators but applies to decision makers in general, including those in business firms. Economists' penchant for assuming away many of the important aspects of real-world behavior in models of business behavior or public sector decision making should not be interpreted as a weakness of economic analysis itself. Properly applied, these techniques are capable of providing improved perspectives on many issues in economics, political science, and many other areas of human decision making.

In addition to the implications of the multiple-reference-group model of decision makers' behavior for purely descriptive analysis and studies of legislators' and regulators' behavior, it can be used as a basis for normative analysis of their behavior, both as a tool for evaluating their performance, and also for motivating behavior by these decision makers that is in accordance with specified normative criteria. Weights could be assigned to the evaluations of different interest groups, based on some normative index of how much of the evaluations of these groups "should" count in decision makers' behavior, and these weights could also be used in determining the reward-penalty incentive system facing any particular type of decision maker whose behavior one wishes to change.

One of the problems facing public- and private-sector decision makers in practice is the lack of any well-defined normative index of whose evaluations of their behavior "should" count. Lacking such an index, even if decision makers wanted to behave in a "socially desirable" manner and to take into account the preferences of those persons whose interests "should" count by some generally accepted notion, they are unable to do so. The diagrammatic multiple-reference-group model provides a heuristic format in which these issues can be recognized and discussed.

Several additional features of the demands, or evaluations, of legislators' behavior by different groups should be noted at this stage. These features are identical to those discussed in Section 5.3. First, the evaluations of a legislator's behavior by different groups may be interdependent; one group's evaluation may depend on another group's evaluation. Second, the legislator may be able to directly influence the evaluations of his or her behavior by providing information to those making the evaluations. This information may or may not be accurate; however, the other sources of information on which people base their evaluations of the legislator's behavior need not be accurate either. Also, the extent to which the legislator can influence the evaluations of his or her behavior by different groups will vary considerably, depending on differences in the amount and sources of information from other sources that the groups possess and on other factors, including their goals. Some people's attitudes on either side of the nuclear power issue are impervious to any amount of information, for example.

The Committee System and Legislators' Behavior. Whether one is dealing with the legislative or monitoring activities of individual legislators, the committee system of decision making generally employed to conduct these activities must be taken into consideration. The committee system itself may profoundly affect the kind of decisions that emerge. Just as legislators have control over the platforms they present to voters, committees of Congress decide which legislative proposals will be voted on. In all human decision processes, an "agenda" is involved that includes what is to be considered; what is to be decided; the objectives being sought; and the method that will be used to reach a decision, such as majority vote, unanimity, consensus, and so on. As Plott and Levine (1978) have emphasized, what is placed on the agenda, and the sequence in which items are to be considered, can affect the outcome of the decision process. Fiorina and Plott (1978) have also demonstrated that the outcome of any decision rule, such as majority vote, depends on the magnitude of the stakes involved for committee members making the decision.

Control over an agenda clearly conveys considerable power to those who set the agenda, since by controlling what is decided and how, they can, to a large extent, structure the agenda to obtain an outcome they prefer. Controlling an agenda is equivalent to restricting the number of competing alternative agendas and is a special kind of entry barrier, *an entry barrier to the formulation of alternatives.* An entry barrier to agenda setting may be far more important in influencing the outcome of a decision process than many of the other aspects of decision processes that are usually emphasized, such as the number of decision makers involved. For example, the traditional concern over entry barriers to new members of the legislature may be misplaced, because even in the absence of such entry barriers restricted entry to the agenda-setting process in congressional committees may preclude many members of Congress from having much impact on the range of legislative proposals actually considered by the legislature.

Many decisions made by legislators concerning the form of regulatory legislation or the dimensions of legislative monitoring of regulatory agencies are made by committees of legislators. In view of the preceding comments, it seems clear that models of legislators' behavior designed to illuminate the relationship between legislators and regulators should include constraints reflecting the legislative committee decision mechanism as one of their central elements. Unfortunately, this prescription has not been followed in the literature dealing with legislative constraints on regulators' behavior. We are unable to say very much about the descriptive or normative implications of these constraints for legislators' behavior connected with the formulation and passage of regulatory legislation or the monitoring of regulatory agencies.

There are few analyses of the legal rule-making behavior of legislators in the literature. In an illuminating article, Erlich and Posner (1974) discussed the normative implications of the degree of precision or specificity with which a legal command is expressed, for the efficiency of the legal process. The specificity with which regulatory legislation defines aspects of behavior that are to be penalized, rewarded, or otherwise regulated is one of the factors that affect the probability that a specific course of action will be penalized or rewarded. This probability, together with the level and structure of penalties or rewards, determines the effect of regulatory constraints on the behavior of regulated decision makers (see Chapter 12). Erlich and Posner point out that the legislator's choice of whether to enact a general standard or a set of precise rules is implicitly a choice between legislative and judicial rule making, because more broadly defined legislation leads to litigation and a need for interpretation by the courts. They also hypothesize that the marginal costs to legislators of activities that produce more specific legislation rise very rapidly. This suggests that regulatory legislation will not be very specific.

Even if a descriptive model of legislators' behavior were developed that included all the constraints that are relevant in determining legislative and monitoring aspects of legislators' behavior, in practice, one major problem would remain. To decide whether these dimensions of legislators' behavior are "optimal" from the point of view of encouraging "optimal" regulation, it is necessary to know what is meant by "optimal" regulation (see Chapter 12). It is sufficient here to point out that it involves knowledge of the following factors: (1) all the goals and constraints that confront regulated decision makers; (2) all the goals and constraints that confront regulators; and (3) existing knowledge concerning the kind of incentive systems that induce decision makers to reveal information truthfully and to adopt "socially optimal" levels of behavior.

Regulated firms and regulators themselves do not generally know all the constraints that confront them. Therefore, one cannot reasonably expect legislators to have this information. If legislators are not aware of concepts of socially optimal behavior by regulators, one cannot expect them to exhibit the kind of behavior that results in socially optimal regulatory legislation and monitoring of regulators' behavior.

5.5   WHY REGULATORS MUST BE REGULATED

In this section we explain why, no matter which concept of "society's satisfaction" is adopted as the criterion for evaluating the behavior of unregulated and regulated decision makers and regulators, the behavior of regulators themselves will need to be regulated. The basic features of the required forms of "regulation of regulators" will be outlined. (See also Chapter 13.)

A useful starting point for understanding why regulators must be regulated is provided by the analysis of benefits and costs of regulation in Chapters 3 and 4. In order for regulation of some of activity A to be at a socially optimal level, the following condition must be met:

$$\sum \begin{pmatrix} \text{society's evaluations} \\ \text{of the benefits and} \\ \text{costs of changes in} \\ \text{activity } A \end{pmatrix} = \begin{pmatrix} \text{costs of changes in} \\ \text{activity } A \text{ to deci-} \\ \text{sion makers per-} \\ \text{forming activity } A \end{pmatrix} + \begin{pmatrix} \text{costs of agen-} \\ \text{cies of regu-} \\ \text{lating activity} \\ A \end{pmatrix}$$

For ease of reference we shall abbreviate the condition above as follows:

$$\Sigma (B - C) = (C_f + C_R)$$

The reader will recall that the B and C concepts depend on *which* members of society are selected as the basis for evaluating activity A. People's evaluations of the effects of regulating activity A are indicated in the rows of Tables 3.2 and 4.1 and may include "equity" weights assigned to each person's monetary evaluations of these effects.

If $\Sigma (B - C) = C_f$ in the absence of regulation, then regulation of activity A is unnecessary, assuming of course that one accepts the definition of individuals whose evaluations are taken to appropriately represent "society's" satisfaction and the weights that are accorded to their evaluations. Given the definition of society's evaluation system used to evaluate activity A if $\Sigma (B - C) \neq C_f$, regulating activity A can increase society's satisfaction as long as $(C_R + C_f)$, the increase in combined total costs of regulatory agencies and regulated firms performing activity A, is less than society's evaluation of the net benefits of a change in activity $A \Sigma (B - C)$.

It should be remembered that the unregulated behavior of decision makers who perform activity A will not be "socially optimal" if (1) they fail to consider some of the people whose satisfaction is affected by activity A, or some of the effects of activity A, and/or (2) the objectives and constraints facing decision makers performing activity A do not lead to choice of characteristics of activity A that maximize society's satisfaction in the sense of ensuring that $\Sigma (B - C) = C_f$.

Socially optimal regulation requires that regulators take into account the people and the effects of activity A omitted by decision makers who perform activity A. There is absolutely no reason why regulators will behave in this way unless they are regulated! If regulators *were* the kind of people whose personal objectives included consideration of society's evaluations, the solution to regulatory problems would be simple and rather obvious: to offer such people sufficient remuneration to have them perform activity A themselves; this would obviously lead to socially optimal characteristics of activity A!

The circumstances under which a regulator's behavior would result in socially optimal regulation provide an indication of the kind of incentives, or regulatory constraints, that are required to induce regulators to behave in a socially optimal manner. A regulator's objective function must include arguments that are *proportional* to the individual elements of the condition $\Sigma (B - C) - (C_f + C_R)$. If the regulator's objective were exactly the same as that condition, behaving in a manner that maximized the regulator's objective would be equivalent to behaving in a manner that maximized society's satisfaction. In addition, the *level* of evaluations by members of society of those effects would be exactly the same as the *regulator's own* personal evaluations of them.

This situation is obviously never likely to occur in practice. As long as the regulator's evaluations of the effects of regulation of activity A are *proportional* to society's evaluations of those effects, however, maximizing the expression $(k_1 b - k_2 c) - (k_3 c_f + k_4 c_R)$ will automatically maximize the expression $(B - C) - (C_f + C_R)$ as long as $k_1 = B/b$, $k_2 = C/c$, $k_3 = C_f/c_f$, $k_4 = C_R/c_R$, where the lowercase letters refer to the regulator's evaluations of benefits and costs of changes in activity A attributable to regulation and the costs the regulatory agency incurs to change activity A.

Again, this is unlikely to happen without special incentives, or regulatory constraints, facing individual regulators. The kind of incentives or regulatory constraints that must confront regulators to induce them to regulate in a socially optimal manner will depend on the regulator's personal objectives and the other constraints that influence the regulator's behavior. In principle, knowledge of these objectives and other constraints will yield information regarding the nature and relative magnitude of the b, c, c_f, and c_R concepts that enter into a regulator's decision-making calculus, directly or indirectly. Knowledge of these concepts would, in turn, permit one to determine the magnitude of the k_1, k_2, k_3, and k_4 magnitudes, which could be used as the basis for the rewards-penalties system confronting the regulator.

Notice that even if a regulator has exactly the same tastes as other members of society, by itself this is not sufficient to result in socially optimal behavior by the regulator. In Chapter 3 it was emphasized that the benefit and cost evaluations of regulation by individual members of society depend not only on their tastes but also on the constraints that confront and determine the effects of regulation on those individuals. The constraints that confront individual regulators will generally differ from those that confront people whose evaluations of regulation are considered appropriate indices of society's welfare. As a result, despite identical tastes, the regulator's evaluations of regulation's effects will differ from those of members of society, and the regulator's behavior will not be socially optimal unless the regulator is regulated.

These principles are valid whether one is dealing with a single regulatory agency decision maker or with many. Obviously, the fact that there are differences in the personal goals or constraints facing different decision makers within a regulatory agency greatly complicates the process of determining the kind of incentives that are required to induce regulatory decision makers, individually and collectively, to act in a socially optimal manner. Some of the constraints that face individual agency decision makers will be represented by the behavior of other decision makers within the agency.

It was also emphasized in Chapter 4 that the output behavior of human inputs and the resulting production function of an organization are endogenously determined by the interaction of their various objectives and constraints. The same thing is true of a regulatory agency.

This means that the system of incentives that is required to induce regulatory agency decision makers to behave in a socially optimal manner, represented by the k's in the preceding exposition, will be a complex matrix of k's representing different incentives for different decision makers within the organization. This k matrix will be determined by the precise nature of the personal objectives and constraints that confront different decision makers within the agency. Obviously, the likelihood that the incentive system that exists in any regulatory agency will result in the k matrix that is required to induce regulators to act individually and collectively in a socially optimal manner is negligible.

Similarly, the likelihood that agency decision makers will search for such an incentive system themselves is negligible, since such search is costly for the organization. More important, just as a redistribution of income or power will increase the satisfaction of some individual members of society and decrease that of others, a change in the incentive system within any organization will generally result in a reduction in satisfaction of some members of the organization and an increase in the satisfaction of others. In any event, it is unlikely that the stimulus or agreement necessary for a system of regulatory agency incentives that is socially optimal will emanate from within the agency itself.

In addition to the problem of inducing regulators to act in a socially optimal manner in the sense of ensuring that $\Sigma (B - C) = (C_f + C_R)$, there is an additional reason why regulators must be regulated. In order to achieve the above condition, regulators must be allocated sufficient resources necessary to enable the agency to achieve this condition. Regulated decision makers, and other members of society who value regulation, will not be motivated to supply accurate information about the $\Sigma (B - C)$ and C_f to regulators unless they themselves are confronted by an incentive system with certain very special "incentive-compatible" characteristics (described in detail in Chapter 12). The same is true of information provided by the regulators to their sponsors, or resource providers. In other words, regulators will generally have incentives to overestimate B and underestimate C, C_f, and C_R when reporting their activities to resource providers, in order to obtain more resources. This is true *irrespective* of the precise nature of the personal objectives of regulatory agency decision makers, since more resources can always be used for purposes that increase the satisfaction of some members of the organization without reducing the satisfaction of others.

Incentives for information distortion on the part of individual decision makers within the agency will also generally exist. These incentives for individual agency decision makers and for the agency collectively to provide inaccurate information regarding their activities and the resulting marginal benefits and costs to society can be overcome only by confronting regulators with special types of incentive designed to induce them to reveal information honestly. The fundamental characteristics of these incentives are very similar to those which must be applied to regulated decision makers by regulatory agencies. They depend on the regulators' goals and constraints, and they can be integrated with the incentives required to induce regulators to act in a socially optimal manner. Again, however, such incentives will not originate with the agency itself. The agency's sponsors, or some other group whose behavior directly or indirectly affects the satisfaction of regulators, must be responsible for enforcing these incentives.

More detailed consideration of the general problem of regulating regulators is postponed until Chapter 13. First, it is necessary to develop a better understanding of how regulation has been conducted in practice in the United States, commencing with regulation of competition among independent firms, then considering regulation of public utilities, and finally regulation of specific dimensions of business behavior. The order of treatment of different types of regulation in Part II roughly reflects the time sequence in which different types of regulation were introduced in the United States, and also the progression from regulation of broad dimensions of business behavior to increasingly detailed regulation of specific dimensions of that behavior.

CHAPTER SIX

Regulating Competition: Antitrust in Theory and Practice

6.1 THE NATURE AND GOALS OF ANTITRUST POLICIES

Government regulation of business has many dimensions. Although they are interrelated, it is necessary to consider some of these dimensions separately in order to gain understanding of the overall relationship among different pieces of the regulatory puzzle. Part I concentrated on providing the reader with an understanding of the links between effects of regulation on individual members of society, evaluations of regulation's effects, and the forces that underlie demands for regulation and the behavior of legislators and regulators. Part II will focus on dimensions of firms' behavior that are regulated in practice, the means of regulation employed, and the rationale of such regulations.

In order to gain perspective on Part II, the reader may find it useful to think in terms of a two-dimensional table like Table 6.1, where each row of the table represents individual dimensions of firms' behavior — costs, prices, profits, sales, input and output quantity and quality, and so on. Each concept could of course be further subdivided; "costs," for example, may be divided into total, average, and marginal cost concepts, as explained in Chapter 3. Similarly, input or output quantities, qualities, and prices may be divided into many input and output dimensions. If each column of the table represents a different firm in the economy, the whole table will represent every conceivable dimension of firms' behavior for every firm in the economy.

The firms in Table 6.1 could be grouped into industries, so that each column would then refer to a different dimension of the behavior of

Table 6.1. Regulated Dimension of Firms' Behavior

	Firm 1	*Firm 2*	*Firm 3 . . . Firm n*
Costs			
Product prices			
Profits			
Sales revenue			
Input quantity			
Input quality			
Output quantity			
Output quality			
Advertising			

a specific industry. We have not adopted this approach, for the following reasons. Grouping firms into industries presents considerable problems, and different groupings are appropriate for different purposes. Depending on how markets and products are defined, multiproduct firms may simultaneously be members of more than one industry. Because of these and other difficulties connected with the problem of delineating market and industry boundaries, explained in more detail in Section 6.2(d) and in Needham (1978, Chap. 5), Table 6.1 refers to the behavior of individual firms. The reasoning and conclusions that involve Table 6.1 can be applied to a similar table representing the behavior of industries, however. Regulators may in practice perform these groupings in many ways, for purposes of deciding which firms are to be subject to particular regulations.

Regulations that apply to a particular dimension of the behavior of every firm in the economy would apply to all the elements in a single row of Table 6.1; pollution or product safety are examples of this kind of regulation. The rationale of many of the more recent forms of regulation of environmental, health and safety, and consumer protection of business behavior are examined in Chapter 10. Chapters 8 and 9 examine the traditional form of public utility regulation in the United States, which involves attempts to regulate the profit returns on capital invested in industries such as electricity, gas, telephone, and communications. This kind of regulation would not apply to every element in the row of Table 6.1 representing the profit/capital dimension of firms' behavior. It would apply only to firms considered to be public utilities.

This chapter deals with government regulation of competition by means of antitrust policies. The appendix to this chapter contains a brief summary of the United States antitrust laws. In the United States, competition was first articulated as a public policy goal with passage of the

Sherman Act in 1890, and was reaffirmed and strengthened by passage of the Federal Trade Commission Act and the Clayton Act in 1914. These acts contain an explicit prohibition of monopolization and of practices that substantially lessen competition. Responsibility for enforcing the acts lies with the Antitrust Division of the Department of Justice and with the Federal Trade Commission. Antitrust policies should properly be included in a study of government regulation of business, for a number of reasons.

Public utility regulation is generally considered to be an appropriate remedy for the control of business behavior only if competition in a particular industry has been deemed to be either impossible or excessive because of structural features of the industry, such as declining average costs of production and distribution, entry barriers, or some other industry characteristics. The same concept of competition that is the focus of antitrust policies will also generally serve as a standard of reference for judging the behavior of industries that are subject to other forms of regulation. Similarly, the kind of firms' behavior that results from "competition" will generally serve as a target in formulating regulatory constraints and other policies that are intended to be substitutes for the lack of competition as an influence on firms' decision making in regulated industries.

Because the concept of competition underlies the rationale of antitrust policies and public utility regulation, it is important to clarify the meaning of this concept at an early stage. The concept of competition that is a crucial determinant of firms' behavior is rival firms' anticipated behavior (see Chapter 7). The normative concept of "desirable" competition is ambiguous, however, and can be defined in a number of ways, each with different implications for normative dimensions of firms' behavior and regulatory policies. For example, in this and the following chapter we shall demonstrate that the belief that "increased competition" will always "improve" firms' behavior is fallacious, irrespective of the concept of competition that is being considered. Given a particular definition of socially optimal firms' behavior and the other constraints that influence individual firms' behavior, only one pattern of competition in the sense of rival firms' anticipated behavior will produce socially optimal behavior on the part of those firms.

A second reason for considering antitrust policies here is that most of the benefit and cost concepts associated with business regulation were originally developed for use in connection with evaluating public policies toward monopoly and competition. The flow of influence between antitrust policies and regulation is not all one way, however. A considerable amount of controversy and confusion that exists in the literature concerning descriptive and normative aspects of the behavior of antitrust agencies can be eliminated if it is recognized that antitrust agencies' and courts' behavior may be analyzed within exactly the same framework as any other regulatory constraint. Some characteristics of this antitrust regulatory constraint have been outlined in Chapter 4, Section 3. Chapter 12 will develop a diagrammatic framework for dealing with a general analysis of the effect of regulatory constraints on regulated firms' behavior.

By viewing antitrust laws and policies as factors that underlie a probabilistic regulatory constraint facing firms, it is possible to clarify the nature of regulatory agency production functions and the relationship between antitrust agencies' and firms' behavior, thereby providing a framework for understanding and improving antitrust policies. In addition, it sheds useful perspective on the vexed subject of the "goals or objectives of antitrust" in practice. Many economists and other people who are puzzled by apparent anomalies in existing antitrust policies, such as the protection of competitors at the expense of allocative or technical efficiency, fail to recognize that, like all regulatory constraints, the behavior of antitrust agencies is a response to demands, or evaluations, of antitrust policies by many interest groups.

As emphasized in Chapter 5, regulators or legislators faced by multiple demands will generally adopt policies that balance these various demands rather than policies that reflect the demands of one group. The demand by economists that antitrust agencies adopt policies that consider only allocative or technical efficiency dimensions of firms' behavior represents only a segment of the demands facing antitrust agencies. It is therefore not surprising that the antitrust policies actually adopted by these agencies and the courts do not include only allocative and technical efficiency as the relevant objectives. Moreover, it is appropriate that antitrust agencies and the courts behave in this way. Chapter 3 emphasized that economists' technical and allocative efficiency concepts contain implicit assumptions about equity weights that determine whose evaluations of antitrust of other public policies ought to be considered. These assumptions were shown to be not the only possible assumptions, and it was pointed out that although equity weights that determine whose evaluations of antitrust and other public or private policies shall be used as an index of "society's evaluations" are unavoidable, these weights should be made explicit.

Admittedly, the equity weights in antitrust agency and court decisions are also often implicit and are not too easy to determine, as Spitzer (1979) has reminded us. However, the fact that existing antitrust policies reflect considerations other than allocative and technical efficiency should not be viewed as evidence that these policies are inferior to policies that include only efficiency considerations. To assume this is to accept the existing income distribution, and to assume that the marginal utility of income of every member of society is the same. The goals of antitrust, as reflected by the response of antitrust decision makers to multiple demands from various segments of society, are as much a part of the political system of determining whose interests, perceptions, and evaluations should prevail in antitrust policy as may be found in any other facet of government activities. Which goals and whose interests "should" be pursued is a matter of one's point of view and value system.

The following two sections closely examine the theoretical justification for competition in traditional economic analysis. It is only recently that some of the explicit and implicit assumptions of this body of analysis have been challenged by economists themselves. Such challenges — or at least illumination of traditional assumptions — are long overdue, since many of the assumptions are highly questionable, and the conclusions that emanate from them are sometimes inappropriate bases for public policies designed to influence competition and to change certain dimensions of decision makers' and firms' behavior. Once these assumptions are exposed and amended appropriately to reflect real-world constraints confronting regulators and regulated decision makers, a much richer theory of competition and a more useful framework for analyzing public policies toward competition and monopoly in both the private and public sectors of the economy emerge.

6.2 LOSSES ATTRIBUTABLE TO MONOPOLY: THEORY AND EVIDENCE

The notion that monopoly imposes costs or losses on society is deeply ingrained in the thinking of most economists, and their conclusions are often used by noneconomists when dealing with problems of monopoly and competition. The models and the reasoning process that underlie economists' conclusions about monopoly and competition will be clarified in this section. This is necessary to develop a better understanding of the economists' conclusions and of their limitations and sensitivity to changes in the assumptions they make when considering monopoly and competition.

The rather detailed analysis and critique of the traditional concept of "monopoly welfare loss" that follows in this and the succeeding section is justified for the following reasons. The same logic and framework of analysis can be applied to the influence of monopoly and competition on other dimensions of firms' behavior in addition to the traditional price-output-level dimensions. Second, concepts of monopoly and competition, and their implications for behavior, are relevant in connection with evaluations of a wide variety of noneconomic dimensions of the behavior of firms and other types of decision maker, such as political dimensions.

The Theory of Monopoly Welfare Losses. The economist's traditional model of the issue of monopoly versus competition may be illustrated

Figure 6.1

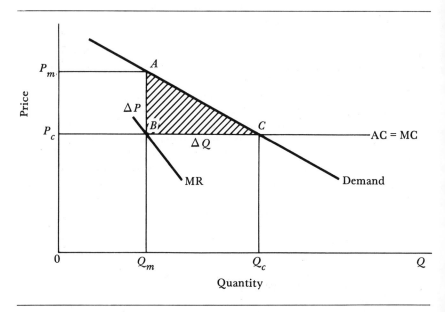

diagrammatically. Figure 6.1 shows the demand and cost curves relating to a particular product. The assumption that the marginal and average costs of the product are equal and constant is made initially for expositional convenience, and will be relaxed later. If the product is produced by profit-maximizing firms that individually assume that the market price of the product will be unchanged by their own output policies, the equilibrium level of industry output and price will be Q_c and P_c, respectively. Individual firms will select an output level where the addition to their total revenues from one more unit of output ("marginal revenue") equals the addition to their total costs caused by producing one more unit of output ("marginal cost").

Because marginal revenue equals the market price of the product when firms assume that their output policies do not affect the market price, individual firms and the industry as a whole produce an output level where the market price of the product equals its marginal cost. Pricing behavior that results in firms' setting product prices equal to marginal costs is termed "perfectly competitive" pricing behavior by economists. Under certain restricted circumstances, this kind of pricing behavior can result in an optimal allocation of society's scarce resources among different products. The reader should be warned against assuming that "perfectly competitive" pricing behavior is desirable in all circumstances, however; later in this section we shall see that such pricing behavior is neither possible nor desirable in a wide range of circumstances found in the real world.

If a single profit-maximizing monopolist produces the product, the price-output level selected by the monopolist will also be where the marginal revenue from the product equals the marginal cost. In this case, however, marginal revenue is less than the market price of the product, because the monopolist must explicitly recognize that an increase in the level of output will reduce the market price that buyers are willing to pay for the product at a larger output level. Marginal revenue is always less than the price of the product in the case of a monopolist, as shown by the curve MR in Figure 6.1.

The profit-maximizing monopolist who is *faced by the same demand and cost conditions as a perfectly competitive group of sellers* will charge a higher price, P_m, and produce a smaller output level, Q_m. The italicized phrase is important because it emphasizes an assumption that is implicit in the diagram and that is vitally important to any conclusions based on the diagram. (We shall later investigate the consequences of relaxing this assumption.) To compare the price and output behavior of a monopolist with a perfectly competitive group of producers, some normative assumptions must be made regarding the demand and cost curves in Figure 6.1. It is usually assumed that the demand curve reflects the value members of society place on increments of output; in other words, the height of the demand curve at any output level shows the value society places on that increment of output. It should be noted that when the product is sold at a uniform price per unit of output, members of society value all units of output except the "marginal" or last unit purchased at that price at a higher level than the price actually paid.

The marginal cost curve shows the additional total costs that must be paid out by the firm or industry to increase output by one unit; these increased total costs are paid to inputs that are required to produce the extra output. *Assuming that the marginal costs of the product exactly equal the value of the alternative outputs that could be produced instead* by the inputs required to produce a marginal unit of the product, the marginal cost curve can be viewed as reflecting the "opportunity costs" of the product to society, which measure society's valuation of the alternative outputs forgone. At this stage, it should be noted that two important requirements must be met in order for the MC curve for a product to accurately reflect the value placed by society on alternative outputs: (1) there must be input mobility among different industries so that the price for any particular input is the same in all sectors; (2) product prices must be set equal to marginal costs in *all* other sectors of the economy.

These assumptions enable us to define the burden, or "welfare loss," as it is conventionally termed, that is imposed on society by the existence of monopoly. The shaded triangle ABC in Figure 6.1 measures this burden on society in money terms. At the monopoly output level Q_m, the value placed by society on an increment of output is shown by the height of the demand curve, while the value placed by society on the alternative outputs that must be forgone to increase output by one unit is shown by the height of the MC curve. The difference between the height of the demand curve and the MC curve, therefore, represents the monetary evaluation of the *net gain in satisfaction* that would be experienced by members of society from expanding the output of the product one unit. A net gain in satisfaction will be experienced by society for each increment of output up to the level Q_c, and adding these increments of satisfaction results in the shaded "welfare-loss triangle" as a measure of the total loss to society of restricting output from Q_c to Q_m. The welfare-loss triangle is normally expressed in money terms, but it can also be expressed as a percentage of total output, or GNP, in an economy.

Empirical Estimates of Monopoly Welfare Losses. Economists have attempted to estimate the welfare loss attributable to monopoly for the United States and other countries. To understand and interpret their findings, however, it is necessary to transform the diagrammatic measure of the welfare loss into an operational measure. One way to accomplish this is to recognize that triangle *ABC* in Figure 6.1 is equal in area to $\frac{1}{2}\Delta Q \Delta P$, where ΔQ and ΔP are the differences in quantity and price of the product under monopoly and perfect competition, respectively. The price elasticity of demand for the product, which indicates the percentage increase in the quantity of the product demanded in response to a 1 percent reduction in the price of the product, is defined symbolically as follows:

$$E_d = \frac{\Delta Q}{\Delta P} \cdot \frac{P}{Q}$$

Substituting this expression into $\frac{1}{2}\Delta Q \Delta P$ yields $\frac{1}{2}\Delta P \, E_d \, \Delta P Q / P$, and multiplying this by $\Delta P / P$ yields the following symbolic expression for the area of the welfare-loss triangle:

$$\text{Monopoly welfare loss} = \frac{1}{2} E_d \left(\frac{\Delta P}{P} \right)^2 PQ \cdot \cdot \cdot \qquad (1)$$

where $\Delta P / P$ is the proportionate excess of price under monopoly over price under competition, E_d is the price elasticity of demand for the monopolist's product, and PQ equals the total sales revenue of the monopoly firm. Expression (1) indicates the magnitude of the welfare loss attributable to monopoly measured in money terms. Dividing this expression by the dollar value of total output in the economy as a whole yields a measure of the welfare loss expressed as a percentage of the total output produced in the economy.

A second approach to measuring the monopoly welfare-loss triangle is related to the monopolist's profits. In Figure 6.1 MR bisects the distance between the price axis and the demand curve, as previously noted. This means that the base of the welfare-loss triangle is equal in length to the level of the monopolist's output Q_m. The side of the welfare-loss triangle is equal to the difference between the monopolist's price and unit cost of the product that is the monopolist's profit per unit of output. It follows that the area of the welfare-loss triangle in the figure is equal to 1/2 the monopolist's profits.

In a seminal article, Harberger (1954) estimated the magnitude of the welfare loss attributable to monopoly in the United States economy using data for the period 1924–28. His estimate of $59 million, or less than 1/10 of 1 percent of the United States GNP at that time, would at first sight appear to relegate the importance of monopoly as a cause of resource misallocation to insignificance. The estimate is probably too low, however, for a number of reasons explained in detail in Needham (1978, Chap. 10). One of these reasons is that Harberger observed low price-cost margins in the monopoly sector and assumed that a low market price elasticity of demand existed for the product of the monopoly sector. As the reader can verify from the welfare-loss formula in expression (1), this ensures a small welfare-loss estimate.

Harberger failed to recognize that price-cost margins are automatically related to price elasticities of demand for the products of individual firms, however. Profit maximization implies that a firm's product-pricing behavior must satisfy the condition $P - \mathrm{MC}/P = 1/E_f$ where E_f is the price elasticity of demand for the firm's product. Low observed price-cost margins in profit-maximizing firms therefore imply that price elasticities of demand facing those firms are high! High price elasticities of demand facing individual firms in a particular industry imply, in turn, that those firms, and the industry as a whole, cannot act like monopolists.

Statistical studies have generally found low price elasticities of total market demand and low price-cost margins. The reader may be wondering how low market price elasticities of demand for the product of a particular industry can coexist with high price elasticities of demand for the products of individual firms in the industry. The explanation is as follows. The price elasticity of demand for the product of an individual firm, E_f, does not depend only on the price elasticity of total market demand for the product, E_m. It also depends on the firm's expectations about how rival firms in the industry will respond to reductions in the price of its product. A low market price elasticity of demand (E_m), combined with a firm's expectations of large increases in its rivals' output in response to price reductions by the firm, will result in high price elasticities of demand for the products of individual firms, E_f, and in low price-cost margins (see Chapter 7).

Market price elasticities of demand, E_m, are the appropriate price elasticity in the welfare-loss formula, because total market demand reflects society's evaluation of the product in question. But firms' subjective estimates of the price elasticity of demand for their respective products, E_f, is the relevant elasticity for determining the magnitude of profit-maximizing price-cost margins.

The relationship between total market demand price elasticities and firm price elasticities, and the implications for welfare-loss measures, may be clarified simply by substituting the profit-maximizing price-cost relationship for a firm's product, $P - MC/P = 1/E_f$, or $\Delta P/P = 1/E_f$, into the welfare-loss formula, as follows:

$$WL = \frac{1}{2} E_m \left(\frac{\Delta P}{P}\right)^2 PQ = \frac{1}{2} E_m \left(\frac{1}{E_f}\right)^2 PQ = \frac{1}{2} E_m \frac{[P - MC]}{E_f} Q \cdots (2)$$

If a single firm controls an industry, $E_m = E_f$, and the welfare-loss formula will be equal to $\frac{1}{2}Q(P - MC)$, which equals half the firm's profits when $MC = AC$ as in Figure 6.1.

Cowling and Mueller (1978) have used a similar approach in estimating monopoly welfare losses for the United States and United Kingdom. They obtain estimates significantly greater than those of previous studies. For the period 1963–66 in the United States they obtain welfare-loss measures for each of 734 firms on the Compustat tape, and a total welfare loss expressed as a proportion of the gross corporate product (GCP) originating in these firms ranging from between 4 and 13 percent of GCP. The annual welfare loss estimated for General Motors, which headed the list, was $1.75 billion, which alone is more than $\frac{1}{4}$ of 1 percent of average GNP during the period and exceeds Harberger's original welfare loss for the entire economy. For the United Kingdom, the aggregate estimates of the welfare loss attributable to the top 103 firms ranged between 4 and 7.2 percent of GCP for the 1968–69 period.

Because Cowling and Mueller assume that each firm is a monopoly in its market, so that $E_m = E_f$, these estimates may overstate the actual magnitude of the allocative welfare loss. Overstatement would occur if E_f, the firm's expectations regarding the response of demand for its product to a price reduction, exceeds E_m, the actual response of demand for the firm's product in response to a price reduction. However, it has not been generally recognized in the literature that it is also possible for E_f to be less than E_m, so that welfare-loss estimates based on observed price-cost margins may understate the allocative welfare loss.

This situation results from the following considerations. When more than one firm produces in an industry, it can be shown that the price elasticity of demand for each firm's product is related to the market price elasticity as follows:[1]

---

[1] The interested reader may consult Needham (1978, Chap. 4) for proof of these propositions.

$$E_f = \frac{E_m + E_r(1 - S_f)}{S_f}$$

where S_f is the firm's share of total market output and E_r is the anticipated rivals' output response to price changes initiated by the firm. The welfare-loss formula for each firm will then be as follows:

$$\frac{1}{2} E_m \frac{(P - MC)}{E_f} Q = \frac{1}{2} \frac{E_m(P - MC)Q_f S_f}{E_m + E_r(1 - S_f)}$$

where Q_f is the output level of any given firm for whom the welfare loss is calculated. Under monopoly no rivals are assumed to exist, and therefore $S_f = 1$ and E_r is zero, reducing the welfare-loss formula to the form discussed earlier, which is similar to that used by Cowling and Mueller in their study.

Although it is not immediately obvious, a closer examination of the relationship between E_f and E_m in the multifirm case will confirm that it is still possible for E_f to equal E_m. For this to occur, the expression E_r must exactly equal $-E_m$. This will result in the following relationship between the firm's price elasticity and the market price elasticity:

$$E_f = \frac{E_m - E_m(1 - S_f)}{S_f} = \frac{E_m S_f}{S_f} = E_m$$

It can be demonstrated that the situation in which $E_r = -E_m$, and firms' price elasticities are equal to market elasticities, is one in which each firm expects its rivals to imitate its price and output policies, and in which each firm's anticipated demand curve is a "constant-share-of-the-market" demand curve. A constant-share-of-the-market demand curve has exactly the same price elasticity of demand as the market demand curve, as is demonstrated by a comparison of the two price elasticity concepts

$$E_m = \frac{\Delta Q_m}{\Delta P} \frac{P}{Q_m} \qquad \text{(market price elasticity)}$$

$$E_f = \frac{\Delta Q_f}{\Delta P} \frac{P}{Q_f} \qquad \text{(firm's price elasticity)}$$

$$I_f \Delta Q_f = \frac{\Delta Q_m}{n} \quad \text{and} \quad Q_f = \frac{Q_m}{n} \qquad \begin{array}{l}\text{where } n \text{ is the number}\\ \text{of firms in the market}\end{array}$$

$$E_f = \frac{\Delta Q_m}{\Delta P \cdot n} \frac{P}{Q_m} \cdot n = E_m$$

When a firm expects its rivals to try to increase their share of the market in response to a reduction in the price of the firm's product, E_f will be less than E_m, and a group of firms acting independently will set prices *higher* than the monopoly level. This possibility has not been adequately recognized in the literature of economics, which usually assumes that monopoly behavior is a limiting case of oligopoly behavior (see Chapter 7). In the present context, such a situation will imply that welfare-loss measures based on the firm's demand elasticities implied by observed price-cost margins will *understate* the magnitude of the actual welfare loss, because the market elasticities are larger than the firm's price elasticities.

The debate concerning the magnitude of monopoly welfare losses continues in the literature. Although most studies have obtained small estimates of the aggregate allocative welfare loss attributable to monopoly in the United States economy, a number of studies have emphasized that the monopoly welfare losses are large in particular sectors of the economy. For example, Siegfried and Tiemann (1974), on the basis of 1963 data, demonstrated that the bulk of the allocative welfare loss in mining and manufacturing was concentrated in five industries. Plastic materials and synthetics, drugs, petroleum refining and extraction, office and computing machinery, and motor vehicles accounted for 67 percent of the total estimated welfare loss; the motor vehicle industry alone was responsible for almost one half of the total loss, 44 percent.

Unit Cost of Production Increases and Welfare Losses. To this point, our discussion of the monopoly welfare-loss concept and its measurement has been based on the assumption that unit and marginal costs of the product are constant. If unit and marginal costs of output increase with scale of output, as shown in Figure 6.2, some modifications of the welfare-loss formulas are required. It is clear, for example, that the welfare loss will now be smaller than one half of monopoly profits. Also, the monopolist's price–marginal cost margin is no longer equal to the difference between the price of the product under monopoly and competition.

It is not difficult to take account of these factors, however, by introducing the slope, or elasticity, of the MC curve, into the formula for the welfare loss. The earlier welfare-loss formula is changed from

$$\frac{1}{2} E_d \left(\frac{\Delta P}{P} \right)^2 PQ \quad \text{and now becomes} \quad \frac{1}{2} E_d \left(\frac{\Delta P}{P} \right)^2 PQ(1 + E_d E_c)$$

where $\Delta P/P$, as before, is the difference in the price of the product under monopoly and perfect competition, and E_c, the "elasticity of marginal cost," is defined as the percentage change in MC in response to a 1 percent change in the quantity of output produced. When MC does not vary with the level of output, $E_c = 0$, and the modified welfare-loss formula reverts to the initial version. The larger E_c is, the steeper the MC curve and the larger the welfare loss associated with any level of product price above P_c.

Figure 6.2

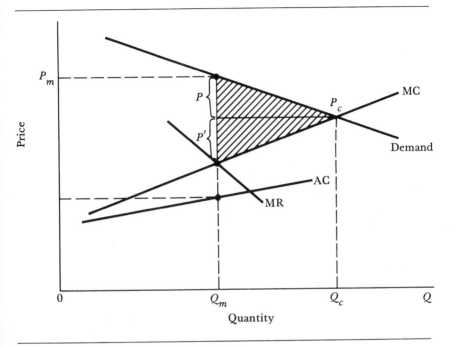

Quantity

For purposes of estimating the welfare loss in the case of increasing marginal costs of output, the monopolist's $(P - MC)/P$ is no longer equal to $\Delta P/P$, the difference between price under monopoly and competition, respectively. However, it can be shown[2] that the relationship between the monopolist's profit-maximizing $(P - MC)/P$, and $\Delta P/P$, is as follows:

$$\frac{(P - MC)}{P} \text{ monop} = \frac{\Delta P}{P}(1 + E_d E_c) \quad \text{or} \quad \frac{\Delta P}{P} =$$

$$\frac{(P - MC)}{P} \text{ monop} \frac{1}{(1 + E_d E_c)} \cdots$$

[2] The monopolist's $(P - MC)$ is equal to $\Delta P + \Delta P'$ in Figure 6.2

$$E_d = \frac{\Delta Q \cdot P}{\Delta P \quad Q}, \quad \text{and} \quad E_c = \frac{\Delta P'}{\Delta Q} \cdot \frac{Q}{P}$$

Therefore, $\Delta P' = \Delta P E_d E_c$, and $(P - MC) = \Delta P (1 + E_d E_c)$.

Substituting this last expression into the welfare-loss formula for the increasing MC case therefore yields the following expression:

$$\text{WL} = \frac{1}{2} E_d \left(\frac{P - \text{MC} \cdot 1}{P(1 + E_d E_c)} \right)^2 (1 + E_d E_c) \quad \text{or}$$

$$\text{WL} = \frac{1}{2} E_d \left(\frac{(P - \text{MC})}{P} \right)^2 \frac{1}{(1 + E_d E_c)}$$

This shows that the larger E_c, the more steeply the MC slopes up at the monopolist's output level, the *smaller* the welfare loss from monopoly. The profit-maximizing price of the monopolist's product will be lower when MC declines as output is reduced below the level Q_c than when MC is constant; the reader may easily verify this by inspection of Figure 6.2. It should also be noted that E_d, the elasticity of market demand, still exerts a net positive influence on the magnitude of the welfare loss, despite the occurrence of E_d in the denominator of the preceding formula.

The preceding analysis of monopoly welfare losses is based on the assumption that monopoly occurs in markets for final outputs. Monopoly pricing of inputs will add two components to the preceding allocative welfare loss. First, it will lead to the use of inefficient input mixes at the next stage of production; the method of dealing with these technical efficiency losses attributable to monopoly will be dealt with in the next section. Second, monopoly pricing of inputs, by reducing the quantity of inputs demanded and employed, reduces total output in an economy; this effect is not captured by the allocative or technical efficiency-loss measures traditionally employed.

6.3 UNSATISFACTORY FEATURES OF EXISTING MONOPOLY WELFARE-LOSS CONCEPTS

In this section we shall focus on a number of aspects of the monopoly welfare-loss concepts and measures discussed in the preceding section that need to be made explicit in order to place such measures in proper perspective. We shall include not only aspects that are controversial in the literature but also some highly questionable assumptions that are generally accepted by those on both sides of the issues. The major topics we shall be concerned with are the following:

(a) Which cost items should be included in the price-cost margin.
(b) Demand and cost curves under monopoly and competition.
(c) The multidimensional nature of monopoly behavior.
(d) Evaluation of monopoly and competition and the relevance of income distribution.

(e) Prices and marginal costs in other sectors of the economy.
(f) Definition and identification of relevant markets and products.

(a) Which Cost Items Should Be Included in the Price-Cost Margin?

Since the allocative welfare loss attributable to monopoly is defined in terms of $(P - MC)$, the difference between society's monetary evaluation of the benefits and marginal cost of a change in the level of the monopolist's output, correct definition of the appropriate marginal cost concept is obviously important. In principle, the proper marginal cost concept is the "opportunity cost," or value in alternative uses, of the inputs required to produce a change in the level of the monopolist's output.

Great care is required in selecting the cost concepts that are used in practice to estimate this opportunity cost concept, for the following reasons. The appropriate $(P - MC)$ concept for measuring the welfare effects of product-price and resulting output-level changes is *not* generally the same as profit per unit of output. Profit per unit of output equals $(P - ATC)$, where ATC (average total cost) includes advertising and other expenditures in addition to production costs, per unit of output. Advertising and any other expenditures that do not change when the firm's product price and output level are changed are "fixed" costs and should not be included in the MC concept for measuring the welfare loss associated with output-level changes. If one is estimating the welfare loss using the "monopoly profits" approach, however, these fixed costs per unit of output must be *added* to profits $(P - ATC)$ in order to obtain a correct measure of the difference between product-price and *average variable production costs*. This can be seen from the following symbolic relationship between ATC and AVC:

$$\text{Profit per unit output} = (P - ATC)$$
$$= (P - [AFC + AVC])$$

Therefore

$$\text{Profit per unit} + AFC = (P - AVC)$$

Figure 6.3 shows the same relationships diagrammatically.

The next important point is that AVC will not be the same as MC, the change in the firm's total variable production costs when output is changed, unless AVC does not change when the firm's output level changes.

When AVC is increasing with level of output, MC is above AVC. However, MC may be either above or below ATC (which includes "fixed" costs that do not vary with output). When MC is above ATC, profit per unit of output *exceeds* $(P - MC)$; therefore, profits per unit of output

Figure 6.3

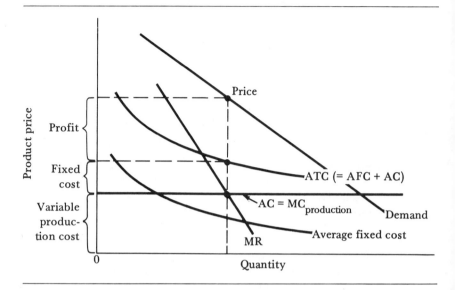

overstates the welfare change resulting from a unit reduction in the level of the firm's output. When MC is below ATC, profit per unit of output *understates* $(P - MC)$, the allocative welfare change from a unit change in the firm's output. However, adding all the fixed costs per unit of output to profit per unit would not be appropriate in these circumstances, since this would lead to an *overstatement* of $(P - MC)$.

Failure to distinguish between $(P - MC)$, $(P - AC)$ the difference between price and unit production cost, and $(P - ATC)$, the difference between price and unit total cost, or profit, has led to a considerable amount of confusion and errors in attempts to estimate allocative welfare losses from available data. Low observed profit rates and low observed market price elasticities of demand are quite compatible with high $(P - MC)$ margins and allocative welfare losses.

"Rent-Seeking" Activities and Welfare-Loss Measures. Tullock (1967), Posner (1975), and a growing number of other writers have argued that the traditional approach understates the welfare cost of monopoly by failing to recognize the costs involved in attempts to gain and retain monopoly power. They argue that competition among firms for the right to earn potential monopoly profits will lead firms to spend on advertising, political lobbying, and similar activities, which are usually termed "rent-seeking" activities in the literature. Expenditures by firms on rent-seeking activities will raise firms' costs under monopoly above the level that would obtain under perfect competition.

It is generally argued (Posner, 1975) that rent-seeking expenditures should be added to the traditional monopoly welfare-loss measures. To the extent that these expenditures are part of the difference between product prices and firms' marginal costs of changing output levels, we have already explained why they should indeed be added to industry profits in estimating the welfare loss $(P - MC)$.

Some writers imply that the reason why advertising, rent-seeking, and similar "fixed" expenditures should be added to firms' profits in measuring allocative welfare losses in the economy is that such expenditures are wasteful or excessive and produce nothing of value for society. This view is incorrect, for the following reasons.[3]

It is impossible to determine whether advertising, or any other type of expenditure, is socially wasteful or excessive without reference to society's evaluation of the effects of that expenditure and of the opportunity costs of the resources purchased by such expenditures. In principle, exactly the same logic and diagrammatic framework that is applied to the traditional problem of determining welfare losses from monopoly-pricing and output levels can also be applied to issues of socially optimal levels of other dimensions of firms' behavior. As we shall argue in Section 6.3(d), such a broader approach to the evaluation of monopoly behavior is needed.

It is illegitimate to attempt to deal with the issues of socially optimal pricing and socially optimal advertising, rent-seeking, or other dimensions of firms' behavior in the same diagram that is used to examine socially optimal pricing behavior and output levels, for several reasons. First, the traditional practice of assuming that the same market demand curve faces monopolists and perfect competitors implicitly assumes an identical and unchanging level of advertising and other nonproduction expenditures for both types of industry. This implicit assumption is inconsistent with a wide body of theory and evidence indicating that the behavior of competitive and monopolistic industries will generally differ in other dimensions of behavior in addition to the traditional product-price and output-level dimensions.

We shall examine the inconsistencies involved in assuming identical advertising and other nonproduction expenditures for monopolists' and perfectly competitive industries in Section 6.3(b). For the present, it is sufficient to emphasize that the traditional approach to the monopoly welfare loss implicitly assumes a constant level of advertising, rent-seeking, and similar "fixed" costs that do not vary when output levels change. It does not show how the level of these "fixed" costs was determined or how the level of any of these types of expenditure is related to society's evalu-

---

[3] More detailed treatment of this issue is contained in D. Needham, "Welfare-Loss Measures, Relevant Elasticities and Price-Cost Margins and Rent-Seeking Activities," *Western Kentucky University College of Business Administration Working Paper Series*, Vol. 1, No. 5, April 1982.

ation of the benefits and marginal opportunity costs of that type of expenditure.

As already noted, the same logic and diagrammatic framework applied to the traditional problem of determining welfare losses from monopoly pricing can be applied to these other types of expenditure. A demand curve indicating society's evaluation of different levels of, say, rent-seeking activities, and a marginal cost curve indicating the opportunity cost of resources used for rent-seeking activities, can easily be envisaged by the reader. The intersection point of these two curves would indicate the "socially optimal" level of rent-seeking activities, for reasons analogous to those underlying the conclusion that output levels where $(P - MC) = 0$ represent socially optimal output levels.

Firms in various types of market structure may not engage in socially optimal levels of rent-seeking activities, depending on their objectives and other constraints. The actual expenditures by firms on rent-seeking activities will not, therefore, generally equal socially optimal levels of those expenditures, and there may be either "excessive" or "deficient" levels of such expenditures from the point of view of society's welfare. The actual level of firms' expenditures on rent-seeking activities will not reflect the opportunity cost of the resources engaged in rent-seeking activities unless rent-seeking activities are at a socially optimal level, as Foster (1981) has emphasized. Except in this case, therefore, the level of expenditures on rent-seeking and other "fixed" costs that do not vary with firms' output level are no guide to whether the expenditures are "excessive" and "wasteful" or deficient.

Despite this conclusion, and irrespective of whether or not firms' rent-seeking and other types of "fixed" expenditure are at socially optimal levels, it is the relationship between the product price and the marginal cost of *changes in output* that is relevant for measuring the welfare change resulting from monopoly product-price and output-level changes. If one is estimating this welfare change from available data on firms' product prices and total costs per unit of output (ATC), rent-seeking and other "fixed" costs have to be *added* to the firms' profits in order to obtain the correct measure of $(P - MC_{output})$ and the associated welfare change.

(b) Demand and Cost Curves under Monopoly and Competition

The traditional approach to comparing monopoly and perfectly competitive pricing employs an unchanged demand curve facing the two types of decision maker. As has been noted, this approach implicitly assumes identical levels of all nonproduction expenditures that affect demand for the product of the monopolist and the group of perfectly competitive firms. It also implicitly assumes that pricing behavior does not affect these nonproduction expenditures. Neither assumption is valid, in general. The fact that pricing behavior will generally affect nonproduction types of expenditure that affect demand for the firm's product can easily be demonstrated by reference to the profit-maximizing condition for a firm's advertising expenditures. A profit-maximizing level of advertising expenditure must satisfy the condition

$$\frac{A}{S} = \frac{(P - MC)E_a}{P}$$

where A and S are the firm's total advertising expenditures and sales, respectively, and E_a is the "advertising elasticity of demand for the firm's product," which is defined as the percentage increase in the quantity of the firm's product demanded in response to a 1 percent change in the level of the firm's advertising expenditure (see Chapter 7).

If $(P - MC)$ is higher under monopoly, the profit-maximizing advertising condition implies that advertising/sales ratios will also be higher than under perfect competition only if E_a, the responsiveness of demand to advertising, is the same in both types of industry. The conclusion that advertising will necessarily be higher under monopoly than under competition is not necessarily valid, however.

No general conclusions regarding the relative level of advertising by a monopoly industry and an industry composed of two or more independent firms emerge from a careful analysis of the determinants of a firm's advertising in the two situations. This remains true even if the $(P - MC)/P$ component of the profit-maximizing advertising condition is higher in a monopoly industry. The reason is as follows: the advertising elasticity of demand for a firm's product, E_a, is related to the response of buyers and rival firms to changes in the level of the firm's advertising in the manner[4]

$$E_a = E_B + E_{conj} \cdot E_{Ar}$$

where E_B is the percentage response of total market demand to a 1 percent change in the firm's advertising, E_{conj} is the anticipated percentage change in rivals' advertising in response to a 1 percent change in the firm's advertising, and E_{Ar} is the percentage change in the quantity of the first firm's product demanded in response to a 1 percent change in the firm's rivals' advertising.

When a firm has no rivals, the last two terms in the expression are zero, and the advertising elasticity of demand for the firm's product depends only on E_B, the response of buyers to the firm's advertising. Where there is more than one firm in an industry, and each firm expects its rivals to increase their advertising in response to increases in its own advertising, the term E_{conj} will be positive in sign. However, if increases

4 See Needham (1978, Chap. 5) for proof of this proposition.

in rivals' advertising reduce the demand for the first firm's product at any level of price and advertising by the firm, E_{Ar} will be negative. This means that the combined effect of rivals' expected reactions (E_{conj}) and the effect of these reactions on the demand for the firm's product (E_{Ar}) will be negative, so that E_a is lower than E_B for individual firms in the industry. However, total industry advertising is the sum of advertising by all the firms in the industry, and, assuming that each firm expects rivals to react in the same way, the advertising elasticity of demand for all the independent firms combined may be represented by the expression

$$E_{a_{industry}} = n(E_B + E_{conj} \cdot E_{Ar})$$

where n is the number of firms in the industry.

It is clear from this expression that whether the advertising elasticity of demand for a monopolist's product is greater or less than the combined advertising elasticities of demand of a group of independent firms in the same industry depends on whether

$$E_B \quad \text{is greater or less than} \quad n(E_B + E_{conj} \cdot E_{Ar})$$

It is intuitively obvious that a sufficiently large negative magnitude for $E_{conj} \cdot E_{Ar}$ can result in a situation where the advertising elasticity of demand facing a group of independent firms is exactly equal to that faced by a monopolist. It can be shown that this situation will in fact result whenever each firm expects its rivals to exactly imitate its advertising policies.

Anticipated increases in rivals' advertising greater than those of the firm initiating the change will result in combined advertising elasticities confronting a group of independent firms that are smaller than those that would be faced by a monopolist facing the same market demand. Given similar pricing policies, this will result in lower levels of industry advertising than under monopoly. On the other hand, anticipated increases in rivals' advertising that are smaller than those of the firm initiating the change will result in combined advertising elasticities facing a group of independent firms that are larger than those that would be faced by a monopolist facing the same market demand. In this case, given similar pricing policies, the result will be higher industry advertising than under monopoly.

The preceding discussion indicates that anticipated rivals' reactions are of prime importance in determining the advertising behavior of a group of independent firms, and no generalizations are possible. Moreover, the dimensions of rivals' reactions that are relevant to firms' advertising are more complex than this brief introduction suggests. However, the same reasoning processes and conclusions may be applied to other types of expenditure that affect the demand for individual firms' products, such as expenditures on quality dimensions of the product. (See Chapter 7.)

(c) The Multidimensional Nature of Monopoly Behavior

The traditional approach to welfare losses from monopoly pricing behavior ignores both the multidimensional nature of a monopolist's behavior and the interdependence that exists among different dimensions of that behavior. Even if welfare losses from monopoly-pricing behavior are insignificant, this does not necessarily mean that other aspects of monopoly behavior cause no welfare losses for society. To focus exclusively on pricing behavior as a criterion for judging monopoly behavior is analogous to judging a Miss Universe contest on the basis of the length of the contestants' noses!

There are scattered signs in the literature of economics that indicate concern for dimensions of monopoly behavior and effects other than price and output effects. For example, Miller (1978) has argued that the existence of monopoly profits may shift demand for assets toward financial assets such as common stock of monopoly firms and away from fixed capital accumulation, with the result that the total stock of capital in the economy, and total output, is lower at any point in time than it would otherwise be. There has also been a long-standing but inconclusive debate in the literature concerning the effect of monopoly on innovation and research and development. The reasons for the inconclusiveness of this controversy are similar to those outlined in Section 6.3(b) in connection with advertising behavior and are explained in Needham (1978, Chap. 6).

In order to determine the effects, costs, and benefits of monopoly, a much wider framework is required, however, than analyses that focus on purely "economic" dimensions of monopoly behavior. The analysis must also be extended to political and other dimensions of decision-maker behavior. Not only is this desirable, because other dimensions of decision-maker behavior than pricing behavior and performance are important in their own right; it is also necessary, because all the dimensions of monopoly behavior are interdependent. Just as pricing and advertising behavior are interdependent, so are economic and political dimensions of behavior. They are simply alternative means by which decision makers may seek to achieve their respective objectives.

Chapter 7 explains how firms can eliminate their rivals without changing their pricing policies and engaging in "predatory" pricing behavior. The same kind of reasoning can be applied to economic and political characteristics of decision-maker behavior. A decision maker may be able to eliminate his or her rivals without changing economic dimensions of behavior simply by changing political dimensions of behavior. Similarly, monopolies can avoid violating prescribed rules of "desirable" market pricing and still achieve their objectives by means of other types of behavior. Jensen and Meckling (1977) have questioned whether the institution of the private corporation can survive in the face of competition with decision makers in the public sector.

In order to understand the determinants and relationship among different dimensions of decision-maker behavior, monopolists or otherwise, models of such behavior that take the multidimensional nature of behavior into account are essential. To evaluate these characteristics of decision-maker behavior, it is also essential that multidimensional evaluation criteria be used. It is not appropriate, for example, to evaluate firms' advertising or other dimensions of behavior solely by reference to their implications for pricing behavior.

There is no doubt that advertising will generally affect pricing behavior via its effect on consumer behavior and demand for firms' products. However, it would be a mistake to assume, for example, that advertising is desirable if it lowers price-cost margins and undesirable if it increases price-cost margins. Yet this is precisely the assumption made by most economic analysts when dealing with advertising. The correct approach is to evaluate advertising itself, and to do this we need to understand how individual members of society view and evaluate advertising. It is presumptuous for an analyst to claim that advertising is "informative" or "persuasive," valuable or wasted, without reference to the evaluations of people affected by advertising.

The essential ingredients of a satisfactory multidimensional model for evaluating the welfare loss attributable to monopoly, or any other form of decision-maker behavior, are two: (1) a vector of different dimensions of decision-maker behavior such as the following: $(P - MC)/P$, TC/TC_{min}, quantity and quality dimensions of output, advertising expenditures, R&D expenditures, expenditures on political activities such as campaign contributions, and so on; (2) a model of decision-maker behavior showing the determinants and relationship among these dimensions of behavior in any given set of circumstances; and (3) a vector of normative criteria for evaluating each of these behavior dimensions.

(d) Evaluation of Monopoly and Competition and the Relevance of Income Distribution

The evaluation vector, or "objective function," as it is usually termed, that has been traditionally used to evaluate monopoly behavior is seriously deficient. It includes criteria for evaluating pricing behavior and the resulting "allocative" welfare loss attributable to monopoly and also criteria for evaluating the "technical efficiency" with which output is produced. Technical efficiency refers to the extent to which particular output levels are produced with the minimum necessary inputs. It can be measured by the ratio between the actual costs of producing a given output and the minimum feasible level of costs, given available technology.

Figure 6.4

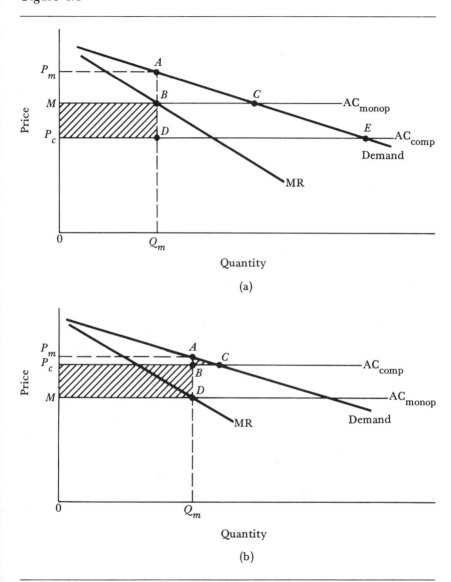

(a)

(b)

If the degree of technical efficiency under monopoly and competition is different, this will imply a different height of the average cost curves relating to output, as demonstrated in Figure 6.4. If technical efficiency is greater under competition than monopoly, as depicted in Figure

6.4(a), the welfare-loss triangle is larger than the monopolists' $(P - \text{MC})$ would suggest. To the allocative welfare loss represented by the large triangle ADE must be added a "technical efficiency loss" equal to the shaded area $MBDP_c$; this shaded area represents the money value of the reduction in inputs required to produce output level Q_m under competition. If technical efficiency is greater under monopoly than competition, as in Figure 6.4(b), the allocative welfare loss attributable to monopoly, shown by the small shaded triangle $ABC,$ is smaller than the monopolists' $(P - \text{MC})$ margin would suggest. In this case, the technical efficiency reduction under competition represented by area P_cBDM must be *subtracted* from the allocative monopoly welfare loss in order to determine the net welfare effect of monopoly on both types of efficiency.

Whether total, average, and marginal production costs are higher under competition or monopoly is obviously important in determining the overall welfare loss attributable to monopoly behavior. As is usual in economics, hypotheses abound on both sides of the issue. The relative strength of pressures for technical efficiency, the ability of decision makers to substitute other goals for profit maximization, and the relative magnitude of incentives to innovate under the two types of market structure are all relevant in this connection. No really convincing theoretical or empirical evidence has been presented to date to show that technical efficiency will be higher or lower under monopoly than under competition.

Whatever the final outcome of the debate over technical efficiency under competition and monopoly, the foregoing discussion indicates that allocative and technical efficiency effects of monopoly might conflict. The same is true of other dimensions of monopoly behavior. For example, advertising behavior by a monopoly industry might be closer to the "socially optimal" level than under "competition." This means that the criteria used to evaluate monopoly and other forms of decision-maker behavior must include much more than a list of "desirable" characteristics of pricing and other dimensions of such behavior. In addition, there must be a set of *relative evaluations* of different dimensions of "socially desirable" behavior that permit an overall evaluation of a decision maker's behavior. Without these relative evaluations of dimensions of socially desirable behavior, it would be impossible to compare the behavior of particular decision makers, particular market structures, or other institutional forms that exhibit varying mixtures of socially desirable behavior.

Satisfactory and generally accepted normative criteria for aspects of decision-maker behavior such as advertising and other economic forms of firms' behavior do not exist to date. The relevance and importance of political and other noneconomic dimensions of firms' behavior for evaluations of monopoly have barely been recognized by economists. Yet, the analytical tools for broadening the range of decision variables and their evaluation are available and are similar to those employed in the traditional analysis of monopoly welfare losses.

In principle, for each dimension of behavior, such as advertising, there is an "evaluation schedule" analogous to the demand curve that is used to evaluate different output levels in the traditional model. Similarly, there is a "cost schedule" indicating the opportunity costs of the sources used for advertising. A "socially optimal" level of advertising may be defined, and "welfare losses" associated with behavior that departs from this level may be conceptually defined in a manner very similar to that involved with output levels. All one is doing, in essence, is expanding the number of behavioral dimensions that are relevant in examining and evaluating decision-maker behavior.

The major caveat that must be borne in mind relates to interdependencies that may exist among different dimensions of behavior. Diagrammatically, this means that the position and shape of the demand and cost curves relating to each dimension of behavior *depend on the level of other dimensions of behavior*. Thus, a general rather than a partial approach to the determinants of individual dimensions of decision-maker behavior must be adopted; the same holds true of an evaluation of that behavior according to some norms of socially desirable behavior.

These comments should enable the reader to place in perspective the importance of income distribution, and other matters, in influencing the evaluation of monopoly and other forms of decision-maker behavior. The demand or evaluation curves employed by economists traditionally represent the money value individuals place on the outputs or activities to which the demand curves apply, as explained in Chapter 3. While the general methodological approach to determining socially optimal levels of output and the other dimensions of decision-maker behavior outlined is quite sound, the assumption that the relevant demand or evaluation curves that "should" be used in this process are *those based on the existing distribution of money income* is not acceptable as a generalization. If we change the distribution of income among individual members of society, this will change the monetary evaluations of the benefits of particular activities by members of society, even if all members' evaluations are included. If we redistribute income to the retired generation from the younger generation, for example, the monetary evaluation of, or demand for, sports cars will tend to fall and the evaluation of hearing aids will tend to rise. This redistribution will raise the socially optimal level of hearing aids and reduce the socially optimal level of sports cars.

Which income distribution, or whose evaluations "should" be used as an index of society's evaluations of particular activities — and therefore of socially optimal levels of decision-maker behavior — cannot be determined in any "objective" way. The best we can do is recognize that different methods of deciding whose evaluations should be employed to evaluate decision-maker behavior will produce different outcomes in terms of what is regarded as socially desirable behavior. Also, this should alert us to the fact that, like any other resource, the right to decide what is socially desirable behavior may itself become the subject of intense competition. The vector of socially desirable behavior can, in fact, be viewed as a special kind of "regulatory constraint." By viewing the index of socially desirable behavior as a regulatory constraint, and applying the tools of analysis and principles that are relevant when dealing with the determinants and effects of any particular regulatory constraint, it is possible to gain considerable insight into whose evaluations actually determine existing indexes of socially optimal behavior and how these indexes can be changed. At the very least, one develops a clearer understanding of why economists' concepts of socially optimal behavior are not often applied in the real world.

(e) Prices and Marginal Costs in Other Sectors of the Economy

In Section 6.3(a) it was explained that in order to use $(P - MC)$ as a measure of the net increase in society's satisfaction from a one-unit increase in output, the marginal costs of the product must exactly equal the value of the alternative outputs that could be produced instead. If inputs are mobile between sectors, this requires that prices of other outputs equal their marginal costs. If the prices of other outputs exceed their marginal costs, it is clear that MC in the sector we are analyzing will understate the value to society of other outputs forgone. This, in turn, means that $(P - MC)$ in any particular sector will tend to overstate the net increase in society's satisfaction from an increase in that sector's output.

In addition, however, when prices exceed marginal costs in other sectors, the traditional welfare-loss triangle *is no longer the only component of the welfare loss* that is attributable to a particular sector's pricing policy. Also, the effect of changes in product price in that sector on demands, supplies, and output levels in other sectors must be taken into account. If prices equaled marginal costs in other sectors, such induced output changes in other sectors would have no welfare effects, since $(P - MC)$, the net change in society's satisfaction from changes in output in those sectors, is zero. In contrast, when prices exceed marginal costs in all sectors, the monetary value of a change in satisfaction, or welfare, of society caused by a change in the price and output of the ith product is equal to the following expression:

$$\text{Welfare change} = (P - MC)\Delta Q_i + \Sigma(P - MC)\Delta Q_j \cdots \quad (3)$$

The changes in output levels in other sectors, represented by ΔQ_j, can be positive or negative depending on whether the goods are complements to, or substitutes for, the ith product. The expression before the plus sign is the traditional welfare-loss triangle representing allocative inefficiency attributable to monopoly. The term that follows the plus sign represents the allocative efficiency effects in j other sectors associated with a change in price and output in the market for the monopolized good. This term will be zero only when price equals marginal cost in all other sectors. Diagrammatically, the expression following the plus sign is the algebraic sum of areas like $ABCE$ in Figure 6.5, which represents $(P - MC)\Delta Q_j$ in one other sector. When the price of product i is raised above its marginal cost, if product j of another sector is a substitute for i, the demand for j will be increased from D to D'. In this case, the shaded area $ABCE$ represents an increase in society's satisfaction as a result of the increase in the price of i above its marginal cost; this increase must be *subtracted* from the traditional welfare-loss triangle representing the excess of P over MC in the market for product i. When the product j is complementary with product i, a rise in the price of product i above its marginal cost will shift the demand for j from D' to D. In this case, the area $ABCE$ represents a decrease in society's satisfaction as a result of the increase in the price of i above its marginal cost; this decrease in satisfaction must be *added* to the traditional welfare-loss triangle in the market for i.

Figure 6.5

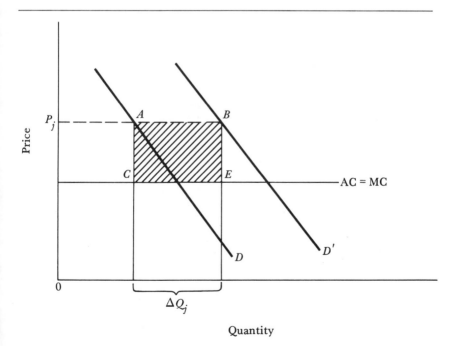

Quantity

Even after recognizing and taking into account the additional welfare effects in other sectors that are associated with a product-price change in one sector, a question still remains: What is the level of $(P - MC)$ in any particular sector that is optimal from the point of view of allocating resources among sectors in such a manner that the satisfaction of members of society is maximized? Until this is known, there is no bench mark for comparing observed $(P - MC)$ margins in particular sectors with "socially optimal" levels of $(P - MC)$ in those sectors. Similarly, without this bench mark, there is no way of knowing whether the expression (1) represents "true" welfare loss attributable to a price above marginal cost in the ith sector. We have explained that MC_i understates the value placed on other outputs that could be produced instead of product i. We cannot use the *observed* price–marginal cost differences of products in other sectors to measure the true value of other outputs forgone, however, unless those prices in other sectors are at *their* "socially optimal" levels. It is therefore essential to determine "socially optimal" levels of price–marginal cost margins in all sectors, then to plug *the socially optimal* price-cost margins into expression (1) when valuing output-level changes caused by a change in the price of the ith product.

The "Theory of Second Best" deals with the nature of welfare-maximizing price–marginal cost rules in situations in which any constraint exists that prevents price from equaling marginal cost in every sector of the economy simultaneously. For an illuminating article on this theory, the reader should consult Baumol and Bradford (1970).

In the presence of any type of constraint, C, which prevents pricing at marginal cost in all sectors, the Theory of Second Best indicates that the condition that must be met to achieve a welfare-maximizing allocation of resources among different sectors is as follows. The ratio of the marginal benefits that two goods yield to the community, expressed in money terms as the ratio of their prices, must equal the ratio of the marginal effects of changes in the output levels of the two goods *on the constraint C*, instead of equaling the ratio of their marginal costs, as is the case in the absence of the constraint C. The logic that underlies this optimal "second-best" condition is quite simple. If the ratio of the marginal benefits that two types of output yield to the community were not equal to the ratio of their marginal effects on the constraint C, it follows automatically that the total satisfaction of the community can be increased without violating constraint C. This can be accomplished by switching some resources from production of the output where the ratio between the marginal benefit (price) and the effect of a marginal output change on the constraint C is lower to increased production of the output where this ratio is higher.

Although the second-best allocative efficiency condition is perfectly general, the precise relationship between price and marginal cost in different firms and sectors of the economy that is necessary to satisfy this

condition will obviously depend on the precise nature of the constraint
C, which prevents price from being set equal to marginal cost in all
sectors simultaneously. *Generalizations* concerning the price–marginal cost
relationships required for allocative efficiency are therefore impossible in
these circumstances, since differing optimal price–marginal cost relationships will be appropriate for different constraints.

Despite this, many of the types of constraint that make it impossible
in practice to set $(P - MC)$ equal in all sectors, such as taxes and decreas-
ing-cost industries and products, result in very similar optimal second-best
pricing rules for the products of individual firms and industries. Space
does not permit full development of these rules; the reader is referred
to the References for this chapter for more detailed treatment. In general,
these second-best pricing rules are of the form[5]

$$\frac{(P_i - MC_i)}{P_i} = \frac{(\lambda)}{(\lambda + 1)} \frac{1}{E_{d_i}} + \Sigma\, CE$$

where E_{d_i} is the price elasticity of demand for the ith product and $\Sigma\, CE$
represents the sum of cross-elasticities of demand between the ith product
and other products. Cross-elasticities of demand affect the direction and
size of the shifts in the demand curves in Figure 6.5. Cross-elasticities of
demand for substitutes are positive in sign and are negative in sign for
complementary goods. The preceding expression indicates that when
other goods are substitutes for the ith product, the welfare-maximizing
excess of $(P - MC)$ of the ith good will tend to be higher, all other things
being the same. This is because as $(P - MC)_i$ increases, causing a "welfare-
loss triangle"; the demand curve for other products in Figure 6.5 shifts
to the right; and the rectangle $ABCE$ must be subtracted from the
welfare-loss triangle, resulting in a smaller net welfare loss. Similar
reasoning leads to the conclusion that welfare-maximizing level of
$(P - MC)_i$ will be lower, the greater the degree of complementarity
between i and other products.

The major implications of the Theory of Second Best for the problem
of defining and measuring the allocative welfare losses associated with
changes in the output level of individual products and industries are as
follows: (1) the proper bench mark for evaluating $(P - MC)$ behavior in
a particular industry is no longer $P = MC$ — the determination of that
bench mark of socially optimal pricing behavior is much more complex,
depending on factors such as price- and cross-elasticities of demand; and
(2) the welfare-loss concepts and measures that are appropriate for calculating changes in society's satisfaction resulting from particular pricing
policies are correspondingly more complex.

[5] See Needham (1978, Chap. 10) for more detailed treatment of these relationships.

(f) Definition and Identification
of Relevant Markets and Products

Any discussion of monopoly and competition in a particular industry or
market implies a definition of the industry or market. A market is
simply a group of buyers and sellers engaging in transactions, or exchanges. Firms are sellers in markets for their outputs, and are buyers in
markets for their inputs. All the firms that sell in a particular market,
or that buy if one is considering an input market, are usually termed an
"industry." It follows that once the boundaries of a market are defined,
all firms that sell in that market, or buy in the case of an input market,
will automatically be defined as constituting the industry.

A firm that sells or buys in a number of different markets may simultaneously be a member of different industry groups; it will then be
described as a "diversified" firm. If, instead, firms serve a number of
different markets that are considered to be within the same broad market,
the products sold in different "market segments" may be considered to
be "differentiated" from each other. Similarly, the products of firms
selling in the same market area may be "differentiated" and become
"different" products sold by firms in "different" industries if market
boundaries are defined more narrowly. All this illustrates that measures
of industry, product diversification, and product differentiation are determined by the definition of market boundaries.

Although the concepts of industry and market are part of everyday
life, when one attempts to define a market or industry operationally,
matters are not so simple (Needham, 1978, Chap. 5).

To define a market or an industry there must be some aspect of the
transactions engaged in by individual sellers and buyers that is similar.
A transaction has many characteristics, however, and there are correspondingly many possible criteria for defining market and industry
boundaries.

Even when the adoption of one of the characteristics of a transaction
yields relatively unambiguous boundaries, other dimensions of the resulting transactions will generally differ between firms. The drawing of
market and industry boundaries is therefore complex, involving consideration of all the many dimensions of a transaction and resulting in
innumerable ways of defining markets, products, and industries.

It is impossible to overemphasize the importance of the market definition, since it will determine the identity and number of sellers and
buyers in the market so defined. The problem of market definition has
both descriptive and normative implications. How firms in practice define
markets in their decision making is obviously important in determining
their output, pricing, and other policies. Since price, advertising, and
other elasticities of demand for firms' products in response to changes in
dimensions of firms' behavior determine the profitability of their oper-

ations, it is natural for firms to emphasize approaches to market definition that are related to these elasticity concepts.

The normative aspects of the problem of market definition are most important from the point of view of analyses of monopoly and competition. Traditionally, economists have been concerned with the efficiency with which "given" products are produced and with the pricing and output level of "given" products. There has been little concern with the normative issue of what the characteristics of products "should" be. This is unfortunate, because the choice of a "product's" characteristics determines which inputs and cost curve are "relevant," and also which market demand curve is "relevant" for analyzing the behavior of firms that produce that product. Similarly, a product has many dimensions, and the analyst's choice of "output" dimension will determine the cost and demand function that is appropriate for analyzing a firm's behavior. Even the choice of what is meant by a "unit" of output influences the evaluation of a firm's behavior, since the price "per unit" of a product that is socially optimal will obviously vary with the way in which a "unit" is defined.

One aspect of the problem of which product concept is appropriate has recently been recognized and dealt with within the traditional framework of economic analysis. This is the so-called problem of bundling. This term refers to the practice of selling a number of separable products or services for a single price. A consumer who purchases the bundle does so because he or she values the bundle of products more than the price charged. The consumer may prefer less of some and more of other individual characteristics than the bundle contains, however. If the products or services in the bundle were priced separately, the consumer could reach a higher level of satisfaction by adjusting his or her level of purchases of the individual characteristics to the preferred combination.

In these circumstances, bundling will result in what is termed "distributive inefficiency," a situation in which the prices of individual product characteristics are not proportional to the satisfaction an individual derives from marginal units of the different characteristics of the products.

Bundling adds another component to the welfare-loss concept, corresponding to the money value of the "distributive inefficiency" that results from any particular bundling policy. This distributive inefficiency measures the gains individuals could experience by trading individual components of the bundled products whenever individuals place a different relative value on the various components of the bundled goods. Bundling may also lead to allocative inefficiency that, as Adams and Yellen (1976) have emphasized, is not captured by the traditional allocative welfare-loss triangle.

A useful way of illustrating this is to consider a situation in which the price of a bundled product equals its marginal cost, so that $(P - MC)$

and the welfare triangle in Figure 6.1 is zero. If the demand and marginal cost curve for the bundled product are now disaggregated into a demand and marginal cost curve for each individual component or characteristic of the bundled product, each pair of curves need not intersect at the output level of the bundled product. Instead, the demand and marginal cost curve for an individual component of the bundled product or service may intersect either to the left or right of the output level of the bundled product, as shown by D_1, MC_1, and D_2, MC_2 in Figure 6.6.

    In the case of the product characteristic to which the demand and associated marginal revenue curves D_1 and MC_1 refer, there is an allocative welfare loss equal to the vertically shaded area. It represents the potential gain in satisfaction to consumers from extending the output level of product characteristic 1 from its present level. In the case of the product characteristic to which curves D_2 and MC_2 refer, there is also an allocative welfare loss, shown by the horizontally shaded area. This is the potential increase in consumer satisfaction resulting from a reduction in the output level of product characteristic 2. This illustrates that with bundling, the output level of particular product characteristics can be

Figure 6.6

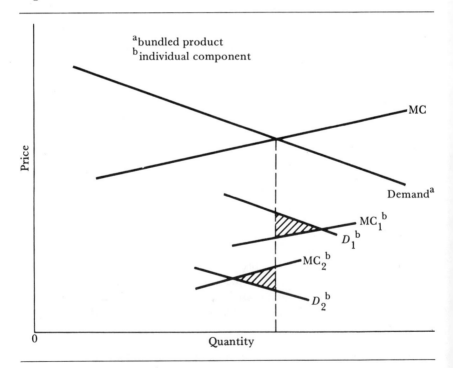

[a] bundled product
[b] individual component

"too large" under perfect competition or any other form of market structure. The two shaded areas must be *added* to obtain the total allocative loss attributable to bundling.

6.4 BEHAVIOR OF ANTITRUST ENFORCEMENT AGENCIES

Whatever the intent of the legislators who originally passed the Sherman Act and other antitrust laws of the United States, the effect of these laws on private sector firms' behavior depends on the manner in which these laws are administered and enforced. This depends on the behavior of existing antitrust agencies, the Department of Justice, the Federal Trade Commission, and the courts in interpreting and administering these laws.

Like other decision makers, the behavior of antitrust agency decision makers and courts depends on the goals and constraints these decision makers consider to be relevant in their decision making. In recent years, a number of studies have attempted to model the behavior of antitrust decision makers and to evaluate their performance. The general consensus has been to award low marks to the antitrust authorities for their role in administering the antitrust laws of the United States. Before we accept these evaluations, however, some investigation of the framework and methodology of the studies is appropriate. Critics of the antitrust agencies often make inappropriate assumptions, or draw unwarranted conclusions. Often, they omit relevant constraints that confront antitrust agencies and courts.

In Section 6.3 it was demonstrated that the task of defining socially optimal concepts of firms' pricing, production, and other dimensions of behavior is not without its problems. Essentially, this task requires the adoption of the preferences or evaluations of all, or some subset, of members of society as a basis for evaluating various dimensions of firms' behavior. The resources and other constraints facing society must also be taken into account. If pricing at marginal cost in every sector is impossible, this will change the characteristics of socially optimal pricing behavior, for example.

Let us assume that a list of socially desirable characteristics of all dimensions of firms' behavior, including market and nonmarket dimensions of behavior, has been agreed upon by members of society. The actual behavior of firms could then be compared with this list. Whenever some dimension of a particular firm's behavior differs from the socially desirable characteristics of that behavior dimension, there will exist a "welfare loss," defined as a potential net increase in society's satisfaction from changing that dimension of the firm's behavior to its socially optimal level. These welfare losses associated with different dimensions of the

174   Regulating Competition

firm's behavior could be expressed in the form of Table 6.2, where the columns represent different firms in the economy.

WL_{11}, the first element in the top row of the table, represents the welfare loss attributable to firm 1's present pricing behavior; WL_{12} represents the welfare loss attributable to firm 1's technical inefficiency, which is higher than the minimum feasible; WL_{13} is the welfare loss resulting from advertising levels that are above or below the "socially optimal" level of advertising for firm 1; and WL_{1i} is the welfare loss resulting from some dimension of firm 1's political activities being above or below socially optimal levels. Some or all the elements in the first row may be zero if the firm is acting in a socially optimal manner in those dimensions of its behavior. The second row represents the welfare loss attributable to various dimensions of firm 2's behavior, and so on, with the number of rows in the table being equal to the number of firms in the economy.

The behavior of antitrust enforcement agencies, or other regulatory agencies concerned with firms' behavior, may be analyzed either from the descriptive point of view or from the normative perspective. Given socially optimal criteria for antitrust agency behavior, the kind of incentives and constraints that are required to move agency behavior toward such socially desirable behavior depend on the nature of the goals and constraints that determine how the agencies behave in practice.

Table 6.2 may be used as a starting point for clarifying both normative and descriptive aspects of antitrust agency behavior. Economists have focused almost exclusively on the first two columns of the table, dealing with the pricing and input-mix behavior of firms and their implications for allocative and technical efficiency welfare-loss concepts. Welfare-loss concepts covering other dimensions of firms' behavior are controversial, and some have not even been considered. The controversy revolves around the nature of the models of firm and consumer behavior that are appropriate, and the issue of whose evaluations are to count in evaluating this behavior.

Table 6.2. Dimensions of Firms' Behavior

	$P - MC$	TC/TC_{min}	Advertising	R&D	Dimensions of firms' political lobbying, etc.
Firm 1	WL_{11}	WL_{12}	WL_{13}		WL_{1i}
Firm 2	WL_{21}	WL_{22}	WL_{23}		WL_{2i}
.					
.					
Firm 3					

A view shared by many economists is that antitrust agencies should identify the largest welfare-loss elements in Table 6.2 and proceed to try to change the behavior of those firms responsible for these elements. This view is erroneous, however, for a number of reasons. First, it ignores the possibility that the costs of detecting the welfare losses may differ for different elements in the table. Resources are required to detect and determine the welfare-loss elements, and the welfare losses associated with some types of behavior, or with different firms, may be more costly to detect than others. If socially optimal antitrust behavior requires maximization of the reduction in total welfare losses from a given amount of antitrust resources, in certain circumstances this objective may be achieved by devoting resources to the detection of welfare losses that are smaller but less costly to detect than other welfare losses.

Second, the detection of welfare losses attributable to firms is only the necessary first step in attempting to reduce the magnitude of such losses. The next step is to try to change the behavior of firms responsible for those welfare losses. This has led a number of writers, including enonomists who have worked on antitrust problems at the Federal Trade Commission and Antitrust Division of the Justice Department, to suggest that welfare-loss elements such as are shown in Table 6.2 must be multiplied by an estimate of the probability of success from agencies' efforts to change firms' behavior.

Other writers have focused on a number of factors that influence this probability and the extent to which agency behavior will change firms' behavior. For example, Elzinga and Breit (1976) have considered the alternative penalties for antitrust violations — fines, jail sentences, re-structuring the industry by dissolution or divestiture, and private actions for treble damages. Posner (1972, 1976) has examined the factors that influence an agency's case selection and prosecution policies, and legal aspects of the behavior of defendant firms. Masson and Reynolds (1977) have emphasized that firms with more to lose by changing their behavior may spend more on defending themselves against antitrust cases, lowering the probability of successful prosecution. In these circumstances, it may be more appropriate for agencies to bring cases against firms with smaller welfare losses and smaller defense efforts resulting in a higher probability of success in winning a case and changing their behavior. This conclusion is strengthened if winning cases sets a precedent and/or increases the probability of successful prosecution in subsequent cases.

Although each of these contributions is relevant and insightful, no satisfactory methodological and analytical framework existed in the literature for integrating these aspects of the antitrust enforcement prob-lem into a logical whole. As a result, the normative implications of conclusions reached by writers concerned with various aspects of antitrust agencies' behavior have limited relevance in practice. In order to over-come this problem, in Chapter 4, Section 3, and in Chapter 12 we develop a general approach to the determinants of the effects of regulatory constraints on firms' behavior that may also be applied to regulatory constraints in the form of antitrust policies. Some implications of this general model for socially optimal antitrust enforcement are quite startling and run counter to many of the conclusions reached by earlier approaches to the problem. It is appropriate, therefore, to briefly sketch the major elements of a satisfactory model of antitrust enforcement and its effects on firms' behavior and welfare losses.

The first major element comprises the potential penalties or rewards that are prescribed for certain kinds of firms' behavior. These are often prescribed by law or determined by the courts, and are to some extent outside the direct control of antitrust agencies, although these agencies may, like other members of society, lobby for changes in these penalties or rewards. For each of the types of behavior represented by the columns of Table 6.2, we can list the applicable penalties or rewards. These may be represented by a scale of penalties or rewards corresponding to different levels or degrees of the behavior dimension in question, rather than a single penalty or reward. Also, the behavior for which the penalties are prescribed may be narrowly or vaguely defined.

The magnitude of these penalties or rewards will play some role in determining whether or not firms behave in a manner that violates required standards of some dimension of their behavior. Even if the probability of detection and successful prosecution of such behavior were 100 percent, firms would not change their behavior if the penalties for violation were less than the gains to firms from violating the standards. Put another way, in order to change firms' behavior, penalties for violating standards must exceed the costs imposed on firms as a result of changing their behavior to meet the required standards. The level of penalties that is sufficient to change firms' behavior in the case of 100 percent certainty of successful prosecution will depend on the nature of the goals and constraints facing the firm's decision makers. These factors determine the "costs," defined as a reduction in the level of the firm's attainment of its objectives, that the firm will suffer as a result of changing its behavior to meet a required standard of behavior that is different from its optimal, unregulated behavior.

One of the major, and rather surprising conclusions that emerges from the analysis contained in Chapter 12 is that the *absolute level* of penalties or rewards for a particular form of behavior is itself far less important as a determinant of the firm's response to the penalties or rewards than the *structure* of the penalties or rewards. By "structure" here we mean the way their absolute level changes with the level of the firm's behavior and the magnitude of violations of any given regulatory standard. A penalty for polluting, for example, will not change the level of a profit-maximizing firm's pollution activities if the magnitude of the penalty is the same at all levels of the firm's pollution activities. Like a "fixed cost" change, it will merely reduce the level of the firm's profits without changing the profit-maximizing level of its activities from their previous levels.

The second major element influencing the response of firms to antitrust enforcement is the probability of detection and successful prosecution, viewed from the firm's point of view. This probability is the product of the three following probabilities (see Chapters 4 and 12).

(i) the probability of the firm's behavior being monitored and violations of required behavior being detected (P_d)
(ii) the probability that a firm whose behavior in violation of required standards will be prosecuted (P_p)
(iii) the probability that a firm that is prosecuted will lose the case and be subject to the penalties prescribed by law (P_f)

These probabilities must be multiplied in order to obtain the overall probability of detection and successful prosecution. This probability must then be multiplied by the penalties prescribed by law to obtain a measure of the "expected value" of the penalties for behaving in a manner that violates required standards of some dimension of behavior. Any or all these probabilities may vary with the level of some dimension of a firm's behavior and the magnitude of the firm's violations of regulatory requirements. Chapter 12 demonstrates diagrammatically that the resulting *structure* of the probabilities, defined as the way in which the probabilities vary with levels of firm's behavior, is more important than the absolute level of the probabilities. For example, if the combined probabilities of detection, prosecution, and loss of case decline with increases in the levels of a firm's violations, this could completely offset the effect of rising penalties for larger violations and even create an incentive for firms to *increase* the level of their violations.

Each of these three probabilities depends on a number of variables. Some of the variables are the decision variables of antitrust agencies. For example, given limited resources, the agency must generally monitor a subset of firms in the economy instead of all firms. The decision rules that describe the agency's monitoring policies will influence P_d, the probability that any aspect of a firm's behavior will be monitored and violations of particular behavior standards detected.

The P_d also depends on aspects of firms' behavior other than the degree to which they violate behavior standards and cause welfare losses. Information required by antitrust agencies in order to monitor firms' behavior must generally come from firms themselves. Firms can be expected to distort this information whenever doing so will reduce the probability of detecting antitrust violations. Chapter 12 explains the conditions that any penalty-reward system must satisfy in order to avoid incentives for firms to provide inaccurate information regarding their actual behavior. These conditions are not met by incentive systems currently in use in antitrust or any other aspect of regulation in the United States. *Misrepresentation of information by firms regarding their behavior is therefore likely to be the rule rather than the exception,* so that little reliance may be placed on the information provided by regulated firms that is needed to detect welfare losses, irrespective of the precise nature of the agencies' standards of socially optimal behavior.

This problem cannot be overcome simply by stepping up the level of antitrust resources devoted to monitoring firms' behavior. Even if every firm and every dimension of behavior in the economy were monitored, the probability of observed violations being successfully prosecuted were 100 percent, and the penalties were huge, violations would continue as long as firms were protected by the information distortion that is unavoidable in absence of a very special kind of "incentive-compatible" penalty-and-reward system described in Chapter 12.

The probability that a firm found in violation of antitrust laws will be prosecuted, P_p, also depends on a number of variables, some of which are under the control of the antitrust agency, and some of which are controlled by firms. The decision rules describing an agency's case selection criteria will determine which firms from among those whose behavior has been found in violation of certain behavior standards will actually be prosecuted. These criteria may include such factors as size of violation and estimated welfare loss, firm size, estimated probability of successful prosecution, and other factors. As this last item suggests, the three probabilities are not necessarily independent of each other. To the extent that firms are aware of an agency's case selection criteria, they may vary aspects of their policies other than violation size, in an attempt to reduce the probability that they will be selected for prosecution.

Other factors outside the direct control of antitrust enforcement agencies and firms will also affect P_p, however. The antitrust laws themselves, and the behavior of the courts in interpreting these laws in particular cases and establishing precedents, will exert an independent influence on case selection. Agencies are unlikely to select cases for prosecution that closely resemble cases previously lost. Whether such cases are lost or not will often depend on the behavior of the courts and other elements of the legal system as much, or more than, on the behavior of the agencies and defendant firms in presenting their respective sides of the issue.

The probability that a firm that is prosecuted will lose the case and be subject to the penalties prescribed by law, P_f, is affected by dimensions of the legal system's behavior as well as by antitrust agency behavior and defendant firm behavior. The amount of resources devoted by agency and defendant, and the expertise of their lawyers and expert advisers, will influence the likely outcome of a case. Where these resources are approximately equal in magnitude and expertise, the decision of the courts will be a deciding factor. Where the law is ambiguous, the courts' decision process will exert an especially important influence on the outcome of a case and the probability of successful prosecution. These decision processes are relatively unknown. To some extent, this may be beneficial, since they may therefore be less subject to manipulation and/or strategic behavior responses by antitrust agencies and defendant firms alike. On the other hand, without knowledge of these decision processes, it is impossible to design antitrust policies to secure a specifically desired effect on firms' behavior. In contrast, manipulation and strategic elements in decision-maker behavior, if they are known, can always be taken into account and allowed for.

To this point we have been concerned mainly with normative aspects of antitrust agency behavior. This is unavoidable if one is to define "socially optimal" antitrust behavior, and such a definition is necessary for evaluating antitrust agency behavior. Like any other type of decision maker, antitrust agency decision makers will not generally act in a "socially optimal" manner (however that term is defined) unless they are properly motivated to do so. In order to know how to provide the necessary motivation, one must first know what kind of antitrust behavior is "socially optimal." In addition, to provide the right kind of incentives and motivations for antitrust decision makers to behave in this manner, it is necessary to know the existing incentives that confront these decision makers. These incentives will depend on the personal goals and constraints that confront individual antitrust decision makers.

In the United States, the goals and constraints that confront the personnel at the Federal Trade Commission and the Antitrust Division of the Department of Justice are relevant in this connection. A growing number of writers have argued that the existing incentives facing these individuals will not produce socially optimal behavior. It must be emphasized that most of these arguments are based on concepts of socially optimal antitrust behavior that have little relevance to the real world, since they ignore most or all the factors we have just discussed. The useful contribution of such studies is therefore in identifying the kind of constraints that face antitrust decision makers in practice, rather than in providing correct normative evaluations of agency behavior. One can hardly blame antitrust agencies for not acting in a socially optimal manner if no one has bothered to explain what that term means, or how to achieve this goal.

The mere existence of a more appropriate and readily accessible body of knowledge for improving antitrust enforcement will not by itself lead to the implementation of its prescriptions by antitrust enforcement agencies. For such implementation to occur, either this knowledge must be capable of enabling these decision makers to reach higher levels of their existing personal goals, or changes must be made in existing incentives facing them.

Such changes may occur from pressures internal or external to the agencies. For example, an improved understanding of concepts of anti-trust enforcement may change the perceptions of various groups whose evaluations of antitrust performance represent pressures and constraints on the antitrust agencies, and this may lead to changes in agency behavior. The direction of these changes, however, is unpredictable, for reasons explained in Chapter 5. There it was emphasized that the behavior of legislators and of regulatory agency decision makers is evaluated by a multiplicity of interest groups in society, not only by "sponsoring" indi-viduals or groups who dole out votes, campaign contributions, or budget allocations to legislators or regulators. It was also explained that, in most situations, the legislators or the regulatory agency decision maker will select a pattern of behavior by weighting the evaluations of these various interest groups and will adopt behavior that is responsive in some degree to each of the evaluations, rather than following a course of action that pleases one group and offends others. The Antitrust Division of the Justice Department is directly responsible to the president, and the Fed-eral Trade Commission to Congress. There is no doubt that these spon-sors' evaluations of agencies' behavior will play a role, and perhaps a major one, in influencing the agencies' behavior. But to suggest that these are the only external groups whose evaluations will affect agency behavior is far from the mark.

The Antitrust Division has sole responsibility for enforcing the Sher-man Act, which declares monopoly, monopolizing, and restraint of trade illegal. The Federal Trade Commission has sole responsibility for section 5 of the Federal Trade Commission Act, which contains a general pro-hibition against unfair methods of competition. Both agencies share responsibility for sections 2, 3, 7, and 8 of the Clayton Act, though the Antitrust Division has in practice left the enforcement of section 2, as amended by the Robinson-Patman Act, which forbids price discrimina-tion, to the FTC.

Much has been made by some writers of the fact that a large pro-portion of antitrust staff are lawyers and that their patterns and motiva-tions may exert undesirable bias to antitrust case selection and procedure. Case selection according to legal precedent rather than novel cases, em-phasis on winning cases rather than maximizing economic efficiency in some sense, and a desire for trial experience rather than attention to the social payoff from cases are examples of this kind of criticism. As we have suggested, these criticisms are largely based on explicit or implicit models of antitrust enforcement that ignore important constraints. When these omitted constraints are taken into account, it is by no means obvious that the behavior of antitrust lawyers is inconsistent with socially optimal norms of antitrust enforcement.

In the two areas of economic analysis that are most relevant to anti-trust enforcement — dealing, respectively, with the mechanism by which antitrust laws and policies influence firms' behavior, and the operational interpretation of the terms "monopoly" and "competition" and their implications for firms' behavior — the literature of economics has provided little guidance for the staff of antitrust agencies until very recently.

Since most of the antitrust laws of the United States are phrased in terms of "monopoly" and "competition," and since the critical issue in many antitrust cases revolves around issues of excessive, unfair, or predatory competition, it is obvious that the precise manner in which these terms are interpreted by antitrust agencies, defendants, and courts will play a major role in shaping the nature of regulatory constraints affecting competition in practice. Economists frequently criticize antitrust rulings on the ground that they protect competitors rather than the type of competition among firms that is in society's best interests. Unfortunately, economists have not been very successful at spelling out, for noneconomists, what the characteristics of socially optimal competition are. A closer look at the concept of competition, and clarification of its different meanings and implications for firms' behavior and society's satisfaction, will be undertaken in the next chapter.

Appendix

SUBSTANTIVE PROVISIONS OF THE UNITED STATES ANTITRUST LAWS

There are three principal antitrust statutes in the United States: the Sherman Act, the Federal Trade Commission Act, and the Clayton Act. Their major provisions, and those of subsequent amending acts, are outlined briefly below.

The Sherman Act

Enacted in 1890, the Sherman Act has two major provisions:

S.1. "Every contract, combination in the form of a trust or otherwise, or conspiracy, in restraint of trade or commerce among the several States, or with foreign nations, is hereby declared to be illegal."

S.2. "Every person who shall monopolize, or attempt to monopolize, or combine or conspire with any other person or persons, to monopolize any part of the trade or commerce among the several States, or with foreign nations, shall be guilty of a misdemeanor."

In 1937 S.1 of the Sherman Act was amended by the *Miller-Tydings Act*, which provides exemption for resale price agreements between manufacturers of products identified by a brand name or trademark and suppliers in states that have their own "fair trade" laws sanctioning resale price agreements.

The Federal Trade Commission Act

This act, passed in 1914, established the Federal Trade Commission to strengthen the observance and enforcement of the antitrust laws. S.5 of the act contained a general prohibition of unfair methods of competition in commerce.

In 1938 the *Wheeler-Lea Act* was passed to extend the commission's jurisdiction to include not only unfair methods of competition that injured competitors but also deceptive or unfair acts in which no competitors were harmed but the public was injured. S.5 of the Federal Trade Commission Act, as amended, provides, in part: "Unfair methods of competition in commerce, and unfair or deceptive acts or practices in commerce, are hereby declared illegal."

In 1952 the *McGuire Act* was passed to exempt from S.5 and allow enforcement of "nonsigners" clauses where the "fair trade" laws of a state permit such clauses in resale price agreements between parties of different states. A "nonsigners" clause requires all retailers in a state, even those who did not sign a contract, to follow the manufacturer's resale price maintenance program once one retailer signs the contract and the other retailers are served notice of this fact.

The Clayton Act

In contrast to the general prohibition against unfair methods of competition that was contained in the Federal Trade Commission Act, the Clayton Act, which was also enacted in 1914, outlawed four specific types of conduct: price discrimination, exclusive and tying contracts, intercorporate acquisitions and mergers, and interlocking directorates.

(i) S.2. Price Discrimination. S.2 of the Clayton Act prohibits sellers from discriminating in price among different purchasers, except where differences in the grade, quality, or quantity of the commodity exist and the resulting lower prices make only due allowance for differences in the cost of selling or transportation, and are offered in good faith to meet competition, where the effect may be to substantially lessen competition or tend to create a monopoly. The original section was designed primarily to prevent large manufacturers from eliminating smaller rivals by temporarily cutting prices in some markets while maintaining prices in other markets.

S.2 was amended in 1936 by the *Robinson-Patman Act*, which was passed in response to the demands of independent wholesalers for added restrictions on the freedom of suppliers to discriminate, and the complaint that chain stores were obtaining from their suppliers advantages in the form of lower prices, greater advertising allowances, and larger discounts than were warranted by lower costs associated with the large volume purchased by chain stores. S.2 of the Robinson-Patman Act provides, in part:

> It shall be unlawful for any person engaged in commerce, in the course of such commerce, either directly or indirectly, to discriminate in price between different purchasers of commodities of like grade and quality, where either or any of the purchasers involved in such discrimination are in commerce, where such commodities are sold for use, consumption, or resale within the United States . . . and where the effect of such discrimination may be substantially to lessen competition or tend to create a monopoly in any line of commerce, or to injure, destroy, or prevent competition with any person who either grants or knowingly receives the benefit of such discrimination, or with customers of either of them.

Like S.2 of the Clayton Act, S.2 of the Robinson-Patman Act allows price differentials that make only due allowance for differences in cost of manufacture, sale, or delivery, and also permits price discrimination if it is justified by the necessity of a seller to meet in good faith the equally low price of a competitor. Other parts of S.2 of the Robinson-Patman Act are directed against arrangements whereby buyers exact price discrimination disguised as brokerage commissions, against discrimination in promotional allowances and services made available to purchasers who buy for resale, and against buyers who use their buying power to extract more favorable treatment from their suppliers than is allowed under the terms of S.2.

(ii) S.3. Tying Arrangements and Exclusive Dealing. The Clayton Act prohibits tying sales where the purchase of one good is made conditional upon the purchase of other goods, exclusive dealing where the purchaser cannot handle competing lines, and requirements contracts that require the purchaser to obtain all or most of his needs from a single supplier, where the effect of such restraints may substantially lessen competition or tend to create a monopoly. S.3 provides, in part:

> It shall be unlawful for any person engaged in commerce, in the course of such commerce, to lease or make a sale or contract for sale of goods, wares, merchandise, machinery, supplies, or other commodities . . . on the condition, agreement, or understanding that the lessee or purchaser thereof shall not use

or deal in the goods, wares, merchandise, machinery, supplies, or other com-
modities of a competitor or competitors of the lessor or seller, where the
effect of such lease, sale, or contract for sale or such condition, agreement, or
understanding may be to substantially lessen competition or tend to create
a monopoly in any line of commerce.

(iii) S.7. Corporate Acquisitions and Mergers. S.7 of the Clayton Act
forbade any corporation to acquire the shares of competing corporations
where the effect may be to substantially lessen competition or tend to
create a monopoly. The effectiveness of S.7 was impaired by subsequent
decisions of the Supreme Court, which effectively barred S.7 from applying in the case of acquisitions of assets, rather than stocks, of a competing corporation. In 1950 the *Celler-Kefauver Act* amended S.7 of the
Clayton Act and broadened this section to cover mergers accomplished
through asset purchases as well as stock purchases. As amended by the
Celler-Kefauver Act, S.7 provides, in part:

No corporation engaged in commerce shall acquire, directly or indirectly,
the whole or any part of the stock or other share capital and no corporation
subject to the jurisdiction of the Federal Trade Commission shall acquire
the whole or any part of the assets of another corporation engaged also in
commerce, where in any line of commerce in any section of the country, the
effect of such acquisition may be substantially to lessen competition, or
tend to create a monopoly.

(iv) S.8. Interlocking Directorates. S.8 of the Clayton Act prohibited
interlocking directorates between corporations engaged in commerce
where one of them has a capital and surplus of more than $1 million and
where the elimination of competition between them would constitute
a violation of any of the provisions of the antitrust laws.

CHAPTER SEVEN

Alternative Concepts of Competition

7.1 IMPLICATIONS OF CONCEPTS OF COMPETITION FOR FIRMS' BEHAVIOR

The concept of competition, perceived as a beneficial invisible hand ensuring socially optimal market-pricing practices and resource allocation, dates back to Adam Smith and the beginning of modern economics. It is enshrined in the economist's model of "perfect competition," where individual firms without power to influence the market price of their inputs or outputs behave in a manner that guarantees socially optimal resource allocation, as evaluated by the members of society on the basis of the resulting income distribution. Preserving market competition in some sense is a basic goal of the antitrust laws and agencies in the United States, and introducing increased competition is a solution frequently advocated for improving a variety of market and nonmarket aspects of human behavior. This procompetition ethic is not without its detractors and opponents, especially among individuals and institutions that perceive themselves to be facing either "too much," "unfair," or "predatory" competition, or all three types.

It is necessary to be able to conceptually define desirable forms of competition, and to be able to recognize these forms of competition operationally, in order to determine and implement any kind of antitrust or other regulatory policies intended to achieve competition. Unfortunately, given the current state of knowledge, it is not easy to determine whether competition exists in practice in any particular industry, profession, or other aspect of human behavior (Preston and King, 1979). Much conceptual discussion of the issue of competition is clouded by a general failure to specify either exactly what is meant by the term "competition," or by the nature of the environment in which competition takes place.

This situation is unfortunate, because different models of competition yield different conclusions.

There is a close relationship between competition and regulation, since one may legitimately view competition as a type of constraint on individual decision makers who are subject to its influence. Moreover, since competition has implications for the behavior of decision makers, it is not surprising that there exists "competition over competition" when concepts of competition are adopted as targets of antitrust or other regulatory policies. Such disputes about which concept of competition is appropriate for public policy are analogous to the political competition between affected interest groups that takes place to influence any other type of regulatory constraint on human behavior. Different parties will try to gain acceptance of their formulation of the appropriate concept and model of competition and its results in order to secure acceptance of their particular conclusions regarding competition. As we emphasized in Chapter 2, Section 4 model building is one of the means by which individuals and interest groups attempt to attain their aims, rather than an antiseptic exercise in the search for truth. In this section we shall examine various concepts of competition and develop a general framework within which the factors that determine competition and its effects can be analyzed and understood.

Behavior versus Determinants of Behavior. At the outset it is necessary to distinguish clearly between the behavior of a firm or other decision maker that results from "competition" defined in some sense, and the forces that cause that behavior. In the economists' model of "perfect competition," for example, the result is equilibrium product prices that equal marginal costs of products; this pricing result has important implications for resource allocation in the economy as a whole. The fundamental cause of the price–marginal cost relationship is a horizontal demand curve facing each firm, reflecting the assumption that each firm's output level does not affect the product's market price. This horizontal demand curve can result from a variety of situations and, contrary to the impression given by many economics texts, has little or nothing to do with the number of rival firms producing the product. As Fama and Laffer (1972) have emphasized, the pricing behavior that is characteristic of the model of perfect competition will emerge irrespective of the number of rival firms if each firm expects its output changes to be matched by offsetting changes in its rivals' output. This kind of pricing behavior can also result under government price-support programs that guarantee sellers a fixed price for their products that is independent of the amount produced.

Behavior is determined by decision-maker goals and all the constraints perceived by the decision maker. Little purpose would be served by defining "competition" in terms of a particular form of behavior, since a specific behavior could result from an infinite number of combinations of objectives and constraints facing the decision maker. In most people's minds, competition has something to do with the existence and influence of rivals' behavior on individual decision makers' behavior. Competition is presumed to exist when, say, the buyers in a particular market are confronted by a number of sellers who act as rivals in attempting to sell their products to buyers. The phrase "acting as rivals" is crucially important, not the number of rivals. If sellers collude in setting the prices and other terms of their products, or divide the total market for their products and do not try to encroach on each other's submarkets, no rivalry or competition in the generally understood sense will occur.

Rivalry and competition between individual sellers will exist only if *individual* buyers are confronted by a range of choices among the products of different sellers. Individual sellers' behavior and the resulting range of choices that confront individual buyers can vary widely, however, even if competition in the sense of rivalry for the custom of individual buyers exists. In other words, the mere existence of competition in the sense of rivalry between sellers (or other types of decision maker) is compatible with innumerable patterns of behavior by the rivals. Some of these patterns may have desirable results for buyers and society as a whole; others may be harmful to buyers, sellers, and society. For example, "cutthroat" competition that periodically eliminates all suppliers from a particular market may be undesirable.

Number of Rivals and Anticipated Reactions of Rivals. By now it should be clear that "the number of rivals" and "the behavior of rivals" are very different concepts. There are general presumptions that increasing the number of rivals will change the behavior of individual rivals and that the resulting changes in behavior will be beneficial to buyers or other members of society. Neither of these suppositions is generally valid, as we shall demonstrate. To do so, we shall start by examining the determinants of the pricing behavior of firms, the traditional focus of competition theory. We shall then extend the analysis to take account of other dimensions of firms' behavior, such as advertising, quality, and other strategies. In the process, we will develop a general theory of the nature and determinants of competition and its implications for decision-maker behavior. This general framework and many of its major implications can be extended to other types of decision maker and other forms of competition.

It was pointed out long ago in the economics literature that the number of rival firms is itself largely *irrelevant* as a determinant of individual and group firm pricing behavior (Archibald, 1959). What matters is *each individual firm's expectations about the way in which its rivals will react to the firm's behavior.* This important message has gone largely unheeded, despite occasional reminders in the economics journals (Stigler,

1964; Needham, 1969, 1978a; Fama and Laffer, 1972). Although a firm's expectations regarding its rivals' behavior may depend on many factors, including the number of rivals, the problem of determining what these factors are in any particular situation remains largely unresolved.

The problem is compounded by the typical textbook treatment of pricing behavior, which deals with pricing behavior in a series of four tautological "market structure" situations — perfect competition, monopoly, and monopolistic competition, and oligopoly, with strong suggestions that the number of firms in each market situation is responsible for producing the different kinds of pricing behavior that are characteristic of each situation.

This is misleading. As has been demonstrated in more detail elsewhere (Needham, 1978a Chap. 4), and as the reader will readily understand from the following discussion, the pricing behavior that results under any of the traditional market structure categories is quite compatible with any number of firms! One can have "monopoly pricing" with one or with many firms; "perfectly competitive" pricing or "monopolistically competitive pricing" can occur with only two firms as well as with "many" firms. Also, the intuitive notion that an increase in the number of rival firms in any industry will cause the price of the industry's product to fall need not be correct. If the demand for each firm's product becomes less price elastic, for reasons that will be explained, then the profit-maximizing price of the industry's products will increase (Satterthwaite, 1979; Rosenthal, 1980).

As we shall explain shortly, the traditional price theory literature has misspecified the theoretical limits of pricing behavior in "oligopolies," situations in which rivals explicitly take into account their rivals' reactions. It is generally assumed that oligopolists will set product prices anywhere between the monopoly and perfectly competitive price levels and that the "worst" one can expect from oligopoly is monopoly pricing. We shall shortly demonstrate that oligopolists may quite rationally charge higher prices than monopolists. The explanation for all these conclusions lies with the nature of the individual firm's expectations regarding its rivals' reactions.

General Model of Determinants of Pricing Behavior. A general model of the determinants of a firm's pricing behavior, which is also operational in the sense that it may be used as a basis for real-world pricing decisions, can be developed quite simply from the familiar marginal revenue-equals-marginal cost conditions of traditional price theory. It is easy to show that the change in total revenue from a change in the price of a firm's product is related to the product price and price elasticity of demand for the firm's product in the manner $MR = P(1 - 1/E_d)$ where E_d, the price elasticity of demand, is defined as the percentage change in the quantity of the firm's product demanded, divided by the percentage change in the price of the product. Equating the marginal revenue from a price change with the marginal cost of producing the product, as is required for profit maximization, yields $P(1 - 1/E_d) = \text{MC}$, which can also be expressed as $P - \text{MC}/P = 1/E_d$.

This last expression indicates that the profit-maximizing relationship between the price and marginal cost of a firm's product will depend on the price elasticity of demand for the firm's product, E_d. Next, it can be shown that E_d depends on three factors that are related to the response of the buyers of the firm's product and to rival suppliers of the product. The formal relationship between the elasticity of demand for the firm's product and these three factors is as follows:[1]

$$E_d = \frac{E_m}{S_f} + \frac{E_r S_r}{S_f}$$

where E_m is the price elasticity of total market demand for the product, S_f is the firm's share of total market output, S_r is the share of total market output produced by the firm's rivals, and E_r is the percentage change in rivals' output expected by the firm in response to a change in the price of the firm's product. Since $S_r = (1 - S_f)$, there are only three factors underlying E_d, not four. By substituting the preceding expression for E_d into the firm's profit-maximizing pricing condition, the relationship between the profit-maximizing price and marginal cost of the firm's product and its determinants is as follows:

$$\frac{P - \text{MC}}{P} = \frac{S_f}{E_m + E_r(1 - S_f)} \qquad (1)$$

Relationship (1) indicates that the level of a profit-maximizing firm's product price will be higher, the larger its market share, the smaller the price elasticity of total market demand, and the smaller the magnitude of E_r. The reader is referred to Needham (1978a) for a diagrammatic illustration of these propositions using the firm's demand and cost curve.

In the present context, it is E_r that is of prime interest to our discussion of competition. Under monopoly a firm has no established rivals, and $E_r = 0$ *provided that the firm has no potential rivals* who might react to its policies by entering the market and producing the product in response to the monopolist's pricing policies. This emphasizes a fundamental element of any theory of competition: the need to include the behavior of *potential* rivals as well as *existing* rivals as a possible influence on decision-maker behavior. Second, it should be clear that even if a firm has existing or potential rivals, E_r may still equal zero if the firm does not expect them to react to changes in its behavior. Whether or

1 See Needham (1978) for detailed proof of these propositions.

not they react will depend on whether they are aware of the firm's actions, and this depends on the ease or difficulty of detecting changes in the firm's policies.

Whether a firm's rivals are one or many, the magnitude of E_r and the firm's resulting pricing behavior will depend on how the firm expects its rivals to react to changes in its product price. It is the *collective* response of rivals that matters; however, one could divide E_r into a series of responses for each of the rivals considered by the firm, and the response of different rivals may be expected to vary. In an article analyzing behavior in the domestic United States coffee-roasting industry, Gollop and Roberts (1979) found evidence suggesting that a firm's conjectures regarding rivals' response to its actions will vary with the rivals' size. Despite this, it is the *collective* response of rivals that matters in determining the magnitude of E_r and the firm's pricing behavior. Separate responses become relevant only if the market for the firm's product is divided into segments or groups of buyers, in which situation product prices in each segment can vary because of barriers to buyer mobility among submarkets. Even here, the analysis applies; the only modification required is that a separate pricing condition would apply to each submarket for the firm's product.

Aggressive Reactions by Rivals. E_r will be negative if rivals respond to a reduction in the price of the firm's product by increasing their output. This response will make the elasticity of demand for the firm's product lower and tend to raise the profit-maximizing price of the firm's product. The more aggressive the expected response of rivals, in terms of the magnitude of their output increases, the higher the price that will be set by the firm. This principle generalizes to other dimensions of a firm's behavior. The more aggressive the competition individual decision makers expect to occur in response to their actions, the less likely it is that such actions will be taken.

When rivals exist, the maximum possible price of the product that may be set by individual firms acting independently is *not* the monopoly level. When there is one firm with no actual or potential rivals, the profit-maximizing price of the product will be given by the expression $(P - MC)/P = 1/E_m$. When rivals exist, the numerator of the optimal pricing condition (1), S_f, is smaller than under monopoly. If rivals are expected to respond to price reductions by increasing their output levels, so that E_r is negative, the expression $E_m + E_r(1 - S_f)$ in the denominator of equation (1) will also be smaller than under monopoly. It is possible for the ratio between S_f and $E_m + E_r(1 - S_f)$ to be higher under "oligopoly," a situation with more than one firm, than under monopoly! It is in fact not difficult to identify the situation, in intuitively understandable terms, where the magnitude of E_r leads to monopoly behavior by a group of rivals in the absence of any collusion among the firms. It will be where the magnitude of E_d facing each firm in the group equals E_m.

It is easy to show (Needham, 1978) that E_d facing each firm in a group of firms will equal E_m whenever firms expect their rivals to exactly imitate their price and output policies. In such a situation, each firm will expect to face a so-called share-of-the market demand curve. If, instead, a firm expects its rivals to react by increasing their output sufficiently to reduce the firm's share of total market output at any given price of the product, the firm's E_d will be less than the market E_m, and the firm will set the price higher than the price a monopolist controlling the whole industry would charge.

Although the total industry profit resulting from a monopoly price is higher than that resulting from either a lower or a higher price, individual firms may not recognize, or be able to agree on, a collective policy of reducing their prices to the monopoly level. Such an occurrence would require each firm to *change* its expectations about rivals' response to its price reduction and to expect a *smaller* output increase by its rivals than before.

It is often pointed out in the literature that mere recognition by a group of firms that they are not collectively maximizing profits is not sufficient to enable them to act collectively in a monopolistic manner. The argument is usually applied to situations where price increases would raise group profits, however, and it has not been adequately recognized that the same logic applies to situations in which prices set by individual decision makers are above rather than below the group-profit-maximizing level. The public policy implications of the possibility that monopoly behavior is not a limiting case of group behavior, and that the welfare losses associated with monopoly behavior no longer set an upper limit on the welfare losses to society resulting from oligopolistic group behavior, are important and wide ranging.

Accommodating Reactions by Rivals. The expected output reactions of rivals, E_r, will be positive, and a firm will set lower prices, if rivals are expected to reduce their output in response to a product-price reduction by the firm. We are not here concerned with the reasons *why* other firms might be expected to reduce their output in response to an increase in output by one member of the group. Our main purpose is to illustrate the counterintuitive implications of expectations of this kind of "accommodating" behavior on the part of a firm's rivals.

The major implication is that expectations of "accommodating" responses by a firm's rivals — in the sense of changes in the levels of their output that are opposite to those of the firm initiating the change — result in lower prices and higher output levels by individual firms and the group. Most people would probably intuitively regard such accommodating responses as "cooperative" rather than competitive; yet the result is lower prices and higher output, the kind of behavior that is generally associated with competition. The accommodating responses of rivals that are expected to *exactly offset* a firm's output increases results in pricing at marginal cost, the pricing behavior of the "perfectly competitive" model, as Fama and Laffer (1972) have demonstrated.

Although most people would probably regard "aggressive" responses by a firm's rivals as competitive, expectations of such behavior from rivals results in higher prices and lower output, a situation that is generally described as less competitive, as we have explained. The situation where firms expect rivals to imitate their actions, which produces a monopoly group solution, would generally be regarded as a competitive situation by most people. The basic cause of mistaken thinking about these issues of competition is a failure to distinguish between the forces that underlie observed behavior and the observed behavior itself. Paradoxically, more competitive pricing and output behavior will be observed when individual decision makers do not expect aggressive competitive reactions from rivals, and less competitive pricing and output behavior will be observed when individual decision makers do expect aggressive reactions from their rivals. These propositions extend to other aspects of a firm's behavior and to other types of decision maker, and understanding them is the key to understanding competition.

Rivals' Anticipated Reactions May Have Multiple Dimensions. Now that we have firmly established that it is *a decision maker's expectations about the reactions of established or potential rivals* that is the key element in determining the influence of "competition from rivals" on that decision maker's behavior, it is important to recognize that there may be more than one dimension of rivals' reactions. In addition to the distinction between established and potential rivals, and the fact that different rivals may be expected to react differently, each rival may be expected to react by changing more than one decision variable. Moreover, these rivals need not necessarily be expected to respond by changing the same decision variable. For example, rivals may be expected to respond to a reduction in the product price of one firm by changing their advertising or some other dimension of their behavior.

Table 7.1 illustrates the various types of rivals' responses that are possible. The columns refer to different dimensions of the expected response of a firm's rivals (price changes, quantity changes, advertising changes, quality changes). Each row of the table refers to the expected response of rivals to a change in the dimension of a firm's behavior shown at the extreme left-hand side of the table.

If the change in the firm's behavior and the rivals' response are expressed in percentage terms, it is easy to relate Table 7.1 to the firm's profit-maximizing pricing condition outlined earlier. If the firm expects its rivals to respond to a change in the price of its product only by changing the level of their output, all the elements in the first row of the table except the second element, E_{12}, are zero, and E_{12} corresponds to the term E_r in the firm's profit-maximizing pricing condition.

Table 7.1. Rivals' Response (expressed in percentages)

Dimension of firm's behavior changed	Price change	Quantity change	Advertising change	Quality change
1% price change	E_{11}	E_{12}	E_{13}	E_{14}
1% quantity change	E_{21}	E_{22}	E_{23}	E_{24}
1% advertising change	E_{31}	E_{32}	E_{33}	E_{34}
1% quality change	E_{41}	E_{42}	E_{43}	E_{44}

If the firm expects its rivals to change any other dimension of their behavior in response to the change in the price of its product, some of the other elements in the first row of the table will also be nonzero. These other nonzero elements indicate the nature and magnitude of rivals' responses. The effect of these responses on the demand for the first firm's product and on the additional total revenue that results from the price change initiated by the first firm must also be taken into account.

The E terms, which are "response elasticities," must be multiplied by the effect of a change in each dimension of rivals' behavior on the demand for the first firm's product. Let R_p, R_Q, R_a, and R_q represent, respectively, the effect of a 1 percent change in rivals' prices, output levels, advertising levels, and quality expenditures on the quantity of the first firm's product demanded at any given price. The combined effect of rivals' response on the demand for the first firm's product, and hence the impact on the firm's marginal revenue from a price reduction, is represented as

$$E_{11} \cdot R_p + E_{12} \cdot R_Q + E_{13} \cdot R_a + E_{14} \cdot R_q \cdots$$

and the first firm's profit-maximizing pricing condition would be changed from

$$\frac{P - MC}{P} = 1/E_d = \frac{S_f}{E_m + E_{12}(1 - S_f)} \quad \text{to} \quad \frac{P - MC}{P} =$$

$$\frac{S_f}{E_m + (1 - S_f) E_{11} \cdot R_p + E_{12} \cdot R_Q + E_{13} \cdot R_a} + \cdots$$

The net effect of taking into account all possible dimensions of rivals' response to one firm's price reduction on that firm's profit-maximizing pricing behavior will depend on the signs and magnitudes of all the response coefficients. If rivals increase their advertising when the firm reduces its product price, this response will tend to reduce the demand for the firm's product at lower prices and will therefore reduce the marginal revenue from a price reduction. This implies that the profit-maximizing price of the firm's product will be higher than if rivals did not change their advertising. This is only one possibility, however; if rivals reduce their advertising in response to a price cut by the firm, the opposite of the previous line of reasoning will apply — the marginal revenue from a price cut will be higher, and the profit-maximizing price of the firm's product will be lower, all other things remaining the same.

Rivals' Anticipated Reactions and Nonprice Dimensions of Behavior. To this point we have dealt with the influence of rivals' reactions on a firm's profit-maximizing pricing behavior; this influence is depicted by only the first row of Table 7.1. A theory of the factors that determine a firm's profit-maximizing pricing behavior *is not an adequate theory of the factors that determine the firm's profits* and provides an incomplete view of the influence of competition from rivals on the firm's behavior and profits. The difference between the price and production cost per unit of the firm's product at a profit-maximizing price level consists of profit *plus* expenditures by the firm on advertising, research and development, or any other nonproduction expenditures, expressed as an amount per unit of output sold at the profit-maximizing product price. Indeed, if these expenditures are large enough, the "profit-maximizing" level of product price may yield zero profits or losses!

A theory of the factors that determine a firm's profits must therefore include the factors that determine the firm's advertising and similar nonproduction expenditures. Including such factors is not difficult to accomplish, and next we shall briefly outline the major elements of a theory of the determinants of a firm's profits. The reader may consult Needham (1978a) for more detailed proof of the resulting propositions. We shall first examine the factors that determine the profit-maximizing level of a firm's advertising, and then show the implications of combining these factors with the firm's pricing behavior for the firm's profits. The conclusions generalize to other types of nonproduction expenditure.

To maximize profits, a firm must select a level of advertising expenditures where the effect of a change in advertising outlays on the firm's total sales revenue just equals the effect on the firm's total costs. If this condition were not satisfied, a change in the level of the firm's advertising would increase the firm's profits. A change in the level of advertising outlays will change the firm's total revenues by an amount equal to the resulting change in the quantity of the firm's product demanded, multiplied by the price of the product. The change in the firm's total costs will equal the sum of the advertising expenditure change itself, plus the increased total cost of producing the additional output demanded. Symbolically, profit maximization requires that $\Delta Q \cdot P = \Delta A + \Delta Q \cdot MC$ and one can easily reformulate this expression

---

[2] See Needham (1978a) for more detailed proof of these propositions.

into the profit-maximizing condition for advertising[2] $A/S = (P - MC/P)\,E_a$ where A/S is the firm's profit-maximizing ratio of advertising expenditure to sales, P is the price of the firm's product, and MC is the marginal production cost of the firm's product. The advertising elasticity of demand for the firm's product, E_a, is defined as the percentage change in the quantity of the firm's product demanded in response to a 1 percent change in its advertising expenditure. It can be demonstrated that E_a depends on the response of buyers and rival sellers to the firm's advertising expenditure change in the manner

$$E_a = E_B + \Sigma(E_{31} \cdot R_p + E_{32} \cdot R_Q + E_{33} \cdot R_a + E_{34} \cdot R_q \cdots)$$

where E_B is the elasticity of buyer response to the firm's advertising, defined as the percentage change in total market demand for the product in response to a 1 percent change in the first firm's advertising expenditures. If rivals do not react by changing the level of their decision variables, the first firm will experience only the first term in the preceding expression, representing the buyer response to its advertising. If rivals respond to the firm's advertising, these responses will also have an impact on the firm in addition to the buyer response. The E terms represent the percentage response of various dimensions of rivals' behavior in the third row of Table 7.1, and the R terms are the same effects of changes in dimensions of rivals' behavior on the quantity of the first firm's product demanded (previously discussed in connection with rivals' response to the firm's pricing behavior).

There is one important difference between rivals' reactions that are relevant to a firm's pricing behavior, and rivals' reactions that are relevant to a firm's advertising behavior, or any other dimension of nonproduction expenditures. With pricing behavior, only rivals' reactions represented by the first row of Table 7.1 are relevant. In contrast, in the case of advertising behavior, in addition to rivals' reactions depicted by the third row of the table, *the rivals' reactions in the first row are also relevant.* In other words, the same rivals' reactions that are relevant in determining the firm's profit-maximizing pricing behavior are also relevant in connection with the firm's advertising behavior. This can be understood by reference to the fact that the term $(P - MC)/P$ in the profit-maximizing advertising condition will be equal to $1/E_d$ if the firm is charging a profit-maximizing price. To select a profit-maximizing level of advertising, a firm must take into account the rivals' reactions that underlie E_a, the firm's advertising elasticity of demand, and *also* the reactions that underlie E_d and, therefore, the profit-maximizing level of the firm's $(P - MC)/P$.

The implications of profit-maximizing pricing and advertising policies for a firm's profits, and the relationship between these profits and rivals' reactions, can be illuminated as follows. Assume that marginal and average cost of producing a firm's product are equal, so that $(P - MC) =$

$(P - AC_Q)$. We have noted that the margin between price and production cost per unit of output includes expenditures on activities other than production, such as advertising, in addition to any profit. Therefore

$$\frac{(P - AC_Q)}{P} = \left(\frac{n}{P} + \frac{a}{P}\right)$$

where n and a are, respectively, profit and advertising cost per unit of output. Multiplying the numerator and denominator of this expression by the profit-maximizing level of the firm's output, Q^*, yields

$$\frac{(P - AC)}{P} = \frac{(n + a)Q^*}{PQ^*} = \frac{\Pi}{S} + \frac{A}{S}$$

where Π/S is the ratio of the firm's total profit to total sales revenue, and A/S is the ratio of the firm's total advertising expenditure to sales. It is clear from this expression that when the profit-maximizing level of A/S equals or exceeds $(P - AC_Q)/P$, the firm's profits are zero or negative, respectively. Given the price elasticity of demand for the firm's product and therefore the profit-maximizing level of $(P - MC)/P$, whether the firm's profits are positive or not depends on the optimal level of the firm's advertising/sales ratio (A/S), which is determined by E_a. Rivals' reactions affect E_a, and the optimal level of the firm's A/S and profits, given $(P - MC)/P$. Similarly, rivals' reactions influence E_d and $(P - MC)/P$, given E_a.

A couple of examples will serve to illustrate the way in which rivals' reactions may affect the firm's profits. If the firm expects rivals to react aggressively to an increase in its advertising, E_a will be smaller than otherwise at any level of advertising by the firm. Since sales of the firm are less responsive to changes in the firm's advertising, the level of A/S will tend to be large at any given level of advertising. At a profit-maximizing level of the firm's advertising, A/S may be so large that $(P - AC_Q)/P = A/S$, and no profits are earned. Note that this is possible irrespective of the level of $(P - MC)/P$ itself; this means that expectations of sufficiently aggressive rivals' reactions to a firm's advertising can result in zero expected profits for a firm, even if $(P - MC)/P$ is positive and large. This emphasizes that firm profits and the level of $(P - MC)$ or $(P - AC_Q)$ are not the same.

Determinants of Rivals' Anticipated Reactions. It should by now be clear that no generalizations are possible regarding the effect of rivals' anticipated reactions on a firm's pricing behavior, on any other dimension of the firm's behavior, or on its profits. The effect of rivals' anticipated reactions on a particular firm's behavior and profits depends on the nature and magnitude of those reactions, which are multidimensional in character. We *can* set out the nature of the reactions that are relevant in determining an individual firm's behavior, which we have done in Table 7.1. We cannot say, however, what *determines* these expectations with any precision, for any particular decision maker.

The literature contains a few exceedingly naive hypotheses regarding the factors that influence these expectations, the most prominent of which is the "seller concentration hypothesis." This hypothesis is that the number and/or some aspect of the size distribution of existing rivals will affect their expectations and will be examined in some detail in Chapter 15.

The seller concentration hypothesis excludes potential rivals' reactions from consideration. Even if there is a systematic link between the number and size distribution of established rivals and their expected reactions, individual decision makers' behavior also depends on their expectations regarding potential rivals' reactions. This implies that the influence of "expected competition from rivals" on behavior can be determined only within a theoretical and empirical framework encompassing potential rivals' behavior as well as established rivals' behavior. The body of economic theory concerned with entry barriers and their effect on potential rival and established rivals' behavior provides such a framework.

Unfortunately, modern entry-barrier theory has not provided more than a modicum of insight into the factors that actually determine a firm's expectations regarding its rivals' reactions. Instead, much time and effort have been expended merely on examining the consequences of alternative types of expectation for established and potential rivals' behavior. The principles involved in entry-barrier theory, and the conclusions, are identical to those explained in this section; entry-barrier analysis merely extends the number of rivals whose behavior is being analyzed to include potential as well as established rivals.

One aspect of rivals' reactions as a factor influencing decision-maker behavior requires special emphasis. It is logical for individual firms to attempt to influence their rivals' expectations regarding their *own* reactions. Obviously, if a firm can change its rivals' expectations about its own reactions to rivals' policies, the firm can influence its rivals' behavior and perhaps achieve a higher level of its own objectives. To change its rivals' expectations about its own reactions, a firm must be able to change the factors that *determine* its rivals' expectations. As we have indicated, researchers do not know very much about how decision makers form their expectations regarding rivals' reactions. We can, however, list the kind of factors that may plausibly underlie decision makers' expectations regarding rivals' reactions. These expectations may be based on a number of possible factors described by the following general relationship:

$$E_{ii} = f [\text{Rivals' Past, Present, or expected Future } market \text{ behavior;}$$
Rivals' Past, Present, or expected Future *nonmarket* behavior; Factors unrelated to rivals' market or nonmarket behavior, including

(a) factors related to the behavior of other reference groups (consumers, regulators, legislators)
(b) factors related to the environment within which decision makers operate.]

This group of factors is by no means exhaustive. Several comments are appropriate regarding the factors that may affect a decision maker's expectations regarding his or her rivals' reactions. First, there is a natural tendency in economics to overlook nonmarket methods by which a decision maker might influence rivals' expectations regarding his or her own reactions. Second, there is a tendency to overemphasize the influence of a decision maker's current or past behavior as a determinant of rivals' expectations about the decision maker's future reactions. The Sylos model of entry-barrier theory that underlies most traditional analyses of effects of entry barriers on firms' pricing behavior epitomizes this tendency. In that model, the current behavior of established firms determines entrants' expectations regarding established firms' future conduct.

Third, there is often a failure to distinguish between a decision maker's *efforts* to influence rivals' expectations and the effects of these efforts on rivals' expectations and behavior. As a result, it is too often automatically assumed that such efforts are successful. Finally, there is insufficient recognition of the two-way nature of efforts to influence rivals' expectations. This is especially true in situations analyzing an entrant's and established firms' behavior, where analysts focus on efforts by established firms to influence an entrant's expectations regarding established firms' reactions to entry. Generally omitted is the fact that an entrant, which may be a large firm well established in other markets, may be engaging in the same process of trying to influence established firms' expectations regarding the entrant's behavior.

The concepts of competition described in this section so far are related to characteristics of "optimal" or "equilibrium" behavior of decision makers, defined as behavior that maximizes the decision maker's objectives in any given situation. We have emphasized the importance of a decision maker's expectations regarding rivals' reactions as a determinant of the decision maker's behavior. A particular pattern of anticipated rivals' responses is analytically equivalent to adding a constraint confronting a decision maker, and the nature of this constraint will therefore influence the optimal levels of the decision maker's behavior dimensions.

In addition to the equilibrium aspects of decision-maker behavior and competition, there are also disequilibrium aspects that describe how decision makers react to situations in which their behavior does not exhibit "optimal" characteristics. The disequilibrium decision rules employed by decision makers in attempting to reach optimal levels of their decision variables have profound implications for the resulting time path of individual and group decision making through time. Among other things, these disequilibrium adjustment rules determine whether or not equilibrium behavior will ever be attained, and the characteristics of disequilibrium and equilibrium behavior.

7.2 IDEAL, EXCESSIVE, PREDATORY, AND UNFAIR COMPETITION

Objectives, Constraints, and Normative Concepts of Competition. The preceding discussion of the meaning of competition and its implications for decision-maker behavior provides a basis for examining a number of normative aspects of competition. "Desirable" competition is the kind of competition that results in decision-maker behavior that exhibits "desirable" characteristics. It is not possible to define desirable forms of competition without some implicit or explicit evaluation of the kinds of decision-maker behavior that are preferred to other kinds of behavior, and this in turn implies the use of some objective to evaluate decision-maker behavior. Behavior that "maximizes society's satisfaction" is one such objective; this objective can be interpreted in many ways, depending on whose preferences are used to represent society's evaluations, which distribution of income or wealth is used as a basis for people's evaluations, and a host of other factors. *The kinds of competition that are desirable because they result in certain kinds of behavior will vary with the objective that is used to evaluate behavior.*

Even when the objective used to evaluate decision-maker behavior is unchanged, the kinds of decision-maker behavior that maximize that objective and the kinds of competition that result in the desired behavior will vary with the nature of other constraints facing society. For example, pricing at marginal cost is not desirable unless all firms in society simultaneously set product prices equal to marginal cost. The Theory of Second Best, which deals with situations in which pricing at marginal cost everywhere in the economy is not possible, indicates that price–marginal cost differences should be related to price elasticities and cross-elasticities of demand for the products of different industries (Baumol and Bradford, 1970). The kind of pricing behavior that would result in the textbook model of "perfect competition" is no longer desirable, and any forms of competition that result in pricing at marginal cost will be undesirable wherever the Theory of Second Best applies — meaning in the real world, since a variety of economic and institutional factors make it impossible in practice for the price-equals-marginal-cost rule to be implemented everywhere in the economy.

Although economists have traditionally focused mainly on firms' pricing behavior, other dimensions of firms' behavior may be equally or even more important in influencing society's welfare. The characteristics of products produced by firms are as important as the prices that firms charge for those products. Unfortunately, existing normative concepts of "desirable" advertising, quality, or other dimensions of firms' behavior in economics and related disciplines are rather unsatisfactory. Such concepts are, again, necessarily based on implicit or explicit assumptions about whose evaluations are to be used in judging these dimensions of firms' behavior, and on models of the behavior of firms and other decision makers that contain assumptions about the objectives and constraints that confront those decision makers.

Some of the implicit valuations and explicit assumptions in these models are highly questionable. A prime example is the assumption that consumer evaluations of firms' behavior constitute the only valid evaluations of the consumers' or society's interests, or that firms' pricing behavior is the most important aspect of firms' behavior from the point of view of consumers. Primeaux (1979) and other writers have emphasized that consumers do not in practice switch from high- to low-price products even when the product is similar and known price differences are wide.

Normative concepts of competition must take into account other dimensions of firms' behavior in addition to pricing behavior. It was demonstrated in Section 7.1 that pricing and production behavior alone do not determine a firm's profits and that price and nonprice dimensions of a firm's behavior are affected by the firm's expectations regarding rivals' reactions. Given any particular normative index of "desirable" dimensions of firms' behavior that includes pricing and other dimensions of firms' behavior, the implications of a firm's expectations regarding *all* dimensions of its rivals' reactions are relevant in determining whether the firm's behavior will correspond to that which is desired.

Concepts of Excessive Competition. The conclusion that there can be "too much" competition follows logically from a recognition that differences in a firm's expectations regarding its rivals' reactions will result in differences in the firm's optimal course of action in any given set of circumstances. If a particular type of behavior is regarded as "desirable" from the point of view of some objective, it follows that only those types of expected reactions of the decision maker's rivals that result in the desired form of behavior are the "desirable" kinds of competition.

It should be emphasized that what is "too much" or "too little" competition cannot be defined without reference to (1) the objective used to evaluate and define "desired" standards of decision-maker behavior and (2) all other factors that influence the decision maker's behavior, such as the decision maker's goals and other constraints. As an example of (1), rivals' reactions that result in firms setting $P = MC$ will constitute "too much" competition if the desired pricing behavior involves setting P above MC, as appropriate in most situations in which the Theory of Second Best is applicable. As an example of (2), given a particular level of $(P - MC)/P$ that is desirable on the ground of securing optimal resource allocation in the economy as a whole, the kind of rivals' expected reactions that will result in such pricing behavior on the part of a firm will depend on the firm's market share (S_f) and the price elasticity of total market demand for the firm's product (E_m). Given E_m, the larger the firm's market share, S_f, the smaller will be the expected increase in rivals' output (E_r) that is required to result in a particular desired profit-maximizing level of the firm's $(P - MC)/P$. The reader may verify this conclusion by referring to profit-maximizing pricing condition (1) in Section 7.1.

Panzar and Willig (1977) have emphasized that there can be too much competition even in the case of monopoly if the market is only large enough to permit one firm to produce and cover minimum costs of production. A policy of *reducing* competition from potential entrants might in these circumstances result in industry output and pricing policies that result in a higher level of satisfaction for members of society.

Concepts of "Unfair" and "Predatory" Competition. The preceding discussion of "excessive" competition may be linked with the vexed issue of what constitutes "unfair" or "predatory" competition. This issue is not limited to monopoly situations, but the principles involved may conveniently be examined in the context of a monopolist's response to the threat of potential entry. Moreover, "potential entry" into an industry is identical analytically to a situation in which one of a number of established firms tries to increase its output level; therefore, the conclusions of an analysis of predatory competition in the case of potential entry can be applied also to predatory competition among established rivals.

The demand curve for an entrant's product depends on the output level the entrant expects the established firm to produce after entry occurs. The entrant's demand curve may therefore be viewed as that portion of the market demand curve in Figure 7.1 that lies to the right of the *post-entry* output level the entrant expects the established firm to produce. The italicized phrase is to emphasize that the current, or preentry, output level of the established firm is in general irrelevant to the entrant and becomes relevant only in the special case in which entrants expect the established firms to try to maintain their output in the face of entry. This last situation has been extensively analyzed in the literature under the heading of the "Sylos Postulate" (we shall examine this model again in Chapter 14). For the present, it is sufficient to point out that in general it is the post-entry price and output level of established firms that determines the position of the entrant's demand curve.

In any model of potential entrant's behavior, there is always a post-entry output level produced by established firms that would result in zero expected profits for the entrant. This "entry-deterring" output level is Q_{ed} in Figure 7.1; it is found by locating the point on the total market demand curve where the resulting entrant's demand curve lies just below the entrant's unit cost curve ($AC_{entrant}$) as shown by $D_{entrant}$. If the entrant expects established firms to produce post-entry output levels below Q_{ed},

Figure 7.1

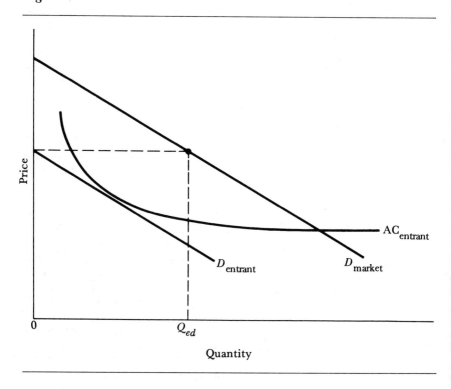

the anticipated demand curve for the entrant's product will lie above the entrant's unit cost curve over some range of output, and the entrant will enter, since profits are expected to be positive. The lower the post-entry output below Q_{ed} the entrant expects established firms to produce, the higher will be the entrant's demand curve, and the entrant's anticipated profits and profit-maximizing output level will be larger also.

If established firms can influence an entrant's expectations about the established firm's post-entry behavior, it is possible for them to deter entry. Even if it is possible to deter entry, however, this will not necessarily be the profit-maximizing strategy for established firms. The profit-maximizing strategy for established firms is determined by choosing the policy that maximizes the established firm's profits or other goals *taking into account potential entrant reactions to the established firm's behavior.* Only in rare cases will this result in complete entry deterrence; a more likely situation is that some entry will be permitted, but the entrant's profits will be lower than if established firms had not taken the entrant's reactions to their behavior into account (Needham, 1978a, Chap. 7).

Given these conclusions, how can "predatory" behavior by established firms be defined? It is clear that the larger the post-entry output produced by established firms, the lower will be the market price of the product and the level of an entrant's profits at any level of the entrant's output. Established firms can always reduce the profits anticipated by an entrant if they can convince the entrant that they will increase their output levels in response to entry. Any actual increase in output by established firms in response to entry will imply lower profits for an entrant at any particular level of the entrant's output. Some economists have suggested, therefore, that actual or threatened increases in output by established firms should be regarded as "predatory behavior." If one shifts one's perspective slightly, however, and applies the same logic to derive the demand for established firms' products, it is clear that the larger the output produced by an entrant, given market demand, the lower will be the demand for established firms' products, and the lower will be the profits associated with any particular level of their output. Who, in other words, should be regarded as engaging in "predatory competition" if the output increase of either party has the same effect on the other firm's profits?

The tendency to view established firms' output increases as predatory and entrants' output increases as "beneficial" is an implicit assumption that entrants should be protected against established firms and that entrants' output is somehow more socially desirable than that of established firms. This is not true; what matters as far as the level of industry price is concerned is the total level of output. Whether a given total output level is produced by established firms or entrants is immaterial as far as its impact on market price is concerned.

The tendency to favor entrants' over established firms' output is often based on an implicit assumption that entrants are small weak firms. This is an invalid perception, since entrants may already be operating in other markets on a larger scale than the firms in the markets entered. If an "output increase" by an already established firm were being analyzed, few economists would suggest that the reactions of other established firms to this output increase should be regarded as "predatory" if they involved increases in output by the other established firms. To do so would be to regard *any* reactions of the type we referred to earlier in Section 7.1 as "aggressive" as "predatory," no matter which firms responded in this way to their rivals' actions.

Yet, this is *exactly* what is being suggested by those who would label established firms' output increases in response to entry as "predatory" behavior. As we have emphasized, there is no analytical difference between "new entry" and an increase in output by one member of a group of established rivals as far as the resulting impact on market price of a product is concerned! Taken to its logical conclusion, the requirement that established firms not be permitted to increase their output in response to entry, thereby raising entrants' profits, can be extended to requiring that established firms reduce their output, thereby permitting entrants to enjoy an even larger share of industry output and profits.

A rule against output increases by established firms, whether in response to new entry or output increases by other established firms, would generally have the effect of changing each individual firm's expectations regarding rivals' output reactions, since it would eliminate the chance of any "aggressive" rivals' output reactions. If attention is confined to price and output policies, the result would be to increase price elasticities of demand and lower price–production cost margins for individual firm's products. In industries in which price-cost margins were previously "too high" for optimal resource allocation among markets, this would be beneficial. In markets where price-cost margins were previously "too low," it would worsen resource allocation, however. The appropriate prescription in the latter type of market would be to *encourage* rather than discourage expectations of "aggressive" reactions from rivals on the part of individual firms. This would reduce price elasticities of demand and raise price-cost margin in those industries. Again, this illustrates that desirable forms of competition cannot be defined without reference to the objectives being sought. Expectations of aggressive rivals' reactions may improve decision-maker behavior in one set of circumstances and worsen it in another.

Multidimensional Aspects of "Predatory" Behavior. Any effective rule against "predatory" decision-maker behavior would have to be multidimensional in character. If output increases by established firms in response to entry were labeled "predatory," established firms could achieve the same effect on an entrant firm's actual or expected profits by engaging in "aggressive" reactions in other types of behavior. For example, if established firms were to increase their advertising in response to entry, this would reduce the effectiveness of any particular level of the entrant's advertising and hence reduce the entrant's profits. It can be demonstrated that there is a level of advertising by established firms that will result in zero profits for an entrant, even if the level of established firms' output does not change in response to entry (Needham, 1978b).

Similar reasoning applies to any other dimension of established firms' behavior that affects the demand for an entrant's product. This implies that rivals' reactions in *all* dimensions of behavior would have to be taken into account in defining "predatory" behavior. In terms of Table 7.1, a rule against "predatory" output increases by a firm's rivals in response to "entry" by the firm would make E_{22} zero. Similarly, a rule against "predatory" increases in advertising by a firm's rivals in response to "entry" would make both E_{33}, the established firm's advertising response to the entrant's advertising, *and* E_{23}, the established firm's advertising response to increases in the entrant's output, zero. The established firms could still make the prospect of entry unprofitable for the entrant by influencing any one or more of the remaining E_s in Table 7.1, however. Thus, any rule designed to prevent established firms from lowering the expected profits of a potential entrant would have to make every E_s in Table 7.1 zero.

But why stop there? By reversing the signs of the E_s and turning expectations of "aggressive" reactions into "accommodating" reactions, the expected profits of an entrant could be raised further. Established firms would be cutting back their output, advertising, and other decision variables, raising the expected demand for the entrant's product at any given level of the entrant's price, advertising, and other decision variables. The obvious result of favoring the entrant over established rivals has already been noted. When "entrant" is replaced by an established rival who increases output, such "predatory" rules have the effect of favoring those established firms which act first in increasing their output or changing other decision variables.

The insoluble chicken-or-egg problem of deciding "who changed their behavior first" illustrates the impracticality of trying to operationalize such "predatory behavior" rules, in addition to their obvious bias favoring particular rivals and their total neglect of whether the effect of any such rule of "predatory behavior" produces the kind of behavior from rivals that is desirable from the point of view of society. On this last point, for example, if the established firms in an industry cut back their output and other decision variables by an amount that exactly offsets an entrant's decision variables, the resulting group behavior of rivals in the industry will not have changed. If the industry were acting monopolistically initially, it would still be doing so after entry!

Operationalizing Rules Against Predatory Behavior. There are a number of other obstacles to attempting to operationalize rules of "predatory" behavior by firms or other types of decision maker. We have already noted that whenever one firm lowers the price of its product, increases its advertising, or changes any other decision variable in an attempt to increase the demand for its product and raise its profits, some other firms *necessarily* suffer a reduction in demand for their products and a reduction in their profits, whether or not the firm takes rivals' behavior into account in its decision making. If "predation" is defined in terms of *"an intent to harm rivals,"* then in order to detect predatory behavior it is necessary to be able to define operationally a decision maker's rivals and to specify the exact nature of the harm that must be intended.

Defining a firm's rivals operationally is exactly analogous to the difficult problem of defining a firm's market (discussed in Chapter 6). Trying to infer which rival firms were taken into account by a decision maker in deciding any particular course of action presents insuperable problems. The behavior of any decision maker depends on all the other constraints faced by the decision maker in addition to a constraint in the form of rivals' reactions. A particular form of behavior may be optimal for a decision maker or firm owing to these other constraints, even if rivals' reactions are ignored. Therefore, to determine whether a decision maker is acting in a predatory manner, it is necessary to be able to distinguish genuine predatory behavior from the same behavior undertaken for other than predatory reasons.

Turning to the problem of defining the nature of the harm or injury to rivals that must be intended in order to substantiate "predatory" behavior, similar problems arise. Rivals' profits depend on all the constraints they face; trying to isolate the effect on those profits of the behavior of a single "predatory" rival is an impossible task. If *intent* to harm rather than *actual* harm is to be the deciding factor in determining whether predation occurred, the decision maker's intentions, again, cannot be inferred from his or her observed behavior unless all relevant constraints facing the decision maker are known, enabling one to determine the behavior that would be optimal for the decision maker in the absence of an intent to harm rivals.

"Driving rivals out of business" is often assumed to be the relevant concept of harm in defining predatory behavior. Even if it were possible to determine whether a particular firm's actions were responsible for driving another firm out of business (rather than the 1,001 other factors that also necessarily affect the level of the defunct firm's profits), there would seem to be no more reason for regarding this result as predatory than a situation in which the same impact of the first firm's actions on its rivals' collective profits occurs without driving any of them out of business. A situation in which the impact of the first firm's actions is felt by one rival, resulting in its demise, and a situation in which the action is spread among a number of rivals, resulting in the same reduction in the combined demands for their products, are the same as far as the impact on industry output and price is concerned.

It may be objected that these two situations are not the same, because rivals who are still in business can increase output more rapidly than a new business can be established, if the first firm attempts to reduce its output and raise the market price of its product after driving out rivals. The idea of "temporary" predatory behavior brings us to the next operational problem: distinguishing between, say, a temporary predatory price reduction designed to eliminate rivals and a price reduction followed by a price increase caused by changes in other constraints such as demand or cost conditions facing a firm.

An excellent illustration of myopic attempts to define concepts of predatory behavior and competition is provided by numerous attempts in the literature to use price-cost relationships as an indicator of predatory behavior. Some writers have suggested that predatory behavior aimed at eliminating rivals may be inferred whenever the price of a firm's product is below the variable cost of the product, resulting in avoidable losses for the firm employing such a pricing strategy. Losses are avoidable in the sense that ceasing production would enable the firm to cease paying out more in variable costs than it is earning in revenues from the sales of the product. The implication is that this will not occur if the firm is trying to eliminate a rival, since the reduction in the firm's output would raise the market price of the product and enable the rival whose demise is intended to earn higher prices for its products.

Several comments are appropriate in response to this line of reasoning. First, setting the price of some products below the marginal and average variable cost of production may be a profit-maximizing policy in multiproduct firms even if there are no rival firms or if the impact of rival firms is ignored by the firm. Such pricing policies may occur when products are complementary with other products produced by the firm, so that lower prices charged for individual products increase the demand and revenues associated with other products. The problem of defining and identifying predatory pricing in multiproduct firms, and the associated issue of cross-subsidization, cannot be determined from information on the price and cost of individual products, as Baumol (1977) has clearly demonstrated.

Second, even in the case of a single-product firm, a particular level of the price-cost margin for the firm's product is compatible with innumerable absolute levels of price and cost. A firm can easily avoid violating any predatory-pricing rule while simultaneously accomplishing the same predatory effect on its rivals by varying other dimensions of its behavior. Our earlier analysis of the determinants of a firm's profitability indicated that advertising and other nonprice policies of a firm's rivals are just as important determinants of the firm's profits as is rivals' pricing behavior. Rules of predatory conduct must therefore be multidimensional if they are to be effective.

Koller (1979) has made one of the most valiant attempts to operationalize predatory-pricing rules by adopting a taxonomic approach to firms' pricing behavior involving the output behavior, the movement of product price, and the resulting relationship between the price and the marginal and average variable cost of the firm's product. In situations of unchanged total industry demand, Koller concludes that predation seems likely to exist if a firm has increased output and the product price has fallen below the short-run marginal or average variable cost of the firm's product. Our comments in the previous paragraph cast some doubt on these findings. Even more interesting is Koller's predatory-pricing rule in situations of declining industry demand, where defendants to a charge of predatory conduct would be required by Koller to establish that they reduced output by an amount that enables rivals to maintain their share of total market output. A rule that encouraged firms to behave in a manner that maintained the market share of their rivals would imply that each firm faces a "share-of-the-market" demand curve. It is not difficult to demonstrate that the behavior of a group of firms, each acting independently on the basis of a "share-of-the-market" demand curve, will correspond to the behavior of a monopolist faced by the same industry demand and cost conditions! (Needham, 1978, Chap. 7). This is a result that was surely not intended by those who seek to develop rules against predatory market behavior.

In stressing the difficulties of making rules against "predatory" behavior operational, we are not denying the fact that certain types of predatory behavior exist, or that they exert an important impact on firms' behavior in practice. The threat of "aggressive" reactions from rival firms reduces the expected profitability of a firm's behavior, as has clearly been demonstrated. Individual firms may therefore try to influence their rivals' expectations by engaging in actions that signal a probably punitive response to actions that encroach on their existing markets. As Williamson (1977, 1979) has emphasized, efforts by firms to influence their rivals' expectations in such a manner as to discipline existing rivals or discourage potential competition require a broader intertemporal view of predatory behavior instead of emphasis only on the effects and period of time during which predatory pricing or other forms of behavior actually occur. Conceptual definition of predatory behavior is one thing; operational identification of such behavior is another matter entirely. Unless the difficulties of implementing rules of predatory conduct are recognized, there is a danger that the actual effects of such rules will be very different from what was intended.

Reasons for Rules Against Predatory Behavior. If, as we have suggested, rules against certain forms of "predatory" behavior are necessarily biased in favor of particular rivals, are impossible to operationalize, and need not result in the kind of behavior from a group of "rivals" that is desirable from some wider point of view such as maximizing some concept of society's satisfaction, why do people persist in trying to define and implement such rules? Part of the reason is undoubtedly an honest belief that such rules can be devised and operationalized to improve society's lot. A more important reason is simply the fact that such rules, like any regulatory constraint, can be used to further the interests of particular rivals and to alter the rules of the competitive game in their favor.

It is impossible to operationalize rules against "predatory" behavior in a manner that makes it possible to detect effective violations of the rules, because to do so would require predatory rules covering every possible dimension of rivals' behavior, political as well as economic. Despite the inherent unenforceable nature of such rules, particular rivals may have a vested interest in seeking implementation of rules against predatory forms of conduct because the rules themselves can be used to harass one's rivals! Even if it is difficult or impossible for antitrust and regulatory agencies to prove violations of particular predatory conduct rules, the process of enforcement may be protracted and costly to a defendant. The defendant's rivals will gain as a result of the time and other costs that are entailed in a defense of the charge of violating particular rules of behavior and acting in a predatory fashion.

The reader should also remember that a firm's "rivals" are not restricted to other firms in the private sector; the term includes any decision makers whose goals may be served by tying up a firm's time and other resources in defending itself against charges of violating particular rules of behavior. Attempts to introduce and apply concepts of predatory competition or other forms of "undesirable" decision-maker behavior must be viewed within this wider framework of competition among different types of decision maker if one is to understand the reasons for their existence. Instead of viewing rules against certain kinds of rivals' behavior as desirable on the ground of "preserving competition," it might be more appropriate to begin with the presumption that such rules represent a foot in the door for rivals who wish to avoid competition in the form of reactions from other decision makers, thereby emphasizing that such rules necessarily favor *particular rivals* over others in any given situation.

Although this chapter has focused on business firms in discussing alternative concepts of competition and their implications for firms' behavior, a similar approach and the principles employed are appropriate for discussing the impact of competition on the behavior of other types of decision maker. In addition to the objectives and other constraints that face any type of decision maker, anticipations regarding the reactions of the decision maker's rivals are an additional constraint influencing the decision maker's behavior. The distinction between established rivals and potential rivals, the meaning of "aggressive" and "accommodating" rivals' reactions, and the multidimensional nature of rivals' reactions are all applicable to any type of decision maker.

Similarly, the discussion of normative aspects of competition between decision makers in this section, and the conclusions, may be applied to other types of decision maker. Moreover, since the behavior of different types of decision maker interacts, it is obviously inappropriate to focus on concepts of competition that apply to only one type of decision maker in attempting to understand real-world situations. The nature of competition among legislators, voters, regulators, and consumers is just as important as competition among firms in determining the kind of world we live in. It may be that these forms of competition are even more important in influencing society's welfare than the competition among firms; we will never know unless we broaden our view of competition to include these additional dimensions of human behavior.

Although some progress has been made in recent years in developing concepts of competition among legislators, voters, and some other types of decision maker, little attempt has been made to integrate these different dimensions of competition. That this is the case is unfortunate, since these dimensions generally represent different methods by which the same individual members of society may try to achieve their objectives, and they are related. Separating the different forms of competition is analytically similar to dealing with competition between firms in terms of only one dimension of firms' behavior, and one element in one row of Table 7.1. Just as firms do not necessarily react to each other's output changes only by changing their output, individuals do not necessarily react to their rivals' economic moves by changing their economic behavior; they may, for example, react by changing political dimensions of their behavior.

CHAPTER EIGHT

Regulating Monopoly
Public Utility Regulation

8.1 REASONS FOR
REGULATING MONOPOLY

The two major reasons for regulating economic activities emphasized in the economics literature are (1) monopoly pricing behavior and (2) external effects of activities or transactions on individuals who are not parties to the activities or transactions in question. More recently, a third broad category of reasons for "transactions failure" has received increasing attention from economists. External effects and transactions failures will be examined in Chapter 10. The present chapter will examine the rationale and effects of regulating monopolies that produce a single product or service.

The traditional economic argument for regulating monopoly is based on analyses which conclude that the product-pricing behavior and input-mix choices of an unregulated profit-maximizing monopolist will not maximize allocative, technical, and distributive efficiency in the economy as a whole. The price of the monopolist's product measures the monetary value that is placed by buyers on a marginal unit of the monopolist's product. In the absence of regulation, this product price will exceed the marginal cost of the monopolist's product, which measures the monetary value placed by society on alternative uses of the inputs required to expand the monopolist's output by one unit of the product. The difference between the price and the marginal cost of the monopolist's product measures the monetary equivalent of the net increase in satisfaction members of society will experience as a result of a one-unit increase in the level of the monopolist's output. This potential net increase, attributable to expanding the output level of the monopolist's product, is depicted in the shaded area of Figure 8.1. It is exactly the

Figure 8.1

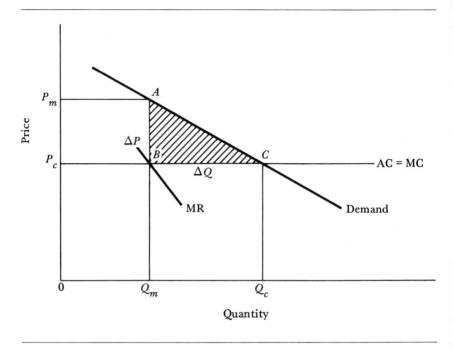

same allocative efficiency "welfare loss" of monopoly that was extensively discussed in Chapter 6.

In Chapter 6 it was also explained that monopoly prices charged by a producer of intermediate goods or services will induce other firms, which purchase and use the monopolist's output as an input, to employ input mixes that result in higher total costs of their products than the minimum feasible level, resulting in technical inefficiency in those firms.

In addition to representing a means of attempting to reduce allocative and technical inefficiencies attributable to monopoly behavior, Koller (1973) and other economists have also advocated regulation as a means of preventing the practice of price discrimination. Price discrimination occurs when different prices are charged to different buyers for the same product, and these price differences do not reflect differences in costs of serving different buyers (Needham, 1978, pp. 64–68). Price discrimination increases the seller's profits but violates the requirement that all buyers must face identical prices for the same product in order for distributive efficiency in an economy to be maximized. Buyers who face different price ratios of any two products could all experience an increase in personal satisfaction by exchanging some of the goods and services they purchase without changing the total amount of any product or service produced in the economy.

One problem with prohibiting the practice of price discrimination on the ground of increasing distributive efficiency is that this practice also generally implies a larger total output level of the discriminating monopolist, which tends to reduce the allocative inefficiency attributable to monopoly pricing behavior. In fact, it can easily be demonstrated that a monopolist who practices perfect price discrimination, and sets product prices equal to the maximum level each buyer is willing to pay for a unit of a product, will produce exactly the same output level as a perfectly competitive industry. This output level maximizes allocative efficiency. Perfect price discrimination of this kind will not usually be possible or profitable in the real world when the costs of discovering the price elasticities of demand of different markets and individuals that would be necessary to practice any kind of price discrimination successfully are taken into account.

In situations in which price discrimination results in distributive inefficiency combined with higher total output and reduced allocative inefficiency, the Theory of Second Best (discussed in Chapter 6) is applicable in determining the kinds of product-pricing behavior that maximizes society's satisfaction. The Theory of Second Best deals with situations in which it is not possible for product prices to be set equal to marginal costs of producing the products for all goods and services in the economy. Price discrimination by a monopolist fits this description, and the Theory of Second Best indicates what kind of product-pricing behavior maximizes total consumer welfare or satisfaction while simultaneously yielding any one level of total profits to a monopolist.

Baumol and Bradford (1970) have lucidly demonstrated that such welfare-maximizing product-price differences are proportional to differences in the price- and cross-elasticities of demand of different markets and buyers. The absolute level of the welfare-maximizing price of the product in every market is lower, and the firm's total profits are lower than under profit maximization. The traditional argument against price discrimination by monopolists or other firms is therefore applicable only in circumstances in which price discrimination does not change the firm's profit-maximizing output level.

Distinction Between Monopoly Behavior and Number of Firms. Although the typical textbook explanation of the rationale of regulating monopoly behavior considers a market in which there is only a single firm, the concept of monopoly behavior must be carefully distinguished from the number of firms selling in a particular market. A group of firms may collectively act like a single monopoly firm. This situation can occur if the firms collude when determining their pricing and other policies. Alternatively, it is also possible for a group of firms in a market to collectively act just like a monopolist, even without explicit collusion, if individual firms' expectations regarding other firms' reactions to their policies exhibit certain characteristics. The important implication of these considerations is that markets that are served by more than one firm are also possible targets for policies aimed at eliminating monopoly behavior.

Even if only one firm serves a particular market, the behavior of *potential* competitors who might react to the firm's policies by entering the market can also act as a constraint on the established firm's behavior and prevent it from adopting monopoly pricing and other policies. The degree to which potential competitors' behavior acts as a constraint on the behavior of established firms serving a particular market depends on the level of "entry barriers" into that market. Traditional analyses that provide a rationale for regulating monopoly implicitly or explicitly assume that the monopolist's behavior is not affected by potential competitors' behavior because of the existence of entry barriers that prevent other firms from entering the monopolist's market.

One of the most significant types of entry barrier is potential entrants' expectations regarding the reactions of firms already selling in a market. This is because a potential entrant's expectations regarding the profitability of entry into a market depends on the nature of the reactions and post-entry behavior it expects from established firms. By influencing these expectations, established firms may be able to have an impact on the level of entry barriers and potential entrants' behavior. Yet, established firms' entry-deterring behavior is not necessarily the most profitable strategy. The best strategy for established firms to adopt is to take into account the relationship between dimensions of their behavior and the profit expectations and resulting behavior of potential entrants, and to select a course of action that maximizes the profits of established firms. Entry deterrence will rarely be the best strategy for established firms (explained in Chapter 14).

Importance of Rivals' Reactions. The occurrence of entry simply means that a larger number of established firms will serve the market in question, and this fact need not change or improve the behavior of the group of firms serving the market. The behavior of an individual firm is determined by its expectations regarding the reactions of other firms to changes in the firm's own policies, not by the number of rival firms. What is important are the implications of potential or actual entry for established firms' behavior and the extent to which market prices and other terms of market transactions between sellers and buyers approximate normative standards of desirable economic, social, and political performance.

In this connection, the important general principles are that (1) the behavior of established firms depends in part on their expectations regarding actual and potential competitors' reactions and (2) the behavior of potential entrants depends in part on established firms' expected reactions to entry. *Both* sets of expectations are relevant in determining the behavior of established firms and entrants, respectively, and in determining the market behavior that results from the interactions between the behavior of these two types of decision maker. The relationship between the behavior of established firms and that of potential entrants is a special case of the general model of competition outlined in Chapter 7. Some aspects of the relationship between these two types of decision maker are worth emphasizing, however, since they have not yet been adequately integrated into the literature on entry barriers.

Multiple Dimensions of Rivals' Reactions. The expected reactions that are relevant in determining the behavior of established firms and potential entrants are multidimensional and include much more than product-pricing and output-level policies emphasized by traditional entry-barrier theory. For example, the implications of "entry" for the profits of established firms and entrants depend on all the dimensions of established firms' and entrants' behavior after entry. Similarly, the dimensions of established firms' behavior that influence potential entrants' expectations regarding the profitability of entry include more than established firms' price and output reactions. Postentry levels of the established firms' advertising, research and development, and other policies will also affect the entrants' postentry profits; and potential entrants' expectations regarding established firms' reactions in these dimensions of behavior are in principle equally important in determining the expected profitability of entry. A monopolist may continue to charge monopoly prices for its products while deterring entry by changing other dimensions of its behavior, such as advertising (Needham, 1976).

Even more important, modern entry-barrier theory has not adequately recognized that the number of dimensions of established firms' behavior that influence potential entrants' expectations of the profitability of entry include *nonmarket* dimensions of behavior, such as whether established firms have a powerful lobby in Congress, or if there is a regulatory agency that might react adversely to an entrant after entry occurs. All dimensions of established firms' market and nonmarket behavior that affect potential entrants' expectations of the profitability of entry must in principle be taken into account in any satisfactory analysis of the relationship between established firms' behavior and the level of entry barriers into the markets they serve. (See Chapter 14.)

The traditional focus and emphasis of antitrust policy has been on policies that encourage competition among firms already operating in particular markets or that reduce entry barriers and result in increased competition from potential competitors, as means of preventing monopoly behavior. In the United States, what is normally called "regulation" refers to the practice of creating regulatory commissions with power to set prices, profits, limitations on entry, and other features of a single industry. This approach to controlling monopoly behavior was adopted in energy, communications, and transportation markets, where competition between established firms or potential competitors either was considered not to be feasible or was judged to be excessive.

A classic situation where regulation is considered to be appropriate is where a particular market could be served by more than one firm only at higher costs of producing and distributing the product. Such a situation exists if there are economies of scale that result in lower unit costs of a product or service as the total output level is expanded. An example is where two local telephone or utility companies could compete only by duplicating distribution lines. These are sometimes referred to as "natural monopoly" situations. Some writers (Primeaux, 1979) have questioned whether conditions cited as characteristics of natural monopolies in economic analysis are in fact present in some of the industries, such as electric utilities, that are generally considered to be prime examples of regulated industries.

Although most of the emphasis in antitrust and regulation is on preventing monopoly behavior, it is recognized that there can be "too much" competition among firms already established in some markets, resulting in prices that are too low relative to costs, or in costs that are higher than necessary (Marris and Mueller, 1980). There can also be too much potential competition, even in the case of markets served by only one firm. If potential entrants expect an established monopolist to maintain the price of its product unchanged, a single-firm monopoly may not be able to survive even if the firm prices its products at cost. Entry will occur if entrants expect to be able to undercut the monopolist by producing a different output level with a lower unit cost, and the post-entry behavior of all firms may result in losses for all firms. In these circumstances, regulation that *prevents* entry may be beneficial to consumers (Panzar and Willig, 1977).

Normative Concepts of Nonprice Dimensions of Firms' Behavior. Multiple dimensions of behavior of established firms and potential entrants are relevant not only from a descriptive perspective concerned with explaining the behavior of both these types of decision maker. Ideally, all dimensions of firms' behavior should be taken into account in formulating normative concepts of desirable firm behavior. The traditional economic analysis of monopoly behavior that provides a rationale for regulating monopoly focuses on pricing behavior, and until recently nonprice dimensions of monopoly behavior were analyzed mainly from the perspective of their implications for product-pricing behavior.

It is now increasingly recognized that, in addition to having implications for firms' pricing behavior, nonprice dimensions of firms' behavior (e.g., advertising, research and development, durability and other product dimensions) all directly affect consumer satisfaction. Regulatory constraints on established firms' or entrants' behavior that are aimed at influencing product-pricing behavior will also generally affect nonprice dimensions of firms' behavior (see Chapters 9 and 11). Moreover, unregulated nonprice dimensions of firms' behavior that diverges from normative standards of desirable performance may justify regulating these dimensions, even if product-pricing behavior does not justify regulation. Regulatory constraints aimed at nonprice dimensions of firms' behavior also influence firms' product-pricing behavior, however.

Therefore, any satisfactory analysis of whether regulation of monopoly is justified, and of the appropriate form of regulatory constraint, requires models of monopoly behavior that include nonprice dimensions of firms' behavior and the effect of regulatory constraints on all dimensions of firms' behavior. Normative criteria of standards of desired performance for nonprice dimensions of firms' behavior will be required in addition to existing concepts of allocative, technical, and distributive efficiency. Moreover, these additional normative standards of firms' behavior should include the *relative* evaluations or weights that are assigned to different dimensions of firms' performance.

Regulated monopoly behavior, or particular regulatory constraints, may imply that some aspects of firms' behavior are closer to standards of desired performance while others are further away from such standards. In these circumstances, where a trade-off exists between the extent to which different desired dimensions of firms' performance are met, relative weights assigned to normative standards of different dimensions of firms' behavior are essential in determining whether, on balance, firms' behavior is closer to, or further away from, an overall measure of performance. Unfortunately, economists have been slow to develop normative criteria of individual nonprice dimensions of firms' behavior and have barely considered the issue of relative normative weights for different dimensions of firms' behavior.

Reasons for Regulation in Practice. The reasons why firms and industries are regulated may have little or nothing to do with the preceding theoretical arguments for regulating monopoly, since even economists have difficulty identifying in practice characteristics of monopoly that justify regulation. Determining whether a firm is charging monopoly prices for its products or services requires detailed knowledge of the firm's production, cost, and demand conditions. Economies of scale in the production of specific products will not necessarily result in monopoly pricing behavior if potential entrants will enter the market if prices exceed costs for established firms. Simply defining the relevant market for a product, which will determine the number of firms in that market, and the nature of the cost and demand conditions for the product, is not without its problems. Trying to infer whether competition exists between established rivals in a market is also exceedingly difficult (Preston and Post, 1979). Finally, monopoly that is based on "economies of scope" underlying multiproduct firms' cost conditions cannot be identified without information concerning production technologies that is very difficult to obtain or that is nonexistent (see Chapter 9).

In view of these considerations, it is not surprising that many existing regulated firms and industries do not exhibit the characteristics that economists consider necessary for justifying regulation on the ground of preventing monopoly behavior. In addition to monopoly, other explanations for the existence of regulation, such as producer protection and wealth transfers, have been advanced by numerous authors. It would be presumptuous for us to attempt to explain the factors that have resulted in regulation of any particular industry in practice, since this would imply having knowledge of the model of demands for regulation and the process of political agenda setting that determine which industries are regulated and which are not.

The true reasons why a particular industry was regulated initially will not usually be evident even from a careful study of the historical record surrounding the passage of regulatory legislation, for a number of reasons. Multiple, sometimes unrecognized factors underlie demands for regulation of a particular dimension of business or nonbusiness organizations. Also, as we have noted in a number of contexts, people will sometimes misrepresent their preferences and the reasons for their behavior whenever doing so enables them to attain a higher level of their objectives than is possible from honest revelation of information. The kind of incentive systems that are necessary to motivate honest revelation of people's preferences and behavior do not exist in the majority of economic and political transactions among individuals. There is no reason that the passage of regulatory legislation should provide any exceptions to this general rule, either now or in the past.

8.2   RATE-OF-RETURN REGULATION: EFFECTS ON TECHNICAL EFFICIENCY AND COSTS

In the United States, the traditional method of regulating a firm whose monopoly power is not restrained by market forces in the form of competition is to limit the maximum profit the firm is allowed to earn on its invested capital. This is often referred to as "fair rate-of-return regulation," since the legal principles that underlie the regulation of public utility companies rest mainly on two Supreme Court cases (Robichek, 1978) that have established that public utilities owners are entitled to earn a return on invested capital that is commensurate with returns on investments in other enterprises facing similar risks. In implementing the legal prescription, the basic approach to the regulatory rate-making process is as follows:

First, the regulatory commission determines a "just and reasonable" percentage rate of return on the regulated firm's fixed-interest and equity capital, respectively, and multiplies this rate of return by the commission's approved estimate of the amount of each of these types of capital employed by the firm, termed the "capital base" or "rate base." Second, the figure of the total allowed after-tax return on equity capital is then multiplied by (1 + profit tax rate) to obtain the amount of profits that would be required before taxes to yield the after-tax allowed rate of return. An approved figure of the firm's operating costs is then added to both of these figures to obtain a measure of the total revenue the firm must earn to cover operating expenses and taxes and to earn the allowed after-tax return on capital.

Finally, after the commission has determined the allowed level of total revenue, it must also regulate the manner in which this total revenue is to be raised by the firm. This is accomplished by approving a schedule of prices or rates for each type of service offered by the regulated firm that will yield the commission's approved total revenue figure. Estimates of demand at different prices for various types of service will be required for this purpose, and such estimates may be based on information supplied by the regulated firm. There will usually be a wide variety of price schedules for different services or classes of consumers that will raise a particular amount of total revenue approved by the commission (see Chapter 9, Section 2). The federal government requires public utilities to meet all demands at the approved regulated rates, and utilities must either be able to provide the service themselves or have firm agreements with other utilities to supply the amount of service demanded at the regulated rates.

The law on regulatory rate making is controversial and commissions have wide discretion in selecting the appropriate concepts of the allowed rate of return on capital, the capital or rate base, allowed operating expenses, and the rate schedule for raising any level of total revenue (see Section 8.4). The remainder of this section will be devoted to an examination of the effect of limiting the amount of profit a firm may earn on its invested capital, on technical efficiency, and the level of production costs in the regulated firm. This aspect of rate-of-return regulation has received more attention, and has generated more controversy in the economics literature, than any other aspect of regulation.

In a seminal article, Averch and Johnson (1962) concluded that if the amount of profit a firm is allowed to earn is dependent on the amount of capital employed by the firm, incentives are thereby created for the firm to use an inefficient input mix with more capital and fewer other inputs than the input mix that minimizes the total cost of producing its output. The reasoning that underlies this conclusion is contained in Section 8.3. More detailed treatment of the conditions that are necessary for this "A-J effect" to be present, is contained in Needham (1978, Chap. 11). By focusing on the behavioral implications of the level of the permitted rate of return, regulated firms' objectives, and uncertainty regarding the constraints that confront regulated firms, one can demonstrate that an *A-J* effect is not an automatic result of rate-of-return regulation; thus, public policy concerning public utility regulation should not be based on an uncritical acceptance of *A-J* effects. These three factors influencing behavior are not the only factors that might invalidate the existence of an *A-J* effect. Other constraints internal to regulated firms could also produce this result.

For example, the addition of conditions that must be met to achieve profit-maximizing levels of dimensions of the regulated firm's behavior other than input mix and output levels may produce such a situation. Constraints that are external to the regulated firm can likewise modify or invalidate the existence of an *A-J* effect. Thus, regulators themselves may use behavioral rules of thumb to enforce the constraint specifying the rate of return they will permit the regulated firm to earn. Davis (1973) has demonstrated that the addition of a disequilibrium adjustment rule that describes how regulators adjust the price of the regulated firm's product when the rate of return differs from the permitted rate will result in an equilibrium input mix and output level by the regulated firm that is different from those predicted by static analysis of the *A-J* effect.

Since an *A-J* effect need not result from regulating firms' return on capital, empirical investigation of the existence and magnitude of this effect in practice is clearly warranted. Spann (1974) and Courville (1974) present evidence that appears to indicate the existence of an *A-J* effect. In contrast to these two studies, Boyes (1976) investigated the overcapitalization hypothesis empirically and found no significant *A-J* effect. A second implication of the *A-J* hypothesis is that, if the allowed rate of return is reduced, a higher level of capital usage will result. Some writers have incorrectly interpreted this observation to mean that the tendency toward excessive use of capital by the regulated firm and the *A-J* effect will be increased when the allowed rate of return is reduced. This need not occur. The effect of reducing the allowed rate of return on the magnitude of the *A-J* effect depends on the exact nature of the regulated firm's production function, and no generalizations are possible. Empirical studies by Smithson (1977) and Hayashi and Trapani (1976) reach conflicting conclusions on this matter.

The controversy over the *A-J* effect is by no means settled. In appraising the results of empirical estimates of the existence and magnitude of the *A-J* effect, however, two important considerations need to be borne in mind. First, an observed failure of regulated firms to minimize total costs and a tendency to use excessive capital inputs can result from factors other than rate-of-return regulation itself (e.g., decision-maker objectives). Eliminating rate-of-return regulation will not therefore necessarily eliminate such inefficiency.

Second, even if *A-J* effects exist and are of considerable magnitude, this does not necessarily mean that total satisfaction in the economy is reduced by rate-of-return regulation. Rate-of-return regulation also affects the firm's output level, as explained in Section 8.3, and the net effect on aggregate satisfaction in the economy depends on the allocative efficiency implications of the resulting output effects as well as on the technical efficiency effects.

8.3   RATE-OF-RETURN REGULATION: EFFECTS ON PRICING BEHAVIOR AND ALLOCATIVE EFFICIENCY

Rate-of-return regulation affects the level of the regulated firm's output and product prices, and these effects will be examined from both a descriptive and a normative perspective.

The conditions that must be met in order for an unregulated firm to maximize the level of profits from its operations provide a logical starting point for understanding these matters.

The impact of hiring an additional unit of labor input on the unregulated firm's profits is shown by the expression $(MR \cdot MPP_L - w)$, where MR is the addition to the firm's total revenue from selling one more unit of output and MPP_L is the increase in the number of units of output resulting from the employment of the additional unit of labor input, usually termed the "marginal physical product" of the input in the literature. Multiplying MR and MPP yields the increase in total revenue of the firm from employing one more unit of labor. W represents the increase in the firm's total costs as the result of employing one more unit of labor (assuming that additional units of labor can be purchased at a constant wage w). The preceding expression can also be written as

$$\left(MR - \frac{w}{MPP_L}\right)MPP_L$$

and the expression w/MPP_L represents the "marginal cost" of increasing the firm's output by one unit by employing more labor.

The impact of hiring an additional unit of capital input on the unregulated firm's profits is shown by either of the following expressions:

$$(MR \cdot MPP_K - i) \quad \text{or} \quad \left(MR - \frac{i}{MPP_K}\right)MPP_K$$

where i is the price per unit of capital input and MPP_K is the increase in the number of units of output resulting from the employment of one additional unit of capital input.

Each of the preceding expressions must be equal to zero in order for an unregulated firm to maximize total profits. This implies that to maximize profits the following condition must be met:

$$MR = \frac{i}{MPP_K} = \frac{w}{MPP_L}$$

The last two terms in the preceding expression represent the necessary condition for minimizing the total cost of the unregulated firm's selected output level.

In the case of a firm that faces a regulatory constraint limiting the amount of profit the firm is permitted to earn per unit of capital employed, the preceding expressions representing the impact of hiring an additional unit of labor and capital on the level of the regulated firm's *actual* profits are the same as in the case of an unregulated firm. In the case of an unregulated firm, however, the additional profit from the last unit of capital or labor input employed must equal zero in order to maximize the firm's profits. In contrast, in the case of the regulated firm, to maximize total profits permitted by the regulatory constraint, the change in actual profits from the last unit of labor or capital employed must equal the change in total permitted profits. In symbolic terms, this requirement is as follows:

$$MR \cdot MPP_L - w = 0 \cdots \qquad (1)$$

$$MR \cdot MPP_K - i + (f - i) = 0 \cdots \qquad (2)$$

Expression (1) is the same as the profit-maximizing condition for hiring labor in an unregulated firm because changes in the quantity of labor input do not change the firm's level of total permitted profits. The change in actual profits from hiring labor must therefore equal zero to maximize permitted profits. Matters are different in the case of capital, however, since a one-unit change in the level of capital input changes permitted profits by $(f - i)$. Even though actual profits may be reduced by an increase in the level of capital input (i.e., $MR \cdot MPP_K - i$ may be negative), total permitted profits will be increased as long as the reduction in actual profit is less than the increase in permitted profit. Total permitted profits will cease to rise only when the reduction in actual profit exactly equals the increase in permitted profit as the capital input is expanded, as occurs in expression (2).

Dividing expressions (2) by (1) yields the following expression:

$$\frac{MPP_K}{MPP_L} = \frac{i}{w} - \frac{(f - i)}{w} \cdots \qquad (3)$$

Since minimizing the total cost of the regulated firm's output occurs only when $i/MPP_K = w/MPP_L$, expression (3) indicates that capital and labor will be used in inefficient proportions as long as $(f - i)$ is positive and permitted profits depend only on the amount of capital employed by the firm. This is the *A-J* effect discussed in Section 8.2. An alternative way to view the reason for excessive use of capital by the regulated firm is as follows. The term $(f - i)$ represents the amount of profit the regulated firm is allowed to earn per unit of capital input employed; $(f - i)$ therefore represents, in effect, a reduction in the effective price of a unit of capital input to the regulated firm. The effective price of a unit of capital input to the firm may therefore be viewed as the expression $[i - (f - i)]$. As long as $f > i$, the effective price of capital is less than i, the actual price of a unit of capital, and the regulated firm will be encouraged to use more capital in its production process than would be employed if the firm's use of capital depended only on the resulting marginal revenue and actual price of capital $(MR \cdot MPP_K - i)$.

The effect of regulation on the firm's product-price and output-level policies can be obtained by adding expressions (1) and (2) and solving for MR, which yields the expression (Scheidell, 1976) that follows:

$$2MR = \frac{w}{MPP_L} + \frac{i}{MPP_K} - \frac{(f - i)}{MPP_K}$$

or, alternatively,

$$MR = MC_{min} - \frac{\frac{1}{2}(f - i)}{MPP_K}$$

since $i/MPP_K = w/MPP_L = MC_{min}$, the minimum cost of expanding the firm's output level by one unit.

Whereas an unregulated firm equates MR and MC_{min} to maximize profits, the regulated firm equates MR with

$$[MC_{min} - \frac{\frac{1}{2}(f - i)}{MPP_K}]$$

which henceforth will be referred to as MC_K^*.[1] Because MC_K^* is less than MC_{min}, this implies that the regulated firm will produce a *larger* level of output than will an unregulated profit-maximizing firm. Owing to the inefficient use of labor and capital by the regulated firm, however, the *actual* marginal cost of the regulated firm's output will be *greater* than MC_{min}.

The determination of the level of the regulated firm's output and product price, Q_r and P_r, and the relationships between MR, MC_{min}, MC_{reg}, and MC_K^* are depicted in Figure 8.2. The regulated firm's output level is higher, and the price of its product is lower, than the levels Q_m and P_m that would be selected by the firm in the absence of regulation of

---

1 MC_K^* can be viewed as the effective marginal cost of expanding the firm's output when the use of capital is in effect subsidized by $(f - i)$ per unit of capital employed.

Figure 8.2

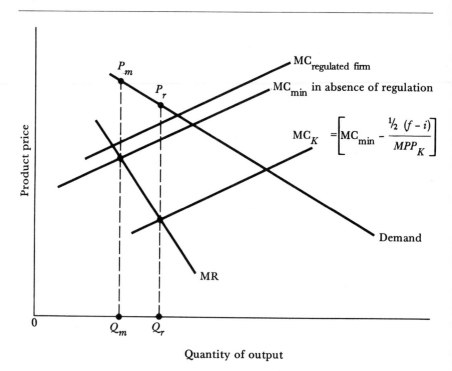

the return on capital employed. The difference between the unregulated and regulated price of the product is

$$P_m - P_r = \frac{\text{MC}_{\min}}{(1 - 1/E_d)} - \frac{\text{MC}_K^*}{(1 - 1/E_d)}$$

since it is easy to show that the price and marginal revenue of any firm's output are always related in the following manner: $\text{MR} = P\,(1 - 1/E_d)$. Since $\text{MC}_K^* = \text{MC}_{\min} - (f - i)/\text{MPP}_K$ this can be written as follows:

$$P_m - P_r = \frac{(f - i)/\text{MPP}_K}{(1 - 1/E_d)} \cdots \tag{4}$$

Expression (4), representing the difference between the unregulated and regulated price of the firm's product, indicates that rate-of-return regulation will lower the price of the firm's product by a larger amount (1), the higher the permitted rate of return to capital f, (2) the smaller the

MPP_K, and (3) the smaller the price elasticity of demand for the firm's product, E_d. The first two of these conclusions are easy to understand. The higher the permitted rate of return, or the larger the MPP_K, the lower is MC_K^* relative to $\text{MC}_{\min}$, and the larger will be the output level at which MC_K^* intersects MR. The excess of f over i represents a subsidy per unit of capital input employed, as already explained, and this subsidy will be larger per unit of output produced by an added unit of capital, the smaller is MPP_K.

Proposition (3) regarding the impact of the price elasticity of demand for the regulated firm's product appears at first sight to be counterintuitive, and requires explanation. The larger E_d, the lower will be P_m and P_r, because a larger E_d implies a higher level of MR at any output level of the firm, irrespective of the position of the $\text{MC}_{\min}$ and MC_K^* curves whose intersections with MR determine P_m and P_r, respectively.

The reason why the *difference* between P_m and P_r is also smaller, the larger the E_d, can be explained with the aid of Figure 8.2 as follows. The slope of the MR curve between Q_m and Q_r, the output levels of the firm in absence of regulation and with regulation, respectively, is directly related to the slope of the demand curve between those two output levels, which shows the difference between P_m and P_r. The flatter the MR curve between Q_m and Q_r, the flatter the demand curve between those two output levels and the smaller the difference between P_m and P_r. A similar conclusion has been demonstrated by Scheidell (1976), using a more rigorous mathematical proof.

The conclusion that P_r will be lower than the unregulated price of the product depends critically on the assumption that f exceeds i. Also, the reader should notice that irrespective of whether f exceeds i or not, the actual marginal and average cost curves for the regulated firm's product, MC_{reg} and AC_{reg}, both lie above the respective unregulated marginal and average cost curves, $\text{MC}_{\min}$ and $\text{AC}_{\min}$, as shown in Figure 8.3. The higher level of marginal and average cost of the product under regulation is the result of the inefficient input mix caused by rate of return on capital regulation.

The higher average cost of the regulated firm's product, depicted by the vertical distance between AC_{reg} and $\text{AC}_{\min}$ at the *unregulated* output level Q_m, implies a corresponding increase in the total cost of producing Q_m, shown by the vertically shaded rectangle in Figure 8.3. This rectangle represents the "technical inefficiency" attributable to rate-of-return regulation. The horizontally shaded area in the figure represents the monetary evaluation of the net increase in satisfaction resulting from expanding the level of the regulated firm's output from Q_m to Q_r. This excess of the price buyers are willing to pay for each additional unit of output produced under regulation over that unit's marginal cost is exactly the same increase in allocative efficiency that was analyzed in Chapter 6 in connection with the welfare loss attributable to monopoly.

Figure 8.3

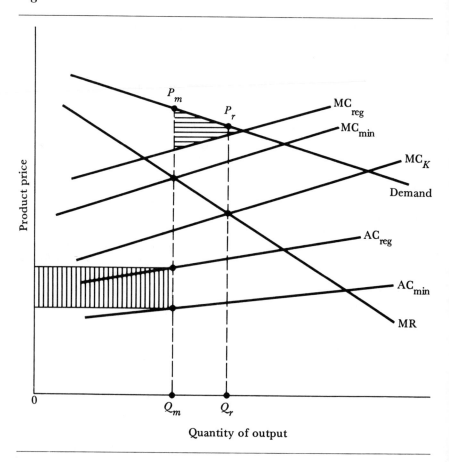

Whether rate-of-return regulation on balance increases or decreases society's monetary evaluation of the satisfaction derived from the regulated product and other products depends on whether the resulting increase in allocative efficiency exceeds the increase in technical inefficiency. These changes in efficiency, shown respectively by the horizontally and vertically shaded areas in Figure 8.3, depend on the effect of rate-of-return regulation on the regulated firm's price and output levels and on the extent of the upward shift of the average cost of the regulated product. These effects depend on the level of the permitted rate of return to capital, f. The level of f, which maximizes the *difference* between the allocative gain and technical efficiency loss areas, would also maximize society's monetary evaluation of the increase in satisfaction attributable to rate-of-return regulation. This level of f has been termed the "socially optimal level" of f, the permitted rate of return to capital in the literature.

One should notice that there is a crucial implicit assumption underlying the whole preceding analysis of the effects of rate-of-return regulation on the regulated firm's price and output levels. *This assumption is that rate-of-return regulation causes no shifts in the demand or cost functions facing the regulated firm.* In practice, such shifts may occur for a variety of reasons, such as changes in the level of other dimensions of the regulated firm's behavior, or in other factors, such as buyers' or rivals' behavior caused by rate-of-return regulation. The implications of such changes for rate-of-return regulation and other forms of regulation will be examined shortly.

First, however, although we have demonstrated that rate-of-return-on-capital regulation is quite compatible with an increase in people's satisfaction despite the existence of A-J effects, it is appropriate to consider briefly how A-J effects could be avoided entirely while the beneficial allocative efficiency effects of regulation could be retained. Some economists (Klevorick, 1966) have suggested that the appropriate solution to this problem is to make the permitted return to capital decline as the level of total capital input employed by a regulated firm increases. This will not eliminate A-J effects, however. This can be seen by reference to the profit-maximizing conditions (1) and (2) for the regulated firm, outlined on p. 222 and reproduced in slightly amended form as follows:

$$\left[\text{MR} - \frac{i}{\text{MPP}_K} + \frac{(f - i)}{\text{MPP}_K}\right]\text{MPP}_K = \left[\text{MR} - \frac{w}{\text{MPP}_L}\right]\text{MPP}_L = 0$$

Whether or not f varies with the level of capital input employed, the regulated firm will not select input levels where $i/\text{MPP}_K = w/\text{MPP}_L$, as is required for minimizing the total cost of the firm's selected output level unless $f = i$ and permitted profits of the firm are zero.

The only way to avoid an inducement for the regulated firm to use an inefficient input mix under rate-of-return regulation is to make the allowed profit rate depend on the firm's total expenditures on all inputs of capital and labor, as follows:

$$\text{Permitted profit} = PQ - (1 + f)(wL + iK)$$

This will change the part of the preceding profit-maximizing condition that refers to the profit-maximizing condition for hiring labor to the following expression:

$$\left[\text{MR} - \frac{w}{\text{MPP}_L} + \frac{(f - w)}{\text{MPP}_L}\right]\text{MPP}_L$$

When this revised condition is combined with the profit-maximizing condition for hiring capital inputs, it becomes necessary, in order to maximize permitted profits, for the regulated firm to select an input mix that satisfies the condition that $i/\mathrm{MPP}_K = w/\mathrm{MPP}_L$, and the total cost of its selected output level will be minimized.

Lack of Incentives to Reduce Total Costs of Output. Even if the incentive for the regulated firm to use an inefficient *mix* of inputs is removed by making its permitted profits depend on total expenditures on all inputs, there may still be a problem with rate-of-return regulation in the form of lack of incentives for the firm to attempt to reduce the minimum total costs of producing its product by increasing the productivities of its inputs.

Even if a regulated firm expects to make additional profits by introducing a cost-reducing innovation, it does not necessarily follow that it will introduce the innovation immediately. In many circumstances a firm may be able to maximize the discounted present value of the additional profits only by delaying, and gradually introducing, the innovation. The rate of introduction of a cost-reducing innovation will affect the time profile of the firm's costs and also the time profile of reactions by regulatory agencies that affect the firm's profits. The rate of introduction that maximizes the present value of profits depends partly on the length of time between regulatory reviews and partly on the rate at which the firm's decision makers discount future profit flows.

To overcome the problem of lack of incentives for regulated firms to attempt to reduce the total costs of producing new products, some economists (Holthausen, 1979) have suggested that regulated firms be allowed to keep a portion of any reductions in total costs. This is analytically equivalent to changing the permitted profit relationship from Permitted profit $= (f - i)K$ under rate-of-return regulation, or Permitted profit $= r \times \mathrm{TC}$ under conventional rate-of-return-on-total-cost regulation, to the following relationship:

$$\text{Permitted profit} = M - r(\mathrm{TC_{actual}} - \mathrm{TC_{min}})$$

where M is a fixed amount of permitted profit. As one can easily confirm by inspecting this condition, any action by the regulated firm that reduces its actual total costs relative to their minimum feasible level will contribute to an increase in the firm's permitted profits. As Loeb and Magat (1979) emphasized, there is a remaining problem that has been overlooked in the regulation literature. The regulated firm may be able to earn higher permitted profits by misrepresenting information regarding $\mathrm{TC_{actual}}$ or $\mathrm{TC_{min}}$. For example, by overstating $\mathrm{TC_{min}}$ or understating $\mathrm{TC_{actual}}$, the regulated firm may be able to earn higher permitted profits under a particular allowed rate of profit. Even more important, by misrepresenting this information the firm may hope to influence the level at which the regulatory agency sets the level of the permitted rate of return.

The nature of the incentive system that will eliminate incentives for regulated firms to misrepresent information regarding their costs, revenues, or other dimensions of behavior and performance is examined in detail in Chapter 12, Section 2. Loeb and Magat (1979) provide an example of a regulatory incentive system that motivates regulated firms to minimize the total costs of their products and that requires no action by the agency when the factors that underlie firms' total costs change. The essential element in their regulatory incentive system is a total subsidy to the firm that increases in magnitude as long as the firm's output is less than the level desired by the regulatory agency. When added to the firm's profits, this subsidy results in a level of combined (profits + subsidy) that reaches a maximum at the output level desired by the agency. In Loeb and Magat's model, this output level is where the price of the regulated product equals the marginal cost of the product, but any other desired relationship between the price and marginal cost of the regulated firm's product can be attained by changing the output level at which the combined (profits + subsidy) reaches a maximum.

The logic of the Loeb-Magat incentive system will become clearer when the reader has mastered the general principles underlying incentive systems in Chapter 12. In the present context, their model is important in emphasizing that under the present system of regulation, regulatory commissions must rely at least partly on regulated firms for information regarding their costs. In such circumstances, constraints that either motivate honest revelation of information by the regulated firm or that reduce the agency's need for cost information will in general be required, in addition to regulatory constraints that achieve the necessary technical and allocative efficiency properties that are stressed in the traditional literature on regulation.

8.4 BEHAVIOR OF REGULATORY COMMISSIONS

The behavior of regulators largely determines the characteristics of regulatory constraints that confront regulated decision makers. These regulatory constraints interact with the other constraints confronting regulated decision makers to produce effects on regulated decision makers' behavior. The analysis of regulators' behavior in Chapter 5 focused on the behavior of regulatory agencies, which differ in a number of respects from the regulatory commissions that are responsible for regulating public utility industries. This section will briefly examine some of the differences between these two types of regulatory institution and the resulting implications for the behavior of regulatory commissions.

In common with all types of decision maker, the behavior of members of regulatory commissions depends on their personal goals and the nature of their perceptions regarding the various types of constraint that confront them and determine the outcome of their actions. The legislative mandate that describes the function or purpose of regulatory commissions is generally vague and leaves wide discretion for commissions to define and implement their own conception of that mandate. For example, the legal principles that underlie the regulation of public utility companies rest mainly on two Supreme Court cases that have established that the owners of public utilities are entitled to earn a return on invested capital that is commensurate with returns on investments in other enterprises that face similar risks (Robichek, 1978).

In implementing this legal prescription, regulatory commissions have wide latitude in selecting both the appropriate concept of the capital base of the utility and the concepts of degree of investment risk and level of earnings earned by comparable unregulated firms. Deciding the appropriate capital base that constitutes the invested capital of the public utility involves distinguishing between operating costs and capital costs and deciding in which category particular items of expenditure such as advertising belong. It also involves valuing long-lived capital assets and deciding whether to use historical purchase costs, current market value, or replacement cost as mēasures of value.

The selection of firms whose activities are purported to be comparable in risk to a public utility firm also leaves wide discretion to regulatory commissions, despite developments in the theory of risk measurement that have provided a conceptual basis for measuring risk. A number of writers (Copeland, 1978) have shown that the average expected return $E(R_i)$ to investors in a risky asset is

$$E(R_i) = R_f + \beta_i[E(R_m) - R_f]$$

where R_f is the return on a risk-free asset (such as Treasury bills), $E(R_m)$ is the expected return to a "market" portfolio consisting of all risky assets, and "beta" (β_i) is a measure of the asset-specific risk of the return on asset i; a "beta-coefficient" may be calculated for any asset, according to the following formula:

$$\beta_i = \frac{\text{covariance } (R_i, R_m)}{\text{variance } (R_m)} = \frac{\Sigma(R_{it} - \overline{R}_i)(R_{mt} - \overline{R}_m)}{\Sigma(R_{mt} - \overline{R}_m)^2} *$$

Although beta is useful as an objective measure of risk for assessing the degree of comparability between regulated public utility firms and non-regulated firms, controversy remains in the literature regarding the question of whether beta is a reliable measure of risk for individual firms;

* Where R_{it} = actual return to investors in asset i in year t
  R_i = average return to investors in asset i over a period $(t = 1, 2, \ldots n)$
  R_{mt} = actual return to investors in the market portfolio of assets in year t
  $\overline{R}_m$ = average return on the market portfolio of assets

some studies suggest that individual betas for relatively short holding periods tend to be unstable (Blume, 1971). Another problem in determining the level of risk associated with investment in public utility firms that is comparable with the level of risk in a selection of unregulated firms is that the degree of investment risk in public utilities itself depends in part on regulation.

Even if the problem of establishing comparability of investment risk in public utilities and other firms is solved, the legal mandate of allowing equity owners of public utility firms to receive a return commensurate with the returns on investments in other enterprises having corresponding risks can be interpreted in many ways. Determining allowed rates of return by comparing individual regulated firms with other regulated firms is obviously inappropriate; if all regulatory commissions used this approach, any level of earnings that regulators collectively approved would be permissible, irrespective of the level of earnings in unregulated firms. The two most widely used approaches used in regulatory proceedings to arrive at "just and reasonable" rates of return to equity holders of public utilities are (1) the "comparable earnings" and (2) "the discounted cash flow" method. The comparable earnings approach is most widely used; its essential elements are to select a sample of firms purported to be comparable in risk to the firm under regulatory review. The average return on the book value of the equity capital for the sample of firms is then taken to be the relevant measure of the required rate of return for the applicant firm and is usually termed the "cost of equity capital" for the regulated firm.

Comparisons of rates of earnings on book values between regulated and unregulated firms may be challenged on the ground that differences in accounting practices make such comparisons meaningless. Even where accounting practices are similar, accounting rates of return in unregulated firms may overstate or understate "true" economic returns owing to the failure of conventional accounting procedures to properly capitalize advertising and research and development expenditures of an investment type.

The discounted cash flow (DCF) method is more recent and is used by only about one third of state utility commissioners, according to Copeland (1978). This method tends to produce a lower estimate of the required return than the actual earned returns of alternative comparable investment opportunities. The basic assumption of the DCF method is that share prices reflect the capitalized value of dividends investors expect to earn in the future. If investors expect current dividends, D, to grow at some constant rate, g, and the investor's discount rate that measures the relative evaluation of \$1 of dividends in the current period to \$1 of dividends in a future period is r, the relationship between the price the investor will pay for a share and these various factors is $P = D/(r - g)$, which may be rearranged as $r = D/(P + g)$.

The last expression indicates that the investor's discount rate, r, is equal to the sum of the dividend yield and the expected dividend growth rate. If the expected return (current yield plus expected growth) is greater than the investor's discount rate, investors will demand more shares, share prices will rise, and yields will fall until the preceding relationship exists. The DCF model is therefore a model of the equilibrium expected return or yield on shares. The investor's discount rate r is a measure of the cost of equity in that it measures the investor's equilibrium required rate of return from purchasing shares. If r is applied to the regulated firm's equity capital, it provides a measure of the total amount of profits that the regulated firm should be allowed to earn in order to yield equity holders a just and reasonable return on their investment.

One advantage of the DCF method is that estimating the investor's current required rate of return automatically takes into account the investment risk of the security, so that it is not necessary to determine "comparability of investment risk." Despite its advantages in taking into account future expected as opposed to past earnings on investment, the DCF approach still leaves room for discretion in determining the investor's discount rate from empirical data on share prices.

Because the legal principles underlying rate-of-return and other forms of regulation are compatible with different interpretations that leave wide discretion for regulatory commissions, it is logical to focus attention on other constraints confronting regulators that might influence the manner in which commissioners select particular courses of action from all those available to them. A variety of models of regulatory commission behavior exists in the literature, and a selection of these is listed in the References for this chapter. In general, these models emphasize that many constraints, such as length of tenure in office, income opportunities during and after regulatory office, size and composition of the regulatory commission, regulators' personal conceptions of the public interest, and pressures from various groups affected by regulators' decisions may affect the behavior of regulatory commissions.

The variety of models of regulatory commission behavior is reflected by a corresponding variety of conclusions, some conflicting. The main virtue of these models is that they emphasize that appropriate assumptions regarding the objectives and constraints facing regulators can generate almost any kind of behavior. A more promising approach is illustrated by empirical studies that attempt to determine the factors that regulatory commissions take into account in their decision making. Joskow (1972), for example, has attempted to estimate empirically the factors that determine the allowed rate of return in a regulatory hearing. Another example is provided by McFadden's (1976) attempt to infer, from the consequences or outcomes of organizational decisions, an implicit choice criterion or decision rule that the organization is following. Although all regulators' behavior may usefully be viewed as a response to demands from multiple reference groups, very little is yet known about either the factors that affect a regulator's choice of reference groups or the weights the regulator assigns to each reference group when deciding between alternative courses of action.

Most of the literature that deals with regulatory commissions' behavior is concerned with the factors that influence the nature and level of the targets that regulators adopt, such as the characteristics of regulated decision makers' behavior that regulators attempt to achieve. There is also increasing recognition, however, that the nature of the decision rules regulators adopt as instruments for achieving these targets plays an independent and equally important role in influencing regulators' behavior and the outcome of regulation. These decision rules have both static and dynamic implications for the behavior of regulators and regulated decision makers.

From a static perspective, such decision rules are often additional aspects of the regulatory constraint itself, and they may therefore change the effects of regulatory constraints on regulated decision makers' behavior. An example is provided by the existence of a time period, or "regulatory lag," before a regulatory agency reacts to a situation in which the profits of a regulated firm exceed the permitted rate of return and compels the firm to reduce the price level of some of its products. Davis (1973) has demonstrated that the existence of a regulatory lag results in a different long-run equilibrium capital-labor choice by the regulated firm than that predicted by the traditional A-J effect analysis, which implicitly assumes instantaneous achievement of regulatory constraints.

The dynamic implications of regulatory decision rules for the behavior of regulators and regulated decision makers are even more profound, since these decision rules determine the nature of the disequilibrium time path of behavior of both types of decision maker and, among other things, also determine whether equilibrium levels of regulators' and regulated decision makers' behavior will ever be achieved. Spann (1976) has emphasized that the disequilibrium path of a regulated firm's product prices that results from the existence of a regulatory lag may imply benefits and costs of regulation for the regulated firm and consumers that are very different from those which would be generated by a model of regulation where regulatory constraints are met and regulators and regulated firms are always in equilibrium. Similarly, Sibley and Bailey (1978) have pointed out that regulatory policy should take into account the disequilibrium behavior of regulated firms and formulate regulatory constraints that constrain those firms to earn the permitted rate of return over a sequence of time periods, even though in individual time periods the disequilibrium rate of return to the regulated firm may exceed, or fall short of, the permitted rate of return.

CHAPTER NINE

Regulating Monopoly in Multiproduct Firms

9.1 IMPLICATIONS OF MULTIPRODUCT FIRMS

The discussion of the rationale of regulating monopoly and the analysis of the effects of rate-of-return regulation on input mixes, product prices, and output levels in Chapter 8 focused on a regulated firm that produced a single product or service. When firms produce multiple products, as occurs in most situations in the real world, a number of additional considerations enter the issue of the rationale and effects of regulating monopoly.

For example, the characteristics of production technology that determine whether a single firm will be able to produce any particular combination of products at a lower total cost than a group of independent firms producing individual products are very different in the multiproduct case from the case of a firm producing a single product. In the traditional analysis of single-product firms, for a single firm to be able to produce a particular level of output at lower total cost than would be possible if more than one firm produced the same total output, production technology has to exhibit "economies of scale." This term refers to a situation in which increases in the output level of a single product lead to less than proportionate increases in total costs, and therefore to a declining unit cost of producing the product as total output level increases.

When firms produce multiple products, economies of scale are neither necessary nor sufficient to create a situation in which a monopolist can produce a particular combination of outputs at lower total cost than a group of independent firms producing the same outputs (Baumol, 1977). In order for monopoly to be the least costly form of productive organization, production technology in the multiproduct case must exhibit "economies of scope." This term, coined by Panzar and Willig (1977), refers to a situation in which joint production of two or more products by one firm is less costly than the combined costs of producing the same level of output of the two products in two or more independent firms. Economies of scope arise from inputs that are utilized jointly in the production of more than one product. The joint input may be imperfectly divisible, so that manufacture of only one or of a subset of the different products that could be produced jointly by the input leaves excess capacity of the input. Or an input may be capable of producing a number of joint products, so that the production of one product will make the input freely available for producing other outputs. For economies of scope to exist there must be some sort of complementarity in the production of different products in a multiproduct firm. If economies of scope exist, a multiproduct monopolist may be able to produce a combination of multiple products at lower total costs than if the products were produced by independent firms, despite the absence of economies of scale in the production of individual products. Conversely, even if economies of scale exist in the production of individual products, a multiproduct monopolist with economies of scope may still be able to produce a vector of outputs at lower total cost than a group of independent firms specializing in individual products if product-specific economies of scale are outweighed by cost savings from joint production. Together, these results imply that the existence or nonexistence of monopoly that is attributable to lower-cost production technology cannot, in the multiproduct case, be inferred from the existence or nonexistence of economies of scale in the production of individual products of the monopolist. In the multiproduct case, only a test for the presence of economies of scope will determine if a monopoly is attributable to lower-cost technology. Unfortunately, as Baumol (1977) has lucidly explained, such a test cannot be performed by reference to production and cost information in the neighborhood of the monopolist's current output mix but requires information about the production technology and cost functions associated with all feasible output mixes. The data required to provide this information will rarely exist in practice.

The existence of economies of scope does not by itself ensure that a multiproduct monopoly is sustainable, since the behavior of potential entrants into the monopolist's markets also needs to be taken into account. Faulhaber (1975) has demonstrated that the only sustainable multiproduct prices that will imply losses for entrants into any of the multiproduct firm's markets are "subsidy-free" prices that involve no cross-subsidization between individual products of the monopolist.

"Subsidy-free" multiproduct prices are prices for each individual product that are lower than the price that could be charged by a firm producing only one, or a subset, of the multiproduct monopolist's products. Whether a multiproduct monopoly firm's product prices are subsidy free or not, therefore, depends on the costs of alternative supply arrangements, and in the case of some types of available production technology there may be no subsidy-free product-price vector for a multiproduct monopolist. Even in situations where a subsidy-free price vector exists, the product prices need not be welfare-maximizing prices; in such circumstances, it may be necessary to restrict entry to a multiproduct firm's markets to enable the firm to charge welfare-maximizing product prices.

When economies of scope are present in the production technology of a multiproduct monopoly firm, Baumol, Bailey, and Willig (1977) have demonstrated that welfare-maximizing product prices will be sustainable, in the sense that such prices will imply losses for any firms that enter all, or any subset, of the monopolist's markets. These are not the only possible sustainable product prices for a multiproduct monopoly firm, but other sustainable price vectors require more knowledge than the demand and cost conditions for output levels in the neighborhood of the monopolist's output mix. Even welfare-maximizing prices need not be sustainable in the absence of economies of scope, since such economies are necessary to ensure that welfare-maximizing prices are subsidy free according to Faulhaber's (1975) definition of sustainable multiproduct prices. The conclusion that a multiproduct monopolist who sets product prices at levels that deter entry will select welfare-maximizing product prices is very similar to the conclusions of traditional analyses of entry-deterring behavior by single-product monopoly firms.

At first sight, these conclusions appear to provide reassurance that the existence of potential entrants into monopoly markets will result in welfare-maximizing product-pricing behavior by single- or multiproduct monopoly firms. Such an inference is invalid, however, for the following reasons. The level of profits that potential entrants expect from entry into any market depends on their expectations regarding established firms' postentry behavior. The previously mentioned analyses of Faulhaber and of Baumol, Bailey, and Willig implicitly assume that potential entrants expect established monopoly firms to keep product prices at an unchanged level if entry occurs. If, instead, potential entrants expect established firms to change product prices in response to entry, established multiproduct monopoly firms may be able to charge product prices that exceed welfare-maximizing product price levels while threatening reductions in those prices if entry occurs. In these circumstances, higher-than-welfare-maximizing product prices will be sustainable. Conversely, welfare-maximizing prices will not deter entry if potential entrant firms expect established firms to reduce the output levels of their products after entry occurs.

The postentry product-price and output levels of established firms are not the only dimensions of established firms' behavior that influence potential entrants' profit expectations. If potential entrants expect changes in other dimensions of established firms' behavior, such as advertising or other nonprice variables, in response to entry, this can deter entry despite established firms' product prices that exceed welfare-maximizing product-price levels.

In short, the mere presence of potential entrants will not guarantee welfare-maximizing behavior by established monopoly firms. What matters as far as potential entrants' profit expectations are concerned is the postentry level of *all* dimensions of established firms' behavior. A variety of combinations of expected postentry product prices, and nonprice dimensions of established firms' behavior, is compatible with zero profits expected by potential entrants, and with entry deterrence. Even if there is a link between the preentry behavior of established firms and potential entrants' expectations regarding established firms' postentry behavior, entry deterrence will not necessarily be the optimal strategy for established firms in the sense that it is the strategy that maximizes the established firms' profits or other objectives.

"Entry" itself is compatible with many levels of output and other dimensions of entrants' behavior, each implying a different level of profits resulting from any given level of established firms' preentry and postentry behavior. Different levels of expected profit, and different optimal preentry and postentry strategies of established firms, will result from established firms' different assumptions about how potential entrants will behave after entry occurs. These entry-related matters will be explored in more detail in Chapter 14, Section 3. For the present, it is sufficient to emphasize that competition between potential entrants and established firms is simply a special case of the general theory of competition (see Chapter 7).

The central proposition of that theory is that the behavior of each rival, and the equilibrium behavior of all rivals, depends on the exact nature of each rival's expectations about how the other rivals will react to its own policies. No determinate conclusions about the impact of competition on firms' behavior are possible without specifying the nature of the reactions of rivals that are expected by each competitor *and* the nature of the objectives and other constraints that confront each competitor. A corollary proposition is that, given the objectives and other constraints that confront an individual firm, only certain types of rivals' reactions expected by that firm will result in behavior by the firm that corresponds to normative standards of pricing or other dimensions of performance. In other words, the *nature* of competition, in the form of anticipated rivals' reactions, is more important than the mere *existence* of competition. In the context of multiproduct monopoly firms, the mere presence of potential entrants is not sufficient to ensure that the monopolist will act in a manner corresponding to normative standards of welfare-maximizing behavior.

9.2 EFFECTS OF REGULATION
ON PRICING
IN MULTIPRODUCT FIRMS

The following discussion of the impact of regulation on pricing in multi-product firms will first briefly describe situations which are generally referred to as "peak-load" pricing situations. Section 9.2(b) examines in detail the effect of rate-of-return regulation on product-price and output-level mixes in multiproduct firms. When regulations limit the amount of profit that a multiproduct firm is permitted to earn, there will generally be many product-price combinations and resulting output mixes that yield the permitted total profit. Some of these price and output mixes will be more desirable than others, from the point of view of maximizing the satisfaction of consumers of the products and society as a whole. We shall examine the factors that are relevant in determining which regulated price-output combination a firm's decision makers will select from the range of feasible alternatives. These factors are important in determining the kind of regulatory constraints that might be required, in addition to limitations on firms' overall profits, in order to ensure that regulated firms select price and output mixes that meet regulatory goals.

(a) Peak-Load Pricing
Problems and Regulation

If demand for a firm's product varies in strength from one period of time to another, as occurs with public transportation, electricity, and telephone calls, for example, there exists what is termed a "peak-load problem." Various writers stress different aspects of this problem, some focusing on the problem of how to price a product in different time periods in the face of fluctuating demand (the pricing problem), others focusing on the question of how much "capacity" to install to meet fluctuating demands. These aspects are related, however, and solutions to all aspects of the problem are interdependent and simultaneously determined.

Much of the unnecessary mystique and confusion that often surround discussions of the peak-load problem can be avoided if it is recognized at the outset that the problem is merely a special case of a firm's general pricing problem, with two characteristics that are usually analyzed separately being combined. Since one characteristic of the peak-load problem is that demand in different periods differs, the demand situation is similar to that found in the traditional treatment of price discrimination in the economics literature.

As far as demand conditions facing the firm are concerned, the only difference is that in the case of price discrimination the firm is confronted at the same time by demands that differ in different markets, whereas the different demands confronting the firm in the peak-load problem situation are associated with different time periods. This distinction leads to another element that is not present in the traditional analysis of price discrimination. Whereas the output sold in different markets in the traditional price discrimination analysis is produced by different units of input, in the peak-load problem, output sold in different periods is produced sequentially by the same capacity. Thus, the peak-load problem is similar to the price discrimination framework but differs in that it also includes "joint-product" problem.

Importance of Objectives in Solving Peak-Load Pricing Problems. The optimal solution to any pricing problem depends on the objectives pursued; whatever the nature of the objectives, however, optimal pricing always requires that price be set in some specific relationship to the marginal cost of output.

Whatever objectives are being pursued, it is always necessary to determine the marginal cost of output sold in any market, or time period, in order to implement the required optimal pricing rules. The marginal cost of output depends on the marginal cost of the inputs required to produce a marginal unit of output. In the case of a peak-load problem, the same units of some inputs — "capacity," as they are usually referred to — produce output in different periods, so that the output produced and sold in these periods is a joint product of capacity. *The key to the solution of all peak-load pricing problems therefore lies in determining which marginal cost of capacity concept should be allocated to units of output produced in different periods.*

As demonstrated in more detail elsewhere (Needham, 1978), whenever an input produces joint products, the cost concept that is appropriate for individual joint products to be able to result in optimal pricing and output-level decisions is an "opportunity cost" concept, which equals the total marginal cost of the input minus the marginal contribution of all other outputs to the decision maker's objective. If the decision maker's objective is profit maximization, the proper marginal cost of each joint product is the total marginal cost of the joint input, minus the sum of the marginal revenues of all the other joint products the input produces.

If the objective is to maximize society's satisfaction, and this requires that product prices equal marginal cost of output produced in every time period, the appropriate marginal cost of the joint input that is allocated to output in each time period is as follows: the total marginal cost of the joint input, minus the sum of the demand prices of all the other joint products.

In a peak-load situation, the effect of regulation on a firm's product prices and output levels in different time periods depends on the form of the regulatory constraint. For example, a regulatory constraint that limits the firm's rate of return on capital will have different effects on product prices and output levels than regulatory constraints that limit a firm's profit per unit of output, or the firm's return on total cost (Bailey 1972; White 1974).

Also, the effect of any particular regulatory constraint on a peak-load pricing situation will depend on the objectives of the regulated firm's decision-makers and on the other constraints that confront them. The interested reader is referred to Needham (1978, Chapter 11, pp. 293–301) for detailed treatment of unregulated and regulated solutions to peak-load pricing problems.

(b) Rate-of-Return Regulation and Multiproduct Price Vectors

Irrespective of whether the costs or demands of the different products of the regulated firm are related, *there will generally be many different price-cost relationships and resulting output mixes that are compatible with a particular level of profit permitted by a regulatory constraint.* The only exception to this rule is where the regulatory constraint is ineffective in limiting the firm's profits, as we shall demonstrate.

One important implication of this is that, irrespective of whether a constraint on profit is related to the amount of capital the firm employs, to the firm's total cost, or to some other dimension of the firm's behavior, *additional* features of the regulatory constraint will generally be required to induce the firm to adopt a particular product-price vector from all those which are compatible with a particular level of total permitted profits of the firm. In the absence of such additional features of regulatory constraints, regulated firms may adopt product-price levels and output mixes that result in lower levels of society's satisfaction than other product-price levels that are compatible with the same level of regulated profits.

A second important implication of the preceding italicized statement is that in order to predict the effect on the level of the firm's product prices of any constraint restricting a multiproduct firm's profits below the maximum level, it is necessary to have information about the firm's decision rule that determines which of the many product-price combinations that are compatible with the regulated profit level will be selected by the firm's decision makers. A third implication is that the effects of regulation on a multiproduct firm's product prices cannot be inferred solely by reference to the resulting effects on the price of individual products, or by reference to the effect of regulation on regulated product prices only, if regulation applies to some of the firm's products and not to others. An explanation of these important propositions follows.

In Figure 9.1(c) the lines labeled *ABCDE* and *abc*, termed "iso-profit" curves, depict all the combinations of prices of two of a firm's products that will result in the same level of total profit for the firm. These lines are derived as follows. The upper portions of Figure 9.1(a) and (b) depict the conventional demand, marginal revenue, and marginal cost curves for two of the firm's products, X and Y. Here, the demand and cost curves of each product are assumed to be independent of the price and output level of the other product. This assumption could be relaxed without changing the shapes of the iso-profit lines in Figure 9.1(c). The lower portions of parts (a) and (b) of the figure depict the total amount of profit the firm earns from each product, at different product prices and resulting quantities demanded. The level of total profit resulting from any price-output combination (a) and (b) is equal to the difference between the areas under the marginal revenue and marginal cost curves, up to the price and output levels in question. The height of the horizontal line through the "profit hills" in the lower portions of (a) and (b) represents a particular level of total profits of the firm equal to Π_1 in magnitude. This level of total profits can be achieved not only by any of the four price-output combinations where the line intersects the two profit hills in parts (a) and (b) of the figure but also by other combinations of the prices of the two products; these different combinations are depicted by lines *ABCDE* and *abc* in Figure 9.1(c).

Segment abc. The combinations of prices of X and Y that result in the same level of total profit shown by iso-profit curve *abc* in Figure 9.1(c) are derived as follows. Starting from the price of product X, $P_{X\max}$, where profit from product X is zero, Figure 9.1(b) shows that there are *two* possible levels of the price of product Y that would result in the total level of profit Π_1, namely P_{Y1} and P_{Y2}. Starting from $P_{X\max}$ and P_{Y1}, shown by point "a" in part (c), it is clear from (a) and (b) that a reduction in the price of product X will increase the profits earned from product X and must therefore be accompanied by an *increase* in the price of Y above P_{Y1} and lower profits from Y to keep the firm's total profits at an unchanged level. The resulting combinations of P_X and P_Y that keep the firm's total profits constant are shown by the segment *ab* of iso-profit curve *abc* in part (c). At P_{X1}, total profits from X equal Π_1, and P_Y must be set at $P_{Y\max}$ so that total profits from Y are zero. The segment *bc* indicates that at prices of Y above $P_{Y\max}$ the price of X must be kept at P_{X1} to maintain total profits of the firm at Π_1.

Segment AB. Segment *ABCDE* of the iso-profit curve results from starting at the combination of product process $P_{X\max}$ and P_{Y2}, shown by point A in Figure 9.1(c). A reduction in the price of product X below $P_{X\max}$ will increase profits from product X and require a reduction in profits from product Y to keep the firm's total profits unchanged. Figure

Figure 9.1

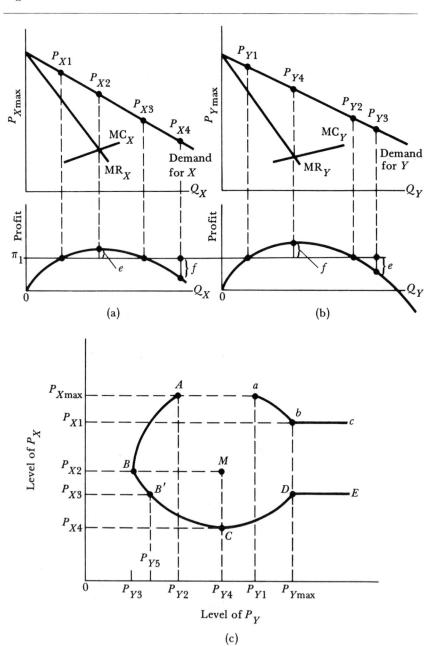

(a)

(b)

(c)

9.1(b) indicates that, starting from P_{Y2}, a reduction in P_Y will be required to reduce profits from Y. The resulting combinations of P_X and P_Y that keep the firm's total profits constant at level Π_1 are shown by segment AB of the iso-profit curve in (c).

Segment BC. When P_X is lowered to P_{X2}, Figure 9.1(a) shows that profits from X cease to increase and start to decline. At P_{X2}, profits from X are greater than Π_1, by an amount e, and therefore profits from Y must be e lower than Π_1; this occurs at P_{Y3}, as shown in (b). As P_X is reduced further, below P_{X2}, and profits from X decline, the price of Y must therefore be *increased* above P_{Y3} to raise profits from Y and to keep total profits constant at level Π_1. The resulting combinations of prices that keep the firm's total profits constant at Π_1 are shown by segment BC of the iso-profit curve in (c).

Segment CD. Eventually, as reductions in P_X below P_{X2} continue to lower profits from X, and increases in P_Y raise profits from Y by a corresponding amount to keep total profits at Π_1, profits from Y reach a maximum at P_{Y4}, as shown in Figure 9.1(b). At P_{Y4} profits from Y are greater than Π_1 by an amount f, and therefore profits from X must be f lower than Π_1; this occurs at P_{X4} as shown in part (a). As P_Y is increased further, above P_{Y4}, and profits from Y decline, the price of X must therefore be *raised* above P_{X4} to raise profits from X and to keep total profits constant at level Π_1. The resulting combinations of prices that keep the firm's total profits constant at Π_1 are shown by segment CD of the iso-profit curve in (c).

Segment DE. As the price of Y is raised and profits from Y are reduced, while the price of X is raised and profits from X are increased by a corresponding amount, eventually the profits from X reach the level Π_1 at P_{X3}. Profits from Y must now equal zero, and $P_{Y\max}$ must be charged as shown by point D in Figure 9.1(c). The segment DE of the iso-profit curve in (c) indicates that at prices of Y above $P_{Y\max}$ the price of X must be kept at P_{X3} in order for the firm to earn the level of total profits Π_1. Recall that we have previously demonstrated that a price level of X of P_{X1} will *also* result in total profits of Π_1 when $P_Y = P_{Y\max}$ and profits from Y are zero. Also, there will be a vertical segment of $ABCDE$ above the point A, and a vertical segment of abc above the point a, indicating that P_{Y2} or P_{Y1} must be charged in order to earn total profits of Π_1 when the price of X is higher than $P_{X\max}$.

Iso-profit curves $ABCDE$ and abc show all the combinations of prices of the two products X and Y that result in total profits of the firm equal to Π_1. If the horizontal line in the lower portions of Figure 9.1(a) and (b) were at a higher level, indicating a higher level of total profits of the firm than Π_1, this would result in another iso-profit curve with a similar shape, lying inside *ABCDE* and *abc*. The highest possible level of profit the firm could earn would be equal to the vertical summation of the highest point of the two profit hills in (a) and (b); this would be earned by the combination of product prices P_{X2} and P_{Y4} shown by the point M in part (c). Horizontal lines implying lower levels of total profit than Π_1 would, similarly, result in iso-profit curves that were outside *ABCDE* and *abc*.

Even if the firm in question produces more than two products, iso-product curves can be constructed for any pair of products, while holding the price and output levels of all other products constant.

Also, it should be noted that whereas the iso-profit curves in Figure 9.1 indicate all product-price combinations that yield the same *total* profits, similar iso-profit curves can be constructed indicating price combinations that yield the same profit/capital ratio. In these circumstances, increases in the level of output of X or Y will require more capital inputs, and a higher absolute amount of profit will be required to earn a given rate of return. Diagrammatically, this merely means that the profit constraint in the lower portion of Figure 9.1(a) and (b) will slope up from left to right instead of being horizontal; otherwise, the method of deriving the iso-profit curves is the same. Similar shapes of the curves will result; the only difference will be that the iso-profit curve corresponding to a particular rate of return will lie farther toward the upper right of the diagram.

The preceding analysis demonstrates why regulation that limits the absolute profits or rate of return on capital that a multiproduct firm may earn still leaves the firm a wide range of pricing options for its products. These options are shown by different points on the iso-profit curve associated with the regulated level of profit or rate of return. It is instructive to examine the implications of the different pricing options that lie on the iso-profit curve.

(a) *Price combinations on segment abc.* These combinations involve higher prices of both products under regulation than the unregulated profit-maximizing price combination M in Figure 9.1(c). Since a limitation on the absolute level of total profits would mean that total profits resulting from product-price combinations on segment *abc* were at the same level as product-price combinations on segment *ABCDE* of the iso-profit curve, it is quite possible that the regulated firm's decision makers might select a price combination on segment *abc*.

In contrast, if the rate of return on capital is limited by regulation, profit-maximizing regulated firms would not select price combinations on segment *abc*, because the higher prices imply lower levels of output and quantities of capital than price combinations on segment *ABCDE*. The absolute level of the firm's permitted profits will therefore be higher on *ABCDE* than on *abc* if profits per unit of capital are regulated. Even so, the assumption that the regulated firm's decision makers' objective is profit maximization is necessary to produce this conclusion; other objectives might lead the firm to operate on segment *abc* even under rate-of-return regulation.

(b) *Price combinations on segment CD.* These involve a lower price of product X and higher price of product Y than in the absence of regulation. Such price combinations are inferior, from the point of view of all consumers of either product, to price combinations on segment *BC*. At any price combination on segment *CD*, a lower price of product Y on segment *BC* at the same price of X will also meet the requirements of the regulatory constraint.

Under regulation that limits the absolute level of the firm's total profits, the firm is no worse off on segment *BC* than on segment *CD* because its absolute profits are the same in either situation. Under rate-of-return regulation, the lower price of Y on segment *BC* at any given level of P_X corresponding to a point on segment *CD* will imply the same level of output of X and a higher output level of Y. Since more capital will be required to produce the extra Y output, the absolute level of the firm's profits permitted by any given level of the rate of return will be higher, and a profit-maximizing firm will therefore also be better off on segment *BC* than on *CD*. Again, this conclusion depends on the assumption that the firm's decision makers wish to maximize profits, subject to the regulatory constraint.

(c) *Price combinations on segment AB.* These combinations involve a lower price of Y and higher price of X than in absence of regulation and are similar to those on segment *CD* in the sense that it is possible to find a price combination on segment *BC* that involves the same price of product Y and a lower price of product X. Again, this would make consumers of both products better off and would not make the regulated firm any worse off.

(d) *Price combinations on segment BC.* These involve lower prices of both products than in the absence of regulation and are superior from the point of view of consumers of the regulated firm's products to price combinations on any other segments of *ABCDE* and *abc*, as already explained. Baumol, Fischer, and Ten Raa (1979) have proved that a price vector that maximizes society's satisfaction when a regulated firm is subject to a profit constraint will normally lie on segment *BC*.

(e) *Price combinations on segment BB′.* These combinations involve lower prices of both products than in absence of regulation, but involve a cross-subsidy in the sense that buyers of product X are required to pay a higher price than they would pay if product Y were priced at $P_{Y\text{max}}$ and were eliminated entirely from the regulated firm's product mix. A price combination on segment *BC* that involves a price of product Y lower than P_{Y5} in Figure 9.1(c) therefore imposes a burden on consumers of product X. It should be remembered that consumers of product X may also consume product Y, however, and the preceding paragraph indicates that welfare-maximizing prices may occur at a price combination on BB' of segment BC.

Whereas rate-of-return regulation reduces the price of the product of a firm producing only one product, the preceding analysis shows that it may raise some product prices and lower others when applied to a multiproduct firm. One cannot therefore determine the full effects of regulation by reference to individual products of a multiproduct firm but must look at the effects on the prices of all products.

In order to know which segment of the iso-profit curve a particular combination of product prices charged by a regulated firm is located on, it is obviously necessary to know the slope of the iso-profit curve through that price combination. Among other things, this information would enable one to determine whether a different combination of product prices that meets the existing regulatory constraint would be superior to the existing price combination. We have already shown that price combinations on the abc, CD, and AB segments are in general inferior to price combinations on segment BC. In addition, the issue of whether existing product prices under regulation involve cross-subsidy requires knowledge, not only of the slope of the iso-profit curve, but also of the product-price combinations on segment BB' of the iso-profit curve that involve cross-subsidy.

Since the iso-profit curve was derived from the demand, marginal revenue (MR), and marginal cost (MC) curves in Figure 9.1, it is obvious that positions and shapes of these curves determine the slope of the iso-profit curve at any particular combination of product prices compatible with a particular level of regulated profits. The position and shape of the demand and marginal revenue curves for the firm's products depend on the price- and cross-elasticities of demand between the firm's products and other firms' products. Rivals' reactions to changes in the price of the firm's products as well as buyer reactions underlie these elasticities. The position and slope of the marginal cost curves for the firm's products depend, similarly, on the elasticities and cross-elasticities of supply of the firm's products.

The costs of gathering information regarding these demand and supply elasticities — to determine the impact of regulation on firms' pricing behavior and to assist in formulating appropriate regulatory constraints — represent an additional constraint that is frequently ignored in discussions of regulation. One noted economist, Ralph Turvey (1969), who has spent a good portion of his career attempting to devise and implement rational pricing systems in the public utility sector, has gone so far as to suggest that when these information and implementation costs are taken into account, regulation that requires firms to set prices equal to marginal costs may still be optimal even in second-best situations.

This view is probably too extreme, however. The same logic could be used to suggest, for example, that where difficulties exist in determining a firm's marginal cost, pricing at average cost, or some other more easily obtainable measure, is appropriate. The correct principle, in deciding whether or not to attempt to apply pricing principles designed to serve any objective, such as allocative efficiency, is whether the cost in terms of the necessary information-gathering and implementation techniques is greater or less than the potential gain in the level of the community's satisfaction that results from the application of particular pricing rules. In the present context, the important point is that none of these issues can be settled without evidence concerning economic performance under alternative pricing systems. This requires practical experimentation to determine the consequences of alternative pricing rules for regulatory policy.

9.3 EFFECTS OF REGULATION ON NONPRICE DIMENSIONS OF FIRMS' BEHAVIOR

Economic analysis of the effects of regulation on firms' behavior has traditionally focused on firms' production and pricing policies. Even where firms' pricing policies are the target of regulation, regulatory constraints will also generally affect the level of other dimensions of firms' behavior, such as the level of advertising expenditures or quality dimensions of output, such as durability. These effects on nonprice aspects of firms' behavior must be taken into account, for at least two important reasons.

First, changes in other dimensions of the regulated firm's behavior may affect the demand and cost conditions facing the firm. If the demand and cost curves that underlie the conclusions of traditional economic analysis are affected by changes in nonprice dimensions of the firm's behavior, this change will generally alter the traditional conclusions regarding the impact of any particular regulatory constraint on the firm's pricing and output behavior.

Second, since people's satisfaction will generally depend not only on the price of regulated firm's products but also on nonprice dimensions of the firm's behavior, the effect of regulation on nonprice aspects of the regulated firm's behavior must be included to determine the overall effect of regulation on people's satisfaction. Finally, the manner in which nonprice dimensions of the firm's behavior are affected by various types of regulatory constraint will determine the type of regulatory constraints necessary to achieve any desired pattern of nonprice behavior on the part of the firm.

Most economics textbook presentations of the determinants of firms' behavior neglect nonprice dimensions of their behavior, and the economics journal literature is characterized by innumerable methodologies and conclusions, many of which are contradictory. This is not surprising, since different models of the determinants of any aspect of decision makers' behavior will produce different conclusions, and there is no way to determine which model is "best" without adopting someone's value judgments regarding the nature of the relationships that should be included in the model.

There are three possible relationships between the level of any non-price dimension of the firm's behavior that affects the firm's total revenues and total costs and the profit-maximizing relationship between the price and marginal cost of the firm's product. These are depicted in Figure 9.2, where the nonprice dimension of behavior is represented by the ratio

Figure 9.2

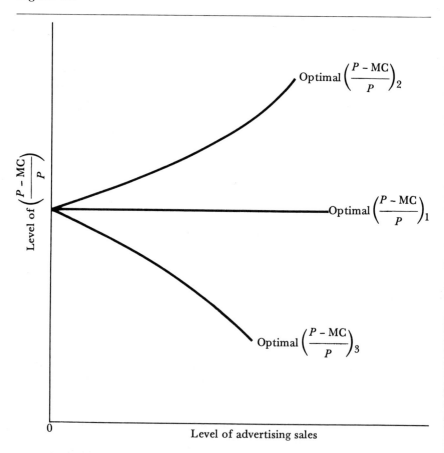

of the firm's advertising expenditures to sales revenue. Any other dimension of the firm's behavior that affects its total revenue and/or total costs could have been selected without changing the subsequent conclusions. (The reasoning that underlies the shape of these curves is presented in Chapter 11.)

Regulatory constraints that affect the marginal revenue or marginal cost of a firm's output will change the optimal level of the firm's output and pricing behavior. This change will be reflected by a shift in the position of the curves in Figure 9.2. The direction in which the curves in Figure 9.2 are shifted depends on the direction in which regulatory constraints change marginal revenue and marginal cost of output.

Under conventional rate-of-return-on-capital regulation, which reduces the effective marginal capital cost of the firm's output as explained in Section 9.2, the profit-maximizing price of the firm's product *at any level of advertising* is reduced, and the curves in Figure 9.2 shift down toward the advertising axis of the diagram. The italicized phrase is extremely important because it emphasizes that the conventional reasoning regarding the effects of rate-of-return regulation on the regulated firm's pricing behavior implicitly assumes that the level of the firm's nonprice decision variables, such as advertising, remains unchanged. Changes in nonprice decision variables would imply shifts in the demand and cost curves in the traditional diagrammatic expositions of the effects of regulation on firms' pricing behavior.

Levels of nonprice decision variables will not generally remain unchanged when regulation affects a firm's pricing behavior, however. This can be seen immediately from the profit-maximizing condition for advertising expenditures, which is[1]

$$\frac{\text{Total advertising expenditures}}{\text{Total sales revenue}} = \frac{(P - MC)}{P} E_a$$

where E_a is the "advertising elasticity of demand," defined as the percentage change in the quantity of a firm's product demanded in response to any given percentage change in the level of the firm's advertising

---

[1] Equating the increase in total revenue from an increase in advertising to the increase in the firm's total costs resulting from the increase in advertising implies

$$P \cdot \Delta Q = \Delta A + MC_Q \Delta Q \quad \text{or} \quad 1 = (P - MC_Q)\frac{\Delta Q}{\Delta A} \frac{\Delta Q}{\Delta A}$$

where ΔQ is the increase in the quantity of the firm's product demanded owing to the increase in advertising ΔA, and MC_Q is the marginal cost of producing one extra unit of output demanded. Multiplying both sides of the expression by A/PQ, the ratio of total advertising to total sales revenue yields

$$\frac{A}{S} = \frac{(P - MC)}{P} \cdot \left(\frac{\Delta Q}{\Delta A} \cdot \frac{A}{Q}\right) \quad \text{and} \quad \frac{\Delta Q}{\Delta A} \cdot \frac{A}{Q} = E_a$$

expenditures. Clearly, if regulation affects $(P - MC)/P$, it will generally affect the profit-maximizing level of the firm's advertising. To understand the resulting implications of regulation for advertising and product pricing, it is necessary to analyze nonprice dimensions of the firm's behavior and then to combine the results of analyzing the separate dimensions of the firm's behavior.

Figure 9.3 depicts the three alternative relationships that may exist between the optimal ratio of a firm's advertising sales and different levels of $(P - MC)/P$. (The reasoning that underlies the shape of these curves is presented in Chapter 11.)

The situation depicted by the curve labeled Optimal $(A/S)_1$ in Figure 9.3 has received much attention in the literature in connection with a firm's choice of the durability of its product, and the effects of

Figure 9.3

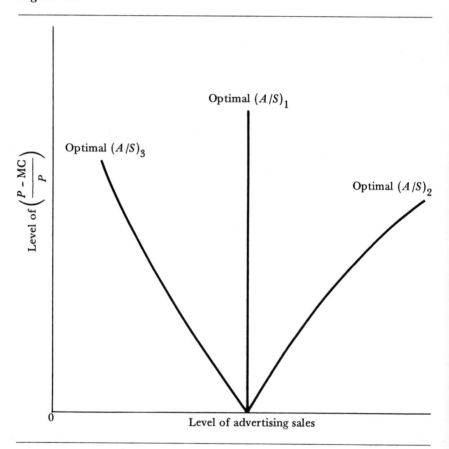

regulation on durability decisions. The interested reader is referred to Schmalensee (1970) for an excellent exposition of the durability issue, and the assumptions that are required to produce the conclusion, sometimes referred to as "the Swan result" (Swan 1971), that a firm's pricing behavior has no effect on a firm's choice of product durability. In terms of our diagrammatic analysis, the essential feature of any model of durability that is necessary to produce the Swan "durability-is-independent-of-pricing" result is that different levels of product price do not affect the marginal revenue or marginal cost of a change in durability.

To determine the effect of regulatory constraints that influence a firm's pricing behavior on the level of its nonprice decision variables, it is necessary to combine the curves in Figure 9.2 with those in Figure 9.3. This is illustrated in Figure 9.4, which depicts the situation where regulation of a firm's pricing behavior reduces the level of the regulated firm's optimal product price $(P - MC)/P$, at any level of the firm's nonprice behavior, such as the ratio of advertising expenditures to sales.

Only one of the three optimal pricing curves in Figure 9.2 will apply to any particular firm, but irrespective of which pricing curve is applicable, the only situation in which price regulation does not change the firm's nonprice behavior is depicted by Figure 9.4(a). This is the Swan result, generalized to any nonprice dimension of the firm's behavior.

If the optimal level of a dimension of nonprice behavior (A/S) falls with reductions in the level of $(P - MC)/P$, as depicted by Figure 9.4(b), regulation that reduces the level of the firm's product price at any level of nonprice behavior will *also* reduce the optimal level of the firm's nonprice behavior.

If the optimal level of a dimension of nonprice behavior rises with reductions in the level of $(P - MC)/P$, two very different situations are possible, as depicted by Figure 9.4(c) and (d). In Figure 9.4(c), the absolute slope of the curve depicting the optimal ratio of advertising to sales (or any other nonprice dimension of the firm's behavior) at different levels of the firm's $(P - MC)/P$ is greater than the absolute slope of the optimal pricing curves. Price regulation that reduces the level of $(P - MC)/P$ at any level of the firm's advertising will in this case also *increase* the optimal level of the firm's nonprice behavior.

In contrast, in Figure 9.4(d), the slope of the optimal advertising curve is less than the slope of the optimal pricing curve labeled Optimal $(P - MC/P)_3$ in absolute magnitude. In this case, regulation that reduces the level of $(P - MC)/P$ at any level of advertising *reduces* the optimal level of the firm's advertising. More startling is the fact that such regulation *increases* the equilibrium optimal level of the firm's $(P - MC)/P!$ The optimal combination of pricing and advertising policies in this case changes from point a to point e.

Figure 9.4 illustrates the dangers of analyzing effects of price regulation on firms' product-pricing policies that ignore the effect of price regulation on nonprice dimensions of firms' behavior. They also emphasize

Figure 9.4

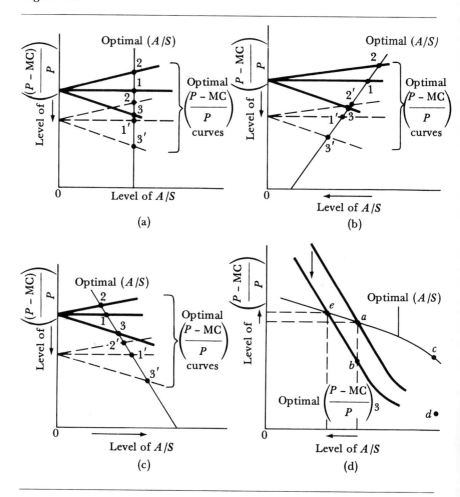

(a)

(b)

(c)

(d)

that product-pricing and nonprice dimensions of regulated firms' behavior are interrelated. The traditional analysis of regulation's effects on pricing behavior is equivalent to determining the direction of the shift of the optimal pricing curve in response to regulation. The direction of this shift will not necessarily correspond to the direction in which the firm's equilibrium pricing behavior is changed by regulation, as Figure 9.4(d) illustrates.

Even in situations in which equilibrium price levels do change in the direction intended by regulators, the magnitude of the change in product prices will depend on the slope of the optimal advertising curves and similar curves that apply to other nonprice dimensions of the regulated firm's behavior. Since the slope of these curves is determined by the factors that determine the optimal levels of nonprice dimensions of the firm's behavior, few reliable conclusions regarding the effects of regulation on pricing policies will be possible without simultaneous determination of whether optimal levels of nonprice dimensions of the firm's behavior increase, decrease, or remain unchanged when the level of the firm's product prices is changed.

This diagrammatic analysis involved product pricing and only one nonprice dimension of the firm's behavior. A similar analysis can be applied to each nonprice dimension of the firm's behavior, so that it is quite possible for regulation to increase some nonprice dimensions of a regulated firm's behavior while simultaneously decreasing others and leaving some unchanged.

If regulation is applied directly to nonprice dimensions of the firm's behavior instead of to product pricing, a similar analysis applies. The only difference is that the curve depicting optimal levels of the regulated nonprice dimension of the firm's behavior will be shifted instead of the optimal product-price curve. In this case, regulation of nonprice dimensions of the firm's behavior will imply changes in the level of the firm's product prices, except in the case where the optimal product-price curve in Figure 9.2 is horizontal.

Again, the direction of the shift in the optimal nonprice behavior curve will not necessarily be the same as the direction of the change in the equilibrium level of the firm's regulated nonprice dimension of behavior, depending on the relative slopes of the optimal product-pricing and optimal nonprice behavior curves.

There is one final complication that has not yet been considered. In the preceding analysis it was assumed that a regulatory constraint affected only the position of either the optimal product-pricing curve or one of the optimal nonprice behavior dimension curves. It is also possible that the same regulatory constraint may simultaneously affect the position of *two* or more of these curves. The resulting implications for the equilibrium levels of the firm's product prices, advertising, and other dimensions of behavior are clearly more complex in this situation. However, it is clear that these effects will always depend on the following factors: (1) the direction and magnitude of the shifts in the curves in Figure 9.4 and (2) the relative slopes of the curves in Figure 9.4.

The major implication of situations in which regulatory constraints simultaneously affect the position of more than one optimal behavior curve is to strengthen the need for considering nonprice and pricing dimensions of the regulated firm's behavior simultaneously in analyses of the effect of regulation on the regulated firm's behavior. In Chapter 11 we shall return to consider the implications of interdependence between different dimensions of regulated firms' behavior for equilibrium behavior of regulated firms and regulators.

There is one very important aspect of the impact of rate-of-return regulation on nonprice dimensions of regulated firms' behavior that has been entirely overlooked in the literature. There is a direct analogy between the analysis of the effects of rate-of-return regulation on product prices in a multiproduct firm and its effects on nonprice dimensions of firms' behavior. A regulatory limitation on the permitted profits, or rate of return, that a firm is allowed to earn is compatible with many combinations of prices of different products, depicted by the iso-profit curve in Figure 9.1. *Similarly, a profit constraint is compatible with many combinations of pricing and nonprice dimensions of regulated firms' behavior,* which can be depicted by an iso-profit curve relating the price of a single product and a dimension of nonprice behavior of the firm, or two dimensions of the firm's nonpricing behavior.

Even in the case of a firm producing a single product, there are many different combinations of the firm's product-price and nonprice dimensions of behavior that are compatible with a particular level of the allowed profit rate. The traditional conclusion, that product prices will be lower, is no longer the only possible outcome; the regulated firm may select a level of advertising and associated profit-maximizing level of product prices that raises the price of the firm's product compared with the unregulated situation. Moreover, without normative criteria of socially optimal advertising behavior, it is not possible to compare these possible price and advertising outcomes of regulation, or to conclude that higher product prices imply on balance a reduction in society's satisfaction as a result of regulation!

9.4   WEAKNESSES IN EXISTING MODELS OF PUBLIC UTILITY REGULATION

Several weaknesses in existing models of public utility regulation were noted in the two preceding sections and in Chapter 8, Section 8.4. This section will briefly list some additional major weaknesses of models of public utility regulation and regulation in general and will indicate chapters that explain how these problems can be solved and the major implications for models of regulation.

Neglected Effects of Regulation on Firms' Environment. Most existing analyses of the effects of regulation on the behavior of regulated decision makers assume that the regulatory constraint does not affect the form of any of the other constraints that determine the regulated decision maker's behavior. This assumption is obviously implicit in all diagrammatic expositions of the effect on a firm's behavior that assume that the position of the firm's demand and cost curves are not affected by the regulatory constraint.

This model of the manner in which regulation affects regulated decision makers' behavior is too restrictive, since *regulatory constraints will also shift the position of the demand and/or cost curves facing the regulated firm whenever regulation affects any of the other constraints that underlie these curves.* The effects of regulation on the regulated firm will then depend on the manner in which these other constraints are affected, and the implications of regulation for the firm's behavior may be qualitatively as well as quantitatively different from those predicted by analyses that omit the effects of regulation on these other constraints.

Although there are many ways in which regulation may affect other constraints facing the regulated decision maker, a prime example is the effect of regulation on the behavior of a regulated decision maker's rivals. If regulatory constraints apply to a firm's rivals, their behavior will generally be changed by regulation, which will imply changes in the demand and/or cost curves facing individual regulated firms.

Chapter 12, Section 12.3, will examine in more detail the implications of regulatory constraints that affect other constraints facing regulated decision makers. It should be noted that it is necessary to consider the implications of regulatory constraints for a firm's rivals' behavior even in situations where only one firm is serving a particular market. The reason is that potential rivals' behavior is an important constraint that may influence the behavior of the "monopolist" serving the market. The theory of rivalry among firms established in a market and potential rivals who may enter the market is simply a special case of the general theory of competition that was developed in Chapter 6. Chapter 14, Section 3, will develop this special case, and the associated theory of entry barriers, in more detail.

Interrelationships among Dimensions of Regulators' Behavior. Section 9.3 emphasized that different dimensions of a regulated decision maker's behavior are related. The existing literature dealing with regulators' behavior does not adequately recognize that regulators' behavior is also multidimensional and does not examine the nature of the interdependence that exists between different dimensions of regulators' behavior. This is unfortunate, because the probability that any particular regulatory constraint will be applied to regulated decision makers depends jointly on the level of different dimensions of regulators' behavior.

In Chapter 4, Section 4.3, and Chapter 6, Section 6.4, it was explained that the probability that the penalties or rewards associated with a particular regulatory constraint will be applied to a regulated firm or decision maker depends jointly on the levels of monitoring and enforcement activities of regulators. Conclusions concerning the effect of changes in the level of individual dimensions of regulators' behavior on the level of this probability, and therefore the effects of the regulatory constraint on regulated decision makers' behavior, will be unreliable unless any interdependence that exists between dimensions of regulators' behavior is taken into account. The same methodological and diagrammatic approach that was used to explain the interdependence between different dimensions of firms' behavior in Section 9.3 can be applied to deal with this problem.

Interactions Between Regulators and Regulated Firms. It is obvious that the regulators' behavior will generally be based on the regulators' expectations of how regulated firms or other decision makers react to their behavior. With a few exceptions, however, such as the paper by Wendel (1976) on interactions between a regulated firm's cost reduction activities and regulation, existing models of regulation neglect the possibility that the behavior of regulated firms and regulators may be interdependent in the sense that the behavior of a regulated firm may be based on the firm's expectations regarding the reactions of regulators to the firm's behavior.

Another type of interdependent behavior that is almost totally neglected in the regulation literature is the possibility that the behavior of different regulatory agencies may also be interdependent. This interdependence may exist whether or not individual agencies recognize and take into account the fact that the response of regulated decision makers to any single agency's actions will depend on other regulatory agencies' actions and on the nature of all the regulatory constraints that simultaneously confront regulated firms or other types of decision maker. The implications of interdependence between regulated firms' and regulators' behavior and between different regulatory agencies' behavior are explained in Chapter 11 and Chapter 12, Section 12.3.

Incentives to Misrepresent Information. Until the early 1970s, the literature of economics merely acknowledged the lack of incentives for individual decision makers to reveal truthful information regarding their own behavior or evaluations of outputs or other outcomes of other people's behavior. Despite considerable progress since that time in developing incentive systems that motivate individuals to reveal information honestly, these developments have barely reached the mainstream literature on regulation. Since regulators will generally have to rely on regulated firms for much of the information regarding these firms' costs and other dimensions of behavior, providing incentives for firms to provide truthful information should obviously be part of the task of devising regulatory constraints.

Chapter 12, Section 12.2, explains the essential characteristics of incentive systems that motivate honest revelation of information by regulated firms. The problem of motivating individuals to supply information honestly is not confined to regulated firms, however. Since the criteria of optimal regulation involve people's evaluation of the benefits or costs of regulated firms' behavior, as well as the resource costs of firms' activities, incentives for honest revelation of information on the "demand" side of the regulatory process are also required. In addition, regulators themselves must be motivated to reveal information regarding their activities honestly. These problems, and their solution, are examined in Chapter 13.

Normative Goals of Regulation. The features of regulation that are inadequately dealt with in the existing literature must be considered irrespective of the normative criteria used to justify and evaluate regulation. In addition, there are some unresolved problems connected with the normative criteria that underlie existing analyses of regulation. Concepts of "optimal" regulation necessarily imply the adoption of someone's evaluations of the benefits and costs of the effects of regulated decision makers' and regulators' behavior (explained in Chapter 3).

The fact that the justification for any regulation, and its precise characteristics, can never be value free is increasingly well understood by economists and other parties to the regulatory process. Less well recognized is the fact that the "demand" and "cost" evaluations that are adopted as the basis of normative analyses of regulation imply acceptance of much more than the choice of whose evaluations should be used or factors such as the existing distribution of income among members of society.

Even if incentives exist for motivating these individuals to reveal their evaluations honestly, such evaluations are necessarily based on the amount of information and on the information-processing abilities possessed by the people whose evaluations are considered appropriate measures of the benefits and costs of regulated decision makers' and regulators' behavior. More important is the fact that this information, and these abilities, will necessarily be influenced by regulated decision makers' and regulators' behavior. Both types of decision maker generally provide information to the people whose evaluations are used as the basis for judging their behavior. Even if incentive systems existed that motivated these decision makers to reveal truthful information, the evaluations of their behavior that form the normative standards for evaluating that behavior cannot possibly be independent of the regulatory process itself!

In short, the conventional view of regulation that it is a means of attempting to implement certain normative criteria of people's behavior that are established independently of the regulatory process is a myth. Regulation and any normative criteria for judging regulation are interdependent and jointly determined by the complex interrelationships between people's behavior and their perceived environment. As emphasized at greater length in Chapter 15, Section 15.2, regulation should be viewed as one of the many instruments people use to attempt to attain their changing personal goals and targets in an uncertain and changing environment, rather than a means of attempting to achieve static criteria of perfect performance according to a fixed normative criterion of economic and political performance.

Regulating Individual Dimensions of Business Behavior: the "New Wave" of Regulations

10.1 THE RISING TIDE OF REGULATION IN THE UNITED STATES

The United States has experienced a massive increase in the number and scope of government regulations and regulatory agencies. The largest increase in regulation occurred in the late 1960s and the 1970s.

Previous forms of regulation focused primarily on issues connected with monopoly and competition in individual industries, as explained earlier. In contrast, much of the "new regulation" is concerned with issues of health and safety, consumer and worker protection, and various types of environmental pollution. The new regulations generally apply to all industries, though their impact on different industries varies with differences between industries' production technologies and marketing practices. More important, each of the newer forms of regulation focuses on individual characteristics of business firms and other, nonbusiness organizations, without regard to effects on other aspects of the firms' operations or profitability. The Environmental Protection Agency, for example, is explicitly forbidden by law to take account of the costs of establishing and enforcing air quality standards.

Three major questions are of interest in attempting to understand the newer forms of regulation: (1) What are the factors that led to demands for, and passage of, these regulations? (2) What are the effects of the new forms of regulation on regulated firms, organizations, and other types of decision maker? (3) What are the benefits and costs, and the resulting evaluations, of the preceding effects of the new regulations on individuals and society as a whole? Possible answers to question (1) will be examined in the remainder of this section; Sections 10.1(b) and (c) will deal, respectively, with questions (2) and (3). In each section, emphasis will be placed on providing the reader with a comprehensive framework for integrating the different factors involved and on factors that are generally omitted, or that are insufficiently taken into account, in the existing literature on regulation.

As was indicated in Chapter 2, a variety of different authors have advanced various theories to explain why government regulation of the behavior of individuals and businesses and other organizations is demanded and supplied. Most of these theories can be viewed as different versions of a more general "interest-group" theory of demands for regulation, each emphasizing the way certain types of regulation may further the interests of particular groups (e.g., producers, consumers, particular social classes). Although these theories of the factors that underlie demands for regulation are often quite compatible, focusing on individual theories tends to obscure a number of features of the real-world behavior of individuals and interest groups that underlie demands for regulation and the process of revealing these demands to legislators and regulators who are in a position to supply regulation.

Some of these factors were noted in Chapter 2, Section 2.2. For example, individuals simultaneously act in a number of roles as producers, consumers, taxpayers, and members of a particular social class. A person's evaluation of particular types of regulation depends on the net impact of the regulations on all these roles and will rarely be correlated in any simple way with any single role or interest group. Another important characteristic of demands for regulation is that they may be revealed in a number of ways. Votes, campaign contributions, direct lobbying, and numerous more subtle means may be used by individuals in attempting to influence the incentive systems that confront and motivate legislators, regulators, and other decision makers whose behavior determines the type of regulation that will be supplied in response to demands for regulation.

It was also noted that suppliers of regulation, such as legislators and regulators, are themselves an interest group whose behavior also influences the demand for regulation. Demands for regulation by different interest groups may be interdependent and influenced by many sources of information, including other interest groups and suppliers of regulation themselves. In these circumstances, economists' conventional practice of assuming "given" demands for regulation and ignoring the process by which demands for regulation are generated, and analyses that assume that the behavior of decision makers on the demand and supply sides of regulatory issues is independent, are inappropriate.

Explaining the factors that underlie demands for particular types of regulation is *not* the same thing as explaining why the total demand and supply of regulation has suddenly grown in the manner experienced recently in the United States and some other countries, even though the factors that underlie demands for regulation and reasons for the growth of these demands may be related. To understand possible reasons for the growth of regulation, it is helpful to examine a number of additional aspects of the process underlying demands for regulation that are shared by all theories of regulation. These factors are issue creation, group-demand formation, interdependence, and disequilibrium aspects of demands for regulation.

(a) Issue Creation

The first important factor that needs to be recognized is that "demands for regulation" are really demands for certain effects of regulation, such as safer products and working conditions or a less polluted environment. Second, demands for regulation are demands for a remedy to some issue or problem that is perceived to exist and that generally takes the form of a discrepancy between people's perceptions of the existing state of some aspect of their general living and working environment and a desired or expected state of that environment.

The mere perception of any problem does *not* itself necessarily indicate which of the possible methods of dealing with the problem should be adopted. In particular, it does not necessarily imply that government regulation should be adopted, as opposed to private sector or market-oriented solutions to the problem.

For some issues, there may be a more or less random event, or "triggering effect," that makes people aware of a specific problem. The regulation literature frequently cites events such as the publication of Rachel Carson's *Silent Spring* and Ralph Nader's *Unsafe at Any Speed* as examples of triggering effects that brought the issues of environmental pollution and automobile safety, respectively, to widespread public attention. The thalidomide tragedy that resulted in the birth of limbless infants is another frequently cited event leading to demands for greater drug screening and safety.

Numerous other examples could be cited of spontaneous events that increased people's awareness of problems and that led to support for increased government regulation of certain activities. It was, however, stressed early in this book that the appropriate solution to any problem depends in large measure on how the problem is defined and that control of the problem formulation stage in any issue therefore conveys considerable control over the nature of the solution that appears to be appropriate. There is a tremendous advantage to any person or group of persons who can monopolize the problem formulation stage in dealing with any issue, since they can thereby obtain the solution they prefer, while appealing to "objectivity" for a justification of that particular solution. Considerable competition among various sides in any issue for control of the problem formulation stage occurs in practice, and problem formulation, rather than problem solving, is the really critical stage that determines how issues are solved.

These points should be kept in mind in considering the process by which demands for regulation are generated. Competing interest groups, including suppliers of regulation, will generally try to influence people's perceptions of any given issue or problem by providing information designed to influence either people's perceptions of the manner in which their welfare is affected by certain aspects of their environment or people's expectations concerning the kind of environment that is desirable. Information from different sources will generally conflict, and the parties providing the information may misrepresent information in such a way that supports their respective positions. Issues connected with nuclear electricity generation, automobile safety, working conditions in asbestos-processing plants, and United States military forces exposed to nuclear radiation are examples of recent issues exhibiting these characteristics.

In addition to providing information that creates issues and problems, interest groups will rarely be indifferent to alternative methods of dealing with particular issues and problems. For example, Enthoven (1980) has documented the very different responses of organized labor, business, the medical profession, hospitals, and the health insurance industry to proposals for universal and comprehensive national health insurance put forward by the Carter administration in 1979. Individuals and groups with more power over private market transactions are likely to formulate issues in a manner that favors private sector solutions. Other groups with more power over political and other nonmarket types of transaction will formulate issues in a manner that favors public sector methods of dealing with issues.

Within the preceding framework of issue creation, several forces may individually or jointly produce an increase in demands for regulation. (1) Increased perceptions of some aspect of people's environment and its effect on their welfare. This in turn may be caused by a variety of factors, such as education, TV and other media, or random occurrences of events that draw widespread attention. (2) Increased expectations of individuals concerning the desired state of certain aspects of their living and working environments. (3) Increased competitive success of individuals and interest groups whose problem formulations favor public sector solutions.

(b) Group-Demand Formation

A second important stage in the process underlying demands for regulation is the mechanism by which the preferences of different individuals are converted into collective, or group demands, for regulation. This stage, which occurs before the group demands are transmitted to legislators and regulators via voting, lobbying, and other demand-revealing methods, has received little attention in the regulation literature. Group-demand formation can usefully be viewed as an additional decision process that transforms different people's perceptions of an issue or problem and their preferred methods of solving the problem into a group demand for a specific solution to the problem.

Recent research in the field of group decision making has clearly emphasized that the outcome of any group decision mechanism will depend on a number of different but related characteristics of the process of group-demand formation. For example, any group decision mechanism necessarily involves an *agenda* that defines what is to be decided; the order in which decisions are to be made; and the method that is to be used by members of the group to decide issues, such as unanimity, majority vote, minimum proportion of total votes cast, and so on. Since the agenda effectively defines the range of alternative outcomes individual members of the group can choose between at any point in the decision process, it influences the voting pattern of each individual in the group and the eventual choice made by the group (Plott and Levine, 1978).

Different agendas will generally result in different choices made by the same group of individuals, so that control of the agenda-setting stage of any group decision mechanism therefore conveys important power over the outcome of group decisions (Romer and Rosenthal, 1978, 1979). Control of agenda setting is analogous to control of problem formulation in the sense that it conveys control over the eventual outcome of the decision process.

Experimental studies (Fiorina and Plott, 1978) have also demonstrated that the *magnitude of rewards or penalties* that confronts individuals will influence the outcome of a group decision process. As the general analysis of competition in Chapter 7 indicated, the behavior of individual members of any group decision process will also be affected by their *expectations regarding the reactions and behavior of other members of the group* as well as by the reactions and behavior of non-members. Coalitions or agreements among group members may occur because of fear of competition from members of other groups rather than because of a desire for cooperation between individual members of the group (Shibata, 1979). As a final example, the outcome of any group decision process will be influenced by the manner in which power to influence the outcome is distributed between members and coalitions within the group. This power is not necessarily proportional to the number of votes controlled by the individuals and coalitions within the group (Fischer and Schotter, 1978).

All the preceding factors are important in influencing the nature of group demands for regulation or other types of solution to problems that are perceived to exist by group members. The same types of consideration also apply to group decision making on the supply side of the regulatory process, such as decisions made by groups of legislators or regulators. (The behavior of these types of decision maker is dealt with in Chapter 5.)

In the present context, what is important is that some of these features of group decision making that underlie demands for regulation may also be relevant in explaining growth of such demands. For example, the expectation of increased involvement of interest groups in activities that lead to demands for regulation that have an adverse impact on other interest groups' welfare may lead members of the latter groups to increase the level of their demands for regulation to protect their interests.

(c) Demands for Regulating Different Types of Business Behavior

Government regulation of business can be viewed as one possible means of attempting to reduce discrepancies between the perceived existing state of some dimension or effects of business behavior and the state, or effects, of business behavior that are desired by certain members of society. Sections 10.1(a) and (b) dealt, respectively, with the process by which these perceptions and desires are initially created and with the process by which they are transformed into interest-group demands for regulation. Although a number of aspects of these processes are capable of generating growing demands for regulating any single aspect of business behavior, interdependence between demands for regulating different aspects of business behavior is most likely to be responsible for growth in the scope of business regulation over time.

Demands for regulating different dimensions of business behavior will generally be related, owing to the interdependencies that exist between different dimensions of business behavior and between the behavior of different types of decision maker, including unregulated firms and regulators as well as regulated firms. These interdependencies take a number of different but related forms (explained more fully in Chapter 11). For example, regulations that affect one dimension of firms' behavior may cause changes in other dimensions of the same firms' behavior that reduce or completely frustrate attainment of the desired effects of regulations. This could occur in a situation in which regulators attempt to regulate the maximum price of a product (or service) if the regulated firm responded by reducing the amount of any of the inputs used to produce the product. The product that is sold at the maximum regulated price will not be of the same quality, and the regulated price of the product, per unit of quality, may be even higher than without regulation. To control the price of a given quality of the product, regulators would need to be able to regulate the amount and quality of all the inputs used to produce the product.

McKie (1960) has christened attempts to extend the scope of regulatory control to capture escaping effects of earlier regulations the "tar-baby effect." Demands for increased scope of regulation due to the tar-baby effect may originate on the supply side as well as on the demand side of the regulatory process. They can occur even if suppliers of regulation do not demand regulations intended to serve their own personal interests but merely attempt to carry out their mandate to enforce regulations demanded by other interest groups in society.

The behavior of regulators themselves will also often be responsible for the failure of attempts to regulate individual characteristics of business behavior, for the following reasons. In the United States, different regulatory agencies are responsible for regulating different dimensions of business behavior. The regulations administered by one agency not only will influence the dimension of a firm's behavior for which the agency is responsible but will also often have effects on dimensions of the firm's behavior that are regulated by other agencies. For example, if regulations designed to protect workers require outside venting of fumes or other substances, this will tend to increase the amount of pollution generated by the firm. The regulatory agency responsible for pollution control may react by changing its regulatory practices in an effort to maintain pollution by the firm within their regulatory standards. This, in turn, will cause changes in the dimension of the firm's behavior that is regulated by the first agency which is responsible for worker health and safety, and these changes may reinforce or offset that agency's efforts. As will be explained in Chapter 11, this process of interaction between the policies of different regulatory agencies can lead to a process of escalating regulation by each agency, which may or may not lead to an equilibrium situation in which each agency is able to achieve its desired effects on the dimension of the firm's behavior for which it is responsible.

The same interdependence between different dimensions of regulated firms' behavior may also stimulate increased demands for regulation on the part of interest groups affected by various unregulated aspects of regulated firms' behavior. If these aspects of firms' behavior are initially at levels desired by individuals and interest groups whose welfare they affect, it follows that any changes in regulated dimensions of firms' behavior that also cause changes in unregulated dimensions of the firms' behavior will produce a discrepancy between the desired and actual levels of unregulated dimensions of firms' behavior. This development may lead to demands for regulation of previously unregulated dimensions of firms' behavior by the interest groups affected by regulation-induced changes in those dimensions of firms' behavior.

The limited resources of regulated firms may result in a situation in which increased use of inputs to expand one dimension of firms' behavior in response to one type of regulation automatically requires a reduction in inputs devoted to other dimensions of firms' behavior. Demands for regulation of different dimensions of firms' operations may therefore result in a process of escalating regulation supported by different interest groups, owing to a failure of earlier regulations to produce the desired effect on the dimension of regulated firms' behavior that is of concern to each interest group. Theories of regulation that assume a monolithic consumer or other interest group overlook these intergroup aspects of the forces underlying demands for regulation.

Interest groups whose welfare will be strongly affected indirectly by effects of regulation of other dimensions of firms' behavior that do not directly concern them will need to be constantly alert and be able to organize to oppose demands for regulating other dimensions of firms' behavior. It may be much less costly for such an interest group to demand creation of a regulatory agency that would in effect act as its agent and perform the function of administering regulations aimed at preserving the dimension of firms' behavior that are of concern to that interest group.

(d) Equilibrium versus Disequilibrium
   Aspects of Demands

In addition to demands for certain *objectives or targets of regulation,* a second, very different type of demand for regulation is also extremely important in determining the disequilibrium behavior of regulators and of regulated and unregulated decision makers. This type of demand is connected with the *instruments* regulators use in their efforts to achieve the objectives or targets of regulation. Regulatory instruments are factors such as types and levels of penalties and rewards and the monitoring and enforcement activities that regulators employ in an effort to influence regulated firms' behavior in the direction of regulatory targets.

The nature of regulatory instruments and the way they are changed when targets are not being achieved influences the disequilibrium time path of regulators' and regulated firms' behavior. Regulatory instruments are just as important as regulatory targets in determining whether or not those targets will be achieved. Moreover, even if targets can be achieved simultaneously, the use of different regulatory instruments will often result in a different disequilibrium path of behavior of regulators' and regulated firms' behavior and in different effects on regulated and unregulated decision makers' welfare.

Although considerable latitude is sometimes given to regulators regarding which instruments they use to try to achieve particular targets, interest groups that demand regulation will rarely be indifferent to the type of instruments regulators employ. Interest groups will generally demand certain types of regulatory instruments and oppose the use of other types, on the basis of the different disequilibrium implications of different regulatory instruments. This aspect of demands for regulation has received very little recognition in the literature on regulation (Buchanan and Tullock, 1975, 1976; Main and Baird, 1976; Yohe, 1976).

The relative neglect of the rationale underlying demands for particular instruments of regulation, as opposed to demands for certain objectives or targets of regulation, in the regulation literature is unfortunate. Instead of opposing demands for regulation aimed at achieving particular targets, opponents might adopt the strategy of demanding regulatory instruments that are likely to result in a failure of the regulatory process to achieve its intended targets!

Growth of demands for regulation can be caused by any number of the factors discussed throughout this section. In view of all the possible explanations, it would be hazardous to speculate on the forces that actually resulted in the upsurge of regulation in the United States since the late 1960s. The only conclusion that appears to be warranted is that any omission of the four major factors discussed in this section from models of the process that generates demands for regulation ignores potentially important features of that process.

10.2 REASONS FOR REGULATING INDIVIDUAL DIMENSIONS OF BUSINESS BEHAVIOR: A GENERALIZED TRANSACTIONS FRAMEWORK

The present section will examine the reasons that underlie demands for regulating dimensions of business behavior. In the United States, in addition to regulations aimed at influencing the rate of return on capital invested in public utility industries, many other features of business behavior are regulated. Regulated aspects of business behavior, and some of the industries in which these regulations apply, include product prices (oil, natural gas, and milk); product costs (hospitals); product quality dimensions such as safety (drugs, automobiles); product information and labeling (food, cigarettes); and production methods, worker safety conditions, and advertising policies in all industries regulated by agencies such as the Environmental Protection Agency (EPA), the Occupational Safety and Health Administration (OSHA), and the Federal Trade Commission (FTC).

Demands for any type of regulation may be viewed as demands for certain desired effects of regulation that are expected to further the interests and objectives of the persons expressing those demands. The type of regulations that will further the interests of an individual or a group will depend on the nature of the objectives and constraints confronting them. Demands for a specific type of regulation therefore imply an underlying model of the objectives and constraints perceived by the parties who demand that type of regulation.

A number of models or theories exist in the economics literature, each purporting to explain why individuals and interest groups such as producers, consumers, and other types of decision maker demand regulation (see Chapter 2). These theories are only a subset of all the possible reasons why regulation may be demanded. Innumerable models of reasons why people demand regulation can be constructed simply by varying the objectives and/or constraints that are assumed to confront individuals and various types of decision maker.

Each of the models underlying demands for different types of regulation can be viewed as permutations on two general themes. Any theory of the rationale for regulation is based on (1) a normative concept of the "desirable" characteristics of some aspect of the behavior of some type of individual or organization and (2) an implicit or explicit model of the determinants of the individual's or organization's behavior that predicts that in the absence of regulation, the behavior will differ from the normative criteria of "desirable" behavior. Much of the difficulty one experiences in trying to identify the reasons that underlie current regulation policies is the result of differences in the normative criteria that different people employ when defining "desirable" characteristics of regulated decision makers' behavior; the other major reason is that different people often use different explicit or implicit models predicting how decision makers' unregulated behavior will diverge from particular normative criteria of "desirable" behavior.

A unifying framework is needed to provide perspective on the many possible reasons for regulating different dimensions of the behavior of individuals and businesses and other organizations. One important reason why such a framework is necessary is that demands for different types of regulation may be related, in ways outlined in Section 10.1. A second reason is that, even if demands for regulating different dimensions of business behavior are unrelated, the regulations aimed at individual dimensions of business behavior may also have effects on other regulated dimensions of firms' behavior, for reasons to be explained in Chapter 11. Third, more than one reason for regulating the same dimension of business behavior may exist simultaneously. Sometimes the different reasons for regulation may reinforce each other. An example is provided by automobile safety regulations. It is often argued (Arnould and Grabowski, 1981) that imperfect information on the part of consumers regarding the benefits of auto safety devices, and external costs imposed on third parties by automobile accidents, will each tend to result in a level of expenditure by individuals on safety devices that is lower than the socially desirable level.

The unifying framework adopted here is a general model of transactions among individuals. In the present context, the term "transaction" will be used to refer to any kind of agreement, or exchange, between two or more people and includes political and social agreements in addition to narrowly defined economic or market transactions. A number of writers have viewed regulation within a transactions framework, but sometimes define transactions in different ways or focus attention on different features of transactions. Consequently, they sometimes arrive at opposite conclusions.

For example, Vogelsang (1980) has argued that regulation may be appropriate in situations in which individuals engage in repeated transactions with certain characteristics, and that regulation will not be appropriate for one-time transactions. In contrast, Telser (1980) has examined the circumstances under which agreements between individuals will be self-enforcing, and his analysis implies that one-time transactions that do not involve contemporaneous performance of each party's obligations may lack the requirement necessary to provide incentives for both parties to perform their part of the agreement. The analyses and conclusions of other writers who have employed a transactions framework for viewing the rationale of regulation are quite consistent with, and may be viewed as special cases of, the more general transactions framework employed in this section.

(a) Important Characteristics of Transactions

The following features of transactions are extremely important in terms of their implications for the behavior of parties to transactions, the resulting terms of transactions between individuals, and possible reasons for transactions failures that lead to demands for regulating some aspects of those transactions.

Multiple Characteristics. The price and quantity of a particular product or service traded by individuals — the focus of traditional economic analysis — represent only two of many possible dimensions of transactions between individuals. In addition, the parties to an agreement need not perform their respective part of the agreement at the same time. Instead, a particular time sequence of behavior by each party may be agreed to, which might imply problems of enforcing the agreement, especially if one party is required to perform its part of the agreement prior to another party, and if expectations of future transactions between the parties cannot be relied on to induce parties to perform agreed-on terms of the transaction (Telser, 1980).

Another important consideration is that transactions may have multiple characteristics that transcend narrowly defined types of transaction, such as economic or conventional market transactions. For example, two or more individuals may agree to support a candidate for political office in return for the candidate's support for policies that convey economic benefits to them. This point is important in connection with understanding possible reasons why regulation is demanded, since rather than constituting a spontaneous event, certain demands for regulation may be part of a prior agreement or transaction between certain individuals.

Transactions with More Than Two Parties. The agreement between a single buyer and a single seller that typifies the transaction of conventional economic analysis is a totally inadequate representation of the number of parties to many real-world transactions. Parties to an agreement may include agents as well as principals, and agents may simultaneously act for more than one principal. Also participating in an agreement may be a third-party enforcer of the terms of the agreement, such as the courts or a regulatory agency. These third parties may simply enforce terms agreed on by the parties to the agreement, or they may represent the interests of nonparticipants in the transaction. For example, a regulatory agency may try to ensure that transactions between producers and consumers of a product do not result in pollution that harms other members of society.

Effects of Expected Reactions of Nonparticipants. The agreed terms of any type of transaction will generally be influenced by the behavior of parties not directly involved in negotiating the terms of the transaction. Established or potential rival sellers' behavior will affect the price and other terms that established sellers offer to buyers. In addition to the reactions of rivals of parties who enter into transactions, the reactions of other types of decision maker, such as the courts or regulatory enforcement agencies, may also influence the terms of transactions, either by ruling out certain terms or by ensuring that certain terms will be enforceable.

Transactions "Failures" and Normative Criteria. All normative concepts of "desirable" characteristics of transactions between individuals are necessarily judgmental and involve the implicit or explicit adoption of someone's evaluations of those characteristics. The person or persons whose evaluations are adopted may be one or more of the parties directly involved in the transaction. In conventional economic analysis, buyer evaluations of the benefits of products or services are used as normative criteria for judging products and services. The costs of products or services are evaluated either by sellers in descriptive models of seller behavior or by buyers in normative models of the social opportunity costs of resources employed in producing the products or services.

The evaluations of benefits or costs of products and services by third parties experiencing external effects are included in economic models that deal with possible reasons for market failures. External effects of transactions on third parties who are not directly involved apply universally to almost every type of transaction. As was explained in Chapter 3, the range of possible normative weights that may be assigned to the evaluations of transactions characteristics or effects is infinite, and there is no objective way of choosing between these alternative normative evaluation systems. It was also emphasized that parties directly involved in, or affected by, particular types of transaction between individuals will not be indifferent to the choice between alternative normative criteria of the "desirable" characteristics of transactions but will prefer those which best achieve their own interests and objectives.

Even transactions that have "perfect" characteristics according to normative criteria of optimally functioning markets in conventional economic analysis may result in transactions failures according to other normative concepts of desirable transactions characteristics. For example, Lane (1978) has pointed out that recent studies of factors that influence people's subjective well-being and happiness suggest that even perfectly functioning economic markets contribute little toward, and may even detract from, human happiness.

In Chapter 2, Section 4, it was stressed that normative choices are also involved in selecting the objectives and constraints that are assumed to confront individuals whose behavior affects the terms of transactions. Given any normative standard of desirable transactions characteristics, whether transactions failure will occur therefore depends on the objectives and constraints assumed to confront such individuals.

(b) Four Basic Types
   of Transactions Failures

In the remainder of this section, we shall focus on a number of types of constraint facing parties to transactions that are often cited in the economics and regulation literature as possible reasons for transactions failure and for regulating particular aspects of transactions. Primary emphasis will be placed on pointing out the often implicit value judgments regarding normative transactions criteria, or models of the behavior of parties to transactions, that are required in order to generate the conclusion that transactions failure occurs and that regulation is an appropriate remedy.

(1) *Monopoly.* If one of the parties to a particular type of transaction has a monopoly of the selling, buying, or some other aspect of the transaction, this may lead to transactions failure. In traditional economic analysis,

monopoly of the sale of a single product results in a higher product price and in lower output levels than those that maximize allocative efficiency (see Chapter 6). In multiproduct monopoly firms, transactions failure may also take the form of a structure of product prices that differs from some normative concept of desirable product-price structure, such as absence of cross-subsidization between individual products (discussed in Chapter 9). A monopoly of the buying side of some market, termed "monopsony" in the literature, may lead to input mixes exhibiting technical inefficiency and product costs above minimum feasible levels. A monopoly of some aspect of noneconomic types of transaction, such as demands or supplies in political or social transactions between individuals, may also result in transactions failures.

It should be noted that the monopoly rationale for transactions failure is itself based on the implicit assumption that costs are involved in devising and enforcing agreements between individuals (Demsetz, 1966). If the costs of reaching agreement between individuals were zero, monopoly would not result in allocative inefficiency because consumers could costlessly agree to bribe monopolists to set their product price equal to the level that maximizes consumer satisfaction. Although a "zero-transactions-cost" assumption is obviously inappropriate in the real world, this aspect of the monopoly rationale for transactions failure emphasizes the fact that the fundamental reasons for all types of transactions failure are connected with the complexities involved in devising and enforcing agreements between individuals.

(2) "External Effects" of Transactions. External effects occur whenever an activity or transaction between parties has effects on third parties who are not directly involved. These external effects may either benefit or adversely affect third parties. An example of the former is the reduced probability of contracting disease experienced by people who do not participate in an immunization program — an external benefit resulting from the immunization of the participants. Reduced air or water quality for society caused by pollutants emitted in the production of goods produced and consumed by a fraction of the populace is an example of negative external effects. According to traditional economic analysis, external effects and monopoly are the two major sources of market failures, and external effects are frequently cited in support of many of the newer forms of regulation of business and other organizations introduced in the United States since the early 1960s.

Unfortunately, the presence of external effects provides little guidance in identifying which activities are or should be regulated. As Shaffer (1979) has lucidly pointed out, external effects are ubiquitous. Almost every type of activity or transaction will have some kind of effects on third parties who are not directly involved in the activity or transaction. The fundamental reason for this is that all individuals' behavior is related by the chain of market and nonmarket transactions that ultimately touches every member of society. The behavior of the parties directly involved in any transaction and the resulting terms and characteristics of the transaction will influence the opportunity set confronting other, nonparticipating individuals.

The real issue is why some types of external effect lead to demands for regulating certain activities or types of transaction while other activities and transactions that often generate large external effects are ignored. Ultimately, the answer to this question is related to the issue of whose interests and evaluations of the characteristics of particular transactions are reflected by the political system of demands and supplies of regulation. The definition of particular external effects itself involves a normative judgment regarding whose interests should be considered in evaluating the activities or transactions that generate the external effects in question.

Although demands for regulation may be a response to certain external effects of transactions, underlying the demands for regulation is a normative issue of whose interests and evaluations of the transaction should count rather than any "objective" characteristic of the transaction itself.

(3) The Frequency, Duration, and Number of Characteristics of Transactions. In economic analysis, the typical transaction is an exchange of a well-defined product or service for money or some other equally well defined product or service, and the items are exchanged at the same time. As Goldberg (1976) and others have emphasized, this type of transaction is inadequate for representing the complexity of many types of transactions that occur in the real world and the reasons why transactions failures may occur in the absence of some type of regulation. Many transactions between individuals involve agreements to exchange items at different points in time, or to perform services over an extended period of time. In addition, where parties agree to deal with each other over a period of time that extends into the future, some elements of the transaction may not be known in advance, and all possible contingencies cannot usually be foreseen and agreed upon in advance.

In a world of complex agreements and transactions between individuals, the frequency, duration, timing, and number of characteristics of a particular type of transaction may individually or collectively affect the extent to which certain terms of the transaction are enforceable by any party to the agreement.

If a transaction involves a sequence of events, such as payment by one party for services to be subsequently rendered by the other party, the first party may be unable to apply any penalties or sanctions if the second party fails to perform its part of the agreement. In these circumstances, some kind of enforcer, such as the courts, may be required to provide incentives for parties to transactions to perform agreed-upon terms. The alternative to third-party enforcement of the terms of an agreement may be no transaction at all — the ultimate form of transactions failure.

(4) Characteristics of Information Flows Confronting Parties to Transactions. Transactions failures, in the sense of characteristics of transactions that diverge from some normative concept of "desirable" characteristics, can occur as a result of a number of characteristics of information flows that confront individual parties to transactions. Before we examine these characteristics, it is appropriate to comment on the meaning of the term "information" and to emphasize the particular interpretation of this term that will be adopted here. "Information" is an elusive, multifaceted concept, and very few writers on the subject have attempted to provide an operational definition of it.

In traditional economic analysis, decision makers are generally assumed to have "perfect" information, which can be interpreted to mean that they are aware of the precise form of their objective function and all the constraints that influence the form of the relationship between aspects of their behavior and the level of that objective function. In practice, a situation of perfect information is impossible, since an infinity of possible constraints confronts any decision maker and influences the form of the relationship between the decision maker's behavior and the level of the decision maker's objective function. Even analysts who assume perfect information in their models of decision-maker behavior content themselves with listing a small subset of constraints they believe the decision maker does or "should" take into account in his or her decision making.

Information influences a decision maker's perceptions of the various constraints confronting the decision maker, and these constraints determine the expected outcome of the decision maker's behavior on his or her other objectives. When faced by uncertainty regarding constraints, a decision maker can either make a decision on the basis of the existing information he or she possesses or postpone making a decision and acquire additional information.

The amount of information any decision maker possesses at any given time is therefore to a large extent under the control of the decision maker. Acquiring more information, however, is costly in time or other resources. From the decision maker's perspective, additional information about any constraint that describes the person's decision environment should be acquired only to the point that the benefits of the added increment of information equal the perceived cost of that information. Yet, even when individual parties to transactions follow this prescription, transactions failures can still occur because of one or more of a number of characteristics of the resulting information possessed by different parties to the transaction.

(c) Transactions Failures
and Quantities of Information

The *quantity of information* possessed by one or more parties to a particular type of transaction may be higher or lower than the optimal amount according to some normative criterion of the "correct" quantity of information. For example, the traditional economics literature has long emphasized that information may have external effects in the form of benefits to parties who did not invest resources in producing the information.

The most obvious example of this principle is found in connection with information regarding new inventions (or principles) that may have potential applications in a much wider area than that for which the invention was originally intended. In the absence of special incentives (e.g., a patent system that protects property rights in new knowledge), individuals will invest resources in producing information in the form of new knowledge only up to the point where the incremental private benefits of the information equal the incremental costs to these individuals. If benefits to third parties occur as a result of the information, the amount of resources invested in producing information and the total quantity of information produced will be lower than the socially optimal level at which incremental benefits to all parties affected by the information are equal to incremental costs of producing the information.

The traditional view of the incentives for producing new knowledge has been challenged by Hirshleifer (1971) and Hirshleifer and Riley (1979). The traditional view overlooks additional pecuniary returns an inventor or person with prior knowledge of information may reap from foreseeable changes in prices of inputs, outputs, and assets as a result of release of the new information. An innovator who possesses prior knowledge of information is in a unique position to forecast and capture some of the pecuniary gains associated with price reevaluations and consequent wealth transfers that result from release and dissemination of the information. It is even possible for the prospect of these gains to be large enough to provide incentives for overinvestment in the production and dissemination of new information. This is because the pecuniary gains are merely transfers of wealth between members of society, as opposed to increases in wealth brought about by the increased technological productive abilities of society by the new knowledge.

Similar principles apply to information regarding market possibilities and to the supply and demand offers of other individuals participating in any type of transaction. Optimizing individuals who are confronted by uncertainty regarding these market or transactions opportunities will invest resources in searching for and acquiring additional information regarding market opportunities up to the point where the perceived incremental benefits of the information, in terms of effects on the attainable level of the individuals' objectives, are equal to the perceived incremental costs of information search and acquisition.

Information regarding market opportunities possessed by individual participants in a market may have potential external benefits to others inside or outside the market that exceed the costs of disseminating the information to them. For example, if an individual acquires information about job opportunities available in an employment market or about product qualities and prices in a specific product market, the dissemination of this information to others may save them time and other resources involved in acquiring the same information themselves.

Although the total potential incremental benefits of information acquired by individual participants in a market may exceed the incremental benefits to them, there may be no incentives for them to disseminate the information to potential beneficiaries. As Grossman and Stiglitz (1980) have emphasized, disseminating information to potential beneficiaries might reduce or eliminate the benefits of information to the individuals who have invested resources in acquiring it, so that there is a fundamental conflict between the efficiency with which markets spread information and the incentives to acquire information facing individuals participating in those markets.

Thus, the cost of producing a given total amount of information regarding opportunities facing participants in a market or transaction may be higher than the minimum feasible cost of producing the same amount of information; this results in technical inefficiency in the production of market information. In addition, the total incremental benefits of the information to participants in the market may be greater or less than the total incremental costs of acquiring the information; this results in allocative inefficiency and "too little" or "too much" information regarding transactions opportunities in a market.

Our main focus at present concerns the reasons for transactions failures. The reasons for technical or allocative inefficiencies in the production of quantities of information relating to particular markets or types of transaction must be clearly distinguished from the possible regulatory or other types of remedy that might be adopted to cope with these situations. It is appropriate to point out, however, that a number of current public policies in the area of information remedies for consumer protection can be viewed in terms of the preceding framework. For example, policies that attempt to establish a system of measurement or a standard of quality for particular items (e.g., meat quality, egg sizes, gas mileage ratings for new cars, or the condition of used cars) may be viewed as policies aimed at reducing the costs of individual consumer search.

If these policies reduce the incremental costs of acquiring information by individual participants in a market, this occurrence will tend to increase the optimal level of resources individuals will invest in acquiring information. If there are external benefits from the information acquired, the amount of allocative inefficiency in the total quantity of market information produced will tend to be reduced. In contrast, if there are no underlying technological benefits of information acquired by individuals, and only pecuniary wealth transfers result, reduced technical inefficiency in the production of a given amount of market information might be accompanied by increased allocative inefficiency and excessive levels of production of such information.

(d) Transactions Failures and Quality of Information

Transactions failures can also occur if the *quality of information* is different from normative standards of the "desirable" quality of information possessed by parties to transactions. A variety of normative concepts that apply to desirable or undesirable aspects of the quality of information can be found in the economics and related literature, including such concepts as "complete," "adequate," "accurate," "deceptive," "misleading," "misrepresented," "false," and "understandable" information.

Each of these concepts, in turn, can be defined in an infinite number of ways, depending on the person whose value system is used to define them or on the model of the objectives and constraints assumed to confront the person whose evaluations are adopted as the basis of definition. Since transactions failure can be attributed to the presence of any of these concepts, and since the absence or presence of any of these concepts will depend on the implicit or explicit models of the behavior of parties engaging in any particular type of transaction, it is not surprising to find a great deal of controversy in the literature that treats these matters. Unraveling and examining these issues cannot be undertaken here in any great detail, but several points are worth noting to provide some perspective.

Given any particular normative standard of desirable quality of dimensions of information possessed by parties to transactions, transactions failures in the form of divergencies of actual quality of information from these normative standards can be caused by the behavior either of the party that provides information, of the recipient or consumer of the information, or of both the provider and the recipient of information.

(e) Incentives to Acquire versus Abilities to Process Information

In considering factors underlying the behavior of recipients of information that can cause transactions failures, it is useful to distinguish between the *incentives* for recipients to acquire information and their *ability* to understand and process the information. In Section 10.2(c) it was pointed out that optimizing individuals will invest resources in acquiring additional information up to the point where the perceived incremental benefits of the information in terms of effects on the attainable level of the individuals' objectives are equal to the perceived incremental costs of acquiring information. It follows that the optimal amount of information acquired by different individuals will vary with differences in the objectives and constraints facing them.

All individuals face a time constraint in the form of twenty-four hours a day that can be allocated among activities including work, leisure, information acquisition, and information processing. Each of these activities results in outputs that yield individuals satisfaction. The amount of output an individual can produce by devoting an hour of time to a particular activity is an index of the individual's "ability" in that activity. Traditional economic analysis of consumer behavior assumes full or perfect information and also perfect information-processing capabilities by all consumers, but neither condition is met in the real world.

In the United States, current government regulatory policies toward consumer product safety and quality strongly favor direct regulatory controls such as product standards and bans on products that fail to meet these standards (Grabowski and Vernon, 1978). This method of dealing with problems of product safety has been criticized by Oi (1973, 1974) and other economists who favor alternative methods such as the dissemination of better information about product safety. However, providing more or better information to consumers may not be an appropriate solution if transactions failure is caused by the fact that consumer information-processing abilities fall below some normative standard that is judged to be necessary to understand the information provided (Goldberg, 1974). Time spent attempting to understand even "improved" or more understandable information implies less time spent on other activities that result in outputs valued by the consumer. A low ability to process information implies a corresponding low relative output of time spent on acquiring and processing information compared with the outputs that would result if that time were devoted to other activities by the individual in question.

The preceding discussion emphasizes the importance of the precise nature of individuals' objectives and perceived constraints in determining whether transactions failures attributable to characteristics of information flows confronting consumers or other types of party to transactions will occur. This, in turn, emphasizes the subjective nature of the problem of determining whether transactions failures occur. A prime example of this subjectivity occurs in connection with deceptive advertising.

In the United States, the courts have generally held that the Federal Trade Commission (FTC) has expert judgment in deceptive advertising cases and have accepted FTC interpretations of how consumers might construe an advertisement. This approach has been challenged increasingly by arguments for the use of research into consumer behavior to determine whether deception has occurred. However, a number of possible approaches can be used to determine whether consumer deception has occurred (Armstrong, Gurol, and Russ, 1979). Measuring deception by asking people if certain advertisements or claims are deceptive is clearly inappropriate, since consumers who perceive an advertisement to be deceptive will not be deceived by it. Instead, some studies have used the "normative belief technique" (NBT), which suggests that the standard against which deceptive advertisements can be judged is the set of beliefs about a particular product's characteristics held by a representative group of knowledgeable consumers.

A different approach is involved in the "salient belief technique" (SBT), which requires not only that consumers perceive and believe false claims that are either made or implied by an advertisement but, in addition, that these claims influence individuals' decisions to purchase the product. According to the SBT, falsely held beliefs about a product or service characteristic are technically a deception but are important only if they influence a person's decision to purchase the product or service, since the decision may be based on criteria other than the false information.

Although the previously cited study by Armstrong, Gurol, and Russ found that the NBT and SBT yielded similar results when applied to Listerine advertising, many unresolved issues remain in defining normative concepts of deceptive advertising and other types of information, and the resulting types of transactions failure that are based on these concepts. Some individuals will misinterpret even the most conscientiously prepared advertisement, and the issue ultimately resolves itself into the question of whose objectives and constraints should be regarded as the proper normative standard for evaluating the terms of transactions.

The cost of time an individual spends on acquiring information (or any other activity) cannot be separated from the individual's objectives that ultimately determine the individual's relative evaluation of the different outputs he or she can produce in a given amount of time.

Recognizing this principle is especially important in connection with government policies that are intended to increase safety by providing consumers with information regarding safety characteristics of products and services, or by restricting certain types of products that have a higher probability of effects that cause accidents, disease, or other life-reducing results.

The benefits of such policies to individuals ultimately depend on how they value length of life or the increased probability of a given length of life.

How any individual values the length of his or her life, or an increase in the probability of a given length of life, depends on his or her objectives. The value of these life-related factors is likely to differ depending on whether the individual's objective is simply maximization of lifetime satisfaction, whether there are constraints on the individual's desired timing of lifetime satisfaction (Masoner, 1979), and whether the length of the individual's lifetime itself depends on the nature and timing of the individual's consumption activities (Hughes, 1978).

(f) Incentives Facing Principals and Agents in Transactions

Traditional economic analysis ignores the possibility that buyers, sellers, and other principal parties engaging in transactions may rely on agents to act on their behalf in gathering information, making decisions, negotiating terms of agreements, and enforcing those agreements. The incentives that confront agents may cause them to behave in a manner that is not "in the best interests of the principal," in the sense of behavior the principal would require if he or she were in possession of the same information and skills as the agent.

If the objectives and constraints confronting an agent were identical to those facing a principal, agent's behavior that maximizes the agent's interests will also maximize the principal's interests. However, in such circumstances there would be little reason for the agency relationship. An agent is generally employed in situations in which the agent has superior ability or more efficient access to information, enabling the agent to perform a given task more efficiently or effectively than the principal.

A number of types of constraint facing principal and agent that may prevent the agent from acting in the best interests of the principal have received attention in the literature. For example, if an agent's attitude to uncertainty is different from that of the principal, the agent will not act in the principal's best interests unless provided with appropriate incentives (Ross, 1973, Shavell, 1979). In principle, however, *any* element of the agent's objective function or constraints that differs from the principal's can lead the agents to behave differently from the way the principal would. Obviously, the types of incentive that are required to induce agents to act in the best interests of their principals are as varied as the number of possible differences between their respective objectives and constraints.

Additional reasons for possible transactions failure involving an agent and a principal can occur if an agent simultaneously acts for more than one principal. In these circumstances, if the objectives and constraints that confront different principals are different, the agent's behavior that is in the best interests of one principal will not be in the best interests of any of the other principals! With multiple principals, additional complications will be involved in defining the meaning of agent's behavior that is "in the principals' best interests" and in designing appropriate incentive systems to motivate the agent to act in the manner so defined.

The incentives that confront *agents* are not the only possible reason for transactions failure, however. *Principals* may have incentives to misrepresent information they provide to agents regarding their objectives and constraints, in order to improve the terms of the agency agreement in the principal's favor, or to mislead the parties the agent deals with. Moreover, sometimes it is not easy to determine which party to a transaction is the agent and which is the principal; and sometimes agents act as principals for themselves and also as agents for other principals in particular transactions. A doctor, for example, in negotiating with a hospital for facilities to perform surgery on one of the doctor's patients, is acting both as a principal and as an agent. It may not always be clear whether the doctor's principal is the patient or the hospital or the doctor!

One feature that has been generally overlooked in the literature on the agency relationship is that simply designating a particular party to a transaction as the agent, and another party as the principal, implies a normative assumption about which party's interests and evaluations of the behavior of the parties to the agency agreement "should" predominate. It is usually automatically assumed that the principal's best interests constitute the proper criterion for judging the agent's behavior. In circumstances in which it is difficult to determine which party to a transaction is an agent or a principal, the criterion of agent's behavior that is in the best interests of the principal, and the nature of the incentive system facing the parties to the agency agreement that will achieve this kind of behavior, will vary with the roles assigned to the parties.

Finally, it must be explicitly recognized that ordinarily the principal and agent will exchange information. The principal must supply the agent with information regarding the objectives and constraints facing the principal for the agent to be able to select a course of action that is in the principal's best interests. Also, the principal needs to have information regarding the consequences of alternative courses of action by the agent in order to motivate the agent to adopt the alternative that is in the principal's best interests. Because the parties to the agency relationship must exchange information, transactions failures in the terms of the agency agreement itself may occur as a result of one or more of the reasons outlined in Section 10.2(b).

(g) Multiple Parties to Transactions

Even in a situation in which all the parties to a single transaction act as principals, there may be more than two parties, such as the buyer and seller in traditional economic analysis of transactions. For example, production in a business firm can be viewed as a series of transactions among inputs, monitored by a residual claimant to the firm's earnings. A monitor who measures input productivity and allocates rewards to inputs is necessary wherever individual productivities cannot be determined by measuring team output (Alchian and Demsetz, 1972).

Jacob and Page (1980) have pointed out that the residual claimant may rely on buyers to perform part of the task of monitoring input productivity. This implies that the traditional boundaries of transactions, viewed as agreements between buyers on one side and sellers on the other, are not necessarily as clearly defined as traditional economic analysis assumes. The interests of residual claimants of a firm's earnings and buyers of a firm's products may be more closely related — both benefit from higher input productivity and lower costs, for example — than are the interests of residual claimants and inputs hired by the firm. Ermer (1979) has cited a similar strategy on the part of bureaucratic organizations that use client groups to monitor the performance of bureau inputs.

The major implication of the existence of multiple parties to any type of transaction is that the objectives and constraints confronting *every* party to the transaction are relevant in determining the resulting characteristics of the transaction. A prime example of this general principle occurs in the case of a transaction among a patient, the patient's doctor, the insurance company, and the hospital. Harris (1977) has argued that a hospital is actually two separate firms, consisting of a medical staff or demand division, and an administration or supply division. Each half of the organization has its own managers, objectives, and constraints; the behavior of the two halves interacts to determine the type and the costs of treatment patients receive.

Current regulatory policies toward hospitals, notably hospital costs, are directed toward the supply side of the organization and may fail to have their intended consequences unless the determinants of the behavior of the doctors on the demand side of the organization are taken into account. Failure to include the behavior of all parties involved in hospital production and cost characteristics is not the sole explanation for failure of regulatory policies in this field. There is considerable controversy in the literature on hospital decision making regarding the nature of objectives of particular types of decision maker, such as hospital administrators.

Some economics models of hospital behavior predict transactions failure in the form of technical inefficiency in hospital production and hospital costs higher than necessary, owing to the use of excessively capital-intensive input combinations. This conclusion ignores the fact that it is in the group interests of admitting physicians for the complementary hospital inputs that doctors use to be supplied at least cost (Bays, 1980). Hospital care is a joint product of the doctor's and the hospital's inputs. Given the demand for hospital care on the part of patients, the higher the hospital component of costs are, the lower will be the residual demand for the doctor component of hospital care, and this will reduce the price doctors can charge for any level of their own services.

In addition, if hospitals are required to earn a particular rate of return on capital invested in hospital facilities, the appropriate model for analyzing hospital behavior is a variant of the rate-of-return-on-capital model of the firm, discussed in Chapter 8, Section 2. If the hospital's administrative decision makers aim at maximizing profits, subject to making a certain required rate of return on invested capital, input mixes will exhibit excessive use of capital inputs, exactly like the A-J effect in traditional analysis of regulated public utility forms. In contrast, if hospital administrators aim at maximizing the total output of a given quality of patient care, input mixes will exhibit excessive use of labor rather than of capital inputs (Bays, 1980).

For each of the multiple parties who engage in a transaction, the behavior of other parties to the transaction is a constraint that will influence the nature of the alternatives open to each participant and the course of action and behavior each participant will select.

The range of possible expectations regarding the behavior of other parties to a transaction, as well as possible reactions by individuals and organizations not directly involved in the transaction, and the different implications for the resulting terms of the transaction and possible transactions failures is large and relatively unexplored in the transactions failure literature.

One example of the importance of taking into account interactions among the behavior of different parties to transactions in regulatory policies designed to remedy transactions failures is provided by the impact of Occupational Health and Safety Administration regulations on worker safety (Viscusi, 1979). OSHA regulations that increase firms' investments in safe working conditions may also lead to a reduction in safety-enhancing worker actions, so that the net effect of regulations on worker safety depends on the relative magnitude of these two offsetting effects. Peltzman (1975) has similarly demonstrated that safety measures such as automobile seat belts that reduce injuries sustained in accidents may increase driving speed and the probability of serious accidents.

Also, just as potential entrant firms may enter a market if the expected terms of transactions are expected to yield profits for them, parties who are not directly involved in a particular transaction may decide to seek direct participation or representation by an agent in the transaction if the terms of transactions affect their interests sufficiently.

The preceding considerations suggest not only that boundaries that define parties to particular transactions will often be blurred but also that those boundaries may shift, sometimes increasing and sometimes reducing the number of parties directly involved in the transactions. In either case, the addition or subtraction of parties and types of decision maker whose behavior is directly involved in determining the terms of transactions may eliminate some previously existing sources of transactions failures and, in other cases, may result in additional sources of transactions failures.

The fact that the objectives and constraints facing each participant are relevant in determining transactions characteristics does not necessarily mean that the terms of observed transactions are always equilibrium terms. Transactions may occur with disequilibrium terms viewed from the perspective of the objectives and constraints that confront some of the parties to the transaction or nonparticipants. This will lead to changes both in these parties' behavior and in the terms of transactions of a particular variety.

It is even possible that there may exist no equilibrium terms of a particular type of transaction, in the sense of terms that simultaneously satisfy the objectives and constraints confronting all parties to the transaction. In the context of the previously cited two-sector model of hospital behavior, for example, Harris (1977) has suggested that the interaction between the behavior of the medical staff and the hospital administration may result in a disequilibrium process in which each party's noncooperative scramble to achieve its own objectives leads to pressures for ever-increasing hospital size. The hospital administration wants the hospital filled, but doctors desire excess capacity in the form of readily available beds and other facilities. As a result, doctors may expand utilization, causing the administration to expand hospital capacity, and so on. This is only one possible model of hospital behavior among many plausible scenarios; it does, however, provide an example of a situation in which equilibrium terms of transactions are nonexistent.

The preceding discussion of possible causes of transactions failure is not exhaustive, and as in the case of automobile safety devices mentioned earlier, more than one reason for transactions failure may exist simultaneously in connection with a particular type of transaction. If each possible cause of transaction failure is viewed as a constraint confronting one or more of the parties to a transaction, the situation is one in which the principles of the Theory of Second Best are applicable. The combined effect of more than one reason for transactions failure on the terms of the transaction, and on the characteristics of transactions failure, may be very different from those which occur when reasons for transactions failure occur in isolation.

The types of policy that are appropriate to deal with the consequences of multiple causes of transactions failures may also differ considerably from those which are appropriate to deal with individual causes of transactions failure. As Section 10.3 will argue in more detail, it is the failure of existing regulatory policies to take into account interactions between different types of transactions failure and between regulatory policies designed to deal with different types of transactions failure that is largely responsible for the poor record of regulation in eliminating transactions failures to date.

10.3   MULTIPLE POSSIBLE ROLES FOR REGULATORS IN A GENERALIZED TRANSACTIONS FRAMEWORK

When government regulation is viewed from the perspective of a generalized transactions framework, regulators are simply an additional group of decision makers whose behavior influences the terms of particular transactions. The first thing that must be clearly understood is that transactions are never completely unregulated. Laws that prescribe penalties for certain types of behavior and that are enforced by the courts are just as much a regulation as a rule administered by a regulatory agency. Taxes influence the behavior of people and organizations, inhibiting some kinds of behavior and providing positive incentives for other kinds of behavior. The statutory and administrative regulations that are generally thought of as regulations are simply a subset of all the different types of regulation that affect transactions between individuals, by influencing the rewards and penalties associated with alternative forms of behavior that individuals and organizations may adopt.

A second extremely important point, which has been emphasized by Wolfe (1979), is that although regulation may be a means of eliminating certain types of transactions failure that might occur in the absence of regulation, regulators' behavior can also just as easily reinforce or create additional transactions failures. Transactions failures, in the sense of characteristics of transactions that fail to conform to some normative criteria of desirable transactions characteristics, occur as a result of the objectives and constraints that confront any of the parties to transactions.

The presence of regulators may affect the behavior of other parties to transactions in ways that create or reinforce existing transactions failures. Moreover, in considering possible transactions failures attributable to regulation, attention must be directed at a much wider class of transactions than the market or nonmarket transactions regulated by a particular agency. For example, as was noted in Chapter 4, the presence of regulation may result in too many resources being devoted toward attempts to influence regulators' behavior. Business firms and other organizations may be induced to switch their activities from competing in the conventional marketplace toward competing in the regulatory marketplace for regulations that advance their respective interests more effectively than market competition.

A third and final point that must be understood is that the appropriate role of regulation in a transactions framework can be viewed in many ways. For example, like the courts, the role of regulators might be to act as an enforcer of terms of transactions agreed on by other parties. Alternatively, regulators may act as agents for one of the parties to a transaction. As agent for buyers, an agency may attempt to prevent monopoly pricing by sellers, for example. As agent for sellers, an agency might act as an enforcer of a collective agreement between sellers. Another possibility is that the regulatory agency may act as agent for different parties to a transaction. A regulatory role that is emphasized in Chapters 12 and 13 is that of administering regulatory constraints that elicit truthful information regarding the costs of regulated firms' activities or the benefits attributed to those activities by affected parties. Another regulatory role stressed in those chapters is that of administering regulatory constraints that ensure that regulated firms' behavior will exhibit certain normative standards of desirable behavior.

Lee (1980) has offered another version of the appropriate role for regulators, one that views regulation as a mutually beneficial exchange between consumers and producers. In this model, enforcement of a monopoly-cartel agreement between sellers is transferred from producers to society. In exchange, producers agree to surrender the power of price determination to a third-party regulatory agency, which sets product prices on the basis of an attempt to balance different interests of members of society. These interests may include those of groups other than producers and consumers of the regulated product; in this respect, the agency acts as agent for third parties who are not directly involved in the production and consumption of the product.

The preceding examples of possible roles for regulation in a transactions framework are not meant to be exhaustive but to illustrate that the ultimate normative problem of deciding whose interests should count, and what criteria should be used to define transactions failures and appropriate remedies, is unavoidable. Different parties to transactions will generally try to influence the choice of normative criteria for evaluating transactions in their favor. To accept uncritically any definition of transactions failure, or a particular role for regulation in a transactions framework, is to accept without question a normative judgment concerning whose interests should count and whose rights should predominate in economic and other types of transaction between individuals.

10.4 REASONS FOR THE FAILURE OF REGULATION

The charge that excessive government regulation is at the root of many of the problems facing the United States economy is a popular theme both in the media and in academic publications. Especially emphasized are the high costs imposed on individuals and organizations in the private sector by regulatory agencies' demands for information and the resources required to meet regulatory standards of performance in dimensions of business behavior, such as worker safety and environmental pollution. Most analysts and commentators see few benefits of regulation that justify these costs of regulation. As Chapters 3 and 4 emphasized, costs and benefits of regulation are subjective; despite this, there appears to be a general consensus, even among those who view the results of regulation more optimistically, that the perceived effects of regulation are quite different from the desired effects.

If the effects of regulation that people desire are viewed as targets of regulation, the exact nature of these targets will vary considerably, depending on the objectives and constraints that confront different individuals and interest groups. In view of the wide variety of regulatory targets that underlies demands for different types of regulation by groups in society, the general failure of regulation to achieve its targets suggests that the reasons for this failure may be much more fundamental than the nature of the individual targets themselves. This possibility implies, in turn, that focusing on regulations that are aimed at a single target may not reveal why that type of regulation has failed to achieve its intended objectives. The remainder of this section will employ a general framework of regulatory targets and instruments to explain several different but interrelated types of reasons why regulation may not attain its targets. These possible reasons for the failure of regulation, and the types of remedy that are appropriate, will then be examined in greater depth in Chapters 11–15, which constitute Part III.

Determinants of Effects of Regulation on Firms. The targets of regulation can be viewed as certain desired effects of regulation. It will be assumed here that these effects are desired levels of some dimensions of business behavior, such as the level of pollutants emitted by a firm or the degree of safety of the firm's working conditions or products. The same principles and conclusions apply to other types of decision maker whose behavior is a target of regulation. To achieve the regulators' target level of some dimension of business behavior, it is necessary to know what factors affect that dimension of behavior. Two sets of relevant factors can be distinguished:

i. the nature of the objectives and constraints facing a firm's decision makers that determine the behavior of the firm in the absence of regulation
ii. the implications of regulators' behavior for the constraints that confront regulated firms' decision makers. Figure 10.1 is a simple diagrammatic representation of these two sets of factors

Curve OO' in Figure 10.1(a) shows the level of attainment of the objective of a firm's decision makers, at different levels of some dimension of the firm's behavior, in the absence of regulation. The firm's decision makers will select level B of that dimension of the firm's behavior, the level that achieves the highest feasible level of their objective in the

Figure 10.1

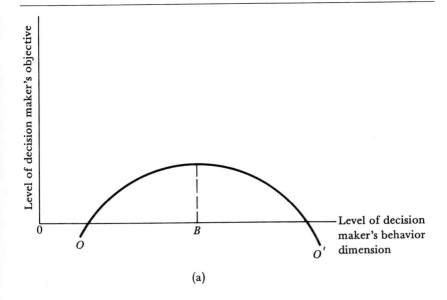

(a)

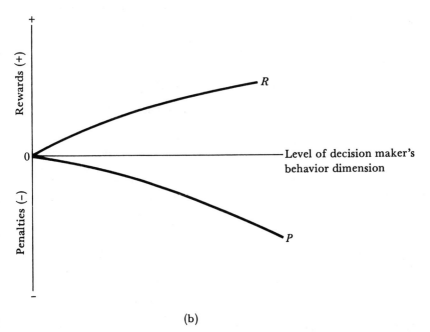

(b)

absence of regulation. In Figure 10.1(b), curve R depicts the level of rewards, and curve P the level of penalties that the regulators' behavior implies for different levels of the dimension of the firm's behavior under regulation. Only one of the R or P curves will exist in any given situation, and these curves can exhibit different shapes from the ones depicted in the figures.

Irrespective of the exact shape of the R or the P curve, when one of these curves is added to the OO' curve, the result is a new curve showing the level of the firm's objective at various levels of the regulated dimension of the firm's behavior. Under regulation, the firm's decision makers will select a level of behavior that results in the highest point on this new curve. Depending on the shape of the R or P curve, this may result in either an increase or a decrease in the level of the regulated dimension of the firm's behavior. The diagrammatic framework provides a suitable basis for understanding a number of related reasons why regulation may fail to have the effects on a regulated firm's behavior that are desired by regulators.

Regulators' Ignorance of Firms' Objectives and Constraints. In order for regulators to achieve a target level of a regulated firm's behavior, they must have information about the position and shape of the firm's OO' curve. This curve depends on the objectives of the firm's decision makers and the perceived constraints confronting those decision makers. Regulated firms' decision makers may misrepresent their objectives and constraints, and therefore the OO' curve, to induce regulators to select R or P curves that yield higher levels of the firms' objectives under regulation. To avoid misrepresentation of information by regulated decision makers, the R and P curves must have very special characteristics, termed "incentive-compatible" characteristics in the literature that deals with this problem. These characteristics will be examined in detail in Chapter 12, Section 2.

One important aspect of the relationship between regulatory instruments and targets that has been largely ignored in the economics and regulation literature is the very likely possibility that regulators' behavior may not only affect the R and P curves but may *also affect the position and shape of the OO' curve itself.* The constraints that confront the firm's decision makers and influence the position and shape of OO' include factors such as levels of other dimensions of the firm's behavior, the behavior of the firm's rivals, and the behavior of the firm's clients or customers. Regulators' behavior may affect one or more of these factors, either directly or indirectly, which will result in a change in the position or shape of the OO' curve owing to regulation. An example of such a situation occurs if the same dimension of behavior of rivals of a regulated firm is also regulated and changes as a result of regulation. Other examples will be examined in Chapter 12. Failure to recognize and take into account such factors will be an important reason why the type and level of regulatory instruments that are required to achieve a specific regulatory target may be incorrectly perceived, leading to a failure of regulation to achieve its intended objectives.

A special case of the general principle discussed in the preceding paragraph occurs if more than one dimension of a firm's behavior is regulated by different regulatory agencies. In these circumstances, the behavior of one of the regulated dimensions of the firm, and the extent to which a particular regulatory target is attained, depend on the level of the regulatory instruments of *all* the regulatory agencies whose policies affect the firm. In other words, the level of one agency's instruments that are necessary to achieve its target level of one dimension of the firm's behavior depends on the level of the regulatory instruments of other regulatory agencies.

There are two major implications of such situations. One implication is that it is necessary to know the form of the relationship between the instruments and targets of *every* regulatory agency whose behavior affects any of the dimensions of regulated firms' behavior in order to select the levels of regulatory instruments in all agencies that will simultaneously achieve the targets of those agencies. Alternatively, each regulatory agency must know how every other agency will react to its own behavior in order to select levels of its instruments that will achieve its regulatory target.

The second implication is that there must generally be at least as many regulatory instruments as there are regulatory targets in order for it to be *possible* to achieve all regulatory targets simultaneously. This proposition is an example of the more general "Theory of Economic Policy" associated with one of the first economists to win the Nobel Prize, Jan Tinbergen. This theory indicates that in any type of decision problem where there are n targets to be achieved, there must normally be at least n instruments that can be varied independently in order for it to be possible to achieve all n targets simultaneously.

Regulators' Ignorance Regarding Determinants of Penalty and Reward Systems. Even if regulators have accurate information concerning the objectives and constraints facing regulated decision makers (and the OO' curve in Figure 10.1), by itself this is not sufficient to permit regulators to achieve a selected target level of the regulated firm's behavior. It is also necessary for regulators' behavior to exhibit the characteristics that result in an R or P curve that, when combined with the regulated firm's OO' curve, results in a new combined curve whose highest point occurs at the level of regulated firm's behavior that corresponds to the regulators' target. Only if this condition is met will regulated decision makers adopt a level of their behavior that corresponds to the regulators' target.

Thus, regulators need to have information on the factors that determine the position and shape of the regulatory reward and penalty curves, R and P. The height and shape of the R and P curves depend in part on regulatory instruments, such as monitoring and enforcement policies of regulatory agencies that affect the regulated decision makers' perceived probability that particular regulatory rewards or penalties will be applied to them. In addition, the perceived probability that regulatory rewards or penalties will be incurred, and therefore the height and shape of the R or P curves, also depends on other factors, such as the behavior of the courts and dimensions of the regulated firm's behavior such as the level of resources devoted to concealing violations of regulatory standards and defending itself against charges of violating these standards.

Unless regulators have information regarding all the factors that influence the shape of the R or P curve that is applicable to the dimension of behavior they are attempting to regulate, they will not know the type and level of regulatory instruments that are required to achieve their target level of the regulated firm's behavior. Existing models of the relationship between regulators' behavior, regulatory instruments, and regulatory targets are grossly deficient in this respect in most areas of regulation practiced in the United States.

A common theme underlying regulators' lack of knowledge is the interdependence that often exists among different dimensions of the behavior of regulators and regulated decision makers. Chapter 11 will examine the nature of these types of behavioral interdependence and their implications for regulation in more detail.

Lack of Appropriate Incentives Facing Regulators. Another reason why regulatory targets may not be achieved is connected with the nature of regulators' objectives and constraints and with the rewards and penalties facing regulators. In general, it is necessary to provide (1) incentives for regulators to truthfully reveal information regarding their objectives and constraints, (2) incentives for regulators to seek information regarding the relationship that exists between regulatory instruments and targets, and (3) incentives for regulators to select levels of regulatory instruments that are compatible with particular regulatory targets. These considerations will be examined in more detail in Chapter 13.

Failure to Consider Disequilibrium Behavior. Uncertainty on the part of regulators concerning the nature of the relationship that exists between regulatory targets and instruments is not the only possible reason for failure of regulation to attain its targets. Even if the form of the relationship between regulatory instruments and targets is known, even if there are at least as many regulatory instruments as there are targets, and even if regulators could be provided with incentives to motivate them to use these instruments to attempt to achieve particular targets, there is an additional set of considerations that may result in a failure of regulation to achieve its intended targets.

These considerations are connected with the disequilibrium behavior of regulators and regulated decision makers, and especially with the way in which individual regulatory instruments are changed when targets are not being achieved. Traditional economic analysis deals mainly with the equilibrium behavior of decision makers, and analysis of disequilibrium behavior is usually restricted to graduate-level economics courses. This approach is unacceptable if one is dealing with possible causes of regulatory failure, because if regulation does not achieve its targets, the resulting situation is one of disequilibrium. Analysis of the causes and consequences of regulatory disequilibrium is therefore unavoidable.

In the presence of uncertainty regarding the relationship that exists between regulatory instruments and targets, levels of regulatory instruments that simultaneously achieve all regulatory targets are not known, so that the levels of regulatory instruments actually selected at a particular point in time will generally result in a failure to achieve at least some targets. Even in the absence of uncertainty, however, the use of a system of regulation that is decentralized, in the sense that different regulatory targets are the responsibility of different regulatory agencies and decision makers, can result in a failure to achieve some or all regulatory targets.

The key considerations are the manner in which regulatory instruments are assigned to regulatory targets and the directions and relative speeds with which regulators change regulatory instruments when targets are not being met. These "regulatory disequilibrium adjustment rules," employed by regulators, together with disequilibrium adjustment rules, used by regulated and unregulated decision makers, interact to determine the disequilibrium time path of regulatory instruments and the extent to which each target is achieved at any given point in time. This disequilibrium time path can take innumerable forms, depending on the exact nature of regulatory targets and the disequilibrium adjustment rules employed by regulators and regulated decision makers.

A major distinction is drawn in economic analysis between disequilibrium time paths that are termed "dynamically stable" and that converge toward levels of the instruments that simultaneously achieve all targets, and disequilibrium time paths that lack this property. However, in the present context it is important to note that whether or not a particular disequilibrium time path of regulatory instruments and targets is dynamically stable, some or all regulatory targets may not be achieved at any particular point in time during the disequilibrium period of adjustment.

Regulatory failures, in the sense of situations in which some regulatory targets are not being achieved, may be a normal characteristic of the regulatory process. Even if the regulatory process is dynamically stable, a situation in which the levels of regulatory instruments converge toward levels that simultaneously achieve all targets may be postponed indefinitely because of changes in the targets themselves or because of changes in regulatory instruments and disequilibrium adjustment rules. Such changes may, in turn, be related to feedback of information regarding the effects of regulatory instruments on targets in previous periods of time.

Neglected Interactions among Methods of Influencing Behavior. There are a number of alternatives to regulation, including deregulation, industrial restructuring, reductions in entry barriers aimed at stimulating more competition, and increased social responsibility on the part of business (see Chapter 14). It is useful to view these alternatives as methods of attempting to achieve the *same* targets as those which regulation and regulatory instruments attempt to achieve. Viewed from this perspective, an important point emerges that has not been sufficiently emphasized to date in the literature dealing with these alternatives to regulation. Although there exists a wider class of potential instruments for attempting to achieve the same targets that regulatory instruments attempt to achieve, those targets still take the form of changes in dimensions of individual and organizational behavior. All the objectives and constraints that confront decision makers, except for the different types of instrument that may be used to influence their behavior, will be the same.

For the same reasons, most of the problems that are encountered in attempting to use government regulation as a means of influencing human behavior will be met when different types of instrument are used to achieve similar targets. Even more important, regulation, deregulation, industrial reorganization, and social responsibility of business should not be viewed as mutually exclusive instruments for achieving targets in the form of certain desired characteristics of the behavior of individuals and firms and other types of organization. A mixture of these instruments may be the only feasible means, or the best means, of achieving a particular set of behavioral targets (see Chapter 15).

Even when different types of instrument are being analyzed as alternatives to regulation, the behavior of decision makers who are the target of those instruments will still be influenced by the nature and magnitude of existing regulatory and other types of instrument. If the main reason for regulatory failure is a lack of information about the relationship that exists among regulatory instruments and targets, simply turning to other types of policies and instruments will not avoid that problem. It merely increases the number of instruments, and their relationship to the targets regulation seeks to achieve, that must be taken into account in designing policies to achieve those targets.

Regulation and other types of policy aimed at influencing the behavior of individual decision makers, and businesses and other types of organization, should be based on models of decision-maker behavior that include the objectives and constraints that actually influence the behavior of decision makers in the real world. This emphasizes the importance of incentives for motivating decision makers to honestly reveal information. Also, although uncertainty facing decision makers should be incorporated into models of determinants of their behavior, the different methods and rules of thumb decision makers use to cope with uncertainty in the real world need to be included. These rules of thumb have important implications for equilibrium and disequilibrium characteristics of people's behavior. Unfortunately, the traditional literature on economics and regulation has devoted little attention to the behavioral implications of different methods of dealing with uncertainty in a dynamic disequilibrium framework.

CHAPTER ELEVEN

Relationships among Different Effects of Regulation

11.1 LINKS AMONG CHARACTERISTICS OF A REGULATED FIRM'S BEHAVIOR

This section will explain why regulation of a single dimension of a firm's behavior will also generally affect its unregulated dimensions. We will also demonstrate the nature of the relationship that exists between regulated and unregulated dimensions of a firm's behavior and the factors that determine the direction and magnitude of the effects of regulation on unregulated dimensions of the firm's behavior. Although the focus will be on the impact of regulation on business firms, the same analytical and diagrammatic framework is applicable to other kinds of organization, and the major conclusions of this section apply equally to the effects of regulation on other kinds of organization.

The starting point for understanding the relationship among different decision variables of any firm, and the impact of regulating one of these decision variables, is the following relationship between the firm's profits, sales revenues, and expenditures on all the different types of input purchased by the firm:

Total profits = Total sales revenue − (total production costs
+ total advertising expenditures + total product quality
improvement expenditures + · · ·)

The change in total production costs that occurs when only the quantity of the firm's product that is produced changes is termed the "marginal cost" (MC) of the firm's product. This MC concept is crucial in determining the profit-maximizing level of the price of the firm's product. It is also relevant in connection with the determination of profit-maximizing levels of advertising, product quality, and other types of expenditure.

Total sales revenues are equal to product price (P) multiplied by quantity of product sold (Q), and total production costs are equal to average production cost per unit of output (AC)[1] multiplied by quantity of output produced (Q). The preceding relationship may therefore be written as follows:

$$\text{Profit} = (P - AC)Q - \text{adv} - \text{product quality exp} - \cdots$$

Dividing both sides of the preceding relationship by the firm's total sales revenue (PQ) changes this relationship to the expression

$$\frac{\text{Total profit}}{\text{Sales}} = \frac{(P - AC)}{P} - \frac{\text{adv}}{\text{sales}} - \frac{\text{product quality exp}}{\text{sales}} - \cdots \quad (1)$$

The relationship in expression (1) is true at all times, whether or not the firm's product price, product quality, and other decision variables are at profit-maximizing levels. The assumption that the firm produces only one product is made solely for expositional convenience at this stage. This assumption will be relaxed later in this chapter and will not change any of the major conclusions reached in the single-product case. Another assumption that will be relaxed later is that the average cost of the firm's product is the same at all levels of output so that $AC = MC$. This situation will occur whenever total production costs change in proportion to changes in the firm's total output level.

In order for a firm to maximize its profits, all the following conditions must simultaneously be satisfied:

$$\frac{P - MC}{P} = \frac{1}{E_p} \cdots$$

the profit-maximizing pricing condition

$$\frac{\text{Adv}}{\text{Sales}} = \frac{(P - MC)E_a}{P} \cdots$$

the profit-maximizing advertising expenditure condition, often referred to as the Dorfman-Steiner condition in the literature

---

[1] It is important for the reader not to confuse AC, which refers only to *production* costs per unit of the firm's product, and the *total* expenditures of the firm per unit of the firm's product. This last concept includes advertising, product quality expenditures, and any other type of expenditure on inputs by the firm. Expression (1) *separates* these types of expenditure from the firm's production costs; $(P - AC)$ refers to profit per unit of product *before* deducting advertising, product quality, and other types of expenditure, per unit of output.

$$\frac{\text{Product quality exp}}{\text{Sales}} = \frac{(P - MC)E_q}{P} \cdots$$

the profit-maximizing product quality expenditure condition, which is similar to the Dorfman-Steiner condition for advertising

The E terms in these conditions are "elasticities," defined as the percentage of change in the quantity of the firm's product demanded in response to a 1 percent change in each of the n types of expenditure by the firm. By substituting these profit-maximizing conditions into expression (1), the following condition that must be met for the levels of *all* the firm's decision variables to be at profit-maximizing levels is obtained:

$$\frac{\text{Total profit}}{\text{Sales}} = \frac{(P - MC)}{P} (1 - E_a - E_q \cdots E_n) =$$

$$\frac{1}{E_p} (1 - E_a - E_q \cdots - E_n) \cdots \qquad (2)^2$$

The reader is cautioned against assuming that the magnitude of each of the various elasticity terms depends solely on the level of the decision variable to which the elasticity measure applies. Generally, the magnitude of each elasticity measure will depend on the level of *all* the firm's decision variables. For example, E_p, the percentage change in the quantity of the firm's product demanded in response to a 1 percent change in the price of the product, will depend not only on the initial price level of the product but also on the existing level of the firm's expenditures on advertising and

---

[2] For expositional convenience, profit-maximizing condition (2) ignores two complications that do not change any of the major conclusions of this chapter. When $AC \neq MC$, the profit-maximizing level of the firm's product price, $(P - MC)$, depends on two other factors in addition to the price elasticity of demand for the firm's product, E_p. These factors are the elasticities of supply, and the productivities of the firm's inputs. See Needham (1980) for more detailed discussion of these factors.

The second complication that is not explicit in condition (2) is that the relevant sales and elasticities are *discounted present values* whenever current expenditures on production, advertising, or product quality result in effects on demand for the firm's product that occur in future periods of time. In these circumstances, the changes in quantities of the firm's product demanded and revenues that are expected to occur in future time periods in response to current expenditures by the firm must be weighted by a "discount rate" that reflects the firm's decision makers' relative evaluation of outcomes in different time periods. The general form of the discount rate is $1/(1 + d)^n$, as explained in Chapter 3, Section 3.2, in connection with people's evaluations of future effects of regulation. When this discount rate is multiplied by an expected future change in quantity of the firm's product demanded, or future sales revenues, the result is a "present-value" equivalent of that future outcome. Since different types of expenditures and actions by a firm's decision makers will generally have dissimilar future outcomes, reducing these outcomes to a common "present value" is indispensable for comparing different expenditures and actions and for deciding on optimal levels of different dimensions of the firm's behavior.

other activities that affect buyers' perceptions of the product. Similarly, the magnitude of E_a, the percentage change in demand for the firm's product in response to a 1 percent change in the firm's advertising expenditures, will depend on the level of the price of the firm's product. The major implication of this is that the profit-maximizing levels of the firm's product price, advertising, product quality, and all other decision variables are interdependent and cannot generally be determined separately. This statement can be clarified by reference to Figure 11.1.

The Effect of Product Quality on Optimal Product Price.[3] Figure 11.1(a) illustrates the effect of an increase in the level of a firm's product quality, from q_1 to q_2, on the conventional "demand curve" that shows the quantity of the firm's product that would be demanded by consumers at different product prices. Curve D_1 is the demand curve for the firm's product at a level of product quality q_1. Since expenditures on improvements in product quality are a "fixed cost" from the point of view of decisions about the quantity of the firm's product, they do not enter into the MC curve, which is relevant for determining the profit-maximizing level of the firm's product price at any particular level of product quality. This marginal cost curve, labeled MC in Figure 11.1(a), is horizontal, owing to the assumption that AC = MC.

Given the level of product quality q_1 and the resulting demand curve D_1, the profit-maximizing price and output of the firm's product are P_1 and Q_1, respectively. At P_1 the increase in total revenue from a price change, shown by the height of the marginal revenue curve (MR), is exactly equal to the change in the firm's total production costs (MC) that are necessary to change the quantity of the product by the amount demanded because of the price change. In other words, MR = MC, which implies that the profit-maximizing pricing condition $(P - MC)/P = 1/E_p$, is satisfied.[4]

An increase in the level of product quality expenditure by the firm from q_1 to q_2 is assumed to increase the quantity of the firm's product demanded at any price and shifts the firm's demand curve from D_1 to D_2.

---

[3] The term "product quality" can refer to any one of a number of dimensions, such as durability, safety, and other features of a product. It may also be used to refer to characteristics of a product that are perceived by buyers of the product, rather than to intrinsic characteristics of the product. Examples of such perceived characteristics are status and style. Expenditures by firms that improve product quality may be on inputs that affect the physical characteristics of a product, such as inclusion of safety belts or air bags in automobiles. Alternatively, such expenditures may be on testing the product, such as drug testing and automobile crash tests. The analysis contained in this section may be applied to any particular dimension of product quality that affects the demand for a firm's product.

[4] It is easy to demonstrate that $MR = P(1 - 1/E_p)$. $MR = MC$ implies that $P(1 - 1/E_p) = MC$, and $(P - MC)/P = 1/E_p$.

Figure 11.1

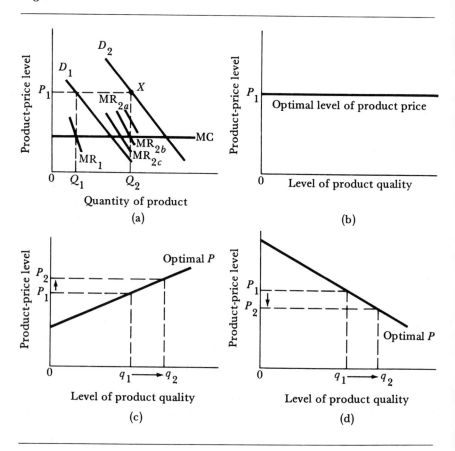

The effect of this increase in the firm's product quality on the profit-maximizing level of the firm's product price depends on the magnitude of the price elasticity of demand for the firm's product at point x in Figure 11.1(a). Point x represents the higher quantity demanded (Q_2) at the *old* profit-maximizing price P_1. If at point x the price elasticity of demand for the firm's product is the same as at P_1Q_1, footnote 4 implies that the change in total revenue (MR_{2b}) from a price change at point x is the same as before the increase in product quality. Since the marginal production cost (MC) is also unchanged, the *new* profit-maximizing price is not changed by the increase in product quality expenditures. The resulting relationship between the profit-maximizing product price and the level of product quality is shown in Figure 11.1(b).

If, instead, the price elasticity of demand for the firm's product at point x is lower than at $P_1 Q_1$, this implies that the marginal revenue (MR_{2c}) from a price change at point x is lower than at $P_1 Q_1$. Since MC is unchanged, the new profit-maximizing level of product price is higher than P_1 at level of product quality q_2. The resulting relationship between the profit-maximizing levels of product price and product quality in this case is depicted by Figure 11.1(c).

Finally, if the price elasticity of demand for the firm's product at point x is higher than at $P_1 Q_1$, this implies that the marginal revenue (MR_{2d}) from a price change is higher than at $P_1 Q_1$. Since MC is unchanged, the profit-maximizing level of product price is lower than P_1 at level of product quality q_2. The resulting relationship between the profit-maximizing levels of product quality and product price in this case is depicted by Figure 11.1(d).

If the assumption that marginal production costs are constant is relaxed, the effect of product quality on the profit-maximizing level of the firm's product price will also depend on whether MC rises or falls as output increases. If MC falls with increases in output, as occurs when there are "economies of scale" in production, the profit-maximizing price at any level of product quality will tend to be lower than when MC is constant as output levels change.

The Effect of Product Price on Optimal Product Quality. The preceding analysis of the relationship between a firm's product quality and profit-maximizing levels of product price is not sufficient to determine which product-quality and product price levels will actually be adopted by the firm, or the nature of the interdependence that exists between product-quality and product-price levels. First, it is necessary to analyze the relationship between the firm's product prices and profit-maximizing levels of product quality. A profit-maximizing level of product quality occurs when the addition to a firm's total revenue from an increase in product quality equals the increase in production costs resulting from the increase in product quality. It is easy to demonstrate that this profit-maximizing product quality condition may be expressed as[5] where S is the firm's

$$\frac{\text{Product quality expenditures}}{S} = \frac{(P - MC)}{P} E_q \cdots \tag{3}$$

total sales revenue and the elasticity of demand E_q measures the percentage increase in the quantity of the firm's product demanded in response to a 1 percent change in product quality expenditures by the firm.

At any particular level of the firm's product price, P, there is a level

[5] The interested reader may consult Needham (1978, Chap. 5) for proof of this proposition.

of product quality expenditures that satisfies the stated condition and maximizes profits *at that level of product price*. At different levels of P, however, the magnitude of E_q associated with a particular level of product quality expenditure may be different. This can be explained by reference to Figure 11.1(a). At different levels of P the horizontal shift of the firm's demand curve shows the increase in the quantity of the product demanded in response to any particular increase in the level of product quality. Dividing this increase in quantity demanded by the initial level of output demanded yields the percentage change in quantity of the product demanded resulting from the increase in product quality. This percentage figure determines the magnitude of E_q associated with a particular percentage increase in the firm's product quality expenditures.

Figure 11.2

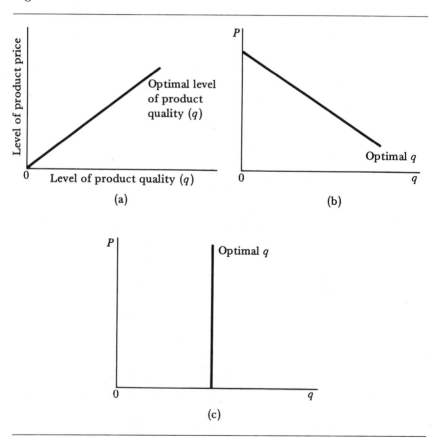

From the profit-maximizing product quality condition (3), it is clear that if the percentage increase in quantity of the firm's product demanded, and the resulting magnitude of E_q associated with an increase in product quality, is larger at higher level of P, this means that the profit-maximizing level of the firm's product quality will also be larger. This relationship between the profit-maximizing level of the firm's product quality and different levels of product price is depicted in Figure 11.2(a).

In contrast, an increase in product quality may shift the firm's demand curve in such a manner that the increase in the quantity of the firm's product demanded, and the magnitude of E_q, is smaller at higher product-price levels. This will imply that the profit-maximizing level of product quality will be lower, the higher the product price P, in condition (3). The resulting relationship between the profit-maximizing level of the firm's product quality and different levels of product price is depicted in Figure 11.2(b). If an increase in product quality shifts the firm's demand curve so that the percentage change in quantity of the product demanded, and the magnitude of E_q, are the same at different levels of product price, the profit-maximizing level of the firm's product quality will be independent of the level of product price. This situation is depicted in Figure 11.2(c).

Joint Determination of Optimal Product Price and Product Quality. To illustrate the determination of and the relationship between the profit-maximizing levels of product quality and product price, Figures 11.1 and 11.2 are combined in Figure 11.3, which adopts a taxonomic approach to all the possible combinations of circumstances shown in Figures 11.1 and 11.2. The curves in Figure 11.3(a)–(c) are not labeled, since in each case either curve could represent the optimal price relationship depicted in Figure 11.1 or the optimal product quality relationship depicted in Figure 11.2. There are therefore actually six possible situations depicted by Figure 11.3(a)–(c). In any of these situations, a shift in one of the curves will result in a new intersection point between the two curves that implies changes in the optimal level of *both* decision variables.

A shift in one of the curves will occur whenever any of the factors that affect the profit-maximizing level of just one of the decision variables are changed, either by regulation or any other changes in the objectives or constraints facing the firm's decision makers. This will also affect the profit-maximizing level of other decision variables in cases (a)–(c), since optimal levels of the other decision variables depend on the level of the decision variable that is initially affected.

In parts (d) and (e) of the figure, the profit-maximizing level of only one of the decision variables depends on the level of the other decision variable. In these cases, changes in the optimal level of one of the decision variables need not therefore affect the optimal level of the other decision variable. It needs to be emphasized that this is true only of *one* of

Figure 11.3

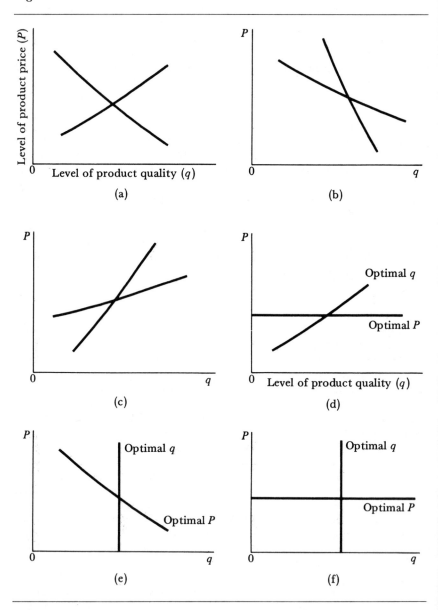

the decision variables, however. In (d), a change in factors that affect the optimal level of product quality at any level of product price will not affect the optimal level of product price. A change in the factors that affect the optimal level of product price at any level of product quality *will*, however, affect the optimal level of product quality! Similarly, in (e), a change in the factors that affect the optimal level of product price at any level of product quality will not change the optimal level of product quality. A change in the factors that affect the optimal level of product quality will, however, affect the optimal level of product price.

The only situation in which the profit-maximizing levels of product price and product quality are truly independent is depicted in Figure 11.3(f). In this case, changes in factors that affect the optimal level of product quality at any level of product price do not affect the *optimal,* or profit-maximizing, level of product price. Similarly, changes in factors that affect the optimal level of product price at any level of product quality do not affect the *optimal* level of product quality. The reader can verify these conclusions by shifting the curves in Figure 11.3 and examining the resulting implications for the intersection points of the curves, which represent optimal levels of both decision variables.

Generalizing the Results to Other Dimensions of Firms' Behavior. In the preceding examples, product price and product quality, and levels of the price- and product-quality elasticities of demand, E_p and E_q, were selected solely for illustrative purposes. The same conclusions would be obtained if any other two decision variables had been selected. Moreover, the preceding analysis implicitly assumed that levels of a firm's decision variables other than product price and product quality remained unchanged. Changes in levels of these other decision variables would shift the position of the optimal product-price curves in Figure 11.1, the positions of the optimal product quality curves in Figure 11.2, and the positions of the curves in Figure 11.3. Changes in levels of other decision variables would, in other words, affect the profit-maximizing levels of product price and product quality.

However, it is equally true that diagrams like Figures 11.1 and 11.2 could be drawn for each pair of the firm's other decision variables and that changes in the level of product price or product quality will generally shift the curves representing optimal levels of other decision variables at given levels of product quality and product price. In other words, a shift in just *one* curve in Figure 11.3, resulting in a change in the optimal levels of product price and product quality, will usually lead to changes in the optimal levels of *all* other decision variables in the firm. The only situation in which a decision variable would not change would be if the optimal level of that decision variable did not depend on the level of any other decision variable in the firm. Such a situation occurs only where — as in Figure 11.3(d) depicting optimal prices unrelated to product quality or as in Figure 11.3(e) depicting optimal product quality unrelated to price — the same horizontal and vertical shapes of the curves continue to hold *for every single decision variable of the firm that is placed on the horizontal axis* (for price independence) *or vertical axis* (for product-quality independence). As one might surmise, such a situation is not likely to occur very often in practice.

Equilibrium versus Disequilibrium Changes in Decision Variables. Although regulatory constraints or other factors that directly affect one dimension of a regulated firm's behavior will generally affect other dimensions of the firm's behavior, the reader is cautioned against automatically assuming that the levels of all the firm's decision variables will be adjusted to their new optimal levels by the firm's decision makers. Even in situations in which a firm's decision makers have sufficient information to determine the exact shape and position of curves like those in Figure 11.3, the levels of the firm's price and product quality decision variables need not be adjusted instantaneously to their new optimal levels. Responsibility for price and product quality decisions may be allocated between different individuals within the firm, and a variety of "disequilibrium adjustment rules" may be used by the firm's decision makers when levels of the firm's decision variables are not optimal. Different disequilibrium adjustment rules will result in different time paths of adjustment of the firm's decision variables from one optimal combination of decision variables to another. These adjustment rules may even result in a situation in which levels of the firm's decision variables do not converge toward the new optimal levels but instead depart increasingly from optimum levels.

Figure 11.4 may be used to illustrate some of these points diagrammatically. If regulation shifts the curve depicting the optimal level of the firm's product price at any level of product quality from P to P', the optimal levels of the firm's product price and product quality change from combination 1 to combination 2. At point 1, representing the initial price- and product-quality combination, product quality is optimal but product price is not. If the firm uses a disequilibrium adjustment rule that requires price to be changed to the optimal level associated with any existing level of product quality, followed by adjustments in product quality to achieve optimal levels of product quality at any given product-price level, the disequilibrium path of product-price and product-quality levels will be shown by the dashed line in Figure 11.4. This path is shown to diverge increasingly from the new optimum combination of product price and product quality depicted by point 2.

This result is not the only possibility, however; if the optimal product-quality line had been drawn with a slope that is steeper than the P lines, the process would have converged to point 2. Similarly, the use

Figure 11.4

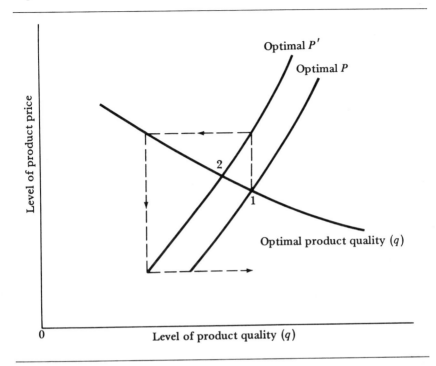

Level of product quality (q)

of a disequilibrium adjustment mechanism that involves simultaneous changes in price and product quality variables would yield a different disequilibrium path of adjustment, which could either diverge from, or converge toward, point 2.

The preceding examples are sufficient to warn the reader against drawing incorrect conclusions based solely on analysis of optimal or equilibrium levels of decision variables. Disequilibrium adjustment rules employed by decision makers are also important.

Analysis of the impact of regulation on optimal levels of regulated and unregulated firms' decision variables is very important, however, because the direction of changes in optimal levels of decision variables will determine what kind of a disequilibrium exists initially. Without disequilibrium there will be no disequilibrium adjustment process. However, analysis of the impact of regulation on optimal levels of firms' decision variables, and analysis of the response of firms to nonoptimal, or disequilibrium, levels of decision variables are *both* necessary in order to determine the effects of regulation on firms' behavior. Traditional analysis of regulation has focused almost exclusively on the first type of analysis; as a result, its conclusions may sometimes have limited relevance to the effects of regulation in practice.

11.2   LINKS BETWEEN DIFFERENT
PRODUCTS AND MARKETS

Section 11.1 emphasized that regulations aimed at changing a particular decision variable of a regulated firm will also generally change the optimal levels of other decision variables of the firm. This section explains why effects of regulation on dimensions of regulated firms' behavior will also generally cause changes in dimensions of the behavior of unregulated firms.

For example, regulations that affect the price of a regulated firm's products will change the relative prices of products produced by regulated firms and unregulated firms. This will cause buyers to reallocate their spending between different firms' products and will increase or reduce the demand for unregulated firms' products. If the goal of regulation is to achieve this change in relative prices of regulated and unregulated firms' products, such effects on unregulated firms may be desirable. In other situations, these and other effects of regulation on unregulated firms' behavior may be undesirable. However, regulation will almost invariably have effects of some kind on unregulated firms, since the behavior of regulated firms directly or indirectly influences the behavior of buyers of unregulated firms' products and suppliers of inputs to unregulated firms.

Fortunately, the same analytical and diagrammatic expository framework employed in Section 11.1 may also be used, with minor modifications, to explain the fundamental characteristics of the relationship that exists between regulated and unregulated firms' behavior in a broad range of regulatory contexts.

If changes in the price of a product Y do not affect the demand for another product X, the relationship between the profit-maximizing price of product X and alternative prices of product Y will be shown by the horizontal line in Figure 11.5(a) labeled Optimal P_X. If increases in the price of Y cause the demand curve for X to shift to the *right*, indicating increased demand for X at any level of the price of X, the relationship between the profit-maximizing price of X and alternative prices of Y will be shown by the upward-sloping curve in Figure 11.5(b) labeled Optimal P_X; X and Y are usually termed "substitutes" for each other in this case. Examples of substitute goods are butter and margarine, automobiles and bicycles, different methods of reducing pollution.

Figure 11.5

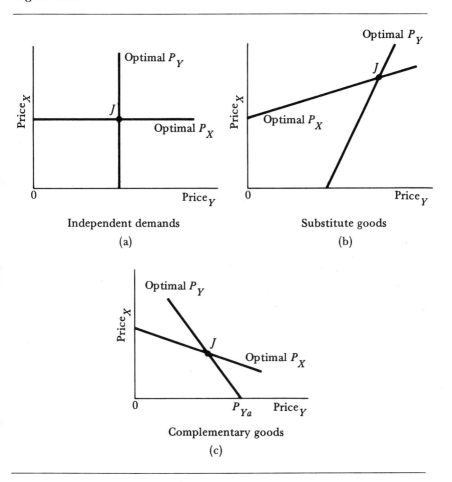

Independent demands
(a)

Substitute goods
(b)

Complementary goods
(c)

If an increase in the price of Y causes the demand curve for X to shift to the *left*, indicating reduced demand for X at any given price of X, the products are termed "complementary goods," and the relationship between the profit-maximizing price of X and alternative prices of Y is depicted by the downward-sloping curve in Figure 11.5(c) labeled Optimal P_X. Examples of complementary goods are tennis balls and racquets, automobiles and gasoline.

If increases in the price of X do not affect the demand for Y, the relationship between the profit-maximizing price of Y and alternative prices of X will be shown by the vertical line in Figure 11.5(a) labeled

Optimal P_Y. If increases in the price of X cause the demand curve for Y to shift to the *right,* the products are substitutes, and the upward-sloping curve labeled Optimal P_Y in Figure 11.5(b) shows the relationship between the profit-maximizing price of Y and alternative prices of X. Finally, if increases in the price of X cause the demand curve for Y to shift to the *left,* the products are complementary, and the curve labeled Optimal P_Y in Figure 11.5(c) depicts the relationship between the profit-maximizing price of Y and alternative prices of X.

The point J in Figure 11.5(a)–(c) represents the combination of prices of product X and product Y that simultaneously satisfy the profit-maximizing conditions in the two firms. At any other combination of product prices, the profit-maximization condition of one or both of the firms producing X and Y will not be met, and some kind of disequilibrium adjustment rules involving changes in product prices or other decision variables will be set in motion for one or both firms.

Commencing from an equilibrium combination of prices represented by point J, regulatory constraints that affect either the marginal cost curve or the demand curve of one of the firms, such as the firm producing X, will shift the curve labeled Optimal P_X. Except in the situation depicted by Figure 11.5(a), this will change the profit-maximizing price level of *both* firms' products, not only the profit-maximizing price of the regulated firm's product. The same conclusion applies if the price of product X is directly regulated, which may be depicted diagrammatically as the introduction of a horizontal line at the regulated price level in Figure 11.5(a)–(c).

The reader is reminded of the important point made at the end of last section: the actual path of adjustment of prices from an initial equilibrium combination of prices J toward or away from the new optimal combination depends on the precise nature of the disequilibrium adjustment rules employed by both firms.

Irrespective of the precise nature of these adjustment rules, however, changes in the level of a regulated firm's product price in response to regulatory constraints imposed on the firm will cause changes in the demand conditions facing unregulated producers of products that are substitutes or complements for the regulated product. This, in turn, will imply that unregulated firms are in disequilibrium, since the changed demand conditions facing those firms will imply new optimal levels of product prices. Moreover, for exactly the same reasons that were explained in Section 11.1 dealing with the response of regulated firms to regulation, changes in profit-maximizing levels of product prices in unregulated firms will imply changes in profit-maximizing levels of other decision variables, such as advertising, and research and development, in unregulated firms.

The preceding analysis indicates that regulation of a single dimension of a regulated firm's behavior will generally cause changes in many other dimensions of the behavior of both regulated and unregulated firms. All regulated firms produce products or services for which there are substitutes or complements, and therefore the effects of regulation will not be confined either to effects on the regulated dimension of behavior or to effects on regulated firms. Although the preceding exposition emphasized relationships between demands for different products, similar conclusions apply if relationships exist between costs of different products.

The effect of regulation on the actual levels of regulated and unregulated firms' decision variables, as opposed to the effects on optimal levels of those decision variables, depends on the precise nature of the disequilibrium adjustment rules employed by regulated firms *and* unregulated firms. In other words, it is necessary to include disequilibrium as well as equilibrium facets of *unregulated* firms' behavior in order to predict the consequences of regulation, even if one is interested only in predicting the effect of regulation on regulated firms! Moreover, as we shall explain in the following section, it is also necessary to include the disequilibrium behavior of regulatory agencies.

11.3 INTERACTIONS AMONG REGULATORY AGENCIES

Sections 11.1 and 11.2 focused on factors that determine the effects of a particular regulatory constraint on the behavior of regulated and unregulated firms. These factors, which underlie the equilibrium and disequilibrium behavior of regulated and unregulated firms, are not the only factors that determine the effects of regulation on these firms. The behavior of regulatory agencies themselves must be included in the analysis, because any particular regulatory constraint administered by one regulatory agency will generally affect the behavior of other regulatory agencies and the nature of other regulatory constraints that influence regulated and unregulated firms' behavior.

Suppose that regulations administered by an agency responsible for worker safety require outside venting of sawdust in furniture factories. This will tend to increase the amount of air pollution by the firm, which may lead another regulatory agency responsible for protecting environmental quality to change its regulatory policies. Furniture-producing firms might, for example, be required to install equipment that extracts sawdust from the air in the factory and that collects the sawdust for removal, rather than using outside venting. The firm's expenditures on this equipment might necessitate curtailment of previous expenditures on other equipment that improved worker safety. In this situation, the actions of the regulatory agencies tend to work against each other. In other situations, the actions of different agencies might reinforce each other.

Before we proceed to analyze the nature of regulatory agency inter-actions in more detail, it is helpful to recall the meaning of the terms "regulatory constraint" and "regulatory agency behavior." The relation-ship between these two terms was briefly examined in Chapter 4, where regulatory agency behavior was described as consisting of various aspects of monitoring and enforcement activity. These activities influence the nature of the regulatory constraint *that is perceived by regulated firms* and that consists essentially of a probabilistic relationship between pen-alties or rewards and various characteristics and levels of a regulated firm's behavior. In other words, various dimensions of regulatory agency monitoring and enforcement behavior affect either the magnitude or the probability that a particular penalty or reward will result from certain behavior exhibited by a regulated firm.

There are many different dimensions of regulatory agency behavior that affect the regulatory constraint, and many of the changes in agency behavior may affect the regulatory constraint *without changing the be-havior of regulated firms*. The relationship between agency behavior, regulatory constraints, and regulated firms' behavior will be examined in Chapters 12 and 13. Here, we shall analyze the effects of regulatory agency behavior, or decision variables that do affect regulated firms' behavior, without specifying precisely the nature of these regulatory decision variables.

Assume that only two regulatory agencies A and B exist and that each agency is responsible for regulating a different dimension of the same regulated firm's behavior. The conclusions of the subsequent anal-ysis would not be different if the regulated dimensions of behavior were those of two different firms, since the behavior of different firms is gen-erally related. Regulatory agency A's goal is to achieve a level $\overline{X}$ of di-mension X of the regulated firm's behavior, and regulatory agency B's goal is to achieve a level of $\overline{Y}$ of dimension Y of the regulated firm's be-havior. If each agency controls a decision variable that influences *only* the dimension of the firm's behavior regulated by that agency, Figure 11.6(a) depicts the relationship between the optimal level of each agency's de-cision variable, defined as that level of the agency's decision variable that achieves the desired level of behavior, $\overline{X}$ or $\overline{Y}$, exhibited by the regulated firm.

Combination J of the two agencies' decision variables simultaneously achieves both dimensions of the regulated firm's behavior, $\overline{X}$ and $\overline{Y}$, desired by each agency. The effect of each regulatory agency's decision variable on the dimension of firm's behavior that is regulated by the agency depends on many factors that underlie the behavior of the regu-latory agency and the regulated firm. These factors are assumed to be given in drawing the relationships labeled $\overline{Y}$ and $\overline{X}$ in Figure 11.6(a).

Figure 11.6

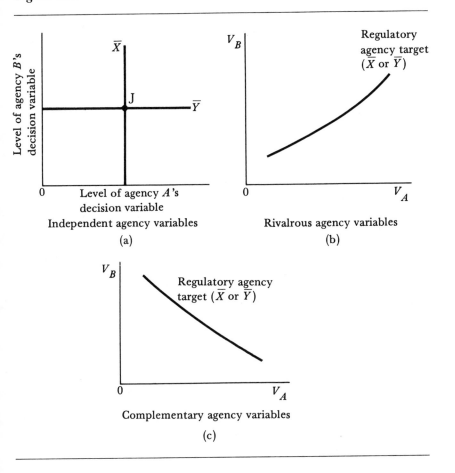

Level of agency B's decision variable

$\overline{X}$

J

$\overline{Y}$

0   Level of agency A's
                decision variable
        Independent agency variables
                        (a)

V_B

$\overline{Y}$

Regulatory
agency target
($\overline{X}$ or $\overline{Y}$)

0 V_A
        Rivalrous agency variables
                        (b)

V_B

Regulatory agency
target ($\overline{X}$ or $\overline{Y}$)

0   V_A
        Complementary agency variables
                        (c)

Changes in any of these underlying factors affecting agency A, for example, will shift the $\overline{X}$ curve and change the optimal level of the decision
variable of agency A. In the situation depicted by Figure 11.6(a), the
optimal level of agency B's decision variable will *not* be changed, since
the Y dimension of the firm's behavior regulated by agency B is not
affected by the behavior of agency A.

Rivalrous and Complementary Relationships among Agencies. The preceding situation is extremely unlikely to occur in practice, because as
Section 11.1 emphasized, all dimensions of a regulated firm's behavior

are generally related, and changes in one dimension of a firm's behavior will usually imply changes in the levels of other dimensions also. In other words, regulation that causes changes in dimension X of a regulated firm's behavior will also generally cause changes in dimension Y, and vice versa. In these circumstances, two general types of relationship between the behavior of different regulatory agencies will exist. These are depicted in Figure 11.6(b) and (c).

In Figure 11.6(b), the level of a regulatory agency's decision variable, such as monitoring or enforcement, that achieves the agency's target level of regulated firm behavior, $\overline{X}$ or $\overline{Y}$, is higher at higher levels of the other agency's decision variable. In this case, the effect of increases in each agency's decision variable on the level of X or Y tend to work in opposite directions. An increase in one agency's decision variable tends to raise (or lower) X or Y, and an increase in the other agency's decision variable tends to lower (or raise) X or Y. This situation will henceforth be referred to as a situation in which agency decision variables are "rivals" as far as their effects on a dimension of the regulated firm's behavior are concerned.

Figure 11.6(c) exhibits the other type of relationship that is possible between regulatory agency decision variables. Here, the level of an agency's decision variable that achieves the target level of the regulated firm's behavior, $\overline{X}$ or $\overline{Y}$, is lower at higher levels of the other agency's decision variable. In this case, the effect of increases in each agency's decision variable on the level of X or Y tends to work in the same direction. An increase in one agency's decision variable tends to raise (or lower) X or Y, and an increase in the other agency's decision variable also tends to raise (or lower) X or Y. This situation will be referred to as one in which agency decision variables are "complementary" as far as their effects on a dimension of the regulated firm's behavior are concerned.

The "rivalrous" and "complementary" relationships between regulatory agency decision variables may be combined in any one of the three possible ways depicted in Figure 11.7. Each of the two curves in any of the diagrams could apply either to regulatory agency A's target $\overline{X}$ or to agency B's target $\overline{Y}$. In reality, therefore, there are six possible relationships, all exhibiting interdependence between the two regulatory agencies.

The points labeled J in each diagram represent the combination of regulatory agency decision variables that simultaneously achieve the level of the dimension of the regulated firm's behavior that is desired by each agency. In each diagram, a shift in one of the curves represents a change in the level of one agency's decision variable that achieves the desired behavior dimension of the regulated firm, $\overline{X}$ or $\overline{Y}$, at given levels of the other agency's decision variable. What is important in the present context is that a shift in one of the curves will change the optimal level of *both* agencies' decision variables.

The intuitive explanation for this is not difficult to understand. As

Figure 11.7

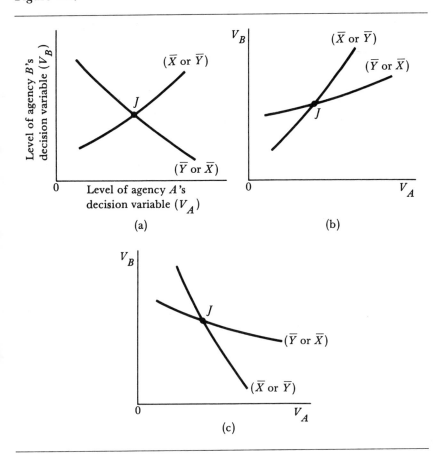

the agency A adjusts the level of its decision variable to the new optimal level resulting from a shift in the optimal policy curve for agency A, this affects the Y dimension of the regulated firm's behavior that is regulated by agency B. This will change the level of agency B's decision variable that is required to keep the firm's Y dimension of behavior at $\overline{Y}$. As can be easily verified by Figure 11.7, some shifts in the optimal policy curve of one agency will change the optimal level of both agencies' decision variables in the same direction. This will occur whenever one of the curves in Figure 11.7(b) shifts in either direction, for example. In this situation the impact of the decision variables of the agencies on either dimension X or Y of the regulated firm's behavior is rivalrous, as already

314 Effects of Regulation

noted. Changes in the level of one agency's decision variable in a particular direction must therefore be matched by changes in the same direction in the other agency's decision variable in order to preserve unchanged levels of the firm's behavior at levels $\overline{X}$ and $\overline{Y}$.

In contrast, in situations depicted by Figure 11.7(c), a shift in the optimal policy curve of one regulatory agency will increase the optimal level of one agency's decision variable and reduce the optimal level of the other agency's decision variable. The intuitive reasoning behind this conclusion is not difficult to understand. The agencies' decision variables are "complementary" in this case, in the sense that an increase in one agency's decision variable will require a decrease in the other agency's decision variable in order to leave regulated firm's X or Y behavior unchanged at levels $\overline{X}$ or $\overline{Y}$.

Equilibrium versus Disequilibrium Levels of Agency Instruments. Changes in the optimal levels of both regulatory agencies' decision variables caused by shifts in the optimal policy lines in Figure 11.7 imply disequilibrium in one or both agencies' decision variables at the previously optimal combination *J*. This fact does *not,* however, imply that the new optimal levels of agency decision variables will be established. The resulting disequilibrium path of the agencies' decision variables depends on the nature of the "disequilibrium adjustment rules" employed by both agencies in an effort to reach optimal levels of their respective decision variables.

Different disequilibrium adjustment rules, defining the directions and relative speeds with which the regulatory agencies adjust their respective decision variables when in disequilibrium, can lead to different paths of adjustment of those decision variables through time. Some of these paths need not converge on optimal levels of the agencies' decision variables. Whether or not optimal levels of the regulatory agencies and other types of decision variable converge to optimal levels can be determined only by considering the disequilibrium adjustment rules used by different types of decision makers, as well as the factors that underlie the positions and shapes of the optimal policy curves of regulatory agencies, regulated firms, and unregulated firms.

One thing should be amply clear: one cannot predict the effects of a particular regulatory agency's policies — either on equilibrium or disequilibrium aspects of regulated and unregulated firms' behavior — without simultaneously considering factors that determine the equilibrium and disequilibrium behavior of other regulatory agencies.

Interactions Between Regulated Firms and Regulators. Interactions between different decision variables within regulated firms were analyzed in Section 11.1; interactions between regulated and unregulated firms were examined in Section 11.2; and interactions between regulatory agencies were analyzed in the present section. There is one other type of interaction that has not been explicitly mentioned and that can be depicted diagrammatically in exactly the same manner as the other types of interaction: the possible interaction between levels of a regulatory agency's decision variables and the levels of the firm's decision variables the agency attempts to regulate. In this and the preceding sections of this chapter it has been assumed that a regulatory agency is able to influence the dimension of the regulated firm's behavior the agency has responsibility for. This implicitly rules out situations depicted by Figure 11.8(a), which illustrates a case in which different levels of a regulatory agency's decision variables have no effect on the optimal level of a regulated firm's decision variable. (Such cases do exist in practice, and the reasons will be explained in Chapter 12.)

Figure 11.8

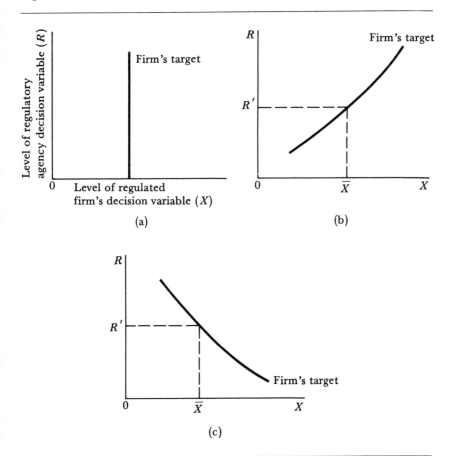

(a)

(b)

(c)

Even in situations where the agency's decision variable affects the optimal level of the firm's decision variable — illustrated by the fact that the firm's optimal policy curve slopes up or down, as in Figure 11.8(b) or (c) — there is an additional implicit assumption in the analysis conducted in this chapter. It is that the regulatory agency is able to select the level of its decision variable that elicits the level of the regulated firm's behavior, $\overline{X}$, desired by the agency. In Figures 11.8(b) and (c), this means the agency is able to set its decision variable at R', which induces the firm to select $\overline{X}$ in order to achieve its own target. This requires that the agency have information on the regulated firm's optimal policy curve, which depends on the objectives and all the constraints that confront the firm's policymakers (see Chapter 12).

In practice, a more likely situation is that, lacking information about the firm's optimal policy curve, the agency may initially select a level of R other than R', and then adjust R in response to the firm's observed response.

11.4   A FRAMEWORK FOR VIEWING THE RELATIONSHIP BETWEEN DIFFERENT TYPES OF REGULATION

The analysis and discussion contained in Sections 11.1–11.3 demonstrate that it is not legitimate to view the effects of regulation as a sequence of effects that occur first on regulated firms, then on unregulated firms. Instead, the effects of regulation on regulated firms and the behavior of unregulated firms and other regulatory agencies interact simultaneously to produce effects on the decision variables of all three types of organization. Two types of effects may be usefully distinguished. First, there are effects on *optimal, or equilibrium, levels of decision variables* in each type of organization. These effects are depicted diagrammatically by changes in the intersection points of the optimal policy curves in Figures 11.3–11.8.

Second, there are effects on *disequilibrium levels of decision variables* in each type of organization. Diagrammatically, these effects are depicted by the disequilibrium path of decision variables from any point in the diagrams that is *not* an intersection point between optimal policy curves. Even if such a point is on *one* of the optimal policy curves, indicating that one of the decision variables is an optimal level, the other decision variable to which the diagram refers will not be at an optimal level. Decision makers who control that decision variable can therefore be expected to change the level of the decision variable, according to some disequilibrium adjustment rule that defines the direction and time rate of change of the decision variable in question.

Except in situations like Figures 11.3(f), 11.5(a), and 11.6(a), where optimal levels of different decision variables are independent, changes in the level of one of the decision variables will affect the outcome associated with any level of the other decision variable, and will imply that any level of that other decision variable that was previously optimal will no longer be optimal. The level of this other decision variable will therefore also be changed in accordance with some disequilibrium adjustment rule used by the decision maker who is responsible for deciding the magnitude of that decision variable. As we have already emphasized, the disequilibrium path of adjustment of decision variables can take many forms and need not converge toward an equilibrium combination of optimal levels of all the decision variables.

The preceding discussion and diagrammatic exposition of the effects of regulation on dimensions of regulated firms', unregulated firms', and regulatory agencies' behavior can be linked up with Tables 3.1 and 4.1 in Chapters 3 and 4, where each row of the tables depicts people's evaluations of one of the effects of regulation. The factors that determined the effects of regulation on regulated and unregulated decision makers were not explained at that early stage of the book, since the emphasis was on explaining what determines people's evaluations of effects of regulation. There was therefore no explanation of the way in which the different effects of regulation depicted by the first column of Table 3.1 and Table 4.1 are related to each other.

The verbal and diagrammatic analyses contained in Sections 11.1–11.3 provide perspective for understanding the determinants and relationship between different effects of regulation on the behavior of regulated and unregulated firms, and also on the behavior of regulatory agencies themselves. Because the diagrammatic analysis is restricted to the effects of regulation on two decision variables only, however, it is useful to provide an additional expository framework that shows all the different effects of regulation on levels of decision variables in the economy, and that can be used to summarize the conclusions reached in each of the preceding three sections of this chapter. Such a framework is provided by Table 11.1, where the rows indicate all possible dimensions of firms' behavior and the columns indicate every firm in the economy.

Table 11.1 assumes that only P_X is regulated, and E_{11} represents the effect of regulating P_X on the level of P_X. In Section 11.1 it was explained that regulations affecting any single dimension of a firm's behavior will generally also affect other dimensions of that firm's behavior. This means that the E terms in the first column are related, and will be zero only in the case depicted by Figure 11.3(f). In Section 11.2 it was explained that regulations affecting the product price or other dimensions of a *regulated* firm's behavior will generally have effects on the product price and other dimensions of *unregulated* firms' behavior. This means that the E terms in the second through nth columns are related to those in the first column, and will be zero only in the case depicted by Figure 11.5(a).

Table 11.1. Effects of Regulating a Particular Dimension of Firms'
Behavior

Dimension of firms' behavior	Firm 1	Firm 2	. . .	Firm n
P_X	$*E_{11}$	E_{12}	. . .	E_{1n}
P_Y	E_{21}	E_{22}	. . .	E_{2n}
.				
.				
.				
Advertising, R&D	E_{31}	E_{32}	. . .	E_{3n}

NOTE The * denotes which firm and which dimension of that firm's behavior is regulated.

The E elements in Table 11.1 can refer either to (1) changes in optimal levels of decision variables caused by regulation, depicted diagrammatically by changes in the intersection points of optimal policy curves labeled J in earlier sections, or to (2) disequilibrium changes in levels of firms' decision variables in response to a particular regulatory policy. As we have already noted, there is no reason why these two elements should bear any relationship to each other, in either sign or magnitude. Disequilibrium responses to regulation by decision makers, and effects of regulation on equilibrium characteristics of decision-maker behavior, are two entirely different aspects of the effects of regulation. Although these aspects are related, it is essential not to confuse equilibrium and disequilibrium effects of regulation.

It is also important to understand that irrespective of whether the E terms in Table 11.1 refer to equilibrium or disequilibrium effects of regulation, information on the E terms alone is insufficient to determine the nature of the underlying process that generates these effects. In the case of regulation's effects on optimal levels of decision-maker behavior analyzed diagrammatically in this chapter, any particular effect of regulation on decision-maker behavior can be produced by a variety of underlying behavior relationships.

This can best be illustrated by an example of the relationship between regulation of advertising and the price of a product. In Section 11.1 it was explained that the profit-maximizing price of any firm's product could either increase or decrease with increases in the level of the firm's expenditures that affect the demand for the firm's product, such as product quality or advertising expenditures. It was also explained that the profit-maximizing level of a firm's expenditures on product quality or advertising could either increase or decrease with increases in the price of the firm's product.

Benham (1972) estimated empirically the relationship between advertising and the price of eyeglasses in states with different degrees of prohibition on the advertising of eyeglasses; he found that the price of eyeglasses was substantially lower in states with fewer restrictions on advertising this product. Benham interpreted this finding as evidence that restrictions on advertising increase the price of eyeglasses and, by implication, that reducing or eliminating these restrictions would reduce prices in those states where restrictions existed.

Figure 11.9 indicates that this inference is not necessarily correct. Figure 11.9(a) and (b) illustrates situations in which profit-maximizing product prices are lower in states that permit unrestricted advertising, shown by the combination of decision variables labeled S_U, than in states with advertising restrictions, shown by the combinations labeled S_R. The implications of eliminating restrictions on advertising for the price of eyeglasses are very different in the two cases, however. In the case illustrated by Figure 11.9(a), prices are lower and advertising is higher in states with fewer advertising restrictions because the firm's profit-maximizing level of price is lower at any level of advertising than in states with restrictions on advertising. This could occur if rivals' reactions to price reductions are expected to be smaller in states without advertising restrictions than in states currently with advertising restrictions. In this case, eliminating restrictions on advertising that increase the optimal level of a firm's advertising at any level of product price will shift the curve labeled Optimal adv in Figure 11.9(a) to the right. As the reader can verify, this would *increase* the profit-maximizing price of the product in that state.

In the case illustrated by Figure 11.9(b), prices are lower and advertising is higher in states with fewer advertising restrictions because the firm's profit-maximizing level of advertising at any particular level of product price is higher than in states with advertising restrictions. This could occur if rivals' reactions to a firm's advertising changes are expected to be smaller in states without advertising restrictions than in states with these restrictions. In this case, eliminating restrictions on advertising that increase the optimal level of a firm's advertising at any level of product price will shift the curve labeled Optimal adv in Figure 11.9(b) to the right, which will reduce the profit-maximizing price of the product.

Partial- versus General-Equilibrium Analysis. Any analysis of the effects of regulation on optimal levels of decision maker A's behavior that implicitly or explicitly assumes that some of the factors that influence A's behavior remain unchanged is termed a "partial-equilibrium" analysis of the decision maker's behavior. A "general-equilibrium" analysis of the effects of regulation on a particular decision maker's behavior permits

320

Figure 11.9

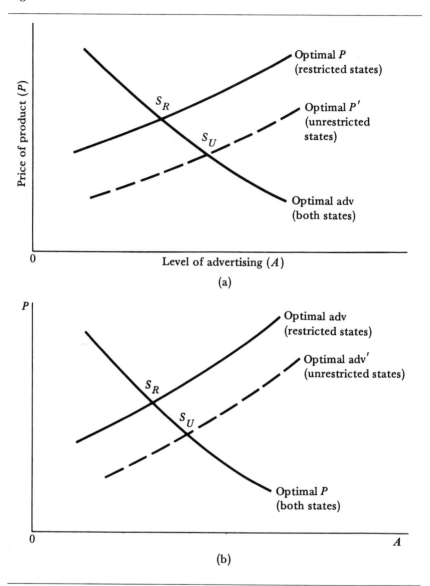

more of the factors that influence the decision maker's behavior to vary in response to regulation. These additional factors become "endogenous," which means that they are to be explained by the analysis, instead of remaining "exogenous," which means that they are determined outside the analysis and taken as fixed and unexplained by the analysis, as occurs in a partial-equilibrium analysis.

The distinction between partial- and general-equilibrium analysis of decision-maker behavior is one of degree. A completely "general" general-equilibrium analysis, which treats every factor that influences a decision maker's behavior as a variable whose magnitude is to be determined by the analysis, is impossible. Such an analysis would have to include the determinants of the behavior of every decision maker who is currently alive, as well as the behavior of preceding generations of decision makers whose decisions resulted in some of the characteristics of the environment that influence the behavior of the generation of decision makers currently alive.

An analysis of the effects of regulation on the position of one of the optimal policy curves in any of the diagrams in this chapter is an example of a partial-equilibrium analysis of the effects of regulation. Such an analysis indicates the direction and magnitude of the effect of regulation on one dimension of decision maker's behavior, at any particular unchanged level of other dimensions of the same or other decision makers' behavior. Introducing a second optimal policy curve, and examining the effect of regulation on the position of both curves and the intersection point that depicts optimal levels of both decision makers' decision variables, is an example of general-equilibrium analysis.

General-equilibrium analysis is important, for it indicates that the consequences of regulation for the direction and magnitude of changes in particular decision variables may in some circumstances be very different from conclusions based on partial-equilibrium analysis, and can focus attention on the type of information required to determine whether these circumstances exist in practice. From time to time, articles have appeared in the economics literature arguing for more general-equilibrium analyses of the effects of regulation on regulated dimensions of decision-maker behavior, and with illustrations of cases in which such analyses reverse conclusions based on partial-equilibrium analysis. For example, Johnson (1969) demonstrated that, contrary to the conclusions drawn from partial-equilibrium analysis, there are circumstances in which a minimum wage law that applies to only part of the productive activities of the economy may benefit workers in all sectors. Similarly, Frenkel and Pashigian (1972) have emphasized that when changes in relative factor prices and income distribution are included in the analysis of regulation of the quantity or price of a particular product, traditional partial-equilibrium conclusions regarding the magnitude of excess demand for the regulated product at the regulated quantity or price may no longer be valid.

Many other articles, and contexts, could be cited where general-equilibrium analysis reverses the conclusions of partial-equilibrium analysis of regulation's effects; all are variations on the same theme, which may be summarized by reference to the diagrammatic framework of this chapter, as follows. Figure 11.10 illustrates six possible ways in which the optimal prices of two goods whose demands or supplies depend on the price of both products may be related. The solid curves represent the situation in absence of regulation; the dashed curves represent the effect of some kind of regulation that *raises* the optimal price of product 1 at any level of the price of product 2. In all six diagrams, any change in the price of product 1 changes the optimal level of the price of product 2, and vice versa.

The intersection point between the dashed curve, representing optimal levels of the price of product 1 at different levels of the price of product 2 when there is regulation, and the solid curve labeled Optimal P_2, represents the combination of prices of both products that are optimal and simultaneously achieve the objectives of decision makers controlling the prices of both products. In Figure 11.10(a)–(d) this intersection point illustrates that regulation raises the equilibrium optimal price of product 1. In contrast, in parts (e) and (f) of the figure, regulation that raises the optimal price of product 1 at any given price of product 2 results in a *decrease* in the equilibrium optimal price of product 1. This perverse result is attributable to the effect of regulating the price of product 1 on the price of product 2, and the difference in the relative slopes of the optimal price curves in cases (e) and (f) in comparison with cases (b) and (c).

In the preceding illustration of the effects of regulation in a general-equilibrium analysis, product prices were selected as decision variables merely for expository convenience. The nature of the interdependence that exists between any two decision variables will always be depicted by one of the six diagrams in Figure 11.10. Therefore, the preceding diagrammatic framework and its implications are applicable to any situation where two or more decision variables are interdependent. For example, Abernathy and Chakravarthy (1979) have emphasized that industrial innovation is affected by a number of government policies, including government investment in research and development, taxation, and regulatory policy variables. These policy variables are controlled by different government decision makers, and optimal levels of each policy variable may depend on the level of one or more of the other policy variables. In these circumstances, changes in one type of policy designed to influence industrial innovation in a particular direction may cause changes in other government policy variables that result in effects on innovation that are very different in sign and magnitude from the effects that were intended.

Figure 11.10

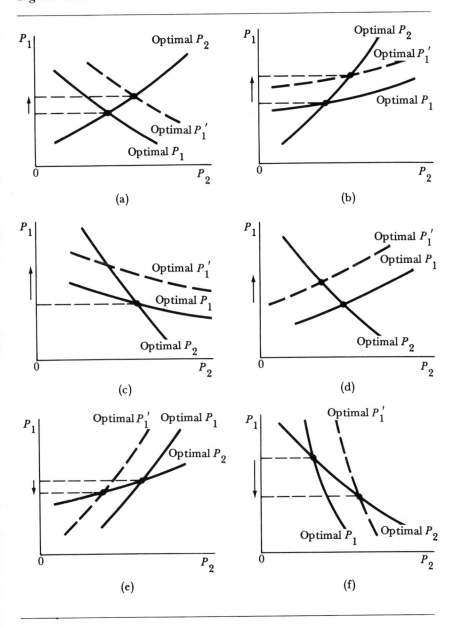

In addition to these implications for the effects of regulation on optimal levels of decision variables, the diagrams in Figure 11.10 also have important implications for the effects of regulation on disequilibrium levels of decision variables and their consequences for decision-maker behavior. For example, Gould and Henry (1967) have pointed out that regulation that reduces the price of a particular product below the level that initially equates demand and supply for the product, and that causes excess demand for the product, does not necessarily imply that this excess demand will "spill over" into markets for substitute products and raise the price of those products. The effect of a reduction in the price of the regulated product in markets for substitute products will depend on changes in both demand and supply of substitute products.

Even if demand for substitutes were to increase, the effect on the state of excess demand for, and price of, the substitute products would depend also on the magnitude and direction of the change in supply of substitute products. Moreover, even if there is no change in the supply of substitute products, Gould and Henry also demonstrate that demand for substitute products need not increase as the result of a reduction in the price of one of the products resulting from regulation. The reason for this is that some buyers who obtain the regulated product at the lower price will reduce their demand for substitutes, while buyers who are unable to satisfy their demand for the regulated product at the lower price will increase their demand for substitute products. On balance, the net effect of these two opposing influences on the demand for the substitute product is indeterminate a priori.

We have thus far focused on the mechanism by which regulation of a single decision variable causes effects on other decision variables, producing the overall effects summarized in Table 11.1. There will be a different set of effects on dimensions of firms' behavior, and a different table, similar to Table 11.1, for each dimension of the firm's behavior that is regulated. The net effect of different regulations aimed at different dimensions of a firm's behavior will therefore depend on the aggregation of all the effects associated with each type of regulation. In some cases, the effects of different types of regulation on particular dimensions of behavior will reinforce each other. In other cases, the effects of different types of regulation on particular dimensions of behavior will tend to offset each other.

These conclusions apply whether one is concerned with the effects of regulation on equilibrium levels of firms' behavior or with effects of regulation on disequilibrium levels of variables and decision-maker behavior. Since the effects of any single regulatory agency's behavior on regulated and unregulated firms' behavior will depend on the behavior of other regulatory agencies as well as on determinants of regulated and unregulated firms' behavior, this raises the important issue of what the proper level of aggregation is for viewing regulation and regulation's effects.

11.5 THE PROPER LEVEL
OF AGGREGATION
FOR VIEWING REGULATION

The literature on regulation has almost totally ignored the problem of deciding the proper level of aggregation at which analysis of regulation's effects is conducted. This problem can be viewed from a number of perspectives, and each perspective has important implications for both descriptive and normative analyses of the effects of regulation. The preceding sections of this chapter provide a useful framework for viewing this problem and understanding its implications. A major conclusion of those sections is that the effect of any regulatory agency's behavior on regulated and unregulated firms' behavior will depend on the behavior of other regulatory agencies as well as on determinants of regulated and unregulated firms' behavior. This means that a decision to analyze the effects of one agency's behavior implicitly accepts the regulatory constraints that result from the behavior of other agencies. All existing analyses of the behavior of individual regulatory agencies and individual regulatory constraints adopt this approach.

We are *not* saying that all existing analyses of particular regulatory agencies ignore the behavior of other regulatory agencies or assume that other agencies do not change their behavior in response to actions by the agency whose behavior is the focus of analysis. A small minority of writers on the subject of regulation have recognized the interdependence that exists between the behavior of different regulatory agencies.

What we *are* saying is that existing analyses of regulation do not usually examine the effects of simultaneous initial changes in the behavior of *two or more* regulatory agencies or regulatory constraints. A rare exception is provided by Winston (1981), who argues that if motor freight rates alone were deregulated, this would increase the amount of surface freight traffic misallocation between road and rail. He argues that deregulation of motor carrier rates *accompanied* by regulated rate reform in rail is a more desirable alternative.

In terms of the diagrams in this chapter, conventional analyses of regulation examine the effect of changing some dimension of a single regulatory agency's behavior on the position of the regulated firm's optimal policy curves. This will indicate very different effects from an analysis that simultaneously changes one or more decision variables of two or more regulatory agencies. If the levels of decision variables in two or more agencies are simultaneously varied at the outset, the resulting implications for the position and intersection points of the various optimal policy curves that depict equilibrium levels of the decision variables of regulatory agencies, regulated firms, and unregulated firms will differ from those which result from initially changing the level of a single regulatory agency's decision variable. In addition, the disequilibrium path of decision variables that results from the use of any particular disequilibrium adjustment rules by the various decision makers will also generally be different.

It may be true that under current regulatory practice decisions by regulatory agencies are made in a decentralized manner. This does not necessarily imply that current practices are the only possible way to do things, any more than the fact that some firms allocate decision-making responsibility for pricing decisions and advertising decisions to different individuals means that combining responsibility for those two decisions in one person is impossible. Our main concern here is to make the reader aware that any analysis of the effects of a single regulatory agency's behavior implicitly accepts the behavior of other agencies as a "proper" constraint in the analysis.

If there are n regulatory agencies, or regulatory constraints, the effects of changing one of these constraints on the behavior of regulated and unregulated decision makers will be very different from the effects of changing two or more of these constraints simultaneously. Similarly, if the perspective of regulatory decision makers is confined to the effects of changing individual regulatory constraints on regulated decision makers' behavior, the perceived effects and related benefit and cost estimates associated with individual regulatory constraints will be very different from those which result from a regulatory perspective that views the consequences of varying individual regulatory constraints as a whole.

From a normative point of view, it is desirable to view different regulatory constraints, and their effects on decision makers' behavior, as a whole, even if regulatory decision making continues to be performed in a decentralized manner. There are circumstances in which decentralized regulatory decision making can work well, and there are others where it cannot. These circumstances are determined by characteristics of the equilibrium and disequilibrium behavior of regulatory agency decision makers considered as a whole. In other words, in order to determine the nature and degree of decentralized regulatory decision making that is compatible with any particular set of regulatory targets, it is necessary to view different regulatory agencies and constraints as a whole. This is true even in circumstances in which an aggregate perspective that includes simultaneous consideration of all regulatory constraints indicates that greater decentralization in regulatory decision making will improve the degree to which a given set of regulatory targets is attained.

Regulators' Perspective versus Firms' Perspective. Another perspective for viewing this problem that is also important is that of regulated firms and decision makers. Even if regulation is conducted in a decentralized manner, this does not necessarily imply that the response of regulated firms to regulation is also based on a decentralized view of different regulatory agencies and regulatory constraints affecting dimensions of regulated firms' behavior. At one extreme, a firm's decision makers may simultaneously consider all the different regulatory constraints that confront the firm jointly and may select the optimal levels of the firm's decision variables in light of this aggregate view of the regulatory constraints that confront the firm.

At the other extreme, the firm may allocate responsibility for reacting to regulatory constraints directed at different dimensions of the firm's operations to different individuals within the firm. In this second situation, three possible cases may be distinguished. In one case, the firm's decision maker who is responsible for reacting to a particular regulatory constraint may consider the impact of the constraint only on the dimension of the firm's behavior that is regulated by that constraint. In the second case, the decision maker may consider the impact of the regulatory constraint on levels of all the firm's decision variables. In the third possible way in which a firm may structure its decision making to deal with regulatory constraints, a particular decision maker may be given responsibility for reacting to *all* the regulatory constraints that impact a particular dimension of the firm's behavior, irrespective of the dimension of the firm's behavior that the regulatory constraints are directed toward.

These three ways in which a firm's decision makers may view and react to regulatory constraints have very different implications for the behavior of regulated firms and the effects of regulation on regulated and unregulated decision makers' behavior.

CHAPTER TWELVE

Guidelines for Improving Regulation: Aspects of Regulated Firms' Behavior

12.1 THE PROBLEM OF INCENTIVES

Many writers have pointed out that the problem of unsatisfactory performance in regulatory and other contexts is that the existing incentives facing decision makers are not appropriate. The problem of determining what kind of incentives are optimal from the point of view of eliciting desired forms of decision-maker behavior, and the problem of how these incentives can be introduced, are related but distinguishable ones.

The existing incentives that confront any decision maker include the objectives the decision maker is trying to accomplish and *all* the constraints the decision maker perceives to be relevant in choosing between alternative courses of action. For these reasons, it is no easy task to determine the incentives facing decision makers; yet this is precisely the information that is required to change existing incentives in a manner that produces the desired changes in the decision makers' behavior. In this section, a number of characteristics shared by all attempts to change decision-maker behavior in particular ways by changing the incentives facing them will be discussed. In Sections 12.2 and 12.3, applications of important principles in designing optimal incentive systems will be applied to regulated firms.

The problem of devising incentives designed to influence decision makers' behavior in a particular desired manner can be divided into two distinct but related problems. One problem is to obtain accurate information from decision makers whose behavior is the object of the incentive system. In most situations, the designer of the incentive system must rely on the decision maker for certain information regarding some of the constraints confronting the decision maker. This information is required because any decision maker's behavior will depend not only on the characteristics of a particular incentive system but also on the other constraints the decision maker considers relevant when deciding how to behave.

If a decision maker who is the object of a specific incentive system can gain by distorting information that is reported to the designer of the incentive system, he or she can be expected to provide inaccurate information. For example, by exaggerating the costs of a particular activity relative to their true level, a decision maker can reduce the apparent "socially optimal" level of that activity. This will reduce the level of the activity that is adopted as a required standard by the regulator who designs the incentive system and will raise the reward, or reduce the penalty, from any given level of decision-maker behavior that differs from the true socially optimal level of the activity. A decision maker may also exaggerate or understate reported behavior relative to the true level in order to raise rewards or reduce penalties from a particular incentive system. Section 12.2 will examine more closely the characteristics that an incentive system must exhibit in order to motivate decision makers to report accurate information regarding their behavior or the constraints they face.

The second problem of devising an appropriate incentive system is that of selecting characteristics of the system in such a manner that decision makers who are the object of the system respond in the desired manner. The "desired manner" depends on the objectives of the "center" that designs the incentive system, and different objectives on the part of this center will generally change the characteristics of an optimal incentive system. Given the objectives of the center, the characteristics of the optimal incentive system will depend on how decision makers respond to variations in particular characteristics of the incentive system, and these responses will in turn depend on the goals and constraints perceived by those decision makers.

In both of these incentive problems, three aspects of the problem of designing an appropriate incentive system need to be clearly distinguished, even though they are related:

1. Which *dimension* of decision-maker behavior should be rewarded or penalized? This includes the choice of whether to apply rewards or penalties to dimensions of the behavior of organizations or to dimensions of the behavior of persons. For example, penalties may be applied to violations of pollution laws by a firm or other organization irrespective

of whose decisions within the firm were responsible for the pollution. Alternatively, penalties may be applied to the persons within the organization whose decisions were responsible for the violations of pollution standards.

2. What *type* of rewards or penalties should be used? This includes the choice between rewards for meeting regulatory standards and penalties for violating those standards.

Although in principle rewards and penalties connected with regulatory standards can take many forms, in practice in the United States penalties are the main type of regulatory sanction, and these are limited in number. For example, penalties for antitrust violations are of three major types: fines and jail sentences, "remedies," and private damage suits. Jail sentences for violations of the Sherman Act of 1890 were not applied until 1959, and only light sentences have been applied in several major cases since that time. "Remedies" are of two types. One is "injunctive relief," which is a prohibition by the courts of certain kinds of behavior. Violations of injunctions automatically lead to penalties applied by the courts. The second type of remedy takes the form of court-decreed changes in company structure, through divestiture, divorcement, or dissolution of certain company operations.

Private damages can be levied by the courts at triple the amount of harm shown to have been caused to an injured party by an antitrust violation. A successful suit by an antitrust agency can therefore trigger private suits by private parties such as overcharged customers or injured competitors. Private damage suits may not be brought if a *consent decree* or *nolo contendere* plea by the violating firm is accepted by the court or prosecuting agency. This limits the potential threat of private damage suits in practice, since nine tenths of antitrust suits are settled by consent decree. The prospect of being able to settle an antitrust suit by consent decree also limits the potential threat of other sanctions such as fines, jail sentences, and remedies.

3. At what *level* should rewards or penalties for certain kinds of behavior be set? This problem can be divided into (a) how the level of rewards or penalties should vary at different levels of a selected dimension of decision-maker behavior that is to be encouraged or discouraged and (b) what the *relative* level of rewards or penalties to different dimensions of the behaviors that are to be encouraged or discouraged should be.

Mention has already been made of the limited use and short duration of jail sentences for violations of antitrust laws in the United States. Criticism has also often been directed at the level of monetary fines that may be imposed for antitrust violations. The $5,000 limit originally established by the Sherman Act was raised to $50,000 in 1955 and to $500,000 for individuals and $1 million for firms in 1974. These fines are often small in comparison with the additional profits firms may earn from violating antitrust laws. The added profits from current violations may often far exceed the discounted present value of even a large fine that is distant in time, and perhaps avoidable. Also, since these maximum fines apply irrespective of the size of firms committing violations, their impact as a potential deterrent to violations of antitrust laws is likely to be smaller for large firms with ample resources than for smaller firms.

Appropriate solutions to the three preceding aspects of the problem of designing an incentive system depend critically on (1) the objectives of the agency that designs the incentive system and (2) the objectives and constraints that determine the behavior of the decision maker who is the object of the incentive system. The following group of some of the more important constraints that determine decision-maker behavior, in addition to the form of any incentive system, will prove helpful in gaining perspective on the problem of devising an appropriate incentive system for any particular type of decision maker.

a. The Decision Maker's Own Objective Function. This describes the variables that yield the decision maker positive or negative satisfaction and the decision maker's own relative evaluation of these different variables.

A decision maker's objective function is clearly important in connection with (2), the problem of which type of rewards or penalties to use to encourage or discourage particular behaviors. If the rewards or penalties that are selected do not enter directly into the objective function of the decision maker, the only way they can possibly affect behavior is by changing one or more of the constraints that confront the decision maker. For example, if a decision maker derives no personal satisfaction directly from profits, raising or lowering the profits associated with particular dimensions of behavior will not change behavior unless it permits other variables in the decision maker's objective function to be changed that are presently constrained because of some limitation on profits.

The nature of a decision maker's objective function is also important in connection with (3), the problem of the appropriate level of rewards or penalties. As will be explained in more detail in Section 12.3, in the presence of uncertainty the response of a decision maker to a specific system of rewards and penalties will depend on how the decision maker values different aspects of uncertainty. If the decision maker ignores risk, which can be defined as the variance, or "spread," of possible outcomes around the expected value or most likely outcome, the decision maker's behavior in response to a particular system of rewards or penalties will differ from the case in which the decision maker is risk averse and places negative values on the spread of possible outcomes around the most likely outcome.

b. The Decision Maker's "Production Function." In economics this concept is used to summarize the relationship between inputs and outputs that are controlled by the decision maker and that may be defined to include the degree of uncertainty regarding the precise form of this relationship. "Input" and "output" are relative terms; what is an "output" viewed from one perspective may be an "input" if a broader definition of "output" is adopted. The scope of a decision maker's responsibility will therefore influence the definition of inputs and outputs that is appropriate in the case of that decision maker.

A production function may link one or more inputs with a single type of output, or there may be a number of outputs simultaneously produced. In addition, the input mix that is used to produce a particular output, or the output mix that is produced from a particular input mix, may be variable. A situation in which particular inputs simultaneously produce more than one output is referred to as a production function exhibiting "joint products," and joint products may be produced in either fixed proportions or variable proportions. These are only a few of the characteristics a production function may exhibit. Together with the prices of inputs, these characteristics determine the monetary costs of producing individual or joint products.

The precise form of a decision maker's production function is extremely important for the design of incentive systems and for the effect of any particular incentive system on the decision maker's behavior. If outputs can be produced only with fixed-input proportions, it does not matter whether inputs or outputs are rewarded or penalized, since in either case input and output dimensions of a decision maker's behavior will change in the same direction by proportionate amounts. If the input combinations that can be used to produce particular outputs are variable, however, rewarding particular inputs may provide disincentives for decision makers to minimize total cost.

In contrast to a situation in which inputs are rewarded, if outputs are rewarded the decision maker has an incentive to combine inputs in an output-maximizing manner. In addition, the decision maker faces some incentive to attempt to determine the form of the production function, since any resulting increases in output from a particular quantity of inputs will increase the rewards to the decision maker. However, the level of rewards yielded by other uses of the decision maker's time is also relevant; that is, whether the rewards yielded by increased time and effort spent determining the form of the production function will be more profitable than other uses of the decision maker's time.

c. The "Budget Constraint" Facing the Decision Maker. All decision makers face a limitation on the overall amount of resources at their disposal. For example, we all face a time constraint of twenty-four hours a day, which cannot be varied. Generally, decision makers can influence the magnitude of some of the budget constraints they are confronted by. A firm can vary the amount of sales revenue it earns by varying product prices or other dimensions of the firm's behavior. Individuals can vary the amount of income they earn by varying the amount of time they spend on leisure and various income-earning activities.

The characteristics of the budget constraint or constraints facing a decision maker have a profound effect on the decision maker's behavior. In conventional economic analysis, the twenty-four-hour budget constraint is frequently ignored, resulting in conclusions regarding decision makers' behavior that are very different from those which follow when the time constraint is included. One of the major practical problems for organizations and individuals is to determine the factors that underlie their budget constraints, in the form of the revenue and cost functions they are confronted by. The same is true for regulatory agencies, whose budget allocations may sometimes be based on characteristics of agency output, much like a firm's customers exchange budget for output characteristics. In other agencies, estimate of costs of performing particular activities may determine budget requests and allocations.

The manner in which a decision-making unit's revenues are determined will determine how the decision maker reacts to an incentive system. For example, if "resource budgets" are awarded on the basis of some dimension of a decision maker's own "absolute" performance, the decision maker's behavior will be different from that which occurs if the budget allocation is based on the decision maker's performance *relative* to that of other decision makers, or relative to the behavior of the decision maker in some past or future period.

d. The Decision Maker's Expectations Regarding Rivals' Behavior. Even if rival decision makers' behavior does not enter directly into the budget allocation process confronting a decision maker, it may do so indirectly. The behavior of a firm's rivals is obviously important in influencing the outcome of any specific action by the firm, since buyers may make their budget allocations in the form of purchases from different firms by comparing the relative performance of rival firms in meeting the buyers' needs. The term "rivals" is used in a broad sense to include decision makers whose activities are similar and whose behavior influences the outcome of each rival's behavior. As was emphasized in more detail in Chapter 7, "rivals" so defined may collectively or individually adopt policies that maximize the joint rewards to the decision makers.

Although the behavior of a decision maker's rivals is important in influencing the results of the decision maker's behavior and the magnitude of the decision maker's objective function, changes in rivals' behavior need not change the *optimal* levels of the decision maker's behavior. The reasons and circumstances under which this will be the case are discussed in greater detail in Section 12.3.

At this stage, however, it is useful to distinguish between two different mechanisms by which rivals' behavior exerts its influence on the decision maker. (1) In deciding on the response to a change in the incentive system a decision maker faces, he or she may take into account possible changes in its rivals' behavior in response to changes in the decision maker's own behavior; this may occur even though the incentive system facing the rival decision makers has not changed. (2) If the incentive system facing the rival decision makers has *also* been changed, each individual decision maker may take into account the change in his or her rivals' behavior that has been brought about by the changed incentive system, even if rivals are not expected to react in response to changes in each other's behavior.

Both of these mechanisms may operate simultaneously. In either of these cases, however, the exact nature of the anticipated change in rivals' behavior is important in determining whether and how these changes affect a decision maker's behavior, and no generalizations are possible.

The preceding listing of constraints that affect decision-maker behavior in response to any incentive system is by no means exhaustive. Care must be taken not to omit any of the constraints that a particular decision maker considers relevant.

In considering the effect of any incentive system on decision-maker behavior, all the objectives and constraints must be combined in order to predict the consequences for decision-maker behavior, because individual constraints may either reinforce or tend to offset each other in terms of their effects on particular dimensions of decision-maker behavior. In the following two sections, a diagrammatic framework is developed that will enable the effects of individual and combined constraints on a decision maker's behavior to be analyzed more clearly and that illustrates many of the factors mentioned in this section. A major weakness in the existing literature on decision makers' behavior is the lack of such an integrating framework. Too much emphasis tends to be placed on the consequences of individual constraints for decision-maker behavior, with insufficient attention devoted to the explicit or implicit assumptions regarding other constraints that are required to validate the conclusions of the analyst. This, in turn, affects empirical testing of hypotheses concerning decision makers' behavior. Attempts to test hypotheses concerning decision-maker behavior in response to any particular constraint must be based on implicit assumptions about the other constraints that influence decision-maker behavior, in order to generate the predicted conditions that are compared with the actual behavior of the decision maker in testing the analyst's hypothesis.

12.2   INCENTIVES FACING REGULATED FIRMS: ENCOURAGING TRUTHFUL REVELATION OF INFORMATION

The task of the regulator is to reduce the discrepancy between the actual behavior of the regulated firms and some normative concept of "desired" behavior of firms; symbolically, the regulator's goal is to reduce

($BS - BA$) where BS is the desired behavior of regulated firm and BA is the actual behavior of regulated firm.

If the regulator were aware of both BS and BA, it could compel the regulated firm to adopt behavior BS by threat of sufficiently large penalties to overcome the costs/loss to the regulated firm of changing behavior from its unregulated level BA to BS. To calculate the magnitude of the penalties that are sufficient to induce the firm to change its behavior, the regulator would have to know the objective function and constraints confronting the regulated firm, since these determine the magnitude of the cost experienced by the firm in changing its behavior from the unregulated level BA to BS.

In practice, the regulator does not generally know either BS or BA in advance and must rely wholly or in part on information provided by the regulated firm in order to determine BS, and also regarding BA. Assume that BS, the regulator's desired level of some dimension of the regulated firm's behavior, is the level at which the marginal benefits to society from changing the behavior dimension equal the marginal costs to society. Part of the costs of changing the regulated firm's behavior are the (marginal) costs incurred by the regulatory agency itself in order to change the firm's behavior; another part of the costs is the resource costs of changing the behavior dimension itself within the regulated firm. The latter component depends on the cost function of the regulated firm, which in turn depends on the technology involved and the supply conditions of the inputs required to produce the behavior dimension.

A regulated firm will generally know more about its own cost factors than the regulator (or will be in a better position to obtain the information than the regulator). Only if the regulator were to become as knowledgeable as the regulated firm about the production function and input supply conditions would the regulator be able to avoid relying on the regulated firm for information regarding the costs of changing the behavior dimension that is the subject of regulation. This information might be obtained by regulators from other firms in the same industry or from other sources of information regarding the production process and input supply conditions in the industry.

If the regulator relies on information provided by a particular firm about the potential costs of changing the firm's behavior, the firm may have an incentive to distort the information provided. If the firm overstates costs, for example, this will reduce the regulator's estimate of BS (given the benefits to society associated with different levels of the behavior dimension) and hence will reduce the extent to which the firm is required to change its existing behavior. On the other hand, additional checking or obtaining information from another source by the regulatory agency will raise the regulatory agency cost component of the total cost of changing the regulated firm's behavior and will also tend to reduce the optimal level of BS.

In addition to providing distorted information on costs of changing the firm's behavior in order to reduce BS, the regulated firm also has an incentive to overstate BA. Given the regulatory rewards to reductions in $(BS - BA)$ or penalties for discrepancies between BS and BA, the regulated firm can clearly increase the rewards or reduce the penalties by overstating BA. In order to prevent, or estimate the magnitude of, such overstatement, the regulatory agency either would have to engage in extensive double-checking of the regulated firm's actual performance or would have to rely on information from an independent third source that has no incentives to over- or understate the information. Again, this will tend to raise the regulatory component of the costs of changing the regulated firm's behavior and reduce BS, and the potential benefits to society of any given change in the regulated firm's behavior.

The incentives for the regulated firm to provide information that reduces BS and overstates BA will clearly be present irrespective of the magnitude of the rewards or penalties applied to a particular level of $(BS - BA)$. These incentives cannot be overcome by rewarding actual performance BA only; in this case, the incentive to overstate BA remains, and the regulatory agency still has to obtain information regarding BS and BA from some source. An independent source may be more costly than the regulated firm, and the regulated firm will have an incentive to overstate its costs in order to reduce BS, unless the rewards to increases in BA exceed the firm's own estimates of the disadvantages of changing its behavior. On the other hand, setting BS too high may discourage regulated firms from trying to achieve BS and encourage evasion of regulatory standards.

Even if there were no incentive for the regulated firm to provide inaccurate information to reduce BS and increase reported BA above actual BA, there would be a *disincentive* for the firm to come up with less costly methods of achieving the particular behavior dimension. This would tend to raise the firm's profits at existing product prices but would also tend to raise BS at any given level of actual performance BA. If rewards to the regulated firm are larger, the smaller $(BS - BA)$, or if penalties are higher, the larger $(BS - BA)$, the firm has a clear incentive not to undertake cost-reducing activities.

The preceding problems associated with the incentives for regulated firms to provide inaccurate information regarding potential changes in behavior, and actual levels of behavior, are referred to as the "incentive-compatibility" problem in the economics and related literature. The problem is not confined to regulatory issues, or even to regulated firms. Regulators themselves may have incentives to distort information they provide to legislators, regulated firms, or other sectors of society (see Chapter 13). However, the nature of the solutions to incentive-compatibility problems existing in a wide variety of situations is remarkably similar, and some of the characteristics of the solutions to the problem of devising suitable incentives for regulated firms will be encountered again in later sections dealing with incentives confronting other types of decision maker. It is worthwhile, therefore, to outline the essential principles involved in solutions to the incentive-compatibility problem that have appeared recently in the literature.

As already noted, if regulated firms are rewarded or penalized on the basis of their performance in meeting some standard $(BS - BA)$, where BS is the desired standard of performance and BA is their actual behavior, these firms have an incentive to provide information or to act in other ways that reduce the level of BS. For example, if regulated firms overstate the true costs of increasing some dimension of their output, such as safety, doing so tends to reduce the social-optimal level of safety and reduces the need for firms to change existing behavior. It also makes it easier for these firms to exceed the standard of safety that regulators judge to be desirable on the basis of the cost data the firms have provided, and thus to appear to be "socially responsible" firms. It should be emphasized that when regulated firms provide information that is used to determine BS, they are already indirectly involved in setting the standard, in addition to deciding on the extent to which they will meet the standard.

The central principle involved in recent attempts to overcome the incentive-compatibility problem is to explicitly permit the regulated firm to select a standard, or target of behavior, for itself, and to evaluate the firm's performance, not only on the extent to which it is successful in meeting this target, but also the level of the target itself. In other words, the "performance index" P, which is used as a basis for rewarding or penalizing the regulated firm, takes the general form

$$P = F + k_1 BT - k\,(BT - BA)$$

where BT is a self-selected target standard of performance of some dimension of the firm's behavior and k_1 and k are positive numbers whose magnitudes will be discussed below.

It should be noted that the firm's self-selected target, BT, used in the determination of regulated firm performance is *not* the same as the socially desirable level of firms' behavior, BS, which regulators use in setting the level of the k coefficients and resulting rewards or penalties in the performance index P. By controlling the k coefficients, regulators can influence the level of both BT and BA of regulated firms. In principle, the regulators' goal is to try to ensure that $BA = BS$, where BS is the level of regulated firm behavior desired by regulators. Even if regulators are successful in selecting the coefficients in the performance index P to ensure that firms' BA equals BS, this does not necessarily imply that BT will equal BS. In other words, it may be optimal for regulated firms to select BT that they cannot actually achieve (explained later in this section).

Measuring a regulated firm's performance on the basis of the level of its BT tends to reduce the incentive for the regulated firm to provide information that understates its true behavior capabilities, since each unit increase in BT adds k_1 to the firm's performance index. Similarly, this also provides some incentive for regulated firms to attempt to reduce existing costs, since doing this will also tend to increase BT. However, since any understatement of BT by one unit will *also* tend to reduce $(BT - BA)$ at any level of BA, and increase P by the amount k, the *relative magnitude* of both k_1 and k is vitally important.

Two situations may be distinguished that result in different required relative magnitudes for k_1 and k. (1) When the regulated firm over-achieves the self-selected target, $(BT - BA)$ is negative; and a one-unit reduction in BT reduces P by $(-k_1 + k)$, and an increase in BT raises P by $(k_1 - k)$. *In this situation,* k_1 *must exceed* k *in magnitude* in order to avoid an incentive for the regulated firm to be able to raise P by under-stating the value of BT and overfulfilling the target. (2) When the regulated firm fails to achieve the self-selected target, $(BT - BA)$ is positive; and a one-unit reduction in BT reduces P by $(k_1 - k)$, and an increase in BT raises P by $(k_1 - k)$. In this case, *in contrast to the preceding situation,* k_1 *must be less than* k *in magnitude* in order to avoid an incentive for the regulated firm to be able to raise P by overstating the value of BT and underfulfilling the target.

Therefore, to avoid any incentives for the regulated firm to over- or understate the value of BT, the performance index that is used to reward or penalize regulated firm behavior must have the following form:

$$P = F + k_1 BT - k_2 (BT - BA) \qquad \text{when } BT \text{ exceeds } BA \text{ (underfulfill-ment of target)}$$

$$P = F + k_1 BT - k_3 (BT - BA) \qquad \text{when } BT \text{ is less than } BA \text{ (overfulfill-ment of target)}$$

where k_2 exceeds k_1, k_3 is less than k_1, and all are greater than 0. This last point requires some elaboration. At first sight, it might seem plausible to argue that an incentive for setting BT too low and overfulfilling the resulting target could be avoided by setting k_3 equal to zero, that is, not rewarding overfulfillment of the target or even penalizing overfulfillment (setting k_3 negative). The problem with this solution is that it would discourage the regulated firm from overfulfilling the target in circum-stances in which this would be desirable; if a cost reduction occurred after the target had been set, for example.

Only if $k_2 > k_1, > k_3$ are set in relation to each other as described will there be an incentive for the regulated firm to set BA as high as possible, and to set BT as high as possible without over- or underestimating BT. This can be demonstrated by rearranging the two preceding performance indexes as follows:

$$P = F - (k_2 - k_1)BT + k_2 BA \qquad \text{for } BT \text{ greater than } BA \text{ (underfulfill-ment of target)}$$

$P = F + (k_1 - k_3)BT + k_3BA$ for BT less than BA (overfulfillment of target)

From these expressions, it is clear that both k_2 and k_3 must be positive in order to provide the firm with an incentive to increase BA as much as possible. It is also clear that only if $(k_2 - k_1)$ is positive (i.e., k_2 exceeds k_1) will an incentive to avoid overstating BT (and underfulfilling the target) exist, and only if $(k_1 - k_3)$ is positive (i.e., k_1 exceeds k_3) will an incentive to understate BT (and overfill the target) be avoided.

In the preceding exposition, BT and BA could be standards of some dimension of output that regulators wish to encourage, such as safety. In this case, the primary problem faced by the regulators is the possibility that regulated firms might find it advantageous to *understate* the standards of performance they can achieve and/or overstate their actual performance in meeting these standards. In contrast to the preceding output standard example, the problem facing regulators may be the possibility that regulated firms might find it advantageous to *overstate* the minimum level of some dimension of their performance, such as costs that they can achieve, and/or to understate their actual cost performance. The form of the performance index that overcomes these incentives for the firm to report estimated and actual costs inaccurately is *almost identical* to the performance index that is required in the output standard case. The only difference is that the *signs* of the three k coefficients must be reversed, but the condition that $k_2 > k_1 > k_3$ in absolute magnitude must be maintained.

The only difference between the two preceding performance indexes was the reversal of the minus and plus signs in front of the k's. This reflects the fact that whereas one is trying to encourage *larger* absolute levels of BT and BA in the output dimension performance indexes, in the case of costs one is trying to encourage lower levels of estimated and actual cost performance. Therefore, the performance indexes in the first case must be an increasing function of both BA and BT, and the second performance indexes must increase with reductions in estimated and actual costs.

These performance indexes can be shown diagrammatically. This will prove extremely useful both for understanding the characteristics of the performance indexes themselves and in explaining their consequences for the behavior of regulated firms' decision makers and other decision makers in subsequent sections.

The horizontal axis of Figure 12.1 depicts different levels of some dimension of a regulated firm's actual behavior, BA. The vertical axis depicts the level of the performance index, P, with negative values of P occurring below the horizontal axis and positive values of P occurring above it. The dimensions of P, which reflect whether behavior is rewarded or penalized with money, jail sentences, or some other kind of reward or penalty, need not concern us here. We shall now "construct" the performance index described on p. 337 in three stages.

The first term F in the performance index is simply a positive or negative number that determines the height of the performance indicator at a level of $BT = BA = 0$; it is shown as a positive number in Figure 12.1(a) for expositional convenience only. The term $+ k_1BT$ in the performance index may be drawn as a straight line radiating from the origin of the diagram, whose slope depends on the magnitude of k_1. Since F does not vary with BT or BA, the amount F may be added vertically to any point on the line k_1BT to result in the straight line labeled $F + k_1BT$ in Figure 12.1(a). This line shows the level of the performance index P at different levels of BT selected by the firm, *assuming that BA = BT*.

The next step in constructing the performance index diagrammatically is to take into account the penalties for underfulfillment (or rewards for overfulfillment) of any level of BT selected by the firm. At any level of BT selected by the firm, say BT' in Figure 12.1(b), when $BA = BT'$ there are no penalties for underfulfillment or rewards for overfulfillment of the target. At levels of BA below BT' penalties for underfulfillment shown by the straight line $BT'U$ are assessed; these penalties are equal to $- k_2(BT' - BA)$ in magnitude. Similarly, at levels of BA above BT' rewards for overfulfillment are earned, shown by the straight line BT'–O; these rewards are equal to $+ k_3(BA - BT')$ in magnitude.

To provide incentives for firms to report information regarding BT and BA truthfully, it was explained earlier that k_2 must exceed k_3 in magnitude. This is reflected by the fact that the slope of line $BT'U$, which equals k_2, is steeper than the slope of line BT'–O, which equals k_3.

The final step in the construction of the performance index is to add the penalty-reward function in Figure 12.1(b) vertically to line $F + k_1BT$ *at the level of BA = BT'*. It follows from the restrictions placed on k_1 relative to k_2 and k_3 that the resulting performance index will be like the dashed line $U'BT'O'$ in Figure 12.1(c). However, the previous italicized phrase is important. There is a whole *family* of performance indexes such as $U'BT'O'$, each one corresponding to a different level of BT selected by the firm. We cannot specify *which* level of BT will be selected by the firm without introducing the firm's objective function and other constraints that influence the firm's behavior in addition to the performance index. We shall do this shortly. First, however, it is useful to visualize the firm's choice, given the F and k terms in the performance index, as the choice of being able to "slide" the kinked penalty-reward line $UBT'O$ along the line $F + k_1BT$ and, by selecting a level of BT, thereby "fixing" the position of the performance indicator.

No matter which level of BT is selected by the firm, however, the incentives for the firm to report this target truthfully can be seen clearly in Figure 12.1(c). Suppose the firm were to understate the true level of its target, and reported BT' instead of, say, BT_2 in order to earn rewards

Figure 12.1

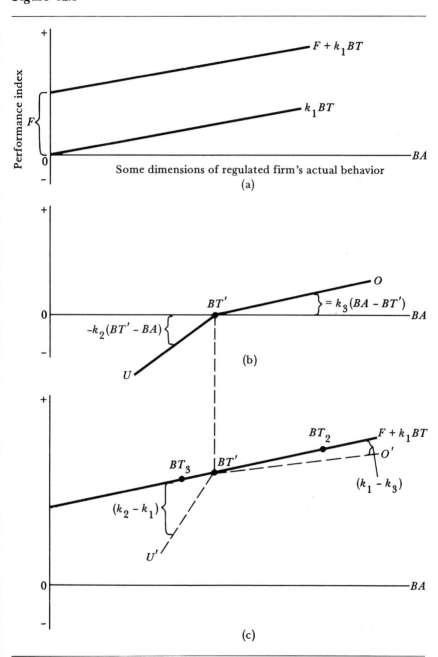

Some dimensions of regulated firm's actual behavior

(a)

(b)

(c)

for overfilling the reported target. The resulting level of the firm's performance indicator at BT_2 will be shown by the point on the dashed line $U'BT'O'$, and will be $(k_1 - k_3(BT_2 - BT')$ unit lower than if the firm correctly reported BT_2 as its target. Similarly, suppose the firm were to overstate the true level of its target and reported BT' instead of BT_3 in order to earn the higher rewards of k_1 per unit of BT. The resulting level of the firm's performance indicator at BT_3 will be shown by the point on the dashed line $U'BT'O'$, and this will be $(k_2 - k_1)$ $(BT' - BT_3)$ units lower than if the firm correctly reported BT_3 as its target.

As Figure 12.1(c) suggests, the penalties for understatement of the true level of BT are higher, the larger the difference $(k_1 - k_3)$, and the penalties for overstatement of the true level of BT are higher, the larger the difference $(k_2 - k_1)$. This may lead one to conclude that these differences should be set as high as possible to encourage truthful reporting. While this conclusion is valid when a firm knows its constraints with certainty, and can therefore ensure that its actual behavior corresponds to its selected target behavior, it is no longer valid if the firm is uncertain about its ability to meet a selected target. In the latter circumstances, the levels of k_2 and k_3 affect the optimal selected level of the firm's target, BT itself. This means that the levels of k_2 and k_3 cannot in general be set solely with the object of inducing truthful reporting of BT in mind but must also take into account the effects of k_3 and k_2 on the level of BT selected by the firm.

As previously noted, the effects of the performance index on the level of BT selected by a firm cannot be determined without introducing the firm's objective function and other constraints that affect its behavior. Figure 12.2 illustrates the total revenue and total cost of an unregulated firm at different levels of its behavior dimension BA. Total revenue (TR) depends on factors such as buyer behavior and rival seller behavior; total cost (TC) depends on the production function exhibiting the relationship between the firm's inputs and BA, and on the input prices. Subtracting TC from TR at each level of BA shows the amount of the firm's profit at each level of BA; profit is assumed to rise, then decline as BA is increased. In the absence of any regulatory constraint, a profit-maximizing firm will select BA' as its optimal level of behavior.

To examine the impact of a regulatory constraint like the performance index on the firm's behavior, we shall again introduce the performance index diagrammatically in three stages in Figures 12.2 and 12.3. If P is expressed in dollars, the level of the firm's profit at each level of BA may be added to the performance index at that level of BA. Consider, first, the effect of adding the firm's profit hill to the component of the performance index P, which is represented by curve F in Figure 12.1. Since F is a horizontal line, the level of BA that maximizes the firm's combined (profit + performance index) would not be changed, since the index would add the same amount to the firm's profits at all

Figure 12.2

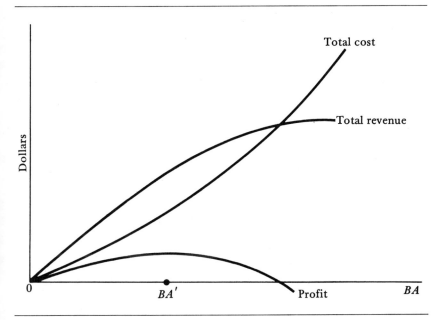

levels of BA. The same conclusion would apply if the performance index were in the negative region of Figure 12.3, reflecting penalties assessed for levels of BA rather than rewards. Changes in the magnitude of F will therefore shift the height of the performance index and the firm's combined (profit + performance index) but will not change the level of BA that *maximizes* the firm's combined (profit + performance index).

This conclusion is very important, for it indicates that the absolute level of rewards or penalties applicable to a particular aspect of a firm's behavior, and the issue of whether the activity is rewarded or penalized, are not by themselves generally relevant in determining the firm's response to the rewards or penalties. The important consideration is how the rewards or penalties *vary* with the level of the firm's behavior.

Consider next the effect of adding the component of the performance index that is represented by $k_1 BT$ to the firm's profits at each level of BA in Figure 12.3. Since a larger absolute amount will be added to the firm's profits, the higher the level of BT, this will imply that the level of BA that maximizes the firm's (profit + performance index) is *higher* than when $k_1 BT$ is ignored. Similarly, it implies that an increase in the magnitude of k_1 will raise the level of BA that maximizes the firm's

Figure 12.3

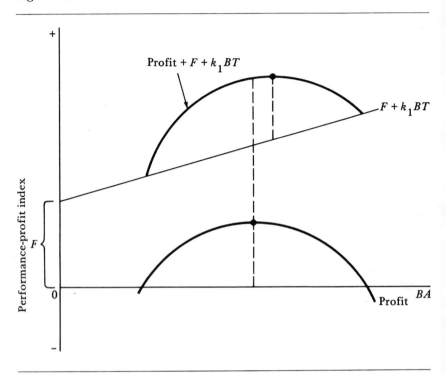

(profit $+ F + k_1 BT$). The impact of adding the $F + k_1 BT$ component of the performance index to the firm's profits is shown in Figure 12.3.

We have examined the effect of introducing only the $F + k_1 BT$ component of the performance index on the firm's behavior. It remains to take into account the implications of the penalties or rewards for under- or overfulfillment of a selected level of BT. Figure 12.4 demonstrates the effect of adding this penalty-reward function. At BA_m the level of BT that would be selected if penalties and rewards for under- or overfulfillment were absent, we could add the corresponding penalty-reward function $U_m O_m$ vertically, resulting in the dashed line labeled mm. Curve mm represents the *actual* position and shape of the combined profit-plus-performance index at different levels of BA if BA_m *were selected as a target by the firm.*

Other levels of BA could be selected as targets by the firm. For example, if the firm selected BA_i as a target, the corresponding penalty-reward function for under- or overfulfillment would be $U_i O_j$ and the

actual position and shape of the combined profit-plus-performance index
would be the dashed line labeled *ii* in Figure 12.4. However, *if the firm
is certain about its constraints and can therefore be certain about meeting
any target it selects,* BA_m is the level of the target that will maximize
the firm's combined (profit + performance index). In this case, the firm
will never under- or overfulfill its selected target; and the coefficients
k_2 and k_3 play no part in determining the level of BT selected by the
firm. They do, however, ensure that the firm will report its optimal
target behavior truthfully; to understate or overstate BT_m compared with
its true value would result in lower levels of the performance index than
if the firm reports BT_m truthfully.

   It must be emphasized that the preceding conclusions concerning
the effects of F and the k coefficients of the performance index on the
firm's choice of target and behavior depend critically on the assumption
that the firm knows the constraints that underlie its profit function with
certainty and is therefore sure that its actual behavior will correspond

Figure 12.4

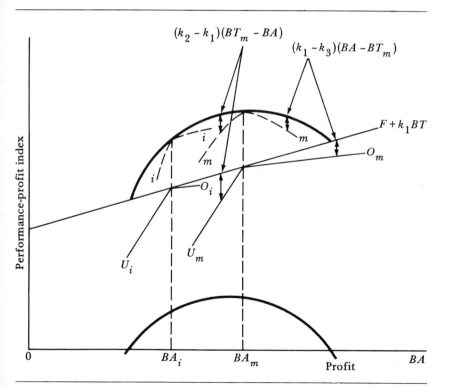

to its selected target. The consequences of relaxing this assumption, and a number of other implicit assumptions underlying the preceding analysis, will be examined in some detail in the next section. First, however, it is helpful to consider one modification of the performance index that has been discussed in the recent literature on incentive systems.

In our exposition of the performance index so far, the regulatory agency sets the F and k terms, and the firm selects its own target behavior BT. The agency itself sets no standards of performance. A slight modification of this performance index would permit the regulators to establish a tentative target BS for regulated firms and to reward regulated firms for the extent to which they achieve this target.

The performance index discussed so far was

$$P = F + k_1BT - k(BT - BA)$$

The amended performance index would be

$$P = F + k_1(BT - BS) - k(BT - BA)$$

By noting that $k_1(BT - BS) = k_1BT - k_1BS$, the only real difference between the two indexes is that the term $- k_1BS$ has been added to the second performance index. This does not affect the incentives for firms to report BT and BA truthfully. However, it is also useful to examine whether the addition of $- k_1BS$ will affect the actual level of BT selected by the firm. A similar term was part of the reformed Soviet incentive system in 1971. Loeb and Magat (1978b) have argued that this does not change the essential incentive properties of the system and are correct as far as the incentives for truthful revelation of information are concerned. However, the presence of the term may in certain circumstances change the level of BT selected by firms.

The term $- k_1BS$ may be visualized as an additional fixed term that is subtracted from F. Analytically and diagrammatically, raising the level of BS is like a reduction in F. It reduces the level of the performance indicator by the same amount at any given level of the firm's behavior. It does not therefore affect the optimal level of behavior selected by the firm. The result of a change in k_1 is now more complicated than before, however. In addition to the upward tilting of the $F + k_1BT$ line previously explained, an increase in k_1 will now also cause a parallel downward shift in the performance indicator at all levels of BA, by an amount equal to $- \Delta K_1BS$. In the model of the behavior of firms analyzed so far, this does not change the optimal level of the firm's behavior, since it subtracts an equal amount from the firms profit-plus-performance index at each level of BA.

Different conclusions may result in a model in which there is uncertainty on the part of firms regarding the profit function, and in which the firm's decision makers value risk reduction. Consideration of such a model is deferred until the next section. Our main purpose here is to establish the general principle that the addition of a term $- k_1BS$, reflecting the presence of penalties for failure to meet a predetermined standard of performance set by regulators themselves, affects only the *absolute height* of the performance index at different levels of the firm's behavior, not the *slope* of the performance index at any given level of the firm's behavior.

Figures 12.1–12.4 illustrate the case of a performance index that is appropriate for encouraging honest revelation of a dimension of a decision maker's behavior that regulators wish to *encourage*. In the case of a dimension of behavior that regulators wish to *discourage,* such as the level of costs or pollution associated with an activity, we explained earlier in this section that the appropriate performance index is identical to the index that was previously analyzed, except that the *signs* of the k coefficients are reversed. Figure 12.5 illustrates this situation.

We have purposely depicted two performance indexes in Figure 12.5, the index $P,$ in the positive quadrant of the diagram, rewards for behavior B that diminish in magnitude as the level of B increases. Index P' in the negative quadrant provides penalties for behavior B that increase

Figure 12.5

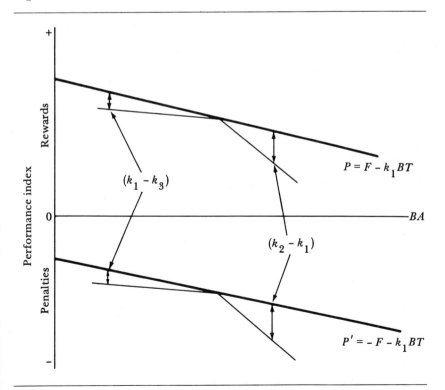

in magnitude as the level of B increases. The discussion earlier in this section indicates that *the incentive effects of these two performance indexes are identical.* The level of performance index P' at any level of B is simply $P - 2F$, where $2F$ is the vertical distance between the two performance indexes that is assumed to be the same at all levels of B. It was also explained earlier that adding or subtracting a fixed term F to the performance index does not change the slope of the performance index at any level of B, and it is the *slope* of the performance index that is responsible for incentive effects that change the level of the regulated dimension of behavior B. Since the slopes of the P and P' performance indexes are identical at any level of B, their incentive effects will be the same.

The identical incentive effects of performance indexes P and P' on the level of BA selected by a firm are illustrated in Figure 12.6. The

Figure 12.6

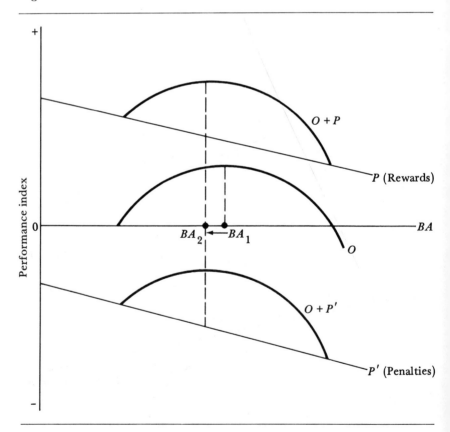

"hinged" segments of each performance index, representing the $(k_2 - k_1)$ and $(k_3 - k_1)$ terms that encourage truthful revelation of information about B by the regulated decision maker, are omitted purely for expositional convenience. Since these terms apply to both performance indexes, their effects on the level of BA will be the same. Given the preceding k coefficients, the effect of the performance index on the level of BA will depend on (1) the slope of the performance index as determined by the magnitude of the $(-)k_1$ coefficient and (2) the slope of the decision maker's objective function at different levels of BA.

At *any* level of BA, the slope of the decision maker's objective function *plus* the slope of performance index at that level of BA will indicate the change in the level of $(O + P)$, the decision maker's objectives *plus* the performance index resulting from a change in the level of B. The best level of BA, from the point of view of the regulated decision maker, will be a level where the level of $(O + P)$ is a maximum; this will be where the combined (slope of O + slope of P) equals zero. At BA_1 the level of BA that maximizes O in the absence of regulation, adding P or P' to the firm's profits will *reduce* the level of (slope O + slope P or P') because the slope of both P and P' is negative. This means that BA_2, the level of BA that maximizes $(O + P)$, will be *lower* than BA_1, the unregulated level of BA.

The *magnitude* of the reduction in the level of BA that is necessary to make (slope O + slope P or P') zero will depend on the slope of O only, if the slope of P and P' is unchanged at different levels of BA as assumed. If the slope of P and P' varies with the level of BA, the magnitude of the change in the level of BA in response to the performance index P or P' will depend also on how the slope of P or P' varies as the level of BA is changed.

The preceding points have extremely important implications for the manner in which most regulatory activities are conducted in the United States, where the relationship between business and government can best be described as adversary in nature. Government regulation usually involves penalties for violations of regulatory standards; that is, the regulatory performance indexes are more like P' than P in Figure 12.5. Actually, this depiction is far too generous to existing regulations, since most existing regulatory constraints are more like the performance index shown in Figure 12.7, with penalties that begin at a level of BA that is regarded as the maximum permissible level of BA or regulatory standard of behavior B_{max} and that frequently do not vary with the magnitude of violations of this regulatory standard. As we have seen, and one can readily verify, such regulatory performance indexes *will not change the level of BA*. If penalties increase with the level of BA beyond the permissible regulatory standard B_{max}, this will imply a performance index like P' that *will* reduce the optimal level of BA for those firms whose objective function reached a maximum above B_{max} in the absence of regulation.

Figure 12.7

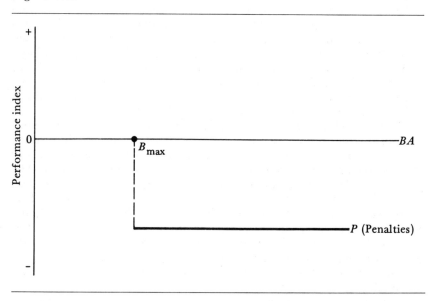

The reasoning that underlies this conclusion was previously explained in connection with Figure 12.6. The conclusion is, however, based on a number of implicit assumptions that will be clarified, and relaxed, in the next section. One of these assumptions is that violations of regulatory standards can be detected with 100 percent probability. This is not generally the case in practice, and even if detection with 100 percent probability is possible, it will be costly. A shift from a system of regulation that employs penalties for violations of regulatory standards, like P', to a system of regulation that provides rewards for meeting regulatory standards, like P, will have much more than cosmetic effects.

Although the incentive properties of both regulatory systems are similar, the costs of monitoring regulated firms and detecting violations are likely to be reduced under the "rewards" or "subsidies" approach, because firms meeting regulatory standards will have to volunteer this information to obtain the rewards or subsidies. Monitoring costs associated with firms whose behavior is found to be in compliance with regulatory standards under the penalties approach to regulation could be avoided under the subsidies approach. The reader is reminded that the incentives for firms to report behavior truthfully is the same under the two performance indicators P and P'; firms are therefore no more likely to overstate performance when claiming subsidies than they are to overstate performance that is penalized under the penalties approach.

The "rewards" or "subsidies" approach to regulation *adds* to the height of firms' objective functions, whereas the penalties approach subtracts from the height of firms' objective functions. Although the incentive effects on *BA* are formally the same, the subsidies approach turns the adversary nature of the relationship between government and business into a more cooperative relationship. The psychological effects of this change on the behavior of government and business decision makers could be profound and might be a further reason for preferring the subsidies approach to the penalties approach. Should one imagine that a subsidies approach to regulation implies a major shift toward a welfare-state-for-business approach to government and business relations, it should be remembered that tax subsidies for business have long been a feature of the United States tax system. If a shift to a subsidies approach to regulation reduces monitoring and enforcement costs associated with regulation, there need be no net increase in the level of government expenditures on regulation.

12.3 OTHER FACTORS INFLUENCING REGULATED FIRMS' RESPONSE

In this section, we shall focus on some of the more important explicit and implicit assumptions that underlie the conclusions of Section 12.2 and consider the implications relaxing those assumptions for regulated firms' behavior and the design of optimal regulatory constraints.

The analysis presented in Section 12.2 was based on the following important assumptions:

i. The firm faced no uncertainty about any of its constraints and the resulting relationship between its behavior and profits.
ii. The firm's constraints (TR and TC curves in Figure 12.2), and hence the profit curve were not related to the performance index itself and were not affected by changes in the characteristics of the performance index.
iii. There was no uncertainty on the part of the firm regarding the performance index itself.
iv. The firm took no account of the possibility that its behavior might influence the form and characteristics of the performance index. In other words, the firm was assumed to believe that changes in its behavior would not change the form of the performance index, only the level of rewards or penalties the firm would earn under a particular performance index.

The consequences of relaxing each of these assumptions for regulated firms' behavior and the design of optimal regulatory incentive systems will now be examined. Attention will be focused on the following important constraints that individually and collectively affect a regulated firm's behavior:

a. the attitude of the regulated firm to uncertainty and risk
b. the behavior of the regulated firm's rivals
c. the behavior of other regulatory agencies
d. additional characteristics of the regulatory constraint
e. the regulated firm's expectations of agency behavior

In regard to item (e), the regulated firm's expectations about the way the regulatory agency administering a particular performance index decides the form of the performance index, is different from item (d), the regulated firm's expectations about the performance index itself. The factors considered in item (d) will influence the behavior of a regulated firm in response to a particular performance index, whereas the factors considered in item (e) will influence the extent to which the regulated firm may try to influence the form of the performance index itself. Of course both sets of factors may operate simultaneously, along with the other constraints also listed. The net result of these interreactions will determine both the form of the performance index and the behavior of the regulated firm. It is necessary to consider the various influences separately, however, in order to develop a better understanding of the regulatory process and how to improve it.

(a) The Attitude of the Regulated Firm to Uncertainty and Risk

The existence of uncertainty on the part of the regulated firm's decision makers regarding any of the constraints that underlie the firm's profit function implies that the exact position of the firm's profit hill depicted in Figures 12.2–12.4 is uncertain. This, in turn, implies that the target level of behavior selected by the firm (BT) may turn out to be different from the level of BA that actually maximizes the firm's profits, given the firm's previously selected target BT. In these circumstances, the firm will either be assessed penalties for failing to achieve its target BT or will earn rewards if the actual profit-maximizing level of BA exceeds the target. In the presence of uncertainty, the resulting nonzero probability of penalties or rewards for under- or overfulfillment of the previously selected target, will change the conclusion of the preceding section that k_2 or k_3 will not affect the firm's choice of target BT.

A lower level of BT will reduce the penalties for underfulfillment, or will increase the rewards to overfulfillment of the target, at any given level of BA. Therefore, the firm's BT will be lower, under uncertainty, the higher are k_2 and k_3, all other things being equal. In other words, the agency can induce more conservative behavior targets from regulated firms, which are more likely to be fulfilled, by raising k_2 and/or k_3. Alternatively, by lowering k_2 and/or k_3 the agency can stimulate more ambitious targets, which are less likely to be fulfilled.

The presence of uncertainty regarding the regulated firm's profit function may also change our previous conclusions regarding the effect of changes in k_1 or the F and BS terms in the performance indicator on the regulated firm's choice of BT. In the presence of uncertainty, the firm's profit at any level of BA ceases to be a single value and becomes a range of possible values, each with a different probability attached by the firm's decision makers. The "expected value" of profit at any given level of BA is defined as the sum of each possible profit outcome multiplied by the probability of its occurrence. If the regulated firm's decision makers base their decisions on the "expected value of profit criterion" only, it can be shown that under uncertainty, increases in k_1 have the effect of increasing the firm's target BT, while changes in F (or BS, if applicable) have no effect on the firm's target BT. In these circumstances, no changes in previous conclusions are necessary despite uncertainty.

Matters are different if the regulated firm's decision makers also consider "risk," defined as the variance of possible profit outcomes around the "expected value." *If the firm's decision makers are "risk averse,"* meaning that they prefer lower risk, all other things remaining the same, this also implies that they are willing to trade off increased profits for reduced risk at a rate determined by their respective evaluations of the satisfaction they derive from increments of profit and risk. In these circumstances, *the effect of an increase in* k_1 *on the firm's choice of* BT *is no longer determinate a priori.* The increase in k_1 now causes two opposing influences to operate on the firm's choice of BT. The level of the firm's performance index at any level of BT will be increased; this "income effect" will tend to reduce the level of BT, since the firm can now earn the same or higher expected (profit + performance index) as before while simultaneously reducing the risk of penalties for underfulfillment. The increase in k_1 also has a "substitution effect," however, which tends to make the firm adopt a higher level of risk and raise BT; this effect takes the form of higher relative rewards to increases in BT, and therefore higher compensation for increases in risk adopted. The strength of these two opposing influences in any situation will determine whether an increase in k_1 will raise or reduce a particular regulated firm's choice of BT, and no generalizations are possible.

In the case of risk aversion on the part of the firm's decision makers, changes in F (or BS) may also affect the level of BT. Again, however, no firm conclusions are possible, since there are two opposing influences at work on the degree of risk adopted by the firm and the resulting choice of BT. On one hand, an increase in F (or a reduction in BS) implies that the firm's performance indicator is higher at any level of BT, and the firm could earn the same expected (profit + performance index) while simultaneously reducing BT and the risk of incurring penalties for underfulfill-

ment of its target. On the other hand, because the firm's expected
(profit + performance index) at the existing level of risk is increased, its
capacity for accepting increased risk without lowering the previous level
of its expected (profit + performance index) is also increased. The effect
of the increase in F (or reduction in BS, where applicable), therefore,
depends on which of these two opposing influences is strongest in any
particular case.

Before we conclude this section, there is one implication of the performance index that needs to emphasized with respect to regulated firms'
behavior in the case of uncertainty. From the point of view of regulators,
it is BA that is the important consideration in attaining socially desirable
behavior on the part of the regulated firms. In the case of perfect certainty, BT and BA will coincide, as already noted. In the more practically
relevant case of uncertainty, however, BT and BA may differ. Moreover,
firms may *consciously* select a level of BT *that they do not expect to be
able to achieve;* that is, situations in which BA is less than BT are not
only those in which regulated firms' expectations are not fulfilled. The
reason why a firm may *consciously* choose to under- or overfulfill its self-
selected target is explained by the fact that after it has selected its target
BT, the firm generally can vary the level of its effort in meeting the
target. As Ekern (1979) has demonstrated, in some circumstances it may
be optimal for the firm to vary effort to meet the target, but not in others,
resulting in a conscious discrepancy between BT and BA.

More important in the present context is the fact that, in circumstances in which regulated firms find it optimal to select BA less than BT,
regulators may have to select magnitudes of the coefficients in the performance index that result in BT exceeding the socially desirable level
of performance. In other words, inducing regulated firms to select targets
of behavior *above* the levels required for socially optimal performance
may be necessary in some circumstances. This will require regulators to
use standards of behavior that *exceed* socially desirable levels, for purposes
of evaluating those firms' performance. It may also require regulators to
provide inaccurate information about "socially desirable" levels of
regulated firms' behavior, since to announce these, and use standards of
behavior selected by firms that were higher, would be open to misin-
terpretation at best, and at worst might cause considerable confusion and
possible loss of confidence in regulators among firms and other parties to
the regulatory process.

(b) The Behavior of the
   Regulated Firm's Rivals

With few notable exceptions, the existing literature dealing with a firm's
response to regulation has neglected the influence of the firm's rivals'
behavior. If a regulated firm does not expect its rivals to change their

behavior either in response to the firm's own response to regulation or directly in response to regulation itself, this omission is warranted. However, the last assumption is obviously unreasonable; regulatory constraints will generally also affect the decision environment of a regulated firm's rivals, though not necessarily in an identical way. The resulting changes in the regulated firm's rivals' behavior change the position of the TR and/or TC curves in Figure 12.2, and may affect the level of the firm's behavior that is "optimal," given any particular regulatory constraint.

For example, if a firm's rivals are all required to install smog-reducing equipment, the costs of all the firms' products will increase, but the firms' relative costs and competitive ability will tend to remain unchanged. The manner in which rival firms are expected to react to a given regulatory constraint may change the reaction of the firm to the regulatory constraint. Moreover, when the influence of a regulated firm's rivals' behavior is added to the factors that determine a regulated firm's response to a particular regulatory constraint, this may not only affect the magnitude of the firm's response to the constraint, but it may even change the direction of the response.

These points may be illustrated with the aid of Figure 12.8, where TR and TC are the total revenue and cost constraints confronting a firm in the absence of regulation. In Section 12.2 these constraints were assumed to remain unchanged when the performance indicator representing the regulatory constraint was introduced. In contrast, we are now considering the possibility that these constraints themselves may change in response to the introduction of the regulatory constraint. We shall assume in what follows that only TR is changed by the regulatory constraint; TR depends on the level of the regulated firm's rivals' behavior. This behavior may change directly in response to the regulatory constraint, as might occur if the regulatory constraint is applied to those firms also.

Alternatively, even if rival firms are not themselves faced by the regulatory constraint, the firm may expect them to behave differently in response to any level of its behavior after the regulatory constraint is applied to the firm. In either situation, TR' will change position, and this will change the position and possibly the shape of the firm's profit function compared with a situation in which rivals' behavior changes are ignored. This, in turn, will change the conclusions regarding the effect of any given regulatory constraint on the firm's behavior.

It is vital to recognize that what matters, as far as the effect of rivals' behavior changes on a profit-maximizing regulated firm's behavior is concerned, is *not* the resulting implications for the absolute height of TR but the implications for the *shape* of TR. Thus, if TR is increased (or reduced) by the same amount ΔTR at each level of the regulated firm's behavior in Figure 12.8, due to a change in rival firms' behavior, *the profit-maximizing level of the regulated firm's behavior will not be changed.* Only the amount of profit at the profit-maximizing level of

Figure 12.8

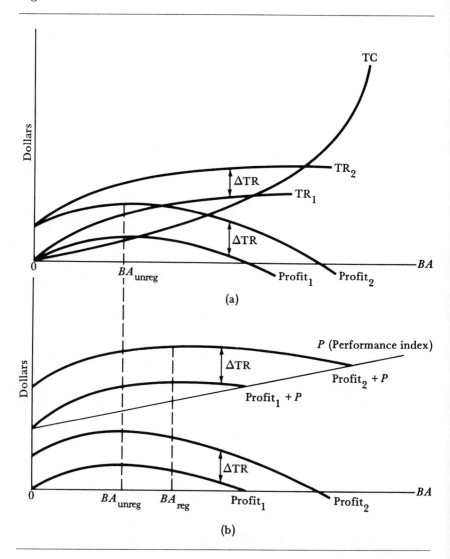

(a)

(b)

behavior would be changed. Parallel shifts in TR affect only the behavior of firms that pursue goals other than profit maximization, subject to a minimum profit constraint. Such firms would experience an increase or decrease in profits at their initial behavior levels and would therefore be in a position to change their behavior without violating the profit constraint. However, we shall confine our analysis of the effect of regulation to profit-maximizing firms, in keeping with traditional practice. More-over, the reader who masters the principles applicable to regulation of profit-maximizing firms will have little difficulty in extending them to firms or non-profit-maximizing enterprises with other objectives.

Returning to our analysis of the effects of shifts in TR on the be-havior of the regulated firm, we can conclude the following. Rivals' behavior changes that steepen the slope of TR (whether TR is shifted up or down is immaterial) at any particular level of the regulated firm's behavior will raise the *marginal,* or incremental, profitability of the firm's behavior at that level. This will tend to increase the profit-maximizing level of the firm's behavior.

The impact of a parallel upward shift in TR on the firm's profit curve, and on the combined (profit + performance index) curve, is shown in Figure 12.8(a) and (b). The parallel shift in TR has no effect on the regulated firm's optimal behavior. In contrast, in Figure 12.9, a change of rivals' behavior that shifts up and steepens the slope of the regulated firm's total revenue curve is shown. The effect is to increase the marginal, or incremental, profit at each level of the regulated firm's behavior and to increase the level of the regulated firm's behavior that maximizes the regulated firm's combined (profit + performance index). The same results would have been obtained if TR had shifted *down,* provided that the *slope* of the new TR curve were higher than previously at each level of the firm's behavior.

A change in the regulated firm's rivals' behavior that flattens the slope of TR (whether TR is shifted up or down) will lower the marginal or incremental profit at each level of the regulated firm's behavior and will reduce the level of the regulated firm's behavior that maximizes the firm's combined (profit + performance index).

To repeat, the main principle involved in determining the effect of a change in the regulated firm's rivals' behavior on the optimal behavior of the regulated firm is as follows. Does the change in rivals' behavior have a different-sized effect on the regulated firm's total revenues (or total costs) at different levels of the regulated firm's behavior? If the answer is affirma-tive, we can conclude that the change in rivals' behavior will affect the regulated firm's response to a particular regulatory constraint. The *direction* of the effect on the regulated firm's behavior will be determined by whether the effect of the rivals' behavior change on the regulated firm's total revenue (or total costs) increases or decreases with levels of the regulated firm's behavior dimension. If the change in total revenue is positive and increases with levels of the regulated firm's behavior dimen-sion, as in Figure 12.9, the optimal level of the regulated firm's behavior will be higher. If the change in total revenue is negative and declines in magnitude with levels of the regulated firm's behavior dimension, the optimal level of the regulated firm's behavior dimension will also be higher.

In order for the shift in TR to cause a reduction in the optimal level

Figure 12.9

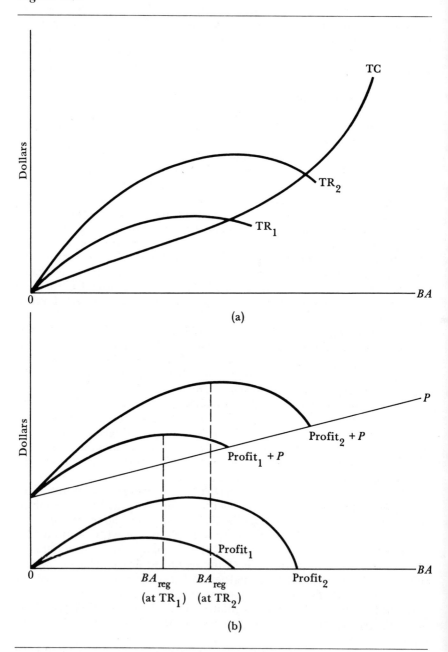

of the regulated firm's behavior, its slope must be reduced. This will occur *either* if TR is increased, but by a smaller amount as the level of the regulated firm's behavior dimension rises, *or* if TR is reduced, and by a larger amount as the level of the regulated firm's behavior dimension rises.

As a test of his or her understanding of the preceding principles, the reader should try to specify the kind of shifts in TC that would raise or lower the regulated firm's response to a particular regulatory constraint. One thing should be clear: it is quite possible for shifts in TR and/or TC to occur in response to the introduction of a regulatory constraint that would *completely offset* a tendency for the regulatory constraint to increase the regulated firm's behavior when these effects are ignored.

(c) The Behavior of Other Regulatory Agencies

As has been stressed, the literature dealing with the response of regulated firms to individual regulatory agencies has generally ignored the impact of other regulatory agencies on the regulated firm's response. This is unsatisfactory, because the behavioral response of a regulated firm to changes in one regulatory constraint depends on *all* the constraints the firm faces, including other regulatory constraints. This is relatively easy to comprehend in a situation in which a number of regulatory constraints administered by different regulatory agencies are applied to the *same* dimension of a regulated firm's behavior. For example, if tax incentives for research and development expenditures already exist, the impact of an additional regulatory constraint designed to affect the firm's research and development behavior will depend on the nature of the existing tax incentives. The same principles apply, however, even if the various regulatory constraints apply to different dimensions of the regulated firm's behavior.

Moreover, these principles apply even if other regulatory constraints do not change when a regulatory constraint is added or changed. An additional element is introduced if other regulatory constraints are changed as a result of the firm's response to the first constraint. For example, a regulatory constraint designed to reduce waste emission by a firm may require changes in the firm's production methods that raise the marginal cost of producing the firm's product and reduce the profit-maximizing level of the firm's output. Another regulatory agency that has the responsibility for trying to increase, or attain certain levels of output (or some other dimension of the firm's behavior that varies with output) may respond by changing the constraint it administers in an effort to restore the firm's output to the previous level.

In this example, the actions of the two agencies are "competitive." The action of the first regulatory agency tends to lower the performance of the second regulatory agency in meeting its targeted impact on the firm's behavior. Other situations in which the actions of different regulatory agencies are "complementary," and that tend to reinforce attainment of the respective agencies' targets for different dimensions of the regulated firm's behavior, are quite possible. However, the second situation is no better than the first, in terms of its implications for the regulated firm's behavior. If each agency ignores the impact of the other agencies on the regulated firm's behavior, they will set their respective regulatory constraints at levels that cause the regulated firm to exhibit *excessive* levels of the two regulated dimensions of behavior. Decreasing pollution and increasing safety use scarce resources that have alternative uses. If the value placed by society on the alternative uses of resources is higher than the value placed on reductions in pollution or increases in safety, there will be "too little" pollution and "too much" safety. The moral of the story is clear: irrespective of whether actions by different regulatory agencies reinforce or offset each other in affecting a particular dimension of a regulated firm's behavior, they must be taken into account in designing individual regulatory constraints.

Diagrammatically, the impact of other regulatory agencies on the way in which a regulated firm responds to one agency's regulatory constraint may be illustrated in *exactly* the same way that the behavior of the regulated firm's rivals was dealt with in Section 12.3(b). The levels of TR and TC at different levels of a particular dimension of the regulated firm's behavior depend on the levels of *all other dimensions of the regulated firm's behavior.* Some of these other dimensions may be affected by other regulatory constraints.

These other constraints may exert their impact on the firm's behavior in two distinguishable ways. First, even if other regulatory constraints do not change, changes in the level of the *BA* dimension of the regulated firm's behavior will imply effects on the TR and/or TC curves associated with other dimensions of the firm's behavior, leading to changes in the profit-maximizing levels of these other behavior dimensions. Diagrammatically, changes in profit-maximizing levels of other decision variables will shift the TR and TC curves applicable to *BA*.

Alternatively, the TR and TC curves applicable to *BA* may be drawn to include and take into account such optimal changes in other dimensions of the firm's behavior as *BA* varies, in which case such behavior changes will influence the *shape* of the TR and TC curves applicable to *BA*. Whichever approach is adopted, it is clear that other regulatory constraints may affect the magnitude of changes in optimal levels of other dimensions of the regulated firm's behavior, and therefore the position and/or shape of TR and/or TC at different levels of *BA*. This, in turn, will influence the impact of a regulatory constraint applied to *BA* on the level of *BA* selected by the firm.

Second, if other regulatory constraints are changed in response to changes in other dimensions of the regulated firm's behavior that occur as a result of a regulatory constraint on BA, this will have an impact on the optimal level of other dimensions of the firm's behavior, which will in turn imply a shift in TR and/or TC associated with BA.

Since the diagrammatic treatment of either of the preceding situations is identical to that involved in analyzing the impact of a regulated firm's rivals' behavior on the regulated firm's behavior, it will not be repeated here. It is well to bear in mind, however, that the impact of the behavior of other regulatory agencies' behavior on the regulated firm's response to regulation of BA does not depend on the consequences of that behavior for the *position* of the TR and/or TC curves that are applicable to the regulated dimension of behavior BA. It depends on the consequences for the *slopes* of TR and/or TC, since it is the slopes that determine the marginal, or incremental, profitability of BA. It is marginal profitability that is relevant in determining the level of BA that maximizes the regulated firm's combined (profit + performance index).

(d) Additional Characteristics of the Regulatory Constraint

Our discussion of the performance index in Section 12.2 omitted several important aspects of regulation dealing with enforcement of the performance index. The characteristics of the performance index P that is used to reward or penalize regulated firms for certain kinds of behavior are by themselves insufficient to determine the regulated firm's response to the performance index, because enforcement of the index will generally be less than 100 percent. Lack of perfect enforcement is attributable to a combination of factors, including the costs of monitoring a regulated firm's behavior and imprecise definition of the characteristics of the firm's behavior that are to be rewarded or penalized. In other words, the BS, BT, and BA terms in the performance index, discussed in Section 12.2, may be capable of a number of interpretations, and different interpretations may be placed on these terms by regulators and regulated firms, leading to legal disputes over whether a particular performance index should be applied to a particular firm or situation. The normative aspects of monitoring and enforcement activities of regulatory agencies will be dealt with in Chapter 13. In this section we shall concentrate on the implications of regulatory agency monitoring and enforcement activities for the response of regulated firms to a particular regulatory constraint.

The costs of monitoring regulated firms' behavior will generally prohibit monitoring 100 percent of firms to which the regulatory constraint applies. In addition, given agency monitoring activities, generally not all violators can be prosecuted, again for cost reasons. Third, even if a regulated firm is prosecuted, there is usually less than 100 percent chance that the agency will succeed; the law does not usually describe regulated firm behaviors that violate a particular regulatory standard of performance in sufficient detail to avoid the need for legal interpretation by the courts. Consequently, the performance index P must be multiplied by three probabilities in order to arrive at an estimate of the rewards and penalties that are associated with a particular level of BT and BA selected by the regulated firm, as follows: $P(BT,BA)_i \times (P_d \cdot P_p \cdot P_f)$, where $(BT,BA)_i$ is a particular self-selected behavior target and level of actual behavior of a regulated firm; $P(BT,BA)_i$ is the reward or penalty to the firm resulting from that behavior in the case of perfect enforcement $(P_d = P_p = P_f = 100\%)$; P_d is the probability of being monitored and of violations being detected; P_p is the probability of being selected by the agency as a candidate for legal prosecution; and P_f is the probability that the firm will lose the case and be subject to the penalties prescribed by law.

Each of these three probabilities depends on a number of variables influenced by regulatory agency behavior *and* on the behavior of regulated firms and other organizations, such as the courts, for reasons explained in Chapter 4, Section 3.

The probabilities P_d, P_p, P_f may differ between regulated firms, so that generalizations about the effect of particular regulatory constraints on regulated firms' behavior may be impossible. A few examples should suffice to illustrate the importance of these additional factors that influence such firms' response to regulatory constraints.

Figure 12.10 is useful in demonstrating the impact of the probability factors on the regulatory constraint and of the resulting regulatory constraint on a regulated firm's behavior. Assume that the performance index $P(BT,BA)_i$ in the certainty case is linear, and slopes up from left to right as shown in Figure 12.10(a). Even if each of the probabilities does not vary with the level of BA, multiplying $P(BT,BA)_i$ by these probabilities will change the position and the slope of the resulting regulatory constraint.

As we have seen earlier in this chapter, it is the *slope* of the regulatory constraint, sometimes referred to as the "structure" of the penalty-reward function, that is crucial in determining the effect of the constraint on the optimal level of the regulated firm's behavior. Only if the slope of the penalty-reward function remains unchanged when the probability factors are added to the analysis are no changes in earlier conclusions required. This would be the case, for example, if the penalty-reward function $P(BT,BA)_i$ were horizontal *and* the three probabilities, when combined, did not vary with BA. In these circumstances, although multiplying the penalty-reward function by the combined probabilities at each level of BA will shift the penalty-reward function downward, its slope will not be changed. Even in these circumstances, however, there may be some

Figure 12.10

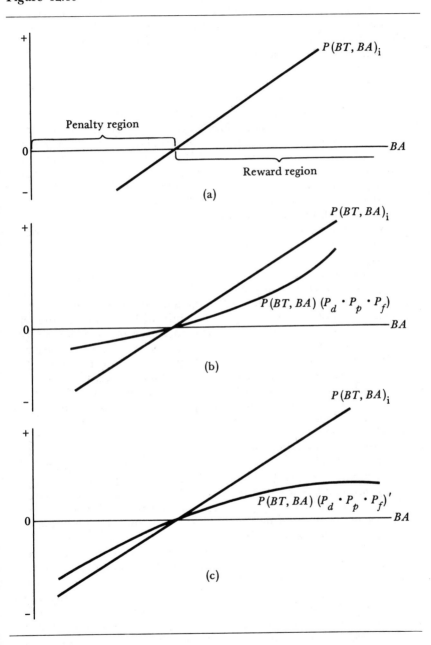

qualifications to the general proposition that such a shift in the penalty-reward function will not change the regulated firm's behavior. The reader is reminded of the ambiguous effects of changes in F or BS on a regulated firm's behavior in the presence of uncertainty and risk aversion on the part of the regulated firm's decision makers, which were discussed in Section 12.3(a).

As was already noted, if the penalty-reward function $P(BT,BA)$ slopes up from left to right, its slope will be reduced when multiplied by the three probabilities, even if these combined probabilities are the same at different levels of the regulated firm's behavior (BA). If the combined probabilities increase with the level of the regulated firm's behavior, the slope of the reward-penalty function will be reduced by less than when the combined probabilities do not vary, as shown by the curve labeled $P(BT,BA)(P_d \cdot P_p \cdot P_f)$ in Figure 12.10(b). This implies that the incentive effects of the penalty-reward system on BA are attenuated less, and may even be increased, by the probability factors. The opposite situation may also occur, however, if the combined probabilities decline with increases in the level of the regulated firm's behavior, as shown by the curve labeled $P(BT,BA)(P_d \cdot P_p \cdot P_f)'$ in Figure 12.10(c). Moreover, it is reasonable to suppose that the monitoring and enforcement efforts of regulatory agencies may often be greater in the case of firms that exhibit lower levels of BA, the activity to be encouraged by regulator. In these circumstances, if the combined probabilities decline sufficiently with increases in the level of firms' behavior, it is possible for this to flatten out the probabilistic penalty-reward function, or even impact a *negative* slope. The negative slope implies an incentive for regulated firms to *reduce* rather than increase the level of their behavior, since it implies declining marginal rewards and increasing marginal penalties as the level of BA increases.

Remember that it is the *combined* probabilities at different levels of regulated firms' behavior that matter. In certain circumstances, individual probabilities may differ at different levels of the firm's behavior, but may vary in opposite directions, so that the combined probabilities do not vary with the level of the firm's behavior. For example, the probability of being monitored may be higher at low levels of performance. However, if firms with low levels of performance are willing to spend more on legal defense of regulatory agency charges than firms with higher levels of performance, the resulting probability of a successful prosecution may be lower at low levels of performance. The poorest performers may, in other words, be the largest spenders on legal defense, with the result that the combined probabilities of detection and successful prosecution are unchanged at different levels of firms' behavior.

There is of course no reason why, in practice, the combined probabilities need vary systematically, either increasing or decreasing as BA varies. As a result, even if the penalty-reward function is linear and upward-sloping, it may exhibit a wavy shape when it is multiplied by the combined probabilities and expressed in probabilistic terms. This implies that the regulatory constraint will have incentive effects that tend to raise the level of *BA* over some ranges of regulated firms' behavior and reduce *BA* over other ranges of *BA*.

The implications of *changes* in the three probability factors for the regulatory constraint, and its impact on a regulated firm's behavior, are similar to the conclusions concerning the effect of the absolute levels of the probability factors. For example, a change in the level of one of the probabilities, or in the combined probabilities, that is the same at different levels of the regulated firm's behavior will change the slope of the probabilistic penalty-reward function unless the penalties and rewards are constant at different levels of the firm's behavior.

Probabilities, it should be remembered, are percentage figures. Thus, a 10 percent increase in the combined probabilities at each level of the regulated firm's behavior will mean a 10 percent downward shift in the probabilistic penalty-reward function. The absolute amount of the shift will vary unless the penalty-reward function, as in the absolute certainty case, is horizontal. A horizontal penalty-reward function — indicating that the size of penalties or rewards does not vary with the level of a regulated firm's behavior — conflicts with the characteristics required for truthful revelation of information and incentives for the firm to increase *BA*, however.

It is important to remember that it is the absolute penalties and rewards *multiplied by* the three probabilities of monitoring, selection, and successful prosecution that is relevant in determining a regulated firm's response to the penalty-reward function. Therefore, even though a regulatory penalty-reward function may exhibit the required shapes discussed in Section 12.2, it need not have this shape once it is multiplied by the three probability factors at each level of a regulated firm's behavior. Clearly, debates about the proper kind of penalties or rewards, and their level, cannot by themselves determine the nature of the regulatory constraint facing regulated firms, and therefore the effect of those penalties and rewards on regulated firms' behavior. It is essential to include consideration of the three probability factors.

Much more attention needs to be given to descriptive analysis of the factors that determine these probabilities in order to provide a basis for normative prescriptions concerning dimensions of regulatory agency behavior that influence these probabilities. Without such knowledge, it is impossible to determine which kinds of agency behavior are necessary to elicit certain desired characteristics of behavior from regulated firms. Similarly, it is impossible to evaluate regulatory agency behavior without such norms or to design appropriate incentive systems for regulators themselves.

It is not possible to consider all the implications of combining an absolute penalty-reward function with the three probability factors in this work. One major implication is quite clear, however. The appropriate framework for viewing particular issues concerning the proper form of regulatory constraints — such as standards versus taxes or subsidies, penalties versus rewards for behavior, the level of rewards or penalties, the specificity with which behavior to be regulated is defined, and a host of other issues — is much more complex than the framework currently employed in the literature.

A second major implication of our analysis of the regulatory constraint is that the *slope* of the probabilistic penalty-reward function is the characteristic of the regulatory constraint that affects the regulated firm's behavior. This slope represents the *change* in the regulated firm's performance index at each level of its behavior, and as explained, a profit-maximizing firm will select a level of behavior BA where the combined (profit + performance index) is a maximum. This will be a level of BA where the (change in profit + change in performance index) equals zero — that is, where a change in BA cannot increase the firm's (profit + regulatory rewards or penalties). Since the slope of the probabilistic regulatory constraint may differ at different levels of the regulated firm's behavior, the incentives provided, and response of regulated firms, may very well differ depending on the existing level of BA in different firms. This should provide a warning to those who assume that a regulatory constraint must always operate in the same way on firms in a particular industry.

The preceding brief exposition of the determinants of the probabilistic reward function $P(BT, BA) \times P_d \cdot P_p \cdot P_f)$ by no means exhausts the list of factors that may affect its shape (or the almost endless list of areas of economic, political, legal, and other fields where the analytical method employed in this section may provide powerful insights). Our main purpose is to provide a framework that can be used to integrate all the factors that affect the penalty-reward function and to emphasize that they must all be taken into account simultaneously in order to determine their implications for the incentives facing decision makers. This framework also provides improved perspective for viewing the work of writers who have focused on individual factors involved such as Polinsky and Shavell (1979), Polinsky (1980), Just and Zilberman (1979), and Harford (1978).

We mentioned earlier in this chapter (and in Chapter 5 when dealing with legislators' behavior) the importance of the specificity with which regulatory legislation is formulated as an influence on the probability of having the penalties of the law applied to one's behavior. The behavior of the legal system also exerts an impact on this probability, in a number of different but related ways. Legal precedents obviously affect the case selection policies of regulatory agencies and also the defense strategies of defendants; both factors play a role in determining the probability that a particular decision maker will have the penalty-reward function applied to them.

We could give additional examples, but this is not necessary. A major point, already emphasized, is that *all* the different factors that underlie the probabilistic penalty-reward function must be considered simultaneously in order to determine their effect on a decision makers' behavior. Another major point is that these factors may be interrelated in the sense that they affect *each other.* For example, efforts to change legal precedents will tend to change case selection policies of regulatory agencies, amounts spent on prosecultion by regulatory agencies, and amounts spent on defense by defendants in regulatory proceedings. Changes between strict liability and negligence rules may have similar effects on a number of factors that jointly determine the position and shape of the probabilistic penalty-reward function facing decision makers. For these reasons, one must be cautious in accepting the conclusions of studies that focus on only one aspect of the penalty-reward function.

One other aspect of all regulatory penalty-reward functions needs to be emphasized here. There will be time delays in the regulatory process of monitoring, detecting, and prosecuting violations, and these delays may sometimes be sufficient to make violations profitable even though eventual penalties exceed the earlier profits from violations. Whenever revenues and costs, or profits and penalties, occur in different time periods, the relevant comparison is between the *discounted present value* of the outcomes that occur in different time periods (see Chapter 3, Section 2). In the present context, the important implication of this principle is that the precise timing of penalties or rewards, and the discount rate used by decision makers who are affected by those penalties or rewards, are also relevant in determining the height and shape of regulatory penalty-reward functions.

In terms of the diagrams that depict the penalty-reward function $P(BT,BA) \times (P_d \cdot P_p \cdot P_f)$, for example, whenever penalties or rewards occur in time periods that differ from the occurrence of the behavior that is penalized or rewarded, the vertical axis of the diagram represents the discounted present value of penalties or rewards, not their absolute magnitude, multiplied by the probabilities of monitoring, detection, and successful prosecution of the behavior in question.

(e) The Regulated Firm's Expectations of Agency Behavior

Section 12.3(c) emphasized the importance of other regulatory agencies' policies as a determinant of the response of regulated firms to a particular regulatory constraint P. In this section, attention is switched to the regulated firm's expectations about the regulatory agency that administers P. In particular, attention will be focused on *the regulated firm's expectations regarding the process by which the regulatory agency determines the regulatory constraint P.*

A number of writers, including Weitzman (1980a), Wendel (1976), and Sappington (1980), have emphasized several different but related implications of situations in which regulated firms take into account the regulators' reaction to their behavior. Moreover, it needs to be emphasized that such a situation is almost inevitable in practice. Because they lack information regarding the relevant constraints that determine how a regulated firm will respond to any particular regulatory constraint, regulators are generally unable to establish at the outset the kind of regulatory constraint that is necessary to elicit the kind of regulated firms' behavior desired by the regulators. A more likely situation is one in which the regulators select particular characteristics of the regulatory constraint, such as levels of the F and k coefficients discussed in Section 12.2, then observe the regulated firms' behavior in response to the regulatory constraint, and then vary the characteristics of the regulatory constraint in an attempt to move closer to desired levels of the firm's behavior. In these circumstances, since the regulatory constraint is affected by the regulated firm's response to the constraint in an earlier period of time, the form of the constraint in any time period depends in part on the regulated firm's behavior in a previous period. If the regulated firm recognizes this, as is likely, it will attempt to take into account the relationship between its behavior and the form of the regulatory constraint P in selecting optimal levels of its behavior in each period of time.

A slightly more formal way to view the same situation is to say that, in our previous analysis of the impact of regulatory constraints on regulated firms, these firms totally ignored the determinants of the performance indicator $P = f(. . .)$. In contrast, we are now considering a situation in which regulated firms take into account that $P = f$(behavior of regulated firms . . .) in selecting optimal levels of their behavior. The behavior of the regulated firms will be different in the two situations, but just how different we cannot say without specifying the precise form of $P = f$(behavior of regulated firms) that *regulated firms* use in their decision making. The italicized term is important, because the regulated firm's *expectations* regarding this relationship need not correspond to the actual relationship that is employed by regulators. Despite this, it is the regulated firms' expectations that are relevant in determining their behavior.

The next point to emphasize is that although regulated firms' behavior may be based on how they expect regulators to respond, regulators can still select the regulatory constraints' characteristics at levels that result in desired behavior on the part of regulated firms. In order to do so, the regulators must *take into account* this additional constraint influencing regulated firms' behavior when selecting characteristics of the regulatory constraint. In principle, there is no more problem than with taking into account the influence of regulated firms' rivals' behavior, or other regulatory agencies, previously discussed. In practice, however, the problem of designing the regulatory constraint is greatly complicated.

One aspect of this complexity is the fact that the incentives for correct revelation of information by regulated firms (in the form of the performance index which was analyzed in Section 12.2) *are no longer appropriate.* The performance index analyzed in Section 12.2 deals with what is termed the "static" problem of incentives for truthful revelation. It does not provide appropriate incentives for truthful revelation of information in a "dynamic" situation involving the behavior of regulated firms in a number of periods, and in which the regulatory constraint in any period depends in part on the behavior of regulated firms in past, present, or future periods. For example, if a regulated firm's decision makers think that regulators will use the firm's current behavior as a partial basis for setting future coefficients in the performance index, they may purposely understate present performance in order to induce the regulators to set higher coefficients for performance in future periods.

Loeb and Magat (1978b) have expressed the basic principle that must be followed to avoid incentives for regulated firms to report inaccurate information in a dynamic incentive situation. Essentially, the performance indicator of each regulated firm must be independent of the firm's own forecasted performance, in order to avoid incentives for the firm to report its forecasted performance inaccurately. Using our earlier terminology, the factors that determine the performance index that is applied to an individual regulated firm must not depend on that firm's own forecasted performance. One way to accomplish this objective might be to base the coefficients in each firm's performance index on the forecasts of *other,* similarly regulated firms, for example. This would be desirable only if the response of different regulated firms were independent; otherwise, a group strategy of misleading the regulatory agency might pay off for regulated firms as a group.

There is one other aspect of the situation in which regulated firms take into account the factors that determine the regulatory constraint $P = f(. . .)$ that has been almost totally ignored in the literature. Simply eliminating the regulated firm's behavior from $P = f(. . .)$ will *not* necessarily eliminate the need for the regulatory agency to take into account the firm's expectations regarding $P = f(. . .)$ in its decision making. Suppose, for example, that one of the factors that determines $P = f(. . .)$ is legislators' behavior. The regulated firm may take this factor into account and try to influence the form of P by influencing legislators rather than by altering its own behavior. In other words, regulators need to take into account *all* the ways in which regulated firms expect to be able to influence P, not only the ways in which their regulated dimensions of behavior may affect P.

We can only point out the nature of the problem, and the nature of the approach that is appropriate, in devising incentive systems that are optimal in a multiperiod situation. Despite increasing interest and a growing number of publications in the professional economics journals dealing with incentive systems, only modest progress has been made to date in devising theoretical and operational incentive systems for the dynamic multiperiod problem. Despite this, it may be that the opportunities for playing games on the part of regulated firms in the multiperiod case are less than is often assumed, even if the "static" performance indicators are used, owing to the complexities of these indicators. At the very least, some attempt to implement and experiment with the statically efficient performance indicators should be encouraged. The experience gained by regulators from such an exercise may be an essential ingredient in providing solutions to the multiperiod incentive problems.

An extreme view of the importance of regulated firms' expectations of regulators' response to firms' behavior is expressed by Smythe (1980). He is of the opinion that the whole apparatus of regulation was itself created with private enterprise support as a means of heading off public ownership between the 1880s and the 1920s.

CHAPTER THIRTEEN

Guidelines for Improving Regulation: Aspects of Regulators' Behavior

13.1 INCENTIVES FACING REGULATORS

The preceding chapter has laid the foundation and provided a framework for considering the problem of setting guidelines, or standards of performance, for regulators' behavior, and for considering the type of incentive systems that are necessary in order to motivate regulators to try to achieve those standards of performance.

Regulation and regulators' behavior are targets of criticism from a variety of sources, and numerous proposals for regulatory reform have been advanced in recent years. Only a few attempts at regulatory reform have actually been implemented, however. For example, in 1974 President Gerald Ford required federal agencies to prepare "inflation impact statements" prior to issuing new regulations, and "economic impact statements" that estimated the costs and benefits of new regulations were required under the Carter administration. In 1978 President Jimmy Carter created a Regulatory Analysis Review Group, headed by the chairman of economic advisors, to review the economic impact of major new regulations. In the same year, the president also created a Regulatory Council, composed of the major regulatory agencies and charged with coordinating common regulatory approaches among agencies with overlapping responsibilities.

These and other reforms of regulation attempted by the executive branch of the United States government appear to have had very little

371

impact. Regulatory commissions such as the Federal Communications Commission and the Interstate Commerce Commission, which are not government departments headed by members of the president's cabinet, may not be subject to presidential control on regulatory matters. Some regulatory agencies, such as the Environmental Protection Agency and the Food and Drug Administration, are prohibited or restricted by the terms of the legislation that created these bodies from giving weight to costs and other economic impacts of their decisions. In addition, even in government agencies where regulatory reforms can be attempted, simply requiring regulators to use different criteria or techniques in their decision making will not usually be sufficient to change the results of regulatory decision processes. In addition, changes in the incentives that confront regulators will generally be needed in order to motivate them to give appropriate consideration and weight to new criteria or techniques in their decision making. In the absence of such incentives, cursory or cosmetic reference to such new criteria or techniques are likely to be the only result, and regulators will make the same decisions they consider optimal given the unchanged penalties and rewards determined by the existing constraints that confront them.

Proposals for legislative reform of regulation are also commonplace. According to Weidenbaum (1981), concern over the cost of regulation alone has resulted in the introduction of more than 150 bills on the subject in Congress. These proposed laws cover a wide variety of approaches that generally embody one or more of the following types of reform.

(a) *Economic impact statements.* All regulatory agencies would be inquired to prepare such statement indicating various effects of proposed regulations, such as costs imposed on businesses and individuals affected by the regulations as well as effects on employment, productivity, product and service prices, competition, and other aspects of the regulated sector and other sectors of the economy.

(b) *Benefit-cost studies.* Regulatory agencies would be required to prepare such studies of proposed regulations and to take these studies into account in their decision making by applying various benefit-cost tests to proposed regulations. Whereas economic impact statements focus mainly on various effects of regulation, benefit-cost studies also give explicit or implicit weights to these effects, and usually attempt to aggregate and compare the various positive effects (benefits) and negative effects (costs) of particular regulations. Under proposed laws, regulators would have to show that proposed regulations generate more benefits than costs. However, as explained in Chapters 3 and 4, there will generally be a number of different but equally plausible models of the effects of particular regulations, and a wide range of choice for assigning different weights to particular effects of regulation predicted by these models.

Weidenbaum (1981, pp. 36–71) provides a detailed example of benefit-cost analysis of the same traffic safety standards performed by two separate bodies, the U.S. Safety Administration and the private National Safety Council. The total costs of motor vehicle accidents in the United States as estimated by these two bodies differed by as much as threefold in some years, and their estimated benefit-cost ratios of particular safety measures such as bus passenger seating and crash protection were widely different.

Unless regulators' choice of models to be used for analyzing effects of particular regulations, and their choice of weights to be applied to the effects of regulation predicted by those models, are also restricted by legislation that mandates cost-benefit analyses, it will usually be possible for regulators to select models and weights that result in the benefit and cost estimates they desire. Since there is no general agreement among economists or specialists in regulation regarding the appropriate models for analyzing effects of regulation, or for assigning weights to these effects, reaching agreement regarding these matters in legislation designed to constrain regulators is likely to be impossible. Even if agreement were reached regarding these matters, incentive systems that motivate regulators to employ the selected models and weights in their decision making would still be required also.

(c) *Limitations on regulatory budgets.* These limitations would include not only the administrative budgets of regulatory agencies themselves but also the amount of costs a regulatory agency could impose on businesses and the nation as a whole. Enforcement of such limitations would require estimates of the total costs that regulations impose on society, and this in turn would require models that could predict the effects of particular regulations, and the assignment of weights to those effects which are considered to be costs to members of society. The same problems of lack of agreement on relevant models, and weights to be assigned to predicted effects of regulations, that were mentioned in connection with benefit-cost tests also apply to cost limitation proposals.

Two additional problems merit special mention. First, limitations on the total costs a regulatory agency may impose on society might prevent regulations from being implemented that exceed the cost limitation but that also would generate even larger benefits. Second, the effects of regulations and actions of individual agencies generally interact with actions of other regulatory agencies (see Chapter 11). The resulting effects of these interacting regulations on the total costs imposed on organizations and members of society are therefore the net result of all regulations and actions taken by regulatory agencies as a whole. Even if effects of all regulations on total costs to society could be estimated, it would be difficult or impossible to allocate these total costs of regulation among different agencies. The situation is similar to the problem of allocating the total costs of an input that produces several joint products in a business firm. There may be no unique way of allocating the total costs imposed by all regulations and regulatory agencies among the individual agencies responsible for particular regulations.

(d) *Legislative vetoes.* There would be wider application of such vetoes by Congress, which in the past has given itself power to veto individual regulations. A prominent example is provided by congressional efforts to limit Federal Trade Commission powers, whose proconsumer regulations in recent years have angered many business groups. In practice, for most regulatory agencies the constraint that is imposed by the probability of attracting a congressional veto is very limited, owing to the vast number of new regulations published in the Federal Register each year. It is impossible for Congress and its committees to review all these regulations. A number of legislative proposals that attempt to widen the application of congressional vetoes to new regulations stipulate an extended time period, usually ninety days, after a new regulation is issued before it becomes effective. During this period, a resolution by either the Senate or the House of Representatives, rather than by both bodies as is required at present, either to disapprove the regulation or to require the issuing agency to reconsider the regulation, would prevent the regulation from becoming effective.

(e) *Sunset laws.* These laws would require periodic reviews of individual regulatory programs or entire regulatory agencies by Congress to determine whether the program or agency should continue in existence. This procedure would provide Congress with a formal opportunity to revise underlying regulatory statutes and to terminate a program or an agency.

When considering the likely effects of these proposed legislative reforms of regulation, existing constraints on legislators' time and incentives for legislators to perform more than perfunctory reviews of regulation must be taken into account. As already noted in connection with reforms of regulatory agencies attempted by previous presidents and members of the executive branch, legislative reforms will not change regulators' behavior unless they are accompanied by effective constraints. Whenever these constraints require legislators to monitor regulators' behavior, it is implicit that changes will also be required in the legislators' behavior. Unless existing incentives facing legislators are changed, their behavior vis-à-vis regulators cannot be expected to change, despite the introduction of legislative reforms such as those outlined in the preceding paragraphs.

To date, none of the procedural reforms described in the foregoing discussion has been enacted by Congress. Since 1975 a number of significant statutes have been passed that attempt to deregulate certain aspects of the securities, natural gas, oil, trucking, and airline industries (see Chapter 14). Also, the executive and legislative reforms of regulation that have been outlined in this section are not the only proposals and approaches spawned by dissatisfaction with regulation. Alternatives to regulation, including industrial reorganization, lowering entry barriers into markets and other types of transactions, and social responsibility of business are discussed in some detail in Chapter 14. As emphasized there, various procedural reforms and alternatives to regulation are not necessarily mutually exclusive.

Lack of agreement on the type of regulatory reforms that are considered appropriate has prevented all but a few legislative reforms from being enacted. Regulatory reforms attempted by the Nixon, Ford, and Carter administrations appear to have had few significant effects on the behavior of regulators and on the upward trend of regulation in the United States. As of this writing, it remains to be seen whether the target of reduced regulation that featured prominently in administrative efforts during the Reagan administration will be achieved. As explained in Chapters 1, 3, and 4, regulation has many dimensions and many effects. Even if administrative efforts to reduce the number of new regulations added annually to the Federal Register, or to reduce the amount of government paperwork, are successful, this does not necessarily imply that the overall costs regulation imposes on society will be reduced. Also, if reduced regulation results in less monitoring and enforcement by regulatory agencies, this may reduce the benefits of regulation by an even greater amount than reductions in costs of regulation.

Following are major considerations that provide perspective on different proposals for regulatory reform and the reasons that underlie disagreements about reform proposals and the failure of such proposals to be enacted or to be effective.

Normative Concepts of Regulators' Behavior. To design appropriate incentives for regulators, one must have some normative concept of improved or optimal regulatory agency behavior that one is seeking to implement. This desired form of regulators' behavior depends, in turn, both on the perceived objectives of regulation and on the constraints that are perceived to confront regulators. Criticism of regulators' behavior, and proposals for regulatory reform, are often based on many different concepts of what regulatory targets should be, and failure to agree on the objectives or targets of regulation explains a good deal of the failure of Congress and other legislative bodies to pass legislative reforms.

The second important consideration is that the kind of regulators' behavior that is appropriate from the point of view of achieving any particular regulatory target depends on the nature of the constraints that actually confront regulators in the real world. Even where the objectives of regulation are not in dispute, different proposals for reform are often based on different perceptions of, and assumptions about, the kind of constraints that confront regulators. Much criticism of regulators' behavior ignores or misperceives the nature of the constraints that determine the environment within which most regulators operate in practice. As

Chapter 12, Section 12.3, indicated, many constraints that face regulated firms and regulators and that determine optimal regulatory behavior are uncertain. Although regulators are often in the best position to determine the form of these constraints, they are rarely faced by the proper incentives needed to motivate them to do so and to report the constraints accurately to those bodies that are responsible for determining the penalties and rewards facing regulators. The remainder of this chapter will be devoted to an examination of the problem of providing incentives for regulators to act in any particular desired manner.

As already noted, in order to design appropriate incentives for regulators, one must have a normative concept of the desired form of regulators' behavior. In economic analysis, the task of regulatory agencies is generally assumed to be the design and administration of regulatory constraints facing regulated firms in such a manner as to produce "socially optimal" behavior on the part of these firms. Modern concepts of socially optimal behavior of regulated firms and regulators include consideration of the regulatory resources required to design and administer regulatory constraints. Regulation is socially optimal if the difference between the marginal benefits and marginal costs experienced by members of society as a whole, as a result of a regulation-induced change in any dimension of firms' behavior, exactly equals the marginal cost of the regulatory resources required to change that dimension of firms' behavior. The marginal cost of regulating any particular dimension of firms' behavior is the cost of the regulatory resources required to design and enforce an incentive system facing regulated firms that changes their behavior in a particular desired manner.

The preceding prescription for socially optimal regulation hides more than it reveals (see Chapters 3 and 4). In those chapters it was emphasized that the benefits and costs of changes in various dimensions of firms' behavior depend critically on whose evaluations are selected to represent society's evaluations. Moreover, even the same group of individuals will evaluate particular changes in firms' behavior differently in monetary terms, depending on the distribution of income, wealth, or power among those individuals. In addition, there may be incentives for individuals and interest groups to report their evaluations of changes in dimensions of firms' behavior inaccurately to regulators (discussed in Section 13.2). It is important to emphasize now, however, that information distortion may be just as characteristic of the "demand" side of regulation as the "supply" side distortion of information by regulated firms. This possibility implies that the normative task of regulation may need to be expanded to include the design and administration of incentive systems confronting individuals and organizations on the demand side of the regulatory process. Accurate information on the benefits and costs to members of society of regulation-induced changes in firms' behavior is indispensable in determining socially optimal dimensions of regulated firms' and regulators' behavior.

The analysis contained in Chapter 12 emphasizes that the characteristics of an optimal regulatory incentive system that elicits truthful reporting of information, and that also results in the kind of regulated firms' behavior desired by regulators, depends on the goals and other constraints that confront regulated firms. The relevant regulatory agency policy variables are factors such as the k and F coefficients in the regulatory penalty-reward function; the types of rewards or penalties facing regulated firms; and various decision variables involved in monitoring, case selection, and case prosecution by regulators. The reader will recollect that the probabilities of being monitored and prosecuted by a regulatory agency, and the probability of winning or losing a case, determine the strength with which any particular reward or penalty system is applicable to any particular regulated firm.

The "socially optimal" levels of the regulatory policy variables are the normative standards by which regulatory agency behavior itself should be judged and rewarded or penalized. Unfortunately, such standards of regulators' behavior are not generally known in advance. In other words, this is a situation that is exactly analogous to that which is involved in the case of regulated firms whose total cost or revenue curves in Figure 12.2 of Chapter 12 are uncertain. In the present context, it is the characteristics of socially optimal behavior of regulators that are not known in advance, and it is regulators who must be relied on to supply much of the information that is required to determine socially optimal regulatory behavior.

The fundamental nature of the problem of providing appropriate incentives for regulators to behave in a socially optimal manner is therefore analytically very similar to the problem of providing incentives for regulated firms to behave in a socially optimal manner. Only the type of decision maker whose behavior is being considered, and the dimensions of that decision maker's behavior, are different in the two cases. The same problems of overcoming incentives for regulators to report information inaccurately, and of providing incentives for regulators to behave in a socially optimal manner in selecting the levels of their policy variables, exist. The same general principles apply to the design of an incentive system facing regulators that solves these problems as are applicable in the case of incentive systems facing regulated firms. Obviously, this implies that some decision-making body will be required to "regulate the regulators" by designing and administering the incentive system that confronts individual regulatory agencies and regulators. Moreover, just as the optimal characteristics of a regulatory incentive system confronting regulated firms depends on the goals and constraints confronting those firms' decision makers, the optimal design of an incentive system for regulators will also depend on the goals and constraints confronting those regulators, since these factors will influence the manner in which regulators respond to any particular incentive system.

The forgoing discussion should enable the reader to place in better perspective the frequent admonitions and prescriptions for regulators to "act in a more socially responsible manner." How *can* they act in this manner if no one, including the regulators, knows what the relevant constraints are that determine the characteristics of socially optimal regulatory agency behavior? Even where these characteristics are known, there are few or no incentives for regulators to act in a socially responsible manner.

Existing incentives facing regulators generally bear little resemblance to the characteristics exhibited by an incentive system designed to elicit socially optimal behavior on the part of regulators. Some characteristics of existing incentives facing regulators are often counterproductive in this regard when viewed in isolation. Budgets are often allocated to agencies on the basis of criteria that conflict with principles of socially optimal agency behavior. For example, budget allocations may be related to the number of cases won by a regulatory agency, even though this criterion may be unrelated to socially optimal agency behavior. Budget allocations to an agency may sometimes be reduced if the agency improves its efficiency in performing particular functions.

There are two reasons why we must be tentative in our conclusions regarding the nature of existing incentives facing regulators. First, existing incentives facing regulators depend on the personal goals and *all* the constraints that are considered relevant by the regulators in their decision making. Despite a good deal of theorizing concerning the incentive properties of certain personal goals and particular constraints facing regulators, and an increasing number of empirical studies of regulatory decision processes, very little is currently known about the kind of goals and constraints that influence regulators' decisions and their consequences for regulators' behavior. Individual constraints that have adverse implications in the form of less than socially optimal levels of certain dimensions of regulators' behavior may be partly or wholly offset by other constraints that, viewed in isolation, have the opposite implications. Much of what we do know about regulators' behavior should be treated with some care and skepticism if the source of the information is the regulatory agency itself. Existing incentive systems facing regulatory agencies do not generally exhibit the properties that are needed to elicit accurate information regarding agency behavior (discussed in Chapter 12, Section 2).

Second, because we do not know much about the personal objectives and constraints facing regulators, it is not possible to specify in advance the characteristics that incentive systems must exhibit to elicit socially optimal behavior on the part of regulators. More information is needed in order to evaluate existing incentive systems facing regulators and to determine the kind of changes in existing incentive systems that are necessary to improve regulators' behavior.

Although we cannot, for the reasons just cited, either specify the existing nature of incentives facing regulators in general or evaluate these incentives in relation to a socially optimal system of incentives facing regulators, it would be very surprising if the two incentive systems bore much resemblance to each other. Even if they were similar, it could hardly be claimed that this similarity was the result of a conscious effort to design optimal regulatory incentive systems. Much of the existing knowledge on the design of optimal incentive systems facing decision makers in general is of relatively recent origin and is understood by relatively few economists and other specialists in behavioral science and by fewer regulatory agency decision makers or their sovereign bodies. In making these comments regarding incentives facing regulators, it should be emphasized that the same comments apply equally to the incentive systems facing most other types of decision maker, including legislators, voters, consumers, and business decision makers. As will be emphasized in Section 13.2, the search for socially optimal regulatory incentive systems must be extended to many of these other types of decision maker.

One argument that is frequently advanced as an explanation for the lack of proper incentives facing regulators is the concept of "lack of appropriability" of any "surplus" analogous to a firm's profits. This, it has been argued, implies absence of appropriate incentives for regulators and decision makers in nonprofit organizations in general, and results in inefficient or otherwise socially undesirable decisions in these organizations. Such reasoning generally leads to prescribed remedies that attempt to introduce some kind of bonus or reward for decision makers that is related to a concept of organizational surplus analogous to profits in a business enterprise. Several points must be mentioned in response to this line of reasoning.

First, appropriability of profits is *not* in fact the feature that produces profit-maximizing behavior on the part of managers in business enterprises. This is obvious in the case of managers who do not receive all or any part of the profits resulting from their firm's operations. Rather than appropriability, it is the linking of managerial performance and rewards to the firm's profits that may encourage profit-maximizing behavior on the part of a manager or other type of decision maker within the organization. Provided that managerial rewards are equal to k(total revenue − total costs), any decisions that increase $(TR − TC)$ will increase the level of managerial rewards.

Similar reasoning may be applied to nonprofit organizations of all types, with appropriate changes in the total revenue and cost concepts to reflect the different "benefit" and "cost" concepts that are applicable in these types of organization. In a regulatory agency, for example, "social benefit" and "social cost" would replace the monetary revenue and cost concepts used in the managerial performance indicator and reward function. Despite this, the notion of linking decision-maker rewards to some measure of organizational "surplus" will not necessarily encourage desirable forms of decision-maker behavior in nonprofit organizations. The same conclusion is true even in profit-oriented organizations, for a number of reasons.

First, the use of such a performance indicator does nothing to overcome incentives for the decision maker to report (total benefits − total costs) inaccurately, in terms of both potential performance and actual performance. For example, the decision maker may overstate total benefits and/or understate total costs when reporting actual performance. Or, if the decision maker is rewarded for actual performance in relation to some estimate or promise of potential performance, he or she may intentionally understate potential performance in order to subsequently exceed the stated potential. (See Chapter 12, Section 2.) Even if the decision maker accurately reports potential or actual performance, alternative courses of action that result in the same level of (TB − TC) but different absolute levels of TB and TC will not change the level of k(TB − TC), and therefore managerial rewards. One of these courses of action may be more desirable than the others from an organizational point of view, however. In the case of a profit-maximizing firm, for example, higher absolute levels of total revenue and total costs that yield the same profits imply a lower profit per unit of cost or capital invested.

The fundamental reason why adopting a managerial reward system that is related to the organization's surplus in the general manner $P = k$(TB − TC) will not necessarily improve decision-maker behavior — even apart from the problem of overcoming incentives for inaccurate reporting of (TB − TC) — is that it completely ignores the goals and other constraints that confront the decision maker. These goals and constraints will influence the decision maker's behavior and resulting levels of (TB − TC) even if the decision maker is confronted by a reward function of the form k(TB − TC). For example, the manager of a firm may prefer increased size of the firm, measured in terms of TR (sales revenue) or TC (expenditure on inputs), even if it reduces profit and the level of his or her managerial bonus that is based on the firm's profits. In order to set k at a level that would overcome such "disincentives," it would be necessary to know the value — expressed in terms of the type of rewards used in the managerial bonus function — placed by the manager on increased size of the firm. The general principles that are relevant in this connection are identical to those already discussed in Chapter 12, Section 2.

While on the subject of simple nostrums for solving problems of organizational decision making, it is appropriate to emphasize that similar reasoning and conclusions apply to the introduction of new "techniques" of decision making as are applicable to attempts to reward decision-maker behavior on the basis of particular characteristics of the resulting decisions, such as (TB − TC) concepts. Even if regulators are provided with the most up-to-date knowledge and techniques for determining relevant constraints and enabling them to behave in a "socially optimal" manner, this does not guarantee that such techniques will be used. That this is so has been amply demonstrated in the case of programming-planning-budgeting techniques introduced into government agencies under the Johnson administration, and more recently in the case of "zero-based" budgeting under the Carter administration. Both have proved to be ineffective in changing decision-maker behavior.

This is not the result of the inherent nature of the techniques themselves, both of which can be powerful aids to improved decision making. Rather, it is caused by the failure to recognize the need to provide incentives for decision makers to use these techniques, and to use them properly. These incentives must include an adequate recognition of the problems and constraints that influence the ability of decision makers to use the techniques. In the case of zero-based budgeting, for example, insufficient regard was paid to the amount of resources and time needed to use the techniques properly, with the result that adequate application of the techniques was impossible even if decision makers tried to implement their use (Herzlinger, 1979).

The factors that enable decision makers to apply such techniques of decision making are only one part of the picture, however. Motivating them to do so is also necessary, and this requires some knowledge of the existing constraints confronting decision makers, which determine the "costs" to the decision maker brought about by changing from existing techniques of decision making. Moreover, adequate attention must be paid to ensuring that techniques are used *properly*. They must not become new cosmetic clothing for doing things in an unchanged manner.

One aspect of this problem that is generally ignored is that new techniques of decision making may not change decision-maker behavior if the *criteria* used for decision making when those techniques are employed remain unchanged. This can be illustrated by reference to zero-based budgeting, which differs from "conventional" budgeting in one important respect only. The *total* expenditures, and resulting effects and benefits of using resources for particular purposes, are analyzed in each budget period, instead of only *incremental* changes in these totals. In a sense, zero-based budgeting increases the concept of "marginal" expenditure until it equals "total" expenditure. Thus, levels of expenditure that would not have been considered under conventional incremental budgeting come under scrutiny.

Even if zero-based budgeting is applied meticulously, it will not result in improved decision making if the criteria for evaluating items of expenditure in budgets, whether zero-based or conventional, are the reason for poor decision-making performance, rather than the levels of expenditure that are scrutinized. If the "benefit" and "cost" concepts used in the evaluation are incorrectly conceptualized or measured, no amount of tinkering with budget techniques will improve the performance of decision makers, judged from the perspective of the correct benefit and cost concepts.

In short, whether one is discussing techniques for decision making or criteria for decision making, incentives are necessary to induce decision makers to adopt these techniques or criteria, and the nature of the necessary incentives cannot be divorced from the goals and constraints confronting the decision makers whose behavior one is trying to change. There *are no* simple or complex "new incentive systems" that can be applied automatically to improve decision-maker behavior according to any particular criteria of decision-maker behavior, without considering such factors.

This does not mean that new incentive systems should not be tried without all the information about constraints currently facing decision makers being first determined. Introducing, a constraint in the form of a new incentive system, and observing the resulting behavior of decision makers in response to this new constraint, may be a method of obtaining information regarding the nature of preexisting constraints facing decision makers. That is, in certain circumstances the information required to design an improved incentive system facing decision makers may be obtained more appropriately by a trial-and-error procedure. This procedure would involve feedback of information and possible modification of the incentive system facing decision makers in order to obtain the desired effects on decision-maker behavior. Whichever approach is adopted, however, the design of an appropriate incentive system facing decision makers must be based on information regarding certain characteristics of their goals and the other constraints that they consider relevant in their decision making.

Normative Concepts of Regulatory Agency Efficiency. It is useful to consider the concept of regulatory agency "efficiency" within the normative framework of regulatory agency behavior developed so far in this chapter. A general definition of "efficiency" involves the output/input ratio, and where multiple inputs or outputs are involved, the definition requires some weighting system for individual inputs and outputs in order to determine how the degree of efficiency has changed in a situation in which multiple changes in inputs or outputs occur. In the case of business firms, inputs and outputs are weighted by their respective prices, so that the concept of efficiency can then be expressed in terms of value of output/ value of inputs, or total revenue / total cost. Output and input prices are appropriate weights in the case of firms with profit-maximizing objectives, since any increases in "efficiency" so defined will imply an increase in profits.

In the case of nonprofit organizations, "efficiency" may also be defined in terms of the ratio of the weighted sum of outputs divided by the weighted sum of inputs. The relevant weights in this case may be different from output and input prices, reflecting different objectives of nonprofit organizations, and the resulting different contributions that particular inputs and outputs may make to those objectives. The relevant input and output concepts themselves may be very different for nonprofit organizations and business firms, respectively.

Increases in efficiency are obviously desirable in any organization, since they imply a higher level of attainment of the organization's objectives from existing resources. Even more important, however, is the requirement that the "proper" efficiency concept be employed. This means that the input and output concepts, and their weights, should be the ones that are appropriate in light of the organization's goals. This is true of organizations in general, and also of regulatory agencies in particular. The issue of determining proper indexes of regulatory agency input and output, and associated measures of regulatory agency efficiency, has received little attention in the literature. Charges of agency inefficiency are the rule rather than the exception. The "paperwork burden" generated by regulatory agencies is an obvious example. The use, by regulatory agencies such as OSHA, of input-related criteria (e.g., the length of ladders or number of exists) in defining safety standards instead of output-related criteria (e.g., the number of accidents occurring) is another example.

These criticisms may or may not be valid, and our purpose here is not to settle the issue. Rather, it is to emphasize that any criticism of an organization's efficiency necessarily implies some implicit or explicit efficiency standard involving a weighted set of outputs and inputs that is used to judge the organization's existing performance. Both the output and input sides must be taken into account in order to make valid inferences regarding an organization's efficiency. One cannot, for example, infer that efficiency has improved as the result of an observed reduction in the quantity or total cost of inputs; output dimensions may also have changed, resulting in a reduction in efficiency. Conversely, a higher quantity total cost of inputs need not imply lower efficiency if the weighted index of outputs has increased more than proportionately.

These considerations are important in evaluating efficiency in regulatory agencies. Increases in the amount of regulatory inputs devoted to monitoring and enforcement activities may increase the probability of detecting or successfully prosecuting firms that violate certain standards of required performance. This may, in turn, result in increases in the extent to which regulated firms' behavior meets socially desirable standards of performance, the "output side" of the regulatory agency efficiency concept, and in an overall increase in the efficiency of the agency's performance. On the other hand, reductions in the total cost of regulatory agency inputs required to achieve given levels of regulated firms' performance will also imply increases in the efficiency of the agency. As these examples suggest, little information regarding the efficiency of a regulatory agency is provided by information regarding regulatory inputs alone. Yet to date there are few serious attempts to define conceptually, or to measure empirically, the output side of regulatory agency activities.

The article by Sabbatier (1977) listed in the references to this chapter is an exception to this generalization.

Even less attention has been devoted to the normative issues involved in defining what the output concepts, and relative weights attributed to different output concepts, should be in the case of regulatory agencies. It follows that little normative significance can be attached to proposals for rewarding or penalizing "efficiency" in regulatory agencies. Such proposals may or may not improve regulatory agency performance, depending on (1) which of the many possible input and output concepts, and their relative weights, is used to define efficiency; (2) how regulatory agency decision makers react to a particular reward system involving a particular efficiency concept, which depends on their goals and the other constraints they face; and (3) which set of regulatory agency goals is adopted for use in evaluating regulatory agency behavior.

Rivalry Between Regulatory Agencies. There is one type of constraint that influences an individual regulator's behavior in response to any particular incentive system — and that therefore must be taken into account in designing an optimal incentive system facing individual regulators — that is generally ignored in both descriptive and normative discussion of regulatory agency behavior. This is the nature of a regulator's anticipations regarding the behavior of other regulators. Different regulatory agencies attempt to influence different aspects of regulated firms' behavior. However, these aspects of firms' behavior are related, so that each regulatory constraint facing the firm will have some impact on the firm's behavior in response to other regulatory constraints (see Chapter 11). When faced by a particular incentive system, the results of a regulator's efforts to change a particular dimension of a regulated firm's behavior, and therefore the "success" of the regulator, will depend on the behavior of other regulators.

We can distinguish two conceptually different mechanisms by which the behavior of other regulatory agencies will exert an impact on the behavior of each individual regulatory agency. First, other regulatory agencies may change *their* regulatory constraints in response to changes in regulated firms' behavior caused by the first regulator's regulatory constraint. Second, other regulatory agencies may change their behavior directly in response to changes in the behavior of the first regulatory agency. For either case, the relevant principles for analyzing competition between agencies are similar to those discussed in Chapter 7, Section 1. The expected reactions of rival agencies are relevant when considering how to devise constraints that will result in "socially optimal" behavior by individual regulatory agencies.

Even if individual regulatory agencies do not recognize and attempt to take into account each other's behavior, their behavior *is* related, and this fact will affect the actual outcome of regulatory agency behavior.

Discrepancies between the expected outcome and actual outcome of regulatory agency policies may result in a dynamic process of change in regulatory instruments. Interdependence between the ways different regulatory agencies behave also needs to be remembered in connection with suggestions that "competition" among regulatory agencies be increased as a means of improving agency performance. These proposals generally envisage the creation of agencies with overlapping responsibility for the same area of regulation. They do not usually recognize or attempt to take into account adequately the relationships already existing between the behavior of regulatory agencies with responsibility for regulating different sectors and aspects of firms' behavior. By ignoring such relationships, proposals to change regulatory agency behavior in particular areas of regulation may have very different effects from those which are intended.

The characteristics of "socially optimal" behavior of different agencies are also automatically related, because the effect of each agency's policies on regulated firms' behavior depends on the behavior and regulatory policies of other agencies. Therefore, whether one is concerned with purely descriptive analysis of regulatory agency behavior, or with the normative problem of setting socially desirable standards of behavior for regulatory agencies, the manner in which each agency's behavior is related to the behavior of other agencies is crucial.

The analytical framework and principles that are applicable to the problem of determining descriptive and normative interrelationships between the behavior of individual regulatory agencies is very similar to the body of economic analysis involved in analyzing the behavior of firms. The decision makers and the decision variables are different, but the links between the principal actors are very similar. Regulatory agencies with responsibility for similar areas of regulation are analogous to firms in the same industry, and regulatory agencies with responsibility for different areas of regulation are analogous to firms in different industries. Just as firms attempt to influence buyer behavior, regulatory agencies attempt to influence the regulated decision maker's behavior. And just as the response of buyers to a particular firm's policies depends on the behavior of other firms in the same and other industries, the response of regulated decision makers to the policies of a particular regulatory agency depends on the policies of other regulators.

These close analogies between firms' behavior and regulatory agency behavior have implications for attempts to improve our understanding of the process of regulation. It is not necessary to reinvent the wheel, and make all the mistakes that have been made in developing the current body of knowledge concerning interrelationships between different dimensions of firms' behavior, in the case of regulatory agency behavior. The central principles of that same body of knowledge may be applied directly to regulatory agencies themselves and, more important, to an analytical framework that combines the behavior of firms, and the behavior of regulatory agencies, as part of the same interrelated process.

The ingredients required to develop improved models of regulation are already available, and the path that must be taken is fairly well designated, even to the extent of recognizing that the behavior of other decision makers, legislators, voters, and individuals in their various decision-making capacities can and should also be included in this process. The result would be a closed behavioral system capable of explaining and improving human decision making in all its interrelated facets. The missing ingredient? An incentive system that motivates specialists in different disciplines to devote time and other resources to its completion.

13.2   THE WIDER PROBLEM OF INCENTIVES

In Chapter 12, and in the preceding section of this chapter, the focus has been the problem of devising appropriate incentive systems that motivate regulated firms and regulators to report information honestly and to behave in a socially optimal manner. The problem of devising appropriate regulatory incentives is actually much broader than this, because there may be incentives for individuals, interest groups, and legislators to misrepresent their evaluations of the benefits or costs associated with dimensions of firms' behavior. As mentioned in Section 13.1, information distortion is as much of a problem on the "demand" side of regulation as is the "supply" side distortion of information by regulated firms or regulators.

In Chapter 5, Section 5.5, it was explained that, irrespective of the value system that is adopted to evaluate the benefits and costs of regulation, the condition that must be met in order for regulation of any dimension of regulated firms' behavior to be at a socially optimal level is as follows:

$$\Sigma (B - C) = (\Sigma C_{fi} + C_R)$$

The expression on the left-hand side of the equation represents evaluations of the effects of a regulation-induced change in some dimension of firms' behavior by individuals whose evaluations are adopted as the relevant measure of the benefits and costs to society. The first term on the right-hand side of the equation represents the additional costs attributable to regulation imposed on regulated firms. The second term represents the costs of regulatory bodies responsible for the regulated dimension of firms' behavior.

In order for regulators to devise appropriate incentive systems facing regulated firms, and in order for regulators themselves to behave in a socially optimal manner, it is necessary for people's evaluations of the effects of regulation-induced changes in dimensions of regulated firms' behavior, represented by the expression $\Sigma\,(B - C)$, to be honest revelations of their evaluations. There is little point in ensuring that only part of the information that is required to achieve socially optimal regulation — that part which relates to the behavior of regulated firms and regulators — is accurate.

The problem of possible misrepresentation of people's preferences for "public goods," defined as any kind of output that simultaneously affects more than one individual, has long been recognized in the economics literature, but possible solutions to the problem are of relatively recent origin, dating back only to the early 1970s. Before we consider the nature of these solutions, it is appropriate to describe several features of the problem of misrepresentation of demand for "public goods." As was emphasized in Chapter 2, the way a problem is formulated automatically determines the nature of the solution that is appropriate, and since this particular problem can be formulated in a number of ways, these formulations may affect the nature of the solution that is appropriate.

The conventional textbook exposition emphasizes nonrevealing, or underrepresentation, of people's demands for public goods. The reason usually given for this is that the effect that an individual's honest revelation might have on the total quantity of the public good demanded and produced is negligible, whereas the individual can obtain a nonnegligible payoff in terms of a reduced payment for these goods by understating his or her true evaluation of the benefits derived from the public good. In contrast, when attention is focused on the way in which demands for public goods are expressed in practice, by political parties, interest groups, and responses to public opinion polls, the opposite tendency is often observed, where people probably overstate their true evaluations of the benefits, or understate the costs, of public goods. The basic reason for this practice is the form in which the issue is presented to individuals; usually the tax increase that is necessary to finance the production of public goods, and its distribution among individuals, is left out of the issue.

In short, whether people's evaluations of the benefits and costs of public goods will over- or understate their true evaluations depends on the manner in which the question is posed, and the rewards or penalties that are attached to the various answers the individual can give to the question. Institutional constraints, such as separation of public expenditure and tax decisions, and the presence or lack of any connection between an individual's evaluations of public goods and responsibility for financing the production of such goods, are all relevant in determining the incentive system that will influence a person's evaluations of public goods.

The incentives for a person to distort evaluations of public goods will obviously depend on whether any payment will be based on the evaluation, and whether that payment will equal, or might be less than, the evaluation. If public goods will be provided as long as "demand" justifies their need, an incentive will exist for people who benefit from such goods to overstate their evaluations of these goods. Both of the preceding situations might occur, with unknown probabilities, when a person is asked to evaluate public goods; in these circumstances, whether a person will under- or overstate his or her evaluations of the benefits or costs of public goods is not clear. Either possibility may occur, depending on the probabilities attached to the outcomes of different answers and on the person's attitude to uncertainty. A person who knows with complete certainty that he or she will gain by misrepresenting evaluations of public goods may not do so in situations of uncertainty about the consequences attached to alternative evaluations.

The alert reader will have noticed the close analogy that exists between the possibility of under- or overestimation of demand for public goods and the possibility that a person's evaluations may differ depending on whether or not there is uncertainty attached to the outcomes of alternative evaluations, and the analysis of regulated firms' behavior in Chapter 12. This analogy is not surprising, since there is no analytical difference between the problem of eliciting honest revelation of costs or other dimensions of behavior from decision makers in firms and the problem of eliciting honest revelation of benefits of public goods from individuals who experience benefits or costs from these goods.

Following seminal work by E. H. Clark (1971) and T. Groves (1969), incentive mechanisms for eliciting truthful revelation of evaluations for public and private goods or "demand-revealing mechanisms," to use the conventional terminology that has been adopted in the literature, have been the subject of considerable attention. There are a number of variants of these demand-revealing mechanisms, but the essential feature that is responsible for eliciting truthful revelations of people's evaluations of public or private goods is the same. Each individual receives a payment, or is assessed a charge, that is independent of the person's own evaluation of the marginal benefits or costs of a public or private good and that depends on the evaluations of the marginal benefits or costs of the good by all *other* individuals. The general form of the demand-revealing mechanism is

$$\text{Charge or payment to } i\text{th person} = \text{MC}_\text{T} - \Sigma \, \text{MB}_j + A$$

where MC_T is the total marginal cost of the private or public good in question, $\Sigma \, \text{MB}_j$ is the sum of the evaluations of the marginal units of the good reported by every other person, and A is some lump sum that can be positive, negative, or zero and that is independent of each person's own reported evaluation.

It should be noted that the problem of eliciting honest revelations of demand is not confined to public goods but also exists in the case of private goods in certain situations. An example is the problem of allocating the cost of joint products — say, beef and hide — in circumstances in which the demand conditions for the individual joint products are known only by different salesmen within a firm (Needham, 1978, Chap. 2).

There are a number of shortcomings of the preceding demand-revealing incentive systems for public and private goods that need to be mentioned. First, all collective decision mechanisms and choice processes are capable of exploitation by suitably designed coalitions of individuals. Second, and more important, the strength of a person's motivation to pay time and attention to evaluating public or private goods, and to participating in the demand-revealing process, may be very small. This occurs in all voting processes in which either the probability of influencing the outcome, or the potential benefit to the individual from influencing the outcome, are very small.

The incentives that the preceding demand-revealing mechanisms provide for honest revelation of people's evaluations are therefore *not* the same as the incentives that the mechanisms provide for people to *participate* in the demand-revealing process. As the magnitude of the payment or charge for participation diminishes, the motivation for taking the trouble to reveal one's evaluations diminishes. Given the magnitude of the payment or charge for revealing one's evaluation honestly, the strength of the incentive to participate will depend on the objectives and all the other constraints that confront the individual. This situation is analogous to the situation discussed in Chapter 12. There it was demonstrated that the form of the incentive system that motivates honest revelation of information (discussed in Section 12.2) has very different effects on the behavior of regulated firms, depending on the nature of their objectives and other constraints (discussed in Section 12.3). Tideman and Tullock (1976) have pointed out how small the incentives to participate in the demand-revealing process for public goods might be, in situations where individuals have only a small influence on the issue or outcome that they are evaluating.

Although it is essential to distinguish between the incentives that a demand-revealing mechanism provides for honest revelation of people's evaluations, and the effect of the mechanism on people's behavior, it is equally important to recognize that these two effects occur simultaneously and are inextricably related. Although the general form of all demand-revealing mechanisms that motivate honest revelation of people's evaluations is similar, the magnitude of the parameters and coefficients in these demand-revealing mechanisms can vary, and may produce very different effects on people's behavior, given the objectives and other constraints

that confront those individuals. Again, there is a direct analogy with the
analysis of Chapter 12, which demonstrated that changes in the k coefficients and the level of F in the performance index that results in honest
revelation of information by regulated firms will result in different levels
of the targeted and actual behavior of those firms.

Another important characteristic that demand-revealing mechanisms
must exhibit, which is analogous to the necessary characteristic of the performance index facing regulated firms discussed in Chapter 12, Section
12.3(e), is that the form of the demand-revealing mechanism facing any
individual must not be changed in response to that person's revealed
evaluations. If the form of the demand-revealing mechanism, and the
magnitude of the payment or charge associated with the evaluation that
is revealed by an individual at a point in time, were related to the level of
the person's evaluations in a past time period, this would motivate
untruthful revelations of the person's demands for public or private
goods.

In the context of public goods, this means that each individual's
share of the tax payments for public goods must not be related to the
individual's evaluations of public goods. Any overall net balance, positive
or negative, of the payments or charges that result from the implementation of a particular demand-revealing mechanism must not be returned
to, or obtained from, the individuals whose preferences are being elicited.
If any net balance collected were returned to the individuals concerned,
the possibility of increasing their share of this balance might destroy the
incentive for them to reveal their evaluations of the benefits and costs of
public goods honestly.

The discussion contained in the previous paragraph emphasizes
another feature of demand-revealing mechanisms. It may not be possible
to select levels of the A term that represent lump-sum payments or charges
in the demand-revealing incentive system facing individuals that will
exactly balance each other in total, or that will achieve a particular
balance in the budget of the authority that has responsibility for administering the demand-revealing incentive system, while *simultaneously*
achieving the desired impact of the incentive system on levels of the
participants' behavior. In other words, many different levels of the A
term are compatible with truthful revelation of people's preferences, but
these different levels of A will imply differences in the behavior of the
individuals who are confronted by the demand-revealing mechanism in
addition to the other constraints that influence their behavior. Given all
other features of the demand-revealing incentive system, only one level of
A will generally result in a particular level of an individual's behavior
that is desired by the authority that administers the incentive system. This
means that in the presence of a need for resources to administer the
demand-revealing incentive system, and a constraint on their magnitude,

it may be impossible to use the demand-revealing mechanism that elicits the desired behavior from participants in addition to honest revelation of information.

In the literature on incentive systems to date, there has been little consideration of the consequences of introducing constraints in the form of limitations on the total amount of rewards that are available for administering demand-revealing and cost-revealing incentive systems and that imply constraints on the magnitude of the A terms in the demand- and cost-revealing incentive systems.

When such limitations exist, and this fact is known by individual participants in the demand-revealing process, this may introduce strategic considerations into the behavior of individual participants that destroy the incentives for revealing information honestly. With a limited total fund of rewards for distribution to participants in a demand-revealing process, for example, individual's may overstate or understate their evaluations in order to obtain a larger share of this limited total.

In addition to destroying incentives for honest revelation of information, such limitations on the total rewards or penalties (e.g., limited prison space) that are available for distribution among individuals may also change the behavior of individuals faced by other constraints.

Despite remaining problems of designing suitable incentive systems for revealing people's evaluations of public and private goods, the strength of the existing demand-revealing mechanisms should not be underemphasized. For example, one of the extremely important characteristics of the demand-revealing incentive system is that it is not necessary to restrict people's evaluations and choices to a single public or private good, or to a single dimension of those goods. In principle, a multidimensional public or private good, several public goods, or public goods plus political candidates can all be dealt with simultaneously. This feature probably makes the demand-revealing process less susceptible to distortion by coalitions, since agreement among individuals is more difficult to achieve, the larger the number of issues that are included in the agreement.

The major remaining task of the incentive system literature is to combine the problem of designing appropriate demand-revealing mechanisms together with the problem of designing appropriate regulatory or other types of incentive system on the supply side of public and private goods. As we have already indicated several times in this section, there are many similarities between the two problems and their solutions. Loeb (1976) has demonstrated that the appropriate incentive systems for achieving honest revelation of information on demand and cost or supply are analytically identical. The only difference between the two types of incentive system is that one is applied to persons demanding a public or private good, and the other is applied to suppliers. Similarly, Loeb and Magat (1978) have demonstrated that the necessary form of any performance indicator that is required to maximize or minimize overall performance by a group of individuals who use a common resource, such as capital, that must be allocated between the individuals, is

$$P_i = P_{ai} + \Sigma P_{fj} - A_i$$

where P_{ai} is the actual performance of the ith individual, and P_{fj} is the sum of the performance forecasted by all other individuals. "Performance" could refer to demand, cost, output, profits, or any other measure of performance. As we emphasized earlier, the preceding performance indicator motivates honest revelation of performance by individuals. The nature and magnitude of the rewards to various levels of the performance indicator P_i will affect the actual and forecasted performance of the various decision makers, and the problem of selecting types and magnitudes of rewards that motivate desired characteristics of behavior and performance on the part of the individuals remains to be solved. It is in connection with this last aspect of the problem of designing appropriate incentive systems that the existing literature is at its weakest.

In a regulatory context, it is necessary to combine the regulatory incentive system facing firms, which is discussed in Chapter 12, with the type of demand-revealing incentive systems that was discussed in this section and that must be applied to those individuals whose evaluations are used as the basis for determining the benefits of a regulated firm's behavior.

The incentive system that is used to elicit honest revelation of the benefits or costs of regulated aspects of the firm's behavior could in principle be administered by a different authority than the regulatory agency itself. The existing literature usually regards legislators as the appropriate decision makers who should estimate and encourage revelation of demands for public goods. However, as the discussion of legislators' behavior that is contained in Chapter 5 indicates, there are many problems involved in devising incentives for legislators themselves to obtain and reveal information honestly to regulatory agency decision makers.

If individuals' evaluations were honestly revealed directly to regulators, this would sidestep many of the problems connected with failure of legislators to obtain and transmit these evaluations to regulators. Of course, even if individuals honestly reveal information directly to regulators, it will still be necessary to provide the proper incentive system that motivates regulators to use this information and to adopt characteristics of the regulatory constraint and demand-revealing incentive systems that result in socially optimal behavior by regulated firms and regulators. An important role for legislators would still remain, therefore, in implementing the type of incentive system facing regulators that would allocate resources to regulators and set penalties and rewards for various characteristics of regulators' behavior at the appropriate levels necessary to elicit socially optimal behavior from regulators.

There is no reason, in principle, why individual members of society's evaluations of a regulated firm's behavior might not be revealed directly to regulatory agencies, provided that the demand-revealing incentive system employed by the agency motivates honest revelation of people's evaluations. In practice, however, taxes and subsidies are the most likely weapons available for use in demand-revealing incentive systems, and these are traditionally the responsibility of legislators, who will not willingly give up this power. For the foreseeable future, therefore, it is likely that any feasible demand-revealing mechanisms will have to be administered by the legislature, or some administrative agency under the direction of Congress, rather than by regulatory agencies who are directly responsible to the executive.

Irrespective of whether or not the same agency administers the regulatory incentive system facing regulated firms and also the demand-revealing mechanisms facing individuals whose evaluations are used to measure benefits or costs of regulated firms' behavior, the information obtained by the two types of incentive system must be combined in designing socially optimal regulatory constraints, as emphasized at the beginning of this section.

Even more important, however, is the need to consider the *combined* effects of the two types of incentive system both on the behavior of regulated firms and on the behavior of individuals whose evaluations of regulated firms' behavior are selected to represent society's evaluations. This problem has been entirely ignored in the literature on incentive systems, which generally deals with the demand and supply sides of the problem of providing proper incentives separately.

It is important to consider incentive systems on the demand and supply sides jointly, because the form of the demand-revealing mechanism may influence not only the behavior of the individuals whose evaluations of regulated firms' behavior are sought but also the behavior of regulated firms themselves. Regulated firms may try to influence the form of the demand-revealing incentive system by influencing the behavior of regulators or other decision makers responsible for administering the system. Alternatively, regulated firms may try to influence the evaluations that individuals reveal in response to a particular demand-revealing mechanism. As we emphasized earlier, these evaluations will depend on the objectives and other constraints that confront the respondents, and regulated firms may be able to influence some of these constraints by providing information to individuals, or by changing the incentives that determine how these individuals will evaluate regulated firms' behavior in response to a particular demand-revealing mechanism.

The possibility that the form of the demand-revealing mechanism may influence, or be influenced by, regulated firms' behavior in the preceding manner is only half of the problem. It is also possible that the form of regulatory incentive systems that confront regulated firms may influence the behavior of individuals who are confronted by a particular demand-revealing mechanism. Again, those individuals may attempt to influence the form of regulatory incentive systems directly, or they may try to change the behavior of regulated firms in response to a particular regulatory incentive system by changing some of the other constraints that confront regulated firms.

In short, it should not be automatically assumed that demand-revealing incentive systems affect only the behavior of individuals on the demand side of regulatory problems, and that regulatory incentive systems affect only the behavior of individuals on the supply side of regulatory problems. Each type of incentive system may affect the behavior of individuals on both sides of the problem; in addition, there may be some causal flows that operate from the behavior of individuals on either side of the problem to the form of the incentive systems themselves. As these complications suggest, we are still a long way from solving all the problems connected with designing regulatory incentive systems that simultaneously exhibit informational and behavioral optimality conditions on both the supply or cost side, and the demand or benefit side, of regulatory problems.

CHAPTER FOURTEEN

Alternatives to Regulation

14.1 DEREGULATION

"Deregulation," like the term "regulation," can mean many things. Legislative deregulation is determined by exactly the same kind of forces that result in regulation; it is the result of demands for deregulation by interest groups in society and by legislators' response to those demands. The reader is reminded of one of the major conclusions of Chapter 5 regarding the behavior of legislators and regulators. There it was explained that the behavior of these types of decision maker will generally take into account and reflect the demands of different interest groups, rather than the demands of a single interest group. In the present context, one important implication of this conclusion is that demands for deregulation will tend to be more successful when a majority of interest groups with power to influence legislators' decisions favor deregulation. The support of regulators, and at least some members of a regulated industry, will generally be required if demands for deregulation are to be successful.

Pressures for reform of regulation led to congressional and regulatory commission actions in the late 1970s that deregulated certain aspects of a number of regulated industries in the United States. Following extensive hearings and studies by Congress and the Securities and Exchange Commission, the SEC ordered securities exchanges to cease the practice of adopting fixed commission rates for brokers. Although substantial changes in fees and some changes in the structure and practices of the brokerage industry followed, the disaster that had been predicted by the industry did not occur.

Much of the great congressional debate over energy policy during 1977–78 centered on the problem of natural gas pricing, and reform of the regulatory structure for natural gas emerged as the centerpiece of the

Carter administration's National Energy plan. Congress remained deadlocked over the issue for eighteen months, and through a highly complex compromise the 1978 Natural Gas Policy Act was finally passed. This legislation transferred regulatory responsibility from the Federal Power Commission to the Federal Energy Regulatory Commission, extended regulation of gas prices to gas sold in intrastate as well as interstate markets, and established a time schedule for the gradual deregulation of new gas and a set of wellhead prices to be in effect during the transition to total deregulation. Gas from existing wells will remain regulated indefinitely.

As these measures indicate, the gas legislation included extensions of regulation in addition to measures for the eventual deregulation of new natural gas prices. Industry reaction was predictably mixed. The Independent Petroleum Association, the principal trade association of small- and medium-sized producers, denounced the bill as a blueprint for disaster, whereas few larger gas producers condemned the bill and some openly endorsed it. All gas producers would have preferred faster and more liberal deregulation of domestic gas prices than provided by the 1978 legislation. Small- and medium-sized producers were, however, probably more affected than large firms by the expanded price controls on gas sold in intrastate markets.

Following Senate hearings on Civil Aeronautics Board practices and procedures, a bill was introduced into Congress early in 1977 that would deregulate the airline industry over a period of years. The bill was initially opposed vigorously by most airlines, but this opposition diminished with the appointment of economist Alfred Kahn as chairman of the CAB. Kahn initiated a procompetition policy that may have persuaded some members of the industry that CAB restrictions on permissible forms of competition in the industry were worse than unregulated competition. By the time the airline bill came to a vote in the fall of 1978, little opposition remained, and the 1978 Airline Deregulation Act passed with large majorities in both houses of Congress. The act phases out regulation of the airline industry by 1985.

The airline deregulation legislation included some protection for special interests that might suffer from deregulation, such as small communities that might have air service curtailed in the absence of regulation. All these factors tended to minimize opposition to deregulation sufficiently to make passage of legislation deregulating the industry possible. This does not necessarily imply that airline deregulation has made everyone better off, despite the increase in discount fares, air travel, and industry profits that initially followed the 1978 act. Panzar (1979) has suggested that business travelers may have been worse off because of higher load factors. The collapse of Braniff airlines in 1982 is also a reminder that individual firms in an industry that has been deregulated may suffer from the cold winds of competition.

Definitive conclusions regarding the effects of deregulation in the airline and other industries should be treated with care, since in order to determine the effects of any form of deregulation, it is necessary to know what would have happened in the absence of deregulation. This depends on other constraints confronting regulated and unregulated decision makers in addition to regulatory constraints. Changes in these other factors, for reasons unrelated to deregulation, may partly or wholly explain observed changes in the behavior of regulated and unregulated decision makers following deregulation measures. For example, a generally depressed economy and airline industry, or factors peculiar to Braniff, may have been more important than deregulation in causing the firm's demise. Such changes must be determined and taken into account before one may isolate the effects of deregulation alone.

In April 1979, President Carter announced his intention of phasing out crude oil price controls by October 1981 in order to allow oil prices to rise to levels that reflected world oil prices and encourage conservation of energy. He also proposed that taxes be imposed on domestically produced oil that had been sold at less than world prices, in order to eliminate the "windfall profit" that would otherwise result from the increased price of this oil. Crude oil produced in the United States had been placed under federal price controls in 1971, and during the 1970s these controls evolved into a complex system that included multiple price levels, an allocation program, regulation of refined product prices, and a system of cross-payments among refiners that combined the high cost of imported oil with the lower cost of domestically produced oil. The regulated price of crude oil depended on many factors, including the date at which production at a particular well began, the amount of oil produced, the location, and the viscosity of the oil. The regulated prices of crude oil and refined products were held below world levels, and only increased oil imports prevented a shortage of crude oil from developing.

Following lengthy congressional debates on oil price regulations and taxes, the Windfall Profit Tax Act was finally passed in April 1980, and the president immediately began to reduce oil price controls in a series of steps designed to allow oil prices to rise to world prices by September 1980. The higher United States prices of oil eliminated the subsidy to oil consumption that existed under price controls, since it eliminated the averaging of prices of controlled domestic crude oil with the price of more expensive imported oil that kept prices below world levels. Allowing the price of domestically produced crude oil to rise increased incentives for domestic production, since the windfall profit tax was designed to provide maximum incentives for increased exploration and United States production while preventing most of the wealth transfers that decontrol of prices would cause.

In a few instances, regulatory reform has been initiated by the regulators of an industry, rather than by outsiders and legislative action. For example, in July 1980 the Federal Communications Commission issued an order eliminating most of its regulation of cable TV, though some aspects of the industry are still regulated at the state and local levels. Similarly, following the appointment of a new chairman to the Interstate Commerce Commission in 1980, and signs that major reforms of regulation of trucking would come from inside the commission, the trucking industry apparently became convinced that it would receive better treatment from Congress than from the ICC. A new trucking bill easily passed through Congress, and the Motor Carrier Act became law in June 1980. Although trucking is still regulated, the act gave individual truckers much more freedom to vary prices without ICC approval; made it easier for truckers wishing to enter new routes to obtain certificates; and eliminated a number of costly restrictions the ICC had previously imposed, such as regulations that imposed circuitous routes, backhaul, and intermediate-stop restrictions. Steps in the direction of deregulation of the railroad industry also occurred when the same session of Congress that enacted new trucking legislation also enacted the Staggers Rail Act, which lessened ICC control of railroad rates and permitted railroads to raise or lower their rates by significant amounts without ICC approval.

In appraising demands for deregulation in general, and the legislative response to those demands, the reader should bear several factors in mind. Deregulation should not necessarily be regarded as a victory for interest groups that initially opposed regulation. There is no reason in principle why the same groups that once demanded regulation might not rationally demand deregulation later. Circumstances and constraints that confront particular decision makers and industries change with the passage of time, and regulation that advances a particular group's interests at one time may cease to do so as conditions change. Another relevant factor is that experience with regulation, and its actual outcome, may differ from what was expected by the same individuals and interest groups that initially demanded regulation. As a result, even if conditions have not changed, the groups that initially demanded regulation may be disappointed with the outcome and may demand deregulation or regulatory reform. The dynamic implications of this relationship between demands for, and effects of, regulation are examined in more detail in Section 2 of Chapter 15.

One of the reasons why the outcome of regulation may differ from what was expected by individuals and interest groups that initially demanded regulation is connected with the multiple-reference-group model of legislators' and regulators' behavior that was discussed in Chapter 5. This model predicts that legislators and regulators will respond to competing demands for regulation by adopting behavior that balances various demands. This process of balancing demands for competing versions of regulation may result in legislation that differs from all of the forms of regulation demanded by particular groups that favor regulation. The same kind of reasoning applied to demands for deregulation suggests that the legislative outcome may also differ from the forms of deregulation demanded by various interest groups. This sobering thought should be borne in mind by anyone who seeks to improve regulatory processes by legislative reform. Given the constraints facing legislators, legislative effort to repeal or reform regulatory legislation may make matters worse. Attempts to change existing regulatory legislation may result in bills representing competing interest groups, and the kind of legislation that will emerge from this process is impossible to predict.

Another extremely important consideration in appraising demands for regulation and the legislative response to these demands is the incentive for individuals and interest groups to misrepresent their preferences and actions. It should be remembered that this incentive applies to all groups in society, including voters, legislators, regulators, and regulated and unregulated decision makers. If interest groups that desire *increased* regulation perceive that their demands will be more effective if couched in terms of "deregulation," the terminology used by various groups involved in the legislative process may be an unreliable guide to the actual content of legislation that embodies regulatory features. From an objective perspective, it is probably more appropriate to use the term "regulatory reform" for all legislation that changes the nature of existing regulatory legislation. Whether the intent behind the legislation is "regulatory" or "deregulatory" in nature will rarely be apparent from the debates that lead up to passage of the legislation, and may not be any clearer in the legislation itself, given the usual propensity of legislators to couch legislation in vague terms.

Whatever the intent and precise form of legislation that is described as "deregulating" an industry or a facet of firms' behavior, the actual effect of that legislation can vary widely, ranging from no effects, effects that are different from those intended, and effects that are the opposite of those intended. A change in regulatory legislation is, after all, a change in just one of the constraints that confront agency decision makers who are responsible for enforcing that legislation. Variations in the goals and other constraints that confront regulators will result in different regulatory agency responses to any particular piece of legislation "deregulating" some facet of regulated decision-maker behavior.

Some of the possible responses of agency decision makers may, paradoxically, increase the effectiveness of preexisting regulations on regulated decision makers' behavior. For example, it was explained in Chapter 12 that the effect of regulation on regulated decision makers' behavior depends on the implications of the behavior of agencies and the courts for the "probabilistic regulatory constraint" that describes the penalties for certain behavior by regulated decision makers multiplied by the probability of detection and successful prosecution of that behavior. It was emphasized that the *slope* of the regulatory constraint, which describes how expected penalties vary with changes in the level of regulated decision-maker behavior, determines the effect of the constraint on decision-maker behavior. The *height* of the regulatory constraint, which describes the magnitude of the expected penalties for certain kinds of behavior, was shown to be relatively unimportant as a determinant of regulated decision makers' behavior.

It was also explained that introducing penalties for certain kinds of behavior would provide incentives for *increases* in the behavior regulation was intended to reduce, if the slope of the probabilistic penalty function did not have the (negative) sign that is necessary to encourage decision makers to reduce the level of a regulated dimension of behavior that is considered undesirable. Moreover, penalties that increase with the magnitude of violations of a regulatory standard of behavior do not guarantee that the magnitude of penalties expected by regulated decision makers will increase with the magnitude of the violations. This is because the probability of detection and successful enforcement could fall with increases in violation size, for a variety of reasons (see Chapter 12, Section 3).

Most kinds of deregulation do not completely eliminate regulatory constraints. A more usual situation is that some aspects of the behavior of regulatory agencies are changed, with implications for the probabilistic regulatory constraint that confronts regulated decision makers. It is impossible to generalize concerning the effects of deregulation on this regulatory constraint, but it is possible to envisage many plausible circumstances in which deregulation produces changes in the slope of the penalty-reward constraint that reinforce the preexisting effects of regulation on regulated decision makers' behavior. This is another reason for caution in assuming that deregulation will reverse the effects of existing regulatory constraints.

Finally, it must be remembered that whatever the effects of legislative deregulation are on regulators and regulated and unregulated decision makers, the benefits and costs of these effects will depend on whose evaluations are adopted as the basis for evaluating deregulation. All the principles and conclusions expounded in Chapters 3 and 4 in connection with benefits and costs of regulation apply equally to the benefits and costs of deregulation. For example, deregulation will change constraints that confront many members of society, and deregulation will always affect some members of society adversely. Effects of deregulation that are evaluated equally in monetary terms by different people will not signify equal changes in satisfaction for the individuals concerned unless the marginal utility of income is identical for those individuals. Implicit or explicit equity weights attached to particular individuals' evaluations of deregulation are unavoidable, and whether such weights are monetary evaluations or votes cast by the individuals affected by deregulation, they reflect implicit value judgments about whose interests should count, and by how much. There can be no value-free evaluation of deregulation. Furthermore, one should remember that deregulation, like regulation, is simply one means by which different individuals and interest groups attempt to further their own self-interests.

14.2 INDUSTRIAL REORGANIZATION

One alternative to government regulation of business behavior that has received increasing attention from economists and legislators in recent years is the concept of reorganizing, or influencing the future course of, industrial structure, particularly measures aimed at reducing the degree of seller concentration in some industries and markets. Proponents of the various measures implicitly believe that restructuring certain characteristics of some industries will increase competition among firms in those industries and that the resulting competitive behavior will improve resource allocation and utilization in the economy.

The 1968 White House Task Force Report on Antitrust Policy proposed a "Concentrated Industries Act" that recommended restructuring of "oligopoly industries," which were defined as relevant economic markets (1) with more than $500 million in annual sales, (2) in which the combined market share of the largest four firms equaled or exceeded 70 percent, and (3) in which the *same* four firms retained this market share over time. The proposed goal of the restructuring was a maximum market share of 12 percent for any single firm. Provision for the justification of higher levels of concentration on the basis of scale economies and greater efficiency was included.

The act would also have prevented mergers between "large firms," defined as firms with $500 million annual sales or $250 million in assets, and between "leading firms," defined as firms that in two recent years had more than 10 percent of their market while four (or fewer) firms had combined shares of more than 50 percent of the same market. These proposals were much more demanding than the merger guidelines issued by the Antitrust Division of the Justice Department in 1968. The latter guidelines give less attention to conglomerate mergers than the proposed "Concentrated Industries Act" proposals and do not have the force of law.

Another proposal, the "Industrial Reorganization Act" introduced by Senator Philip Hart in 1972, declared the possession of monopoly power unlawful and presumed that monopoly power exists when *any one* of the following conditions obtains: (1) the corporate rate of return on net worth after taxes is above 15 percent over a substantial time period; (2) there has been no substantial price competition; (3) the combined market share of the four largest firms is 50 percent or more.

A bill introduced in the Senate by Senator Edward Kennedy on March 8, 1979, would have prohibited companies with more than $2.5 billion of sales or $2 billion of assets from merging with one another. Companies with $350 million of sales or $200 million of assets would have to prove that a merger would be procompetitive or yield economies of scale or other efficiencies. Those restrictions would also apply to mergers between companies with more than $100 million of assets if their combined assets amounted to more than $1 billion.

In some proposals for industrial reorganization, the limits on a firm's size are absolute, rather than being dependent on a firm's size expressed either in relation to its total market or to the market share of its rival firms. Thus, firms with large absolute size but small market shares could be prevented from merging under proposals limiting absolute size. Conversely, firms with small absolute size, but with very large combined market shares, might be prevented from merging under such proposals.

The preceding examples of proposals that would change present or future industrial structure by reducing the market shares, or absolute size, of individual firms are by no means exhaustive. However, our main purpose in this section is not to describe proposals for industrial restructuring but to examine the logic underlying such proposals. In particular, the theoretical and empirical justification for such proposals will be examined. We shall emphasize the mechanism by which industrial structure may affect firms' behavior, and the factors that are relevant in determining the nature of any resulting changes. This examination will provide a framework for evaluating proposals for industrial restructuring, for choosing among different proposals, and for devising even better proposals.

Why, for example, should proposals limiting firm size or market share stop at the $2.5 billion sales or 50 to 70 percent combined market share of the four largest firms? If smaller firm size or market share are beneficial on grounds of promoting competition or otherwise improving firms' behavior, why not further reduce the limits of maximum size? What, in other words, is the analytical or empirical justification for a particular size limitation? These and other issues can be tackled only within a model that shows the links between individual firms' behavior and industrial structure.

Proposals for industrial restructuring are explicitly or implicitly based on the notion that certain features of industry structure influence individual firms' behavior. The industry structure-behavior-performance relationship is the essence of that branch of economics known as industrial organization. The feature of industry structure that has received more attention than any other is "seller concentration," a term that refers to the number and size distribution of firms selling in a specific market. A large number of statistical studies conducted over many years suggest that a price-cost margin of an industry's product, and the ratio of firm and industry profit to equity or assets, increase as the degree of seller concentration increases. This positive relationship between profits and seller concentration has, in turn, been interpreted as implying that reduced concentration will reduce profits and that the reason for the reduction in profits will be increased price competition among firms in the industry and reduced price-cost margins.

On closer inspection, the preceding line of reasoning contains an alarming number of questionable assumptions and interpretations. Since they go to the heart of the issue over whether industrial reorganization will change firms' behavior, it is necessary to review these assumptions. Anticipating our conclusions, we shall find, among other things, that the hypothesis that seller concentration affects pricing behavior is questionable on theoretical and empirical grounds. Moreover, even if changes in seller concentration do affect firms' behavior, the mechanism is probably more complicated and the implications for firms' behavior more complex than is generally perceived.

Our conclusions regarding the impact of other features of industry structure, market share, and firm size are more positive. Market share can be shown to be theoretically and empirically important in determining a firm's behavior; again, however, the implications of market share for firms' behavior are more complex than is generally recognized. Changes in market share may simultaneously affect a number of dimensions of a firm's behavior, some in desirable directions and others in undesirable directions. In such cases, even if industry restructuring is feasible, its desirability may be open to question.

Moreover, most of the proposals for industry restructuring are imprecise, requiring further interpretation by the administrative agencies or courts responsible for administering the proposals. It is impossible to predict how these interpretations will turn out without additional information on the goals and other constraints confronting the decision makers who will be responsible for such interpretations. In other words, any proposal for industry restructuring would, if enacted, introduce some new "rules of the game," but the exact nature of the rules of the game would still be open to influence by all parties interested in the eventual outcome of the game. The rules of the economic and political power struggle between individuals and interest groups in society are themselves influenced by this power struggle (Samuels, 1975). To try to predict what the eventual outcome of any aspect of this power struggle will be, in terms of the interpretations placed on new legislation governing restructuring of industry, is hazardous.

Seller Concentration and Pricing Behavior in Theory. Surprisingly, there is little support in economic theory for the proposition that seller concentration affects a firm's pricing behavior. Articles in the professional literature have repeatedly emphasized that *analytically* the number or

size distinction of a firm's rivals is *irrelevant;* what matters is the *nature
of the reaction the firm expects from its rivals* in response to changes in
its own behavior.

This can be demonstrated by reference to the profit-maximizing
product-pricing condition for an individual firm, $(P - \mathrm{MC})/P = 1/E_d$,
where E_d is defined as the percentage change in the quantity of the firm's
product demanded in response to a 1 percent change in the price of the
firm's product, P is the price of the firm's product, and MC is the marginal, or incremental, cost of producing one more unit of the product
(see Chapters 6 and 7). It can be easily demonstrated that E_d itself depends
on the following three factors:[1]

(i) the firm's market share (S_f)
(ii) the price elasticity of total market demand for the product (E_m)
(iii) the reactions of rival sellers anticipated by the firm (E_s)

The formal relationship between these factors is indicated by the
expression

$$E_d = \frac{E_m}{S_f} + \frac{(E_s S_r)}{S_f}$$

where S_r is the combined market share of all the firm's rivals, which
equals $(1 - S_f)$, and E_s is a measure of the change of a firm's rivals' output
in response to a change in the price of the firm's product. The "elasticity
of supply of rival firms' output," termed E_s, is defined as the percentage
change in the quantity of rival firms' output that occurs in response to a
1 percent change in the price of the first firm's product. The term E_s can
be positive or negative in sign, depending on whether rival firms reduce
or increase their output in response to a reduction in the price of the
firm's product.

The profit-maximizing price–marginal cost relationship can therefore be represented as follows:

$$\frac{P - \mathrm{MC}}{P} = \frac{1}{E_d} = \frac{S_f}{E_m + E_s(1 - S_f)}$$

This relationship implies that the profit-maximizing product price
will be higher, the larger the firm's market share, given the price elasticity
of market demand and the reaction of rival sellers anticipated by the
firm. If MC = AC, where AC is the cost per unit of output, or if MC
and AC are linearly related, increases in $(P - \mathrm{MC})$ imply increases in
profit per unit of output. Statistical studies (Shepherd, 1972a,b); indicate

---

[1] Readers who desire a fuller treatment of these matters should read Needham
(1978, Chap. 4).

that a firm's market share is not only positively associated with a firm's profit rate but is a *major* determinant of its profit rate. While this finding lends support to the concept of limiting the market share of individual firms as a means of attempting to reduce product prices, the implications of absolute firm size for pricing behavior are ambiguous. Holding market price elasticity and rivals' anticipated reactions constant, an increase in absolute firm size will imply a larger market share and higher price if total market demand remains unchanged. If total market demand also increases when a firm's output increases, the firm's market share could remain unchanged or even decline.

"Seller concentration," a term used to refer to the number and size distribution of a firm's rival sellers, appears nowhere in the profit-maximizing pricing condition. This reflects the point already mentioned that, analytically at least, any particular number or size distribution of rival sellers is compatible with a particular "anticipated reaction of rivals" and resulting value of E_s.

Seller Concentration and Industry Profitability. From a theoretical point of view, it is possible to construct innumerable plausible models of firm pricing behavior in which rivals' anticipated reactions are related to the number and/or size distribution of a firm's rivals. Unfortunately, theoretical models that link E_s to the number and/or size distribution of a firm's rivals are inconclusive. Empirical studies of the relationship between seller concentration and the pricing behavior of individual firms are essential in order to settle the issue, and many studies have been undertaken with this object in mind. There is apparent agreement between the findings of a majority of these studies — that seller concentration is positively but weakly associated with profit rates in firms and industries. Even if one accepts these findings, the support they provide for restructuring industries in order to change the degree of seller concentration is very weak. If changes in seller concentration have only a small impact on firm and industry behavior and profits, it follows that relatively large changes in the degree of seller concentration would be needed to achieve any given change in firm and industry behavior.

Even if a very strong positive relationship between seller concentration and firm profits were observed, this would not necessarily provide more support for the industrial deconcentration argument. To understand why, it is necessary to examine briefly the methodology of the statistical studies of the relationship between seller concentration and industry profitability.

These statistical studies usually use data on some index of seller concentration and either profit rates or price-cost margins existing in a group of different industries in order to infer the nature of any underlying relationship between the degree of seller concentration and industry pricing behavior.

Since the profit-maximizing price-cost margin and resulting profit also depend on the firm's market share, S_f, and the price elasticity of market demand, E_m, ideally these other explanatory factors should be included in statistical studies, and their effects taken into account in determining whether any relationship between seller concentration and firms' behavior remains after their influence has been removed. Unfortunately, the price elasticity of market demand has rarely been included as an explanatory variable in statistical studies of the concentration-profitability relationship, despite its analytical and empirical significance as a determinant of the profit-maximizing $(P - \text{MC})$ relationship (Pagoulatos and Sorensen, 1981).

A more serious problem for the interpretation of observed concentration-profitability studies is connected with the index that is used to measure seller concentration. Most statistical studies of concentration have used the combined market share of the four largest firms in an industry or market, termed the "four-firm concentration ratio" (CR_4), to measure seller concentration. There are many other ways to measure seller concentration. In the present context, the exact nature of these alternative measures of seller concentration is not important. What is important is that *the basic difference between different concentration indexes lies in the weights that are assigned to the market shares of firms in the definition of the respective indexes.* Concentration indexes are of the following generic form:[2]

$$\text{Seller Concentration Index} = \Sigma\, w \cdot S_{f_i}$$

where S_{f_i} is the market share of each of the firms in an industry and w is the weight that is assigned by a particular index to the market share of each firm.

Since every possible measure of seller concentration uses the market share of some firms in an industry, this implies that each and every concentration index will *automatically* be correlated with the market shares of those firms whose shares are used to calculate the index. Moreover, since both analysis and statistical studies indicate that the market share of a firm will exert a strong positive impact on the magnitude of the firm's profits, all seller concentration indexes will *automatically* be positively associated with a firm's profits even in the absence of any *independent* influence of seller concentration on E_s, the firm's expectations regarding its rivals' reactions. The exact nature of this automatic relationship will vary for different concentration indexes, however, owing to their different weighting schemes.

Even when statistical regressions include the market share of firms as a separate explanatory variable, an observed positive association between seller concentration measures and profits may merely reflect the

[2] Interested readers are referred to Needham (1978, Chap. 6) for more detailed treatment of these matters.

preceding automatic influence of market shares that are used to calculate the concentration index. In view of the wide differences between the data base, sample size, industry definitions, other explanatory variables included in the study, profitability concepts, and statistical methodology employed by different investigators, the general consensus regarding the existence of a weak positive association between concentration and industry profitability is remarkable. The fact that almost all statistical studies of the concentration-profitability relationship use as a measure of concentration the market share of the four largest firms in industries studied (CR_4) reinforces the suspicion that this consensus may be attributable to the automatic positive correlation between CR_4 and profitability that occurs because market shares of the four largest firms in an industry and CR_4 are identical.

Another unsatisfactory feature of existing statistical studies of the relationship between seller concentration and profitability is that they focus on the relationship between seller concentration and *industry* profitability rather than on profitability in individual firms. This masks possible differences in the effect of seller concentration in a particular industry on different firms in the industry. There is much to be gained by shifting the focus of analysis from the industry to the individual firms in the industry, since the behavior of an industry is simply the sum of the behavior of individual firms in that industry.

Gollop and Roberts (1979) attempted to measure the magnitude of individual firms' expectations regarding rivals' output reactions, E_s, in the United States coffee-roasting industry. They found that although individual firms in that industry do take rivals' behavior into account, that is ($E_s \neq 0$), they do not expect the same kind of reactions from each of their rivals. Firms expected different reactions from rival firms in different sized classes. This study indicates that the pattern of E_s in individual firms is an important determinant of the relationship between industry concentration and industry behavior and profits.

Relationships between industry dimensions of behavior and seller concentration cannot reveal the relationship between seller concentration and the behavior of individual firms in the industry. Different firms may respond differently to a change in seller concentration or some other aspect of industry structure. In some circumstances, the net result could be no change in industry behavior, even though there are offsetting changes in individual firms' behavior.

Implications of Profits for Firms' Behavior. A firm's profits depend on all dimensions of its behavior, not just on product prices. Although a few statistical studies have used price-cost margins as the dependent variable, which is desirable if one is interested in determining the relationship between seller concentration and firm or industry pricing behavior, most studies instead use data on firm profit-equity ratios as the dependent variable.

It is well known in the literature that profit-equity or profit-asset ratios are not the same as price-cost margins and that the relationship between these may be expressed as follows:[3]

$$\frac{\text{Profit}}{\text{Equity}} = i + \frac{S}{E}\frac{(P - \text{AC})}{P}$$

where S is total sales, E is equity or net assets of a firm, P is the price of the product, and AC is the unit cost of the product. Thus, if S/E is the same for different firms or industries, P/E ratios and $(P - \text{AC})$ margins will be correlated, and any observed relationship between concentration and P/E will have the same sign as the relationship between concentration and $(P - \text{AC})$. In practice, firms and industries with higher profit rates also have smaller ratios of S/E (Qualls, 1977). Therefore, the positive association that is observed between seller concentration and industry or firm profits is weaker than the relationship between concentration and $(P - \text{AC})$.

Seller Concentration and Other Dimensions of Firms' Behavior. What is not generally taken into account in analyzing the relationship between seller concentration and profitability is that seller concentration may influence profits by influencing other dimensions of firms' behavior in addition to pricing behavior. In these circumstances, it is necessary to interpret observed data on concentration and profits within an analytical framework that takes into account the possible influence of concentration on multiple dimensions of firms' behavior. This analytical framework, and the form of the appropriate statistical regressions that attempt to determine the nature of the relationship that exists in practice between concentration and firms' behavior and profits, are different from those discussed to this point in this section.

The model of a firm's pricing behavior discussed previously is as follows:

$$\frac{P - \text{MC}}{P} = \frac{S_f}{E_m + E_s(1 - S_f)}$$

The issue is whether seller concentration affects pricing independently, by influencing the magnitude of E_s, the firm's expectations about its rivals' reactions to changes in its own pricing policies.

Here we shall assume that the only other decision variable the firm controls is the level of its expenditures on advertising. The conclusions may be generalized to other dimensions of the firm's behavior. When a firm is able to influence the demand for its product by advertising, the profit-maximizing condition for advertising is[4]

---

[3] See Needham (1978) for a fuller treatment of this proposition.

[4] Interested readers may consult Needham (1978, Chap. 5) for proof of these propositions.

$$\frac{A}{S} = \frac{(P - MC)}{P} \cdot E_a$$

where E_a, the advertising elasticity of demand for the firm's product, is defined as the percentage increase in the quantity of the firm's product demanded in response to a 1 percent increase in the level of the firm's advertising expenditure. In turn, E_a depends on three other factors:

(i) the response of total market demand to a change in (the firm's) advertising expenditures on the product (E_A)
(ii) the response of the firm's rivals' advertising to changes in the firm's advertising $(E_{\text{conj } A})$
(iii) the effect of an increase in the firm's rivals' advertising on the quantity of the firm's product demanded (E_{Ar})

When rivals increase their advertising in response to increases in the firm's advertising, $E_{\text{conj } A}$ will be positive, $E_{\text{conj } A}$ will be negative. Generally E_{Ar} will be negative — that is, increases in rivals' advertising will generally reduce the demand for the firm's product.

The formal relationship between these factors can be shown to be as follows:

$$E_a = E_A + E_{\text{conj } A} \cdot E_{Ar}$$

The profit-maximizing relationship between a firm's advertising outlays and sales of its product may therefore be written as follows:

$$\frac{\text{Advertising outlays}}{\text{Sales}} = \frac{P - MC}{P} \cdot E_a = \frac{P - MC}{P} \cdot (E_A + E_{\text{conj } A} \cdot E_{Ar})$$

The level of seller concentration may affect the profit-maximizing level of a firm's advertising by affecting E_{conj}, the expected *advertising* reactions of a firm's rivals to changes in the firm's advertising. Despite a great deal of theorizing, the a priori nature of this relationship is indeterminate; that is, raising seller concentration may be associated with higher or lower profit-maximizing levels of firm and industry advertising. In order to infer the relationship between seller concentration and E_{conj} from empirical data, it will be necessary to take account of the possible influence of seller concentration on pricing behavior.

In fact, if the firm sets $(P - MC)/P$ at a profit-maximizing level, $(P - MC)/P = 1/E_d$, and the firm's profit-maximizing advertising condition can be rewritten in the following form:

$$\frac{A}{S} = \frac{E_a}{E_d} \quad \text{or} \quad \frac{A}{S} = \frac{(E_A + E_{\text{conj } A} \cdot E_{Ar})}{E_m/S_f + E_s(1 - S_f)/S_f}$$

The preceding expression indicates that seller concentration may affect advertising *both* by affecting $E_{\text{conj } A}$ (and therefore E_a), and also by affecting E_s (and therefore E_d). Moreover, it is quite possible that the effects of seller concentration on E_{conj} and E_s, and therefore on E_a and E_d, may either reinforce each other or cancel each other entirely. For example, if higher concentration reduces E_d by causing expectations of more aggressive output-level reactions from a firm's rivals in response to product-price cuts *and* also reduces E_a by causing expectations of more aggressive advertising-level reactions from rivals, proportional changes in E_a and E_d would leave the profit-maximizing level of the firm's advertising unchanged.

There are many other possibilities. In order to determine the impact of seller concentration on a firm's behavior, it is necessary to distinguish between the impact of concentration on *different* dimensions of the firm's rivals' reactions. For example, in the preceding example, it is necessary to try to estimate the relationships $E_a = f(E_A, E_{ar}, \text{SC})$ and $E_d = f(E_m, S_f, \text{SC})$ *separately*, in order to determine how concentration affects different dimensions of the anticipated reactions of a firm's rivals, and hence the firm's behavior. The general principle that "a firm's behavior depends on the nature of expected reactions from rivals" is not changed; the dimensions of the expected reactions are merely increased in number.

Reverse Causality Between Dependent and Explanatory Variables. Many theoretical and statistical models of the relationship between industry structure and firms' behavior and profits have ignored the possibility that the flow of causation may run in the opposite direction. For example, high profits may lead to high advertising expenditures that drive some firms from an industry and result in higher concentration. Once it is recognized that causation between the various factors may run in either direction, it becomes apparent that single-equation models of this process are no longer adequate.

What is required in the statistical analysis of relationships between industry structure and firms' behavior is a simultaneous-equation model with equations that represent all possible causal influences linking the variables. Statistical estimation of the coefficients in simultaneous-equation systems will provide more accurate indications of the directions and strength of the relationships involved.

The weak positive association between seller concentration and industry profitability that is found in many single-equation statistical studies disappears completely in some simultaneous-equation studies. Market share continues to be a major explanatory factor underlying profit rates in most studies, however. At first sight, this appears to strengthen the argument for a policy of limiting or reducing firms' market shares as a means of reducing profits and improving firms' pricing behavior. Unfortunately, knowledge of how changes in firms' market shares alone affect firms' behavior is not an adequate basis for legislation or policies that limit or change firms' market shares. The reason for this is that we cannot be sure that other factors influencing firms' behavior would remain unchanged. Nor can we be sure that such policies would leave unchanged the behavior of other decision makers in the private and public sectors whose behavior interacts with and influences firms' behavior. Thus, what appears at first sight to be support for industrial restructuring in the form of policies to influence firms' market shares has on close inspection less justification.

14.3   REDUCING ENTRY BARRIERS

The discussion in Section 14.2 provides useful background for viewing another alternative to regulation that is frequently advocated as a means of increasing competition and improving decision-maker behavior and performance, namely proposals for reducing entry barriers.

Proposals for reducing entry barriers are sometimes viewed as proposals for changing industry structure, since traditional entry-barrier theory emphasizes firms' cost conditions, scale economies, and other factors normally considered to be elements of industry structure. As this section will demonstrate, however, firms' expectations regarding their rivals' reactions are a major factor underlying the profitability of entry and the height of entry barriers into an industry. Whether these expectations are related to dimensions of industry structure is a largely unresolved issue. Although statistical studies of the rate of entry into certain industries suggest that features of industry structure such as cost conditions, growth, and diversification are associated with entry, these studies suffer from many of the same limitations as existing studies of concentration and profitability. Omission of possibly relevant explanatory variables and directions of causality between variables, lack of proper specification of relationships between variables, and other problems combine to provide a very shaky foundation on which to base public policies.

Although the focus of this section is on the implications of entry barriers for the behavior of firms and industries in the private sector, the same analytical framework and general principles are applicable to other sectors of the economy and to other dimensions of decision makers' behavior. For example, the issue of entry barriers and their impact on decision makers' behavior is equally relevant to political issues such as the impact of increases in the number of parties or candidates for political office on the behavior of individual legislators and parties, and the issue of restrictions on political campaign spending by incumbent and potential candidates.

The fundamental assumption that underlies proposals for reducing entry barriers is that doing so will increase competition. However, two related but different mechanisms by which lower entry barriers will increase competition are often distinguished. In one mechanism, lower entry barriers are expected to increase the number of firms actually competing in a market; in the other mechanism, the number of potential competitors is expected to increase and influence established firms' behavior despite the absence of actual entry. We shall examine each of these mechanisms more closely in order to underline the implicit or explicit assumptions required to validate each mechanism and to investigate the consequences of each mechanism for established firms' behavior.

In addition, attention will be focused on the meaning of "entry barriers" themselves, and on the operational problem of lowering entry barriers. It will be demonstrated that some of the factors that are generally assumed to be entry barriers are not necessarily entry barriers, while other, neglected factors may be potentially serious entry barriers. Even if we are able to determine the factors that can be legitimately viewed as entry barriers, the forces that determine these entry barriers must be known in order to permit one to lower or raise the level of these entry barriers.

The consequences of entry barriers for firms' behavior, and the determinants of entry barriers, must be distinguished conceptually in order to decide (1) the level and characteristics of entry barriers that are desirable on grounds of encouraging certain characteristics of firms' behavior and (2) the methods of achieving the desired entry-barrier characteristics.

Traditional Entry-Barrier Theory. "Entry" into an industry can be defined in several ways. In economic analysis, entry into a particular industry is usually viewed as the addition of new productive facilities by a decision-making entity not previously operating in that industry. The purchase of an existing firm by a new decision maker that changes the control over the firm already existing in the industry can, however, also change the behavior of the industry. This will occur if the new decision maker acts differently from the previous controller of the firm, or if other existing firms *expect* the new decision maker to behave differently. Thus, the traditional view that "entry" must increase the number of independent decision makers in an industry if it is to change the behavior of firms in the industry is not necessarily valid.

Entry barriers are factors that inhibit new firms from entering an industry or line of activity. In many regulated industries, such as trucking, communications, and taxicabs, entry barriers take the form of licenses that are required in order to operate in those industries. In these circumstances, the phrase "reducing entry barriers" may refer to a change in legislation or regulatory commission policies that make it easier for new entrants into the industry to obtain licenses. The Motor Carrier Act of 1980 made it easier for truckers wishing to enter new routes to obtain certificates, for example.

Even if licenses to operate in a regulated industry are easier to obtain, or are totally unnecessary, this does not necessarily mean that entry barriers into the industry have been reduced, however. Other entry barriers may remain that present effective barriers to entry despite the absence of licensing.

For these reasons, it is necessary to begin our discussion of the policy of reducing entry barriers by examining all the factors that are relevant in determining whether a firm's decision makers will enter a line of activity or a new market. Also, it should be noted that a potential entrant firm may be a giant firm that is already producing in other markets. This emphasis is needed to offset the common tendency for people to assume unconsciously that new entrants are small firms starting from scratch, with limited resources, that automatically face entry barriers. Second, it is necessary to point out that the essential characteristic of an entry barrier is a *difference* between the cost or revenue conditions confronting established firms and potential entrant. All firms entering an industry for the first time require resources and face innumerable problems of organizing these resources and commencing production. These kinds of problems are *not* what is generally meant by the term "entry barriers" in economic analysis.

The profits a potential entrant anticipates from entering a market already occupied by other firms depend on the entrant's costs of producing the product and the demand conditions the entrant anticipates he or she will face if he or she enters the market. These demand conditions depend on (1) the entrant's expectations regarding the total market demand for the product and (2) the postentry behavior of firms already established in the market. These factors may be clarified by reference to the profit-maximizing price–marginal cost relationship for the potential entrant's product

$$\frac{P - \text{MC}}{P} = \frac{1}{E_d} = \frac{S_f}{E_m + E_{r\ \text{est}}\,(1 - S_f)}$$

where S_f is the share of the market the entrant expects to occupy after entry, E_m is the price elasticity of total market demand, and $E_{r\ \text{est}}$ is the expected change in established firms' output in response to entry.

Much of the existing theory of entry barriers is based explicitly or implicitly on the assumption, usually referred to as the Sylos postulate, that entrants expect established firms to maintain their output at an unchanged level in response to entry. This means that the term $E_{r\ \text{est}}$ in the potential entrant's profit-maximizing pricing condition equals zero, which reduces the preceding relationship to the expression $(P - \text{MC})/P = S_f/E_m$.

Since $S_f = 1 - S_r$, where S_r is the share of total market demand supplied by established firms, a sufficiently large S_r will imply zero anticipated profits for the entrant. However, unless established firms have lower unit costs than the potential entrant, owing to scale economies or other factors, the level of S_r that results in zero anticipated profits for the potential entrant would also result in zero profits for established firms. Unless costs differ, entry-deterring behavior by established firms would not be plausible, and there would be no entry barriers, since there would be no difference between established firms and the entrant.

When $E_{r\,\mathrm{est}} = 0$, as is assumed by the Sylos postulate, potential entrants will expect entry to be profitable whenever the existing market price of the product exceeds unit costs in established firms by more than the difference between the unit cost of producing the product in established and entrant firms, or by more than an amount that is directly related to scale economies and market price elasticity of demand. In these circumstances, information concerning scale economies and absolute cost differences alone would enable one to rank industries in terms of the factors that determine the height of entry barriers.[5]

These cost-related entry barriers will influence the level of the industry's product price, whether or not established firms attempt to deter entry into their industry. Under the Sylos postulate it is always *possible* for established firms to deter entry by setting the market price and quantity of their output at an entry-deterring level, because potential entrants are assumed to believe that the established firms' postentry output level will remain at the preentry level. Entry-deterring behavior need not be *optimal*, however, in the sense of achieving the highest profit level for established firms, *taking into account the reactions of potential entrants* to established firms' choice of price and output levels (see Needham 1978, Chap. 7).

Entry-Barrier Theory When Established Firms React to Entry. The conclusions of traditional entry-barrier analysis hinge on the Sylos postulate, which assumes $E_{\mathrm{est}} = 0$ in a potential entrant's profit-maximizing pricing condition. If potential entrants assume that established firms will change the level of their output in response to entry, $E_{\mathrm{est}} \neq 0$ and it is the *postentry* output of established firms that determines the anticipated price at which the entrant can sell any given output level. The *preentry* price and quantity sold by established firms become relevant to the entry decision only in special cases in which established firms' postentry behavior is determined by the preentry behavior, as the Sylos postulate assumes.

If potential entrants expect established firms to change their output in response to entry, the anticipated profitability of entry depends not only on cost-related factors but also on the sign and magnitude of established firms' output-level reactions (E_{est}). For example, if potential entrants anticipate entry-deterring behavior by established firms, they will not enter an industry even though the market price of the product

[5] The propositions contained in this paragraph are developed in detail in Needham (1978, Chap. 7).

exceeds production costs in established firms by much more than would be possible if established firms behaved as the Sylos postulate assumes. Conversely, if potential entrants expect established firms to reduce output in response to entry, entry may occur even though the preentry price of the established firms' product did not exceed unit costs by more than the production cost difference between established firms and potential entrants.

Since a potential entrant's expectation about established firms' reactions to entry (E_{est}) is not directly observable, some operational index is required that would reflect the reactions to entry and profitability of entry anticipated by potential entrants, and which would express the ease or difficulty of entry, into an industry.

Attempts have been made to estimate statistically the kind of factors that influence the rate of entry into industries. Orr (1974a), for example, in a study of entry into Canadian manufacturing industries, found that the rates of entry were negatively associated with capital requirements, high concentration, and ratios of industry advertising/sales and research and development/sales, and were positively associated with industry size, past profit rate, and past industry growth rate. In another study, L. Deutsch (1975) also found the rate of entry to be negatively associated with industry advertising intensity and industry diversification, but differed from Orr in finding a positive association between industry concentration and the rate of entry.

Entry barriers can be reduced, in the sense of raising the expected profitability of any given level of entry, by a number of methods. For example, new entrant's costs may be subsidized to reduce a differential cost advantage possessed by established firms, or public policies may be adopted that reduce the probability of "entry-deterring" reactions by established firms. It should be noted that even if these policies do not increase the number of firms actually entering an industry, they can still affect the behavior of established firms, *provided* that established firms take potential entrants' behavior into account in deciding their policies.

If established firms *do not* consider potential entrants' behavior in their decision making, reducing entry barriers and increasing the profitability of entry will *only* affect industry pricing policies (1) to the extent that actual entry occurs and (2) if actual entry changes the combined behavior of the previously established firms and the new entrant.

The second point requires emphasis, because actual entry need not change industry behavior. In connection with our discussion of seller concentration in Section 14.2, we saw that the number of firms is less important than the expectation each firm has regarding its rivals' reactions. If established firms in an industry were to reduce their output by an amount equal to a new entrant's output, industry output and price will not change. Nor is collusion necessary to produce this result. It is easy to demonstrate that if each firm in a particular industry has an identical cost function and expects every other firm to exactly match its own price and output strategies, the resulting pricing behavior of the industry will correspond to a monopoly profit-maximizing solution, irrespective of the number of firms in the industry.[6]

Nonprice Dimensions of Firms' Behavior and Entry Theory. Up to this point our discussion of entry barriers has assumed that the only decision variable for potential entrants and established firms is the level of their output. This assumption conforms to the traditional approach to entry barriers found in the economics literature. In practice, entrants also select levels of other decision variables, such as advertising or research and development expenditures, and established firms may respond to entry by changing the level of these other decision variables in addition to, or instead of, output levels. The traditional one-dimensional theory of entry barriers must be expanded to incorporate these other decision variables. This can be accomplished by recognizing that the profitability of entry depends on the anticipated postentry level of these other decision variables for both the entrant firm and established firms. In other words, to the previous list of absolute cost, scale economy, and established firms' output reactions must now be added the potential entrant's anticipations regarding the established firms' reactions in any other dimensions of established firms' behavior that affect the profitability of the entrant's behavior.

Again, it is generally *possible* for established firms to increase some dimension of their behavior, such as advertising outlays, sufficiently to make entry unprofitable.

This does not mean that it is the *most profitable* strategy for established firms or that it is the response that potential entrants consider most likely to occur. Once the traditional emphasis on price and quantity is replaced by a more general theory of firm behavior encompassing other decision variables, such as advertising, the relevant concept of entry barriers becomes a vector or matrix of expected reactions of established firms instead of a single–quantity-reaction dimension. This vector or matrix of reactions is just like Table 7.1 in Chapter 7. This considerably complicates the problem of determining the level of entry barriers in any particular situation, and the effect of those entry barriers on potential entrants' and established firms' behavior.

For example, a number of combinations of expected reactions by established firms may be compatible with the same consequences for an entrant's expected profits. Also, since the expectations of the potential entrant are not directly observable, it is necessary to determine the operationally observable factors that influence those expectations, in order to be able to "reduce entry barriers" and change a potential entrant's behavior.

6 See Needham (1978, p. 168) for proof of this proposition.

The nature and magnitude of established firms' reactions anticipated by potential entrants are the real entry barriers; not only do they determine whether or not entry will occur, but they also determine the profit-maximizing *levels* of the entrant's decision variables.

Measuring Entry Barriers in Practice. The distinction between existing levels of established firms' decision variables, and *changes* in response to entry as possible entry barriers, has important implications for attempts to measure entry barriers into different industries by reference to *levels* of decision variables. It is well known that firm and industry profit rates tend to be higher in firms and industries with higher advertising sales ratios. This is often interpreted as evidence that advertising is an entry barrier, reducing entry in markets where the advertising levels of established firms are high, and permitting them to earn higher profits. Such an interpretation is unwarranted. As demonstrated in more detail elsewhere (Needham 1978, Chap. 7), a positive association between profit rates and advertising sales ratios implies that in the following profit-maximizing advertising condition applicable to individual established firms:

$$\frac{A}{S} = \frac{(P - MC)}{P} E_a = \frac{E_a}{E_d}$$

(1) E_d is lower in firms and industries with higher profits and advertising,

and

(2) E_a may be the same, higher, or lower in firms and industries with higher profit and advertising rates, depending on whether profit rates are observed to increase proportionately, less than proportionately, or more than proportionately with increases in advertising/sales ratios.

Since[7]

$$\frac{E_a}{E_d} = \frac{E_A + (E_{\text{conj est}} + E_{\text{conj ent}}) \cdot E_{Ar}}{\dfrac{E_m}{S_f} + (E_{r\text{ est}} + E_{r\text{ ent}}) \dfrac{(1 - S_f)}{S_f}}$$

where $E_{\text{conj est}}$ and $E_{r\text{ est}}$ represent the expected reactions of a firm's existing rivals, and $E_{\text{conj ent}}$ and $E_{r\text{ ent}}$ represent the expected reactions of the firm's potential entrant rivals, it follows that there are *three* possible explanations for the observed positive associations between firm and industry profit rates and advertising/sales ratios: (1) differences in *buyer reactions*, represented by E_A and E_m, the price and advertising elasticities

---

[7] Needham (1978, Chap. 7).

of market demand; (2) differences in the anticipated *reactions of established rivals,* represented by $E_{\text{conj}_{\text{est}}}$ and $E_{r\text{ est}}$, may account for the differences in E_a and E_d and resulting profit/advertising ratios in different firms and industries; (3) differences in the established firms' anticipations regarding the *reactions of potential entrants* may account for the observed profit/advertising relationship.

Only the third explanation involves entry-barrier considerations in explaining a positive association between profit rates and advertising/sales ratios. Moreover, even if differences in the expected behavior of potential entrants do explain all or part of this relationship, it does *not* automatically follow that such differences are related to the *current* advertising policies of established firms! It is the anticipated postentry behavior of established firms that determines potential entrants' behavior. In order for potential entrants' behavior to be affected by the current advertising policies of established firms, there must be a positive association in the minds of potential entrants between the current advertising behavior of established firms and *some* aspect of the *postentry* behavior of established firms. For example, the magnitude of expected increases in the level of established firms' advertising, or some other dimension of their behavior, in response to entry, would have to be positively associated with the preentry level of the established firms' advertising.

As the preceding remarks suggest, we are a long way from being able to conclude that heavy advertising, or other types of expenditure, by established firms automatically represent a barrier to entry. As we stressed at the beginning of this section, the essence of an entry barrier is a *difference* between the cost or revenue conditions confronting established firms and potential entrants. If an entrant firm must spend more on advertising or other activities to achieve a given level of sales, this results in a higher advertising cost per unit of the entrant's output, and a lower rate of profit for the entrant at any given market price of the product. Combined with a sufficiently aggressive expected output response by established firms, this cost difference may deter an entrant. However, the expected response of established firms may be insufficient to deter entry.

More important, we cannot simply *assume* that established firms have an advantage in terms of a higher advertising elasticity of demand and greater sales response to any given level of advertising than potential entrants, since potential entrants may be large firms already operating in other markets with experience and expertise in advertising. The fact that firms already established in a market have spent funds on advertising to influence buyer behavior does not necessarily create an advantage in terms of greater effectiveness of advertising for established firms. The effect of established firms' prior advertising on buyer behavior wears out or depreciates with the passage of time, and has to be renewed. In general, there is no reason why established firms should necessarily have greater response to their advertising than new entrants.

Implications of Multiple Potential Entrants. As a final complication in the entry-barrier analysis, we must now consider the impact on potential entrants' and established firms' behavior of the existence of *more than one potential entrant.* It is usually assumed that "the more potential entrants the better," and that the probability of entry will increase as the number of potential entrants increases. We shall now show that this assumption is not necessarily valid and explain why.

The impact of more than one potential entrant on the behavior of individual potential entrants can easily be incorporated into our earlier analysis by adding another term, E_{ent}, to the potential entrant's profit-maximizing pricing condition, as follows:

$$\frac{P - \text{MC}}{P} = \frac{S_f}{E_m + (E_{r\text{ est}} + E_{r\text{ ent}})\,(1 - S_f)}$$

The term we have added to this expression, $E_{r\text{ ent}}$, represents a particular potential entrant's expectations regarding the reaction of *other potential entrants* to entry by the firm. If, for example, other potential entrants *also* enter in response to the firm's entry, this is analogous to a larger increase in output by established firms, and the expected profitability of entry to the individual entrant will be reduced. In other words, more potential entrants may *reduce* the profitability of entry to any single potential entrant. This is only one possibility, however. Each potential entrant will, in principle, take into account the reactions of established firms and all other potential entrants, in deciding whether or not to enter the industry. The resulting behavior of the *group* of potential entrants, in terms of the number of firms entering the industry, will depend on the net result of these interacting expectations.

The effect of the number and size distribution of potential entrants on the expectations of individual potential entrants is indeterminate a priori. The situation is analytically identical to that involved in trying to establish the effect of seller concentration on *established rivals'* expectations and behavior. The matter can be settled only by empirical study of the way in which potential entrants form their expectations of each other's reactions to discover whether and how their number affects these expectations.

Increasing the number of potential entrants will also have implications for the behavior of established firms that take into account the reactions of potential entrants in deciding their policies. In principle, the established firms are now faced by a number of potential entrants whose behavior is considered by the established firms. The anticipated behavior of all the potential entrants will determine the established firms' profit-maximizing strategy. No generalizations are possible regarding the impact of adding more potential entrants on the optimal behavior of established firms, however. The likelihood of entry into the industry, and the magnitude of entry at any given level of established firms' decision variables, may increase, decrease, or remain unchanged as a result of a change in the total number of recognized potential entrants.

In terms of the profit-maximizing pricing condition for established firms

$$\frac{P - \mathrm{MC}}{P} = \frac{S_f}{E_m + E_{r\ \mathrm{ent}}\ (1 - S_f)}$$

$E_{r\ \mathrm{ent}}$ may be increased, reduced, or remain unchanged with changes in the number of potential entrants. Although we have discussed the implications of changes in the number of potential entrants for firms' output and pricing behavior, the number of potential entrants may of course affect expectations of entrants and established firms regarding advertising or other dimensions of behavior.

Entry-Barrier Analysis, Competition, and Established Firms. In a recent development in the economics literature, the analytical framework and principles of entry-barrier theory have been applied to explaining the behavior of *established rivals* (Porter and Caves, 1977; Porter, 1979). Just as the threat, or expectation, of aggressive reactions by established firms may deter a new firm from entering the market of established firms, they may similarly deter established rivals from attempting to enter or expand their share of submarkets currently served by other established firms. "Entry" by a firm new to the industry and an expansion of output by another established rival are *identical* in their impact on each individual established firm. Therefore, the rationale for treating rivalry between established firms in the same analytical framework as rivalry between entrant firms and established firms is obvious.

The analytical similarity between rivalry among established firms and potential rival firms also serves to emphasize the importance of anticipated rivals' reactions in determining patterns of firm behavior, as explained in Chapter 7. Simply by changing one's definition of the boundaries of markets, an analysis of the behavior of firms that are "established" firms and "potential" entrants under one market definition becomes an analysis of the behavior of two "established" firms in the same market.

There is one particular dimension of rivalry between firms serving submarkets of the same market that tends to be overlooked, or insufficiently stressed, by conventional entry-barrier analysis. This is the possible existence of threats of "reverse entry" into the market of the entrant firm as a possible deterrent to entry. Decision makers in different submarkets of the same industry, or in different industries, may collectively or individually decide not to enter each other's markets, even if the apparent height of cost-related and other entry barriers into each market are very low. Viewed from this perspective, the threat of entry into other decision makers' markets becomes a *double-edged* strategy, one that can be used "adversely" as a threat to prevent entry into one's own market.

This fact illustrates the need for caution in interpreting "low" entry barriers as being conducive to more competition. If the entry barriers into potential entrant A's existing market are high, then the threat of "reverse" entry by established decision makers in market B will be *less* likely to act as a deterrent to A's entry into B. Lower rates of entry and higher profit rates have been observed in industries in which established firms are diversified (Rhoades 1973, Deutsch 1975). One possible reason for this may be that diversified firms are in a better position than specialized firms to counter by "reverse entry" into potential entrants' existing markets.

In principle, a reduction in the level of entry barriers may be viewed as *anything that reduces the magnitude of the response of established firms' decision variables that is anticipated by potential entrants* in response to entry, since this will imply an increase in the entrant's expected profits from entry. However, since entry barriers are a vector of expected reactions, rather than a one-dimensional concept, the phrase "lowering entry barriers" can be interpreted in many ways, each with different implications for the entrant's behavior and for market behavior.

Even if operational concepts of entry barriers are developed, and the effects of changing the level of entry barriers on firms' market behavior are predictable with reasonable accuracy, it does not necessarily follow that a reduction in entry barriers into narrowly defined economic markets will improve firms' behavior. The example mentioned in connection with "reverse entry" indicated that raising entry barriers may be appropriate in certain circumstances. However, entry-barrier analysis is not only relevant in connection with the behavior of regulated and unregulated firms in the private sector of the economy, but it also applies to the behavior of other types of decision maker, including legislators and regulatory agencies. The entry barriers that may need to be changed to improve the performance of regulated decision makers may, for example, include entry barriers into certain areas of legislative or regulatory agency decision making. The behavior of those three types of decision maker is closely interrelated, and it is myopic to assume that the only entry barriers that should be changed in order to improve the outcome of the regulatory process are those facing regulated firms. A good deal of theory and empirical evidence indicates that entry barriers into legislative and regulatory decision making are much higher than entry barriers into regulated industries. In the case of single-member legislative districts, the entry barriers are unsurmountable during the incumbent's term of office; entry into the decision making of congressional committees is severely restricted.

Our perspectives need to be widened so that attention is simultaneously focused on entry barriers into *all* types of decision making and on their consequences for decision-maker behavior. In this wider perspective, it should be remembered that it is the *relative* height of entry barriers that is relevant in determining resource allocation between different sectors of the economy. Deciding whether entry barriers into a particular type of decision making are "too high" or "too low" can be determined only by reference to the height of entry barriers into other sectors. Instead of lowering entry barriers into a particular sector, an alternative way of changing *relative* entry barriers might be to *raise* entry barriers into other sectors. If resources flow in response to the relative height of entry barriers into different activities, as is usually assumed, raising the height of entry barriers in other sectors would tend to divert resources into the relatively lower entry-barrier sectors.

14.4   SOCIAL RESPONSIBILITY OF BUSINESS

The idea of social responsibility on the part of business is not new. It can be found, for example, in the writings of Berle and Means (1932) and was more fully discussed in A. A. Berle's *The Twentieth Century Capitalist Revolution* (1954), where the author stressed the need for "the growth of conscience in the corporation of our time." Interest in the concept grew and developed major momentum in the late 1960s and has continued up to the present time. The basic reason for this increased emphasis on social responsibility may be traced to a widening gap between business behavior and the expectations of a widely assorted collection of individuals and interest groups in society regarding the kind of behavior business "should" exhibit. There are, therefore, strong normative overtones in any concept of social responsibility.

The reasons for this widening gap between business behavior and society's expectations of business have been attributed to a number of forces, including education, changing life-styles, improved communications, and the media. On one thing most people are agreed: business has *not* become less socially responsible in any absolute sense. On the contrary, a large number of examples and much evidence could be cited to indicate that the business sector as a whole is undertaking activities that would be considered more socially responsible compared with business sector behavior in preceding periods of time.

Despite an absolute increase in socially responsible characteristics of business behavior that would be acknowledged by all but the most biased of observers, society's expectations of business behavior have increased even faster, resulting in a widening gap that has created a heightened state of tension between business and society. As a result, in recent times the call for increased social responsibility by business has become louder, even strident. Some of the response to these demands has been predictable, with business as a whole adopting a generally defensive stance, and government usually lining up on the side of advocates of increased social responsibility of business, often as a prelude to government intervention as an alleged "remedy" for the failure of business to exhibit sufficient social responsibility in some facet of its behavior.

Even among more impartial observers, however, there are wide differences in conclusions regarding the current status and desired characteristics of socially responsible business behavior. Among economists, for example, Milton Friedman (1963) condemns the doctrine of social responsibility and argues that if firms depart from their traditional goal of profit maximization to serve social interests, the very foundations of private sector competitive activity would be eroded. Friedman argues that in a free society there is only one social responsibility of business, namely to use its resources to increase the profits of its owners as long as it stays within the rules of the game, which he says is to engage in open and free competition without deception or fraud. Friedman correctly points out that the social responsibility doctrine is vaguely defined and could be used to justify a role for business in any and every sphere of economic and social life. It could be added that the same statement applies to the terms "profit," "free and active competition," and "the rules of the game" used by Friedman.

An example of the opposite point of view is provided by Bowen's (1953) view that the duty of business in a democracy is to follow the social obligations that are defined by the whole community. A more recent example in the same vein is the work of Preston and Post (1975), two of the few economists who have attempted to define the social responsibility doctrine in operational terms, which they term "the principle of public responsibility."

Regulation and Social Responsibility Compared. Our purpose in this section is not to attempt to resolve the dispute over whether businesses are, or should be, socially responsible, or to take sides in the issue. Instead, it is to provide a framework for viewing the issue of social responsibility and for integrating it with a wider view of business-society relationships, including regulation of business. Indeed, since the regulation of business by government agencies is a means of reducing discrepancies between business behavior and some concept of "socially desirable" business behavior, it is necessary to place regulation and proposals for increased social responsibility of business in perspective in relation to each other. They are, to some extent, alternative approaches to the same perceived problem. Government intervention and direct regulation of business behavior have increased considerably since the early 1960s. To some people, including a large number of business decision makers, further increases in government control of business to ensure that certain perceived social needs are met might be avoided if businesses themselves became more socially responsive and took account of these wider interests in their decision making.

Government regulation and increased social responsibility of business are two alternative approaches to changing business behavior. There are differences, however, between regulation and social responsibility problems and between their respective solutions.

For example, the characteristics of business behavior that the social responsibility approach considers relevant are considerably wider than those generally considered in the traditional regulation approach to business behavior. Some versions of social responsibility include characteristics of a firm's behavior and problems that are completely outside the firm's current operations but that the firm could help to alleviate, directly or indirectly. Charitable contributions, for example, may be solicited from firms for a wide variety of problems that the firms themselves have not caused, ranging from the alleviation of world hunger to cancer research to a variety of religious projects.

Even where the perceived social responsibility problem covers the same dimensions of firms' behavior as the regulation problem, the solutions that are appropriate may differ. This seems obvious when the two approaches are compared in terms of the degree of government involvement in attempts to reduce discrepancies between firms' existing behavior and certain perceived socially desirable behavior characteristics. However, some proposals for achieving increased social responsibility would entail as much, if not more, direct government involvement in their implementation than traditional government regulation.

Even if business decision makers were more involved in attempts to achieve socially desirable business behavior than would be the case under government regulation that had the identical behavioral objectives for firms, the appropriate solutions would generally differ. If we regard "regulation" and "social responsibility" as two types of additional constraints or incentive systems that are added to those already facing business decision makers, in order to elicit certain specific desired changes in business behavior, it is legitimate to ask *why* these constraints and incentives might differ depending on whether they were administered by a government regulatory agency or by a "private sector regulatory agency." One reason is that private sector firms' decision makers who are subject to the constraints or incentives might react differently, even if the constraints or incentives themselves were identical, depending on whether "public sector" or "private sector" decision makers administered them. This may seem "unreasonable" or illogical to some readers; if so, ask yourself how you would react to a request to show your driver's license from (1) a uniformed policeman and (2) a plainclothes policeman, or to a request to strip naked from (1) a doctor in a white coat and (2) a doctor in street clothes.

Operationalizing the Concept of Social Responsibility. The thesis of the "social responsibility of business" appears to have been adopted by an increasing number of people, including a large part of the business community and many academics. Yet, no common position can be found among its many advocates, and few attempts have been made to examine carefully and to integrate the idea in any systematic way with either economic theory or other disciplines involving organizational and human behavior. Indeed, it can be argued that it is precisely this vagueness that has facilitated its acceptance in many quarters. Who could disagree with the concept of "social responsibility" and risk being labeled an advocate of "social irresponsibility"? Who, when faced with the term "social responsibility," will not put a positive connotation on the term, even if that person's particular interpretation of the term may be different from everyone else's?

Like the terms "freedom," "motherhood," and "the flag," the term "social responsibility" is a wonderful ploy for evading all the important issues involved and disarming all but the most persistent opposition. How else can one explain the widespread defensiveness, even guilt evident among members of the business community when faced by the issue of social responsibility, even in situations in which particular businesses have made considerable strides in the direction of increased social responsibility? In the remainder of this section we shall examine the concept and problem of social responsibility more closely in an effort to emphasize that, like all problems, the conceptualization stage in large part determines the nature of the solution that is appropriate. There are many variants of the social responsibility concept, with different solutions, and at all stages great care must be taken to unearth the unavoidable value judgments that are implicit in any particular version of the concept and associated solution.

The first step is to focus on the meaning, in operational terms, of "socially responsible" business behavior. The term may cover particular dimensions of a firm's behavior, and even particular levels of those dimensions. It may cover characteristics of inputs — for example, how many minorities are employed by a firm — as well as outputs. It may cover outputs currently produced and affecting buyers of the firm's products (e.g., the safety of the product); third parties (e.g., pollution suffered by nonconsumers of the firm's product); or outputs that are not currently produced but that "should" be (e.g., an everlasting lightbulb, an electric car).

Once a particular definition of the characteristics of firms' behavior and performance that should be regarded as socially desirable is accepted, one has accepted a particular version of "the problem of social responsibility"! A good deal of the controversy in the literature revolves around this fundamental issue. What is not always recognized, or admitted, is that this is basically a normative issue about whose evaluations of business behavior should count, and by how much. In other words, the debate about what is socially responsible behavior is part of the struggle between individuals and interest groups to determine whose interests and evaluations should dominate in influencing business behavior.

The interests of firms' owners have traditionally dominated profit-maximizing firms' behavior; these interests remained largely dominant even after hired managers replaced owner-managers. The interests of firms' customers were represented, via the purchasing power they exercised in the marketplace. Other groups in society, which might be affected by firms' behavior directly or indirectly, exerted little influence on firms' policies and behavior. Demands for increased social responsibility stem from a desire by certain interest groups for more influence over business decision making and the resulting characteristics of business inputs, processes, and outputs.

From the point of view of descriptive analysis, one can attempt to model and explain the process that results in a particular definition of "socially responsible" business behavior at a particular point in time. The direction of calls for social responsibility has tended to change with the passage of time. In the 1960s, advocates of corporate social responsibility demanded safer products and working conditions and increased minority employment. In the 1970s, attention turned increasingly to environmental problems and to women's rights and employment opportunities.

The media have had an extremely important influence in terms of providing information about perceived problems. This information is not always unbiased, as one would expect in a situation in which sensational news gets the most attention from individuals. The risk of getting cancer from decaffeinated coffee receives much more emphasis in the media than the fact that a human being would have to drink 50 million cups of decaffeinated coffee every day for his entire lifetime to receive the amount of the cancer-causing agent that was fed to laboratory animals.

Factors Underlying Demands for Social Responsibility. Emphasis on the process that generates particular demands for social responsibility serves several useful purposes, including revealing whose evaluations are involved, and why. It also forces one to recognize that the information underlying demands for particular versions of social responsibility may be inaccurate. This inaccuracy may be the result of ignorance on the part of individuals and groups that place certain values on various aspects of business behavior. For example, if people who require 100 percent pollution-free air were aware that eliminating the last 5 percent of pollutants would double the cost of the products they consume, thereby halving their real income in the process of achieving the 5 percent reduction in the pollution, a different set of relative values might be placed on various characteristics of business behavior.

On the other hand, the information underlying different relative evaluations of business behavior and concepts of social responsibility might be purposely distorted by parties who find it in their own self-interests to provide this information. The deliberate information distortion could occur on both sides of the social responsibility issue — by business itself or by particular groups demanding or opposing variants of "business responsibility."

In short, the problems of obtaining accurate information from individuals and interest groups regarding their evaluations of different characteristics of business behavior constitute simply a special case of the incentive-compatibility problem discussed in Chapter 12.

Another reason for investigating the process by which concepts of socially responsible behavior are defined is connected with the nature of the solution that is appropriate. For example, if expectations of business behavior were generated by a process that made expectations a function of the degree of success made by business in meeting past demands for social responsibility, the gap between business behavior and social expectations might be an ever widening one if business increased its rate of response. In these circumstances, the appropriate strategy for business would be to widen the gap between its expected performance and its actual performance. The analogy with the problem of appropriate incentives for regulated firms discussed in Chapter 12, Section 2, is almost identical. Social responsibility targets that are set "too high" may result in lower rather than higher efforts by firms to attain those targets.

To this point, we have tried to emphasize that, from an analytical perspective, demands for social responsibility of business are similar to demands for regulation, in terms of both the individual and group interests that generate such demands and the problems and characteristics that such sociopolitical demand-revealing processes exhibit. Even if information regarding accurate evaluations of different characteristics of business behavior could be obtained, this information by itself would not be sufficient to permit one to define the characteristics of "socially responsible behavior."

For one thing, such demands and evaluations of business behavior will not usually be cognizant of, and reflect, the absolute and relative resource costs of changes in various dimensions of business behavior. Given the overall limitation on resources available to the business sector, more resources devoted to expanding some dimensions of business behavior will mean less resources devoted to other dimensions. The feasible trade-offs between the alternative uses of resources will not usually be known to interest groups evaluating different dimensions of business behavior. Indeed, firms themselves may not know the trade-offs involved. In this respect, part of the problem of defining appropriate concepts of socially responsible behavior is exactly analogous to that involved in setting targets of performance for regulated firms, and it involves motivating firms to obtain and transmit accurate information regarding the costs of changes in dimensions of business behavior.

A second requirement in defining socially responsible behavior is knowledge of the "monitoring and enforcement costs" involved in changing firms' behavior toward socially responsible levels. These costs determine whether particular dimensions of firms' behavior can be changed without the combined resource and enforcement costs of such changes exceeding the valuations attributed by society to the resulting changes in firms' behavior. In other words, like the concept of socially optimal regulation defined in Chapter 5, Section 5, concepts of socially responsible behavior are not independent of the means and costs of available methods of reducing discrepancies between firms' behavior and desired dimensions of firms' behavior.

Incentives for Increased Social Responsibility. There is very little discussion in the social responsibility literature regarding the operational methods that would be used to make firms more socially responsible, irrespective of the particular concept of social responsibility that is employed. In principle, changes in the behavior of a firm's decision makers can be achieved by means of two fundamentally different approaches. One approach is to try to change the firm's decision makers' own value systems and objectives, adding or increasing the weight attributed by those decision makers to aspects of the firm's behavior that affect the degree of social responsibility of the firm. The second approach is to introduce socially desirable characteristics of the firm's behavior as constraints on the pursuit of managers' existing goals. The choice between these two approaches is much more important than may be apparent. In general, the resulting behavior of the firm's decision makers, and the degree of social responsibility exhibited, will differ, depending on which approach is adopted.

In Chapter 2 it was explained that treating a particular aspect of decision-maker behavior as a constraint in effect raises the implicit valuation of the constrained variable above other variables that contribute to the decision maker's objectives. In other words, "meeting the constraint" on some dimension of the firm's behavior becomes more important than "violating the constraint in order to achieve a higher level of the decision maker's objective," such as profits. Moreover, this statement is true *no matter what the level of attainment of the decision maker's objective.* For example, if the constraint is "zero pollutants emitted," this constraint has to be met whether the firm is making high profits or no profits!

It is not entirely accidental that proponents of social responsibility prefer the "constraint" approach to that of including socially responsible aspects of the firm's behavior in the decision maker's objective function. In the latter situation, faced by a choice between resource uses that increase either socially responsible aspects of the firm's behavior or profits, the choice will depend on the decision maker's relative evaluations of an increase in the firm's social responsibility or profits. These evaluations, and the choice made, will tend to vary with the existing levels of social responsibility and profits.

If the firm is making satisfactory profits, for example, the decision maker's evaluation of extra profits may be low relative to the valuation the decision maker places on an increase in the social responsibility dimensions of the firm's behavior. In contrast, if the firm is making small or negative profits, increased profits and survival may take precedence over increases in social responsibility. Some people may feel that a firm "*should* go out of business if it cannot meet standards of socially responsible behavior." Others would disagree, especially if the standards of socially desirable behavior were arbitrary, excessively high in relation to feasibly attainable levels of performance, or based on a subset of society's members' evaluations.

It is possible to construct the type of constraints on firms' behavior that exhibit the incentive properties required to induce decision makers to act in a socially responsible manner. The principles involved are very similar to those outlined in Chapter 12 dealing with the appropriate incentive system for regulated firms. The problem of achieving the "right" degree of social responsibility is a good deal more complex than the literature suggests, no matter which version of social responsibility is adopted as a criterion.

Even if the goal of increasing a particular version of social responsibility is accepted by policymakers and business itself, there remains the problem of ensuring that business behavior responds. Monitoring and enforcement policies of some kind will be required, even if the business sector itself, rather than some public sector agency, administers these policies. Individual firms may have incentives to evade socially responsible behavior, especially if socially responsible dimensions of behavior are introduced as a constraint on the decision maker's behavior rather than as part of the decision maker's own value system and objective function.

The expectations of individual firms regarding the socially responsible dimensions of their rivals' behavior are just as relevant in determining each firm's own level of social responsibility as are other dimensions of rivals' behavior, such as product prices or advertising expenditures. For example, if all firms in an industry install expensive antipollution devices, the cost of these devices will be included in the costs of firms' products, and no change in relative costs of the products of different firms will occur. In contrast, if one firm is able to evade installing the devices, the costs of its products will be reduced relative to those of its rivals, enabling it to earn higher profits at any given level of industry product prices, or permitting it to reduce the price of its products in order to increase its market share of the product.

Corporate Social Audit as an Incentive Device. In the literature on social responsibility, a considerable amount of attention has been devoted to the "corporate social audit." Current accounting systems focus on providing information regarding a firm's revenues, costs, and profit and are insufficient to meet the requirements of a system of measuring and monitoring such a firm's performance in meeting any specified measures of socially responsible behavior. As is to be expected from the lack of any agreement on the meaning of socially responsible behavior, no standard procedure or form of the social audit, or report, has emerged. The common feature of these reports is an attempt to present a firm's social performance systematically by looking at the various aspects of the firm's behavior that are considered relevant from the point of view of social responsibility and assessing the firm's strengths and weaknesses in each area.

Although some type of information on firms' social performance is indispensable to monitoring and enforcing any system of incentives designed to increase firms' social responsibility, by themselves such social audits are unlikely to change firms' behavior. The information provided by firms can be distorted, and social performance can easily be exaggerated. Also, some of the information required to determine "optimal" characteristics of socially responsible behavior must necessarily be provided by firms themselves, providing them with opportunities to overstate the costs and understate the benefits of particular dimensions of socially responsible behavior. For these reasons, ideally any social audit or reporting system should incorporate the type of incentives for reporting of accurate information that were discussed in Chapter 12, Section 2.

Overview of Social Responsibility. In concluding, it is useful to draw together the threads of the points made in this section, and to view the the issue of social responsibility in light of the perspectives provided. Contrary to the general impression, the need for increased social responsibility should not be accepted unquestioningly. Essentially, the target of social responsibility is a list of firm behaviors, with values assigned by someone, that are to be used in evaluating firms' actual behavior. Whose perceptions and valuations are involved, and whether these perceptions are based on accurate knowledge of the costs and benefits of the various dimensions of firms' behavior, are important considerations in evaluating existing demands for increased social responsibility, and also in deciding the normative issue of whose perceptions and evaluations "should" count in the definition of a concept of social responsibility that is to be implemented in practice.

Once a specific concept of social responsibility is adopted as a valid criterion for judging firms' performance, all the problems of motivating firms to improve their performance in terms of this criterion remain to be solved. These problems are analytically identical to those involved in attempting to change regulated firms' behavior. The basic difference between social responsibility and regulation is the focus of the administration of the monitoring and enforcement system. The business sector is generally assumed, implicitly, to perform this task of increasing social responsibility. Alternatively, under some versions a public sector agency might be involved.

From an analytical standpoint, one can view dimensions of a firm's social responsibility in an analogous fashion to any of the more traditional facets of a firm's behavior, such as product-price or output levels. Just as a firm may serve different markets, or groups of buyers, who value traditional product concepts, the dimensions of the firm's product can be expanded conceptually to include dimensions valued by other groups in society in addition to traditional consumer-purchaser groups. These groupings of individuals will very often overlap, reflecting the fact that individuals often occupy a number of roles simultaneously, such as those of consumer, environmentalist, and shareholder.

One of the great virtues of the price mechanism is that it forces individuals to reveal the value they place, expressed in monetary terms, on the consumption benefits of certain kinds of output. For other kinds of output, generally defined as "public goods" where output simultaneously affects a number of individuals, it is well known that this demand-revealing mechanism need not accurately reveal people's evaluations. It should be noted that even "private" goods are often a composite of different dimensions that a person may value individually but that must be purchased in the fixed proportions offered by the firm. Here also, a demand-revealing mechanism that would convey accurate information about individuals' valuations of different dimensions of the product may be lacking. The problem of social responsibility need not be confined to dimensions of firms' behavior outside the traditional private-good sphere.

The basic problem of social responsibility of business is one of attempting to elicit accurate revelations of people's evaluations of all dimensions of a firm's behavior, and evaluating the nature of the trade-offs, or opportunity costs, between different dimensions of the firm's behavior, in order to *define* the concept of socially responsible behavior. It is naive to assume that this concept is self-evident or to ignore the fact that the concept will depend on, and vary with, changes in whose evaluations and perceptions are used, or to ignore the fact that different individuals and groups will gain or lose depending on which concept of social responsibility is used to evaluate the firm's behavior.

The task of defining the social responsibility of business has scarcely begun. Moreover, the problem of motivating firms to respond to some standard of socially responsible behavior cannot be divorced from the problem of defining that standard itself, since firms must inevitably supply much of the information needed to establish the nature of feasible and optimal characteristics of socially responsible business behavior.

CHAPTER FIFTEEN

Choosing Between Regulation and Other Alternatives

15.1 INTERACTIONS AMONG APPROACHES TO CONTROLLING BUSINESS BEHAVIOR

Discussions of regulation and regulatory reform, industrial reorganization, and the social responsibility of business generally focus on one of these methods of changing business behavior while ignoring the others. This approach obscures the nature of the relationship that exists between the alternative approaches and frequently leads to erroneous conclusions. Irrespective of the concepts of desirable business behavior these alternative approaches seek to implement, a framework that integrates regulation and other methods of influencing business behavior is useful for a number of reasons.

Such a framework clarifies both the nature of the choices available to society for achieving particular forms of business behavior and the implicit or explicit assumptions involved in selecting one approach rather than another. More important, it helps to emphasize that the approaches need not be mutually exclusive and that, in certain circumstances, the success of any approach may hinge critically on a combined and coordinated use of more than one approach.

As a starting point for our discussion of these factors, assume that the relationship between some aspect of business behavior and regulation, industry structure, and social responsibility is represented by the following expression:

$$\text{Dimension of firms' behavior } B = aR + bI + cS \ldots$$

The R, I, and S terms might represent a single dimension of regulation, industry structure, social responsibility constraints, or some combination of dimensions or constraints for each of these factors that influence the dimension of business behavior in question.

If the general form of the relationship is known, it follows that any particular level of firms' behavior dimension, B, or a change in this behavior dimension, could be achieved either by varying R, by varying I, by varying S, or by some combination of changes in R, I, and S. The a, b, and c coefficients would determine by how much R, I, or S would have to be varied in order to achieve the desired change in firms' behavior. Only if one of these coefficients were zero would the corresponding approach to changing firms' behavior be ineffective. In these circumstances, what criteria might be used to choose between the alternative methods of changing business behavior?

One approach is to consider the relative costs of changing R, I, and S. If the costs of changing one of these variables are lower than the costs of changing the other variables, a given change in firms' behavior could be achieved at lower total cost by using just one method of changing business behavior. A more likely situation in practice is that the costs of changing R, I, and S vary as the magnitude of these variables is changed. The general principle that should be followed to minimize the total costs of achieving a particular change in firms' behavior by varying R, I, and S is to equate the marginal cost of each method of changing firms' behavior. If the marginal cost of changing firms' behavior by increasing R exceeds the marginal cost of achieving the same change in firms' behavior by means of increasing I, the total costs of achieving the change can be reduced by substituting an increase in I for a reduction in R.

One important implication of the preceding principle is that regulation, industry reorganization, and social responsibility need not be mutually exclusive methods of changing business behavior, and in certain circumstances a mix of these policies may be a less costly method of attempting to achieve changes in firms' behavior than exclusive reliance on a single approach. Curiously, the literature on public policies toward business behavior scarcely even mentions the possibility of combining approaches. A rare exception is provided by a paper by Trebing (1979) in which the author argues that the perspective and powers of regulatory commissions should be broadened to include changes in market structure in addition to traditional regulation of profits and prices.

A second important implication of the preceding analysis is that knowledge of the relative effectiveness of different approaches to changing firms' behavior, represented by the coefficients a, b, c, is insufficient by itself to permit optimal choice between the approaches. The costs of the different methods of changing business behavior are also relevant in determining this choice.

As emphasized in Chapter 4, however, the term "cost" cannot be divorced from the goals and constraints that confront the persons making the cost evaluation. Different individuals and interest groups in society may evaluate the costs of any particular method of controlling business behavior differently, and will prefer the method of controlling business behavior that they perceive will be the most likely method of advancing their own particular objectives. The marginal costs associated with different methods of controlling business behavior will therefore depend on whose evaluations of these different methods are adopted as the relevant basis for choosing between the different methods. Agreement between groups with different objectives, or facing different constraints, regarding the approach that should be taken to controlling business behavior is unlikely. Each group will attempt to secure adoption of the approach it prefers, and each group is likely to misrepresent the relative costs of the different approaches in order to secure implementation of its preferred approach.

The preceding considerations do not make the task of choosing between alternative approaches any easier, but we should at least recognize that these complications exist. The existing tendency among academic analysts to deplore the lack of "rational" or "optimal" approaches to the social control of business behavior or any other aspect of the human environment, without adequately recognizing the nature of the real-world constraints that inhibit or prevent the adoption of such approaches, contributes little or nothing to social progress, however that term is defined.

Up to this point we have assumed that the form of the relationship among business behavior, regulation, industry structure, and social responsibility constraints is known, as is described by the relationship depicted earlier in this section. In the absence of such knowledge, the choice among approaches to influencing business behavior encounters a number of formidable new obstacles. If the underlying relationship is like the one previously described, lack of knowledge regarding the form of this relationship would not be too serious a matter. In these circumstances, if research into the determinants of business behavior uncovered the relationship between, say, regulation and business behavior, as described by the coefficient a, this knowledge would provide sufficient information regarding the impact of regulation on business behavior. Business behavior could be changed in certain predictable ways without knowledge of the relationship between industry structure and business behavior. Regulation might not be the least costly way to change business behavior, but lacking knowledge of the means or costs of other methods, it would at least provide one predictable means of changing business behavior.

All the conclusions in the preceding paragraph are heavily dependent on the assumed form of the underlying relationship that exists between business behavior and its determinants (1). This relationship may be described as "additive," in the sense that the influence of each of the three determinants of a firm's behavior, R, I and S, is separate from the other determinants, and the combined effects of all the determinants of a firm's behavior may be obtained by adding the separate influences aR, bI, cS. If, instead, the relationship between business behavior and its determinants is "interactive," matters are very different, and none of the preceding conclusions is necessarily valid. An "interactive" relationship is one in which individual determinants of the firm's behavior are themselves related. The following example of an interactive relationship among regulation, industry structure, and firms' behavior is only one of many possible interactive forms but serves to exemplify a number of important general conclusions:

$$B = aR + bI \cdots \tag{1}$$

$$R = c + dI \cdots \tag{2}$$

$$I = e + fR \cdots \tag{3}$$

Relationships (1)–(3) indicate that firms' behavior depends on regulation and industry structure, as in the previous case. In contrast to the previous case, the amount of regulation depends on industry structure, and industry structure depends on regulation. The complex nature of the interacting relationship between firms' behavior, regulation, and structure can be clarified by substituting relationship (3) for the term I in relationship (2), to obtain the following expression:

$$R = c + d(e + fR) \quad \text{or} \quad R = \frac{c + de}{1 - df} \cdots \tag{4}$$

Similar substitution of relationship (2) for the term R in relationship (3) yields:

$$S = e + f(c + dI) \quad \text{or} \quad I = \frac{e + fc}{1 - df} \cdots \tag{5}$$

Finally, substituting (4) and (5) for R and I in relationship (1) yields the following expression:

$$B = a\left(\frac{c + de}{1 - df}\right) + b\left(\frac{e + fc}{1 - df}\right) \cdots \tag{6}$$

The last relationship is termed the "reduced form" of the relationship between firms' behavior, regulation, and industry structure. The reader will note that the terms R and I do not appear explicitly in the reduced-form equation. This is because the levels of R and I are themselves determined by the interaction between the two relationships (1) and (2). The determination of R and I is shown diagrammatically in Figure 15.1,

Figure 15.1

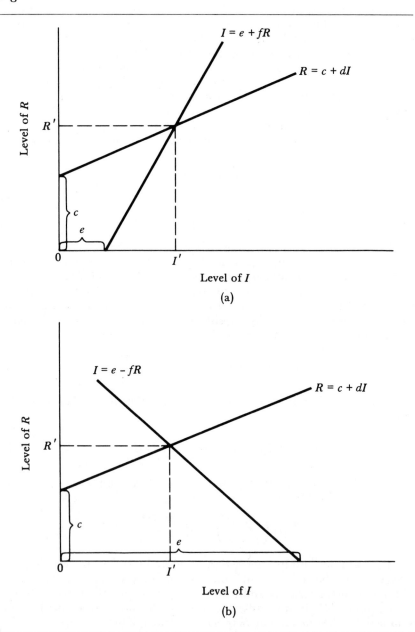

(a)

(b)

where the two curves represent relationships (2) and (3), and the intersection point between the two curves determines the levels of regulation, R', and industry structure, I', which will result from the interaction of these two relationships. The level of B is then found by substituting R' and I' for R and I, respectively, in relationship (1). The diagram clearly shows that R, I, and B are jointly determined by the coefficients a, b, ... f and that changes in any of these coefficients will shift one or more of the curves in Figure 15.1 and change the levels of R, I, and B.

A crucial difference between the interactive relationship and the additive relationship discussed at the beginning of this section is that a change in either of the coefficients c or d in relationship (2) that describes the determinants and level of regulation will affect firms' behavior by changing R and I. Similarly, a change in either of the coefficients e or f in relationship (3) that describes the determinants and level of industry structure will affect firms' behavior by changing I and R. This can be understood by noting that both terms within parentheses in (6) contain the coefficients c, d, e, and f; only the form of the two expressions in parentheses differs. Alternatively, the reader can confirm from Figure 15.2 that a change in one coefficient will shift one of the two curves and change the combination of R and I where the new curves intersect.

The important implication of this is that the effect of a change in R on firms' behavior cannot be determined without knowledge of the form of relationship (3), which describes the determinants of the industry structure dimension I. This situation is therefore very different from the case of the additive relationship, where the effect of a change in R on firms' behavior could be predicted without knowledge of the determinants of I and the relationship between I and firms' behavior. In that case, the choice between controlling business behavior by changing R or I could be based on knowledge of the determinants of either R or I and the relationship between one of these variables and firms' behavior (i.e., the a or b coefficients). This is no longer possible in the case of the interactive relationship; in this case, the determinants of *both* R and I must be known in order to determine the effect of a change in R, or I, on firms' behavior.

The signs and relative magnitudes of the coefficients a, b, c, d, e, and f will determine whether an increase in R or I will increase or reduce B. When the signs of all these coefficients are positive, increases in R will cause increases in I owing to the effect of the f term in relationship (3), and increases in I will cause increases in R owing to the effect of the d term in relationship (2). In this case, the changes in R and I will reinforce each other in changing firms' behavior, as can readily be verified by shifting one of the curves in Figure 15.1(a). This will also be true if both a and b have a negative sign.

In contrast to the preceding situations, if any of the coefficients c, d, e, or f differ in sign, changes in R and I will tend to work in opposite directions in influencing B, and the net effect of a change in any of the coefficients on firms' behavior will depend on the relative magnitudes of all the coefficients. This can be seen by shifting the R curve upward in Figure 15.1(b); the effect will be to increase R but reduce I. In these circumstances, even if a is positive, changes in c or d that increase R need not increase B; the signs and relative magnitude of e and f would also have to be known in order to know how B would be affected. Similar conclusions apply to changes in e or f, which affect the level of I and firms' behavior.

Some readers may wonder why there is a minus sign in the denominator of the terms in parentheses in the reduced-form relationship (6), even when all the coefficients in the three underlying relationships (1), (2), and (3) are positive. The explanation is connected with the interaction between the d and f coefficients in relationships (2) and (3), and with the concept of a geometric progression. Any change in R will affect I by f times the change in R, as relationship (3) indicates; similarly, any change in I will affect R by d times the change in I, as relationship (2) indicates. Irrespective of whether c, d, e, or f changes, this will set in motion a series of changes in R and I that cumulatively add up to the eventual total effect on B. For example, an initial change in $R = \Delta R$ because of a change in c will cause the following stream of effects *on R:*

$$\Delta R + \Delta R f d + \Delta R (fd)^2 + \Delta R (fd)^3 \cdots + \Delta R (fd)^n$$

The second term in the preceding expression is obtained as follows: The initial change in R is multiplied by f to obtain the change in I that results from the initial change in R. The change in I is then multiplied by d to obtain the "feedback" effect of the initial change in R on R itself, via the resulting effect on I. The third term is obtained by taking the second term, Rfd, and repeating the preceding process; first multiplying by f to get the change in I, then multiplying by d to get the feedback effect on R of the second-stage change in R. By repeating this process for each term, one obtains the forgoing expression, which describes the *total* effect on R of an initial change in R. The expression is a geometric progression, since each successive term is equal to the preceding terms multiplied by fd. It can be shown that the sum of terms in any geometric progression is equal to: 1 minus the ratio between any two successive terms in the progression. In this example, this sum is $1/(1 - fd)$, and the total effect on R owing to the initial change in R is therefore equal to the following expression:

$$\Delta R \left(\frac{1}{1 - fd} \right)$$

A similar process of reasoning can easily demonstrate that the total change in I owing to any initial change in the level of I is equal to the following expression:

$$\Delta I\left(\frac{1}{1 - df}\right)$$

Any change in I, multiplied by d, yields the change in R caused by the change in I; when this change in R is multiplied by f, the result is the change in I owing to the feedback effect of the initial change in I on R. Repeating this process generates geometric progression identical to the one previously considered in connection with a change in R. The terms df and fd are of course identical. The larger the magnitude of f or d, the larger the feedback effects of changes in R on I, and changes in I on R, and the larger the total change in R and I that will result from any initial change in R or I, owing to changes in any of the coefficients in relationships (2) and (3). The reader should remember that f or d can be negative, so that changes in R and I need not be of the same sign; such a situation is illustrated in Figure 15.1(b), where f is negative.

The major implication of the preceding interactive relationship is that independent changes in regulation, industry structure, or other factors influencing business behavior are impossible. Changes in one of these factors will automatically imply changes in the other factors. The joint effects of different approaches to controlling business behavior must be considered and, in certain circumstances, carefully coordinated in order to achieve the desired effects on business behavior. In these circumstances, much of the controversy in the literature concerning different approaches to controlling business behavior becomes irrelevant and futile.

Interactive relationships between firms' behavior and alternative methods of influencing that behavior also have important implications for statistical studies that attempt to determine the nature of relationships among firms' behavior, regulation, and other determinants of firms' behavior. Unless these studies are very carefully formulated, and employ methods that attempt to determine the coefficients in the simultaneous relationships involved, their results may be misleading.

For example, if attention is focused only on the relationship between firms' behavior and dimensions of regulation, the coefficients in the statistical relationship linking regulation and firms' behavior may include both the *direct* impacts of regulation on firms' behavior and also the *indirect* impacts of regulation on firms' behavior that operate via the effect of regulation on industry structure or other determinants of firms' behavior. In these circumstances, the statistical coefficients are in effect combining coefficients such as a and the coefficients in parentheses in relationship (6), and are compatible with innumerable possible combinations of the underlying coefficients and relationships between regulation and other factors that determine firms' behavior. To change the impact of regulation on business behavior in any particular manner, it is necessary to know the underlying relationships in an interactive relationship; knowledge of the outcome of underlying interactions, in the form of statistical regression coefficients reflecting the net effects of the inter-actions, is of little use for this purpose.

Before concluding this section, it is necessary to point out that the criteria for choosing between alternative methods of influencing business behavior may include other factors in addition to the *feasibility* and *costs* of changing particular constraints or relationships that underlie business behavior, or the amount of *existing knowledge* about how these changes will change the behavior of firms. Other factors that may be relevant include the relative enforceability of different methods; their flexibility in response to changing conditions; and, perhaps most important of all in a political democracy, public acceptability.

In closing this section, the reader is reminded that industrial re-organization, reductions in entry barriers, and social responsibility of business are not the only possible means for influencing business be-havior. Taxes, government ownership, and moral suasion are a few of the many other possible means of influencing business behavior that can be and have been used in the United States and other countries. How-ever, each of these other means of influencing business behavior can also be viewed as additional constraints confronting business decision makers, and essentially the same analytical framework we have employed to discuss regulation and alternatives to regulation in this book may also be used to analyze these other means of influencing business behavior. Accordingly, the comments, principles, and conclusions contained in this section also apply to these other alternative means of influencing business behavior.

15.2   CONCLUDING COMMENTS

In this final section we shall adopt a broad perspective on the material that has been covered in this book and attempt to underline some of the major features of regulation our analysis has revealed and their implica-tions for future research aimed at improving our understanding of regulation. To accomplish this task, the discussion will be related to the accompanying diagrammatic relationship among several major character-istics of regulation.

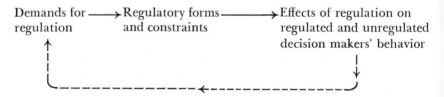

The direction of the solid arrows in the diagram reflects the tradi-tional view of the direction in which the forces that influence regulation typically flow.

A significant feature of traditional analyses of regulation is the general omission of the feedback of information regarding the effects of existing regulations and the implications of this information for the process by which demands for regulation are formed. This missing link is shown by the dashed-line arrows in the diagram. The most important implication of this link is that it transforms regulation from the static phenomenon that is implicit in virtually all traditional analyses of regulation to an evolving process that changes with the passage of time. The resulting shift of emphasis from a static to a dynamic view of regulation increases the number of factors that are relevant in determining the characteristics of regulation at any particular point in time, but it also provides additional insights that simplify the task of attempting to understand the determinants and effects of regulation.

The necessity of studying political processes in order to understand the mechanism by which demands for regulation are articulated is well known. The demand for regulation will reflect not only the preferences of individuals and interest groups but also their ability to influence the behavior of legislators and regulators who supply regulation. There are many means by which individuals may reveal their demands for regulation; and analyses of the political demand-revealing mechanism that include only voting, or political contributions, are likely to be seriously misleading. How people's preferences for regulation are initially formed has not been treated satisfactorily in the literature to date. Analyses of demands for regulation that assume "given" preferences for regulation are misleading, since the effects of existing regulations will usually influence people's preferences. Chapter 2 emphasized that people's demands for regulation will depend on their objectives and the constraints they face, and these constraints will, in turn, depend on the various roles people occupy. The list of possible objectives and constraints confronting individuals is infinite in number and form, however.

A more useful approach is to recognize that individuals face uncertain constraints, and the effects of existing and proposed regulatory constraints are correspondingly uncertain. In addition, people's perceptions about the effects of regulation will be influenced by information from a variety of sources that stand to benefit or lose from regulation, in addition to information from "neutral" sources. This information will often conflict and will often be a misrepresentation of the actual effects of regulation as perceived by the parties who provide the information. The process by which individuals form preferences and demands for regulation is obviously quite complicated when viewed from the preceding perspective. When feedback of information regarding the effects of existing regulations is added to the scenario, however, this constrains the behavior of parties to the regulatory process and influences the demand for regulation in a more predictable manner.

In the absence of feedback regarding the effects of existing regulations, there may be little connection between what legislators or regulators promise the people who demand regulation and what is delivered. There are a number of possible reasons for this. For example, in Chapter 5 it was explained that legislators and regulators may select regulations that are a compromise between the demands of different individuals and groups. Also, given the lack of information on the part of legislators and regulators regarding the constraints that determine how particular regulations will affect the behavior of regulated decision makers, even regulations that are adopted as a means of attempting to implement the wishes of groups who demand regulation will rarely have the intended consequences.

Once the feedback of information regarding the effects of existing regulations is taken into account, however, if the perceived effects of regulation differ greatly from the effects that were desired by the people who initially expressed demands for regulation, this can be expected to lead to changes in people's demands for regulation. In other words, the effects of regulation are not only an output but are also a major input into the evolving process of demands for regulation. According to this view of the relationship between the effects of existing regulations and demands for regulation, one would expect those regulations which are relatively successful in achieving the results people desire to survive, and to be followed by demands for similar types of regulation. Regulations that do not have the consequences desired by people who demand regulation will result in demands for regulatory reform, or even in demands for deregulation in cases of extreme dissatisfaction. Another important implication of this view is that demands for regulation will change with the passage of time.

In addition, it may be more helpful to view demands for regulation as demands for certain desired effects of regulation. Individuals cannot be expected to know all the effects of any particular regulatory constraint, or what kind of regulatory constraint is needed in order to achieve certain effects. Instead, people will usually demand regulation that achieves some limited set of effects desired by those people. These desired effects are not necessarily confined to the effects usually listed in textbooks on regulation. Regulation should not be viewed solely as a response to "market failures" such as the classic cases of monopoly or the presence of externalities that occur whenever transactions between two or more individuals affect third parties who do not participate in the transaction. Externalities are ubiquitous, in the sense that any action by one person always has effects on innumerable other people. This is true even in the case of market transactions where externalities of the traditional variety are completely absent; for example, if one person reduces his or her demand for a commodity, this reduces the market-clearing price of the product and benefits every other purchaser of the commodity!

Because externalities are associated with almost every action by any person, the existence of regulation cannot be explained solely by reference to the presence of externalities. Instead, regulation and regulatory constraints should be viewed as one of many alternative, but not mutually exclusive, means by which individuals may attempt to further their own personal objectives. Moreover, market transactions and political transactions between individuals occur side by side, and may be complementary rather than alternative means of achieving a person's objectives. Regulatory constraints on market and political dimensions of people's behavior affect the opportunities that are available to individuals, and the extent to which people participate in market and political transactions.

Economic and political markets are related and are never unregulated; the only relevant choice that confronts any society is a choice between different kinds of regulation, not between regulation or no regulation. From a descriptive point of view, the important question is not which activities have external effects. Rather, it is which external effects of certain activities are behaviorally relevant, in the sense that they motivate individuals sufficiently to reveal demands for regulating those particular effects and activities. From a normative point of view, the central issue is whose evaluations of the effects of activities "should" be used to evaluate the benefits and costs of those activities and to design appropriate regulatory constraints aimed at influencing the activities.

In focusing on information regarding the effects of existing regulations as a major determinant of people's evolving demands for regulation, we are not suggesting that this information is the only factor that underlies people's demands for regulation. People's objectives, roles, political and economic ideology, and other factors all will influence their demands for regulation at any point in time. However, any discrepancy between people's desired effects of regulation and the perceived effects will be the major factor that underlies *changes* in their demands for regulation.

The effects of regulation that people desire may usefully be viewed as "targets," and people's political and market behavior as the "instruments" people may change in order to achieve their targets. When the perceived effects of regulation differ from the effects people desire, there is a disequilibrium situation, and people will change some dimensions of their political or market behavior in an effort to remove this disequilibrium situation. The resulting disequilibrium path of people's political and economic behavior — including the type of regulations demanded and the effects of regulation at any particular point in time — will depend on the nature of the political and economic "disequilibrium adjustment rules" that describe how people change political and economic aspects of their behavior when existing effects of regulation differ from desired effects. The reader should note that the preceding view of the relationship between regulation and economic markets is the opposite of that which is contained in conventional approaches to regulation, which regard economic markets as the object of regulation. According to the preceding view of regulation as an evolving dynamic process resulting from feedback of information regarding effects of existing regulations, political and economic aspects of behavior are instruments that are used to change regulation in an effort to achieve people's desired effects of regulation.

The importance of feedback of information regarding the effects of existing forms of regulation greatly increases the importance of incentives for people to reveal information honestly. Information about the effects of regulation that is provided by regulated and unregulated decision makers, regulators, legislators, and analysts of regulation will not be reliable in the absence of incentive systems that motivate honest revelation of information by these individuals. Irrespective of the value system that is used to evaluate effects of regulation, the regulatory process can be improved by introducing incentive systems that motivate individuals to honestly reveal information regarding the effects of existing regulations.

Incentives for honest revelation of information are also important in connection with the normative problem of deciding whose value system should be used to evaluate the effects of activities and regulation. As we emphasized in Chapters 3 and 4, this problem is inescapable when evaluating effects of any activities or forms of regulation that simultaneously affect different people, and all types of regulation fall into this category. Irrespective of whose evaluations are adopted as the appropriate measure of the benefits and costs of regulation, it is desirable that these people be motivated to provide honest revelations of their evaluations of the effects of regulation.

Even when people's evaluations of the benefits and costs of regulated activities and regulation are honestly revealed, it should be remembered that these evaluations are based on the objectives and all the constraints that confront those individuals. These constraints include the degree of uncertainty regarding the precise form of the constraints that face each individual. They also include the individual's ability to process and evaluate conflicting information regarding the effects of regulation and their implications for the person's welfare. This information comes from a variety of sources that seek to influence the individual's evaluations of specific effects of certain activities or regulation of those activities. Any normative significance that is placed on people's evaluations therefore implicitly accepts all these constraints.

A major implication of the preceding points is that when regulation is viewed as a dynamic process that results from people's attempts to improve their personal satisfaction in a world of uncertainty and change, a shift of emphasis is required from static analyses of people's behavior to disequilibrium and dynamic analyses of their behavior. Much more attention needs to be devoted to the ways in which people react when information regarding the effects of existing regulations indicates that the effects that are desired by those individuals are not being achieved. These disequilibrium adjustment rules, together with the factors that underlie people's choice of targets describing their desired effects of regulation, are the two key aspects of behavior that determine the dynamic sequence of demands for regulation and effects of regulation through time.

As long as analyses of regulation continue to focus on static models of optimizing behavior under certainty regarding constraints, or omit the influence of feedback of information on the degree of uncertainty in models of behavior that incorporate uncertainty facing decision makers, progress toward understanding regulation will be slow. As Vickers (1979–80) has emphasized, only when uncertainty exists do individuals have any real choice. In the absence of any uncertainty regarding the constraints that confront an individual decision maker, the behavior that maximizes the individual's objectives is uniquely determined. The resulting process of human behavior has been described by McKenzie (1978, p. 639) as the theoretical equivalent of the walls of a rat maze through which the individual must run. Incorporating uncertainty regarding constraints in models of decision-maker behavior is not sufficient, however. In addition, it should be explicitly recognized that the degree of uncertainty is modified by feedback of information from the consequences of the individual's behavior in previous periods of time. The addition of feedback of information regarding the consequences of past behavior, together with the targets and disequilibrium adjustment rules employed by individuals, results in a behavioral system that underlies the dynamic process of behavior through time. This important principle has not been adequately recognized and incorporated into the existing literature on regulation.

References

CHAPTER 1

Blankenship, L. V. "The Social Context of Science." *Behavioral Models and Market Analysis,* edited by F. M. Nicosia and Y. Wind, chap. 2. Hinsdale, Ill.: Dryden Press, 1977.

Caldwell, B. "Positivist Philosophy of Science and the Methodology of Economics." *Journal of Economic Issues* (March 1980).

MacAvoy, P. W. *The Regulated Industries and the Economy.* New York: W. W. Norton, 1979.

McKie, J. W. "Regulation and the Free Market: The Problem of Boundaries." *Bell Journal of Economics and Management Science* (Spring 1960).

Mitnick, B. "The Concept of Regulation." *Bulletin of Business Research,* Center for Business and Economic Research, Ohio State University (May 1978).

Samuels, W. "Normative Premises in Regulatory Policy." *Journal of Post-Keynesian Economics* (Fall 1978).

U.S. Commission on Federal Paperwork. Final Summary Report. Washington, D.C.: U.S. Government Printing Office, 1977.

U.S. Government Accounting Office. *Federal Paperwork, Its Impact on American Businesses: Report to the Comptroller General of the United States.* Washington, D.C.: U.S. Government Printing Office, 1978.

Weidenbaum, M. L. *Business, Government and the Public.* 2d ed. Englewood Cliffs, N.J.: Prentice-Hall, 1981.

CHAPTER 2

Abrams, B. A., and R. F. Settle, "The Economic Theory of Regulation and Public Financing of Presidential Elections." *Journal of Political Economy.* Pt. 1 (April 1978): 245–257.

Archibald, G. C. " 'Large' and 'Small' Numbers in the Theory of the Firm." *Manchester School of Economic and Social Studies* (January 1959).

Argyris, C. "Ineffective Regulating Processes." *Regulating Business: The Search for an Optimum,* edited by C. Argyris et al. San Francisco: Institute for Contemporary Studies, 1978.

Auster, R., and M. Silver, "Collective Goods and Collective Decision Mechanisms." *Public Choice* (Spring 1973).

Bhagwati, J. "Lobbying and Welfare." *Journal of Public Economics* (December 1980).

Blankenship, L. V. "The Social Context of Science." In *Behavioral Models and Market Analysis*, edited by F. M. Nicosia and Y. Wind, chap. 2. Hinsdale, Ill.: Dryden Press, 1977.

Brennan, T. J. "Explanation and Value in Economics." *Journal of Economic Issues* (December 1979).

Brun, A. Review of "Property, Power, and Public Choice: An Inquiry into Law and Economics," by A. Schmid. *Journal of Economic Issues* (September 1979): 747–749.

Buchanan, J. "Towards an Analysis of Closed Behavioral Systems." In *The Economic Approach to Public Policy*, edited by R. C. Amacher, R. D. Tollison, and R. D. Willett. Ithaca, N.Y.: Cornell University Press, 1976.

Caldwell, B. "Positivist Philosophy of Science and the Methodology of Economics." *Journal of Economic Issues* (March 1980).

Caldwell, B. "A Critique of Friedman's Methodological Instrumentalism." *Southern Economic Journal* (October 1980).

Churchman, C. W. "Epilogue." In *Behavioral Models for Market Analysis*, edited by F. M. Nicosia and Y. Wind. Hinsdale, Ill.: Dryden Press, 1977.

Clark, E. H. "Multipart Pricing of Public Goods." *Public Choice* (Fall 1971).

Cohan, A. B. "Classification of the Reinvestment Assumption in Capital Analysis: Classification, Comment, Query." *Journal Business Research* (January 1975).

Elliot, J. E. "Fact, Value, and Economic Policy Objectives." *Review of Social Economy* (April 1980).

Ellis, M. G. "The Psychology of Learning Economics: A Dissatisfied Economist's View." *Journal of Economic Education* (Spring 1979).

Feldman, A. "Manipulating Voting Procedures." *Economic Inquiry* (July 1979).

Fiorina, M. P. and Noll, R. G. "Voters, Legislators and Bureaucrats: A Rational Choice Perspective on the Growth of Bureaucracy," *Journal of Public Economics* (April 1978).

Fisher, D., and A. Schotter, "The Inevitability of the Paradox of Redistribution in the Allocation of Voting Weights." *Public Choice* (1978): 49–67.

Friedman, Milton. "The Methodology of Positive Economics." In *Essays in Positive Economics*. Chicago: University of Chicago Press, 1953. Pp. 3–43.

Fusfeld, D. R. "The Conceptual Framework of Modern Economics." *Journal of Economic Issues* (March 1980).

Garner, C. A. "Academic Publication, Market Signalling, and Scientific Research Decisions." *Economic Inquiry* (October 1979).

Jarrell, G. A. "The Demand for State Regulation of the Electric Utility Industry." *Journal of Law and Economics* (October 1978).

Jordan, W. A. "Producer Protection, Prior Market Structure, and the Effects of Government Regulation." *Journal of Law and Economics* (April 1972).

Kapteyn, A., T. Wansbeck, and J. Buyze, "Maximizing, or Satisficing?" *Review of Economics and Statistics* (November 1979).

Lee, L. W. "A Just Theory of Regulation." *American Economic Review* (December 1980).

McGuire, T., Coiner, M., and L. Spancake, "Budget-Maximizing Agencies and Efficiency in Government." *Public Choice* 34 (1979): 333–357.

Machlup, F. *Methodology of Economics and Other Social Sciences.* New York: Academic Press, 1978. Chap. 17.

McKean, Roland N. "Collective Choice." In *Social Responsibility and the Business Predicament,* edited by J. W. McKie. Washington, D.C.: Brookings Institution, 1974.

McKenzie, R. B. "The Economic Basis of Departmental Discord in Academe." *Social Science Quarterly* (March 1979).

McKenzie, R. B., and H. H. Macaulay, "A Bureaucratic Theory of Regulation." *Public Choice* 35 (1980).

Mason, W. E. "Some Negative Thoughts on Friedman's Positive Economics." *Journal of Post-Keynesian Economics* (Winter 1980–81).

Mayer, T. "Economics as a Hard Science: Realistic Goal or Wishful Thinking?" *Economic Inquiry* (April 1980).

McKie, J. W. "Regulation and the Free Market: The Problem of Boundaries." *Bell Journal of Economics and Management Science* (Spring 1970).

Mieszkowski, P. "On the Theory of Tax Incidence." *Journal of Political Economy* (1967): 250–262.

Migue, J. L. "Controls versus Subsidies in the Economic Theory of Regulation." *Journal of Law and Economics* (April 1977).

Needham, D. *The Economics of Industrial Structure, Conduct and Performance.* Eastbourne: Holt, Rinehart & Winston Ltd., 1978. Pp. 61–63.

Nisbett, R. E., and T. D. Wilson, "Telling More Than We Can Know: Verbal Reports on Mental Processes." *Psychological Review* 84, no. 3 (May 1977).

Owen, B. M., and R. Braeutigam, *The Regulation Game: Strategic Use of the Administrative Process.* Cambridge, Mass.: Ballinger Publishing Co., 1978.

Peltzman, S. "Towards a More General Theory of Regulation" and "Comments" by J. Hirschleifer and G. Becker. *Journal of Law and Economics* (April 1972).

Phillips, A. "Introduction," In *Promoting Competition in Regulated Markets.* Washington, D.C.: Brookings Institution, 1975.

Posner, R. A. "Theories of Economic Regulation." *Bell Journal of Economics* (Autumn 1974).

Posner, R. A. "Taxation by Regulation." *Bell Journal of Economics* (Spring 1971).

Samuels, W. "Normative Premises in Regulatory Policy." *Journal of Post-Keynesian Economics* (Fall 1978).

Sandler, T., and J. T. Tschirhart, "The Economic Theory of Clubs: An Evaluative Survey." *Journal of Economic Literature* (December 1980).

Shaffer, J. D. "Observations on the Political Economics of Regulations." *American Journal of Agricultural Economics.* Pt. 2 (November 1979).

Shibata, H. "A Theory of Group Consumption and Group Formation." *Public Finance.* No. 3 (1979): 395–413.

Silberman, J., and G. Yochum, "The Market for Special-Interest Campaign Funds." *Public Choice* 35 (1980): 75–83.

Smythe, D. W. "Discussion." *American Economic Review,* Papers and Proceedings (December 1979): 403.

Stigler, G. J. "The Theory of Economic Regulation." *Bell Journal of Economics and Management Science* (Spring 1961).

Stigler, G. J. "Free Riders and Collective Action: An Appendix to Theories of Regulation." *Bell Journal of Economics* (Autumn 1974).

Tarascio, V. J., and B. Caldwell, "Theory Choice in Economics: Philosophy and Practice." *Journal of Economic Issues* (December 1979).

Tversky, A., and D. Kahneman, "Judgment Under Uncertainty: Heuristics and Biases." *Science* 185 (September 1974): 1124–1131.

Wald, H. P. "Comment: Normative Premises in Regulatory Theory." *Journal of Post-Keynesian Economics* 1 (1979): 126–129.

Weaver, P. H. "Regulation, Social Policy, and Class Conflict." In *Regulating Business: The Search for an Optimum,* edited by Chris Argyris et al. San Francisco: Institute for Contemporary Studies, 1978.

Weidenbaum, M. L. *The Future of Business Regulation: Private Action and Public Demand.* New York: Amacom, 1979.

Weitzman, M. L. "The Soviet Incentive Model." *Bell Journal of Economics* (Spring 1976).

Welch, W. P. "The Allocation of Political Monies: Economic Interest Groups." *Public Choice* 35 (1980): 97–120.

Wiles, P. "Ideology, Methodology, and Neoclassical Economics." *Journal of Post-Keynesian Economics* (Winter 1979–80).

Wilson, J. Q. "The Politics of Regulation." In *Social Responsibility and the Business Predicament,* edited by J. W. McKie. Washington, D.C.: Brookings Institution, 1974.

Wolfe, C., Jr. "A Theory of Non-Market Failure: Framework for Implementation Analysis." *Journal of Law and Economics* (April 1979).

CHAPTER 3

Adams, W. J., and J. L. Yellen, "Commodity Bundling and the Burden of Monopoly." *Quarterly Journal of Economics* (August 1976).

Baumol, W. J. "On the Discount Rate for Public Projects." In *Public Expenditure and Policy Analysis,* 2d ed. edited by R. H. Haveman and J. Margolis. Chicago: Rand-McNally, 1977.

Boadway, R. "The Welfare Foundations of Cost-Benefit Analysis." *Economic Journal* (December 1974).

Boadway, R. "Integrating Equity and Efficiency in Applied Welfare Economics." *Quarterly Journal of Economics* (November 1976).

Brent, R. J. "Distinguishing Between Money Income and Utility Income in Cost-Benefit Analysis." *Public Finance Quarterly* (April 1980).

Burns, M. E. "A Note on the Concept and Measure of Consumers' Surplus." *American Economic Review* (1963).

Canterberry, E. R., and H. P. Tuckman, "Reflections on the Income Distribution as a Pure Public Good." *Quarterly Journal of Economics* (May 1973).

Cohan, A. B. "Clarification of the Reinvestment Assumption in Capital Analysis: Clarification, Comment, Query." *Journal of Business Research* (January 1975).

Crean, J. F. "The Income Redistributive Effects of Public Spending on Higher Education." *Journal of Human Resources* (Winter 1975): 116–123.

Gramlich, E. M., and M. J. Wolkoff, "A Procedure for Evaluating Income Distribution Policies." *Journal of Human Resources* (Summer 1979).

Hansen, W. L., and B. A. Weishrod, "Distributional Effects of Public Expenditure Programs." *Public Finance* (1972): 414–420.

Harberger, A. C. "Three Basic Postulates for Applied Welfare Economics: An Interpretive Essay." *Journal of Economic Literature* (September 1971).

Harberger, A. C. "On the Use of Distributional Weights in Social Cost-Benefit Analysis." *Journal of Political Economy* 86 no. 2, pt. 2 (1978): S87–121.

Hettich, W. "Distribution in Benefit-Cost Analysis: A Revenue of Theoretical Issues." *Public Finance Quarterly* (April 1976): 123–149.

Hochman, H. M., J. D. Rodgers, and G. Tullock, "On the Income Distribution as a Public Good." *Quarterly Journal of Economics* (May 1973).

Jones-Lee, M. W. "The Value of Changes in the Probability of Death or Injury." *Journal of Political Economy* (July–August 1974).

Lane, R. E. "Markets and the Satisfaction of Human Wants." *Journal of Economic Issues* (December 1978): 799–827.

Layard, R., and L. Squire, "On the Use of Distributional Weights in Social Cost-Benefit Analysis" and "Reply" by A. C. Harberger. *Journal of Political Economy* (October 1980).

Linnertooth, J. "The Value of Human Life: A Review of the Models." *Economic Inquiry* (January 1979): 52–73.

Lyon, K. S. "Consumers Surplus When Consumers Are Subject to a Time and an Income Constraint." *Review of Economic Studies* (June 1978).

Mishan, E. J. *Economics for Social Decisions: Elements of Cost-Benefit Analysis,* New York: Praeger, 1972.

Mishan, E. J. *Cost-Benefit Analysis: An Introduction,* rev. ed. New York: Praeger, 1976.

Mishan, E. J. "How Valid Are Economic Evaluations of Allocative Changes?" *Journal of Economic Issues* (March 1980).

Mohring, H. "Alternative Measures of Welfare Gains and Losses." *Western Economic Journal* (December 1971): 42–52.

Morawetz, D. "The Social Rate of Discount, Targets and Instruments." *Public Finance* (1972).

Needham, D. *The Economics of Industrial Structure, Conduct and Performance,* Eastbourne: Holt, Rinehart, & Winston Ltd., 1978.

Pauly, M., and T. D. Willett, "Two Concepts of Equity and Their Implications for Public Policy." In *The Economic Approach to Public Policy,* edited by R. D. Amacher, R. D. Tollison, and T. D. Willett. Ithaca, N.Y.: Cornell University Press, 1976.

Ramsey, J. B. "The Marginal Efficiency of Capital, Internal Rate of Return, and Net Present Value: An Analysis of Investment Criteria." *Journal of Political Economy* (September–October 1970).

Schelling, T. C. "Ergonomics, or the Art of Self-Management." *American Economic Review,* Papers and Proceedings (May 1978): 290–294.

Silberberg, E. "Duality and the Many Consumer's Surpluses." *American Economic Review* (December 1972): 942–952.

Solomon, E. "The Arithmetic of Capital Budgeting Decisions." *Journal of Business* (April 1956).

Thurow, L. C. "The Income Distribution as a Pure Public Good." *Quarterly Journal of Economics* (May 1971).

Turvey, R. "Present Value versus Internal Rate of Return: An Essay in Third Best." *Economic Journal* (March 1963).

Weishrod, B. A. "Distribution Effects of Collective Goods." *Policy Analysis* 5, no. 1 (Winter 1979).

Westfield, F. M. "Methodology of Evaluating Economic Regulation." *American Economic Association,* Papers and Proceedings (May 1971): 211–217.

Whitaker, G. P. "Who Puts the Value in Evaluation?" *Social Science Quarterly* (March 1974).

Williams, A. "Cost-Benefit Analysis: Bastard Science? and/or Insidious Poison in the Body Politick?" *Journal of Public Economics* 1, no. 2 (August 1972): 199–226.

CHAPTER 4

Alchian, A. A. "Costs and Outputs." In *The Allocation of Economic Resources,* edited by M. Abramovitz. Palo Alto, Calif.: Stanford University Press, 1959. Reprinted in *Readings in Microeconomics,* edited by W. Breit and H. M. Hochman. New York: Holt, Rinehart & Winston, 1968.

Baumol, W. J., and A. G. Walton, "Full Costing, Competition, and Regulatory Practice." *Yale Law Journal* (March 1973).

Blois, K. J. "A Note on X-Efficiency and Profit Maximization." *Quarterly Journal of Economics* (May 1972).

Buchanan, J. M., and R. L. Faith, "Trying Again to Value a Life." *Journal of Public Economics* (October 1979): 245–247.

Dewey, D. "The Ambiguous Notion of Average Cost." *Journal of Industrial Economics* (July 1962).

Feldman, A. "Manipulating Voting Procedures." *Economic Inquiry* (July 1979).

Foster, E. "The Treatment of Rents in Cost-Benefit Analysis." *American Economic Review* (March 1981).

Hanushek, E. A. "Conceptual and Empirical Issues in the Estimation of Educational Production Functions." *Journal of Human Resources* (Summer 1979): 351–388.

Hirschleifer, J. "The Firm's Cost Function: A Successful Reconstruction?" *Journal of Business* (July 1962).

Latham, R. W., and D. Peel, "The Cost Function." *Bulletin of Economic Research* 28 (November 1976).

Leibenstein, H. "Allocative Efficiency vs. X-Efficiency." *American Economic Review* (June 1966).

Leibenstein, H. "Comment on the Nature of X-Efficiency." *Quarterly Journal of Economics* (May 1972).

Leibenstein, H. "Competition and X-Efficiency: Reply." *Journal of Political Economy* (May–June 1973).

Leibenstein, H. "Aspects of the X-Efficiency Theory of the Firm." *Bell Journal of Economics* (Autumn 1975).

Leibenstein, H. "X-Inefficiency Exists — Reply to an Exorcist." *American Economic Review* (March 1978a).

Leibenstein, H. L. "On the Basic Proposition of X-Efficiency Theory." *American Economic Review,* Papers and Proceedings (May 1978b): 328–332.

Littlechild, S. "Marginal Cost Pricing with Joint Costs." *Economic Journal* (June 1970).

McCain, R. A. "Competition, Information, Redundancy: X-Efficiency and the Cybernetics of the Firm." *Kyklos* 28 (1975): 286–308.

Needham, D. "Cost Conditions." In *The Economics of Industrial Structure,* Con-

duct, and Performance, chap. 2. Eastbourne: Holt, Rinehart, & Winston Ltd., 1978.

Pfouts, R. W. "Some Cost and Profit Relationships in the Multiproduct Firm." *Southern Economic Journal* (January 1973).

Primeaux, W. J., Jr. "An Assessment of X-Efficiency Gained Through Competition." *Review of Economics and Statistics* (February 1977).

Primeaux, W. J., Jr. "Some Problems with Natural Monopoly." *Antitrust Bulletin* (Spring 1979).

Pustay, M. W. "Industry Inefficiency Under Regulatory Surveillance." *Journal of Industrial Economics* (September 1978).

Smalls, I. S. "Hospital Cost Controls." *Management Accounting* (March 1973).

Turvey, R. "Marginal Cost." *Economic Journal* (June 1969).

Vaughn, K. I. "Does It Matter That Costs Are Subjective?" *Southern Economic Journal* (January 1980).

Weil, R. L. "Allocating Joint Costs." *American Economic Review* (December 1968).

Whitin, T. M. "Output Dimensions and Their Implications for Cost and Price Analysis." *Journal of Business* (April 1972).

Selected List of Cost-Benefit Studies

Felton, J. R. "The Costs and Benefits of Motor Truck Regulation." *Quarterly Review of Economics and Business* (Summer 1978): 7–20.

Ippolito, R. A., and R. T. Masson, "The Social Cost of Government Regulation of Milk." *Journal of Law and Economics* (April 1978): 33–65.

Moore, T. G. "The Beneficiaries of Trucking Regulation." *Journal of Law and Economics* (October 1978): 327–343.

Morici, P., Jr. "The Benefits and Costs of Crude Oil Price Regulations." *Journal of Energy Development* (Spring 1978): 366–377.

Porter, R. C. "A Social Benefit-Cost Analysis of Mandatory Deposits on Beverage Containers." *Journal of Environmental Economics and Management* 5 (1978): 351–375.

Zerbe, R. O., Jr. "The Costs and Benefits of Early Regulation of the Railroads." *Bell Journal of Economics* (Spring 1980).

CHAPTER 5

Abrams, B. A., and R. F. Settle, "The Economic Theory of Regulation and Public Financing of Presidential Elections." *Journal of Political Economy.* Pt. I (April 1978): 245–257.

Allewelt, W., Jr. "Bureaucratic Intervention, Economic Efficiency, and the Free Society: An Episode." Report Paper No. 5, Institute for Economic Research (May 1977).

Amacher, R. C., and W. J. Boyes, "Politicians and Policy: Responsiveness in American Government." *Southern Economic Journal* (October 1979).

Amacher, R. C., Tollison, R. D., and T. D. Willett, "A Budget Size in Democracy: A Review of the Arguments." *Public Finance Quarterly* (April 1975).

Bennett, J. T., and M. H. Johnson, "Paperwork and Bureaucracy." *Economic Inquiry* (July 1979a).

Bennett, J. T., and M. H. Johnson, "The Political Economy of Federal Government Paperwork." *Policy Review* 7 (Winter 1979*b*).

Blin, J. M., and M. A. Satterthwaite, "Strategy-Proofness and Single-Peakedness."
Public Choice (1976): 51–58.

Breton, A., and R. Wintrobe, "The Equilibrium Size of a Budget-Maximizing
Bureau: A Note on Niskanen's Theory of Bureaucracy." *Journal of Political
Economy* (February 1975).

Brock, W. A., and S. P. Magee, "The Economics of Special Interest Politics: The
Case of the Tariff." *American Economic Review,* Papers and Proceedings
(May 1978): 246–250.

Caleb, T. S. "Bureaucratic Performance and Budgetary Reward: A Test of the
Hypothesis with an Alternative Specification." *Public Choice* (Fall 1977).

Chan, K. S. "A Behavioral Theory of Bureaucracy." *Southern Economic Journal*
(April 1979).

Crain, W. M. "On the Structure and Stability of Political Markets." *Journal of
Political Economy* (August 1977): 829–841.

Cremer, J. "A Partial Theory of the Optimal Organization of a Bureaucracy."
Bell Journal of Economics (Autumn 1980).

Diver, C. S. "A Theory of Regulatory Enforcement." *Public Policy* (Summer
1980).

Duncan, W. J. "Organizations as Political Coalitions: A Behavioral View of
the Goal-Formation Process." *Journal of Behavioral Economics* (Summer
1976).

Eckert, R. D. "On the Incentives of Regulators: The Case of Taxicabs." *Public
Choice* (Spring 1973).

Erlich, I., and R. Posner, "Economic Analysis of Legal Rule Making." *Journal
of Legal Studies* (January 1974).

Ermer, V. "Strategies for Increasing Bureaucratic Responsiveness." *Policy Analysis*
(1979).

Feldman, A. "Manipulating Voting Procedures." *Economic Inquiry* (July 1979).

Ferejohn, J. A., and R. G. Noll, "Uncertainty and the Formal Theory of Political
Campaigns." *American Political Science Review* (June 1978).

Fiorina, M. P., and R. G. Noll, "Voters, Legislators, and Bureaucrats: A Rational
Choice Perspective on the Growth of Bureaucracy." *Journal Public Economics* (1978).

Fiorina, M. P., and C. R. Plott, "Committee Decisions under Majority Rule: An
Experimental Study." *American Political Science Review* (June 1978): 492–
505.

Fischer, D., and A. Schotter, "The Inevitability of the Paradox of Redistribution
in the Allocation of Voting Weights." *Public Choice* (1978): 49–67.

Forte, F., and A. di Pierro, "A Pure Model of Public Bureaucracy." *Public
Finance* 35, no. 1 (1980): 91–100.

Gibbard, A. "Manipulation of Voting Schemes: A General Result." *Econometrica*
(July 1973).

Goodin, R. E. "The Logic of Bureaucratic Back-Scratching." *Public Choice*
(Spring 1975).

Guttman, J. M. "Understanding Collective Action: Matching Behavior." *American Economic Review,* Papers and Proceedings (May 1978): 251–255.

Haveman, R. H. "Policy Analysis and the Congress: An Economist's View." In
Public Expenditure and Policy Analysis, edited by R. Haveman and J. Margolis. Chicago: Rand-McNally, 1977.

Heclo, H. "Political Executives and the Washington Bureaucracy." *Political Science Quarterly* (Fall 1977).

Hettich, W. "Bureaucrats and Public Goods." *Public Choice* (Spring 1975).

Hilton, G. W. "The Basic Behavior of Regulatory Commissions." *American Economic Review*, Papers and Proceedings (May 1972).

Holcombe, R. G., and E. O. Price, III. "Optimality and the Institutional Structure of Bureaucracy." *Public Choice* (1978): 55–58.

Jensen, R. C., and W. H. Meckling, "Can the Corporation Survive?" Reprint Paper No. 6, Institute for Economic Research (July 1977).

Johnson, R. J. "Campaign Spending and Votes: A Reconsideration." *Public Choice* 33 (1978): 83–92.

Jones, Bryan. "Competitiveness, Role Orientation, and Legislative Responsiveness." *Journal of Politics* (November 1973): 924–947.

Leibowitz, A., and R. Tollison, "A Theory of Legislative Organization: Making the Most of Your Majority." *Quarterly Journal of Economics* (March 1980).

McFadden, D. "The Revealed Preferences of a Government Bureaucracy: Empirical Evidence." *Bell Journal of Economics* (Spring 1976).

McGuire, T., M. Coiner and T. Spancake, "Budget-Maximizing Agencies and Efficiency in Government." *Public Choice* 34 (1979): 333–357.

Mackay, R. J., and C. L. Weaver, "In the Mutuality of Interests Between Bureaus and High Demand Committees: A Perverse Result." *Public Choice* 34 (1979).

McKean, Roland N. "Collective Choice." In *Social Responsibility and the Business Predicament*, edited by J. W. McKie. Washington, D.C.: Brookings Institution, 1974.

McKenzie, R. B., and H. H. Macaulay, "A Bureaucratic Theory of Regulation." *Public Choice* 35 (1980).

McKie, J. W. "Regulation and the Free Market: The Problem of Boundaries." *Bell Journal of Economics and Management Science* 1, no. 1 (Spring 1960).

Margolis, J. "Comment: Bureaucrats or Politicians," *Journal of Law and Economics* (December 1975).

Miller, G. J. "Bureaucratic Compliance as a Game on the Unit Square." *Public Choice* (Spring 1977).

Mohr, L. B. "The Concept of Organizational Goal." *American Political Science Review* (June 1973).

Niskanen, W. A. "The Peculiar Economics of Bureaucracy." *American Economic Review* (May 1968): 293–305.

Niskanen, W. A. *Bureaucracy and Representative Government*. Chicago: Aldine-Atherton, 1971.

Niskanen, W. A. "Bureaucrats and Politicians." *Journal of Law and Economics* (December 1975).

Peltzman, E. "Towards a More General Theory of Regulation." *Journal of Law and Economics* (August 1976).

Plott, C. R., and M. E. Levine, "A Model of Agenda Influence on Committee Decisions." *American Economic Review* (March 1978): 146–150.

Posner, R. "The Behavior of Administrative Agencies." *Journal of Legal Studies* (June 1972).

Romer, T., and H. Rosenthal, "Political Resource Allocation, Controlled Agendas, and the Status Quo." *Public Choice* 33 (1978): 27–43.

Romer, T., and H. Rosenthal, "The Elusive Median Voter." *Journal of Public Economics* (October 1979).

Rycroft, R. W. "Bureaucratic Performance in Energy Policy Making: An Evalua-

tion of Output Efficiency and Equity in the Federal Energy Administration."
Public Policy (Fall 1978).

Sabbatier, P. A. "Regulatory Policy Making: Toward a Framework of Analysis."
Natural Resources Journal (July 1977).

Sandler, T., and J. T. Tschirhart, "The Economic Theory of Clubs: An Evaluative Survey." *Journal of Economic Literature* (December 1980).

Satterthwaite, M. A., "The Existence of a Strategy Proof Voting Procedure: A
Topic in Social Choice Theory," Ph.D. Dissertation, University of Wisconsin,
1973.

Schwert, G. W. "Public Regulation of Natural Security Exchanges: A Test of
the Capture Hypothesis." *Bell Journal of Economics* (Spring 1977).

Stockfisch, J. A. *The Political Economy of Bureaucracy*. New York: General
Learning Press, 1972.

Thompson, E. A. Book review of *Bureaucracy and Representative Government*
by W. A. Niskanen. *Journal of Economic Literature* 11, no. 3 (September
1973): 950–953.

U.S. General Accounting Office, *Federal Paperwork: Its Impact on American
Business: Report by the Comptroller General of the United States*. Report
No. GGD-79-4. (Washington, D.C.: U.S. Government Printing Office, 1978).

Warren, R. S., Jr. "Bureaucratic Performance and Budgetary Reward." *Public
Choice* (June 1975).

Williamson, O. E. *Markets and Hierarchies: Analysis and Antitrust Implications*.
New York: The Free Press, 1975.

Williamson, O. E. Markets, Hierarchies: Some Elementary Considerations."
American Economic Review, Papers and Proceedings (May 1977).

Wilson, J. Q., ed. *The Politics of Regulation*. New York: Basic Books, 1979.

Wittman, D. "Candidates with Policy Preferences: A Dynamic Model." *Journal
of Economic Theory* (February 1977): 180–189.

Wittman, D. A. "Parties as Utility Maximizers." *American Political Science
Review* (June 1978).

Wolf, C., Jr. "A Theory of Nonmarket Failure: Framework for Implementation
Analysis." *Journal of Law and Economics* (April 1979): 107–139.

Wright, C. L. "A Note on the Decision Rules of Public Regulatory Agencies."
Public Choice (Spring 1973).

CHAPTER 6

(i) *Antitrust Laws, Policies, and Agencies*

Asch, P. "The Determinants and Effects of Antitrust Policy." *Journal of Law and
Economics* (October 1975).

Blair, R. D., and D. Kaserman, "Market Structure and Costs: An Explanation
of the Behavior of Antitrust Authorities." *Antitrust Bulletin* (Winter 1976).

Bork, R. H. "The Goals of Antitrust Policy." *American Economic Review,* Papers
and Proceedings (May 1967).

Comanor, W. S. "The Nader Report and the Limits of Antitrust." *Public Policy*
(Summer 1972).

Demsetz, H. "Economics as a Guide to Antitrust." *Journal of Law and Economics*
(August 1976).

Elzinga, K., and W. Breit, *The Antitrust Penalties: A Study in Law and Economics.* New Haven: Yale University Press, 1976.

Kauper, T. E. "The Goals of United States Antitrust Policy — The Current Debate." *Zeitschrift f.d. gesamte Staatswissenschaft* 136, no. 3 (September 1980).

Lee, L. W. "Some Models of Antitrust Enforcement." *Southern Economic Journal* (July 1980).

Long, W., R. Schramm, and R. Tollison, "The Economic Determinants of Antitrust Activity." *Journal of Law and Economics* (October 1973).

Masson, R. T., and R. J. Reynolds, "Statistical Studies of Antitrust Enforcement: A Critique." *American Statistical Association Proceedings,* Business and Economics Section, Pt. I (1977): 22–28.

Menzines, B. J. "The Robinson Patman Act: Current Developments." *Antitrust Bulletin* (Winter 1979).

Nann, H. M., and J. Meehan, "Policy Planning for Antitrust Activities: Present Status and Future Prospects." In *The Antitrust Dilemma,* edited by Dalton and Levin. Lexington, Mass.: D.C. Heath, 1974.

Posner, R. A. "Oligopoly and the Antitrust Laws: A Suggested Approach." *Stanford Law Review* (June 1968).

Posner, R. A. "A Statistical Study of Antitrust Enforcement." *Journal of Law and Economics* (October 1970).

Posner, R. "The Behavior of Administrative Agencies." *Journal of Legal Studies* (June 1972).

Posner, R. A. *Antitrust Law: An Economic Perspective.* Chicago: University of Chicago Press, 1976).

Reynolds, R., and B. Reeves, "The Economics of Potential Competition." In *Essays in Industrial Organization* in Honor of Joe S. Bain, edited by Masson and Qualls. Cambridge, Mass.: Ballinger, 1976.

Rowe, F. M. "Political Objectives and Economic Effects of the Robinson-Patman Act: A Conspicuous U.S. Antitrust Policy Failure." *Zeitschrift f.d. gesamte Staatswissenschaft* (September 1980).

Siegfried, J. J. "The Determinants of Antitrust Activity." *Journal of Law and Economics* (October 1975).

Spitzer, M. L. "Multicriteria Choice Processes: An Application of Public Choice Theory to Bakke, the FCC, and the Courts." *Yale Law Journal* (March 1979): 717–779.

Weiss, L. W. "An Analysis of the Allocation of Antitrust Division Resources." In *1973 Benefit-Cost Analysis,* Chap. 16. Chicago: Aldine, 1974.

(ii) *Theory and Measurement of Monopoly Welfare Losses*

Adams, W. J., and J. L. Yellen, "Commodity Bundling and the Burden of Monopoly." *Quarterly Journal of Economics* (August 1976).

Baumol, W. J., and D. F. Bradford, "Optimal Departures from Marginal-Cost Pricing." *American Economic Review* (June 1970).

Bergson, A. "On Monopoly Welfare Losses." *American Economic Review* (December 1973). "Reply" (December 1975).

Comaner, W. S., and H. Leibenstein, "Allocative Efficiency, X-Efficiency, and the Measurement of Welfare Losses." *Economica* (August 1969).

Cowling, K., and D. C. Mueller, "The Social Costs of Monopoly Power." *Economic Journal* (December 1978): 727–748.

Foster, E. "The Treatment of Rents in Cost-Benefit Analysis." *American Economic Review* (March 1981).

Friedland, T. S. "The Estimation of Welfare Gains from Demonopolization." *Southern Economic Journal* (July 1978).

Goldberg, V. P. "A Note on the Costs of Monopoly." *Antitrust Bulletin* (Summer 1972).

Goldberg, V. P. "Welfare Loss and Monopoly: The Unmaking of an Estimate." *Economic Inquiry* (April 1978).

Harberger, A. C. "Monopoly and Resource Allocation." *American Economic Review* (May 1954).

Hause, J. C. "The Theory of Welfare Cost Measurement." *Journal of Political Economy* (December 1975).

Jensen, M. C., and W. H. Meckling, "Can the Corporation Survive?" Reprint Paper #5, *International Institute for Economic Research* (July 1977).

Krueger, A. O. "The Political Economy of the Rent-Seeking Society." *American Economic Review* (June 1974).

Miller, E. M. "Effect of Monopoly on Income, Interest, and Capital." *American Journal of Economics and Sociology* (October 1978).

Mueller, G. E. "Lawyers' Guide to the Welfare-Loss Concept: An Introduction." *Antitrust Law and Economics Review* (Spring 1972).

Needham, D., "Welfare-Loss Measures, Relevant Elasticities & Price-Cost Margins and Rent-Seeking Activities," *Western Kentucky University College of Business Administration Working Paper Series,* Vol. 1, No. 5, April 1982.

Needham, D. *The Economics of Industrial Structure, Conduct and Performance.* Eastbourne: Holt, Rinehart, & Winston Ltd., 1978. Chap. 10, pp. 229–249.

Posner, R. A. "The Social Costs of Monopoly and Regulation." *Journal of Political Economy* (August 1975).

Satterthwaite, M. "Consumer Information, Equilibrium Industry Price, and the Number of Sellers." *Bell Journal of Economics* (Autumn 1979).

Schwartzman, D. "The Expected Profits Methods of Locating Monopoly Power." *Antitrust Bulletin* (Winter 1972).

Shepherd, W. G. "The Yields from Abating Market Power." *Industrial Organization Review* 1 (1973).

Siegfried, J. J., and T. K. Tiemann, "The Welfare Cost of Monopoly: An Interindustry Analysis." *Economic Inquiry* (June 1974).

Skogh, G. "The Social Costs of Monopoly and Regulation: Some Comments." *Journal of Political Economy* (December 1976).

Tullock, G. "The Welfare Cost of Tariffs, Monopolies and Theft." *Western Economic Journal* (June 1967).

West, E. G. "The Burdens of Monopoly: Classical versus Neoclassical." *Southern Economic Journal* (April 1978).

Worcester, D. A. "New Estimates of the Welfare Loss to Monopoly in the U.S. 1959–1969." *Southern Economic Journal* (October 1973).

Worcester, D. A. "On Monopoly Welfare Losses." *American Economic Review* (December 1975).

(iii) *Relevant Market Definition*

Dorward, N. "Market Areas, Buyer Behavior and Industrial Concentration in a Product Differentiated Market." *Applied Economics* (1978).

Dorward, N. M., and M. J. Wise, "Market Areas in Product Differentiated Industries: Some Conceptual and Empirical Approaches." *Economic Geography* (January 1978).

Elzinga, K. G., and K. Hogarty, "The Problem of Geographic Market Delineation in Antimerger Suits." *Antitrust Bulletin* (Spring 1963).

Huff, D. L., and R. R. Batesell, "Delimiting the Areal Extent of a Market." *Journal of Marketing Research* (November 1977).

Needham, D. *The Economics of Industrial Structure, Conduct, and Performance.* Eastbourne: Holt, Rinehart, & Winston Ltd., 1978. Chap. 5.

Pace, J. D. "Relevant Markets and the Nature of Competition in the Electric Utility Industry." *Antitrust Bulletin* (Winter 1970).

Raab, R. L. "Delineating the Relevant Market from Census Industry Classifications." *Antitrust Bulletin* (Fall 1977).

Schnabel, M. "Defining a Product." *Journal of Business* (October 1976).

Schwartzman, D. "The Cross-Elasticity of Demand and Industry Boundaries: Coal, Oil, Gas, and Uranium." *Antitrust Bulletin* (Fall 1973).

Wind, Y. "Issues and Advances in Segmentation Research." *Journal of Marketing Research* (August 1978): 315–337.

Young, S., L. Ott, and B. Feigin, "Some Practical Considerations in Market Segmentation." *Journal of Marketing Research* (August 1978): 405–412.

CHAPTER 7

(i) *Alternative Concepts of Competition*

Anderson, F. J. "Market Performance and Conjectural Variation." *Southern Economic Journal* (July 1977).

Archibald, G. C. "Large and Small Numbers in the Theory of the Firm." *Manchester School of Economics & Social Studies* (January 1959).

Bernhard, R. C. "Competition in Law and Economics." *Antitrust Bulletin* (1967).

Bernhard, R. C. "Divergent Concepts of Competition in Antitrust Cases." *Antitrust Bulletin* (Spring 1970).

Enthoven, A. C. "How Interest Groups Have Responded to a Proposal for Economic Competition in Health Services." *American Economic Review,* Papers & Proceedings (May 1980): 146–156.

Fama, E. F., and A. B. Laffer, "The Number of Firms and Competition." *American Economic Review* (September 1972).

Gollop, F. M., and M. J. Roberts, "Firm Interdependence in Oligopolistic Markets." *Journal of Econometrics* (August 1979): 313–331.

Grether, E. T. "Competition Policy in the U.S.: Looking Ahead." *California Management Review* (Summer 1974).

Jacoby, N. H. "Antitrust or Pro Competition?" *California Management Review* (Summer 1974).

Jensen, M. H., and W. H. Meckling, "Can the Corporation Survive?" International Institute for Economic Research, Reprint Paper No. 6 (July 1977).

Kalish, L., H. J. Cassidy, and J. Hartzog, "Potential Competition: The Probability of Entry with Mutually Aware Potential Entrants." *Southern Economic Journal* (January 1978).

Lambin, J. J., P. A. Naert, and A. Bultez, "Optimal Marketing Behavior in Oligopoly." *European Economic Review* (April 1975).

McCormick, R. E., and R. D. Tollison, "Rent-Seeking Competition in Political Parties." *Public Choice* 34 (1979): 5–14.

Marris, R., and D. C. Mueller, "The Corporation and Competition." *Journal of Economic Literature* (March 1980).

Needham, D., *Economic Analysis and Industrial Structure* (New York: Holt, Rinehart & Winston, 1969).

Needham, D. *The Economics of Industrial Structure, Conduct and Performance.* Eastbourne: Holt, Rinehart, & Winston Ltd., 1978*a*. Chap. 4 (pp. 61–63), chaps. 5 and 7.

Needham, D. "Pricing Behavior, Seller Concentration and Entry Barriers: An Analytical Framework." *Industrial Organization Review* 6 no. 1 (1978*b*).

Nutter, G. W., and J. H. Moore, "A Theory of Competition." *Journal of Law and Economics* (April 1976).

Panzar, J., and R. Willig, "Free Entry and the Sustainability of Natural Monopoly." *Bell Journal of Economics* (Spring 1977).

Phillips, A., ed. *Promoting Competition in Regulated Markets.* Washington, D.C.: Brookings Institution, 1975.

Porter, M. E., and J. F. Sagansky, "Information, Politics, and Economic Analysis: The Regulatory Decision Process in the Air Freight Cases." *Public Policy* (Spring 1976).

Preston, L. E., and B. King, "Proving Competition." *Antitrust Bulletin* (Winter 1979).

Primeaux, W. J., Jr. "Some Problems with Natural Monopoly." *Antitrust Bulletin* (Spring 1979).

Pustay, M. W. "The Transatlantic Airline Market: Exploring the Myths of Excessive, Unfair, and Predatory Competition." *Quarterly Review of Economics and Business* (Summer 1979).

Rosenthal, R. W. "A Model in Which an Increase in the Number of Sellers Leads to a Higher Price." *Econometrica* (September 1980).

Satterthwaite, M. "Consumer Information, Equilibrium Industry Price, and the Number of Sellers." *Bell Journal of Economics* (Autumn 1979).

Sherman, R. "Competition over Competition." *Public Policy* (Fall 1972).

Sherman, R., and T. D. Willett, "Potential Entrants Discourage Entry." *Journal of Political Economy* (August 1967).

Stigler, G. J. "A Theory of Oligopoly." *Journal of Political Economy* (February 1964).

Van der Weide, J. H., and J. H. Zalkind, "Deregulation and Oligopolistic Price-Quality Rivalry." *American Economic Review* (March 1981).

(ii) *Predatory Pricing and Competition*

Areeda, P., and D. F. Turner, "Predatory Pricing and Related Practices Under Section 2 of the Sherman Act." *Harvard Law Review* (February 1975): 697–733.

Areeda, P., and D. F. Turner, "Scherer on Predatory Pricing: A Reply." *Harvard Law Review* (1976): 891–900.

Areeda, P., and D. F. Turner, "Predatory Pricing: A Rejoinder." *Yale Law Journal* (July 1979).

Baumol, W. J. "On the Proper Tests for Natural Monopoly in a Multiproduct Industry." *American Economic Review* (December 1977).

Baumol, W. J. "Quasi-Permanence of Price Reductions — A Policy for Prevention of Predatory Pricing." *Yale Law Journal* (1979).

Joskow, P. L., and A. K. Klevorick, "A Framework for Analyzing Predatory Pricing." *Yale Law Journal* (December 1979).

Koller, R. H. "When Is Pricing Predatory?" *Antitrust Bulletin* (Summer 1979).

McGee, J. S. "Predatory Pricing Revisited." *Journal of Law and Economics* (October 1980).

McGee, J. S. "Predatory Price-Cutting: The Standard Oil (N.J.) Case." *Journal of Law and Economics* (October 1958): 137–169.

Scherer, F. M. "Predatory Pricing and the Sherman Act: A Comment." *Harvard Law Review* (1976):869–890.

Scherer, F. M. "Some Last Words on Predatory Pricing." *Harvard Law Review* (1976): 901–903.

Stiglitz, J. "Potential Competition May Reduce Welfare." *American Economic Review, Papers and Proceedings* (May 1981): 184–189.

Telser, L. G. "Cutthroat Competition and the Long Purse." *Journal of Law and Economics* (October 1966): 259–277.

Williamson, O. E. "Predatory Pricing: A Strategic and Welfare Analysis." *Yale Law Journal* 87 (1977).

Williamson, O. E. "Williamson on Predatory Pricing II." *Yale Law Journal* (May 1979).

CHAPTER 8

(i) *Rationale of Regulating Monopoly*

Green, M., and R. Nader, "Economic Regulation vs. Competition: Uncle Sam the Monopoly Man." *Yale Law Journal* (April 1973).

Koller, R. H. H. "Why Regulate Utilities? To Control Price Discrimination." *Journal of Law and Economics* (April 1973).

Marris, R., and D. C. Mueller, "The Corporation and Competition." *Journal of Economic Literature* (March 1980).

Needham, D. "Entry Barriers and Non-Price Aspects of Firms' Behavior." *Journal of Industrial Economics* (September 1976).

Needham, D. *The Economics of Industrial Structure, Conduct and Performance.* Eastbourne: Holt, Rinehart & Winston Ltd., 1978. Chap. 10, pp. 229–240.

Panzar, J., and R. D. Willig, "Free Entry and the Sustainability of Natural Monopoly." *Bell Journal of Economics* (Spring 1977).

Preston, L. E., and J. Post, "Proving Competition." *Antitrust Bulletin* (Winter 1979).

Primeaux, W. J. "Some Problems with Natural Monopoly." *Antitrust Bulletin* (Spring 1979).

Telser, L. "On the Regulation of Industry: A Note." *Journal of Political Economy* (November 1969) and "Reply" by H. Demsetz and "Rejoinder" by Telser (March–April 1971) and "Correction" by Telser (July–August 1971).

(ii) *Effects of Rate-of-Return Regulation on Technical Efficiency and Costs*

Averch, H., and L. L. Johnson, "Behavior of the Firm Under Regulatory Constraints. *American Economic Review* (December 1962).

Bailey, E., and R. D. Coleman, "The Effect of Lagged Regulation in an A-J Model." *Bell Journal of Economics and Management Science* (Spring 1970).

Bailey, E. E., and J. C. Malone, "Resource Allocation in the Regulated Firm." *Bell Journal of Economics and Management Science* (Spring 1970).

Baumol, W. J., and A. K. Klevorick, "The A-J Thesis: Input Choices and Rate of Return Regulation: An Overview of the Discussion." *Bell Journal of Economics and Management Science* (Autumn 1970).

Boyes, W. J. "An Empirical Examination of the Averch-Johnson Effect." *Economic Inquiry* (March 1976).

Callen, J., G. F. Mathewson, and H. Mohring, "The Benefits and Costs of Rate of Return Regulation." *American Economic Review* (June 1976).

Corey, G. R. "The A-J Proposition: A Critical Analysis." *Bell Journal of Economics and Management Science* (Spring 1971).

Courville, L. "Regulation and Efficiency in the Electric Utility Industry." *Bell Journal of Economics and Management Science* (Spring 1974).

Cross, J. G. "Incentive Pricing and Utility Regulation." *Quarterly Journal of Economics* (May 1970).

Das, S. P. "On the Effect of Rate of Return Regulation Under Uncertainty." *American Economic Review* (June 1980): 456–460.

Edelson, N. M. "Resource Allocation and the Regulated Firm." *Bell Journal of Economics and Management Science* (Spring 1971).

Hayashi, P. M., and J. M. Trapani, "Rate of Return Regulation and the Firm's Equilibrium Capital-Labor Ratio: Further Empirical Evidence on the Averch-Johnson Hypothesis." *Southern Economic Journal* (January 1976).

Holthausen, D. M. "A Model of Incentive Regulation." *Journal of Public Economics* (August 1979).

Johnson, L. L. "Behavior of the Firm Under Regulatory Constraint: A Reassessment." *American Economic Review,* Papers and Proceedings (May 1973).

Kafoglis, M. Z. "Output of the Restrained Firm" *American Economic Review* and "Comment" (September 1969).

Kahn, A. E. "The Graduated Fair Return: Comment." *American Economic Review* (March 1968).

Klevorick, A. "The Graduated Fair Return: A Regulatory Proposal." *American Economic Review* (June 1966).

Loeb, M., and W. Magat. "A Decentralized Method for Utility Regulation." *Journal of Law and Economics* (1979): 399–404.

Peles, Y. C., and J. L. Stein, "The Effect of Rate of Return Regulation Is Highly Sensitive to the Nature of Uncertainty." *American Economic Review* (June 1976).

Peterson, H. C. "An Empirical Test of Regulatory Effects." *Bell Journal of Economics and Management Science* (Spring 1975).

Smithson, C. W. "The Degree of Regulation and the Monopoly Firm: Further Empirical Evidence." *Southern Economic Journal* 79, no. 3 (1977): 568–580.

Spann, R. M. "Rate of Return Regulation and Efficiency in Production: An Empirical Test of the A-J Thesis." *Bell Journal of Economics and Management Science* (Spring 1974).

Wichers, C. R. "The Graduated Fair Return: Comment." *American Economic Review* (September 1971).

Zajac, E. E. "Geometric Treatment of Averch-Johnson's Behavior of the Firm Under Regulatory Constraint." *American Economic Review* (March 1970) and "Comment" by R. J. Stonebraker, and "Reply" by Zajac, *American Economic Review* (March 1972).

Zajac, E. E. "A Note on 'Gold-Plating' or 'Rate-Base Padding.' " *Bell Journal of Economics and Management Science* (Spring 1972).

(iii) *Effects of Rate-of-Return Regulation on Pricing Behavior and Allocative Efficiency*

Baumol, W. J., and D. F. Bradford, "Optimal Departures from Marginal Cost Pricing." *American Economic Review* (June 1970).

Bergson, A. "Optimal Pricing for a Public Enterprise." *Quarterly Journal of Economics* (November 1972).

Boiteux, M. "On the Management of Public Monopolies Subject to Budgetary Constraints." *Journal of Economic Theory* (September 1971).

Coase, R. H. "The Theory of Public Utility Pricing." *Bell Journal of Economics and Management Science* (Spring 1971).

Craven, J. "On the Choice of Optimal Time Periods for a Surplus-Maximizing Utility Subject to Fluctuating Demand." *Bell Journal of Economics and Management Science* (Autumn 1971).

Craven, J. "Space-Time Pricing for Public Utilities." *Bell Journal of Economics and Management Science* (Spring 1974).

Goddard, F. O. "On the Effectiveness of Regulation of Electric Utility Prices: Comment." *Southern Economic Journal* (July 1971).

Joskow, P. L. "Pricing Decisions in Regulated Firms: A Behavioral Approach." *Bell Journal of Economics and Management Science* (Spring 1973)

Klevorick, A. "The Optimal Fair Rate of Return." *Bell Journal of Economics and Management Science* (Spring 1971).

Moore, C. G. "Has Electricity Regulation Resulted in Higher Prices?" *Economic Inquiry* (June 1975).

Moore, T. G. "The Effectiveness of Regulation of Electric Utility Prices." *Southern Economic Journal* (April 1970).

Needy, C. W. "Social Cost of the A. J. W. Output Distortion." *Southern Economic Journal* (January 1976).

Pelzman, S. "Pricing in Public and Private Enterprises: Electric Utilities in the U.S." *Journal of Law and Economics* (April 1971).

Ramsey, F. P. "A Contribution to the Theory of Taxation." *Economic Journal* 37 (March 1927): 47–61.

Rees, R. "Second-Best Rules for Public Enterprise Pricing." *Economica* (August 1968).

Scheidell, J. M., "The Relevance of Demanded Elasticity for Rate-of-Return Regulation," *Southern Economic Journal* (October 1976).

464

References

(iv) *Behavior of Regulatory Commissions*

Blume, M. "On the Assessment of Risk." *Journal of Finance* 26 (March 1971).

Breen, W. J., and E. M. Lerner, "On the Use of β in Regulatory Proceedings." *Bell Journal of Economics and Management Science* (Autumn 1972).

Copeland, B. L., Jr. "Alternative Cost-of-Capital Concepts in Regulation." *Land Economics* (August 1978): 348–361.

Davis, E. G. "A Dynamic Model of the Regulated Firm with a Price Adjustment Mechanism." *Bell Journal of Economics and Management Science* (Spring 1973).

Eckert, R. D. "On the Incentives of Regulators: The Case of Taxicabs." *Public Choice* (Spring 1973).

Hagerman, R. L., and B. T. Ratchford, "Some Determinants of Allowed Rates of Return on Equity to Electric Utilities." *Bell Journal of Economics* (Spring 1978).

Hilton, G. W. "The Basic Behavior of Regulatory Commissions." *American Economic Review,* Papers and Proceedings (May 1972).

Joskow, P. L. "The Determination of the Allowed Rate of Return in a Formal Regulatory Hearing." *Bell Journal of Economics and Management Science* (Autumn 1972).

Levy, R. A. "On the Short-Term Stationarity of Beta Coefficients." *Financial Analysts Journal* (November–December 1971).

McFadden, D. "The Revealed Preferences of a Government Bureaucracy: Empirical Evidence." *Bell Journal of Economics* (Spring 1976).

Pettway, R. H. "On the Use of β in Regulatory Proceedings: An Empirical Examination." *Bell Journal of Economics* (Spring 1978).

Roberts, R. B., G. S. Maddala, and G. Enholm, "Determinants of the Requested Rate of Return and the Rate of Return Granted in a Formal Regulatory Process." *Bell Journal of Economics* (Autumn 1978).

Robichek, A. A. "Regulation and Modern Finance Theory." *Journal of Finance* (June 1978).

Russell, M., and R. B. Shelton, "A Model of Regulatory Agency Behavior." *Public Choice* (Winter 1974).

Sibley, D. S., and E. E. Bailey, "Regulatory Commission Behavior: Myopic versus Forward Looking." *Economic Inquiry* (April 1978).

Solomon, E. "Alternative Rate of Return Concepts and Their Implications for Utility Regulation." *Bell Journal of Economics and Management Science* (Spring 1970).

Spann, R. M. "The Regulatory Cobweb: Inflation, Deflation, Regulatory Lags and the Effects of Alternative Administrative Rules in Public Utilities." *Southern Economic Journal* (July 1976).

Wright, C. L. "A Note on the Decision Rules of Public Regulatory Agencies." *Public Choice* (Fall 1979).

CHAPTER 9

(i) *Multiproduct Firms and the Rationale of Regulation*

Baumol, W. J. "On the Proper Tests for Natural Monopoly in a Multiproduct Industry." *American Economic Review* (December 1977).

Baumol, W. J., E. E. Bailey, and R. D. Willig, "Weak Invisible Hand Theorems on the Sustainability of Prices in a Multiproduct Monopoly." *American Economic Review* (June 1977).

Faulhaber, G. R. "Cross-Subsidization: Pricing in Public Enterprises." *American Economic Review* (December 1975).

Panzar, J., and R. Willig, "Free Entry and the Sustainability of Natural Monopoly." *Bell Journal of Economics* (Spring 1977).

Willig, R. "Multiproduct Technology and Market Structure." *American Economic Review*, Papers and Proceedings (May 1979).

(ii) *Product Pricing and Regulation in Multiproduct Firms*

Bailey, E. J. "Peak-Load Pricing Under Regulatory Constraint." *Journal of Political Economy* (July–August 1972).

Baumol, W. J. "Optimal Depreciation Policy: Pricing the Products of Durable Assets." *Bell Journal of Economics and Management Science* (Autumn 1971).

Baumol, W., D. Fischer, and T. Ten Raa, "The Price-Iso Return Locus and Rational Rate Regulation." *Bell Journal of Economics* (Autumn 1979).

Boiteux, M. "Peak-Load Pricing." *Journal of Business* (April 1960).

Crew, M. A., and P. Kleindorfer, "Marshall and Turvey on Peak Load or Joint Producing Pricing." *Journal of Political Economy* (November–December 1971).

Crew, M. A., and P. Kleindorfer, "Recent Contributions to the Problem of Marginal Cost Pricing: The Problem of Peak Loads." *Economic Journal* (December 1971).

Crew, M. A., and P. R. Kleindorfer, "On Off-Peak Pricing: An Alternative Technological Solution." *Kyklos* 28 (1975): 80–93.

Hirshleifer, J. "Peak Loads and Efficient Pricing: Comment." *Quarterly Journal of Economics* (August 1958).

Joskow, P. L., et al. "Symposium on Peak-Load Pricing." *Bell Journal of Economics and Management Science* (Spring 1976).

Landon, J. H. "Pricing in Combined Gas and Electric Utilities: Comment" and "Reply" by B. M. Owen. *Antitrust Bulletin* (Spring 1973).

Littlechild, S. C. "Marginal Cost Pricing with Joint Costs." *Economic Journal* (June 1970).

Littlechild, S. C. "Peak-Load Pricing of Telephone Calls." *Bell Journal of Economics and Management Science* (Autumn 1970).

Mann, P. C., and E. J. Siegfried, "Pricing in the Case of Publicly Owned Electric Industries." *Quarterly Review of Economics and Business* (Summer 1972).

Mohring, H. "The Peak-Load Problem with Increasing Returns and Pricing Constraints." *American Economic Review* (September 1970).

Needham, D. *The Economics of Industrial Structure, Conduct, and Performance.* Eastbourne: Holt, Rinehart & Winston, 1978. Chap. 2 pp. 42–45, Chap. 11.

Sappington, D. "Strategic Firm Behavior Under a Dynamic Regulatory Adjustment Process." *Bell Journal of Economics* (Spring 1980).

Steiner, P. O. "Peak Loads and Efficient Pricing." *Quarterly Journal of Economics* (November 1957) and "Comments" by J. Hirschleifer (August 1958) and J. M. Buchanan (August 1964).

Turvey, R. "Peak-Load Pricing." *Journal of Political Economy* (January–February 1968).

Turvey, R. "The Second-Best Case for Marginal Cost Pricing." In *Public Economics,* edited by J. Margolis and H. Gutton. New York: St. Martin's Press, 1969.

Vickrey, W. "Responsive Pricing of Public Utility Services." *Bell Journal of Economics and Management Science* (Spring 1971).

Vickrey, W. "Maximum Output or Maximum Welfare? More on the Off-Peak Pricing Problem." *Kyklos* (March 1971).

Vogelsang, I., and J. Finsinger, "A Regulatory Adjustment Process for Optimal Pricing by Multiproduct Monopoly Firms." *Bell Journal of Economics* (Spring 1979).

Waverman, L. "Peak-Load Pricing Under Regulatory Constraint: A Proof of Inefficiency." *Journal of Political Economy* (June 1975).

Whinston, A., and E. A. Loehman, "A New Theory of Pricing and Decision Making for Public Investment." *Bell Journal of Economics and Management Science* (Autumn 1971).

White, L. J. "Reversals in Peak and Off-Peak Prices." *Bell Journal of Economics and Management Science* (Spring 1974).

Williamson, O. E. "Peak-Load Pricing: Some Further Remarks." *Bell Journal of Economics and Management Science* (Spring 1974).

Williamson, O. E. "Peak-Load Pricing and Optimal Capacity Under Indivisibility Constraints." *American Economic Review* (September 1966).

Wilson, G. W. "The Theory of Peak-Load Pricing: A Final Note." *Bell Journal of Economics and Management Science* (Spring 1972).

(iii) *Effects of Regulation on Nonprice Dimensions of Regulated Firms' Behavior*

Bailey, E. E. "Innovation and Regulation." *Journal of Public Economics* (August 1974).

Grabowski, H. G., J. M. Vernon, and L. G. Thomas, "Estimating the Effects of Regulation on Innovation: An International Comparative Analysis of the Pharmaceutical Industry." *Journal of Law and Economics* (April 1968).

Magat, W. A. "Regulation and the Rate and Direction of Induced Technical Change." *Bell Journal of Economics* (Autumn 1976).

Schmalensee, R. "Regulation and the Durability of Goods." *Bell Journal of Economics and Management Science* (Spring 1970).

Spence, A. M. "Monopoly, Quality and Regulation." *Bell Journal of Economics and Management Science* (Autumn 1975).

Swan, P. L. "The Durability of Goods and Regulation of Monopoly." *Bell Journal of Economics and Management Science* (Spring 1971).

(iv) *Weaknesses in Existing Models of Utility Regulation*

Davis, E. G. "A Dynamic Model of the Regulated Firm with a Price Adjustment Mechanism." *Bell Journal of Economics and Management Science* (Spring 1973).

Wendel, J. "Firm-Regulator Interaction with Respect to Firm Cost Reduction Activities." *Bell Journal of Economics* (Autumn 1976).

Westfield, F. M. "Methodology of Evaluating Economic Regulation." *American Economic Review,* Papers and Proceedings (May 1971).

CHAPTER 10

Alchian, A. A., and H. Demsetz, "Production, Information Costs, and Economic Organization." *American Economic Review* (December 1972).

Argyris, C. "Ineffective Regulating Processes." In *Regulating Business: The Search for an Optimum,* edited by C. Argyris et al., chap. 8. San Francisco: Institute for Contemporary Studies, 1978.

Armstrong, C. M., and M. N. Gurol, F. A. Russ, "Detecting and Correcting Deceptive Advertising." *Journal of Consumer Research* (1979): (December 1979).

Arnould, R. J., and H. Grabowski, "Auto Safety Regulation: An Analysis of Market Failure" *Bell Journal of Economics* (Spring 1981).

Auster, R., and M. Silver, "Collective Goods and Collective Decision Mechanisms." *Public Choice* (Spring 1973).

Baron, D. P. "Price Regulation, Product Quality, and Asymmetric Information." *American Economic Review* (March 1981).

Bays, C. W. "Prospective Payment and Hospital Efficiency." *Quarterly Review of Economics and Business* (Spring 1980).

Beales, H., R. Craswell, and S. Salop, "Information Remedies for Consumer Protection." *American Economic Review,* Papers and Proceedings (May 1981): 410–413.

Breyer, S. "Analyzing Regulatory Failure." *Harvard Law Review* (January 1979).

Buchanan, J., and G. Tullock, "Pollutors' Profits and Political Response: Direct Control versus Taxes." *American Economic Review* (March 1975) and "Reply," *American Economic Review* (December 1976): 983–984.

Colantoni, C. S., O. A. Davis, and M. Swaminuthan, "Imperfect Consumers and Welfare Comparisons of Policies Concerning Information Regulation." *Bell Journal of Economics* (Autumn 1976).

Crawford, V. P. "A Self-Administered Solution to the Bargaining Problem." *Review of Economic Studies* (January 1980).

Dardis, R. "The Value of Life: New Evidence from the Marketplace." *American Economic Review* (December 1980): 1077–1082.

Deacon, R. T. "An Economic Analysis of Gasoline Price Controls." *Natural Resources Journal* (October 1978).

Demsetz, H. "Some Aspects of Property Rights." *Journal of Law and Economics* (October 1966).

Enthoven, A. C. "How Interest Groups Have Responded to a Proposal for Economic Competition in Health Services." *American Economic Review,* Papers and Proceedings (May 1980): 142–156.

Erickson, E. W., W. L. Peters, R. M. Spann, and P. J. Tese, "The Political Economy of Crude Oil Price Controls." *Natural Resources Journal* (October 1978).

Ermer, V. "Strategies for Increasing Bureaucratic Responsiveness." *Midwest Review of Public Administration* (April/July 1975).

Feldman, P. H., and R. J. Zeckhauser, "Sober Thoughts on Health Care Regulation." In *Regulating Business: The Search for an Optimum,* edited by C. Argyris et al., chap. 5. San Francisco: Institute for Contemporary Studies, 1978.

Fiorina, M. P., and C. R. Plott, "Committee Decisions Under Majority Rule: An Experimental Study." *American Political Science Review* (June 1978): 492–505.

Fischer, D., and A. Schotter, "The Inevitability of the 'Paradox of Redistribution' in the Allocation of Voting Weights." *Public Choice* 33, no. 2 (1978).

Fusfeld, D. R. "The Conceptual Framework of Modern Economics." *Journal of Economic Issues* (March 1980).

Goldberg, V. P. "The Economics of Product Safety and Imperfect Information." *Bell Journal of Economics and Management Science* (Autumn 1974).

Grabowski, H. G., and J. M. Vernon, "Consumer Product Safety Regulation." *American Economic Review,* Papers and Proceedings (May 1978): 284–289.

Gronau, R. "Leisure, Home Production, and Work — The Theory of the Allocation of Time Revisited." *Journal of Political Economy* (December 1977): 1099–1123.

Grossman, S. J., and J. E. Stiglitz, "The Impossibility of Informationally Efficient Markets." *American Economic Review* (June 1980).

Harris, J. "Internal Organization of Hospitals: Some Economic Implications." *Bell Journal of Economics* (Autumn 1977).

Hirschleifer, J. "The Private and Social Value of Information and the Reward to Inventive Activity." *American Economic Review* (September 1971).

Hirschleifer, J., and J. G. Riley, "The Analytics of Uncertainty and Information — An Expository Survey." *Journal of Economic Literature* (December 1979).

Holton, R. H. "Advancing the Backward Art of Spending Money." In *Regulating Business: The Search for an Optimum,* edited by C. Argyris et al., chap. 6. San Francisco: Institute for Contemporary Studies, 1978.

Hughes, W. R. "Lifetime Utility Maximization When the Consumer's Lifetime Depends on His Consumption." *Economic Record* (April 1978): 65–71.

Jacob, N. L., and A. N. Page, "Production, Information Costs, and Economic Organization: The Buyer Monitoring Case." *American Economic Review* (June 1980).

Jensen, M., and W. Meckling, "Theory of the Firm: Managerial Behavior, Agency Costs, and Ownership Structure." *Journal of Financial Economics* (October 1976): 305–360.

Johnson, W. R. "Substitution in Household Production and the Efficiency of In-Kind Transfer." *Public Finance Quarterly* 6, no. 2 (April 1978).

Kapteyn, A., T. Wansbeek, and J. Buyze, "Maximizing or Satisficing?" *Review of Economics and Statistics* (November 1979).

Keiser, K. R. "The New Regulation of Health and Safety." *Political Science Quarterly* (Fall 1980).

Kotowitz, Y., and F. Mathewson, "Advertising, Consumer Information, and Product Quality." *Bell Journal of Economics* (Autumn 1979).

Krattenmaker, T. G. "The Federal Trade Commission and Consumer Protection." *California Management Review* (Summer 1976): 89–104.

Kraus, M. "On Pareto Optimal Time Allocation." *Economic Inquiry* (January 1979).

Lane, R. E. "Markets and the Satisfaction of Human Wants." *Journal of Economic Issues,* no. 4 (December 1978).

Lee, S. "A Just Theory of Regulation." *American Economic Review* (December 1980).

Leland, H. E. "Quacks, Lemons and Licensing: A Theory of Minimum Quality Standards." *Journal of Political Economy* (December 1979): 1328–1346.

Linnertooth, J. "The Value of Human Life: A Review of the Models." *Economic Inquiry* (January 1979).

MacAvoy, P. W. "Health and Safety Regulations." *The Regulated Industries & the Economy.* New York: W. W. Norton, 1979. Chap. 3.

Main, R. S., and C. W. Baird, "Pollutors' Profits and Political Response: Direct Control versus Taxes: Comment." *American Economic Review* (December 1976): 979–980.

Masoner, M. "The Allocation of Time: An Extension." *Journal of Post Keynesian Economics* 1 (1979): 107–223.

McKie, J. "Regulation and the Free Market: The Problem of Boundaries," *Bell Journal of Economics and Management Science* (Spring 1960).

Mead, W. J. "The Political-Economic Problems of Energy — A Synthesis." *Natural Resources Journal* (October 1978).

Morici, P., Jr. "The Benefits and Costs of Crude Oil Price Regulations." *Journal of Energy Development* (Spring 1978): 366–377.

Murphy, M. "The Value of Time Spent in Home Production." *American Journal of Economics and Sociology* (April 1976).

Needham, D. "The Economics of Reducing Faculty Teaching Loads: Comment." *Journal of Political Economy* (February 1975): 219–223.

Needleman, L. "The Valuation of Changes in the Risk of Death by Those at Risk." *Manchester School of Economic and Social Studies* (September 1980).

Newhouse, J. P. *The Economics of Medical Care.* Reading, Mass.: Addison-Wesley, 1978.

Oi, W. Y. "The Economics of Product Safety." *Bell Journal of Economics and Management Science* (Spring 1973).

Oi, W. Y. "The Economics of Product Safety: A Rejoinder." *Bell Journal of Economics and Management Science* (Autumn 1974).

Owen, B. M., and R. Braeutigam, *The Regulation Game: Strategic Use of the Administrative Process.* Cambridge, Mass.: Ballinger, 1978.

Pauly, M. V. "The Ethics and Economics of Kickbacks and Fee Splitting." *Bell Journal of Economics* (Spring 1979).

Peltzman, S. "The Effects of Automobile Safety Regulation." *Journal of Political Economy* (August 1975).

Peterson, M. B. *The Regulated Consumer.* Ottowa: Green Hill Publishers, 1971.

Plott, C. R., and M. E. Levine, "A Model of Agenda Influence on Committee Decisions." *American Economic Review* (March 1978).

Pollak, R. A., and M. L. Wachter, "The Relevance of the Household Production Function and Its Implications for the Allocation of Time." *Journal of Political Economy* (April 1975).

Pollak, R. A., and M. L. Wachter, "Reply: Pollak and Wachter on the Household Production Approach." *Journal of Political Economy* (October 1977): 1083–1086.

Porter, R. C. "A Social Benefit-Cost Analysis of Mandatory Deposits on Beverage Containers." *Journal of Environmental Economics and Management* (1978): 351–375.

Romer, T., and H. Rosenthal, "Political Resource Allocation, Controlled Agendas, and the Status Quo." *Public Choice* 33 (1978): 27–43.

Romer, T., and H. Rosenthal, "Bureaucrats versus Voters: On the Political Economy of Resource Allocation by Direct Democracy." *Quarterly Journal of Economics* (November 1979).

Ross, S. "The Economic Theory of Agency: The Principal's Problem." *American Economic Review* (May 1973).

Rothschild, M. "Models of Market Organization with Imperfect Information: A Survey." *Journal of Political Economy* (November–December 1973).

Shaffer, J. D. "Observations on the Political Economics of Regulations." *American Journal of Agricultural Economics.* Part 2 (November 1979).

Shavell, S. "Risk Sharing and Incentives in the Principal and Agent Relationship." *Bell Journal of Economics* (Spring 1979).

Shibata, H. "A Theory of Group Consumption and Group Formation." *Public Finance,* Vol. 34 no. 3 (1979): 395–413.

Simon, H. A. "On How to Decide What to Do." *Bell Journal of Economics* (Autumn 1978).

Simon, H. A. "Rational Decision-Making in Business Organizations." *American Economic Review* (September 1979).

Simon, M. J., "Imperfect Information, Costly Litigation, and Product Quality." *Bell Journal of Economics* (Spring 1981).

Smith, R. S. "The Impact of OSHA Inspections on Manufacturing Injury Rates." *Journal of Human Resources* Vol 14 No 2 Spring 1979.

Taylor, A. K. "Government Health Policy and Hospital Labor Costs." *Public Policy* (Spring 1979): 203–225.

Telser, L. G. "A Theory of Self-enforcing Agreements." *Journal of Business* (January 1980).

Tinbergen, J. *On the Theory of Economic Policy,* 2d ed. Amsterdam, North-Holland, 1966.

Viscusi, W. K. "A Note on 'Lemons' Markets with Quality Certification." *Bell Journal of Economics* (Spring 1978).

Viscusi, W. K. "The Impact of Occupational Safety and Health Regulation." *Bell Journal of Economics* (Spring 1979).

Vogelsang, I. "The Design of Regulatory Rules." In *Regulated Industries and Public Enterprise: European and United States Perspectives,* edited by B. M. Mitchell and P. R. Kleindorfer, chap. 2. Lexington, Mass.: D.C. Heath, 1980.

Ward, R. A. *The Economics of Health Resources.* Reading, Mass.: Addison Wesley, 1975.

Weitzman, M. L. "Is the Price System of Rationing More Effective in Getting a Commodity to Those Who Need It Most?" *Bell Journal of Economics* (Autumn 1977).

Wenders, J. T., and L. D. Taylor, "Experiments in Seasonal Time of Day Pricing of Electricity to Residential Users." *Bell Journal of Economics* (Autumn 1976).

White, L. W. "Quality Variation When Prices Are Regulated." *Bell Journal of Economics* (Autumn 1972).

Williamson, O. E. *Markets and Hierarchies: Analysis and Antitrust Implications.* New York: Free Press, 1975.

Williamson, O. E. "Markets, Hierarchies: Some Elementary Considerations." *American Economic Review,* Papers and Proceedings (May 1977).

Williamson, O. E. "Transactions-Cost Economics: The Governance of Contractual Relations." *Journal of Law and Economics* (October 1979).

Wolfe, C. L., Jr. "A Theory of Nonmarket Failure: Framework for Implementation Analysis." *Journal of Law and Economics* (April 1979): 107–139.

Yohe, G. W. "Pollutors' Profits and Political Response: Direct Control versus Taxes: Comment." *American Economic Review* (December 1976): 981–982.

CHAPTER 11

Abernathy, W. J., and B. S. Chakravarthy, "Government Intervention and Innovation in Industry: A Policy Framework." *Sloan Management Review* (Spring 1979).
Adam, C. M. "On the Estimation of Reaction Functions for Several Economic Policy Makers," *Economic Inquiry* (October 1980).
Balantine, J. G., and I. Eris, "On the General Equilibrium Analysis of Tax Incidence," *Journal of Political Economy* (June 1975).
Benham, Lee. "Advertising and the Price of Eyeglasses." *Journal of Law and Economics,* vol. 15 (October 1972): 337–352.
Dorfman, R., and P. O. Steiner, "Optimal Advertising and Optimal Quality." *American Economic Review* (December 1954).
Frenkel, J. A., and P. Pashigian, "Regulation and Excess Demand: A General Equilibrium Approach." *Journal of Business* (July 1972).
Gould, J. R., and S. G. B. Henry, "The Effects of Price Control on a Related Market." *Economica* (February 1967).
Harberger, A. C. "Three Basic Postulates for Applied Welfare Economics." *Journal of Economic Literature* (September 1971).
Johnson, H. G. "Minimum Wage Laws: A General Equilibrium Analysis." *Canadian Journal of Economics* (November 1969).
Kraus, M. B. "Tax Burden, Excess Burden, and Differential Incidence Revisited: Comment and Extensions." *Public Finance,* Vol. 29(3) (1974): 404–415.
Kraus, M. B., and H. G. Johnson, "The Theory of Tax and Expenditure Incidence: A Diagrammatic Analysis." *Public Finance,* Vol. 31(3) (1976): 340–361.
McKie, J. W. "Regulation and the Free Market: The Problem of Boundaries." *Bell Journal of Economics and Management Science* 1, no. 1 (Spring 1970).
McLure, C. E. "General Equilibrium Incidence Analysis: The Harberger Model after Ten Years." *Journal of Public Economics* (February 1975).
Mieskowski, P. M. "On the Theory of Tax Incidence." *Journal of Political Economy* (June 1967).
Needham, D. "Market Structure and Firm's R&D Behavior." *Journal of Industrial Economics* (June 1975).
Needham, D. "Entry Barriers and Non-Price Aspects of Firms' Behavior." *Journal of Industrial Economics* (September 1976).
Needham, D. "Non-Price Behavior." In *The Economics of Industrial Structure, Conduct, and Performance,* chap. 4. Eastbourne: Holt, Rinehart, & Winston Ltd., 1978.
Needham, D. "Seller Profitability and Input Market Structure: Theory and Implications." James Madison University, Department of Economics and Center for Economic Education Working Papers, no. 80–6, 1980.
Schmalensee, Richard. "Market Structure, Durability, and Quality: A Selected Survey." *Economic Inquiry* (April 1979).
Winston, C. "The Welfare Effects of ICC Rate Regulation Revisited." *Bell Journal of Economics* (Spring 1981).

CHAPTER 12

Alchian, A. A., and H. Demsetz, "Production, Information Costs, and Economic Organization." *American Economic Review* (December 1972): 777–795.

Bonin, J. P. "On the Design of Managerial Incentive Structures in a Decentralized Planning Environment." *American Economic Review* (September 1976).

Bonin, J. P., and A. J. Marcus, "Information, Motivation, and Control in Decentralized Planning: The Case of Discretionary Managerial Behavior." *Journal of Comparative Economics* (June 1979).

Diver, C. S. "A Theory of Regulatory Enforcement." *Public Policy* (Summer 1980).

Dumas, L. J. "Armament, Disarmament and National Security: A Theoretical Duopoly Model of the Arms Race." *Journal of Economics Studies* (May 1979).

Ekern, S. "The New Soviet Incentive Model: Comment." *Bell Journal of Economics* (Autumn 1979).

Fan, L. S. "On the Reward System." *American Economic Review* (March 1975).

Groves, T. "Incentives in Teams." *Econometrica* (July 1973).

Harford, J. D. "Firm Behavior Under Imperfectly Enforceable Pollution Standards and Taxes." *Journal of Environmental Economics and Management* (March 1978).

Harris, J. E. "Taxing Tar and Nicotine." *American Economic Review* (June 1980).

Jacob, N. L., and A. N. Page, "Production, Information Costs, and Economic Organization: The Buyer Monitoring Case." *American Economic Review* (June 1980): 476–478.

Just, R. E., and D. Zilberman, "Asymmetry of Taxes and Subsidies in Regulating Stochastic Mishap." *Quarterly Journal of Economics* (February 1979): 139–148.

Kleindorfer, P. R., and M. R. Sertel, "Profit-Maximizing Design of Enterprises Through Incentives." *Journal of Economic Theory* (June 1979).

Loeb, M., and W. A. Magat, "Soviet Success Indicators and the Evaluation of Division Management." *Journal of Accounting Research* (Spring 1978a): 113–121.

Loeb, M., and W. A. Magat, "Success Indicators in the Soviet Union: The Problem of Incentives and Efficient Allocations." *American Economic Review* (March 1978b).

McKenzie, R. B. "The Economic Basis of Departmental Discord in Academe." *Social Science Quarterly* (March 1979).

Miller, J., and J. Thornton, "Effort, Uncertainty, and the New Soviet Incentive System." *Southern Economic Journal* (October 1978).

Mirrlees, J. "The Optimal Structure of Incentives and Authority Within an Organization." *Bell Journal of Economics* (Spring 1976).

Myerson, R. B. "Incentive Compatibility and the Bargaining Problem." *Econometrica* (January 1979): 61–73.

Needham, D. "Student Effort, Learning, and Course Evaluation." *Journal of Economic Education* (Fall 1978).

Nikolai, L. A., and R. Elam, "The Pollution Control Tax Incentive: A Non-Incentive." *Accounting Review* (January 1979).

Polinsky, A. M. "Notes on the Symmetry of Taxes and Subsidies in Pollution Control." *Canadian Journal of Economics* (February 1979): 75–83.

Polinsky, A. M. "Strict Liability versus Negligence in a Market Setting." *American Economic Review*, Papers and Proceedings (May 1980): 363–367.

Polinsky, A. M., and S. Shavell, "The Optimal Tradeoff Between the Probability and Magnitude of Fines." *American Economic Review* (December 1979): 880–891.

Posner, R. A. "An Economic Analysis of Legal Rulemaking." *Journal of Legal Studies* 3 (January 1974).

Sappington, D. "Strategic Firm Behavior Under a Dynamic Regulatory Adjustment Process." *Bell Journal of Economics* (Spring 1980).

Shavell, S. "Strict Liability versus Negligence," *Journal of Legal Studies* (Jan. 1980).

Simon, M. J. "Imperfect Information, Costly Litigation, and Product Quality." *Bell Journal of Economics* (Spring 1981).

Smythe, D. W., "Discussion: Changing Role in the Market in Utilities Regulation," *American Economic Review*, Papers & Proceedings (May 1980).

Snowberger, V. "The New Soviet Incentive Model: Comment." *Bell Journal of Economics* (Autumn 1977).

Thomson, W. "Eliciting Production Possibilities from a Well-Informed Manager." *Journal of Economic Theory* (June 1979).

Van Winden, F. "The Interactions Between State and Firms." *Oxford Economic Papers* (November 1980).

Viscusi, W. K., and R. J. Zeckhauser, "Optimal Standards with Incomplete Enforcement." *Public Policy* 27, no. 4 (Fall 1979): 437–456.

Weitzman, M. L. "The Soviet Incentive Model." *Bell Journal of Economics* (Spring 1976).

Weitzman, M. L. "Optimal Rewards for Economic Regulation." *American Economic Review* (September 1978).

Weitzman, M. L. "Efficient Incentive Contracts." *Quarterly Journal of Economics* (June 1980*b*).

Weitzman, M. L. "The 'Ratchet Principle' and Performance Incentives." *Bell Journal of Economics* (Spring 1980*a*).

Wendel, J. "Firm–Regulator Interaction with Respect to Cost-Reduction Activities." *Bell Journal of Economics* (Autumn 1976).

Yohe, G. W. "Comparisons of Price and Quantity Controls: A Survey." *Journal of Comparative Economics* 1, no. 3 (September 1977).

CHAPTER 13

Caleb, T. S., "Bureaucratic Performance & Budgetary Reward: A Test of the Hypothesis with Alternative Specification," *Public Choice*, Fall 1977.

Clark, E. H. "Multipart Pricing of Public Goods." *Public Choice* (Fall 1971).

Clark, E. H. "Some Aspects of the Demand-Revealing Process." *Public Choice*, Supplement (Spring 1977).

Demski, J. S. and Feltham, G. A., "Economic Incentives in Budgetary Control Systems." *Accounting Review* (April 1978).

Diver, C. S. "A Theory of Regulatory Enforcement." *Public Policy* (Summer 1980).

Feldman, A. "Manipulating Voting Procedures." *Economic Inquiry* (July 1979).

Goldberg, V. P. "Regulation and Administered Contracts." *Bell Journal of Economics* (Autumn 1976).

Green, J., and J. J. Lafont, "An Incentive Compatible Planning Procedure for Public Good Production." *Scandinavian Journal of Economics*, vol. 80(1), 1978.

Groves, T. "The Allocation of Resources Under Uncertainty: The Informational Incentive Roles of Prices and Demand in a Team," Center for Research in Management Science, Reprint No. 1, University of California-Berkeley (Aug. 1969).

Groves, T., and J. O. Ledyard, "Some Limitations of Demand Revealing Processes." *Public Choice,* Supplement (Spring 1977).

Hammond, P. J. "Straightforward Individual Incentive Compatibility in Large Economies." *Review of Economic Studies* (April 1979).

Herzlinger, R. E., "Zero-Based Budgeting in the Federal Government: A Case Study." *Sloan Management Review* (Winter 1979).

Keating, B. P. "Prescriptions for Efficiency in Non-Profit Firms." *Applied Economics* (September 1979): 321–332.

Lane, R. E. "Markets and the Satisfaction of Human Wants." *Journal of Economic Issues* (December 1978).

Lewis, T. R. "Bonuses and Penalties in Incentive Contracting." *Bell Journal of Economics* (Spring 1980).

Loeb, M. "Alternative Versions of the Demand Revealing Process." *Public Choice* (Spring 1976).

Loeb, M. and W. A. Magat, "Success Indicators in the Soviet Union: The Problem of Efficient Allocations," *American Economic Review* (March 1978).

Mitnick, B. "The Theory of Agency: The Policing Paradox and Regulatory Behavior." *Public Choice* (Winter 1975).

Needham, D. *The Economics of Industrial Structure, Conduct and Performance.* Eastbourne: Holt, Rinehart, & Winston Ltd., 1978.

Nitzan, S., J. Paroush, and S. I. Lampert, "Preference Expression and Misrepresentation in Points Voting Schemes." *Public Choice* 35 (1980): 421-436.

Roberts, J. "The Incentives for Correct Revelation of Preferences and the Number of Consumers." *Journal of Public Economics* (November 1976).

Roberts, J. "Incentives in Planning Procedures for the Provision of Public Goods." *Review of Economic Studies* (April 1979).

Ross, S. "The Economic Theory of Agency: The Principal's Problem." *American Economic Review* (May 1973).

Sabbatier, P. A. "Regulatory Policy Making: Toward a Framework of Analysis," *National Resources Journal,* Vol. 17 (July 1977).

Schoumaker, F. "Incentives in Planning with Private Goods." *Review of Economic Studies* (April 1979).

Schultze, C. L. "The Role of Incentives, Penalties and Rewards in Attaining Effective Policy." In *Public Expenditures and Policy Analysis,* 1st ed., edited by R. H. Haveman and J. Margolis, chap. 6. Chicago: Rand-McNally, 1977.

Shavell, S. "Risk Sharing and Incentives in the Principal and Agent Relationship." *Bell Journal of Economics* (Spring 1979).

Tideman, T. N., and G. Tullock, "A New and Superior Process for Making Social Choices." *Journal of Political Economy* (December 1976).

Tideman, T. N., and G. Tullock, et al., in a special issue of *Public Choice* devoted to "Demand-Revealing Processes" (Spring 1977).

Walker, M. "On the Nonexistence of a Dominant Strategy Mechanism for Making Optimal Public Decisions." *Econometrica* (September 1980).

Warren, R. S., Jr. "Bureaucratic Performance and Budgetary Reward." *Public Choice* (June 1975).

Warren, R. S., "Bureaucratic Performance and Budgetary Reward: A Reply and Reformulation." *Public Choice* (Fall 1977).
Weidenbaum, M. L. *Business, Government and the Public,* 2d ed. Englewood Cliffs, N.J.: Prentice-Hall, 1981.

CHAPTER 14

Berle, A. A. *The Twentieth-Century Capitalist Revolution.* New York: 1954.
Berle, A. A., and G. Means. *The Modern Corporation and Private Property.* New York: Macmillan, 1932.
Bowen, H. R. *Social Responsibilities of Businessmen.* New York: Harper, 1953.
Deutsch, L. L. "Structure, Performance and the Net Rate of Entry into Manufacturing Industries." *Southern Economic Journal* (January 1975).
Friedman, M. *Capitalism and Freedom.* Chicago: University of Chicago Press, 1963.
Gollop, F. M., and J. M. Roberts. "Firm Interdependence in Oligopolistic Markets." *Journal of Econometrics* (August 1979): 313–331.
Needham, D. *The Economics of Industrial Structure, Conduct and Performance.* Eastbourne: Holt, Rinehart & Winston, 1978.
Orr, D. "The Determinants of Entry: A Study of Canadian Manufacturing Industries." *Review of Economics and Statistics* (February 1974).
Orr, D. "An Index of Entry Barriers and Its Application to the Market Structure–Performance Relationship." *Journal of Industrial Economics* (September 1974).
Pagoulatos, E., and R. Sorenson. "A Simultaneous Equation Analysis of Advertising, Concentration and Profitability." *Southern Economic Journal* (January 1981): 728–741.
Panzar, J. C. "Regulation, Deregulation, and Economic Efficiency: The Case of the CAB." *American Economic Review* (December 1979): 311–315.
Porter, M. E. "The Structure Within Industries and Companies Performance." *Review of Economics and Statistics* (May 1979).
Porter, M. E., and R. E. Caves. "From Entry Barriers to Mobility Barriers: Conjectural Decisions and Contrived Deterrence to New Competition." *Quarterly Journal of Economics* (May 1977).
Preston, L. E., and J. E. Post. *Private Management and Public Policy.* Englewood Cliffs, N.J.: Prentice-Hall, 1975.
Qualls, P. D. "A Note on the Lerner Measure of Monopoly Versus the Rate of Return in Structure-Performance Studies." *Industrial Organization Review,* vol. 5 (1), 1977.
Samuels, W. J. "The Industrial Reorganization Bill: The Burden of the Future." *Journal of Economic Issues* (June 1975).
Shepherd, W. G. "The Elements of Market Structure." *Review of Economics and and Statistics* (February 1972).
Shepherd, W. G. "Elements of Market Structure: An Interindustry Analysis." *Southern Economic Journal* (April 1972).
White House Task Force Report on Antitrust Policy. Washington, D.C.: U.S. Government Printing Office, 1968.

Index